*War Office, 25th April,* 1807.

THE following Collection will be found to include the principal Regulations connected with the business of the War Office, that have at different times been circulated for the guidance of the Army; and that still remain in force. The original object of the Collection did not extend beyond the mere republication of Documents of the above description: in the execution of the plan, however, the convenience of the Military has been further consulted, by occasionally annexing Notes to Passages that appeared liable to misconstruction; by printing some decisions on particular questions which have not before been made known to the Army at large; and, in a few instances, by comprizing in a Memorandum the substance of various detached Orders, or stating in the same form, the established practice of Office upon points concerning which no express Regulation exists.

The Notes and other additional articles so introduced, are to be considered as having the authority of official communications.

Several

Several Regulations that have, in part, or entirely, ceased to be in force, are, notwithstanding, included in the Collection; being inserted either for the sake of preserving useful information as to the origin and principle of the existing Rules; or because the later and amended Regulations are framed with such an immediate and verbal reference to those which they supersede, as not to be intelligible without a previous perusal of the latter. In these cases, the obsolete parts, besides being pointed out by the Notes, are generally printed in a smaller type, and enclosed between brackets.

The intimate relation between many of the Army Services renders it difficult to distribute the Regulations into well defined classes; and a further difficulty in classing them arises from the circumstance of there being sometimes more than one subject adverted to in the same Regulation. On these accounts, among others, the arrangement is imperfect: but any inconvenience that might proceed from this defect will be, in a great measure, obviated by the use of the *Index;* in forming which, particular attention has been paid to the bringing together, under their proper heads, articles relating to the same subject that are accidentally separated in the Collection.

The extent of the operation of the several Regulations

*WAR OFFICE, 25th April,* 1807.

# A COLLECTION

OF

# ORDERS, REGULATIONS,

AND

# INSTRUCTIONS,

FOR THE

# A R M Y;

ON MATTERS OF FINANCE

AND

POINTS OF DISCIPLINE

IMMEDIATELY CONNECTED THEREWITH.

PUBLISHED BY ORDER OF THE

Secretary at War.

SOLD BY T. EGERTON, AT THE MILITARY LIBRARY, NEAR WHITEHALL.

*Price* 8s. 6d. *bound in Calf Skin: and* 6s. 6d. *in Boards.*

The Naval & Military Press Ltd

Published by
**The Naval & Military Press Ltd**

## The Naval & Military Press ...

...offer specialist books for the serious student of conflict. The range of titles stocked covers the whole spectrum of military history with titles on uniforms, battles, official histories, specialist works containing Medal Rolls and Casualties Lists, and numismatic titles for medal collectors and researchers.

The innovative approach they have to military bookselling and their commitment to publishing have made them Britain's leading independent military bookseller.

*In reprinting in facsimile from the original, any imperfections are inevitably reproduced and the quality may fall short of modern type and cartographic standards.*

gulations is, for the most part, explained in their titles. It may be observed generally, that they do not necessarily apply to the Forces serving in the *East Indies*, unless where particularly expressed; nor to those in *Ireland*, unless where they have been extended, under the immediate authority of the Lord Lieutenant, to the Establishment of that part of the United Kingdom.

In circulating future Instructions to the Army it is intended to print them in a form corresponding to that of the present Collection; and with references to the pages thereof to which they may relate.

# TABLE OF CONTENTS.

## SECTION I.

*Pay of the Officers and Men of the several Corps of the Army; including the Allowances issued in the Shape of Pay.*

25 *Jan.* 1798.—Circular relative to the Pay of Field Officers and Captains — — — — Page 3

27 *June*, 1797.—Circular to the Colonels of Cavalry Regiments, relative to issuing the Pay of Subalterns, &c. — 6

27 *June*, 1797.—Ditto—Infantry Corps — — 7

10 *June* 1802.—Extract of a Circular stating the Footing of Adjutants in the Cavalry — — — 9

———————Ditto—in the Infantry — — 10

25 *May*, 1797.—Warrant for encreasing and regulating the Pay and Allowance of Non-commissioned Officers and Private Men of Corps of Cavalry serving at Home — — 11

25 *May*, 1797.—Ditto—Infantry serving at home — 15

5 *July*, 1797.—Ditto—Corps of Cavalry and Infantry serving out of Great Britain — — — — 20

6 *Feb.* 1799.—Warrant declaring the Deductions to be taken from the Pay of Soldiers under various Circumstances of Service — — — — 23

5 *Dec.* 1798.—Circular relative to the Stoppage from Soldiers while Prisoners of War — — — 25

30 *March*, 1803.—Extract of a Circular explaining the Footing of Armourers in the Militia — — 26

9 *Jan.* 1805.—Circular relative to the Enlistment of Boys in the Second Battalions for limited Service — — 27

8 *Nov.* 1805.—Circular relative to the Pay of Boy Recruits 28

28 *Feb.*

## CONTENTS.

28 *Feb.* 1806.—General Orders relative to the Pay of Boys enlisted for the Purpose of being trained as Drummers or Fifers 29

15 *July*, 1806.—Circular to the Cavalry relative to the additional Allowance to Corporals and Privates after certain Periods of Service, &c. — — — 30

29 *July* 1806.—Ditto to the Cavalry at home, explaining the above — — — — — 32

29 *July*, 1806.—Ditto to the Cavalry on Foreign Stations, 34

15 *July*, 1806.—Circular to the Colonels of the Foot Guards, relative to the Encrease of Pay and Allowances — 35

15 *July*, 1806.—Ditto—Marching Regiments of Foot — 37

29 *July*, 1806.—Ditto—to marching Regiments of Foot on the Home Station, explaining the above — — 40

29 *July*, 1806.—Ditto—on Foreign Stations — 42

15 *July*, 1806.—Circular to the Commandants of Militia Corps relative to encreasing the Pay and Allowance of Subalterns, &c. — — — — 43

25 *July*, 1806.—Circular to the Paymasters of Militia Corps, relative to issuing the additional Allowance — 45

Memorandum referring to the Authorities for the Pay of various Appointments — — — 46

States of the Rates of Pay of the Officers and Men of the several Corps of the Army — — — 47 to 55

# SECTION II.

*Annual or Contingent Regimental Allowances.*

27 *May*, 1803.—Extracts of Circulars relative to the Allowance to Field Officers in lieu of their Troops or Companies 59

11 *Oct.* 1806.—Letter relative to the Appropriation of ditto 60

Regulation of Allowances for Captains and Riding Masters, &c. 61

11 *Feb.* 1806.—General Orders relative to the Appropriation of the Contingent Allowance, in the absence of Captains 62

13 *July*

## CONTENTS.

13 *July* 1799.—Circular relative to an Allowance for the Maintenance of Adjutants' Horses — — 63

22 *July* 1797.—Letter stating the Rates of Lodging Money for Officers in North Britain — — — 64

25 *May* 1795.—Ditto—South Britain — — 65

17 *March*, 1800.—Warrant granting an Allowance in lieu of Small Beer to the Troops at Home, &c. — — 66

20 *Nov.* 1800.—Circular relative to placing the Supply of Bread under the Commissary General — — 69

25 *March* 1801.—Circular relative to the Extra Price of Meat 71

4 *Aug.* 1803.—General Orders relative to ditto — 72

13 *Aug.* 1803.—Circular relative to ditto — 74

21 *July*, 1806.—Act for the Relief of Innkeepers — 75

18 *March*, 1795.—Circular limiting the Supply of Hay and Straw by Innkeepers — — — 79

15 *Aug.* 1801.—Circular placing the Supply of Oats under the Commissary General — — — 81

29 *June*, 1799.—Circular relative to the Purchase of Troop Horses — — — — 84

23 *May*, 1803.—Ditto — — — 85

15 *July*, 1802.—Circular relative to the Extra Allowance for Farriers — — — — 87

20 *Aug.* 1803—Ditto — — 88

23 *Aug.* 1803.—Circular relative to an Allowance for Saddle Water Decks, and Corn Sacks — — 89

25 *Feb.* 1784.—Regulation for Regimental Contingencies 91

29 Nov. 1785.—Circular relative to ditto — 93

Regulation for ditto, applying to Regiments on Foreign Stations 94

12 *Dec.* 1792.—Instructions relative to ditto, for Corps of Embodied Militia — — — 95

6 *Dec.* 1797.—Circular respecting an additional Allowance to Agents for Postage and Stationary — — 97

20 *June*, 1801.—Circular respecting the Hire of Waggons for Troops on a March — — — 98

8 *Nov.*

8 *Nov.* 1802.—Circular relative to Allowances for the Carriage of Regimental Baggage in the Cavalry — 99

8 *Nov.* 1802.—Ditto—in the Infantry — — 101

7 *April*, 1803.—Ditto—in the Militia — — 102

19 *April*, 1803.—Circular relative to additional Rates for the Hire of Carriages — — — 104

21 *July*, 1803.—Circular respecting the Rates of Allowance for the Carriage of the Baggage of Field Officers — 105

# SECTION III.

*System of Regimental Accompts.*

## PART I.
### *General Instructions.*

27 *June*, 1805.—Extract of the Act of 45th Geo. III. Cap. 58, relative to the Mode of issuing and accounting for Monies for Army Services — — — 109

10 *July*, 1760.—Circular relative to the Responsibility of Colonels for their Agents — — — 114

## PART II.

*Series of Instructions to Paymasters, &c. in regard to the Forms of the Accompts commencing from 25th December*, 1797.

18 *Nov.* 1797.—Circular relative to the Appointment of Paymasters in the Regular Cavalry and Infantry — 116

6 *Dec.* 1797.—Ditto——ditto — — 119

5 *Dec.* 1797.—Ditto—in the Militia — — 121

12 *Oct.* 1799.—Circular relative to the Military Duties to which Paymasters of Militia and Fencibles are liable — 123

19 *Jan.* 1798.—Instructions for Paymasters — 124

9 *Feb.* 1798.—Circular relative to the Appointment of Paymasters to Corps of Militia and Fencibles, consisting of fewer than three Companies — — — 133

## CONTENTS.

24 *Dec.* 1798.—Circular to Regimental Paymasters, relative to the Mode of balancing their Accompts — 135

29 *May*, 1801.—Circular to Colonels, adverting to the Duty of Agents in regard to Paymasters — — 136

11 *May*, 1801.—Additional Instructions and Regulations respecting the Conduct of Regimental Paymasters and others 138

30 *Nov.* 1802.—Explanatory Directions for the Information and Guidance of Paymasters and others, enclosed to Commanding Officers — — — — 144

5 *March*, 1803.—Continuation of Explanatory Directions for the Information of Paymasters and others — — 165

25 *Sept.* 1802.—General Orders on the Subject of the punctual Payment for Articles of subsistence furnished to Soldiers 168

6 *Nov.* 1805.—Table of Fees payable on Army and Regimental Commissions, signed by the King — — — 169

25 *April*, 1805.—Explanatory Directions for the Information of Paymasters and others.—Continued from *page* 167 — 170

24 *Sept.* 1806.—Circular relative to the Payment of the Bounty of Men who volunteer for extended Service — 183

22 *Aug.* 1806.—Explanatory Directions for the Information of Paymasters and others.—Continued from page 182 — 185

27 *Feb.* 1804.—Circular relative to an Arrangement for the regular and punctual Settlement of Regimental Accompts 195

28 *Feb.* 1804.—Circular to Agents, communicating ditto — 197

29 *Feb.* 1804.—Circular relative to the regular Transmission of Pay Lists, &c. — — — — 198

13 *Aug.* 1804.—General Orders respecting ditto — 199

31 *Dec.* 1804.—Circular to Commandants of Militia Corps, relative to the Adoption of Quarterly Pay Lists — 200

15 *March*, 1805. — Circular respecting the Transmission of ditto — — — — — 201

3 *Jan.* 1806.—Circular relative to a more compendious Form of Monthly Accompts, &c. — — — 202

27 *Jan.* 1806.—Circular to Agents, referring to ditto, and directing Monthly Abstracts to be made up as usual — 204

## CONTENTS.

29 *Jan.* 1806.—Circular to Colonels of Cavalry, and Regular and Fencible Infantry at home, relative to the Adoption of Quarterly Pay Lists — — — — 205

29 *Jan.* 1806.—Ditto to Corps on Foreign Stations — 206

14 *Feb.* 1806.—Circular to Paymasters of Regular and Fencible Corps at home, relative to the Preparation of new Monthly Accompts — — — — 207

14 *Feb.* 1806.—Ditto to Corps on Foreign Stations — 208

9 *April,* 1806.—Circular to Agents, enclosing the new Form of Quarterly Accompts — — — 209

19 *March,* 1806.—Circular to Commanding Officers, relative to the periods of transmitting the Quarterly Pay Lists 210

19 *March,* 1806.—Memorandum for the Guidance of Paymasters of Militia, in making up the New Quarterly Accompts — — — — 211

## PART III.

*Series of Instructions to Paymasters of Recruiting Districts.*

3 *Feb.* 1798.—Original Instructions to Paymasters of Recruiting Districts — — — — 213

31 *August,* 1798.—Circular containing further Instructions to Paymasters of Recruiting Districts — — 217

22 *April,* 1799.—Circular containing additional Instructions 219

13 *Nov.* 1800.—Circular relative to the Allowance for Postage and Stationary for ditto — — — 220

30 *June* 1806.—Circular to Inspecting Field Officers of Recruiting Districts, enclosing Forms of Quarterly Accompts 221

13 *June,* 1806.—Memorandum for the Guidance of Paymasters of Districts in making up the New Quarterly Accompts 222

## PART IV.

*Instructions to Paymasters of the additional Battalions formed for Limited Service.*

1 *October,* 1804.—Extract of a Circular, relative to the Appointment of Paymasters to Additional Battalions, raised under the Defence Act — — — 226

6 *Nov.*

6 *Nov.* 1804.—Circular relative to ditto — 227

26 *Nov.* 1804.—Circular relative to Paymasters of Additional Battalions formed from the Army of Reserve — 228

25 *April*, 1805.—Letter relative to the Succession of Paymasters of Second Battalions, to the Paymastership of First Battalions — — — — 229

5 *Feb.* 1805.—Extract of a Circular, relative to Charges for Men volunteering for extended Service, &c. — 230

30 *Dec.* 1805.—Circular relative to Charges for Recruits raised for First Battalions serving abroad — — 233

PART V.

*Miscellaneous Instructions relative to Accompts.*

20 *Feb.* 1799.—Regulation relative to the Effects and Credits of Soldiers who die — — — 235

23 *Dec.* 1800.—Circular respecting ditto — 238

6 *May*, 1799.—Circular establishing a Check on the Issues of Provisions, &c. on Foreign Stations — — 240

23 *October*, 1802.—Circular relative to the Transfer of Regiments to and from the Irish Establishment — 241

27 *October*, 1802.—Extract of a Letter to the Irish Government, enclosing ditto — — — 246

21 *May*, 1803.—Regulation for subsisting Men, belonging to Regiments in Ireland, and left behind in Great Britain 247

23 *Nov.* 1805.—Circular to Agents, relative to the mode of charging Fees — — — 251

—Declaration required to be made by Regimental Paymasters, previously to their Appointment — — 252

# SECTION IV.

*Regulations for the Government of certain distinct Departments, or Branches of Service.*

12 *July*, 1806.—Regulations relative to the Pay, &c. to be in future granted to Corps of Volunteer and Yeomanry Cavalry, formerly subject to the Regulations of June, 1803 — 255

## CONTENTS.

12 *July*, 1806.—Regulations relative to Corps of Volunteer and Yeomanry Cavalry, accepted subsequently to the 3d August, 1803 — — — — 259

12 *July*, 1806.—Abstract of the Regulations and Allowances applicable to Corps of Volunteer Artillery and Infantry, formerly subject to the Regulations of June, 1803 — 262

12 *July*, 1806.—Abstract of Regulations applicable to Corps of Volunteer Artillery and Infantry, accepted subsequently to the 3d August, 1803 — — — 272

25 *October*, 1806.—Regulations and Instructions for carrying on the Recruiting Service — — — 274

29 *Sept.* 1802.—General Orders respecting the Bounty of Recruits deserting before final Approval — 302

31 *May*, 1805.—Ditto relative to the Bounty of Boys, enlisted for the purpose of being trained as Drummers or Fifers 303

9 *June*, 1803.—Circular relative to an Allowance for certain Articles of Equipment for Cavalry Recruits — 304

13 *October*, 1806.—Instructions to Officers, and other Persons specially appointed to recruit for the Infantry — 306

—Form of Bond to be given by ditto — — 309

1 *Sept.* 1801.—Regulation respecting Deserters, comprehending the several points of their Apprehension, Inspection, Escort, &c. — — — — 311

—Form of Route for escorting a Deserter — — 316

14 *April*, 1806.—Circular relative to Charges for the Subsistence of Deserters on the march — — — 318

23 *Sept.* 1796.—Warrant for the gradual abolition of Regimental Chaplaincies, and making more effectual provision for the performance of religious duties throughout the army 319

30 *Sept.* 1796.—Extract of a Circular to the Colonels of Regular Regiments, respecting the Abolition of Regimental Chaplaincies — — — — 323

30 *Sept.* 1796.—Extract of a Circular to the Chaplains of Regiments, respecting ditto — — — 324

3 *Feb.* 1797.—Circular from the Chaplain General in explanation of the Warrant for abolishing Regimental Chaplaincies — — — — 325

9 *Oct.*

9 *Oct.* 1798.—Circular from the Chaplain General in further explanation of ditto — — — 326

9 *Oct.* 1798.—Ditto—to Militia Corps — — 329

8 *Aug.* 1806.—Extract from the Instructions given to the Agent for paying the allowances to Retired and Officiating Chaplains — — — 330

## SECTION V.

*Pay and Allowances of General and General Staff Officers.*

State of the Rates of Pay borne on the Establishment for certain Classes of General and General Staff Officers 339

State of the Rates of Forage Money allowed in time of War to Officers serving on the Home Staff — 341

11 *Aug.* 1803.—Extract of a Circular, relative to the Forage and Lodging Money of the Staff — — 342

13 *Dec.* 1804.—Regulation relative to the Contingent Accompts of General and other Staff Officers — 344

24 *Jan.* 1805.—Circular specifying the Articles of Stationary permitted to be charged in the Contingent Accompts of General and Staff Officers — — — 348

## SECTION VI.

*Medical Department of the Army, including the Veterinary Branch.*

12 *March,* 1798.—New Arrangement of the Medical Department of the Army — — 351

19 *March* 1801.—Letter to the Principal Officers of the Army Medical Department, relative to the term of Service, entitling Medical Staff Officers to be placed on Half Pay — 356

12 *Jan.* 1801.—Circular granting an Additional Allowance of one shilling a-day to Assistant Surgeons of Cavalry — 357

27 *June,* 1803.—Circular relative to the appointment and situation of Surgeons Mates in the Militia — 358

22 *May*

## CONTENTS.

22 *May*, 1804.—Regulation for encreasing the Advantages, and improving the Situation of Medical Officers of the Army 359

28 *May*, 1804.—Circular to Corps of Regular Cavalry, enclosing ditto, and pointing out the nett daily pay of Surgeons and Assistant Surgeons — — — 363

28 *May*, 1804.—Circular to Corps of Regular Infantry—ditto 364

28 *May*, 1804.—Circular to Corps of Militia—ditto — 366

14 *Nov.* 1805.—Circular to Corps of Infantry of the Line and Militia, relative to the Pay of Regimental Surgeons 368

State of the Rates of Forage Money allowed in time of War to Officers of the Medical Staff at Home —— 369

Ditto—Lodging Money—ditto —— —— 370

Ditto—of the Number of Horses allowed to be kept up by ditto 371

15 *Aug.* 1803.—Letter to the Surgeon General, stating the Allowances of Lodging Money, and for Travelling Expences, to Officers of the Medical Staff —— —— 372

24 *Nov,* 1803.—Letter to the Surgeon General relative to the Allowances for Travelling Expences to ditto —— 375

5 *June*, 1805.—Ditto—Lodging Money for ditto —— 376

9 *Dec.* 1805.—Ditto—relative to Recommendations for Travelling Expences for ditto —— —— —— 377

1 *Jan.* 1806.—Extract of the Regulations for Regimental Hospitals; with a General Order prefixed —— 378, 379

3 *Feb.* 1803.—General Orders relative to Leaves of Absence to Medical Officers —— —— —— 387

31 *Aug.* 1802.—General Orders relative to the Stoppage from Pay of Men in Regimental Hospitals —— 389

31 *March,* 1800.—Extract of the Instructions for General Hospitals; with a General Order prefixed —— 390, 391

30 *April,* 1800.—Regulations relative to Pay and other Charges for Soldiers in General Hospitals —— 397

20 *Jan.* 1801.—Letter to the Surgeon General relative to Contracts for Supplies for General Hospitals —— 399

8 *July,* 1801.—Letter to the principal Officers of the Army Medical Department relative to Boards of Inspection, &c. 401

12 *Sept.*

12 *Sept.* 1801.—Letter to the Surgeon General, containing Instructions relative to the Disposal of condemned Hospital Stores, &c. —— 404

23 *Feb.* 1804.—General Orders relative to the Stoppage from the Pay of Soldiers in General Hospitals —— 406

22 *Jan.* 1806.—General Orders relative to the Supply of Bread and Meat to Soldiers in Regimental Hospitals —— 407

12 *Nov.* 1805.—General Orders relative to the Stoppage from the Pay of Boys in General Hospitals —— 408

24 *July,* 1806.—General Orders relative to the Accommodation of the Sick of the Ordnance Department Abroad —— 409

24 *May,* 1796.—Circular relative to the Appointment of Veterinary Surgeons in the Cavalry —— 412

21 *Sept.* 1796.—Ditto — ditto —— 413

26 *May,* 1803.—Circular relative to the Supply of Horse Medicines, &c. —— 416

# SECTION VII.

## *Regimental Field Allowances.*

Memorandum relative to the Field Allowances of Regiments serving in Great Britain, or embarking therefrom for Foreign Service —— 421

20 *Sept.* 1803.—Extract of a Circular to Corps in Great Britain, relative to the Mode of foraging Bât Horses —— 424

Ditto, relative to the Ration of Forage for Bât Horses 426

SECTION

## SECTION VIII.

*Clothing and Appointments.*

15 *Aug.* 1781.—Warrant establishing certain Regulations with respect to Clothing and Regimental Appointments  429

22 *Apr.* 1803.—Regulation for the Clothing and Appointments of the Army  433

8 *Aug.* 1803.—Regulation for the Clothing of the Embodied Militia  459

12 *Jan.* 1804.—Circular relative to the Contribution to be made out of the Off-reckonings towards the Cost of Great Coats for Serjeants of Infantry  466

12 *Jan.* 1804.—Circular respecting a new Rate of Clothing Allowance for Serjeants of Militia  467

11 *Feb.* 1805.—Letter explaining how Paymasters' Clerks and Armourers, in the Militia, are to be clothed  468

15 *April,* 1805.—Warrant for altering the Rate of Compensation to Infantry Soldiers, in lieu of Clothing  469

18 *April,* 1805.—Circular to Corps of Cavalry and Infantry enclosing an amended Copy of the Clothing Regulations  470

18 *April,* 1805.—Ditto—to the Militia, enclosing ditto  471

24 *May,* 1805.—Circular relative to the Provision of Great Coats for Regiments of Infantry  472

28 *Nov.* 1805.—Regulation for the Supply of Bear Skin Caps to the Grenadiers of Militia Corps  473

19 *Mar.* 1806.—Regulation for the Inspection of Great Coats  474

5 *May,* 1806.—Circular relative to ditto  476

Form of Certificate when Great Coats are required to be replaced  477

11 *Sept.* 1806.—Circular relative to the Clothing to be taken with Men transferred from one Corps to another  478

2 *Oct.* 1806.—Ditto—Caps—ditto  479

20 *Oct.* 1806.—Circular respecting the Discontinuance of lacquered Felt Caps  480

27 *Oct.* 1806.—Circular relative to the Distinction to be made in the Great Coats of Non-commissioned Officers — 481

## SECTION IX.

*Miscellaneous Orders.*

6 *April*, 1802.—Circular relative to Allowances to Deputy Judge Advocates — 485

11 *July*, 1798.—Rules to be observed by the Medical Department in granting Certificates of Expences for the Cure of Wounds — 487

Allowances and Regulations in Cases where Officers lose an Eye, or a Limb; or are killed in Action — 489

1 *March*, 1796.—Regulation for the Indemnification of Losses of Baggage, &c. sustained on actual Service — 490

8 *May*, 1797.—Circular to Generals commanding Abroad, relative to ditto — 493

15 *July*, 1805.—Circular to Colonels, relative to Indemnification for Appointments lost on Service — 494

1 *July*, 1805.—General Orders respecting Indemnification for the Loss of Appointments belonging to Glandered Horses 496

1 *May*, 1799.—Circular enclosing Regulations to be observed relative to the Mode of obtaining Issues of Arms — 497

25 *June*, 1806.—Extract of His Majesty's Warrant containing Instructions for the Paymaster of Pensions to the Widows of Officers of the Land Forces and Marines — 500

Forms of Certificates, &c. required for placing a Widow on the Pension, and for receiving the same — 503 to 505

Rates of Pensions for certain Widows of Officers, as encreased from 25th June, 1806 — 506

19 *April*, 1800.—Letter from the Adjutant General, relative to Officers absent without Leave — 507

24 *July*, 1805.—Circular relative to the Pay of Gentlemen first obtaining Commissions — 508

7 *Aug.*

## CONTENTS.

*7 Aug.* 1800.—Circular relative to Leaves of Absence for Paymasters of Regiments, when stationed abroad — 509

*9 Sept.* 1805.—Circular relative to the Advance of Pay to Officers embarking for Service — — 510

*6 June,* 1806.—Circular respecting the Pay of ditto 511

*31 Oct.* 1806.—Circular relative to the Nature of the Services to be defrayed by Deputy Paymasters General on Foreign Stations — — — 512

*29 Oct.* 1800.—General Orders respecting the Number of Women to accompany Regiments ordered abroad, &c. 513

*6 June,* 1805.—Circular relative to the Mode of defraying the Expence of the Hire of Ground for Encampments 514

*31 July,* 1805.—Circular containing further Information respecting ditto — — — 516

*13 April,* 1800.—General Orders relative to Men sleeping out of Quarters — — — 517

*4 Sept.* 1801.—General Orders containing further Instructions relative to ditto — — — 518

*14 May,* 1805.—Circular relative to the Accommodation of Officers proceeding to India, on Board the Company's Ships 519

*1 Aug.* 1806.—Regulations under which Soldiers are allowed to send and receive Letters at a low Rate of Postage 522

*12 Sept.* 1804.—Circular relative to the Mode of addressing Applications to the War Office — — 524

# APPENDIX.

*23 Sept.* 1806.—Circular relative to the Description of previous Service entitling Soldiers to additional Allowances, &c. 529

*7 Oct.* 1806.—Warrant establishing certain Orders and Regulations for improving the Condition of Soldiers — 534

*24 June,* 1805.—Circular relative to allowing an Augmentation or Diminution of the Feed of Cavalry Horses, in certain cases 540

*31 Oct.* 1805.—Circular referring to ditto, and enclosing the Copy of a Clause inserted in the new Contracts for the Supply of Forage to Cavalry in Barracks — 544

*31 Dec.*

## CONTENTS.

31 *Dec.* 1806.—Circular enclosing Forms of Returns, &c. for stating the Length of Service of Soldiers — 546

25 *June*, 1803.—Regulations to be observed in supplying the Troops with the Articles furnished under the Direction of the Commissary General, in Home Encampments — 551

5 *Aug.* 1803.—General Orders relative to Soldiers acting as Musicians — 557

8 *Dec.* 1806.—General Orders relative to the Mode of conducting the Recruiting Service of Second Battalions — 558

14 *Jan.* 1807—General Orders relative to the Enlistment of Lads — 560

22 *Aug.* 1806.—Circular respecting an Alteration in the Mode of receiving and communicating His Majesty's Decisions on the Proceedings of Courts Martial — 561

15 *Dec.* 1806.—Letter relative to the Supply of Forge Carts 562

6 *April*, 1803.—Circular respecting the Transmission of Adjutants' Rolls from Regiments in India, &c. — 564

20 *Sept.* 1803.—Extract of a Letter relative to an Allowance to the Inhabitants of North Britain, upon whom Soldiers may be quartered — 565

Memorandum stating some Peculiarities in the Situation of Soldiers in North Britain — 566

24 *July*, 1799.—Circular to Generals commanding on Foreign Stations requiring the Transmission of Half Yearly Returns of the Staff — 567

7 *Feb.* 1807.—Circular relative to the Allowances to Field Officers employed in superintending the Recruiting Service of Second Battalions — 569

1 *Feb.* 1807.—General Orders substituting new Regulations for those formerly in force relative to the Incidental Expences of Officers employed on the Recruiting Service — 571

21 *Feb.* 1807.—Circular relative to the General Registry of the Army being kept in the War Office — 577

3 *March*, 1807.—Circular limiting the Period within which Agents are to furnish the Explanations required, on the Examination of their Accounts — 578

24 *Feb.* 1800.—Circular to Agents, relative to the Repayment of Advances made by Persons in Public Trust. — 579

1 *August,* 1800.—General Orders relative to the Accompts of Soldiers, who are sent to General Hospitals; or who become Prisoners of War — — — 580

23 *June,* 1801.—Memorandum pointing out the Authority upon which Payments for Hospital Contingencies are to be made — — — 581

18 *August,* 1803.—Circular to Agents relative to the Mode of crediting the Allowances issued on account of Great Coats; and of Saddle Water Decks and Corn Sacks — 582

5 *March,* 1804.—Circular relative to the regular Transmission of District Pay Lists — — 583

19 *February,* 1805.—Extract of a Circular to Commanding Officers of Militia Corps, requiring a Monthly Distribution of the Men in support of the Charges for Innkeepers Allowance 584

14 *Jan.* 1806.—Circular to Paymasters of Militia Corps, relative to the Adoption of a New Form of Monthly Accompt, &c. 585

19 *Feb.* 1807.—Circular relative to the Mode of issuing the Half Pay of Officers employed on the Extraordinary Recruiting for the Infantry — — 586

13 *May,* 1801.—General Orders issued to the Troops in North Britain, relative to the Extra Price of Meat, Bread, Oatmeal, Corn, &c. — — 587

28 *Sept.* 1801.—Circular to Agents pointing out the Forms of Accompts to be rendered by them — 588

17 *December,* 1802.—Circular relative to the Issues of Pay, and Contingencies for the Recruiting Staff in Great Britain 591

31 *March,* 1804.—Circular respecting the Allowance to be granted to Men enrolled for Militia Corps, and rejected at Head Quarters; to carry them back to their homes — 592

18 *January,* 1805.—Circular enclosing a Memorandum respecting the New Forms of Monthly Accompts for Militia Corps — — — 593

12 *August,* 1805.—General Orders relative to Officers of Second Battalions becoming, from Promotion or other Causes, effective in the First Battalions of their Regiments — 595

CONTENTS. xvii

30 *October*, 1805.—General Orders, relative to the Recruiting for First Battalions on Foreign Service; in Cases where the Second Battalions are for limited Service — 597

17 *December*, 1805.—Circular from the Adjutant-General, relative to the Provision of a New Description of Pioneers' Accoutrements — — — 599

10 *February*, 1806.—General Orders relative to Men transferred from Regular Regiments to Veteran Battalions — 601

1 *July* 1806.—General Orders requiring Quarterly Returns to be made of the Names of Officers whose Pay has been suspended, in consequence of their having been absent without Leave 603

13 *March*, 1794.—Circular relative to Advertising Deserters in the Hue and Cry — — 605

9 *July*, 1805.—Circular from the Military Secretary to the Commander in Chief, relative to the Stoppages to be made from the Pay of Soldiers in General Hospitals abroad — 607

16 *March*, 1807.—Circular relative to the Allowance of Pay, and Marching Money, to be granted to Soldiers discharged from the Veteran Battalions — — 608

24 *March*, 1807.—Circular to Paymasters of Recruiting Districts, relative to Charges for Stamps on Bills drawn upon Agents, to the Mode of crediting the Effects and Credits of Soldiers of Recruiting Parties, &c. — — 609

Additional Notes — — 611

Index — — — 615

Errata — — — 641

# SECTION I.

# PAY

OF THE

# OFFICERS AND MEN

OF THE

SEVERAL CORPS OF THE ARMY;

INCLUDING

*THE ALLOWANCES*

ISSUED IN THE SHAPE OF PAY.

# COLLECTION

OF

# *REGULATIONS, &c.*

---

*Circular Letter from the Secretary at War, to the Colonels of Dragoon Guards, Dragoons, and Infantry of the Line, and to the Colonels or Commandants of Fencible Cavalry, Militia, and Fencible Infantry, relative to exonerating the Field Officers and Captains from general Responsibility for the future Accompts of their respective Corps; and for establishing a new Daily Rate of Pay for the said Officers; abolishing the Distinction between Subsistence and Arrears.*

*War Office, 25th Jan.* 1798.

SIR,

I HAVE received His Majesty's commands to acquaint you, that in those corps wherein the new system regarding Paymasters has been established, the Field Officers and Captains will not be held generally responsible, as such, for the future regimental accompts of their respective corps.

The establishment of the said system has enabled His Majesty, with safety to the public, to shew a further instance of his royal consideration for the Field Officers and Captains above mentioned, by ordering that their whole pay shall in future be issued monthly, instead of being divided

vided into subsistence and arrears; and be subject only to the usual deductions on account of poundage, hospital, and agency.

You will be pleased to take the earliest opportunity of making known these marks of His Majesty's gracious attention to the Field Officers and Captains of the regiment under your command; and of acquainting them with the respective rates of their pay as it is hereafter to be issued by His Majesty's order, according to the annexed state, *in which you will observe that the Surgeon is also comprehended:*[*] these daily rates have been calculated upon the total amount per annum of the sums which the officers have heretofore received under the denomination of subsistence and nett arrears; excluding minute fractions, which would have greatly tended to complicate the general accompts of the regiments, as well as the particular accompts of the officers themselves.

I am to add, that in the issue of pay to be made by the pay-office on the 24th of next month, the difference between the old and new rates for the two preceding months, (viz. from the 25th of December, 1797, to the 23d of February, 1798,) will be included.

    I have the honor to be,
      Sir,
       Your most obedient humble servant,
         W. WINDHAM.

Colonel of the
Regiment of

---

[*] The words in *italics* were omitted in the letters to the Fencibles.

## RATES OF PAY

To be issued to the Field Officers and Captains of the Dragoon Guards; Dragoons; Fencible Cavalry; Infantry of the Line; Militia; and Fencible Infantry; and to the Surgeons of Dragoon Guards, Dragoons, and Infantry of the Line: commencing from the 25th December, 1797.

| Dragoon Guards, Dragoons, and Fencible Cavalry. | Per Diem. £. s. d. | For 365 Days. £. s. d. |
|---|---|---|
| Colonel | 1 12 10 | 599 4 2 |
| Lieutenant Colonel | 1 3 0 | 419 15 0 |
| Major | 0 19 3 | 351 6 3 |
| Captain | 0 14 7 | 266 2 11 |
| *Surgeon of Dragoon Guards, and Dragoons | 0 11 4 | 206 16 8 |

| Infantry of the Line, Militia, and Fencible Infantry. | | |
|---|---|---|
| Colonel | 1 2 6 | 410 12 6 |
| [Lieutenant Colonel | 0 15 11 | 290 9 7 |
| Major | 0 14 1 | 257 0 5 |
| Captain | 0 9 5 | 171 17 1 |
| *Surgeon of the Line | 0 9 5 | 171 17 1] |

*War Office*, 25th *January*, 1798.

By His Majesty's command.

W. WINDHAM.

---

\* The pay of Regimental Surgeons has been altered by His Majesty's subsequent regulation, bearing date the 22d May, 1804. See Section VI.
For the New Rates of Pay and Allowances to Officers of Infantry commencing 25th June, 1806, see page 37.

*Circular Letter from the Secretary at War to the Colonels of Dragoon Guards, Dragoons, and Fencible Cavalry, relative to issuing the Pay of Subalterns, &c.*

War Office, 27th June, 1797.

SIR,

THE King having taken into consideration the difficulties to which the Subalterns of the line have been subjected, by not receiving their Arrears for a length of time after the same have become due; and being desirous of improving their situation, as far as may be consistent with the circumstances of the country; His Majesty is graciously pleased to direct, that the whole Pay borne on the establishment shall in future be issued, at the same times and in the same manner as Subsistence is now issued, to each Lieutenant, Cornet, Ensign, Adjutant, and Quarter-master of Dragoon Guards, Dragoons, Marching Regiments of Foot, Embodied Militia, Fencible Infantry, and Invalids: and, as a further instance of His Majesty's attention, it is his Royal Pleasure, that the said Pay be issued free from the deductions heretofore made therefrom, on account of poundage, hospital, and agency.

You will be pleased to take the earliest means of making known these marks of His Majesty's gracious consideration to the Officers of the Regiment under your command.

I have the honour to be,

SIR,

Your most obedient humble servant,

W. WINDHAM.

Colonel of the
Regiment of

*Circular Letter from the Secretary at War to the Colonels of Marching Regiments of Foot, and Commandants of Embodied Militia, Fencible Infantry, and Invalids, relative to issuing the Pay of Subalterns, &c. and granting an Allowance in addition thereto.*

War Office, 27th June, 1797.

SIR,

THE King having taken into consideration the difficulties to which the Subalterns of the line have been subjected, by not receiving their Arrears for a length of time after the same have become due; and being desirous of improving their situation, as far as may be consistent with the circumstances of the country; His Majesty is graciously pleased to direct, that the whole Pay borne on the establishment shall in future be issued, at the same times and in the same manner as Subsistence is now issued, to each Lieutenant, Cornet, Ensign, Adjutant, and Quartermaster, of Dragoon Guards, Dragoons, Fencible Cavalry, Marching Regiments of Foot, Embodied Militia, Fencible Infantry, and Invalids: and as a further instance of His Majesty's attention, it is His Royal Pleasure that the said Pay be issued free from the deductions heretofore made therefrom, on account of poundage, hospital, and agency.

His Majesty having also adverted to the low rate of pay assigned to the Subalterns of Infantry, and which, notwithstanding the advantages above stated, would still be inadequate to the unavoidable expences of their respective situations, is graciously pleased to order, that, from the 25th of this month, an Allowance of one shilling *per diem*, shall be made to each Lieutenant, Ensign, *Adjutant*,* and Quarter master of his Marching Regiments of Infantry, Embodied Militia, Fencible Infantry, and Invalids, not holding another commission.

It is at the same time to be clearly understood, that the additional Allowance is not to give the Officers any title whatsoever to an increase of half pay, in case of reduction.

---

\* The above additional allowance of 1s. a day to *Adjutants* ceased of course when the pay of adjutants was augmented in the year 1802.

You will be pleafed to take the earlieft means of making known thefe marks of His Majefty's gracious confideration to the Officers of the Regiment under your command.

   I have the honour to be,

     SIR,

      Your moft obedient humble fervant,

        W. WINDHAM.

Colonel of the
Regiment of

*Extract from a Circular to the Regiments of Dragoon Guards and Dragoons, dated 10th June, 1802, stating the future Pay and Footing of Adjutants in the said Corps.*

" I AM further to acquaint you, His Majesty has been pleased to direct, that from the 25th instant the Pay annexed to the appointment of Adjutant, shall, in the Dragoon Guards and Dragoons, be encreased to 10s. a day: Adjutants, who now hold other Commissions, are, from the above date to cease to receive Pay for the same; but are to be borne as Supernumerary in the rank they possess, retaining their seniority in their respective corps, and their claim to promotion by virtue thereof. To such Adjutants as do not at present hold other appointments, the rank of Cornet (without pay) is to be given, taking date from the 25th instant; and they are to rise according to seniority, in their respective corps and in the Army."

*Instructions concerning the Pay and Footing of Adjutants in the Infantry, extracted from the Secretary at War's Circular relative to the Reduction which took place in the Regimental Establishments from the 25th June, 1802.*

"I AM further to acquaint you, His Majesty has been pleased to direct, that from the commencement of the new Establishment, the Pay annexed to the appointment of Adjutant, shall, in the Infantry, be encreased to [eight shillings a day]* the allowance of a Shilling a day being discontinued: and that from the said period Adjutants who now hold other regimental commissions, are to cease to receive Pay for the same, but are to be borne as supernumerary in the rank they possess, retaining their seniority in their respective Corps, and their claim to promotion by virtue thereof: to such Adjutants as do not at present hold other Appointments, the Rank of Ensign (without Pay) is to be given, taking date from the 25th instant; and they are to rise according to seniority in their respective Corps and in the Army."

---

* Further encreased by an allowance of 6d. a day, from 25th June, 1806. See page 37.

*Warrant*

*Regimental Pay and Daily Allowances.* 11

*Warrant for increasing and regulating the Pay and Allowance of Non-commissioned Officers and Private Men, of Corps of Cavalry, serving at Home, dated 25th May, 1797.*

## GEORGE R.

WHEREAS WE, having been pleased to take into OUR consideration the various pecuniary Allowances, as well permanent, as incidental, or temporary, which have been granted to the private soldiers of OUR Regiments of *Dragoon Guards, Dragoons,* and *Fencible Cavalry,* serving at home, viz. the consolidated allowance, the allowance for escorting deserters, and of the extra price of bread and meat; and finding, not only that the application of the same is from sundry causes intricate and difficult, but also that the amount thereof is insufficient fully to answer the purposes for which they were given; have thought fit to substitute, in lieu of the said Allowances, one fixed Allowance at a daily rate; and to increase the same by a nett addition of *two pence per diem* to each soldier:

WE do therefore most graciously signify OUR WILL AND PLEASURE, that, in addition to the Pay of *eight pence per diem,* now borne on the establishment, the further sum of *seven pence per diem,* in lieu of the said several Allowances, shall be borne thereon, making the Pay and fixed Allowance of a Private Man belonging to OUR Corps of *Dragoon Guards, Dragoons,* and *Fencible Cavalry,* serving at home, equal, together, to *one shilling* and *three pence per diem:* out of which a sum not exceeding [*four shillings* and *sixpence* a week]* (unless he shall himself choose to appropriate a further part of his Pay and Allowance for this purpose) shall be applied to the expence of his mess, including vegetables, &c.; a sum not exceeding *two shillings* and *seven pence halfpenny* a week shall be retained for necessaries, to be accounted for every two months; and the remainder, being *one shilling* and *seven pence halfpenny,* shall be paid weekly to himself, subject to the accustomed deduction for

---

* Altered to *five shillings and one penny* a week by His Majesty's Warrant, granting an allowance in lieu of small beer, bearing date the 17th March, 1800. See Section II.

washing

washing and for articles to clean his clothing and appointments.

[To prevent any doubts respecting the species and quantity of necessaries to be provided by stoppage from the pay of the soldiers of OUR Regiments of *Dragoon Guards*, *Dragoons*, and *Fencible Cavalry*, WE are pleased to order an exact list of them to be annexed to this OUR Warrant.

If in the course of the year any of the articles specified in the said list should not be wanted for the soldier's use, the money stopped for such articles shall be repaid to him: but if any of those, which have been furnished to him, should be lost or destroyed, he shall be liable to a further stoppage to replace them.]\*

OUR WILL AND PLEASURE also is, that, by a similar alteration and increase of Allowance, the daily Pay and fixed Allowance of a *Trumpeter* in OUR said Corps shall be *one shilling* and *sevenpence*, whereof *two pence* is a nett addition: of a *Corporal*, *one shilling* and *sevenpence halfpenny*, whereof *twopence halfpenny* is a nett addition: and of a *Serjeant*, *two shillings* and *two-pence*, whereof *three-pence* is a nett addition.

From the 25th of this instant May inclusive, when the allowance before-mentioned commences, the soldier is to defray the whole expence of his bread and meat; with this exception, that if meat of the quality proper to be provided for him should exceed the price of *sixpence* a pound, or if bread of the household quality should exceed the price of *three halfpence* a pound, such excess of price shall be allowed to him upon a quantity not exceeding three quarters of a pound of meat, and one pound of bread a day, for each man.

[And whereas of late an allowance has been granted to publicans for small beer and sundry other articles furnished to OUR troops, at the rate of *two-pence per diem* for each man quartered on them, WE are hereby pleased to direct, that when any soldier, having orders to be quartered, shall be permitted by his commanding officer to find his own lodging, and shall provide himself with the several articles referred to above, he shall receive the said regulated allowance, which would otherwise have been paid to the publican.

In barracks, the daily supply of small beer will be made as before.

In camps, where small beer is not provided, but where six pounds of bread are furnished to the soldier every four days, he paying only *five pence* towards the expence thereof, OUR WILL AND PLEASURE is, that an allow-

---

\* Later orders in regard to the necessaries to be provided by stoppage from the pay of soldiers are contained in His Majesty's Regulation for the Clothing of the Army, bearing date the 22d April, 1803. See Section VIII.

## Regimental Pay and Daily Allowances. 13

allowance of *five pence farthing* be made to him weekly, as an equivalent for the difference.]*

And Whereas WE think it reasonable to grant to other descriptions of OUR troops a similar increased Allowance, OUR WILL AND PLEASURE is, that the following rates of Pay and fixed Allowance do take place, from the date before-mentioned, in OUR two Regiments of *Life Guards*, and OUR Royal Regiment of *Horse Guards*, viz.

In OUR Regiments of *Life Guards*;    s.   d.
    Of a Private Man   -  -   1  $11\frac{1}{4}$
    Of a Corporal   -  -  -   2  $6\frac{1}{4}$

In OUR Royal Regiment of *Horse Guards*;
    Of a Private Man   -  -   1  $8\frac{1}{4}$
    Of a Trumpeter   -  -   1  $8\frac{1}{4}$
    Of a Corporal   -  -  -   2  $3\frac{1}{4}$

Given at OUR COURT at ST. JAMES's, this 25th day of May 1797, in the 37th year of OUR reign.

BY HIS MAJESTY'S COMMAND.

W. WINDHAM.

---

* Altered by the Regulation of 17th March, 1800. See Section II

[List of Necessaries to be provided by Stoppage from the Pay of the Soldiers of Regiments of Dragoon Guards, Dragoons, and Fencible Cavalry, referred to in the preceding Warrant.

Per annum.

| | l. | s. | d. |
|---|---|---|---|
| For one pair of leather, or two pair of shag breeches, in two years, value 1l. 6s. | 0 | 13 | 0 |
| For stable jacket and trowsers, and foraging cap, in two years 15s. | 0 | 7 | 6 |
| Feeding bag, 1s. Watering bridle, 3s. 6d. Collar and log, 6d. in six years, 5s. | 0 | 0 | 10 |
| Three shirts and turnover, 6s. 6d. each | 0 | 19 | 6 |
| One stock and clasps | 0 | 1 | 0 |
| Two pair of worsted stockings at 2s. 5d. each pair | 0 | 4 | 10 |
| Two pair of thread or cotton ditto, 3s. each; and two pair of short gaiters, 1s. 8d. each: or two pair of long black gaiters, 4s. 8d. each pair | 0 | 9 | 4 |
| Two pair of shoes, 7s. each pair | 0 | 14 | 0 |
| Mending shoes | 0 | 3 | 0 |
| Two shoe brushes, 6d. each | 0 | 1 | 0 |
| Powder, pomatum, soap, combs and razors | 0 | 12 | 0 |
| Knee buckles | 0 | 0 | 6 |
| Clothes brush, worm and picker, emery, oil, pipe clay, whiting and blacking | 0 | 16 | 9 |
| Washing and mending | 1 | 6 | 0 |
| Mane comb, 6d. Curry comb and brush 3s. 8d. in two years | 0 | 2 | 1 |
| Tailor's bill | 0 | 2 | 9½ |
| £. | 6 | 14 | 1¼ |

The actual expenditure for horse cloths and surcingles, not exceeding *one shilling* and *eight pence per annum* for each man, will be defrayed by the public, as expressed in a former warrant.]*

---

* N. B. This list is superseded by the schedule annexed to the Clothing Regulation of 22d April, 1803. See Section VIII. It is reprinted here merely for the sake of giving information as to former practice, and the *probable* cost of the several articles of necessaries.

*Warrant*

## Regimental Pay and Daily Allowances. 15

*Warrant for increasing and regulating the Pay and Allowance of Non-commissioned Officers and Private Men, of Corps of Infantry serving at Home, dated 25th May, 1797.*

## GEORGE R.

WHEREAS we, having been pleased to take into our consideration the various pecuniary allowances, as well permanent, as incidental, or temporary, which have been granted to the *Private Soldiers* of our *Marching Regiments of Foot*, and of our *Corps of Embodied Militia* and *Fencible Infantry*, as also of our *Foot Guards*, serving at Home, viz. the consolidated allowance, the allowance for escorting deserters, and of the extra price of bread and meat; and finding, not only that the application of the same is from sundry causes intricate and difficult, but also that the amount thereof is insufficient fully to answer the purposes, for which they were given; have thought fit to substitute, in lieu of the said allowances, one fixed allowance at a daily rate; and to increase the same by a nett addition of *two pence per diem* to each soldier:

We do therefore hereby most graciously signify our will and pleasure, that, in addition to the pay of *sixpence per diem* now borne on the establishment, the further sum of *sixpence per diem*, in lieu of the said several allowances, shall be borne thereon, making the Pay and fixed allowance of a *Foot Soldier* belonging to our *Marching Regiments, Embodied Militia*, and *Fencible Infantry*, serving at home, equal, together, to *one shilling per diem:* out of which a sum not exceeding [*four shillings* a week]* (unless he shall himself choose to appropriate a further part of his Pay and Allowance for this purpose) shall be applied to the expence of his mess, including vegetables, &c.:—a sum not exceeding *one shilling* and *sixpence* a week shall be retained for necessaries, to be accounted for monthly, as required by our Regulation of 1st September, 1795:† and the remainder,

being

---

\* Altered to *four shillings and seven pence* a week by the Regulation of 17th March, 1800. See Section II.

† Extract from the Regulation of 1st September, 1795, above referred to:

" Each Serjeant, Corporal, Drummer, Fifer, and Private, of Infantry, shall be most exactly and regularly accounted with respectively for the

whole

being *one shilling* and *sixpence*, shall be paid weekly to himself, subject to the accustomed deduction for washing and for articles to clean his clothing and appointments.

[To prevent any doubts respecting the species and quantity of necessaries to be provided by stoppage from the Pay of the Soldiers of our Regiments of *Foot*, *Militia*, and *Fencible Infantry*, we are pleased to order an exact list of them to be annexed to this our warrant.

If in the course of the year any of the articles specified in the said list should not be wanted for the Soldier's use, the money stopped for such articles shall be repaid to him: but if any of those which have been furnished to him, should be lost or destroyed, he shall be liable to a further stoppage to replace them.]\*

Our will and pleasure also is, that, by a similar alteration and increase of allowance, the daily pay and fixed allowance of a *Drummer*, in our said corps, shall be *thirteen pence three farthings*, whereof *twopence* is a nett addition: of a *Corporal*, *fourteen pence farthing*, whereof *twopence halfpenny* is a nett addition: and of a *Serjeant*, *eighteen pence three farthings*, whereof *threepence* is a nett addition.

In like manner, our will and pleasure is, that, in addition to the pay of the Private Men, Drummers, and Non-commissioned Officers, of our *Regiments of Foot Guards*, serving at home, and in lieu of the several allowances heretofore granted, there be borne on the establishment a fixed daily allowance for each,

---

whole of their said consolidated allowance, on the 24th day of each month; and shall, without exception, have the money accruing thereby paid into their hands: especial care being taken at the same time that they are provided with necessaries according to the schedule annexed.

Each soldier shall be accounted with for the difference or balance of his Pay, and shall receive the same, at the times and under the conditions before prescribed for his receipt of the allowance.

It shall be certified on the back of the monthly returns, that these regulations have been strictly complied with at the time and in the manner specified.

If it shall appear that in any corps these Regulations have not been complied with, as hereby directed and ordered, the Commanding Officer of such corps shall be reported to us, and made to answer for his disobedience of our orders."

The like orders apply to the Cavalry; except that the settlement is required to be made only once in two months.

\* Later orders in regard to the necessaries to be provided by stoppage from the pay of Soldiers are contained in the Clothing Regulations of 22d April, 1803. See Section VIII.

## Regimental Pay and Daily Allowances. 17

including the fame nett additions of twopence, twopence half-penny, and threepence, to the refpective ranks, viz.

|   |   | d. |
|---|---|---|
| For a Private Man | - - | 6 |
| For a Drummer | - - | 5¾ |
| For a Corporal | - - | 6¼ |
| For a Serjeant | - - | 6¾ |

fo that the daily pay and fixed allowance together fhall be

|   |   | s. | d. |
|---|---|---|---|
| Of a Private Man | - - | 1 | 1 |
| Of a Drummer | - - | 1 | 2¼ |
| Of a Corporal | - - | 1 | 4¾ |
| Of a Serjeant | - - | 1 | 10¾ |

And out of the daily pay and fixed allowance of one fhilling and one penny to the Private Soldier in our *regiments of Foot Guards*, a fum not exceeding one fhilling and one penny a week fhall be retained for neceffaries, to be accounted for monthly, as required by our regulation of 1ft September, 1795.*

From the 25th of this inftant May inclufive, when the allowance before-mentioned commences, the Soldier is to defray the whole expence of his bread and meat; with this exception, that if meat, of the quality proper to be provided for him, fhould exceed the price of fixpence a pound, or if bread, of the houfehold quality, fhould exceed the price of three-halfpence a pound, fuch excefs of price fhall be allowed to him upon a quantity not exceeding three quarters of a pound of meat, and one pound of bread a day, for each man.

[And whereas of late an allowance has been granted to Publicans for fmall beer and fundry other articles furnifhed to our troops, at the rate of *twopence per diem* for each man quartered on them, we are pleafed hereby to direct, that when any Soldier, having orders to be quartered, fhall be permitted by his Commanding Officer to find his own lodging, and fhall provide himfelf with the feveral articles referred to above, he fhall receive the faid regulated allowance, which would otherwife have been paid to the publican.

In barracks, the daily fupply of fmall beer will be made as before.

In camps, where fmall beer is not provided, but where fix pounds of bread are furnifhed to the Soldier every four days, he paying only *fivepence* towards the expence thereof, our will and pleafure is, that an allowance of

---

* See the note, page 15.

*fivepence farthing* be made to him weekly, as an equivalent for the difference.]*

And whereas we think it reasonable to grant to our corps of invalids a similar increased allowance, our will and pleasure is, that the following rates of pay and fixed allowance do take place therein from the date before-mentioned.

|  | | | s. | d. |
|---|---|---|---|---|
| Of a Private Man | - | - | 0 | 11¼ |
| Of a Drummer | - | - | 1 | 1¼ |
| Of a Corporal | - | - | 1 | 1¾ |
| Of a Serjeant | - | - | 1 | 6¼ |

Given at our Court at St. James's, this 25th day of May, 1797, in the 37th year of our reign.

By His Majesty's Command,

W. WINDHAM.

---

* Altered by the Regulation of 17th March, 1800. See Section II.

# Regimental Pay and Daily Allowances. 19

[List of Necessaries to be provided by stoppage from the Pay of the Soldiers of Regiments of Foot, Militia, and Fencible Infantry, referred to in the preceding Warrant.

|  | Per Annum. |  |  |
|---|---|---|---|
|  | *l.* | *s.* | *d.* |
| For two pair of black cloth gaiters, at 4s. per pair | 0 | 8 | 0 |
| For a second pair of breeches | 0 | 6 | 6 |
| One hair leather | 0 | 0 | 2½ |
| Two pair of shoes at 6s. per pair | 0 | 12 | 0 |
| Mending ditto | 0 | 4 | 0 |
| One pair of stockings, or two pair of socks | 0 | 1 | 6 |
| Two shirts, at 5s. 6d. per shirt | 0 | 11 | 0 |
| A foraging cap | 0 | 1 | 3 |
| A knapsack, at 6s. once in six years | 0 | 1 | 0 |
| Pipe clay and whiting | 0 | 4 | 4 |
| A clothes brush, at 1s. once in two years | 0 | 0 | 6 |
| Three shoe brushes, at 5d. per brush | 0 | 1 | 3 |
| Black ball | 0 | 2 | 0 |
| Worsted mitts | 0 | 0 | 9 |
| A powdering bag and puff, once every three years, at 1s. 6d. | 0 | 0 | 6 |
| Two combs at 6d. per comb | 0 | 1 | 0 |
| Grease and powder for the hair | 0 | 3 | 0 |
| Washing, at 4d. per week | 0 | 17 | 4 |
|  | £ 3 | 16 | 1½ |

The charge for watch coats at the rate of *one shilling per annum* each man, the actual expenditure for altering clothing, not exceeding *two shillings* and *sixpence per annum* each man, and for articles to clean the arms, not exceeding *two shillings* and *ninepence per annum* each man, will be defrayed by the public, as expressed in former warrants.]*

---

* This list is superseded by the schedule annexed to the Clothing Regulation of 22d April, 1803: see Section VIII. It is reprinted here merely for the sake of giving information as to former practice, and the *probable* cost of the several articles of necessaries.

*Warrant*

*Warrant for increasing and regulating the Pay and Allowance of Non-commissioned Officers and Private Men of Corps of Cavalry and Infantry, serving out of Great Britain, dated 5th July, 1797.*

## GEORGE R.

WHEREAS we, having taken into our consideration the various pecuniary allowances, as well permanent as incidental or temporary, which had been granted to our troops at home, have thought fit to substitute, in lieu of the said allowances, one fixed allowance at a daily rate, and to increase the same by a nett addition of *three-pence per diem* to each serjeant, *two-pence halfpenny per diem* to each corporal, and *two-pence per diem* to each trumpeter, drummer, fifer, and private man: and whereas we are graciously pleased to extend the said regulation, and to grant the like nett additions to the pay of our forces serving out of Great Britain: our will and pleasure therefore is, that from the 25th day of May last, the daily pay and fixed allowance of our non-commissioned officers and soldiers wheresoever serving abroad, or on board ship, shall be borne on the establishment as follows:

### DRAGOONS.

|                  | s. | d.             |
|------------------|----|----------------|
| Of a Serjeant    | 2  | 2              |
| Of a Corporal    | 1  | $7\frac{1}{2}$ |
| Of a Trumpeter   | 1  | 7              |
| Of a Private Man | 1  | 3              |

### INFANTRY.

|                       | s. | d.             |
|-----------------------|----|----------------|
| Of a Serjeant         | 1  | $6\frac{3}{4}$ |
| Of a Corporal         | 1  | $2\frac{1}{4}$ |
| Of a Drummer or Fifer | 1  | $1\frac{3}{4}$ |
| Of a Private Man      | 1  | 0              |

[And with respect to the application of the said daily pay and fixed allowance, our will and pleasure is, that in situations where the troops find their provisions at their own expence, in like manner as at home, they shall

## Regimental Pay and Daily Allowances. 21

receive their pay according to the rates above specified, without deduction: but on stations where they do not themselves defray the charge of their provisions, such deductions shall be made therefrom as to leave the exact nett additions of *three-pence*, *two-pence halfpenny*, and *two pence*, to the pay of the respective ranks, over and above what they received at the former rates of pay and allowances; agreeably to the schedule hereunto annexed.

And we do hereby declare it to be our intention, that whenever our soldiers, from whom the aforesaid deductions are herein directed to be made on account of provisions, shall be removed to other stations where they are to supply themselves with provisions, they shall immediately thereupon be entitled to receive their full pay without deduction, according to the establishment.

Lastly, our will and pleasure is, that our land forces, when employed as marines on board our ships of war, shall not be liable to any deduction from their pay for provisions supplied to them at the public charge.]*

GIVEN at our Court at St. James's, this 5th day of July, 1797, in the 37th year of our reign.

By His Majesty's Command.

W. WINDHAM.

---

* New regulations respecting the deductions to be taken from the pay of troops, under various circumstances of service, were established by His Majesty's Warrant of 6th February, 1799. See page 23.

[SCHEDULE *referred to in the preceding* WARRANT.

| STATIONS. | CORPS. | RANKS. | Former Pay and Allowance. | Former Deduction. | Nett former Pay and Allowance. | Full Pay, | Deduction, | Nett Pay, |
|---|---|---|---|---|---|---|---|---|
| | | | | | | *Commencing from 25th May, 1797.* | | |
| | | | s. d. | s. d. | s. d. | s. d. | s. d. | s. d. |
| NORTH AMERICA, and those Stations in the *West Indies*, or elsewhere, at which Provisions are supplied by the Public, and a Stoppage is made from the Troops on that account - - | DRAGOONS | Serjeans | 1 6 | 0 2½ | 1 3½ | 2 2 | 0 7½ | 1 6½ |
| | | Corporal | 1 0 | 0 2½ | 0 9½ | 1 7½ | 0 7½ | 1 0 |
| | | Trumpeter | 1 0 | 0 2½ | 0 9½ | 1 7 | 0 7½ | 0 11½ |
| | | Private - | 0 8 | 0 2½ | 0 5½ | 1 3 | 0 7½ | 0 7½ |
| | FOOT - | Serjeant | 1 0 | 0 2½ | 0 9½ | 1 6¾ | 0 6¼ | 1 0½ |
| | | Corporal | 0 8 | 0 2½ | 0 5½ | 1 2¼ | 0 6¼ | 0 8 |
| | | Drummer | 0 8 | 0 2½ | 0 5½ | 1 1¾ | 0 6¼ | 0 7½ |
| | | Private - | 0 6½ | 0 2½ | 0 4 | 1 0 | 0 6 | 0 6 |
| JAMAICA - - - - | DRAGOONS | Serjeant | 1 6 | None. | 1 6 | 2 2 | 0 5 | 1 9 |
| | | Corporal | 1 0 | | 1 0 | 1 7½ | 0 5 | 1 2½ |
| | | Trumpeter | 1 0 | | 1 0 | 1 7 | 0 5 | 1 2 |
| | | Private - | 0 8 | | 0 8 | 1 3 | 0 5 | 0 10 |
| | FOOT - | Serjeant | 1 0 | | 1 0 | 1 6¾ | 0 3¾ | 1 3 |
| | | Corporal | 0 8 | | 0 8 | 1 2¼ | 0 3¾ | 0 10½ |
| | | Drummer | 0 8 | | 0 8 | 1 1¾ | 0 3¾ | 0 10 |
| | | Private - | 0 6½ | | 0 6½ | 1 0 | 0 3½ | 0 8½ |
| GIBRALTAR - - - - | | | *The same as* JAMAICA, *the Loss by Exchange continuing as before.* | | | | | |
| NEW SOUTH WALES - - - | | | *The same as* JAMAICA. | | | | | |
| EMBARKED in Transports, or in Ships of War, but not serving as Marines - | DRAGOONS | Serjeant | 1 6 | 0 3 | 1 3 | 2 2 | 0 8 | 1 6 |
| | | Corporal | 1 0 | 0 3 | 0 9 | 1 7½ | 0 8 | 0 11½ |
| | | Trumpeter | 1 0 | 0 3 | 0 9 | 1 7 | 0 8 | 0 11 |
| | | Private - | 0 8 | 0 3 | 0 5 | 1 3 | 0 8 | 0 7 |
| | FOOT - - | Serjeant | 1 0 | 0 3 | 0 9 | 1 6¾ | 0 6¾ | 1 0 |
| | | Corporal | 0 8 | 0 3 | 0 5 | 1 2¼ | 0 6¾ | 0 7½ |
| | | Drummer | 0 8 | 0 3 | 0 5 | 1 1¼ | 0 6¾ | 0 7 |
| | | Private - | 0 6½ | 0 3 | 0 3½ | 1 0 | 0 6½ | 0 5½ |

N. B. This SCHEDULE was cancelled by the Warrant of the 6th of February, 1799. See page 23.

## Regimental Pay and Daily Allowances. 23

*Warrant declaring the Deductions to be taken, under various Circumstances of Service, out of Great Britain, and in general Hospitals at Home and Abroad, from the full Pay of Non-commissioned Officers and Soldiers of the Life-Guards, Royal Regiment of Horse-Guards, Dragoon-Guards, Dragoons, Fencible Cavalry, Foot-Guards, Infantry of the Line, Militia, Fencible Infantry, and Invalids, dated 6th Feb. 1799.*

## GEORGE R.

WHEREAS we think it expedient, as well for the sake of uniformity, as with the view of simplifying the accompts of the non-commissioned officers and men of our forces, and of facilitating the settlement thereof, to order, that the deductions to be taken in certain cases, from the pay of our said Non-commissioned Officers and Men, shall hereafter be the same for all ranks, and in all corps, under the like circumstances of service: our will and pleasure is, that instead of the several deductions specified in the schedule annexed to our warrant of the fifth day of July, one thousand seven hundred and ninety-seven, and in any subsequent regulations issued from the office of our Commander in Chief, or Secretary at War, there shall be taken a deduction of *six-pence a day* from the full pay of every serjeant, corporal, trumpeter, drummer, fifer, and private man of our regiments of *life-guards*, royal regiment of *horse-guards*, regiments of *dragoon-guards, dragoons, fencible cavalry, foot-guards, infantry of the line, militia* and *fencible infantry*, and companies of *invalids*, when serving out of Great Britain, on stations at which provisions are supplied by the public; also, when embarked in transports, or other vessels (except while serving as marines, or during their passage to and from India, at the expence of the East India company); also, when prisoners of war, and maintained at the expence of Great Britain; [and likewise when in general hospitals, either at home or abroad:]* in which several cases a stop-

---

* The deduction in *general hospitals* has been encreased to 10d. a day. See Section VI.

page from the pay of our troops, on account of provisions, has always been made.

And it is our will and pleasure, that there shall be taken a deduction of *three-pence halfpenny a day* from the full pay of each serjeant, corporal, trumpeter, drummer, fifer, and private man of our said corps, when stationed in Jamaica, in New South Wales, at Gibraltar, (the loss by exchange at the latter place continuing as before), and while on their passage to and from India, at the expence of the East India Company; in which several cases no stoppage has heretofore been made on account of provisions.

It is our further will and pleasure, that while any of the non-commissioned officers and men shall serve as marines, they shall not be liable to any deduction whatsoever from their full pay, on account of provisions.

And it is our will and pleasure, that the deductions aforementioned shall be considered as commencing, in regard to the troops at home, from the twenty-fifth day of February, one thousand seven hundred and ninety-nine, inclusive; and in regard to the troops abroad, from the twenty-fifth day of April, one thousand seven hundred and ninety-nine, inclusive; or as soon thereafter as this our warrant shall have been received by the respective officers commanding on foreign stations, and shall have been given out, in general orders, according to the custom of our service.

Given at our court at St. James's, this sixth day of February, one thousand seven hundred and ninety-nine, in the thirty-ninth year of our reign.

By His Majesty's command.

W. WINDHAM.

*Circular*

*Circular Letter to Commanding Officers of Regiments of Cavalry and Infantry relative to the Stoppages from Soldiers while Prisoners of War.*

*War Office, 5th December,* 1798.

SIR,

I HAVE it in command from the King, to signify to you that the practice which has obtained of allowing to men, returned from being Prisoners, in the earlier years of the present war, their Pay, without any deduction on account of victualling during the time of their captivity, and which practice was occasioned by its having been generally understood that they had been either not supplied at all, or very inadequately supplied with provisions during that period, is not to be continued beyond the 23d of February last, inclusive; from and after which day, to the date of landing in this country, every Non-commissioned officer and Soldier returned from captivity is to be subject to the respective deductions specified in the [Schedule annexed to His Majesty's Warrant of the 5th July, 1797, " for encreasing and regulating the Pay and Allowance of Non-commissioned Officers and Soldiers serving out of Great Britain.]\* This country and France having taken upon themselves the maintenance of the Prisoners belonging to them respectively, and the operation of that agreement being considered to have commenced on the part of Great Britain from the 24th February last, inclusive.

I have the honor to be,

SIR,

Your most obedient

Humble servant,

W. WINDHAM.

---

\* The Warrant referred to was superseded by the subsequent Regulation of the 6th February, 1799, by which the Rate of Stoppage is now governed. See page 23.

*Extract*

*Extract from a Circular Letter to Commanding Officers of Militia Regiments, dated 30th March, 1803, relative to the Appointment and Pay of Armourers.*

"It being thought proper, that in every Militia Corps, confisting of not lefs than three Companies, a perfon fhould be employed as Armourer, in the fame manner as in a Regiment of Infantry of the Line, I have the honour to acquaint you therewith, and to fignify to you the King's Pleafure, that you do felect for the above employment one of the Non-commiffioned Officers or Private Men borne on the eftablifhment of the Corps under your Command, and properly qualified for the Appointment. If a Serjeant, he will continue to receive Pay as fuch: if a Corporal, or Private Man, his Pay will be made up to that of Serjeant."

*Circular to the Colonels of Regiments of Infantry having Second Battalions for limited Service, relative to the Enlistment of Boys.*

*War Office, January 9th, 1805.*

SIR,

I HAVE the honor to acquaint you His Majesty has been pleased to direct, that Ten Boys shall be included in the numbers of each Company of the Second Battalion of the Regiment under your command.

The Boys are not to exceed the age of sixteen, nor to be under five feet high; and are to be enlisted for General Service.

A Bounty of Half a Guinea is to be given to each Boy on his being attested, and his Necessaries are to be found by the Public; the Paymaster is therefore to charge Two Guineas for each Boy actually enlisted, to complete him with Necessaries; and the Parents or Bringers of each will receive, on his attestation, Two Guineas.

Until each Boy recruited is able to do the duty of a Soldier, his daily Pay is to be [Eight Pence.]*

I have the honor to be,

SIR,

Your most obedient

Humble Servant,

W. DUNDAS.

Colonel of the
 Regiment of Foot.

---

\* Subsequently encreased to Tenpence. See p. 28.

*Circular to Colonels of Regiments of Infantry having Second Battalions for limited Service, relative to the Pay of Boy Recruits.*

*War Office,* 8*th November,* 1805.

SIR,

I HAVE the honor to acquaint you, that in confequence of the reprefentations which have been made of the inadequacy of the Pay of Eightpence a day, allowed to Boy Recruits, agreeably to my Letter of the 9th January laft, His Majefty has been pleafed to order, that the Pay of Recruits of the faid defcription fhall be increafed to Tenpence a day, from the 25th ultimo, inclufive.

I have the honor to be,

SIR,

Your moft obedient

Humble fervant,

W. DUNDAS.

Colonel of the
   Regiment of Foot.

## Regimental Pay and Daily Allowances. 29

*General Orders relative to the Pay of Boys.*

*Horse Guards, 28th February,* 1806.

SOME doubts having arisen respecting the Rate of Pay to be allowed to Boys, who, by the special permission of the Commander in Chief, are enlisted into Regular Regiments of Infantry, under the General Orders of the 31st of May, 1805,* for the purpose of being trained as Drummers, or Fifers, His Royal Highness has directed it to be made known, that Boys of this description are not to receive a greater rate of pay, than Ten Pence per diem, until they are sufficiently qualified to be placed as Drummers, or have attained sufficient strength to be placed as Private Soldiers, upon the Establishment of their respective Regiments.

By Order of His Royal Highness

The Commander in Chief.

HARRY CALVERT,
Adjutant General of the Forces.

---

* See Section IV.

*Circular*

*Circular to Colonels of Regiments of Dragoon Guards and Dragoons, relative to an additional Allowance to Corporals and Privates.*

*War Office*, 15th *July*, 1806.

SIR,

THE King having had under His Royal confideration the fituation of the Army in refpect of Pay, with the view of improving the fame, fo far as may be confiftent with a due regard to Public economy in the prefent circumftances of the country; I have the honor to acquaint you, His Majefty is gracioufly pleafed to order, that the Corporals and Privates of his Regiments of Dragoon Guards and Dragoons, fhall, after certain periods of fervice, receive an additional allowance at the Rates undermentioned: viz.

[The Rates are omitted, the Scale being cancelled by the Letter of 29th July. See page 32.]

The faid additional allowances are to commence from the 25th of laft month inclufive.

Further inftructions, in regard to the mode of iffuing the additional allowances, will be tranfmitted to you with as little delay as poffible.

His Majefty has at the fame time been pleafed to fignify his intention of making a more competent Provifion for the Widows of certain Ranks of Officers of the Land Forces, by augmenting their Penfions to the Rates fpecified in a paper herewith * tranfmitted; and of extending the faid Penfions to the Widows of Officers reduced, or placed on Half Pay in confequence of being incapable of further fervice: and it is alfo His Royal intention to increafe the Out-penfion of Chelfea Hofpital.

I have great pleafure in being the channel of communicating to you thefe inftances of His Majefty's gracious confideration;

---

* See Section IX.

and I request that you will use the earliest means of making the same known to the Regiment under your command.

I have the honor to be,

SIR,

Your most obedient

Humble Servant,

R. FITZPATRICK.

Colonel of the
  Regiment of

---

MEMORANDUM.

Similar Letters were addressed to the Life Guards and Royal Regiment of Horse Guards, except that in these Corps the *Privates* only receive the additional allowance.

*Circular to Commanding Officers of Regiments of Dragoon Guards and Dragoons on the Home Station, relative to the Claims of Corporals and Privates to the additional Allowances depending upon Length of Service.*

*War Office,* 29*th July,* 1806.

SIR,

REFERRING to my Letter (Circular) of the 15th inftant, I have received His Majefty's commands to acquaint you, that the directions therein contained, in regard to the Periods of Service after which Corporals and Privates become entitled to additional allowances, are to be confidered as cancelled; and that the faid allowances are to be granted according to the following Scale, viz.

|  | *Nett Additional Allowance per Diem.* |
|---|---|
| Corporals after Seventeen Years Service | two-pence. |
| Ditto from Ten to Seventeen Years | one penny. |
| Privates after Seventeen Years Service | two-pence. |
| Ditto from Ten to Seventeen Years | one penny. |

I have further to acquaint you with the following particulars for your guidance in adjufting the claims of the men of your Regiment to the faid additional allowances.

Previous fervice in any Corps of Regulars, or in any Fencible Corps liable to ferve out of Great Britain, Ireland, and the Iflands in the Channel, is to be taken into account in eftimating the claims of the men to the faid additional allowances:* and it is to be underftood that men difcharged at the late peace, or at any other period, and who have fince entered into the Army, are entitled to claim the benefit of their antecedent fervice in Corps of the above defcription.

But fervice in the Militia, or in any Corps of Fencibles not liable to ferve out of Great Britain, Ireland, and the Iflands in

---

\* Previous fervice in the Royal Artillery or Marines alfo gives a claim to the additional Allowances in queftion.

Service under the terms of the Army of Referve Act, and the Additional Force Act, does not give a claim to the faid additional Allowances.

the

## Regimental Pay and Daily Allowances. 33

the Channel, is not to be confidered as making any part of the fervice entitling the men to the faid additional allowances.

Former defertion is not in any refpect to affect a man's claim to the allowances in queftion, but defertion occurring fubfequently to the 25th ultimo, will deprive a Soldier of all title to the faid allowances arifing from antecedent fervice.

In the cafe of men formerly difcharged and recommended to Chelfea, and who have fince entered into the Army, the time during which fuch men were on the Chelfea penfion is to be taken into account in eftimating their claim to the additional allowances, two years thereof being reckoned as one of actual fervice; and the fame in proportion for any longer or fhorter period.

The additional allowances abovementioned, to Corporals and Privates, may be immediately iffued and charged with their pay in the accompts from the 25th *June* laft.

Should any cafe occur in which the claim to the above allowances cannot be exactly afcertained, payment thereof is to be fufpended until the neceffary information, or a fpecial authority from this Office, in confequence of a reprefentation through you, fhould have been obtained.

The tranfmiffion of the general abftract of the public accompts to the 24th inftant, may be poftponed in the prefent inftance, for ten or twelve days, if found requifite.

I take this opportunity of apprizing you, that it being intended to keep in the War Office an exact Regifter of the Period of Service of the Men of each Regiment, and of the Cafualties among the fame, fome further directions will be given on the fubject as foon as the neceffary forms are printed.

I have the honor to be,

SIR,

Your moft obedient,

Humble Servant,

R. FITZPATRICK.

Officer Commanding the
 Regiment of Dragoon

*In the Letter to Dragoons on Foreign Stations the Four laſt Paragraphs ſtood as follows:*

The additional allowances may be immediately iſſued, and for the intermediate period from the 25th June laſt to the termination of the laſt Monthly Eſtimate tranſmitted from your Corps, are to be ſtated diſtinctly in a manuſcript Supplementary Eſtimate. Theſe allowances to the period to which the accounts ſhall have been already made out, on the receipt of this letter, are to be charged in a Supplementary Abſtract and Supplementary Pay-liſts reſpectively: the ſubſequent payments thereof are to be ſtated with the pay.

The neceſſary Forms of the Supplementary General Abſtract and Pay Liſts, as alſo of Monthly General Abſtracts and Quarterly Pay Liſts, altered ſo as to provide for the inſertion of the additional charges, will be forwarded to each Regiment as ſoon as printed.

Should any caſe occur in which the claim to the above allowances cannot be exactly aſcertained, payment thereof is to be ſuſpended until the neceſſary information, or a ſpecial authority from this Office, in conſequence of a repreſentation through you, ſhould have been obtained.

I take this opportunity of apprizing you, that it being intended to keep in the War Office an exact Regiſter of the Periods of Service of the Men of each Regiment, and of the Caſualties among the ſame, ſome further directions will be given as ſoon as the neceſſary forms are printed.

*Letter to the Colonels of the Foot Guards, relative to the Encreafe of Pay.*

*War Office,* 15*th July,* 1806.

SIR,

THE King having had under his Royal confideration the fituation of the Army in refpect of Pay, with the view of improving the fame, fo far as may be confiftent with public economy in the prefent circumftances of the country, I have the honor to acquaint your Royal Highnefs, His Majefty is gracioufly pleafed to order, that the Pay and Allowance of the effective Non-commiffioned Officers and Privates of his Regiments of Foot Guards, fhall be augmented as fpecified in the enclofed State; and that the augmentation fhall take place from the 25th of laft month inclufive.

His Majefty has further been pleafed to direct that the Lieutenant Colonel and Majors of each Regiment fhall have an Allowance for the forage of one horfe each; fimilar to the Allowance now granted to Adjutants of Infantry.

Further inftructions in regard to the mode of iffuing the encreafe of Pay and Allowance, will be tranfmitted to you with as little delay as poffible.

His Majefty has at the fame time been pleafed to fignify his intention of making a more competent provifion for the Widows of certain claffes of Officers of the Land Forces, by augmenting their Penfions to the rates fpecified in the enclofed State,* and of extending the faid Penfions to the Widows of Officers reduced or placed on Half Pay, in confequence of being incapable of further fervice. And it is alfo his Royal intention to encreafe the Out-Penfion of Chelfea Hofpital.

I have great pleafure in being the channel of communicating to your Royal Highnefs thefe inftances of His Majefty's gracious confideration, and I requeft that you will ufe the earlieft

---

* See Section IX.

means of making the same known to the Regiment under your Royal Highness's command.

I am, with the most profound respect,

SIR,

Your Royal Highness's

Most obedient and

Most humble Servant,

R. FITZPATRICK.

Colonel of the
Regiment of Foot Guards.

---

*STATE referred to in the Secretary at War's Letter of 15th July, 1806.*

## FOOT GUARDS.

| | Present Pay. | | Encreased Pay. | |
|---|---|---|---|---|
| | s. | d. | s. | d. |
| Serjeant Major and Quarter Master Serjeant | 2 | 4¾ | 2 | 8 |
| Serjeant | 1 | 10¾ | 2 | 0 |
| Corporal after 14 Years Service | | | 1 | 7 |
|     from 7 to 14 | 1 | 4¾ | 1 | 6 |
|     below 7 | | | 1 | 5 |
| Private after 14 Years Service | | | 1 | 3 |
|     from 7 to 14 | 1 | 1 | 1 | 2 |
|     below 7 | | | 1 | 1 |

## Regimental Pay and Daily Allowances.

*Circular to Colonels of Marching Regiments of Foot, relative to an Increase of Pay and Allowance, &c.*

*War Office,* 15th *July,* 1806.

SIR,

THE King having had under his Royal confideration the fituation of the Army in refpect of Pay, with the view of improving the fame fo far as may be confiftent with a due regard to public economy, in the prefent circumftances of the country; I have the honor to acquaint you, His Majefty is gracioufly pleafed to order, that the Pay and daily Allowance of certain claffes of Commiffioned Officers, Non-commiffioned Officers, and Privates, of his Marching Regiments of Foot, fhall be augmented to the rates fpecified in the enclofed State; and that the augmentation fhall have effect from the 25th of laft month inclufive.

It is effential to explain that this increafe of Pay and Allowance is granted under the fame reftrictions as the Allowance of One Shilling a day added to the Pay of Subalterns in 1797; and confequently that the difference between the former and the increafed rates is not in any cafe to be received by an Officer holding more than one Military Commiffion or Appointment, nor to give a claim to any higher rate of Half Pay on Reduction.

Further inftructions, in regard to the mode of iffuing the increafe of Pay and Allowance, will be tranfmitted to you with as little delay as poffible.

His Majefty has at the fame time been pleafed to fignify his intention of making a more competent provifion for the Widows of certain ranks of Officers of the Land Forces, by augmenting their Penfions to the rates fpecified in a paper* herewith tranfmitted; and of extending the faid Penfions to the Widows of Officers reduced, or placed on Half Pay in confequence of being incapable of further fervice: and it is alfo his

---

* See Section IX.

royal intention to increafe the Out Penfion of Chelfea Hofpital.

I have great pleafure in being the channel of communicating to you thefe inftances of His Majefty's gracious confideration for the army; and I requeft that you will ufe the earlieft means of making the fame known to the Officers and Men of the Regiment under your command.

I have the honor to be,

SIR,

Your moft obedient

Humble fervant,

R. FITZPATRICK.

Colonel of the
  Regiment of Foot.

MARCHING

## Regimental Pay and Daily Allowances.

## MARCHING REGIMENTS OF FOOT.

STATE REFERRED TO IN THE SECRETARY AT WAR'S LETTER (CIRCULAR) OF THE 15th JULY, 1806.

| REGIMENTAL RANK. | Rate of Pay and Allowance, per Diem, nett; previous to 25th June, 1806. | | Rate of Pay and Allowance, per Diem, nett; commencing from the 25th June, 1806. | |
|---|---|---|---|---|
| | s. | d. | s. | d. |
| Lieutenant Colonel - - - - - | 15 | 11 | 17 | 0 |
| Major - - - - - - - - | 14 | 1 | 16 | 0 |
| Captain - - - - - - - | 9 | 5 | 10 | 6 |
| Further Allowance to Captains having the Brevet of Major, or any superior Rank - - - - - | — | | 2 | 0 |
| Lieutenant - - - - - - - | 5 | 8 | 6 | 6 |
| Further Allowance to Lieutenants of above Seven Years standing - | — | | 1 | 0 |
| Ensign - - - - - - - - | 4 | 8 | 5 | 3 |
| Adjutant - - - - - - - | 8 | 0 | 8 | 6 |
| Quarter Master - - - - - | 5 | 8 | 6 | 6 |
| Serjeant Majors, and Quarter Master Serjeants - - - - - | 2 | 0¾ | 2 | 6 |
| Serjeants - - - - - - - | 1 | 6¼ | 1 | 10 |
| Corporals, after 14 Years Service | | | 1 | 6 |
| Ditto from 7 to 14 - - - - | 1 | 2¼ | 1 | 5 |
| Ditto below 7 - - - - | | | 1 | 4 |
| Privates after 14 - - - - | | | 1 | 2 |
| Ditto from 7 to 14 - - - - | 1 | 0 | 1 | 1 |
| Ditto below 7 - - - - - | | | 1 | 0 |

Officers commanding Battalions, to have an Allowance of 3s. per diem each, in addition to their Regimental Pay.

Lieutenant Colonels and Majors, serving with Battalions at home, to have an Allowance for the Forage of one Horse each; similar to the Allowance now granted to Adjutants of Infantry.*

---

N. B. The difference between the present and increased rates of Pay and Allowance, is not in any case to be received by an Officer holding more than one military commission or appointment; nor is it to give any claim to a higher rate of Half Pay on reduction.

---

* See Section II.

*Circular*

*Circular Letter to Commanding Officers of Regiments of Foot on the Home Station, relative to the Claims of Officers and Men to the additional Allowances depending upon length of Service.*

*War Office,* 29*th July,* 1806.

SIR,

REFERRING to my letter (Circular) of the 15th instant, I have the honor to acquaint you with the following particulars for your guidance in adjusting the claims of the Officers and Men of your Corps to the additional allowances depending upon length of service.

To entitle a Lieutenant to the additional allowance of one shilling a day, he must have been seven years commissioned as Lieutenant in the Regular Army. Should he have been on Half-pay for part of the said period, either in consequence of reduction, or of exchange *without taking the difference*, his claim to the allowance is not to be affected thereby. But if he went on Half-pay *taking the difference*, his standing as Lieutenant is to be considered as only commencing from the date of his re-entering the Service.

In regard to the additional allowances to Corporals and Privates, after seven and fourteen years service respectively, it is to be understood, that previous service in any corps of Regulars, or in any Fencible corps liable to serve out of Great Britain, Ireland, and the islands in the Channel, is to be taken into account in estimating the claims of the Men to the said additional allowances.* It is also to be understood that Men discharged at the late peace, or at any other period, and who have since entered into the Army, are entitled to claim the benefit of their antecedent service in Corps of the above description.

But service in the Militia, or in any Corps of Fencibles not liable to serve out of Great Britain, Ireland, and the islands in

---

* Previous service in the Royal Artillery or Marines also gives a claim to the additional allowances in question.

Service under the terms of the Army of Reserve Act, and the Additional Force Act, does not give a claim to the said additional Allowances.

the

the Channel, is not to be confidered as making any part of the fervice entitling the men to the faid additional allowances.

Former defertion is not in any refpect to affect a man's claim to the allowances in queftion: but defertion occurring fubfequently to the 25th ultimo will deprive a Soldier of all title to the faid allowances arifing from antecedent Service.

In the cafe of Men formerly difcharged and recommended to Chelfea, and who have fince entered into the Army, the time during which fuch Men were on the Chelfea penfion is to be taken into account in eftimating their claim to the additional allowances; two years thereof being reckoned as one of actual fervice; and the fame in proportion for any longer or fhorter period.

The additional allowances above-mentioned, to Lieutenants, and to Corporals and Privates, may be immediately iffued and charged with their pay in the accompts from the 25th June laft.

Should any cafe occur in which the claim to the above allowances cannot be exactly afcertained, payment thereof is to be fufpended until the neceffary information, or a fpecial authority from this Office, in confequence of a reprefentation through you, fhall have been obtained.

The tranfmiffion of the general abftract of the public accompts to the 24th inftant, may be poftponed in the prefent inftance, for ten or twelve days, if found requifite.

I take this opportunity of apprizing you, that it being intended to keep in the War Office an exact regifter of the periods of Service of the Men of each Regiment, and of the cafualties among the fame, fome further directions will be given on the fubject as foon as the neceffary forms are printed.

I have the honor to be,

SIR,

Your moft obedient

Humble fervant,

R. FITZPATRICK.

Officer Commanding the
        Regt. of Foot.

*In the letter to the Infantry on foreign stations, the words, " in any respect," in the fifth paragraph (regarding Desertion) were omitted, and the four last paragraphs of the Letter stood as follows:*

" The additional allowances may be immediately issued, and for the intermediate period from the 25th June last to the termination of the last monthly estimate transmitted from your corps, are to be stated distinctly in a supplementary estimate, agreeably to a form of which    copies are enclosed. These allowances to the period to which the accompts shall have been already made out, on the receipt of this letter, are to be charged in a supplementary abstract, and supplementary pay-lists respectively: the subsequent payments thereof are to be stated with the pay.

" The necessary forms of the supplementary general abstract and pay-lists, as also of monthly general abstracts and of quarterly pay lists, altered so as to provide for the insertion of the additional charges, will be forwarded to each regiment as soon as printed.

" Should any case occur in which the claim to the above allowances cannot be exactly ascertained, payment thereof is to be suspended until the necessary information, or a special authority from this Office, in consequence of a representation through you, shall have been obtained.

" I take this opportunity of apprizing you, that it being intended to keep in the War Office an exact register of the periods of service of the Men of each Regiment, and of the casualties among the same, some further directions will be given on the subject as soon as the necessary forms are printed,"

*Circular*

# Regimental Pay and Daily Allowances. 43

*Circular to the Commandants of Militia Corps, relative to increasing the Pay and Allowance of Subalterns, &c.*

*War Office,* 15th *July,* 1806.

SIR,

THE King having had under his royal confideration the fituation of the Army in refpect of pay, with the view of improving the fame fo far as may be confiftent with a due regard to public economy, in the prefent circumftances of the country; I have the honor to acquaint you, his Majefty is gracioufly pleafed to order, that the pay and daily allowance of certain claffes of Commiffioned Officers in his Militia Regiments, fhall be augmented to the rates fpecified in the enclofed ftate; and that the augmentation fhall have effect from the 25th of laft month inclufive.

It is effential to explain that this increafe of pay and daily allowance is granted under the fame reftrictions as the allowance of one fhilling a day added to the pay of Subalterns in 1797: and confequently that the difference between the former and the increafed rates is not in any cafe to be received by an Officer holding more than one military commiffion or appointment.

Further inftructions, in regard to the mode of iffuing the increafe of pay and allowance, will be tranfmitted to you with as little delay as poffible.

His Majefty has alfo been pleafed to fignify his intention of making an addition to the out-penfion of Chelfea Hofpital.

I have great pleafure in being the channel of communicating to you thefe inftances of His Majefty's gracious confideration; and I requeft that you will ufe the earlieft means of making the fame known to the Corps under your command.

I have the honor to be,

SIR,

Your moft obedient,

humble fervant,

R. FITZPATRICK.

Commandant of the
Militia.

MILITIA.

## MILITIA.

*State referred to in the Secretary at War's Letter, (Circular) of the 15th June, 1806.*

| RANKS. | Rates of Pay and Daily Allowance, nett: previous to 25th June, 1806. | | Increased Rates of Pay and Daily Allowance, nett; commencing from the 25th June, 1806. | |
|---|---|---|---|---|
| | *s.* | *d.* | *s.* | *d.* |
| Lieutenant - - - | 5 | 8 | 6 | 6 |
| Ensign - - - - | 4 | 8 | 5 | 3 |
| Adjutant - - - - | 8 | 0 | 8 | 6 |
| Quarter Master - - | 5 | 8 | 6 | 6 |

N. B. The difference between the former and the increased rates of pay and allowance, is not in any case to be received by an Officer holding more than one military commission or appointment.

*Circular*

## Regimental Pay and Daily Allowances. 45

*Circular to the Paymasters of Militia Corps, relative to the Issue of the Additional Allowances granted from the 25th June, 1806.*

*War Office, 25th July, 1806.*

SIR,

REFERRING to the Secretary at War's Circular Letter of the 15th of July, 1806, to the Colonels and Commandants of Militia, I am directed to acquaint you that the additional allowances thereby granted to Lieutenants, Ensigns, Adjutants, and Quarter Masters, not holding another military appointment, may be immediately issued to them, and charged in your accompts.

I am,

SIR,

Your most obedient servant,

W. MERRY.

**The Paymaster of the**
          Regiment of Militia.

MEMORANDUM.

## MEMORANDUM.

THE original authorities for the prefent Pay of Paymafters and Paymafters' Clerks will be found in the Section relating to the mode of ftating the Regimental Accompts; and for that of Surgeons, Affiftant Surgeons, Surgeons' Mates, and Veterinary Surgeons, in the Section comprehending the Regulations for the Medical Department.

---

The following States fhew the exifting Rates of Pay of the Officers and Men of the feveral Corps of the Army.

# Regimental Pay and Daily Allowances. 47

*Rates of the Pay and Daily Allowance of the Officers and Men of the Life Guards.*

|  | Gross Pay and Allowance per Diem as borne on the Establishment. | | | Subsistence per Diem nett. | | |
|---|---|---|---|---|---|---|
|  | *l.* | *s.* | *d.* | *l.* | *s.* | *d.* |
| Colonel | 1 | 16 | 0 | 1 | 7 | 0 |
| Lieutenant Colonel | 1 | 11 | 0 | 1 | 3 | 3 |
| Major | 1 | 6 | 0 | 0 | 19 | 6 |
| Captain | 0 | 16 | 0 | 0 | 12 | 0 |
| Lieutenant | 0 | 11 | 0 | 0 | 8 | 3 |
| Cornet | 0 | 8 | 6 | 0 | 7 | 3 |
| Adjutant | 0 | 13 | 0 | 0 | 13 | 0 |
| Quarter Master | 0 | 6 | 0 | 0 | 4 | 9 |
| Surgeon | 0 | 12 | 0 | 0 | 9 | 0 |
| Assistant Surgeon  7 6 }  Allowance for a horse  1 0 } | 0 | 8 | 6 | 0 | 8 | 6 |
| Veterinary Surgeon | 0 | 8 | 0 | 0 | 8 | 0 |
| Corporal Major |  |  |  | 0 | 3 | $6\frac{1}{4}$ |
| Armourer, as Corporal |  |  |  | 0 | 2 | $6\frac{1}{4}$ |
| Sadler, as Corporal |  |  |  | 0 | 2 | $6\frac{1}{4}$ |
| Corporal |  |  |  | 0 | 2 | $6\frac{1}{4}$ |
| Trumpeter |  |  |  | 0 | 2 | 6 |
| Kettle Drummer |  |  |  | 0 | 2 | 6 |
| Private |  |  |  | 0 | 1 | $11\frac{1}{4}$ |
| Do. after 10 years service |  |  |  | 0 | 2 | $0\frac{1}{4}$ |
| Do. after 17 do. |  |  |  | 0 | 2 | $1\frac{1}{4}$ |

N. B. The Gross Pay of the Officers (except the Adjutant, Assistant Surgeon and Veterinary Surgeon) above-stated is subject to the deductions of Poundage (1s. in the pound), Hospital (one day's pay in the year), and Agency (2d. in the pound). Of the sum remaining, part is issued as *subsistence* at the rates expressed in the second column; and the remainder as *arrears* when the clearing warrant of the Regiment is made out and acted upon.

*Rates of the Pay and Daily Allowance of the Officers and Men of the Royal Regiment of Horse Guards.*

|  | Gross Pay and Allowance per Diem as borne on the Establishment. | | | Subsistence per Diem nett. | | |
|---|---|---|---|---|---|---|
|  | l. | s. | d. | l. | s. | d. |
| Colonel | 2 | 1 | 0 | 1 | 11 | 0 |
| Lieutenant Colonel | 1 | 9 | 6 | 1 | 2 | 6 |
| Major | 1 | 7 | 0 | 1 | 1 | 6 |
| Captain | 1 | 1 | 6 | 0 | 16 | 6 |
| Lieutenant | 0 | 15 | 0 | 0 | 11 | 6 |
| Cornet | 0 | 14 | 0 | 0 | 11 | 6 |
| Quarter Master | 0 | 8 | 6 | 0 | 6 | 6 |
| Adjutant | 0 | 10 | 0 | 0 | 10 | 0 |
| Surgeon | 0 | 12 | 0 | 0 | 9 | 0 |
| Assistant Surgeon  7 6 <br> Allowance for a horse  1 0 | 0 | 8 | 6 | 0 | 8 | 6 |
| Veterinary Surgeon | 0 | 8 | 0 | 0 | 8 | 0 |
| Corporal Major |  |  |  | 0 | 3 | $3\frac{1}{4}$ |
| Armourer, as Corporal |  |  |  | 0 | 2 | $3\frac{1}{4}$ |
| Sadler, as Corporal |  |  |  | 0 | 2 | $3\frac{1}{4}$ |
| Corporal |  |  |  | 0 | 2 | $3\frac{1}{4}$ |
| Trumpet Major |  |  |  | 0 | 1 | $8\frac{1}{4}$ |
| Trumpeter |  |  |  | 0 | 1 | $8\frac{1}{4}$ |
| Kettle Drummer |  |  |  | 0 | 1 | $9\frac{1}{4}$ |
| Private |  |  |  | 0 | 1 | $8\frac{1}{4}$ |
| Ditto, after 10 years service |  |  |  | 0 | 1 | $9\frac{1}{4}$ |
| Ditto, after 17 ditto |  |  |  | 0 | 1 | $10\frac{1}{4}$ |

The nature of the deductions, and of the division of the Pay into subsistence and arrears, is explained in the memorandum annexed to the state for the Life Guards.

## Regimental Pay and Daily Allowances. 49

*Rates of the Pay and Daily Allowance of the Officers and Men of the Dragoon Guards and Dragoons.*

|  |  | Pay and Allowance per Diem, nett. |
|---|---|---|
|  |  | *l. s. d.* |
| Colonel | | 1 12 10 |
| Allowance to do. per troop, for 1 Warrant man 1s. 2d. | | |
| Do. do. for 1 Hautbois, 1s. 6d. | | |
| Lieutenant-Colonel | | 1 3 0 |
| Major | | 0 19 3 |
| Captain | | 0 14 7 |
| Lieutenant | | 0 9 0 |
| Cornet | | 0 8 0 |
| Paymaster | | 0 15 0 |
| Adjutant | | 0 10 0 |
| Surgeon | | 0 11 |
| Assistant Surgeon | 7s. 6d. ⎫ | 0 8 6 |
| Allowance for a horse | 1s. ⎭ | |
| Veterinary Surgeon | | 0 8 0 |
| Quarter Master | | 0 5 6 |
| Serjeant Major | | 0 3 2 |
| Paymaster Serjeant | | 0 2 2 |
| Serjeant Sadler | | 0 2 2 |
| Serjeant Armourer | | 0 2 2 |
| Serjeant | | 0 2 2 |
| Corporal | | 0 1 7½ |
| Do. after 10 years service | | 0 1 8½ |
| Do. after 17 do. | | 0 1 9½ |
| Trumpeter | | 0 1 7 |
| Private | | 0 1 3 |
| Do. after 10 years service | | 0 1 4 |
| Do. after 17 do. | | 0 1 5 |

D   *State*

*State of the Rates of the Pay and Daily Allowance of the Officers and Men of the Royal Waggon Train.*

|  |  | Pay and Allowance per Diem nett. |
|---|---|---|
|  |  | *l. s. d.* |
| Colonel | — | 2 0 0 |
| Lieutenant Colonel | 15s. 11d. ⎫ | 0 17 11 |
| Allowance for a horse | 2s. ⎭ | |
| Major | 14s. 1d. ⎫ | 0 16 1 |
| Allowance for a horse | 2s. ⎭ | |
| Captain | 9s. 5d. ⎫ | 0 11 5 |
| Allowance for a horse | 2s. ⎭ | |
| Lieutenant | 5s. 8d. ⎫ | 0 7 8 |
| Allowance for a horse | 2s. ⎭ | |
| Cornet | 4s. 8d. ⎫ | 0 6 8 |
| Allowance for a horse | 2s. ⎭ | |
| Paymaster | — | 0 15 0 |
| Adjutant | — | 0 10 0 |
| Surgeon | — | 0 11 4 |
| Assistant Surgeon | 7s. 6d. ⎫ | 0 8 6 |
| Allowance for a horse | 1s. ⎭ | |
| Veterinary Surgeon | — | 0 8 0 |
| Quarter Master | — | 0 4 0 |
| Serjeant Major | — | 0 3 2 |
| Paymaster Serjeant, or Serjeant | — | 0 2 2 |
| Corporal | — | 0 1 7½ |
| Trumpeter | — | 0 1 3 |
| Artificer, &c. | — | 0 3 0 |
| Private | — | 0 1 8 |

*Rates*

## Regimental Pay and Daily Allowances.

*Rates of the Pay and Daily Allowance of the Officers and Men of the Foot Guards.*

|  | Gross Pay and Allowance per Diem as borne on the Establishment. | | | Subsistence per Diem Nett. | | |
|---|---|---|---|---|---|---|
|  | l. | s. | d. | l. | s. | d. |
| Colonel | 1 | 19 | 0 | 1 | 10 | 0 |
| Lieutenant Colonel | 1 | 8 | 6 | 1 | 1 | 6 |
| Major | 1 | 4 | 6 | 0 | 18 | 6 |
| Captain | 0 | 16 | 6 | 0 | 12 | 6 |
| Lieutenant | 0 | 7 | 10 | 0 | 6 | 0 |
| Enfign | 0 | 5 | 10 | 0 | 4 | 6 |
| Adjutant | 0 | 10 | 0 | 0 | 10 | 0 |
| Quarter Mafter — 4s. 8d. } Allowance — 1s. } | 0 | 5 | 8 | 0 | 5 | 8 |
| Surgeon Major | 1 | 0 | 0 | 0 | 16 | 8 |
| Battalion Surgeon | 0 | 12 | 0 | 0 | 10 | 0 |
| Affiftant Surgeon | 0 | 7 | 6 | 0 | 7 | 6 |
| Solicitor | 0 | 4 | 0 | 0 | 3 | 0 |
| Deputy Marfhall | 0 | 1 | 0 | 0 | 0 | 9 |
| Serjeant Major | — | — | — | 0 | 2 | 8 |
| Quarter Mafter Serjeant | — | — | — | 0 | 2 | 8 |
| Armourer, as Serjeant | — | — | — | 0 | 2 | 0 |
| Serjeant | — | — | — | 0 | 2 | 0 |
| Corporal | — | — | — | 0 | 1 | 5 |
| Do. after 7 years fervice | — | — | — | 0 | 1 | 6 |
| Do. after 14 years fervice | — | — | — | 0 | 1 | 7 |
| Drum Major | — | — | — | 0 | 1 | 0 |
| Drummer | — | — | — | 0 | 1 | $2\frac{1}{4}$ |
| Hautbois | — | — | — | 0 | 1 | 0 |
| Fifer | — | — | — | 0 | 1 | $2\frac{1}{4}$ |
| Private | — | — | — | 0 | 1 | 1 |
| Do. after 7 years fervice | — | — | — | 0 | 1 | 2 |
| Do. after 14 years fervice | — | — | — | 0 | 1 | 3 |

The nature of the deductions, and of the divifion of the Pay into Subfiftence and Arrears, is explained in the Memorandum annexed to the ftate for the Life Guards.

*Rates of the Pay and Daily Allowance of the Officers and Men of the Marching Regiments of Foot.*

| RANK. | Pay per Diem, Nett. | | | Additional Pay or Allowance per Diem, Nett. | | | TOTAL. | | |
|---|---|---|---|---|---|---|---|---|---|
| | *l.* | *s.* | *d.* | *l.* | *s.* | *d.* | *l.* | *s.* | *d.* |
| Colonel | 1 | 2 | 6 | 0 | 0 | 0 | 1 | 2 | 6 |
| Allowance for one Warrant man per Company, each 6d. | | | | | | | | | |
| Lieutenant Colonel | 0 | 15 | 11 | 0 | 1 | 1 | 0 | 17 | 0 |
| Major | 0 | 14 | 1 | 0 | 1 | 11 | 0 | 16 | 0 |
| Captain | 0 | 9 | 5 | 0 | 1 | 1 | 0 | 10 | 6 |
| Do. having the brevet of Major, or any superior Rank | 0 | 9 | 5 | 0 | 3 | 1 | 0 | 12 | 6 |
| Lieutenant | 0 | 4 | 8 | 0 | 1 | 10 | 0 | 6 | 6 |
| Do. of above 7 years standing | 0 | 4 | 8 | 0 | 2 | 10 | 0 | 7 | 6 |
| Ensign | 0 | 3 | 8 | 0 | 1 | 7 | 0 | 5 | 3 |
| Paymaster of a Regiment for General Service | 0 | 15 | 0 | 0 | 0 | 0 | 0 | 15 | 0 |
| Do. of a Battalion for limited Service | 0 | 10 | 0 | 0 | 0 | 0 | 0 | 10 | 0 |
| Adjutant | 0 | 8 | 0 | 0 | 0 | 6 | 0 | 8 | 6 |
| Quarter Master | 0 | 4 | 8 | 0 | 1 | 10 | 0 | 6 | 6 |
| Surgeon* | 0 | 11 | 4 | 0 | 0 | 0 | 0 | 11 | 4 |
| Assistant Surgeon | 0 | 7 | 6 | 0 | 0 | 0 | 0 | 7 | 6 |
| Serjeant Major | — | — | — | — | — | — | 0 | 2 | 6 |
| Quarter Master Serjeant | — | — | — | — | — | — | 0 | 2 | 6 |
| Paymaster Serjeant | — | — | — | — | — | — | 0 | 1 | 10 |
| Armourer Serjeant | — | — | — | — | — | — | 0 | 1 | 10 |
| Serjeant | — | — | — | — | — | — | 0 | 1 | 10 |
| Corporal | — | — | — | — | — | — | 0 | 1 | 4 |
| Do. after 7 years service | — | — | — | — | — | — | 0 | 1 | 5 |
| Do. after 14 years | — | — | — | — | — | — | 0 | 1 | 6 |
| Drummer or Fifer | — | — | — | — | — | — | 0 | 1 | $1\frac{3}{4}$ |
| Private | — | — | — | — | — | — | 0 | 1 | 0 |
| Do. after 7 years service | — | — | — | — | — | — | 0 | 1 | 1 |
| Do. after 14 years | — | — | — | — | — | — | 0 | 1 | 2 |
| Officers commanding Battalions | — | — | — | 0 | 3 | 0 | 0 | 3 | 0 |

N. B. The difference between the present and increased rates of Pay and Allowance is not, in any case, to be received by an Officer holding more than one military commission or appointment; nor is it to give any claim to a higher rate of Half-pay on reduction.

*Memo-*

---

\* For the additional Pay granted to Surgeons after certain periods of service, see Sec. VI.

## Regimental Pay and Daily Allowances.

*Memorandum relative to the Pay of special Corps of Infantry.*

Battalions raifed under the Army of Reserve and additional Force Acts. { Men ferving in thefe Battalions, and not attefted for Unlimited Service, receive only the old rates of Pay. See page 55.

Royal Veteran Battalions (except the 7th) and the Weft India Regiments. } The fame as the Line, including the additional Pay.

7th Royal Veteran Battalion { The Officers have the fame Pay as thofe of the Line, and the Men as thofe of the Foot Guards.

Regiments of Fencible Infantry for Service abroad. { The fame as the Line, including the additional Pay; with the exception of the Paymafter, and Surgeon's Mate, who are on the footing of Militia.

*State of the Rates of the Pay and daily Allowance of the Officers and Men of the Royal Staff Corps.*

|  | Pay and Allowance per Diem, nett. | | |
|---|---|---|---|
|  | *l.* | *s.* | *d.* |
| Lieutenant Colonel Commandant | 1 | 3 | 0 |
| Allowance for one Warrant Man per Company at — — — 6d. each | | | |
| Lieutenant Colonel | 1 | 3 | 0 |
| Major | 0 | 19 | 3 |
| Captain | 0 | 14 | 7 |
| Lieutenant | 0 | 9 | 0 |
| Ensign | 0 | 8 | 0 |
| Paymaster | 0 | 15 | 0 |
| Adjutant | 0 | 10 | 0 |
| Quarter Master | 0 | 5 | 8 |
| Surgeon | 0 | 11 | 4 |
| Assistant Surgeon | 0 | 7 | 6 |
| Serjeant Major, or Quarter Master Serjeant | 0 | 3 | 0 |
| Serjeant Overseer | 0 | 2 | 6 |
| Bugle | 0 | 1 | 3 |
| Private of the 1st Class | 0 | 2 | 0 |
| Ditto 2d ditto | 0 | 1 | 6 |
| Ditto 3d ditto | 0 | 1 | 3 |

*Rates*

# Regimental Pay and Daily Allowances.

### State of the Rates of the Pay and Daily Allowance of the Officers and Men of the Militia, and the Corps of Fencible Infantry, not liable to serve abroad.

|  | Pay per Diem. | | | Additional Pay or Allowance per Diem. | | | Total. | | |
|---|---|---|---|---|---|---|---|---|---|
|  | *l.* | *s.* | *d.* | *l.* | *s.* | *d.* | *l.* | *s.* | *d.* |
| Colonel | 1 | 2 | 6 | — | — | — | 1 | 2 | 6 |
| Allowance in lieu of the Pay of One Warrant Man per Company, at 6d each |  |  |  |  |  |  |  |  |  |
| Lieutenant Colonel | 0 | 15 | 11 | — | — | — | 0 | 15 | 11 |
| Major | 0 | 14 | 1 | — | — | — | 0 | 14 | 1 |
| Captain | 0 | 9 | 5 | — | — | — | 0 | 9 | 5 |
| Lieutenant | 0 | 4 | 8 | 0 | 1 | 10 | 0 | 6 | 6 |
| Ensign | 0 | 3 | 8 | 0 | 1 | 7 | 0 | 5 | 3 |
| Adjutant | 0 | 8 | 0 | 0 | 0 | 6 | 0 | 8 | 6 |
| Quarter Master | 0 | 4 | 8 | 0 | 1 | 10 | 0 | 6 | 6 |
| Surgeon | 0 | 11 | 4 | — | — | — | 0 | 11 | 4 |
| Surgeon's Mate, if holding also another Appointment in the Regiment | 0 | 3 | 6 | — | — | — | 0 | 3 | 6 |
| Ditto, not holding another Appointment in the Regiment | 0 | 5 | 0 | — | — | — | 0 | 5 | 0 |
| Serjeant Major | — | — | — | — | — | — | 0 | 2 | $0\frac{3}{4}$ |
| Quarter Master Serjeant | — | — | — | — | — | — | 0 | 2 | $0\frac{3}{4}$ |
| Serjeant | — | — | — | — | — | — | 0 | 1 | $6\frac{3}{4}$ |
| Corporal | — | — | — | — | — | — | 0 | 1 | $2\frac{1}{4}$ |
| Drummer | — | — | — | — | — | — | 0 | 1 | $1\frac{3}{4}$ |
| Private | — | — | — | — | — | — | 0 | 1 | 0 |

The Paymaster in a Militia Corps, being one of the Subalterns, has the Pay of his Rank made up to 15s. a day.

The Paymaster's Clerk must be one of the Serjeants, or Rank and File, on the establishment. If a Serjeant, he receives the Pay of that Rank; if a Corporal or Private, his Pay is made up to that of Serjeant.

The Armourer is on the same footing as the Paymaster's Clerk.

N. B. The additional Pay or Allowance is not, in any case, to be received by an Officer holding more than one military commission or appointment.

# SECTION II.

# ANNUAL

OR

# CONTINGENT

## *REGIMENTAL ALLOWANCES.*

## SECTION II.

## ANNUAL OR CONTINGENT REGIMENTAL ALLOWANCES.

*Extract of a Circular to Colonels of Regiments of Cavalry and Infantry, dated War Office, 27th May, 1803.*

" THE King having been pleased to order, that in future each Troop and Company throughout the Army shall have an effective Captain, and therefore, that the Colonels, First Lieutenant Colonels, and First Majors, in the respective Regiments, shall no longer have Troops or Companies; I have the honour to acquaint you therewith, and that three additional Captains will accordingly be borne upon the establishment of your regiment, from the 25th instant inclusive.

*(To the Cavalry.)*

The Field Officers ceasing to hold troops, in consequence of the present arrangement, are to continue to be paid as Field Officers and Captains; and will also be allowed Twenty Pounds per annum each, in lieu of the emoluments arising from the contingent allowance which Captains of Troops receive."

*(To the Infantry.)*

" The Field Officers ceasing to hold companies, in consequence of the present arrangement, are to continue to be paid as Field Officers and Captains; and will also be allowed Twenty Pounds per annum each, in lieu of the non-effective allowance which Captains of Companies receive."

*Letter from Lieutenant Colonel Gordon to the Deputy Secretary at War, respecting the Appropriation of the Allowance to Field Officers, in Regiments that have Two Battalions.*

*Horse Guards,* 11th *October,* 1806.

SIR,

IN reply to your Letter of the 9th instant, transmitting one from Lieutenant Colonel Johnstone, of the 28th Regiment, herewith returned, I am directed to acquaint you, for the Secretary at War's information, that the Commander in Chief considers the two senior Lieutenant Colonels of every Regiment having two Battalions, as entitled to the Allowance granted to Field Officers in lieu of their Companies, whether actually serving with their respective Battalions or not.

I have the honor to be,

SIR,

Your most obedient

Humble servant,

J. W. GORDON.

F. Moore, Esq.

---

N. B. The like Rule is understood to apply to the two senior *Majors* of Regiments having two Battalions.

## Regimental Allowances.

*Regulation of Allowances for Captains, and Riding Masters, &c. as usually annexed to the annual Establishments.*

### Dragoon Guards and Dragoons.

| Number of Privates per Troop, on the Establishment. | Annual Allowance per Troop. Captain. | Riding Master, &c. |
|---|---|---|
| | £. | £. s. d. |
| Where less than 40 | 30 | 18 1 0 |
| From 40 to 49 | 30 ⎫ | |
| 50 to 69 | 40 ⎬ | 23 6 0 |
| 70 and upwards | 50 ⎭ | |

### Infantry of the Line, Fencible Infantry, and Militia.

| Number of Privates per Company on the Establishment. | Annual Allowance to each Captain. |
|---|---|
| | £. s. d. |
| When 50, or under | 38 5 0 |
| From 51 to 75 | 47 7 6 |
| 76 and upwards | 56 10 0 |

#### MEMORANDUM.

The Captains of Troops in Dragoon Regiments, on *foreign stations*, receive an additional allowance according to the following scale, viz.

| Number of Privates per Troop on the Establishment. | £. |
|---|---|
| From 50 to 59 | 50 |
| 60 to 69 | 60 |
| 70 to 79 | 70 |
| 80 to 89 | 80 |
| 90 to 99 | 90 |
| 100 and upwards | 100 |

*General*

*General Orders relative to the Appropriation of the Contingent Allowance, in the Absence of a Captain of a Troop or Company.*

*Horse Guards,* 11th *February,* 1806.

SOME doubts having arisen with regard to the appropriation of the Contingent Allowance, in the absence of a Captain of a Troop or Company; the Commander in Chief has received His Majesty's commands to declare, that, in such cases, the Subaltern or other Officer, who takes on himself the command and payment of the Troop or Company, and becomes responsible for the same, is entitled to the Contingent Allowance for the time being, and the same is to be appropriated accordingly, under the authority of the Commanding Officer of the Regiment.

His Royal Highness desires it may be clearly understood, that the proportion of the Captain's Allowance in the Infantry Service, which is termed " *Non-effective Allowance,*" viz. 20 *l.* per year, can be received only by the Captain of the Company.

By order of His Royal Highness the Commander in Chief.

HARRY CALVERT,
Adjutant-General.

## Regimental Allowances.

*Circular to the General Officers commanding in Districts, relative to an Allowance for the Maintenance of Adjutants' Horses, dated War Office, 13th July, 1799.*

Sir,

THE Commander in Chief having referred to me two memorials from the adjutants of militia corps, relative to the expence to which they are subjected for the maintenance of the horses, which they are under the necessity of keeping for regimental duty, in pursuance of His Majesty's orders; and the situation of the said officers, and (equally) of the adjutants of the infantry of the line, and fencible infantry, appearing to be well entitled to relief; I have the honor to acquaint you, that His Royal Highness concurs with me in the propriety of granting to each adjutant of infantry of the line, militia, and fencible infantry, in Great Britain, an allowance for the maintenance of one horse, where forage is not issued in kind, at the same rate as is made, in the like case, to the general and staff officers in districts, which at present is two shillings per diem.

This regulation is to commence from the 25th of last month, inclusive, after which time, the adjutants are not to make any charge for the sums which they may pay the innkeepers when their horses are billeted.

The allowance is to be charged monthly, when paid, in the pay lists of the respective corps, and by his Royal Highness's express desire, a certificate is to be annexed thereto, from the commanding officer, declaring upon honor, that the horse kept by the adjutant, is actually his property, and necessarily kept for regimental duty, and that it has been so during the whole of the period for which the allowance shall have been charged.

I have the honor to be, Sir,

Your most obedient humble servant,

W. WINDHAM.

General the commanding in District.

*Letter stating the Allowances for Lodging Money to Officers in North Britain.*

*War Office, 22d July,* 1797.

MY LORD,

HAVING taken into consideration the circumstances mentioned in your Lordship's Letter of the 8th instant, in regard to Officers of Regiments quartered in North Britain, for whom billets, entitling them to quarters as Officers, cannot be obtained, nor any accommodation provided in barracks, I am to acquaint you that an allowance may be made to each Officer so circumstanced, at the same rates as in England, viz.

|  | s. | d. |  |
|---|---|---|---|
| For a Field Officer | 10 | 6 | }per Week. |
| For a Captain - | 8 | 0 | |
| For a Subaltern - | 6 | 0 | |

This allowance is to depend, in every instance, upon your Lordship's special permission, in full confidence that you will take special care that it shall not be extended to any Officer who might be accommodated in Barracks, or who shall not have been under the necessity of hiring Lodgings. And the payment is to be made by the Assistant Barrack Master General in North Britain, upon proper Returns and Certificates signed by your Lordship.

I have the honor to be

Your Lordship's

Most obedient humble servant,

(Signed) W. WINDHAM.

General Commanding in
North Britain.

## Regimental Allowances.

*Letter stating the Rates of the Allowance for Lodging Money to Officers in South Britain.*

*War Office,* 25*th May,* 1795.

SIR,

I AM directed to acquaint you, that where there are no Barrack Apartments for Officers, and the impossibility of billeting them is ascertained; the actual expenditure for Lodging, not exceeding the sums undermentioned, will be allowed, viz.

|                    | s. | d. |           |
|--------------------|----|----|-----------|
| For a Field Officer | 10 | 6  | }         |
| For a Captain      | 8  | 0  | per Week.* |
| For a Subaltern    | 6  | 0  | }         |

I have the honor to be,

SIR,

Your most obedient

Humble servant,

(Signed) M. LEWIS.

Officer Commanding
   the       Regiment of

---

* The above Allowances are paid by the Barrack Department.

*Warrant, granting an Allowance in lieu of Small Beer to the Troops serving at Home; and containing further Regulations on various Matters directed by His Majesty's Warrants of the 25th May, 1797, "For encreasing and regulating the Pay and Allowance of Non-commissioned Officers and Private Men of Corps of Cavalry and Infantry serving at Home." Dated 17th March, 1800.*

## GEORGE R.

WHEREAS it hath appeared expedient for our service to discontinue the supply of small beer to our troops when stationed in barracks, and when billeted in settled quarters, and to grant a pecuniary compensation in lieu thereof; our will and pleasure therefore is, that in all such situations where small beer has been hitherto supplied, and where the supply thereof shall have been discontinued as aforesaid, an allowance of one penny a day, in addition to his pay, shall be made to each serjeant, corporal, trumpeter, drummer, fifer, and private man, of our regiments of life guards, royal regiment of horse guards, regiments of dragoon guards, dragoons, fencible cavalry, foot guards, infantry of the line, embodied militia, and fencible infantry, and companies of invalids.

And whereas it is judged expedient, with the view of simplifying the accounts of our said non-commissioned officers, and private men, that the like allowance of one penny a day shall be made to them when billeted on a march, notwithstanding they will then still continue to receive small beer from the innkeepers as part of their diet, we are hereby pleased to direct, that, the said allowance being accordingly continued to them, a proportionate encrease be made in the rate payable out of the subsistence of the soldier on a march, for his diet and small beer; so as that each dragoon shall pay seven pence per diem, instead of six pence; and each foot soldier five pence per diem, instead of four pence.

As in consequence of this regulation it has become necessary to revise our warrants of the 25th May, 1797, "for increasing and regulating the pay and allowance of non-commissioned officers and private men of corps of cavalry and infantry serving at home;" we are hereby pleased to

declare

declare our royal will and pleasure as follows, touching the several points contained in our said warrants, which are connected with the measures herein directed.

The proportion of the pay of each non-commissioned officer and soldier, directed by the said warrants to be applied to the expence of his mess, having been limited to four shillings and six pence a week in the dragoons, and four shillings a week in the infantry, at which time the man was not liable to the expence of small beer; and it being necessary to fix a new rate under that head; it is our will and pleasure, that the proportion of each man's pay, to be set apart for his mess under the present regulation, shall be limited to five shillings and one penny a week in the dragoons, and to four shillings and seven pence a week in the infantry; unless (as declared in our said warrants) he shall himself choose to appropriate a further part of his pay and allowance for this purpose.

Where any soldier, having orders to be quartered, shall be permitted by his commanding officer to find his own lodging, and shall provide himself with small beer and the other articles alluded to in our said warrants, he shall continue to receive the present allowance of two pence a day; in which it is, however, to be clearly understood, that the pecuniary compensation in lieu of small beer is included.

In North Britain, where our troops are provided with quarters in the houses of the inhabitants, but are not furnished with any of the articles supplied to the billeted soldier in England, the allowance to each man shall be one penny halfpenny a day, beer money included.

But no soldier embarked in ships or coasting vessels, [in hospital],* in prison, on furlough, or absent without leave, shall be entitled to receive either, or any part, of the three before specified allowances.

And whereas it was ordered by our said warrants, that, " in camps, where small beer is not provided, but where six pounds of bread are furnished to the soldier every four days, he paying only five pence towards the expence there-

---

* This expression was not construed to apply to men in *regimental* hospitals, who were always, and are still, allowed beer money.

From the 22d February, 1804, beer money has been equally allowed to men in *general* hospitals. See Section VI.

of, an allowance of five pence farthing should be made to him weekly, as an equivalent for the difference;" we are graciously pleased, instead of the said allowance of five pence farthing a week, to grant to the soldiers encamped, the like allowance of one penny per diem as is made to them in barracks, the stoppage for bread continuing as before.

Lastly, it is our royal will and pleasure, that this regulation do commence and take place from the 25th instant inclusive. Given at our court at St. James's this 17th day of March, 1800, in the fortieth year of our reign.

By His Majesty's command.

W. WINDHAM.

*Circular*

*Circular to the Commanding Officers of Regiments, relative to placing the Supply of Bread to the Troops in England under the Commissary General.*

*War Office, November 20th,* 1800.

SIR,

I HAVE it in command to acquaint you that from the 25th instant inclusive, the supply of Bread to His Majesty's forces in England, is to be made under the directions of the Commissary General, and to signify to you the King's pleasure, that the following instructions which have been suggested by the Commissary General as indispensably necessary for the due execution of this service, be strictly and invariably observed by the Regiment under your command.

1. That Officers commanding Corps or Detachments are to sign Returns of their effective Non-commissioned Officers and Privates for whom they demand Bread, and to direct a Commissioned Officer to receive, and give a receipt for the same.

2. That Commanding Officers, Adjutants, and Paymasters are to sign the Contractor's Monthly Accompts, according to the Form expressed in the printed paper, No. 1, enclosed herewith.*

3. That no Bread is to be received from the Contractors, but what shall be in weight and quality conformable to the contract, and on no consideration is any compensation whatever to be admitted in lieu of Bread.

---

* It has not been thought necessary to reprint the Form. The Certificate annexed thereto is as follows:

"We do hereby certify upon honour, that the Non-commissioned Officers and privates, for whom a charge is made in the above account, were effective and present at the periods specified, and that the quantities of Bread, as stated, were actually delivered to them according to the rates and prices therein specified,

Dated at  
this    day of    180  

Commanding Officer.  
Paymaster.  
Adjutant."

To which is to be added a Declaration from the Contractor. Vide 36th Article of the Explanatory Directions of 5th March, 1803. (Section III.)

4. That

4. That in case the Contractors or their Agents shall not duly supply Bread according to the contract, the Officer commanding is to make immediate complaint to the Commissary General in London, and to report the same to the General Officer commanding the district.

5. That the regimental Paymasters are to pay the Contractors monthly, according to the stipulations in the printed paper, No. 1, being the conditions of the contract: the sixpence per loaf therein mentioned, is of course the four days stoppage from the pay of the Soldier.

To guard against abuse in this material branch of public expenditure, the Commissary General has been ordered to keep a separate correct accompt with every regimental Corps, and from time to time to have it checqued with the number of their effective Non-commissioned Officers and Privates.

The printed paper, marked No. 2, transmitted herewith,* contains a list of all the post towns in England and Wales, arranged under their respective counties, and specifies against each, the names of the Contractors, their Agents and Bakers, who are to supply the Troops with Bread in the respective situations.

            I have the honour to be,

        SIR,

           Your most obedient humble servant,

                W. WINDHAM.

To the Officer commanding

---

\* Not reprinted.

*Circular*

*Circular to the Commanding Officers of Regiments in Great Britain, relative to the Allowance for the extra Price of Meat.*

*War Office, 25th March, 1801.*

SIR,

THERE being reason to believe that the Orders formerly issued, relative to the Allowance of the extra price of Meat to the Non-commissioned Officers and Privates of His Majesty's Regiments of Cavalry and Infantry, are either not generally known or have not been sufficiently adverted to, I have the honour to enclose to you a Form of an Account, with the Certificate to be annexed thereto,* to be transcribed on one of the blank leaves of the Regimental Pay Lists, by which the expenditures under that head will uniformly be required to be vouched, before they can be admitted as a charge against the Public.

I am at the same time to recommend to you in the strongest manner to watch over the application of the said Allowance, and to give the utmost attention to prevent any excess of Expenditure, by taking care that no higher price is given than is absolutely necessary for procuring good and wholesome Meat, such as Soldiers are used to have, and that no extravagance be admitted in the quality thereof.

I have the honor to be,

SIR,

Your most obedient,

Humble Servant,

C. YORKE.

Officer Commanding the
Regiment of

---

* This Form is not reprinted, an amended Form having since been circulated. See page 74*.

*General Orders relative to the extra Price of Meat allowed to Soldiers, dated Horse Guards, 4th August, 1803.*

It appearing to the Commander in Chief, that His Majesty's gracious Intentions, in allowing to Soldiers the *extra price of Meat* beyond a certain rate, as declared by His Majesty's Regulations of the 25th of May, 1797, and enforced and explained by the Secretary at War's Circular Letter, bearing date the 25th March, 1801, have not been universally understood, and acted upon with a due regard to œconomy; but that, in some Instances, through the judicious interference of the General Officers commanding in the Districts, certain Regulations have been so properly and effectually established on this head, that the interests of the Public have been entirely guarded from imposition, while the comfort and welfare of the Soldiers have at the same time been duly provided for; and His Royal Highness having been informed, that, in other districts, where the same salutary interposition had not been exerted, the charges for the *extra price of Meat* have been made at so high a rate, as not only to manifest a material defect in the interior œconomy of the regiment, but to shew an obvious misconception of the principles on which alone such charges should properly be admitted against the Public; the effect of which misconception has evidently been to raise the price of Meat upon the inhabitants in general: the Commander in Chief thinks it proper to call the particular attention of all the General Officers on the Staff to this important object, and desires that they will signify to the Commanding Officers of Regiments, and instruct them to explain in the clearest and most explicit manner to the Non-commissioned Officers and Soldiers, that, although care is to be constantly taken, that the Meat provided for the Soldiers shall be at all times good and wholesome, it never was His Majesty's intention to burden the Public with the excess of price for Meat, of a quality superior to that, which the men were accustomed to purchase for themselves, before this bounty was extended to them; much less was it intended to authorise their purchase of the prime pieces exclusively; and that their persevering in this practice, which seems to have too generally prevailed, may tend to bring in question the propriety of the Allowance being any longer continued to them.

His Royal Highness desires, that the General Officers will further

further inftruct the Commanding Officers of Regiments, that the carcafs, the fide, or quarter, of the beaft, (according as circumftances may require,) fhould be purchafed together: the excefs, if any, being of courfe charged on the average price of the whole.

The Commander in Chief is further pleafed to order, that the certificates in fupport of the charges made in the regimental accompts for the excefs of the price of meat beyond 6d. per pound, fhould hereafter (in conformity to a form which will be circulated from the War Office,) be authenticated in all Regiments ferving in Brigade, or in Garrifon or Cantonments, by the *additional fignature of the General or other Officer commanding*: and His Royal Highnefs moft confidently looks to the perfonal interference and exertion of General Officers commanding Diftricts, and all other General Officers on the Staff, for fuch an improvement of this branch of the public expenditure, as may prevent the fubject from being again brought under His Royal Highnefs's notice.

By order of His Royal Highnefs the Commander in Chief.

HARRY CALVERT,
Adj. Gen. of the Forces.

*Circular*

*Circular Letter to Officers commanding Regiments stationed in Great Britain, enclosing Forms of Accompt for the Charge of the Extra Price of Meat.*

*War Office,* 13th August, 1803.

Sir,

IN pursuance of the intimation given in the General Order of His Royal Highness the Commander in Chief, dated the 4th Instant, I enclose herewith the *Forms of Accompt and Certificates which will be hereafter required in support of the charges made on account of the extra price of meat. These Forms will be furnished from this office with the regimental pay lists, and you will be pleased to cause the same to be affixed thereto, after being signed by the General Officer, or Officer commanding, as directed by the order above mentioned.

I have the honor to be,

SIR,

your most obedient

humble Servant,

CHARLES BRAGGE.

Officer commanding the
 Regiment of

---

\* These Forms are not reprinted, others having been substituted in their stead. See page 74\*.

74*

ACCOMPT of MEAT purchased for the Non-commissioned Officers, Trumpeters, Drummers, Fifers, and Privates, of the _____ Regiment of _____ between the 25th _____ and the 24th of _____ 1806, both days inclusive.

| Places where supplied. | Dates when supplied | No. of days for which supplied. | PARTICULARS OF THE MEAT SUPPLIED AT EACH DELIVERY. | | | | | | | | | REMARKS. |
|---|---|---|---|---|---|---|---|---|---|---|---|---|
| | | | Number of Non-commissioned Officers, Trumpeters, Drummers, Fifers, and Privates, present and not on the March. | | No. of Pounds of Meat delivered for Soldiers not in hospital, at a Pound each per diem. | Expence of the Pound. | Total Expence of the Meat supplied for Men not on a March nor in Hospital. | | | Amount of Charge to Government, after deducting 6d. per pound, to be defrayed out of the Pay of the Soldier. | | | |
| | | | In Regimental Hospital. | Not in Hospital and supplied with Meat. | | d. | £. | s. | d. | £. | s. | d. | |
| | | | | | | | | | | | | | |
| Totals. | | | | | | | | | | | | | |

WE CERTIFY upon *Honour*, that the Non-commissioned Officers, Trumpeters, Drummers, Fifers, and Privates, for whom a Charge is made in this Return, were effective and present, and *were not victualled by the Innkeepers*, nor *in Hospital*, at the respective periods herein specified; that the Quantity of Meat as stated, was actually delivered to them agreeably to His Majesty's Regulations, according to the Rates and Prices charged; and that every possible care has been taken to obtain the Meat on the most reasonable Terms, and in strict conformity to the General Order of the Commander in Chief, dated 4th August, 1803.

_____ COMMANDING-OFFICER, _____ ADJUTANT, _____ PAYMASTER.

I confirm the above Charge as being fair and reasonable, according to the information which I have obtained of the Price of Meat in the part of the Country where the Corps was stationed at the time.

_____ { *Commanding the Brigade, or in the District.* }

N. B. The word "Trumpeter," should be struck out in the Accompts made out for Infantry, and the words, "Drummer and Fifer," in those for Cavalry.

*An Act for increasing the Rates of Subsistence to be paid to Innkeepers and others on quartering Soldiers, dated 21st July, 1806.* [46 Geo. III. Cap. 126.]

WHEREAS by an Act passed in the present session of Parliament, for punishing Mutiny and Desertion, and for the better Payment of the Army and their Quarters, certain rates are established in that part of the United Kingdom of *Great Britain* and *Ireland* called *England*, the dominion of *Wales*, and the town of *Berwick-upon-Tweed*, for the payment of innholders and others on whom Non-commissioned Officers and Private Soldiers are quartered and billetted, who shall be furnished with diet and small beer at their quarters; and an option is given to such innholders and others, to furnish certain articles *gratis*, in lieu of diet and small beer, at the rates prescribed: and whereas the rules prescribed for furnishing Soldiers with necessaries are, in many instances, become from the high price of provisions, inadequate, and are productive of distress to such innholders and others; may it therefore please your Majesty that it may be enacted; and be it enacted by the King's most Excellent Majesty, by and with the advice and consent of the Lords Spiritual and Temporal, and Commons, in this present Parliament assembled, and by the authority of the same, that every Non-commissioned Officer and Private Soldier who shall be furnished with diet and small beer within the aforesaid parts of the United Kingdom, by the innholders or other persons on whom such Non-commissioned Officers or Private Soldiers shall be quartered and billetted by virtue of the said act, shall pay and allow for the same One Shilling and Four-pence *per diem*; and that the accounts of the same shall be rendered, and payment thereof made, in like manner as is directed in the said act now in force touching the former rates of Seven-pence *per diem* for the Cavalry, and Five-pence *per diem* for the Infantry.

II. And be it further enacted, that in case any innholders or other persons on whom any Non-commissioned Officers or Private Men shall be quartered within the aforesaid parts of the United Kingdom, shall, by virtue of the said option in the said act,

act, furnish such Non-commissioned Officers or Soldiers with the articles therein mentioned, in lieu of furnishing diet and small beer, at the rates prescribed by this act, such innholders or other persons on whom such Non-commissioned Officers or Soldiers are quartered, and by whom the said articles shall have been so supplied, shall receive, in consideration thereof, one halfpenny *per diem* for each Non-commissioned Officer and Soldier, instead of furnishing the same *gratis*, as required by the said act; which sum of one halfpenny *per diem* shall be accounted for and paid in like manner as is directed touching the rates aforesaid.

III. And be it further enacted, that the sum to be paid to the innholder or other person within the aforesaid parts of the United Kingdom, on whom any of the horses belonging to His Majesty's forces shall be quartered by virtue of the said act, for hay and straw, shall be One Shilling and Two-pence *per diem* for each horse, instead of Six-pence *per diem* as directed in the said act.

IV. And whereas the provisions contained in the said recited act, with respect to the manner of dieting within the aforesaid parts of the United Kingdom, Non-commissioned Officers and Soldiers on a march, or employed in recruiting, and likewise the Recruits by them raised, have been productive of much inconvenience, as well to the troops, as to the innholders; be it further enacted, that so much of the said recited act as relates to the manner of furnishing Non-commissioned Officers and Soldiers on a march, or employed in recruiting, and likewise the Recruits by them raised, with diet or other provision, be, and the same is hereby repealed.

V. And be it further enacted, that all Non-commissioned Officers and Soldiers shall be entitled to receive their diet and small beer from the innholders or other persons on whom they may be billetted, within the aforesaid parts of the United Kingdom, at the rates herein-before prescribed, while on the march, as also on and for the day of their arrival at the place of their final destination, and on the two subsequent days, unless either of the two subsequent days shall be a market day in and for the town or place where such Officers or Soldiers shall be billetted, or within the distance of two miles thereof; in which case it shall and may be lawful for the innholder, or other person as aforesaid, to discontinue, on and from such market day, the supply of diet and small beer, and to furnish in lieu thereof the articles

## Regimental Allowances.

articles in the said recited act specified; and at the rate hereinbefore prescribed.

VI. Provided always, that if any victualler or other person liable by the said recited act to have Soldiers billetted or quartered on him or her, shall pay any sum or sums of money to any Non-commissioned Officer or Soldier on the march, in lieu of furnishing in kind the diet and small beer to which such Non-commissioned Officer or Soldier is entitled under the said act, every such victualler or other person may be proceeded against and fined in like manner as if he or she had refused to furnish or allow according to the directions of the said recited act, the several things respectively directed to be furnished to Non-commissioned Officers or Soldiers so quartered or billetted on him or her as aforesaid.

VII. Provided also, that if any Regiment, Troop, Company, or Detachment, when on the march, shall be halted, either for a limited or indefinite time, at any intermediate place, the Non-commissioned Officers and Soldiers belonging thereto shall be entitled to receive their diet and small beer from the persons on whom they shall be billetted at such intermediate place, for such time only for which they would be entitled to receive the same after arriving at the place of their final destination, according to this act.

VIII. Provided nevertheless, that whenever it shall happen that any Regiment, Troop, Company, or Detachment, when on their march, shall be halted, and it shall appear by the marching orders, that it is not intended that such Regiment, Troop, Company, or Detachment, shall halt for any longer time than one entire day after the day of their arrival at the place of halting, and the day after such arrival shall be such market day as aforesaid, it shall not be lawful for the innholders or other persons, on whom the Non-commissioned Officers and Soldiers shall be billetted, to discontinue on such market day, the supply of diet and small beer to any such Officers or Soldiers; but that all such Officers and Soldiers shall be entitled to receive their diet and small beer from such innholders and other persons aforesaid, upon such market day as aforesaid, at the rates herein-before prescribed, in like manner as they would have been entitled thereto, if such day had not been a market day; any thing herein-before contained to the contrary hereof notwithstanding.

IX. And be it further enacted, that all Non-commissioned Officers and Private Men employed in recruiting, and the Recruits

cruits by them raised, shall, while on the march, and for two days after the day of their arrival at any recruiting station, be entitled to the same benefits as are herein-before provided in regard to troops upon the march; but no Recruit enlisted after the two days subsequent to the arrival of the party at their Recruiting station, shall be entitled to be supplied with diet and small beer at the rate herein-before prescribed, except at the option of the person on whom he shall be quartered: provided also nevertheless, that in case any such Recruiting Party, with the Recruits by them raised, shall remove from their station, and after a time shall return to the same place, they and the Recruits by them raised, so returning, shall not be again entitled to the supply of diet and small beer for such two days as aforesaid, unless the period between the time of their removal from such place, and their return thereto, shall have exceeded twenty-eight days.

X. And be it further enacted, that this act shall have continuance from the twenty-fourth day of *March*, one thousand eight hundred and six, until the twenty-fifth day of *March*, one thousand eight hundred and seven.

*Circular*

*Circular Letter from the Secretary at War, to the Commanding Officers of Cavalry, relative to limiting the Quantity of Hay and Straw supplied by the Innkeepers.*

*War Office,* 18*th March,* 1797.

SIR,

In order to remove a constant source of dissatisfaction among the Cavalry, and the innkeepers on whose houses they are billeted, the former complaining of the insufficiency of Hay and Straw supplied to their horses, and the latter of the unnecessary consumption and waste of those articles by the troops, it has frequently been proposed, that the quantity should either be limited by the Mutiny Act, or fixed by an official regulation: but, as yet, it has not been judged expedient to adopt a general measure of this kind; not from any doubts as to the quantities which might reasonably be required of the innkeeper, and which (if supplied fairly and of good quality) ought to be deemed sufficient for the daily consumption of the horses; but from difficulties to be apprehended in the execution of the measure, which, unless very particularly provided against, might be productive of material injury to His Majesty's service; namely, the difficulty of ascertaining in all cases, that the innkeeper actually delivers the quantity of Hay and Straw he is bound to do, and of good quality; and that of finding proper places wherein to secure the same when delivered, from the depredation of the servants or guests of the innkeeper.

The experiment, however, has been tried in a few places, under the orders of the Generals commanding in districts; and no inconvenience, as far as I can learn, has resulted from it to the troops; owing to a due observance, on the part of the innkeepers, of those conditions which had been prescribed for the protection of the service.

I have, therefore, thought it my duty to bring the subject under the consideration of the Duke of York; and, with His Royal Highness's concurrence, have submitted the same to His Majesty, who is graciously pleased to order, that from the 25th day of this month inclusive, a limitation of Hay and Straw shall be generally established for the horses of the Cavalry, whereever billeted, under the following regulations; it being at the

same

same time clearly underſtood, that if any innkeeper ſhould fail to perform his part of the engagement, or, in the mode of performing it, ſhould wilfully and unneceſſarily create embarraſsment to the troops, the order, as far as reſpects ſuch innkeeper, will be thereupon revoked.

The regulations to be obſerved are theſe:

1ſt. The quantity to be ſupplied by the innkeeper for each Dragoon horſe, *per diem*, ſhall be eighteen pounds of good Hay, ſo long as the preſent ration of corn is allowed by Government, and ſix pounds of good Straw.

2dly. The deliveries ſhall be either for one day, or for a certain number of days at one time, according as the Commanding Officer ſhall approve; and they ſhall be made at ſuch hours, and in the preſence of ſuch deſcription of Officers or Non-commiſſioned Officers, as he ſhall appoint.

3dly. The articles, after being weighed out, ſhall be depoſited in ſtore rooms, of which the troops ſhall have the keys; and to which no other perſon ſhall have acceſs without their concurrence.

4thly. Separate ſtables, into which no horſes, beſides thoſe of the Dragoons, are to be put, ſhall be aſſigned, wherever it is practicable.

I have the honour to be,

SIR,

Your moſt obedient humble ſervant,

W. WINDHAM.

Officer commanding
the            Regt. of

*Circular*

## Regimental Allowances.

*Circular Letter to the Commanding Officers of Regiments of Cavalry at home, placing the Supply of Oats under the Commissary General.*

*War Office,* 15*th August,* 1801.

SIR,

I HAVE it in command to acquaint you, that, from the 25th instant inclusive, the supply of *oats* to His Majesty's Regiments of Cavalry, *stationed in England and Wales, when not in barracks or encamped,* is to be made under the directions of the *Commissary General*; who, in consequence of orders from the Lords Commissioners of the Treasury, has entered into contracts with persons for the supply of that article in the respective counties. The contractors are to have an agent in every market town, with his name, and the words " *Purveyor of Oats to the Army*," painted over his door, by which the Regiment under your command will be informed where to apply, and they are directed in all ordinary cases to issue, at each delivery, the quantity necessary for *three days consumption*. The contractors, or their agents, are at each settlement to produce to the Paymasters *the Commissary General's certificate, expressing the price to be paid for the oats* for the four weeks last past in each respective county.

The enclosed copy of a contract made for one of the counties will shew you more fully the conditions of the contract, as also the forms of accompt and certificate, which it has been thought necessary to establish generally for the purpose of carrying this measure into execution;* and I am

---

\* It has not been thought necessary to reprint the forms of the contracts and accompts. The forms of the Certificates are as follows:

" I hereby certify, that to the best of my knowledge and belief, this account of oats is justly stated as to the quantity actually supplied to the horses present; that the quality of the oats was conformable to what is required by the contract, and that the price charged agrees with the rate certified by the Commissary General, for the period of this account.—And I further certify, that no charge is made herein for oats supplied for horses, not *bona fide* the property of the Officers, as belonging to whom they were mustered, or

am to signify to you His Majesty's pleasure, that the same be strictly and invariably observed by the Regiment under your command.

It is scarcely necessary for me to add, that, from the 25th instant inclusive, no charge is to be made in the Pay Lists of the Regiment on account of the *extra feed of oats*; the horses of Officers as well as the troop horses, are however to be mustered and their numbers placed on the Pay List as heretofore.

To obviate any possible future misconception as to the rules by which the demands of oats for the Regiment under your command are to be regulated, I think it right to annex hereto a memorandum on the subject, which has been communicated officially to the Commissary General. A copy of this letter will shortly be transmitted with the Pay Lists, for the use of the Paymaster, and you will be pleased to take care that it be duly recorded in the manner pointed out by the last paragraph of the 14th article of the additional Instructions and Regulations respecting the conduct of regimental Paymasters and others, dated the 11th of May, 1801.

I have the honor to be,

SIR,

Your most obedient

Humble servant,

C. YORKE.

The Officer commanding the
    Regiment of            Dragoons.

---

or that exceeded for each Officer the number limited by the King's Regulations.

Commanding Officer."

" I hereby declare upon my honour, that after the most careful enquiry, and having checked this account by the receipts given for the separate issues, the price certified by the Commissary General for the period of this account, and by the number of horses borne on the Pay List, I verily believe the same to be just and true; and I have therefore paid the contractor the total amount above stated, without any deduction whatever.

Paymaster."

To which is to be added a Declaration from the Contractor.—Vide 36th Article of the Explanatory Directions of 5th March, 1803.

*Memo-*

## Regimental Allowances.

*Memorandum relative to the Extra Feed.*

The allowance of *extra feed* is from the 1st of March to the 30th of September, both days inclusive, 8 pounds *of oats per diem*; and from the 1st of October to the last day in February, both days inclusive, 7 pounds *of oats, per diem,* for each troop horse *present in quarters*: towards the expence whereof is to be *credited* 2½*d per diem*, for each ration, being the proportion of the subsistence of the troop horse applicable to the purchase of oats.

The like allowance of oats is made, and the like credit taken, for each effective horse of the commissioned and warrant Officers *present*, not exceeding the regulated proportion for each rank as specified below.

The part of the cost of each ration, not drawn for upon the Commissary General, viz. 2½d. per diem for each horse of the Officers, as also for each troop horse, is to be paid to the contractor in the manner specified in the contract.

| | |
|---|---|
| Field Officer, having a regimental commission as such | 4 horses |
| Captain, ditto | 3 |
| Captain Lieutenant | 3 |
| Subaltern | 2 |
| Adjutant | 2 |
| Surgeon | 1 |
| Assistant Surgeon | 1 |
| Veterinary Surgeon | 1 |
| Paymaster | 1 |
| Quarter Master | 1 |

*Circular to Commanding Officers of Regiments of Cavalry, relative to the Purchase of Troop Horses.*

*War Office,* 29*th June,* 1799.

SIR,

IT being understood, that the King's Regulation, respecting the price of troop horses for Corps of Cavalry, has on some recent occasions been represented as bearing a sense not conformable to His Majesty's intentions, I have it in command to declare His Majesty's pleasure, that no Officer whatsoever is to derive any pecuniary benefit from the purchasing or contracting for such horses, but that in every instance the sums actually and bonâ fide paid to the dealers, with the other necessary expences previous to delivery at Head Quarters, are to be the sums charged to the Public, provided the same do not exceed the amount of Twenty-five Guineas for each horse.

The whole of the money received for cast horses, which are in every instance to be disposed of at the best advantage, is to be credited in the public accompts.

I am further to signify to you His Majesty's pleasure, that this letter be without delay entered in the Orderly Book of the Corps, and that a copy thereof be forthwith delivered under your orders to the Regimental Paymaster.

I have the honor to be,

SIR,

Your most obedient

Humble servant,

W. WINDHAM.

*Circular*

*Circular to Commanding Officers of Regiments of Cavalry, relative to the Purchase of Troop Horses.*

*War Office, 23d May,* 1803.

SIR,

IT having been represented, that the present allowance for the purchase of horses for the Cavalry is unequal in the case of Regiments stationed at a distance from the places where they are usually procured, as also generally insufficient for obtaining such as are perfectly proper for His Majesty's service, I have the honor to acquaint you, that, after full consideration of the subject, the following regulation has been recommended by his Royal Highness the Commander in Chief, and that, having been submitted to the King, it has received His Majesty's royal approbation, viz.

The actual price paid to the dealers, not exceeding twenty-five guineas, will be allowed for each horse delivered at the head quarters of the Regiment, and approved by the Commanding Officer; and a further allowance of two shillings and sixpence for every such horse will be made to the dealer, for every complete eighteen miles which the horse shall have been marched on the direct road from the place where he was purchased by the Officer to the head quarters, except the first eighteen miles, for which the dealer is not to have any allowance. The said purchase money and allowance are to be paid by the regimental paymaster, under the instruction of the Commanding Officer, by a bill upon the Agent at thirty days sight, in favor of the dealer; and a statement, showing the particulars of the charge for which each bill shall be given, is to be annexed to the pay list.

I am further to acquaint you, that His Majesty has been pleased to grant to the Officers sent from the Regiment for the purpose of inspecting and purchasing horses, an allowance of travelling expences at the rate of eighteen pence per mile, both in going to, and returning from the places to which they shall be ordered on this duty; provided the number of approved horses procured by the Officer, and joining the Regiment at one time, shall amount to ten or upwards; and provided also, that the total annual amount of the said allowance shall not exceed twenty shillings for each horse actually recruited by the said Officers in the course of the year; which is to be shewn by a

detailed

detailed yearly account, certified by the Commanding Officer, and annexed by the Paymaster to his supplementary pay list.

I am to add, that the above regulation is to commence from the 25th instant.

I have the honor to be,

SIR,

Your most obedient,

Humble servant,

C. YORKE,

Officer Commanding
    the       Regiment of

*Circular*

*Circular Letter from the Deputy Secretary at War to the Colonels of Regiments of Cavalry, relative to the Extra Allowance to Farriers.*

*War Office,* 15*th July,* 1802.

SIR,

IN the absence of the Secretary at War I have the honor to acquaint you, in pursuance of instructions from His Royal Highness the Commander in Chief, that from the 25th ultimo inclusive, only* one Farrier per Troop will be allowed in the Regiment of         under your command.

I am at the same time to communicate to you the following particulars in regard to the allowances that will be made for farriery, from the above period, viz.

During the time that the Regiment shall be serving at home, the Farriers are to receive an allowance of three farthings per diem for each effective troop horse, one halfpenny thereof being payable out of the subsistence of the horse, and the remainder being to be charged by the Paymaster as an extra expence. This allowance is clearly to be understood as including the sum of Three Shillings per annum, to be paid by the Farriers for medicines supplied by the principal Veterinary Surgeon.

During the time that the Regiment shall be stationed abroad, no charge of an extra allowance to the Farriers is to be made in the public accompts; but in cases where the Farriers shall find the regular allowance of one halfpenny per diem, paid out of the subsistence of the horse, to be insufficient, they are to address their applications for relief through the Commanding Officer of the Regiment, to the General Officer commanding on the station, who will grant such relief as he shall think proper, and charge the amount in his contingent account with the Treasury.

I have the honor to be, &c. &c.

(Signed)     M. LEWIS.

---

\* See the following Circular of 20th August, 1803.

*Circular Letter to Colonels of Dragoon Guards and Dragoons on the Home Station, relative to the Extra Allowance for Farriery.*

*War Office, 20th August, 1803.*

SIR,

I N pursuance of a communication from Head Quarters, I have the honor to acquaint you, that in consequence of the augmentation of the Regiment under your command, commencing from the 25th June last, two Farriers per Troop will be allowed to be employed therein; and that from the above period, the extra allowance for farriery may be charged accordingly, at the rate of one halfpenny per day.

I have the honor to be, &c.

C. YORKE.

Colonel of the
  Regiment of

*Circular*

## Regimental Allowances.

*Circular to Colonels of Regiments of Cavalry on the British Establishment, relative to an Allowance for Saddle Water Decks and Corn Sacks.*

War-Office, 23d August, 1803.

SIR,

It having been represented to the King, that it would be both advantageous to the service, and useful to the men, if each Non-commissioned Officer, Trumpeter, and Private, of the Regiments of Cavalry were to be constantly in possession of a saddle water deck, for the preservation of his baggage and necessaries; and of a corn sack, for the conveyance of the supplies of oats, which are frequently required to be carried from one station to another; I have the honor to acquaint you that His Majesty is pleased to approve of the above articles being immediately furnished to the Regiment under your command, and you are hereby authorised to order the same to be provided, for the complete establishment of the corps, according to a pattern lodged in the office of the Adjutant General. The actual cost of the said articles not exceeding 7s. 6d. for the water deck, and 3s.* for the corn sack, with the expence of the package and carriage, will, in the first instance, be allowed by warrants from this Office, upon the bills of the tradesmen being given in, accompanied by certificates from the Commanding Officer, that the articles have been furnished and forwarded to the Regiment; and that they are conformable to the approved patterns, which being previously sealed by the inspectors of clothing, should be forwarded to the Regiment.

I am further to acquaint you, that the water deck being expected to last six years, and the corn sack three years, an allowance of 2s. 3d. per annum, will be made for each Non-commissioned Officer, Trumpeter, and Private Man, borne on the establishment of your Regiment, from the 25th December next, inclusive, which will be issued half-yearly into the hands of the Agent, and will constitute the fund for supplying, under

---

* The rate of allowance for the corn sack having been found inadequate, the first supply of corn sacks has in several instances been made from the public stores.

the superintendence of the Commanding Officer, the deficiencies that may occur in the above articles in the usual course of service; but it being thought proper, that both the saddle water decks, and the corn sacks, should be deemed to be regimental necessaries, any extraordinary wear and tear thereof, occasioned by the neglect of the men, is to be made good at their expence.

In case of an augmentation of the establishment of the corps, you will order the proper quantity of the said articles to be provided for the additional numbers, and cause the accompts to be rendered to this Office, as above-mentioned.

You will be pleased to direct your Agent to prepare, and transmit to this department, annual accompts, made up to the 24th December, properly certified by the Commanding Officer, of the amount of the fund assigned for the supply of saddle water decks and corn sacks, and of the appropriation thereof; and you will take care, that a particular report of the numbers, and condition of the articles in the possession of the corps, be invariably made to the General Officers, who may, from time to time, be appointed to inspect, or review your Regiment.

If your Regiment is at present in possession of any of the above articles, you will cause them to be expended for the use of the Corps, before the new articles, now ordered, are delivered out.

    I have the honor to be,

     SIR,

      Your most obedient,

       Humble servant,

        (Signed)  C. BRAGGE.

Colonel of the
    Regiment of

*Extract*

*Extract of a Regulation for Contingent Accounts of Regiments of Dragoon Guards, Dragoons, and Foot, on Home Service, from the 25th of December, 1783. Dated War Office, 25th February, 1784.*

" VARIOUS regulations having been eftablifhed by an act paffed in the laft feffion of Parliament, refpecting iffues of public money for the pay and contingent demands of the Army; and it being found expedient, and for the good of the fervice, in conformity to the views of the faid act, that certain fixed allowances fhould be granted for fuch of the ordinary contingent expences of Regiments on Home Service, as, though ufually allowed, have not hitherto been provided for in that manner, viz.

Stationary and poftage for Regiments of Dragoon Guards and Dragoons:

And ftationary, poftage, guard rooms, and ftore rooms, for Regiments of Foot:

It is His Majefty's pleafure, that the following allowances be granted to, and charged by them in future in their refpective contingent accompts, viz.

[1ft, An annual allowance of 12*l* to each Regiment of Dragoon Guards and Dragoons, for poftage and ftationary, taken together;

2dly. An annual allowance of 30*l* to each Regiment of Foot, for poftage, ftationary, guard rooms, and ftore rooms taken together.*]

Thefe allowances to commence from 25th of December, 1783, inclufive, being the commencement of the act before mentioned; and no extra charge from that period to be admitted for regimental books, returns, atteftations, difcharges, or any other article whatfoever falling under the general head of ftationary; or for poftage paid by Officers on recruiting or other fervices; or for guard rooms or ftore rooms on marches or in quarters.

It is His Majefty's further pleafure, that the former allowance of [1s. per mile to each troop or company for carriage of baggage,]†

---

* This allowance was encreafed by a fubfequent order, fee p. 93.
† Increafed to 1s. 6d. See p. 99, &c.

together

together with the actual expence, if any, of warrants for impressing waggons; as likewise the allowances of 6d. *per diem* for fire and candle for guards, and of 10l. *per annum* for carriage of ammunition in Regiments of Dragoon Guards, Dragoons, and Foot, be continued as usual.

All the ordinary regimental contingencies being considered as comprised under the foregoing heads, and included in the allowances hereby granted for them; it is the King's pleasure, that, with respect to any others, which may arise either at distant periods, or upon extraordinary occasions, application be made, and the particular circumstances stated, to the Secretary at War by the respective Commanding Officers, before any expence is actually incurred (sudden and unavoidably pressing emergencies excepted), in order that the same may be duly considered, and such directions given thereupon as shall be thought proper."

*Circular Letter to Colonels of Cavalry and Infantry, respecting an additional Allowance for Postage and Stationary.*

*War Office, 29th November, 1785.*

SIR,

THE encreased rate of postage, together with the stamp duties on various articles of stationary, having created a difference in the amount of the necessary expenditure under these heads, since the present regimental allowances were settled; I have the honour to acquaint you, that the King has been graciously pleased to take the same into consideration, and to direct, that an extra allowance of six pounds *per annum* be granted to each Regiment of Dragoons and Foot at home.

This allowance is to be stated as a separate charge in the contingent bill of each Regiment, and to take place from the 25th of December, 1783, the commencement of the present contingent regulation for Regiments in Great Britain.

I have the honor, &c.

GEO. YONGE.

N. B. The letter to the Colonel of the        Regiment, stationed in Jersey and Guernsey, had the following additional paragraph, viz.

" The islands of Jersey and Guernsey having been represented as subject to some peculiar expence in the article of postage, His Majesty is pleased to grant a further allowance of 2l. *per annum* for the Regiment stationed in those islands for the time being, which is also to take place from the same period."

*Extract of a Regulation for Contingencies of Regiments on Foreign Stations.*

Per Annum.

For Regiments in the West Indies, from the 25th of June, 1784. } Stationary and postage    20*l.*

For Regiments in North America, and Gibraltar, from the 25th of June, 1785. } Stationary and postage    20*l.*

N. B. The rate of allowance for Regiments at the Cape of Good Hope is 12*l.* a year.

    No other charges whatsoever are to be incurred for Regiments abroad, without the special direction of the Governors or Officers commanding in chief, in whose accompts all extra charges are to be inserted.

*Instructions relative to the Contingent Allowances to Corps of Embodied Militia, extracted from the " Rules and Orders," dated 12th December, 1792.*

THE following sums shall be granted, as contingent allowances to corps of 360 men, or upwards, as embodied, viz.

Thirty pounds per annum for postage, stationary, guard-rooms and store rooms taken together.

Six pounds per annum, as an extra allowance, in consideration of the additional imposts on stationary and postage.

[One shilling per mile to each company on a march, having regimental stores necessarily with it.
Nine pence per mile to detachments under the same circumstances.]*

The actual expence, if any, of warrants for impressing waggons.

Six pence per day for fire and candle for guards.

Ten pounds per annum for carriage of ammunition.

For Corps not amounting to 360 privates, as embodied,

Twenty pounds per annum for postage, stationary, guard and store rooms taken together; and four pounds extra allowance: allowances for marching, fire and candle, and carriage of ammunition, the same as before stated: except,

For Corps not having any Field Officer, ten pounds per annum for fire and candle and carriage of ammunition taken together.

The actual expence of package and carriage of clothing, arms, and accoutrements from the packer, to Head Quarters, properly vouched, shall be allowed.

All the ordinary Regimental Contingencies, incident to our embodied corps of Militia, being comprized under the foregoing heads, it is our will and pleasure, that, with respect to any others which may occur upon extraordinary occasions, ap-

---

* Altered. See p. 102.

plication

plication be made, and the particular circumſtances ſtated to our Secretary at War by the reſpective Commanding Officers, before any expence is actually incurred, (ſudden and abſolutely unavoidable emergencies excepted, in which caſes the ſaid Commanding Officers are to remain reſponſible) in order that the ſame may be duly conſidered, and ſuch directions given thereupon as ſhall be thought proper.'

*Circular*

*Circular respecting an additional Allowance to Agents for Postage and Stationary.*

*War Office, 6th December,* 1797.

GENTLEMEN,

YOUR memorial relative to the inadequacy of the present allowance to the Agents having been taken into consideration, I am to acquaint you the following additional allowances under that head will be granted, to commence from the 25th December, 1793, and to continue until a year after the termination of the war.

10*l.* per annum for every corps of Dragoons, regular or fencible, consisting of more than five troops; and 5*l.* per annum for every corps not consisting of more than five troops.

15*l.* per annum for every battalion of Foot, Regular, Fencible, or Militia, consisting of more than eight companies; and 10*l.* per annum for every corps consisting of not more than eight, nor less than five companies.

I am, &c. &c.

(Signed) W. WINDHAM.

The Agents
of Corps on the Establishment of Great Britain.

*Circular to Commanding Officers of Regiments in Great Britain respecting the Hire of Waggons for Troops on a March.*

*War Office, 20th June,* 1801.

SIR,

IT appearing from some representations lately made to this Office, that Constables have in many instances insisted upon payment of a higher rate than One Shilling per mile for Waggons impressed on the marches of the troops, although the same had not been previously fixed and ordered by the Justices of the Peace assembled at any General Sessions of the Peace for the county or district, in which case alone the increased rates can be demanded according to the provisions of the Mutiny Act, I have the honor to acquaint you therewith, and to desire you will give orders, that no sum beyond the ordinary rates of One Shilling per mile for Waggons, Ninepence for Carts, and so in proportion for lesser carriages, be paid in any case where the Constable shall not produce a copy of the Order of the Justices in the General Sessions warranting his further demand, the date of which Orders should be quoted in the Receipt to be given by the Constable.

I am to add, that these Receipts must in future be invariably annexed to the Pay Lists, as Vouchers for the Charges that shall be made therein for the above head of service;—they should also be transmitted in support of the Charges made in Pay Lists already sent to this Office.

I have the honor to be,

SIR,

Your most obedient,

Humble servant,

C. YORKE.

Officer Commanding the
Regiment of

*Circular*

## Regimental Allowances.

*Circular to Officers commanding Regiments of Cavalry in Great Britain respecting Allowances for the Carriage of Regimental Baggage.*

*War Office, 8th November, 1802.*

SIR,

FREQUENT representations having been lately made of the inadequacy of the present Allowance for the carriage of Regimental Baggage, which, upon enquiry, appear to be well founded; I have the honor to acquaint you, that the following increased rates will be allowed for the above service, from the 25th ultimo inclusive, to continue so long as the establishment of the Corps shall not be less than 40 rank and file, per troop, viz.

### For the Regiment.

| s. | d. | |
|---|---|---|
| 1 | 6 | per mile for each troop. |
| 0 | 9 | per mile for additional Field Officers, and occasionally for supernumerary Officers. |
| 2 | 0 | per mile for the Adjutant, Pay-master, Surgeon, Veterinary Surgeon, Assistant Surgeons, Hospital Stores, and for the Armourer. |
| 1 | 0 | per mile for the Sadler's apparatus, and for spare stores and appointments. |

### For Detachments.

| | | |
|---|---|---|
| 0 | 9 | per mile for a detachment with one or two Subalterns. |
| 1 | 0 | per mile for a Captain's detachment. |
| 0 | 3 | per mile for every twenty Men of larger detachments. |

The above being granted as a commuted Regimental Allowance, no proof of the expenditure will be required, except in the instance hereafter mentioned; but the Charge must of course be supported by a reference to the Route by which the March shall be made, and by a Statement of the Number of Miles marched by each Division:—In the case of Detachments, a Certificate of the *Numbers* of which they shall respectively consist must be produced, in addition to the other vouchers above prescribed.

I am further to acquaint you, that these Allowances are made upon the supposition that the owners of carriages only receive the customary rates of hire, viz. One Shilling per Mile for each Waggon, and Ninepence per Mile for each Cart, and so in proportion for lesser carriages; but if in pursuance of, and in conformity to, the provision introduced of late years into the Mutiny Act, admitting in certain cases a further charge to the extent of 4d. a mile for each carriage, any additional sums should be demanded and paid, the amount of such additional payments for the number of carriages actually employed (not exceeding the proportions upon which the increased Allowances above specified are calculated) will be admitted in the Public Accompts of the Corps, upon the same being vouched in the manner prescribed in the Circular Letter from this Office, dated 20th June, 1801:—the expence of Warrants for impressing carriages, not exceeding One Shilling for each Warrant, will be allowed as usual.

I am to add, that the above Allowances being considered both at Head Quarters and in this department, to be fully sufficient for the conveyance of the Baggage and Stores which the Regiment or Detachments should properly carry with them on a march, no application for a further Allowance will be complied with; especially as it is to be expected that there will arise savings on some occasions, which will of course be applicable to any accidental excess of expenditure on others.

I take this opportunity of mentioning, in reference to the additional sums that may be demanded for the hire of carriages as above stated, that the Constables demanding such additional rates should be required to produce a Copy of the Order of the Magistrates in General Session by which the same may have been authorised, and that no such Order can be considered as in force beyond the General Sessions next ensuing after the date thereof.

> I have the honor to be,
> SIR,
> Your most obedient servant,
> C. YORKE.

The Officer commanding
   the               Regiment of

---

N. B. Further Instructions in regard to the mode of charging the allowance for the carriage of baggage, are to be found in the Explanatory Directions for Paymasters.—(Section III.)

*Circular Letter to Officers commanding Regiments of Infantry in Great Britain respecting Allowances for the Carriage of Regimental Baggage.*

*War Office,* 8*th November,* 1802.

SIR,

FREQUENT representations having been lately made of the inadequacy of the present Allowance for the Carriage of Regimental Baggage, which, upon enquiry, appear to be well founded, I have the honour to acquaint you, that the following increased Rates will be allowed for the above service, from the 25th ultimo inclusive, to continue so long as the establishment of the Corps shall not be less than 40 Rank and File per Company, viz.

*For the Regiment.*

| s. | d. | |
|---|---|---|
| 1 | 6 | per Mile for each Company. |
| 0 | 9 | per Mile for additional Field Officers, and occasionally for Supernumerary Officers. |
| 2 | 0 | per Mile for the Adjutant, Pay-Master, Surgeon, Assistant Surgeons, Quarter-Master, Hospital Stores, and for the Armourer. |

*For Detachments.*

| | | |
|---|---|---|
| 0 | 9 | per Mile for a Detachment with one or two subalterns. |
| 1 | 0 | per Mile for a Captain's Detachment. |
| 0 | 3 | per Mile for every Twenty Men of larger Detachments, |

&c. [as in the Circular to the Cavalry, page 99, to the end.

*Circular to Commanding Officers of Militia Regiments, respecting Allowances for the Carriage of Regimental Baggage.*

*War Office, 7th April,* 1803.

SIR,

IT having been thought proper, since the disembodying of the Militia, to augment the Allowance for the carriage of the Regimental Baggage, I have the honour to acquaint you therewith, and that in pursuance of the new Regulation on that head, the following increased rates will be allowed, for the above service, to the embodied Militia, from the time of their assembling, and will be continued so long as the Corps shall consist of not less than *forty* effective Rank and File per Company, viz.

### For the Regiment.

*s. d.*
- 1  6 per Mile for each Company.
- 1  0 per Mile for three or four Field Officers without Companies. ⎫
- 0  9 per Mile for two Field Officers without Companies ⎬ According to the Establishment of the Corps.
- 0  6 per Mile for one Field Officer without a Company. ⎭
- 2  0 per Mile for the Adjutant, Paymaster, Surgeon, Surgeon's Mates, Quarter Master, Hospital Stores, and for the Armourer.

### For Detachments.

- 0  9 per Mile for a Detachment with one or two Subalterns.
- 1  0 per Mile for a Captain's Detachment.
- 0  3 per Mile for every Twenty Men of larger Detachments.

The above being granted as a commuted Regimental Allowance, no proof of the expenditure will be required, except in the instance hereafter mentioned; but the charge must of course be supported by a reference to the Route by which the march shall be made, and by a Statement of the number of miles marched by each Division:—In the case of Detachments, a Certificate of the *Numbers* of which they shall respectively consist must be produced, in addition to the other vouchers above prescribed.

I am

## Regimental Allowances.

I am further to acquaint you, that these Allowances are made upon the supposition that the owners of carriages only receive the rates of hire, specified in the Mutiny Act of the present year, viz. One Shilling per mile for each Waggon, Ninepence per mile for each Cart carrying not less than Fifteen hundred weight, and Sixpence per mile for each lesser Cart; but if in pursuance of, and in conformity to, the provision contained in the said Act, (admitting in certain cases a further charge to the extent of 4d. 3d. or 2d. a mile, according to the size of the carriages) any additional sums should be demanded and paid, the amount of such additional payments for the number of carriages actually employed (not exceeding the proportions upon which the encreased Allowances above specified are calculated) will be admitted in the Public Accompts of the Corps, upon the same being vouched in the manner prescribed in the Circular Letter from this Office, dated 20th June, 1801:—the expence of Warrants for impressing carriages, not exceeding One Shilling for each Warrant, will be allowed as usual.

I am to add, that the above Allowances being considered, both at head quarters and in this department, to be fully sufficient for the conveyance of the Baggage and Stores which the Regiment or Detachments should properly carry with them on a march, no application for a further Allowance will be complied with; especially as it is to be expected that there will arise savings on some occasions, which will of course be applicable to any accidental excess of expenditure on others.

I take this opportunity of mentioning, in reference to the additional sums that may be demanded for the hire of carriages as above stated, that the Constables demanding such additional rates should be required to produce a Copy of the Order of the Magistrates in General Session by which the same may have been authorized, and that no such Order can be considered as valid unless the period for which it is to be in force be specified therein, which period is not to exceed ten days beyond the next General Sessions to ensue after the date of the Order.

I have the honour to be,
SIR,
Your most obedient servant,
C. YORKE

The Officer commanding
the    Militia.

*Circular to Commanding Officers of Regular Regiments in Great Britain relative to the additional Rates for the Hire of Carriages.*

*War Office*, 19th *April*, 1803.

SIR,

REFERRING to the Regulation of the 8th November laſt, reſpecting the carriage of Regimental Baggage, I think it proper to call your particular attention to the proviſions contained in the 51ſt and 54th Sections of the Mutiny Act of the preſent year, concerning the further ſums which the Juſtices, at a General Seſſions of the Peace, may order to be paid under certain circumſtances for the hire of carriages, and to intimate the propriety of your enforcing the ſtricteſt obſervance of the Rules preſcribed in the ſaid Sections, in order that no unneceſſary expence may be brought upon the Public, by the irregular and unauthoriſed demands of Conſtables and others.

You will obſerve that, by the ſaid 51ſt Section, other additional rates are fixed, beſides that of Fourpence per mile, mentioned in the Regulation above referred to; and that the order of the Magiſtrates allowing ſuch additional rates, muſt ſpecify the period for which it is to be in force, which may extend to ten days beyond the next General Seſſions, to enſue after the date thereof.

I have the honor to be, &c.

(Signed)     C. YORKE

Officer commanding

*Circular*

*Circular to Commanding Officers of Regiments of Cavalry and Infantry, stating the Variations in the Allowances for the Carriage of Baggage of the Field Officers, in consequence of their removal from the Command of Troops and Companies.*

*War Office,* 21*st July,* 1803.

SIR,

I HAVE the honor to acquaint you, that, in consequence of the removal of the Field Officers from the command of Troops and Companies, the following variations will be made in the Allowances for the carriage of the Baggage of the Field Officers, viz.

   *s.  d.*
   1  0  per Mile for three or four Field Officers;
   0  9  per Mile for two Field Officers; and
   0  6  per Mile for one Field Officer.

It is however to be clearly understood that the above rates will only be allowed for the Field Officers who are present, except when the Officer's Baggage actually remains at the regiment, and is necessarily conveyed with it; in which case the charge will be admitted upon its being especially certified by the Commanding Officer.

             I have the honor to be,

                SIR,

                    Your most obedient

                        Humble Servant,

                            C. YORKE.

The Officer Commanding the
  Regiment of

# SECTION III.

## SYSTEM

### OF

## REGIMENTAL ACCOMPTS.

( 109 )

# SECTION III.

## PART I.

### GENERAL INSTRUCTIONS

IN REGARD TO

### REGIMENTAL ACCOMPTS.

*Extract from the Act of the* 45 *Year of the Reign of His present Majesty, Cap.* 58. *relative to the Mode of issuing and accounting for the Monies required for Army Services.*
[27 *June,* 1805.]

XIX. AND, for the better Prevention of the issuing from the Exchequer any more Monies than shall be necessary for the Purposes recited in this Act; be it enacted, That, from and after the passing of this Act, the Secretary at War shall, and he is hereby directed and required, from time to time, to transmit to the Office of the Pay-Master General of His Majesty's Forces, Accounts of the Sums, necessary to be issued for the several Services of His Majesty's Regular and Fencible Forces and embodied Militia, according to the effective Strength and the actual Expenditure thereof, distinguishing each Corps severally; and the said Pay-Master General shall, and he is hereby directed and required, to form his Memorials and Requisitions to the Treasury, and to issue his Drafts on the Bank as aforesaid, according to the said Accounts.

XX. And be it further enacted, That, from and after the
passing

passing of this act, the several Allowances now borne or hereafter to be borne on the Regimental Establishments shall be made, namely, the Allowances to Captains of Troops and Companies, and to certain Field Officers not having Troops or Companies; the Allowance for the use of the Riding Masters and Rough Riders, and for immediate Expences relating to the same; the extra Allowances for Farriery, and the Allowances for Great Coats: for which said Allowances the Pay-Master General of His Majesty's Forces, shall and he is hereby directed and required to form his Memorials and Requisitions, and to issue his Drafts as aforesaid, as soon after the Twenty-fourth Day of *June* and the Twenty-fifth Day of *December* in every Year, as the same can conveniently be done, in equal Payments, and to charge the same to the Account of each Corps as aforesaid.

XXI. And be it further enacted, That the Agents of all Regiments, Troops, and Companies of His Majesty's Regular and Fencible Forces and embodied Militia, shall and they are hereby directed and required to make up annual Accounts of every Regiment, Troop, and Company for the preceding Year, ending the Twenty-fourth Day of *December* in every Year; the Accounts of the Forces and Militia serving in *Great Britain* to be made up within Six Months after the Expiration of the Year, and the Accounts of the several Corps on Foreign Service within Nine Months after the Expiration of the Year, unless the Pay Lists from those on Foreign Service shall not have been received and settled, so as to enable the Agents to make up such Accounts; and in the said accounts the several Imprests or Monies received, including every Receipt which ought to be brought to the Credit of the Publick, in the accounts of the respective Corps, and the several disbursements or Monies paid, including Agency, shall be properly distinguished under the several Heads of Service; and the Balance which shall be due to or from the Public on account of every Regiment, Troop, and Company shall be struck; and such Agents shall transmit the said Accounts within the times limited as aforesaid, together with proper Vouchers, agreeably to the present Standing Regulations, or any future Regulations which His Majesty shall be pleased to establish, to the Office of the Secretary at War, and a Copy thereof to the Office of the Pay-Master General of His Majesty's Forces; and on failure herein, or in any other of the Regulations prescribed to

Agents

Agents by this act, every Agent so offending shall forfeit the sum of one hundred pounds for every offence, to be recovered by any person or persons who shall sue for the same; and the Secretary at War, or such other person or persons as shall be duly authorized by His Majesty for that purpose, shall, and he or they is or are hereby directed and required to examine and settle, or cause to be examined and settled, the aforesaid annual Accounts, within three months after the Receipt of the said Accounts respectively, and when settled, to transmit Certificates of the several Charges allowed in the said Accounts, to the Office of the Pay-Master General of His Majesty's Forces, with Warrants signed by His Majesty, directing and authorizing the said Pay-Master General to form memorials and requisitions, and to issue his drafts as aforesaid, for the balance or Nett monies due to each Regiment, Troop, and Company of His Majesty's Regular Forces, and embodied Militia, for Clearings; and to charge the same to the account of the said Regiment, Troop, and Company; and the said Warrants shall authorize and direct the Pay-Master General to make the excess which shall arise upon the several establishments, after deducting therefrom the Monies so disbursed and paid as aforesaid, a Saving, and to carry it to the credit of the Public, and to charge every deficiency which shall arise from the several establishments not being able to discharge the disbursements paid on account as aforesaid, to the general account of Contingencies, or to such other fund as may be applicable thereto.

XXII. And be it further enacted, That whenever a Balance shall in any Agent's account so to be transmitted as aforesaid, be admitted to be due to the Public, and also whenever it shall appear from the Warrants so transmitted to the Pay-Master General, that a Balance is due to the Public from any Agent on any of his Accounts aforesaid, it shall be lawful for the Pay-Master General for the time being, to require such Agent forthwith to pay such Balance into the Bank of *England*, to the account of the Pay-Master General of His Majesty's Forces, of which Payments, Certificate shall be granted to the parties making the same, by the Cashier or Cashiers of the Bank of *England*, and the said Certificate shall be a sufficient discharge to the said Parties for the sums expressed therein; and in case such Agent shall for the space of one Calendar Month after being required so to do, refuse or neglect to pay such Balance into the Bank of *England* as aforesaid, the Amount of
the

the Balance fo admitted to be due by fuch Agent, or fo appearing due from the faid Warrant, fhall from the time of fuch requifition be deemed and confidered to be a Debt to His Majefty on Record, and be recoverable as fuch by His Majefty, His Heirs, and Succeffors, with full cofts of fuit, and all other charges attending the fame, by the like procefs as by the laws of that part of the United Kingdom wherein fuch Agent fhall refide, any debt to His Majefty arifing within the fame may be recovered.

XXIII. Provided always, and be it further enacted, That where any Perfon fhall be Agent for more than one Regiment, Troop, or Company, by reafon whereof it may happen that a Balance may be due from fuch Agent to the Public on account of fome or one of fuch Regiments, Troops, or Companies, and a Balance may be due from the Publick to fuch Agent on account of others of them, every fuch Agent fhall and he is hereby required annually to tranfmit to the Pay-Mafter General of His Majefty's Forces, together with the Copy of his annual Accounts hereby required to be tranfmitted, a general Abftract thereof, including all the Regiments, Troops, or Companies for which he is Agent, in order that it may appear to the Satisfaction of the Pay-Mafter General, whether, upon the whole of fuch Accounts, a Balance fhall be due to or from the Public; and in every cafe in which fuch Abftract as by this Act is required fhall be tranfmitted, it fhall not be lawful for the Pay-Mafter General to require fuch Agent to pay into the Bank of *England*, a fum greater on the whole on the Account of fuch Balances which may be due from him on account of the refpective Regiments, Troops, or Companies for which he is Agent, than fhall appear to be in his hands upon the whole of the faid Accounts: Provided always, that fo long as any fuch Balance fhall remain due from fuch Agent to the Public on the whole of the faid Accounts, no Monies fhall be iffued by the Pay-Mafter General to fuch Agent, on account of any Regiment, Troop or Company.

XXIV. And be it further enacted, That all Monies whatever which may at any time become payable by any perfon or perfons whomfoever to the Pay-Mafter General of His Majefty's Forces, fhall be paid into the Bank of *England*, to the Account of the Pay-Mafter General of His Majefty's Forces; and Certificate of fuch Payments, which fhall be fufficient Difcharges to the perfons paying fuch Money,

fhall

Part I.]  *Regimental Accompts.*  113

shall be granted in like manner as is herein directed in cases of Balances paid by Agents into the Bank of *England*; and all Monies when so paid into the Bank of *England*, as well by Agents or any other person or persons, shall be placed to the same account, and be drawn for in the same Manner, as if the same had been issued from the Exchequer in pursuance of any Memorial presented by the Pay-Master General, according to the directions of this Act.

XXV. Provided always, and be it further enacted, That it shall be lawful for the Secretary at War, and also for the Pay-Master General of His Majesty's Forces, whenever they shall think fit to require any Agent or Agents to make up in the course of any Year such Account or Accounts as the Secretary at War, or the Pay-Master General of His Majesty's Forces, may have occasion for, and also to require any person or persons who shall have been an Agent or Agents, but who shall have ceased to be such, or the representatives of such Agent or Agents, to make up and transmit such accounts for the whole or any part of the periods during which he or they shall have been an Agent or Agents, and which shall not have been finally settled, as the Secretary at War or Pay-Master General may have occasion for; and any such Agent or Agents, or person or persons having been an Agent or Agents, or the Representatives of any such Agent or Agents refusing obedience to such requisition or requisitions, or neglecting for the space of three calendar Months after the same shall have been made to obey the same, shall for every offence be liable to the like penalty, and to be recoverable in the like Manner as is herein-before provided in case of failure to transmit such annual Accounts as aforesaid: Provided also, that nothing herein contained shall extend to exonerate the Colonel or Commandant of any Regiment, Troop, or Company, or the representatives of any such Colonel or Commnadant, from any responsibility to which he or they is or are or may be liable, for any failure or deficiency of the respective Agents, of such Regiments, Troops, or Companies.

XXVI. And be it enacted, That this Act shall not extend or be construed to extend to the making any Alteration in the present Mode or Regulation of the Two Regiments of Life Guards, the Royal Regiment of Horse Guards, or the Three Regiments of Foot Guards, but the same shall continue in the practice of the same mode and regulations as they would otherwise have done had this Act not been made.

*Circular relative to the Responsibility of Colonels for their Agents.*

*War-Office,* 10th *July,* 1760.

SIR,

THE King, being desirous to prevent the inconveniencies, which may arise upon the Death of Agents to. Regiments, was pleased to direct the Board of General Officers to take this matter into consideration, and to report their opinion, in what manner the said inconveniencies may best be guarded against; and the Board accordingly have reported to His Majesty, that they have not been able to discover any better Method of obviating the inconveniencies, the foresight of which occasioned this reference, than by the Colonel's taking a sufficient Security by a Deposit of Money, or by the Agent vesting a Sum in the Public Funds, in the Names of Trustees, applicable upon demand of the Colonel to make good any deficiency arising from the failure or Death of the Agent.

The Board being further directed to consider, what Sums of Money an Agent should deposit or vest in the Public Funds, as a security for the several Corps in His Majesty's Service, report, that they have not been able to fix any certain Sum, which may be adapted to the several circumstances that may occur; and have submitted it to His Majesty, as their opinion, that the Sum to be deposited by the Agent cannot be so properly determined by any Person as by the Colonel of each Corps, whose interest, as well as regard for the service, must induce him to require a sufficient security.

When I had the honor to lay this Report of the Board of General Officers before the King, His Majesty was pleased to order, that the same should be communicated to the Colonels of the several Corps in His Service; that, if any of them have omitted to require sufficient security from their Agents, they may be apprized of the necessity of their speedily taking that precaution; as, in case of any accident, His Majesty, agreeably to the opinion of the Board, must look upon the Colonel as the only Person accountable, not only for the Pay of his Regiment, the Regimental Funds, and other Money with which the Agent is usually entrusted;

but

but alſo for every Obſtruction and Inconvenience which may arife to His Majeſty's Service, from the death or failure of the faid Agent.

I am Sir,

Your moſt obedient

Humble ſervant,

BARRINGTON.

Colonel of the
 Regiment of

( 116 )

# SECTION III.

## *PART II.*

### SERIES OF INSTRUCTIONS

TO

### *PAYMASTERS, &c.*

IN REGARD TO THE FORMS OF THE ACCOMPTS COMMENCING FROM 25th DECEMBER, 1797.

---

*Circular Letter to Colonels of Regular Regiments of Cavalry and Infantry of the Line, relative to the Appointment of Paymasters.*

*War Office,* 18*th November,* 1797.

SIR,

IT having appeared to the King upon mature confideration, that the appointment of Officers of Regiments to act as Paymafters thereto, is detrimental both to the difcipline, and to the economy of the army; and His Majesty having, in confequence, determined that all fuch appointments fhall ceafe on the 24th December next, am commanded to fignify the fame to you, and that it is His Majefty's pleafure, you do recommend fome perfon properly qualified, and for whofe character and circumftances you will confider yourfelf refponfible, to be nominated to the paymafterfhip of the Regiment under your command, and to act in that capacity from 25th December

next

## Regimental Accompts.

next inclufive: for which a fpecial military commiffion will be granted to him (if approved) under the fign manual.

The perfon holding fuch commiffion [is to rank as Captain in the Corps according to the date thereof,]* but he is not to be liable to regimental duty: nor is he to affume any military command, or to expect any military promotion.

Pay at the rate of Fifteen Shillings a day is to be annexed to the commiffion, and the fame baggage and forage money is to be allowed, when abroad,† as to Captains without Companies.

The Paymafter will be allowed a clerk, who is to be an enlifted foldier, to have the Rank and Pay of a Serjeant, and to be borne as fuch on the ftrength of the Regiment, in addition to the eftablifhment of Serjeants.

The Paymafter will alfo be allowed Twenty Pounds per annum for ftationary and poftage.

The Half-pay Lift and the reduced Regiments the King confiders as furnifhing the proper objects of choice for this occafion; and I am accordingly commanded to direct your attention thereto, in felecting fuch perfon as you may fubmit to His Majefty's confideration.

In cafe, however, you fhould think proper to recommend in preference to any other perfon, the prefent Paymafter of your Regiment for the new appointment, there will be no objection; but it is to be underftood, that when the appointment takes place, he muft refign his regimental commiffion, the regulated value of which he will, if he purchafed, be allowed to receive from the Officer fucceeding thereto.

You will be pleafed to report to me, as foon as poffible, the name of the perfon whom you would wifh to be propofed for this appointment; and who muft be prepared to give fecurity to the Secretary at War for the time being, himfelf in the fum of Two Thoufand Pounds, and two fureties in the fum of One Thoufand Pounds each. Which fums fhall be forfeited on proof of malverfation, criminal neglect of duty, or if it fhall appear that any valu-

---

\* Afterwards revoked.—See page 120.
† The words " *when abroad*," were not inferted in the Circular to the *Infantry*.

able confideration has been directly or indirectly given in order to obtain the appointment.

In cafe of demife of either of the fureties, you are forthwith to give notice thereof to this Office, and to require your Paymafter to provide another without delay; on acceptance of whom the reprefentatives of the deceafed furety will be difcharged from further refponfibility.

I enclofe herewith for your further information a paper ftating the duties of regimental Paymafters under the new fyftem, and containing fundry provifions relative thereto.*

I have the honour to be,

SIR,

Your moft obedient humble fervant,

W. WINDHAM.

---

* This paper was fuperfeded by the more complete inftructions afterwards prepared, and is therefore not reprinted.


*Copy*

Part II.] *Regimental Accompts.* 119

*Copy of a Circular Letter to Colonels of Regular Regiments of Cavalry and Infantry.*

*War Office, 6th December,* 1797.

IN addition to my Circular Letter of the 18th ultimo, I have it in command from the King to acquaint you with the following decisions which have taken place, in regard to particular cases which may occur in the appointment of Paymasters under the new Regulation.

When the Colonel of a Regiment is on foreign service, and his Regiment at home, the Paymaster is to be proposed by the first Lieutenant Colonel, or next senior Officer of the Regiment, at home, in conjunction with the agent.

When the Colonel is abroad, and his Regiment abroad also, on a different station, no nomination is to be made, until the Colonel or Commanding Officer of the Regiment can be consulted by the agent.

When the Colonel is disposed to recommend the present Paymaster, his Regiment being abroad, a reasonable time is to be allowed to give an opportunity for the Colonel to communicate with his Regiment.

In each of the latter cases, instructions are to be immediately sent out for the present Paymaster to act upon the new system, until a regular appointment can take place, or for establishing an intermediate Committee of Paymastership, if the present Paymaster should decline to act.

An allowance of Ten Shillings a day, in addition to his regimental pay, will be made to the Paymaster for such period as he shall continue to do the duty beyond the 24th instant; and the same allowance, in case of his declining to act, may be appropriated to the Committee of Paymastership, in such manner as the Commanding Officer of the Regiment shall think fit.

This allowance will be provided for in the estimate of pay for the new Paymasters: who will not be permitted to receive any part of the pay of their appointments but from the respective periods of taking upon themselves the duties thereof, except in the instance of the Regiments being stationed abroad, in which case they will be allowed to receive

H 4 pay

pay at the rate of Five Shillings a day from the respective dates of embarking to join.

I have it further in command to acquaint you, that His Majesty has thought fit to revoke that part of the Regulation which grants to the new Paymasters the rank of Captain. They are to have the choice of quarters according to their standing in the Regiment with respect to the Captains, but in no shape whatever are they to have any claim to military rank in the army.

I have the honor to be, &c.

W. WINDHAM.

*Circular*

*Circular Letter to Commandants of Militia Corps, relative to Regimental Paymasters.*

*War Office, 5th December,* 1797.

THE King having thought fit to extend to his Regiments of Militia such parts of the new Regulations respecting regimental Paymasters as His Majesty hath deemed applicable thereto; I have it in command to transmit to you the inclosed paper, stating the duties of regimental Paymasters in the Militia under the new system, and containing sundry provisions relative thereto.*

His Majesty is pleased to order, that the present Paymaster of your Regiment (provided he is not a Staff Officer therein) be continued in that appointment, unless you shall have special reasons to assign for his removal; he giving security to the Secretary at War for the time being, in the manner, and to the amount, herein-after mentioned.

In order that he may give that degree of attention to his duty, as Paymaster, which the additional importance of it will require, he is to be exempted from all duties with arms:† and, in order that he may be put on an equal footing, in regard to pay, with the Paymasters of the Line, the pay of the commission he may hold in your Regiment will be made up to Fifteen Shillings a day; he will also be allowed        Pounds a year for postage and stationary, and a Clerk with pay equal to that of a Serjeant.

It is to be fully understood, that the present allowance to Paymasters is to cease on the 24th instant; the intended system being to commence on the 25th.

The Paymaster will be required to give security, himself in One Thousand Pounds, and two sureties in Five Hundred Pounds each, which sums are to be forfeited on proof of malversation, criminal neglect of duty, or if it shall appear that any valuable consideration has been directly, or indirectly, given, in order to obtain the appointment.

---

* Not reprinted for the reason mentioned in page 118.
† On the subject of this exemption see the following Circular.

In case of demise of either of the sureties, you are forthwith to give notice thereof to this Office, and to require your Paymaster to provide another without delay; on acceptance of whom the representatives of the deceased surety will be discharged from further responsibility.

You will be pleased, with as little delay as possible, to acquaint me with the name and rank of your Paymaster; and in case of his being a Staff Officer, you will, at the same time, transmit the name and rank of some other Officer in your Regiment, whom you may think proper to recommend, as well qualified for the appointment in question.

I have the honor to be,

SIR,

your most obedient

humble Servant,

W. WINDHAM.

---

### MEMORANDUM.

A like Circular, dated the 8th December, 1797, was addressed to the Commandants of Fencible Corps.

*Circular*

*Circular Letter from the Adjutant General's Office to Generals Commanding in Districts, relative to the Military Duties to which Paymasters of Militia and Fencible Corps are liable.*

*Horse Guards, October 12th, 1799.*

SIR,

SOME doubts having arisen in regard to the duties to which Paymasters of the Militia and Fencible Forces, being at the same time Regimental Officers, are liable, I have received General Sir William Fawcett's directions to inform you that it is considered that the Paymasters of Regiments of Militia or Fencibles, may in their capacities of Captains or Subalterns (as the case may happen) without material inconvenience to their business as Paymasters, or departure from the original Regulations respecting Regimental Duties therein required of them, be held liable to sit on courts martial, to attend all regimental parades, to act as officers of the day, to serve on working parties (not detached) or on other duties usually termed duties of fatigue. In order to prevent any further misunderstanding, Sir William Fawcett has thought it proper to direct me to transmit this decision to the General Officers commanding in districts, and I have his commands to desire you will be pleased to circulate the same throughout the Militia and Fencible Forces under your orders.

I have, &c.

(Signed) W. WYNYARD,

Deputy Adjutant General.

General
  Commanding in

*Instructions for Regimental Paymasters of Regulars, Fencibles, and Militia, dated 19th January, 1798.*

I. THE Paymaster is to make out [Monthly Pay-Lists of the Corps he belongs to, to the 24th of each Month inclusive,*] being the day to which the men are required to be accounted with, according to the King's Regulations.† He is also to make up [Monthly,] under their respective heads, accounts of the different Regimental Services, for which payments have been made within the period.

II. The Paymaster, whose office includes that of Mustermaster, is also to muster the Corps he belongs to [by his pay-list,] on the 24th of each month. The Adjutant is to produce, at the said musters, monthly rolls, made up by himself, which are to be compared with the pay-lists, and to be certified, by the Commanding Officer.

III. The Paymaster's [monthly] lists and Adjutant's monthly rolls, are to be made out by Troops or Companies, in the following order, viz.

[1st. The Colonel's Troop, or Company, in which the Field Officers not having Troops or Companies, and the Staff Officers, as such, are to be stated.

2d. The Lieutenant Colonel's Troop or Company.

3d. The Major's Troop or Company. ‡]

After which the other Troops or Companies, are to be placed, according to the seniority of rank in the regiment, of the respective Captains, by which they are commanded.

IV. The names of the Serjeants, Corporals, Trumpeters, Drummers, and Privates, are each to be arranged, in their several Troops or Companies, in alphabetical order, without any regard to the period, whether complete or broken, for which they may have been paid.§

---

\* In pursuance of recent orders, Regimental Pay Lists and Accompts of other Services, are to be made up *Quarterly* instead of *Monthly*. See the subsequent Circulars dated in 1806.

† For a particular Exception, respecting the Cavalry, see Note to Clause VII. of these Instructions. Page 125.

‡ As Field Officers now serve without Troops or Companies, the above Instructions no longer apply.

§ In the Militia, the names of the Men are now stated alphabetically throughout the Regiment, and those paid for broken periods are separated.

Part II.] *Regimental Accompts.* 125

V. The Officers and Men abfent are to be ftated in their proper place accordingly in the Paymafter's lift, as well as in the Adjutant's rolls. No charge, however, is to be inferted in the Paymafter's lifts, but for perfons and times, for which Payment has actually and *bona fide* been made by the Paymafter, within the period of the account.

VI. Oppofite to the name of each individual, for whom a charge is made, are to be inferted the dates from, and to, and the number of days for, which, he has been paid; as alfo the amount paid to him.*

VII. The pay iffued to Commiffioned Officers prefent is to be feparately vouched by their fignature in the column of "Remarks," oppofite to the fum charged for each of them refpectively †: and the amount of pay of the Non-Commiffioned Officers and Privates of each Troop or Company, by certificates figned by the Officers commanding the fame refpectively, and the fum is to be inferted, in words at length, in their own hand writing.‡

VIII. In the column of "Remarks" all perfons of the Regiment abfent, or charged for broken periods, as well as thofe whofe names, as belonging to the fame Troop or Company, have not appeared in the preceding, or are likely not to be found in the fubfequent Pay Lift, are to be particularly accounted for. When Men are charged for the firft time in the Paymafter's Lift, the ground on which the charge is made to commence from the date ftated muft be fhewn; and if fubfifted before, it muft be fpecified at what place, and by whom.§

IX. No transfers of Men from one Troop or Company to another, are to be permitted to take place, but on the

---

\* This does not now apply in the Militia, as to Men effective for the whole period.

† The remainder of this Article has ceafed to apply to the Militia.

‡ Note annexed to the Original Inftructions. In the Cavalry where permiffion has been given to make the Settlement with the Men only once in Two Months, the following Exception may be added to the Certificates of the Officers commanding the refpective Troops, in the Pay Lifts of the intermediate months when the fettlement does not take place, and may follow the printed words "as above ftated," viz. "Except in regard to ftoppages from the men, for which they are to be accounted " with on the 24th of           next."

§ This article is not applicable to the prefent forms of Militia Pay Lifts.

25th day of the month, being the period of commencement of each monthly account.

[X. Paymasters of Regiments at Home are to supply all the Recruiting Parties of the Corps to which they belong, with money for Subsistence and other services, as the Officers commanding the said parties will not be allowed to draw on the agent.

The Paymasters may issue Subsistence for the said Parties monthly in advance; the issues for the other branches of the Recruiting Service are to be made from time to time, and to such amount only as occasion may require, and as shall be approved and certified, by the Officer commanding the Regiment.

The Officers commanding the several Recruiting Parties are to transmit to the Head Quarters of the respective Corps to which they belong, in time to be annexed to the Paymaster's Monthly Pay-Lists,\* and to be included in his General State, Monthly Accounts of their Recruiting Disbursements, distinguishing, under their several heads, the sums actually paid by them within the month. The Attestations of all Recruits raised within the month, and the Certificates of intermediate approbation, if any, are also to be transmitted with the said Monthly Recruiting Accounts. These accounts are to be vouched by certificates from the Officers commanding the parties respectively, in like manner as the Monthly Accounts for the several Companies, and are to be further authenticated by the signature of the Officer commanding the Regiment.]†

XI. Paymasters of regiments serving abroad are to take Recruits into their Pay-List only from the time, to which they shall have been subsisted on embarkation: a Paymaster will be appointed to each Recruiting District at home, who is to account for them, and for the respective Parties within the same, until their arrival at [Chatham,]‡ or to their embarkation.

XII. To each [Monthly]§ Account is to be annexed, a state of the effects and credits, or debts of the Non-Commissioned Officers and Private Men deceased, or who may have deserted within the said [Month.]

XIII. When any deductions are to be made from the soldier on account of victualling, either at stations abroad,

---

\* Now, Abstracts.

† Parties of Regiments at home, as of those abroad, are now supplied with money, and render their accompts through the district Paymasters, except in the instances mentioned in the Recruiting Instructions, where Recruits are permitted to be sent at once to the Head-Quarters of the Regiment for final approval—to such parties this article will still apply.

‡ The Depôt, now in the Isle of Wight.

§ Monthly, as to Parties on the Recruiting Service---Quarterly as to Regiments.

or

or on the paſſage thereto, the Paymaſter is to charge only the nett ſubſiſtence paid to the men, [agreeably to the rates ſpecified in the Schedule annexed to the Regulation of the 5th of July 1797, reſpecting the pay of Corps ſerving out of Great Britain, which rates are ſtated therein under the head of " Nett Pay."]*

XIV. The [Monthly]† Pay-Liſts and Accounts are to be vouched by certificates from the Commanding Officer and Adjutant, and by an affidavit from the Paymaſter, in the words aſſigned for each of them reſpectively in the printed forms ſent herewith. The ſums, and in cavalry regiments the number of [Troop Horſes]‡ alſo, are to be inſerted in the Paymaſter's affidavit in words at length in the hand writing of the Paymaſter, and without any eraſure; after which, the affidavit is to be taken before the mayor, or chief magiſtrate of the town where the regiment is ſtationed, in the preſence of the Commanding Officer and Adjutant, and to be further authenticated by their ſignatures, as witneſſes.

XV. [Monthly Pay-Liſts and Accounts,]§ of the ſame kind, are alſo to be made up for diſtant detachments and parties‖ at the above-mentioned period by their reſpective Commanding Officers, who are to be reſponſible in the firſt inſtance for the ſaid liſts and accounts, and to tranſmit them, authenticated by themſelves, to head-quarters, where they are to be annexed to the regimental liſts and accounts.

[XVI. The Paymaſter's liſts and accounts are to be tranſmitted regularly, and by the earlieſt opportunities, to the agents: from regiments at home, they are to be diſpatched on, or before the firſt day of the month ſubſequent to that in which they terminate. They are to be ſent, in an open envelope, under cover to the Secretary at War, accompanied by a duplicate of the general ſtate, for the immediate uſe of the War Office: the Adjutant's Rolls are to be tranſmitted to the War Office at the ſame times, as the Pay Liſts and Accounts, but under ſeparate covers.

XVII. The Paymaſters of Regiments ſtationed abroad are to tranſmit, by the earlieſt opportunities of a ſeparate conveyance, duplicates of all

---

\* The Regulation of the 5th July, 1797, was annulled, as far as relates to the rates of " Nett Pay," by the Warrant of 6th Feb. 1799. See Page 23.
† Monthly Abſtracts; and Quarterly Pay Liſts and Accompts.
‡ The Troop Horſes are now ſtated in the Affidavits on the Monthly Abſtracts.
§ Monthly Abſtracts and Quarterly Pay Liſts and Accompts.
‖ See a ſpecial direction to Recruiting Parties--Article X. Page 126

the Monthly Pay-Lists and Accounts for the Agents, and of the General States for the use of the War Office. These duplicates are to be addressed in like manner as the originals.]\*

XVIII. The Pay-Lists thus made out and authenticated, will be deemed to have the full credit and authority of Muster Rolls, and to be entire and incontrovertible vouchers. The accounts will be settled upon them finally; and no subsequent appeal will be admitted on those parts to which they extend. As to the other parts, no alteration will be allowed after settlement.

XIX. [Specimens of Paymaster's Lists and of Adjutant's Rolls, with the Certificates and Affidavit required, are hereunto annexed. These Specimens extend to Two Troops or Companies only, the form being the same for every Troop or Company, except the Colonel's.]†

Orders have been given from this Office for the supply of Paymaster's Lists and Adjutant's Rolls, adapted to the different establishments, upon application from the respective Agents: and the expence thereof not exceeding the numbers hereafter mentioned, will be allowed to be charged in the Public Accounts, viz.

> Two books of Paymaster's Lists, two of Adjutant's Rolls, and one separate copy of the General State, per month, for each of the Regiments stationed at home. (N. B. One of the books of Paymaster's Lists, and one of the Adjutant's Rolls, are intended to be kept at the Head Quarters of the respective Regiments; and strict care must be taken to have them made up in conformity to the originals.)
>
> Three books of Paymaster's Lists, two of Adjutant's Rolls, and two separate copies of the General State, per month, for each Regiment stationed abroad.]‡

XX. Paymasters of Regiments, whether at home or abroad, are not to advance or issue any money for services not provided for by the King's Regulations, unless a special direction shall have been previously obtained by the Commanding Officer from the Secretary at War, if the Corps is at home, or if abroad, from the General or other Officer, Commanding in Chief on the station; with this exception, that, if the services should be so sudden and pressing as not to admit of the previous application, in that case the Paymaster may advance or issue, the sum required, on a

---

\* The practice in regard to transmitting and disposing of the Pay-Lists, &c. now differs in various particulars from the rules above laid down. Vide subsequent Regulations.

† The specimens above mentioned and other forms occasionally referred to, are not reprinted—the forms actually in use being regularly furnished from the War-Office.

‡ These Directions are in various respects inapplicable to present circumstances.

positive

Part II.] *Regimental Accompts.*

politive order in writing from the Commanding Officer of the Corps; such Commanding Officer engaging to be responsible for the same, until the consent of the Secretary at War, or of the General, or other officer commanding in chief, as aforesaid, shall have been obtained. It is further to be observed, that in requisitions of this kind, on foreign stations, the charges, when consented to, are not to be placed in the accounts of the corps, but are to be defrayed by the respective officers commanding in chief, and charged in their accounts with government.

XXI. If a corps shall be stationed in any place abroad, for which there is no acting Deputy Paymaster General, the Paymaster shall be responsible for negociating his bills at the most favourable rate of exchange that can be obtained, and at the least possible commission. He shall note on each bill the course of exchange at which the same is drawn. He will also be held accountable for all the money he shall procure for bills negociated by him as aforesaid, and shall give credit for the same in the regimental accounts of the period: annexing, as his voucher for the amount, a certificate or certificates, under the signature of two respectable merchants. In case of actual loss, the amount shall be charged and certified, in like manner.

XXII. As to all points not specially provided for in these instructions, the Paymaster is to have recourse to the previous regulations respecting pay, allowances, recruiting and contingent disbursements; and as it must be well known, in every corps, what parts of the several regulations, relative to these heads of service, had ceased to be in force prior to the 24th of December last, it is expected and required, that any inexperienced Paymaster, who may be appointed under the new system, shall be furnished with all necessary information in this respect by, or by order of the Commanding Officer of the Corps to which he may belong. Should any further enquiry be found requisite, the Paymaster is to apply to the regimental agent, who can refer to the War-Office, if there should be occasion.

XXIII. The Paymaster is to be amenable, in the ordinary course, to martial law for every part of his conduct, which may appear inconsistent with military discipline, the rules of the service, or the obedience due to the colonel, or commanding Officer of the corps, or other his superior officer; but he shall not be liable to receive orders touching the manner of making up his pay-lists and accounts, unless under a special instruction in writing, from the Officer Commanding in Chief on the station if abroad: or, if at home, from the King, through the Commander in Chief of the forces, or the Secretary at War.

XXIV. In cafe of imputed mifdemeanour in the execution of his office, it fhall be in the power of the Commanding Officer in Chief on the ftation, if abroad, (but of no other) to fufpend him from duty, until proper enquiry can be made into the charges alleged againft him, and to provide, in fuch manner as he, the faid Officer Commanding in Chief, fhall think fit, for the temporary fupply of the department.

XXV. In cafe of the Paymafter's death, or incapacity from accident, his papers of accounts fhall be taken into the poffeffion of the Major, (if prefent; if not, of the Commanding Officer), and the two Officers next in feniority, who are to act as a Committee of Paymafterfhip, and to make up and tranfmit the feveral pay-lifts and accounts above fpecified, at the fame periods, and under the like regulations, as are prefcribed for the Paymafter, until further provifion.

XXVI. The Paymafter once appointed, fhall not be removeable except by command of the King, or by the fentence of a General Court Martial.

XXVII. Paymafters of regular regiments, not being allowed to hold regimental commiffions, will receive a fpecial military commiffion, under the fign manual. They will be entitled to the fame baggage and forage money as Captains without companies, and to the choice of quarters according to their ftanding with refpect to the Captains in the regiments they belong to; but they are in no fhape whatever to have claim to any military rank in the army.

XXVIII. Pay at the rate of fifteen fhillings a day* will be annexed to the Paymafter's commiffion, but is to commence only from the time of his joining. Till his arrival at head-quarters, the perfon or perfons executing the duties of the Paymafterfhip, according to the prefent regulations, will receive ten fhillings a day from the commencement of fuch duty: and the Paymafter himfelf, if his corps is ferving abroad, will receive five fhillings a day from the date of his embarkation to join.

XXIX. Each Paymafter will be allowed twenty pounds per annum for poftage and ftationary; and a clerk, who is to be

---

* A different rate of Pay has fince been affigned to the Paymafters of Battalions raifed for limited fervice.

Part II.] *Regimental Accompts.* 131

an enlifted foldier, to have the rank and pay of a ferjeant, and to be borne as fuch on the ftrength of the regiment, in addition to the eftablifhment of ferjeants.

XXX. In regiments of Fencibles and Militia, where officers are to hold the Paymafterfhip with their regimental commiffions, they are to be exempted from all duties with arms, and their daily pay will be made up to fifteen fhillings, the difference being placed as an extra charge under the head of Paymafter, with this exception, that where a Paymafter of Fencible Cavalry is alfo Captain of a Troop, he is to have his daily fubfiftence made up to fifteen Shillings, and likewife to retain his right to the amount of his ordinary arrears as captain. The rate of baggage and forage money,* and the choice of quarters, will be regulated, in every inftance, by the Paymafter's regimental commiffion.†

XXXI. Till the appointment of a Paymafter takes place, the Officer, or Officers executing the duties of that department, according to the new regulations, will have the former allowance continued to them.

XXXII. A charge will be admitted in the accompts of the refpective regiments for the Paymafter's ftationary and poftage, according to the rates hereafter fpecified :

INFANTRY—In each Corps confifting of 500 Private Men, or upwards, twenty pounds per annum.

In Corps confifting of 360 Private Men and upwards, but lefs than 500, fifteen pounds per annum.

In Corps of 180 Private Men and upwards, but lefs than 360, ten pounds per annum.

CAVALRY—In each Corps of Regular Cavalry, twenty pounds per annum.

In Corps of Fencible Cavalry, confifting according to the prefent eftablifhment, of not lefs than 222 Private Men, fifteen pounds per annum.

In Corps of Fencible Cavalry, confifting of lefs than 222 Privates, ten pounds per annum.

XXXIII. A Clerk will alfo be allowed, who is to receive pay equal to that of a Serjeant, but is not to be borne as fuch in addition to the prefent eftablifhment of the Corps. One of

---

* The Paymafter's Baggage and Forage Money is made up to the fame rate as that allowed to a Captain.
† According to the prefent Militia Law a Captain in the Militia is not eligible to the fituation of Paymafter.

the established Serjeants may however be employed by the Paymaster as his Clerk, [and receive additional pay as such,]† provided the Commanding Officer shall see no objection thereto.

> Given at the War Office, this 19th day of January, 1798.
>
> By His Majesty's Command.
>
> W. WINDHAM.

---

† Additional Pay is no longer allowed to a Serjeant acting as Paymaster's Clerk—See the following Extract of a Circular to Colonels of Militia, dated 30th March, 1803.

"I am further to acquaint you with His Majesty's pleasure, that notwithstanding the orders contained in the Instructions to Paymasters, dated the 19th January, 1798, the Paymaster's Clerk, who may be selected by the Paymaster from among the Non-commissioned Officers and private men, subject to the approval of the Commanding Officer, is to be precisely upon the same footing with the Armourer, as to pay and allowance, (viz. if a Serjeant, to continue to receive pay as such: if a Corporal or Private Man, to have his pay made up to that of Serjeant.)

I take leave to observe, that although a Serjeant may be appointed to be Armourer or Paymaster's Clerk, yet that it would interfere less with the discipline of the Regiment if both individuals were to be taken from among the rank and file; and I make no doubt of your attending to this suggestion, if there should happen to be Corporals or Private Men in your Regiment properly qualified for the above employments."

*Circular*

# Part II.] *Regimental Accompts.*

*Circular to the Commandants of Militia and Fencible Corps, consisting of fewer than three Companies, relative to the Appointment of Paymasters.*

*War Office, 9th February,* 1798.

SIR,

THE King having thought fit to extend to his Militia and Fencible Corps that had not from the smallness of their establishment been hitherto allowed a Paymaster, such parts of the system recently adopted respecting Regimental Paymasters as his Majesty hath deemed applicable thereto, I have it in command to acquaint you therewith, and to desire that you will be pleased, with as little delay as possible, to acquaint me with the name and rank of some Officer of the Corps under your command, not being a Staff Officer, whom you may think proper to recommend as well qualified for the appointment of Paymaster to your Corps; who will, if approved, be required to give security to the Secretary at War for the time being, himself in 500*l.* and two sureties in 250*l.* each; which sums are to be forfeited on proof of malversation, criminal neglect of duty, or if it shall appear that any valuable consideration has been directly or indirectly given in order to obtain the appointment.

The Paymaster to your Corps will be allowed pay at the rate of     * per month, in addition to the pay of his Regimental Commission: and he will also receive     † a year as an allowance for stationary and postage.

The accompts on the new system are to be made up from the 25th Dec. last inclusive.

In case of the demise of either of the sureties, you are forthwith to give notice thereof to this Office, and to require your Paymaster to provide another without delay; on acceptance of whom, the representatives of the deceased surety will be discharged from further responsibility.

---

\* In Corps of two Companies 4*l.* 5*s.*
       of one Company 2*l.* 10*s.*
† In Corps of two Companies 7*l.*
      of one Company 5*l.*

For your information and guidance I enclose herewith a printed copy of Instructions for the conduct of Regimental Paymasters.*

[There being several parts in the last mentioned Instructions applicable to the Regiments and Battalions of Fencibles and Militia, but which cannot be extended to the Corps under your command, the same are distinguished by a circumflex and the word " inapplicable."]†

I have, &c.

(Signed) W. WINDHAM.

---

\* See page 124.
† This distinction is not made in the present Publication.—The passages marked were those which relate to the Rate of Pay of the Paymaster and his Allowance for Postage and Stationary: and to the *Paymaster's Clerk*,—no such appointment being allowed in these small Corps.

Part II.] *Regimental Accompts.*

*Circular Letter to Regimental Paymasters.*

*War Office, 24th December, 1798.*

SIR,

I AM directed to acquaint you, that the [Monthly] General State of Regimental Public Accompts is not to be balanced every [Month] as at first proposed, and the difference carried to the next General State; but a memorandum of the balance due to, or from, the Paymaster, may be stated in the face of the Accompt, in any convenient space, not otherwise occupied, in the following manner:

" *The balance due to* [or *from*, as the case may happen]
" *the Paymaster is £*

The totals on the debtor and creditor side are to be carried over from the General State of one [Month] to that of the succeeding [Month,] and added therein at the foot of the accompt, on the respective sides, to the totals of that period, (as has, some time since, been pointed out, by the printed forms supplied to the Paymasters) and so on, from [Month] to [Month,] to the accompt terminating on the twenty-fourth of December in each year; which accompt is to be exactly balanced.

In the first accompt of the new year no totals are to be brought over from the preceding year.

I am,

SIR,

Your most obedient servant,

(Signed) R. TAYLER.*

---

* The directions in this Circular now apply to the General States of the Monthly General Abstracts, and of the Quarterly Pay Lists.

*Circular to Colonels of Regiments, adverting to the Duty of Agents in regard to Paymasters, and enclosing additional Instructions for the Conduct of Paymasters and others.*

*War Office,* 29th *May,* 1801.

SIR,

It appearing from a variety of representations that have been made to this Office, that many Paymasters entertain an opinion that they are entitled to draw for whatever sums they may think proper, without being subject to the interference of the Agents, I think it right, in order that you may cause the necessary explanation to be given to the Paymaster of your Regiment, to acquaint you, that the opinion above mentioned is not founded upon any just interpretation of the Rules and Orders that have been established for carrying into effect the new system of regimental accompts; but that, on the contrary, it is the duty of the agents acting in the name of the Colonels, to watch over the expenditures for the different services of the Corps, and to check every irregularity or excess that they may perceive either in the nature or amount of any charge that may be made by Paymasters, or others, receiving public money through the agent's hands.

With the view of facilitating the execution of this duty, as well as of preventing the draughts of Paymasters from being made to a greater amount than the several regimental services shall actually require, I have caused certain additional Regulations and Instructions for the conduct of Paymasters and others in these respects to be prepared; and having laid the same before the King, I have the honor to acquaint you that His Majesty has been pleased to approve thereof.

I cannot doubt but that your agent will receive from you and from the Officers from time to time commanding your Regiment, every proper assistance and support for accomplishing in the most effectual manner the important object proposed by the said Regulations and Instructions; and I beg leave to assure you of the prompt and decisive interference of this department whenever it shall be required.

Part II.]   *Regimental Accompts.*   137

Copies of the said Regulations, and of the papers thereunto annexed are enclosed herewith for your information.*

I have the honor to be,

SIR,

Your most obedient,

humble servant,

C. YORKE.

Colonel of the
Regiment

* See page 138.

---

COPY.

*War Office*, 29th May, 1801.

SIR,

I AM directed to transmit, for your information and guidance, the annexed copy of a Circular Letter from the Secretary at War to the Colonels of the Regiments of Regulars, Fencibles, and Militia, and the enclosed copy of the Additional Regulations and Instructions for the Conduct of Paymasters and others therein mentioned.†

I have the honor to be,

SIR,

Your most obedient

Humble servant,

W. MERRY.

The Officer Commanding the
Regiment of

---

† See above, and page 138.   *Additional*

*Additional Instructions and Regulations respecting the Conduct of Regimental Paymasters and others, dated War Office, 11th May, 1801.*

It is the King's will and pleasure, that the following Instructions and Regulations, respecting the conduct of regimental Paymasters and others, be strictly observed, in addition to those heretofore signified by His Majesty's command: viz.

*For all Regiments of the Line, Militia, and Fencibles, in Great Britain and the adjacent Islands.*

I. Every Regimental Paymaster shall, between the 14th and 17th of each month, lay before the Commanding Officer an Estimate, according to the form hereunto annexed,\* of the sums that shall appear to be necessary for the services of the Regiment, to be defrayed by the Paymaster, during the period commencing on the 25th of that month and ending on the 24th of the month following, both inclusive, distinctly stated under each head of service; and he shall, at the same time, add, or deduct, at the foot of the Estimate, as the case may require, the probable amount of the sum that will remain in his hands, or be due from the public, on the 24th of the month in which the Estimate shall be prepared.—The Paymaster will also insert in the column allotted for that purpose, the names of the Officers, and the number of Non-commissioned Officers and Private Men, belonging to the Regiment, who are not expected to be paid through the Paymaster for the same period.

The Commanding Officer shall examine the said Estimate; and, if satisfied as to the numbers and other circumstances upon which the same shall have been formed, he is to sign the Certificate subjoined thereto; and to cause the Estimate, and a duplicate thereof, to be transmitted to the Secretary at War, so that the same may be received at the War Office, in due course of post, on, or before, the 23d of the month.

II. If, after the said Estimate shall have been transmitted as before directed, unexpected occurrences should make it appear

---

\* Not reprinted; the form having been materially altered.

## Form of Draft on Account of the Services included in the [*Monthly*] Estimate.

| Regt. of _____ | £. | s. | d. |
|---|---|---|---|
| Pay of { Officers ......... | | | |
| { Men ......... | | | |
| Extra Allowance to Farriers ..... | | | |
| Extra Allowance to Innkeepers } | | | |
| and in lieu of Beer, &c. ..... | | | |
| Extra Price of Meat........... | | | |
| Recruiting ............... | | | |
| Contingencies ............. | | | |
| ............. | | | |
| ............. | | | |
| ............. | | | |
| Total £ | | | |

£. _____ _____ 180

At _____ after sight, pay to the Order of _____ the Sum of _____ on Account of the Services specified in the Margin, which are included in my [Monthly] Estimate to the 24th _____ 180

} Pay-Master _____
  Regt. of _____

To _____

London.

## Form of Draft for Services specified in a *Supplementary* Estimate.

_____ Regt. of _____

| | £. | s. | d. |
|---|---|---|---|
| Extra Allowance to Innkeepers, &c. | | | |
| Contingencies—Marches . . . . . . | | | |
| . . . . . . . . | | | |
| . . . . . . . . | | | |
| . . . . . . . . | | | |
| . . . . . . . . | | | |
| . . . . . . . . | | | |
| . . . . . . . . | | | |
| Total £. | | | |

£. _____  180

At _____ after sight, pay to the Order of _____ the Sum of _____ on Account of the Services specified in the Margin, and explained in my Supplementary Estimate to the 24th of _____ 180 , dated on the _____ Instant.

} Pay-Master _____
  Regt. of _____

To _____
    London.

that the total amount of the Eſtimate would be inſufficient to defray the ſervices of the period, a Supplementary Eſtimate of the further ſum wanted for that purpoſe, in which ſhould be fully explained the occaſion of the deficiency, is to be prepared and certified as above-mentioned, and, together with a duplicate thereof, to be ſent off, under the orders of the Commanding Officer, who is to be reſponſible for its being done, before any bills ſhall be drawn on account of ſuch deficiency.

III. The drafts or requiſitions of the Paymaſters, founded upon the ſaid Eſtimates, ſhall be made for ſuch ſums only, and at ſuch intervals within the month, as ſhall be abſolutely neceſſary to enable them to defray the ſervices regularly, and at the periods, when, by the cuſtom of the army, they are uſually defrayed.

If at any time it ſhall appear to the Agent, that this rule is not duly attended to, the Agent is to make a repreſentation thereupon to the Commanding Officer, who will, without loſs of time, enquire into the circumſtances that may have rendered it expedient for the Paymaſter to encreaſe the amount of his drafts beyond the uſual proportion; and will, with all convenient diſpatch, communicate to the Agent the reſult of his enquiries, with his opinion relative thereto, in order that the ſame may, if neceſſary, be laid before the Secretary at War.

IV. No draft or requiſition whatever ſhall be deemed valid and of proper authority by the Agent, unleſs expreſſing all the ſervices for which it ſhall be made (diſtinguiſhing the proportion for each,) and referring to the particular Eſtimate in which ſuch ſervice ſhall have been included: ſpecimens of the Forms to be uſed for draughts, in the reſpective caſes of ſums included in the Monthly and Supplementary Eſtimates, are annexed.

V. The Paymaſter's drafts on the Agents ſhall not in future be made payable after *date*; but at the greateſt number of days after *ſight* at which the Paymaſters may be able to negociate their bills at par.

If, upon particular occaſions, it ſhould be found abſolutely neceſſary to draw at ſight, the Paymaſters are hereby required to ſend letters of advice to the Agents, one day, at leaſt, before that on which they ſhall iſſue their drafts, ſpecifying in the ſaid letters the total amount of each bill to be drawn, and the proportional ſum, included therein, for each head of ſervice; and the Paymaſters will be held reſponſible for any detriment that His Majeſty's ſervice may ſuffer, in conſequence of the

non-

non-payment of any bill of which the Agent shall not have been advised as above directed; unless in any particular instance, wherein it shall be proved that it was impossible to give such previous advice.

VI. The services charged in each month shall be invariably and completely liquidated within the same, out of the monies drawn or remitted for them; and the Captains of Troops and Companies, or the Officers duly appointed to pay Troops and Companies, are hereby required to attend particularly to this rule, as they are, and will be, held severally responsible for any misapplication, or defalcation in the amount, of the sums issued to each of them by the Paymaster, in regular course, for the use of their respective Troops or Companies.

VII. In every Pay List the Paymaster shall give credit distinctly and separately, for all the sums drawn by, or required to be remitted to, him for the services of the [month] for which the Pay List is made, distinguishing therein the estimated sum drawn, or required to be remitted, for each head of service, the date of each draught or requisition, the period when payable, and to whom; he shall also constantly notice them in like manner, in his Abstracts for the Agent; and in the last paragraph of his affidavit, shall accordingly include the sums that shall have been required to be remitted, as well as those received.*

[VIII. The Paymaster shall keep a book, in which shall be regularly entered, on one side, the total sums charged in each month; and on the opposite side, all the drafts and requisitions made by him on the public service of the Regiment; the amount of each draft or requisition; the period when, and the persons to whom payable; classing them in both instances under the respective heads of service, as drawn, or paid.

IX. The said several sums are to be added up correctly in the book by the Paymaster, as soon as may be after the termination of each of the monthly periods of account, in the manner pointed out in the form sent herewith; so as to shew, at one view, the total amount of the payments and receipts from the 25th of December, up to the latest period in each year; the said books are to be always open to the inspection of the Commanding Officer; and to that of any Inspecting General Officer, if demanded; and a duplicate thereof, signed by the Paymaster, is to be transmitted to the Secretary at War with the Supplementary Pay List required by the 12th Article of these Instructions.]†

---

* These directions now apply to the Monthly Abstract and Quarterly Pay List respectively.

† In consequence of later Regulations the keeping of the books mentioned in Articles VIII. and IX. will be dispensed with after the expiration of the year 1806, as the Monthly General States will enable the Commanding Officer to judge of the State of the Paymaster's Accompts.

X. When

Part II.] *Regimental Accompts.* 141

X. When Officers, or Parties, not having been subsisted through the Regimental Paymaster, shall join in the course of the month, the Paymasters shall give immediate notice thereof to the Agent, specifying the name of each Officer, and the number of each party, and shall require information as to the periods to which they may have respectively been subsisted by the Agent, or district Paymaster, in order that he may issue their pay accordingly.*

XI. When Officers or Parties shall leave the Regiment in the course of the month, the Paymaster shall give immediate notice thereof to the Agent, specifying the name of each Officer, and the number and destination of each party, and shall inform the Agent to what periods they shall have been respectively subsisted by him; and from whom, and in what manner, they are to receive their subsistence in future. The Agent will, without delay, make the necessary communication to the district Paymaster accordingly.*

XII. In regard to services, which, from particular circumstances, may not have been defrayed before the termination of the year to which they belonged, and cannot therefore be included in the last [Monthly] Pay List of the year, they are to be charged distinctly in a Supplementary [Manuscript]† Pay List, to be vouched in like manner as the [Monthly] Pay Lists, as to the actual payment of the sums charged, in conformity to the Regulations: the said Supplementary Pay List to be closed and exactly balanced; and to be transmitted, with a duplicate of the General State thereof, for the use of the Agent, immediately after the 24th of March ensuing.

Estimates of the sums wanted for these services are to be prepared and transmitted, at the earliest opportunity: and drafts and requisitions for the same are to be made, according to the rules prescribed in Articles II. and V. of these Instructions.

XIII. When any Regiment, or detachment, shall be ordered to embark for service abroad, the Paymaster shall prepare an Estimate, under the directions of the Commanding Officer, of the advance of pay that shall appear necessary to enable the

---

* Refer to No. 41 of the Explanatory Directions.
† Printed Forms of Supplementary Pay Lists are now supplied annually from the War Office to Corps of Regulars and Fencibles.

Officers to lay in provisions for the voyage, and to provide a sufficient stock of necessaries for the men, stating therein the nett pay only of the Non-commissioned Officers and Men, agreeably to His Majesty's Regulation of the 6th of February, 1799; and deducting the customary stoppage for provisions from the Commissioned Officers at three-pence for each ration: the said Estimate and a duplicate thereof are to be signed by the Commanding Officer and Paymaster, and to be transmitted as before directed. The advance of pay is, however, not to exceed the usual proportions, according to the destination of the corps, viz.

| | |
|---|---|
| For the East Indies | Six Months.* |
| For the Cape of Good Hope | Four Months. |
| For America, the West Indies, and the Mediterranean | Three Months. |
| For Portugal and Gibraltar | Two Months. |

XIV. It frequently happening that either through inexperience or inadvertence, charges are made in the [Monthly] Pay Lists, which either do not properly belong thereto, or are not supported by the specific vouchers required by the King's Regulations, it is intended, with the view of correcting and preventing such irregularities, to notice them from time to time in short additional Articles of Instruction.—These occasional notices will be numbered in the order in which they shall be framed, and will be circulated with the [Monthly] Pay Lists; all Paymasters are hereby strictly enjoined, and required, to pay particular attention to their contents, and to acknowledge the receipt thereof, as also of these, and all other, Instructions from the War Office, relative to accompts, by a memorandum on one of the leaves of the Pay List of the [month] in which they shall have been received.

They are to transcribe the said Instructions and occasional notices into their own Regimental Book, and also into a book, which is to be kept in the possession of the Commanding Officer, in order that recourse may be had thereto, in the event of any accident happening to the Paymaster's book.

---

\* For the *Non-commissioned Officers and Men* of a Regiment embarking for India, the advance is Four Months Pay only.

Part II.] *Regimental Accompts.* 143

*For Regiments on Foreign Service.*

XV. All bills drawn by Regimental Paymasters abroad shall specify the particular services for which they are drawn, and they shall all state the exact rate of exchange, as prescribed in Clause XXI. of the Instructions for Regimental Paymasters, dated the 19th of January, 1798. If any bill *whatsoever* is defective in either of these particulars it will be returned, and the consequences will fall upon the drawer. The Paymasters are hereby required to take the earliest opportunity of sending to the Agent, by different conveyances, letters of advice of all such bills, specifying in the said letters the total amount of each bill, and the proportional sum included therein for each head of service.

XVI. In every station, where there is an acting Deputy Paymaster General, the Paymasters are to receive from him, all sums that they shall require for the Pay of the Regiment, as well for Officers as for Men.* If, from unavoidable circumstances, they should not be able to obtain the necessary supplies of money from the Deputy Paymaster General, they may draw upon the Agent: but on every such occasion they are to acquaint the Secretary at War therewith, by the earliest opportunity, and to give at the same time a particular explanation of the cause of their having drawn upon the Agent.

XVII. When Officers, or parties, return home, the Paymaster shall, by the same conveyance if practicable, or if not, by the earliest subsequent opportunity, notify to the Agent the period to which they shall have been subsisted; and when Officers, or parties, arrive at the Regiment from home, the Paymaster shall commence their subsistence according to the advice he shall receive from the Agent, or Officer by whom they shall have been previously paid, who are hereby respectively required to furnish the Paymaster with correct information on this head.

XVIII. Of the Articles in the foregoing Instructions for Regimental Paymasters on Home Service, the whole of the 6th, 7th, 8th, 9th, and 14th, as also the first paragraph of the 12th, are to be considered as applying equally to the Paymasters of Regiments on Foreign Stations.

Given at the War Office this 11th day of May, 1801.

C. YORKE.

---

\* This has been erroneously construed to extend to the half yearly allowances to Captains of Companies—which should not be issued by the Deputy Paymaster General. See a Circular in the Appendix, dated 31st Oct. 1806.

*Circular*

*Circular to Commanding Officers of Regiments, enclosing Copies of Explanatory Directions for Paymasters and others.*

*War Office, 30th Nov. 1802.*

SIR,

I ENCLOSE herewith, two printed copies of some Explanatory Directions, for the information and guidance of Paymasters, and others, one of which you will be pleased to cause to be delivered to the Paymaster of the Regiment under your command.

I am further to acquaint you, that when circumstances shall render it necessary to issue any additional Explanations upon particular points connected with the present system of Regimental Pay Lists, they will be published and circulated as a continuation of the series of numbers of the Explanatory Directions above-mentioned; and I am to desire that you will *yourself* fully apprize the Paymaster, that whatever charges he may hereafter make, contrary to these, or future similar directions, will be peremptorily and absolutely *disallowed*, without any other explanation or remark than a reference to the number of the article that shall have been *disregarded*.

I have the honor to be,

SIR,

Your most obedient

humble servant,

C. YORKE.

Officer Commanding
Regiment of

*Explanatory*

Part II.] *Regimental Accompts.* 145

*Explanatory Directions for the Information and Guidance of Paymasters and others. Dated War Office, 30th Nov. 1802.*

PAY.

No. 1. Mode of drawing for the Pay of Corps at home and abroad.

1. IN explanation of the 3d clause of the Additional Instructions and Regulations dated 11th May 1801, Paymasters are hereby apprized, that, *in the case of Corps on the home station*, they may draw at the beginning of the month, for the Pay of such of the Commissioned and Warrant Officers as receive the same from them, for the whole month.

The Pay of the said Officers may be issued to them at once for the complete period; and if it should afterwards appear that the Officer was not regularly entitled thereto, the Paymaster will be indemnified, upon shewing that he had used every proper endeavour, without success, to recover the over-payment for the public; provided, however, that the circumstances by which the same may have been occasioned shall have been clearly and satisfactorily explained to the Secretary at War, and without unnecessary delay.\*

With regard to the Pay of the Non-Commissioned Officers and men, Paymasters are to draw for such sums only as shall be sufficient to enable the Captains of Troops and Companies at the Head Quarters of the Regiment to settle with their men once a week; for those on detachment, if at any distance, an advance for fourteen days or a month may be made, if thought necessary by the Commanding Officer.

No exception from this rule can be allowed, but by the express direction of the Commanding Officer, who, in giving such order to the Paymaster, will state therein the grounds on which he considers the further advance to be requisite.

The proportion of the Pay of the men appli-

---

\* These Explanations should be given through the Commanding Officer.

K cable

cable towards defraying the charge for bread is of course to be drawn for only at the times when the persons supplying the article are entitled to be paid; the draughts on account thereof are always to be made payable to the order of the said persons, when it can be done without inconvenience to the service.

The same rule is to be observed, as far as practicable, in regard to the draughts to be given for meat furnished by contract, or otherwise; as also, in the Cavalry, in regard to such payments for forage, both in barracks and in quarters, as are drawn for on the agent.

The agents will pay particular attention, to the requiring a due observance of the above directions.

The Instructions in this article are considered as applying to *Corps on foreign stations*, so far as respects the issue of the Pay of Commissioned and Warrant Officers.

No. 2, Vouchers for the Pay of Officers.

2. Whenever a Charge is made by the Paymaster, of the Pay of a Commissioned or Warrant Officer, it is invariably to be supported by the signature of the Officer himself upon the Pay-list, or by his separate receipt to be annexed thereto, specifying the precise period for which the Pay is issued; a duplicate receipt in regard to corps at home, being also taken and annexed to the duplicate Pay-list, which is required to be kept at Head Quarters; and duplicate and triplicate receipts for Corps abroad. Officers signing for their Pay in the original Pay-list, should also sign in the duplicate Pay-list, and in the triplicate Pay-list, if abroad.

No. 3, Officers removed from one Corps to another.

3. When an Officer is removed from one Corps to another, he is not to commence receiving Pay in the Corps into which he shall have been transferred, until the Paymaster, or Agent thereof, shall be satisfied as to the period to which the Officer's Pay had been issued in the former Corps; and the Paymaster or Agent, upon receiving satisfactory information on the subject, is to reimburse in the first instance, to

the

the Paymaster or Agent of the Corps from which the Officer was removed, the amount of the Pay that may have been advanced to him beyond the day preceding the date of his new Commission, and is to make the charge from the date thereof accordingly, producing the acknowledgment of such Paymaster, or Agent, as his voucher for the sum so re-imbursed.

If both Corps should be on the same station, the remittance is preferably to be made to the Paymaster, or Agent, by whichever the sum was over-issued; but when the Corps are on different stations, it is to be made to the Agent only.

The Paymaster, or Agent, having made the over-payment, or the Agent, in all cases where the Regiment, from which the Officer was removed, is stationed abroad, will of course be expected to take the proper steps for giving the necessary information on the subject; and in case the sum overpaid should have been charged in the public accounts, they will take care to deduct the same regularly when received back, in their [monthly]* Pay-lists, or Abstracts; or in their supplementary accompts, if the year to which the charge belonged shall have elapsed.

Officers joining their Regiments are to take with them a certificate from their Agents of the periods to which they have been paid by them.

No. 4. Officers having been absent without leave.

4. Every charge made by an agent, or Paymaster, on account of the Pay of an Officer for a period during which he shall have been absent without leave, is to be invariably vouched by a reference to the date of the official order conveying the sanction of the Commander in Chief for allowing the same agreeably to the tenor of the Adjutant General's† letter of the 19th April, 1800.

No. 5. Rates of Pay of soldiers

5. It apppears necessary to state for the information of Paymasters and Agents, in ex-

---

\* Now, in their monthly and quarterly public accompts.
† See Section IX.

planation

Serving abroad, when not liable to a stoppage for provisions.
planation of the King's Warrants of 5th July 1797, and 6th February 1799, that the Pay of soldiers serving abroad, when not liable to a stoppage for provisions;* (except while doing duty as Marines on board His Majesty's Ships of War) is to be issued at the following rates only, viz.

### Cavalry of the Line.

|  | s. | d. |
|---|---|---|
| Serjeant Major | 2 | $10\frac{1}{2}$ |
| Serjeant, Paymaster Serjeant, Armourer and Sadler | 1 | $10\frac{1}{2}$ |
| Corporal | 1 | 4 |
| Trumpeter | 1 | $3\frac{1}{2}$ |
| Private | 0 | $11\frac{1}{2}$ |

### Infantry of the Line.

|  | s. | d. |
|---|---|---|
| Serjeant-Major and Quarter-Master Serjeant | 1 | $9\frac{1}{4}$ |
| Serjeant, Paymaster Serjeant, and Armourer | 1 | $3\frac{1}{4}$ |
| Corporal | 0 | $10\frac{3}{4}$ |
| Drummer | 0 | $10\frac{1}{4}$ |
| Private | 0 | $8\frac{1}{2}$ |

The like rates are to be issued in cases where soldiers are *employed* in a General Hospital, established on a foreign station, so as to be properly entitled to rations of provisions free of stoppage.†

No. 6. Stoppages for rations, &c.
6. The Paymaster will observe that the *stoppage for provisions*, where the man is liable thereto, is $2\frac{1}{4}$d. a day, in all situations when

---

* That is to say, when serving on foreign stations at which (as explained in the warrant of 6th February, 1799) a stoppage for provisions was not customary prior to the establishment of the new rates of Pay in 1797.

† The encrease of Pay granted from 25th June 1806, occasions an alteration in some of the above rates.

deducted

deducted from the rates of the Pay of *soldiers abroad*, specified in the preceding article: thus leaving for each rank the same nett rate that remains after making the deduction of 6d. per diem from the *full pay* of the soldier *at home*, in the cases mentioned in the regulations of the 6th February 1799, above referred to.

Soldiers doing duty as Marines receive the same rates of *full pay* as when serving at home.

The stoppages payable for rations of provisions supplied at the public expence to Officers and *to their servants not being Soldiers*, viz. three-pence for each ration supplied on board ship, and two-pence halfpenny for each ration supplied on shore, (which are to be paid by the Officers) are to be taken by the Paymasters and Agents, respectively, and are to be brought in aid of the expenditures of the Corps, in the accompts of the period, by being deducted from the charge under the head of Pay.

The Paymasters will be responsible that the proper stoppage for every such ration be duly accounted for as before mentioned, in all cases where the Pay of the persons liable thereto is issued through them, for the respective periods of the supply, (except in the case of parties returning home as hereafter-mentioned,) as also where the Officers being present with the Corps, and being supplied with rations of provisions at the public expence, shall have made their option to draw for their own Pay immediately from the Agent.

The Commanding Officers of Parties, and individual Officers, going out to join their Regiments on foreign stations, are, on their arrival, to account to the Regimental Paymaster for the stoppages for rations of provisions supplied to them, while on their passage, at the public expence: the Commanding Officers of Parties, and individual Officers, coming home from their Regiments, are to account with the Agent for the proper amount of the like stoppages.

The Paymasters and Agents will be held responsible

sponsible for requiring the proper credits on this head, and for accounting for the same to the public, when received; and are to annex to the accompts of the period, certificates upon honor from the Commanding Officers of Parties, or individual Officers, (as the case may require) specifying the particulars and amount of the stoppages paid to the Paymaster and Agent respectively.

No stoppage is required for rations of provisions supplied to the wives, widows and children of soldiers.

No. 7. Soldiers taken from their Corps as Officers servants.

7. When an Officer of a Regiment shall be permitted by the Commanding Officer to take away a soldier of the Regiment to which he belongs, for a time, as his servant, the Officer is to settle with the man for his Pay, *at the proper rate*; and is to be re-imbursed by the Paymaster if the Corps is stationed at home, or by the Agent, if the Corps is serving abroad, such man being considered on the same footing as a man on furlough and being accounted for in the Paylists accordingly.

The charge of course, is only to be made in [a monthly or supplementary accompt*] of the year for which it is due; and the man's receipt is to be annexed to the accompt as a voucher.

## EXTRA ALLOWANCE TO FARRIERS.

No. 8. Charges how to be made.

8. The charges for the extra allowance to Farriers are to be made in the accompts of Corps of Cavalry *at home*, in strict conformity to the new regulation on that head, dated 15th July, 1802.†

No charge whatever is to be made for this service in the Pay-lists of Corps serving *abroad*.

---

\* The public Accompts.
† See page 87.

ALLOWANCES

Part II.]  *Regimental Accompts.*  151

## ALLOWANCES TO COMMISSIONED OFFICERS.

No. 9. How to be charged, when the Command of a Company is vacant.
9. The *Non Effective* proportion of the allowance to Captains of Companies, viz. 20*l.* per annum, is not chargeable for the period of the command of the Company being vacant: the *Contingent* proportion may be issued to the Officer paying the Company during the vacancy.

No. 10. Allowances to 24th June, how to be charged & particularized.
10. The allowances under this head, for the half year to the 24th of June, are to be particularized in the Pay-list [to the 24th of July enfuing, or in that of the fubfequent Month,] in which the same shall be issued by the Paymaster: (such Pay-list being of course, necessarily one of the year to which the allowances belong.)

The statement thereof is to be according to the following form, being the same as is adopted in the Supplementary Pay-lists for the allowances of the latter half year.

Statement

Statement of the Allowances paid by the PAYMASTER to CAPTAINS of TROOPS, and for RIDING MASTERS, &c. [*in the Infantry*, to CAPTAINS of COMPANIES] for the Period from ———— to ————

| Head of Service. | Troops [*or Companies*] by whom commanded. | Officers to whom paid. | Periods for which Payment has been made. | | No. of days. | Rate per Annum. | Amount paid. | | |
|---|---|---|---|---|---|---|---|---|---|
| | | | From. | To | | | £ | s. | d. |
| Allowance to CAPTAINS of TROOPS, [or COMPANIES.] | | | | | | | | | |
| Allowance for RIDING MASTERS, &c. *Applies to the Cavalry only.* | | | | | | | | | |
| | | Total (carried to the General State.) | | | | | | | |

Part II.]  *Regimental Accompts.*  153

## RECRUITING.

No. 11. Reasons and Authority for Discharging Men,

II. When a man is discharged, the reason of the discharge, and the authority for it, are to be invariably stated against his name in the Pay-list, in the column of Remarks.—If a substitute or substitutes should have been procured in his stead, his or their names should also be specified.

And Casting Horses.

When a horse is cast, the cause of his being cast, and the authority for it, are to be stated in the Pay-list, and the sum for which the horse is sold is to be shewn by the Auctioneer's accompt, verified by the certificate of the Officer who may be directed to attend the sale.

Paſſage of the Eſcort of Deſerters to and from the Iſle of Wight.

12. The expence of the passage to, and from, the Isle of Wight, of the escort of deserters sent to the *Army Depôt* for General Service, will be paid by the Paymaster of the *Depôt;* no charge is therefore to be made on account thereof by the Paymaster or Agent of the Corps furnishing the escort.

## CONTINGENCIES.

Carriage of Baggage, how to be charged.

13. The charges for the carriage of Regimental Baggage, which are to be made in strict conformity to the late Regulation, dated 8th November, 1802,* are to be stated particularly in one of the blank leaves of the Pay-list of the [Month] in which the same are incurred. The statements of particulars are required to shew:

1st. The number of the route or order, (as

---

\* See Section II.      mentioned

mentioned in the statement of marches, &c.) and if the route should not have been issued immediately from the War-Office, the route itself, or an authenticated copy thereof should accompany the Pay-list.

2dly. The place from, and to which the march was made.

3dly. The number of Troops or Companies, or the numbers of the Detachments.

4thly. The number of miles marched.

5thly. The rate of charge per mile, according to the rules prescribed in the Regulation above referred to, and

6thly. The amount thereof.

In the case of the payment of the additional sums, which (as mentioned in the said Regulation) may be occasionally demanded and paid, a copy of the order of the magistrates authorising the claim, and the receipts of the constables for the sums paid are invariably to be annexed to the Pay-list in support of the extra charges.

In the estimates for these expenditures the above particulars are to be explained as far as practicable.

The amount of the charge is of course to be added to the accompt of contingent disbursements, in the Pay-lists.

No. 14. Allowances for Altering Clothing, and for Cleaning Arms.

14. The allowances for altering clothing and for articles for cleaning arms are granted only to Corps of *Infantry* on the *home station*—the charges on the former head are to be made as follows, viz. the clothing is to be altered so as to fit the men who shall be effective at the time of the delivery thereof; and the actual expence of the alteration is to be stated in an accompt to be vouched by the certificates of the Commanding Officer, Paymaster, and Quartermaster, in the following form—

" We certify upon honour that        suits
" of clothing were actually and necessarily altered
" to fit the effective men of the         Regiment
" of            and delivered to them on the
                                                      " :—that

## Regimental Accompts.

"             :—that the expence neces-
" sarily incurred of the alteration of the said
" clothing has amounted to the sum of [*The
" amount to be inserted in words and not in
" figures*] and that no deduction has been made
" from the pay of the men on account thereof—

————Commanding Officer
————Paymaster
————Quartermaster."

When any additional Men join the Regiment in the course of the year, *(the Corps still remaining at home)* and are furnished with clothing which requires to be altered, the expence of the alteration is to be stated from time to time as the same shall be incurred, the expenditure being vouched in the manner above specified.

When a Corps is abroad at the proper time for the delivery of the annual clothing, no charge is to be made for the alteration thereof; but in the event of the Corps returning home in the course of the year, and of its being necessary to furnish clothing for additional numbers joining the Corps after its return, the expence of altering such clothing may be stated as before directed.

The actual expenditures for articles for cleaning arms are to be stated half yearly, in the [Monthly] and Supplementary Pay-Lists as mentioned in No. 29 of these Explanatory Directions; and accompts thereof certified by the Commanding Officer, Paymaster, and Quartermaster, are to be inserted in the said Pay-Lists in the following form, viz.

"              Regt. of
" Accompt of Expenditures for Articles for
" cleaning arms from             to

          *Articles.*            *Amount Paid.*
" For Brushes and Pickers ......... £.
" For Turn-screws and Worms.
" For Emery and Brick-dust ..
" For Oil ............

                       Total £.

" *Memorandum of the effective No. of Rank and
" File in the above period.*
          Corporals ⎫  *for the*
          Privates   ⎬  *whole*
          Total      ⎭  *time.*
          *Days of broken periods.*".

" We certify upon honour that the sum *of*
" [*The sum to be inserted in words and not in
" figures*] has been actually and necessarily ex-
" pended by the             Regiment of
"              for the articles above speci-
" fied, during the period of this accompt; and
" that no deduction has been made from the
" pay of the men in respect thereof."

                ———Commanding Officer."
                ———Paymaster."
                ———Quartermaster."

When a Corps is on the home station only for a part of the half year, the accompt is to be made out and certified in like manner for the broken period.

It is to be clearly understood that, though the expenditure should exceed the established allowances for the respective services above-mentioned, the full amount thereof is nevertheless to be stated as above-directed; but the Paymaster's charge is, in all such cases, to be confined, in regard to the altering of clothing, to the rate of 2s. 6d. for each suit altered; and for the articles for
                              cleaning

Part II.] *Regimental Accompts.* 157

cleaning arms, to the proportion of 2s. 9d. per annum for each effective rank and file, according to the period of the regiments being on the home service.

The accompts are to be stated distinctly on one of the blank pages of the Pay-list, and the charges are to be made under the head of contingencies.

No. 15. Allowances for Fire and Candle, for Carriage of Ammunition, and for Horse Cloths and Surcingles.
15. The half-yearly allowances for fire and candle for guards, for carriage of ammunition, and, in the cavalry, for horse cloths and surcingles, are applicable only to Corps on the *home station*.

No. 16. Postage and Stationary for Regiments serving Abroad.
16. The allowance for regimental postage and stationary on foreign stations is 20*l.* per annum for Corps of Infantry, consisting as established of 360 private men or upwards, and 12*l.* per annum for a Corps of *Cavalry* consisting of three Troops or more.

No. 17. Medical Expences.
17. No charge on account of Regimental Medical expences is to be inserted in the Pay-lists of Corps of the Line on the home station, unless previously approved by the Inspector-General of Army Hospitals, if the Corps be stationed in England or Wales or in the islands of Jersey, Guernsey and Alderney; or by the Principal Officer of the Medical Staff in Scotland, if the Corps be stationed in that part of the Kingdom.—The particulars of the charges on this head, in the Pay-lists of Corps serving abroad, are to be stated in an accompt to be made up by the Surgeon, and verified by his affidavit as to the whole of the expences charged having been actually, and necessarily incurred, for articles provided for the use of the sick, and not chargeable against the pay of the men.—The bills and receipts for the several charges are of course to be annexed to the accompt.

In special cases when it may be necessary to make an advance, or advances of money to the Surgeon of a Regiment of the Line before the termination of the half-year, the Paymaster may

issue

issue such sum or sums, on account, as shall be approved by the Commanding Officer; which will of course be accounted for by the Surgeon in his half-yearly contingent account.

These advances are always to be estimated by the Paymaster under the head of Contingencies.

No. 18. Discount, and Stamps on Bills.
18. No charge is to be made of discount on the bills of Paymasters in Great-Britain:—if a Paymaster should find a difficulty in negociating his bills at *par*, he is to apply in the first instance, to the Collectors of the Revenue at, or nearest to the place, and in case they should not be able to furnish him with cash or bank notes, he is to require the agent to remit bank notes, who will forward the same accordingly, observing the usual precautions of dividing them in halves, and sending them by different posts.

The Paymaster may charge the actual expence of the stamps upon his bills drawn on the agent for the public service of the Corps, stating in future, the particulars, under the head of Contingencies, in the same account where the draughts themselves are credited: the expences that have already been incurred for stamps on such bills since the *present system* of accompts, and have not yet been brought against the public, may be charged in the supplementary account for the year 1802; statements of the particulars of the stamps used for the bills credited in the Pay-lists of each [Month,] certified by the respective Paymasters by whom they were paid for, being annexed to the supplementary account.*

No. 19. Taxes upon Horses of Officers.
19. Charges made by Officers for taxes paid for horses actually and necessarily kept by them for the public service only, and not exceeding the prescribed numbers, may be paid, and inserted in the Regimental Pay-lists, upon being vouched by the receipts of the Collectors, (who are instructed to make them out in a particular form) and by certificates from the Officers to whom the horses belong, in the following terms; viz.—

---

* The stamps on bills drawn in favour of Contractors employed by the Commissary General, are liable to be paid by the Contractors.

"I do

" I do certify upon honour that the number
" of horses for which I have paid the sum of
"                        being the amount of duties
" from
" to
" were actually and *bonâ fide* kept by me for
" the public service only."

It is however to be clearly understood, that in cases where the rate of the tax upon each horse shall have been increased in consequence of the Officers keeping other horses than those employed solely on the public service, the charge is of course to be inserted at no higher rate than would have been payable for the number so employed, had the officers not kept any others.

No. 20. Allowances to Officers and Men in Ireland.

20. Officers and Men belonging to Regiments upon the British Establishment are to receive, while stationed in Ireland, the same allowances as are granted to his Majesty's Troops serving in that part of the United Kingdom, and no other: and the charges are to be made in the public accompts accordingly.

No. 21. Extraordinary Expences not to be incurred without Authority.

21. No expence not strictly warranted by law, or by the existing regulations, is to be incurred, without previously obtaining an authority from the War-Office, unless in very special cases, where the exigency of the service may be such as to render it impossible to apply for, and receive such previous authority.

In all these cases an immediate report is to be made to the Secretary at War, explaining the grounds of the necessity for incurring the expence, and the reasons why an official authority could not be applied for, and received in time; and the charge is not to be made until the Secretary at War's sanction shall have been obtained. In making charges of this description, the date of the authority, or sanction, is to be invariably quoted.

Should any charges be inserted contrary to this direction, the Paymaster will of course be
considered

## EXTRA ALLOWANCE TO INN-KEEPERS, &c.

**No. 22. Charges how to be inserted and vouched.**

22. When a charge is made of the allowance to inn-keepers for a man, (or of the allowance to the man himself in Scotland or the Isle of Man,) as being in stationary quarters, the place where he is quartered is to be specified against his name in the Column of Remarks. When the charge is made for a man as being on a march, reference is to be made in the same Column to the number of the route under which he shall have marched.—These routes are to be numbered accordingly, and to be described in the printed form allotted to that purpose, in the Pay-list.

If the route shall have been issued immediately from the War-Office, it will be sufficient to specify the date thereof, and the other particulars pointed out in the said form; but if it shall have been granted by a General Officer commanding in a district, the original order, or an authenticated copy thereof, is to be annexed to the Pay-list.

**No. 23. Men returned "Absent, Sick."**

23. When a Man is returned "absent, sick," it is to be stated against his name whether he is in the Regimental or a General Hospital. He is entitled to the allowance in lieu of beer in the Regimental Hospital at home, [but not in a General Hofpital.]

N. B. Since the 25th February, 1804, the allowance in lieu of beer has been extended to men in General Hospital. See Section VI.

Part II.]  *Regimental Accompts.*  161

## DIRECTIONS WHICH CANNOT BE CLASSED UNDER ANY PARTICULAR HEAD OF SERVICE.

No. 24. Payment for articles of subsistence to be made punctually.

24. Paymasters are desired to pay the strictest attention to the subject of the General Order lately given by His Royal Highness the Commander in Chief, dated the 25th Sept. 1802,* relative to the regular and punctual payment of the demands of persons who furnish Articles of Subsistence for the Men and Horses of the Corps.

No. 25. Additions and Deductions, how to be made at the foot of the General States.

25. When any *additions* or *deductions* are to be made in the [General Monthly States,] † either, in consequence of errors discovered in former Pay-Lists, or in pursuance of directions from the Secretary at War, or otherwise, the sums to be added, or deducted, are to be inserted at the foot of the General State, as shewn by the new printed forms thereof, lately adopted in the Regimental Pay-Lists, in the following manner, viz.

If an *over charge* has been made against the Public, the amount is to be deducted from, and if an *under charge*, it is to be added to, the total of the *expenditures*;—if a *short credit* has been given, the amount is to be added to, and, if an *over credit*, it is to be deducted from, the total of the *receipts*.

The particulars of the sums so added or deducted, are to be fully described, and classed under their proper heads of service in a separate statement, (similar to the one which accompanies the new form of Supplementary Pay-List hereafter mentioned) to be inserted in, or annexed to, the Pay-Lists.—In this statement reference is to be made to the [Monthly] Pay-Lists in which the

---

* Printed at the end of this series of Explanatory Directions. p. 168.
† This now applies to the Monthly Abstracts and Quarterly General States.

L                                                        erroneous

erroneous charges or credits had been originally inserted, as also to the authority, or direction, if any, by which the correction shall have been made.

The sums so added, and deducted, are of course to be placed in the General States under the respective Heads of Service to which they belong, in order that the proper amount of the regimental disbursements or receipts for each service accounted for by the Paymaster, may be shewn, at the termination of each period of accompt.

The like rules are to be observed in making out the Supplementary Accompts: printed forms, adapted to the cases that are likely to occur, will be furnished from the War-Office.

No. 26. Fees of Commissions.

26. An Officer obtaining a commission in any Corps of Cavalry or Infantry of the Line or Fencible Corps, is to be charged with the fees thereof by the Regimental or District Paymaster, or by the Agent, accordingly as he shall commence receiving the pay of his new appointment from the one or the other.—Where the fees, or a proportion thereof, shall have been received by the Paymaster, he is immediately to remit the same to the agent.

Should the Paymaster or Agent by whom the Officer's pay shall have been first issued, cease to issue the same previously to the payment of the full amount of the said fees, he is immediately to signify what proportion thereof shall have remained unpaid, to the Paymaster, or Agent, by whom the Officer's pay is likely to be issued in future; who is to receive the same accordingly, and to remit it to the Agent by whom the fees shall have been paid.

A Table of Fees, to be paid on Regimental Commissions signed by The King, is annexed.*

---

\* For an amended Table of Fees, see the end of this series of Explanatory Directions, p. 169.

27. When

## Part II.] Regimental Accompts. 163

No. 27. Men in Confinement.

27. When a Man is in confinement, not regimental, the cause and place thereof are to be specified against his name in the Pay-Lists.—In that situation he is not entitled to any part of the allowances of beer, &c. charged under the head of Extra Allowances to Innkeepers, &c.; nor is he entitled to pay or regimental allowances, if imprisoned for debt, or under conviction of a criminal offence.

The charges on account of Deserters are to be made in strict conformity to the regulations in force on that head.*

No charge is to be made of cash advanced to Deserters, or to Men of other Regiments, without a special authority for that purpose from the Secretary at War.

No. 28. Mustering and paying Detachments.

28. When a Detachment, in consequence of its being at a distance from the Regiment, or of other special circumstances, cannot be mustered by the Paymaster, the Officer commanding the Detachment is, on the 24th of the month, to muster the same; and the Pay-Lists, (which he is to make up, in conformity to the 15th clause of the Instructions to Paymasters, &c. dated 19th January, 1798,) are to be vouched by a special certificate from the said Commanding Officer, to the same purport as the affidavit of the Paymaster, as well in regard to the fact of the muster having been taken, as to the correctness of the charges.

The said Pay-Lists, when received at Head-Quarters, are to be examined by the Commanding Officer of the Regiment, and Paymaster, and the proper corrections are to be made therein, previously to their being annexed to the Regimental Pay-Lists.

The necessary sums for pay, and other services, are in such cases to be supplied by the Regimental Paymaster, who is to take care that the requisite information as to the forms of Pay-Lists and Accounts be given to the Commanding Officer of the Detachment.

---

* See section 4.

**No. 29.**
Draughts for Half-Yearly Allowances.

29. The draughts of the Paymasters for the regulated half-yearly allowances are to be made separately, and are not on any account to include other services. They are not to be drawn until after the 24th of June, and 24th of December.

[The charges on those heads for the first half year, are preferably to be stated, if paid, in the Pay-List to the 24th of July,]* and for the last half year they are of course to be included in a Supplementary Pay-List.

The Agents will understand, that the draughts so made for the said half-yearly allowances, are to be regularly paid, provided, in the case of the Regiment being at home, the Paymaster shall have furnished the proper Estimates thereof, as required by the existing regulations.

**No. 30.** Vouchers not to be altered, or erased, and Duplicates to be taken.

30. No voucher will be admitted in which there shall be any *erasure, interpolation*, or *alteration*, affecting the nature or amount of the expenditure, or the time of payment; and it will be proper, in every instance where practicable, to take duplicate receipts, or other vouchers, in order that the duplicate Pay-Lists and accompts retained at the Regiment, may, in every respect, be complete, and ready to be produced, if required, for the same purposes as the original.

For Regiments on foreign stations, triplicate vouchers should in like manner be taken.

**No. 31.** Clothing not to be charged in the Pay-Lists.

31. No other charge than that for altering clothing (as described in Article 14.) is to be made on account of clothing, accoutrements, or horse appointments, in the Pay-Lists of Regular or Fencible Corps.

In the Pay-Lists of the Embodied Militia, the expences of altering clothing, and of the carriage of clothing and accoutrements from the

---

\* This now applies to the Monthly Abstract to 24th July, and Quarterly Pay-List to 24th September.

packers

packers to the Head-Quarters of the Corps, may be properly inserted.

No charge is to be made in any Pay-Lists for bât, baggage, or forage money, unless in special cases, where an authority for that purpose shall have been previously received from the Secretary at War.

No. 32. Bills drawn at *par* from a Foreign Station to be certified.
32. When a Paymaster's bill upon the Agent, drawn at a foreign station, is negociated at *par*, it is necessary (in conformity to the meaning of the 21st Article of the Instructions to Paymasters of the 19th of January, 1798, and of the 15th Article of the additional Instructions, &c. dated 11th May, 1801) that the certificate of two respectable merchants, who are not interested in negociating the bill, should invariably be annexed to the Pay-List in which the draft is credited, stating the rate of exchange with London at the *exact* period when the bill shall have been negociated.

Given at the War-Office this 30th day of November, 1802.

CHARLES YORKE.

---

## CONTINUATION OF EXPLANATORY DIRECTIONS:

*Dated War-Office, 5th March*, 1803.

### PAY.

No. 33. Officers absent without leave.
33. In order that the Regimental Agents may be duly apprized of the names of the Officers absent without leave, the Paymasters are to annex Lists of such Officers to the Monthly Estimates for Corps at home, and to the [Monthly General States of their Pay-Lists]* for Corps abroad,

---

* Now applicable to the Monthly Abstracts and Quarterly General States.

transmitted,

transmitted for the use of the Agents, specifying therein the periods of the Officers having been so absent.

No. 34. Officers and Men on Recruiting Service.
34. When Officers and Men are returned "*Recruiting,*" the places where they are respectively stationed, are, if known to the Regiment, to be specified against their names in the Pay-Lists.

No. 35. Men on Furlough.
35. When Men are returned "*On Furlough,*" the periods for which their Furloughs are granted, and the dates of their leaving the Regiment, are to be stated against their names in the Pay-Lists; and when Men return from Furlough, the dates of their joining are to be specified in like manner.

No. 36. Sums payable out of Subsistence for Men and Horses.
36. The Paymaster of a Corps stationed in Great-Britain, is to annex to the Pay-Lists, duplicates of the accompts required to be made out by the Contractors, who supply bread and forage under the superintendance of the Commissary General, to which are to be subjoined declarations from the Contractors, or their Agents, stating, whether the proportions of their claims, payable out of the subsistence of the Men and Horses, have been received in cash, or by bills upon the Regimental Agents. The Paymaster is reminded, that these payments are always to be made by bills upon the Agent, in favour of the Contractors, where it can be done without inconvenience to the service.

## CONTINGENCIES.

No. 37. Allowance for Great Coats.
37. The allowance for *great coats* is not to be brought into the Public accompts of the Paymaster, the same being intended to form a fund in the hands of the Agent, for the supply of that article, under the direction of the Commanding Officer.

DIRECTIONS

## DIRECTIONS WHICH CANNOT BE CLASSED UNDER ANY PARTICULAR HEAD OF SERVICE.

No. 38. In cases of payments made after the 24th of the month, but previously to closing the Pay-Lists.

38. It being possible that a Paymaster may, from necessity, make payments, or draw bills, after the 24th of the month, for services belonging to the period of his Pay-List; he will, in such case, make the following alteration in the form of his Affidavit, namely, instead of the words, "*total sum paid for the said services within the period of the said accompts,*" he will, in that part which relates to his payments, insert the words, "*total sum paid for the services charged in the said Muster-Roll and Pay-List;*" and in that part which relates to his receipts, instead of the words, "*Total sum received, drawn for, or required to be remitted for the said services within the same period,*" he will insert the words, "*Total sum received, drawn for, or required to be remitted on account of the said services,*" with similar alterations on the Credit-side of the General State. It is to be clearly understood, that the full amount of the sum so stated to have been paid or received, must have been actually paid; or received, drawn for, or required to be remitted, previously to the time of the Paymaster swearing to his Pay-List.

War-Office, 5th March, 1803.

C. YORKE.

*General Orders on the subject of the punctual Payment for Articles of Subsistence furnished to Soldiers.*

It having frequently occurred that the Paymasters of Regiments have drawn for the full pay of their respective Corps, and neglected to satisfy the just demands of persons who have furnished Articles of Subsistence for the Men and Horses during the current month, from which practice much discredit has arisen to the service, as well as much embarrassment and inconvenience both to the Public and to Individuals, His Royal Highness the Commander in Chief has been pleased to direct that in future, Officers in the Command of Regiments shall, at the end of each month, and previously to their certifying the Pay-Lists of that month, make the most particular enquiry whether every demand of the above description has been properly satisfied up to the 24th of the month inclusive; and in case of any neglect on this head on the part of the Paymaster, to report the same to the Adjutant-General, for the information of the Commander in Chief, in order that proper notice may be taken of the conduct of such Paymaster.

By order of His Royal Highness

The Commander in Chief.

HARRY CALVERT,
Adjutant General.

*Horse-Guards, 25th Sept.* 1802.

*Table*

*Table of Fees payable on Army and Regimental Commiffions, figned by the King*:

To be fubftituted for that referred to in Article XXVI. of the Explanatory Inftructions for Paymafters.

*War-Office*, 6th Nov. 1805.

| RANK. | In the Army. | | | In the Dragoon Guards and Dragoons. | | | In Infantry Regiments. | | |
|---|---|---|---|---|---|---|---|---|---|
| | *l.* | *s.* | *d.* | *l.* | *s.* | *d.* | *l.* | *s.* | *d.* |
| Colonel | 11 | 5 | 6 | 12 | 7 | 6 | 11 | 5 | 6 |
| Lieutenant colonel commandant | - | - | | 11 | 1 | 6 | 10 | 6 | 6 |
| Lieutenant-colonel | 10 | 6 | 6 | 10 | 13 | 6 | 9 | 18 | 6 |
| Major | 10 | 2 | 6 | 10 | 5 | 6 | 9 | 14 | 6 |
| Captain | - | - | | 9 | 15 | 6 | 9 | 4 | 6 |
| Lieutenant | - | - | | 8 | 2 | 6 | 6 | 13 | 10 |
| 2d Ditto | - | - | | - | - | | 6 | 11 | 10 |
| Cornet | - | - | | 6 | 0 | 6 | - | - | |
| Enfign | - | - | | - | - | | 4 | 11 | 10 |
| Pay-mafter | - | - | | 10 | 2 | 6 | 10 | 2 | 6 |
| Adjutant | - | - | | 4 | 14 | 6 | 4 | 12 | 6 |
| Ditto with rank of Cornet or Enfign | - | - | | 8 | 12 | 0 | 7 | 8 | 0 |
| Ditto with rank of Lieutenant | - | - | | 11 | 0 | 3 | 9 | 9 | 4 |
| Quarter-Mafter | - | - | | - | - | | 4 | 13 | 10 |
| Surgeon | - | - | | 5 | 7 | 2 | 5 | 7 | 2 |
| Affiftant Surgeon | - | - | | 4 | 19 | 6 | 4 | 19 | 6 |
| Veterinary ditto | - | - | | 5 | 0 | 6 | - | - | |

WM. DUNDAS

N. B. The principal alteration in the Rates, being an increafe of five Shillings on each ftamp, took place in October, 1804.

*Continuation*

*Continuation from Page* 167, *of Explanatory Directions, for the Information and Guidance of Paymasters and others: dated War Office,* 25*th April,* 1805.

PAY.

No. 39. Surgeon of Infantry *while in Camp.*

Article 39. According to the tenor of the Circular Letter of the 28th May, 1804, by which the Surgeon of Infantry, keeping a Horse for the performance of his Regimental duty, is to be on the same footing in regard to pay as the Surgeon of Cavalry, no deduction will be required to be made from the additional pay of the Surgeon of Infantry, on account of forage supplied for his Horse by the Commissary General *while in Camp.* Where such a deduction has actually taken place in the Pay-Lists, the amount thereof may of course be accounted for to the Surgeon, and recharged against the Public.

No. 40. Stoppages for Soldiers in the Hospital of Corps to which they do not belong.

40. In the event of Soldiers being in the Regimental Hospital of a Corps to which they do not belong, the Surgeon of such Hospital is to draw the stoppages for them from the Paymaster of his own Corps, who will obtain repayment from the respective Paymasters of the Corps to which the Men belong.* The proper charges on account of pay and beer money are of course to be made in the accompts of the last-mentioned Corps; but those for the extra price of bread and meat may (in order to obviate the inconvenience that would arise in ob-

---

\* That is to say, *in case the Corps is on Home Service.* If the Corps is embarked for Foreign Service, the re-payment is then to be obtained from the Paymaster by whom the subsistence of the Soldier on his proceeding from the Hospital will next be issued; and from the Agent, in the event of the death of the Soldier.

taining

## Regimental Accompts.

taining distinct vouchers) be included in the accompts of the Regiment to which the Hospital belongs; due care being, however, taken to distinguish in these accompts the number of Men of each Regiment so supplied, and the quantity of bread and meat delivered to them.

*No. 41. Parties and Recruits proceeding from one Station to another,*

41. So much irregularity and confusion in the accompts, as well as such frequent double charges of pay and allowances are found to have arisen from the respective Agents and Paymasters not having duly attended to the rules prescribed in the 10th and 11th Articles of the additional Instructions to Paymasters, &c. dated the 11th May, 1801, that it is found necessary to

*how to be accounted with for their Pay and Allowances.*

establish the following regulation on this head: viz. When Parties or Recruits are sent from the district to join their Regiment, or *vice versâ*, or from one district to another, the pay of the Officers is to be advanced to the ensuing 24th of the month; but the pay and allowances of the Non-Commissioned Officers and Men are to be issued only up to the day preceding their march, inclusive; and the Paymaster of the Regiment or district from which the Party marches, is to make up his accompts accordingly; he will then furnish the Officer Commanding the Party with a distinct sum,* according to the probable expenditure for their pay, increased rates to innkeepers, &c. until their arrival at the place of their destination; and will make a report to the Paymaster, by whom the Party is next to be paid, of the date to which the pay of each individual has been issued, and of the sum advanced, desiring the said Paymaster to remit to him the precise amount of the advance by a bill in his favour upon the regimental Agent: this sum is to be remitted accordingly; and being thus reimbursed, is of course not to be charged by the Paymaster by whom it was first advanced. The Officer Commanding the Party will, immediately on his arrival at the place to which the Party shall have marched, deliver to the

---

* This may be an even sum upon account.

Paymaster, by whom the Pay of the party is next to be issued, an account of the expenditure of the sum so advanced, and will settle the balance with the said Paymaster; who will include in his public accompts the proper charges for such expenditures, and will give credit for the bill remitted as above-mentioned; annexing to his Pay-list the accompts of the Officers, and the reports of the other Paymasters.

In the case of recruits sent to the Depôt in the Isle of Wight, the Pay and allowances of the party and recruits are however to be advanced as heretofore, to the day of arrival at Southampton only, in conformity to the Recruiting Regulations.*

Parties and recruits coming from Ireland, are to have an advance on account of their Pay and allowances made to them in like manner by the district Paymaster, or Paymaster of detachments, by whom their Pay shall first be issued, subsequently to their landing in Great Britain; which advance is to be reimbursed to the said Paymaster in the manner before-mentioned, by the Paymaster, by whom their Pay will be issued on arrival of the party at the place of its destination.†

Parties and recruits proceeding to Ireland by way of Bristol or Liverpool, are to have a similar advance to carry them to Bristol or Liverpool respectively, which advance is to be reimbursed by the Paymaster of detachments at either of these places, who will settle for the expenditure of the parties to the day of embarkation for Ireland.‡

42. Regi-

---

* It has since been ordered that the accompts of expenditure should be rendered accordingly through the Paymaster at that station.

† It will follow from the direction alluded to in the preceding note, that for parties proceeding to the Depôt in the Isle of Wight, the advance is to be reimbursed by the Paymaster at Southampton.

‡ It should be understood that no authority was intended to be given to the Paymasters of detachments to reimburse advances to parties that shall not have rendered to him the accompts of expenditures of such advances. The

## Part II.] *Regimental Accompts.* 173

No. 42. Rates of Pay of men not on foreign service, when victualled on board ship at the public charge.

42. Regimental and district Paymasters will be aware that men *victualled at the public expence,* while on board ship on their passage from Ireland and Scotland to England, and *vice versâ,* or coastwise, are only entitled to the rates of nett Pay hereafter specified.

Serjeant

---

The following additional instructions in reference to advances to parties proceeding to, and returning from Ireland have since been issued to the Paymasters of detachments at Liverpool and Bristol.

"It has not been usual to make any advance to parties embarking for *Ireland,* but if it should be found necessary, the Paymaster of detachments may do so, drawing for the precise amount upon the Regimental Agent, or General Agent for recruiting, in London, accordingly as the Corps shall be on the British or Irish establishment, and in order to obviate the inconvenience that would attend in this case, a reimbursement through the General Agents for recruiting, in London and Dublin, the amount so drawn is to be charged in the accompts of the Paymaster of detachments, as an advance to be accounted for by the Paymaster by whom the party is next to be paid on its arrival in Ireland, and who of course should be mentioned in the said accompts.

The Paymaster of detachments will, however, in such case, take the precaution of obtaining two receipts for the said advance from the Officer commanding the party, in the following form annexed.

*Bristol,* 180

"RECEIVED of the Paymaster of detachments at Bristol, the
"sum of £          British, sterling, which sum being an
"advance made by him on account of the Pay and other expenditures
"of the Recruiting party (or detachment) under my command, pro-
"ceeding from          to          I promise to
"account for with the district Paymaster at          (*or*
"*Paymaster of the Regiment of*          *as the case may be)*
"by deducting the value thereof in Irish currency at par, in the next
"accompts of the Pay of the said party. I have signed two receipts
"for the said sum of this tenor and date."

One of these receipts to accompany the charge of the sum advanced in the Paymaster's General State, and the other he is immediately to transmit by the post to the Paymaster, who will have to pay the party after landing in Ireland; giving the said Paymaster by the same conveyance (and also by a report to be sent with the party) the necessary information of the advance so made on account. The said Paymaster to cause the value thereof in Irish currency at the par of exchange, to be regularly accounted for to the public in the first accompt, to be rendered by him of the Pay and allowances of the said party. This should preferably be done by his deducting the advance from the total of expenditure for the said party, if the amount will admit of it, and by his charging against the public the excess beyond the sum advanced, which alone he will have paid.

Should

|  | Dragoon Guards, and Dragoons. per Diem. | | Infantry of the Line. per Diem. | |
|---|---|---|---|---|
|  | s. | d. | s. | d. |
| Serjeant Major | 2 | 8 | 1 | 6¾ |
| Quarter Master Serjeant | - | - | 1 | 6¾ |
| Serjeant | 1 | 8 | 1 | 0½ |
| Corporal | 1 | 1½ | 0 | 8¾ |
| Trumpeter | 1 | 1 | - | - |
| Drummer or Fifer | - | - | 0 | 7¼ |
| Private | 0 | 9 | 0 | 6* |

No. 43. Officers and men stated for the first time in the Pay-lists.

43. Paymasters of regiments or districts, taking into their accompts the names of Officers and men who had been previously paid through another channel, are invariably to specify in the column of Remarks by whom the Pay of such Officers and men had been last issued. Any neglect of this rule will subject the Paymasters to the deduction of the Pay charged without such reference.

---

Should a party coming *from* Ireland have received on embarkation there, an advance on account, the Paymaster of detachments will in like manner be reponsible for causing the same to be accounted for by the Officer commanding the party, and for deducting the amount from the charge in his General State in British currency, at the par of exchange, taking care to specify by what Paymaster the advance was made."

* Including the additional allowances granted from the 25th June, 1806, the rates will be

|  | Dragoon Guards, and Dragoons. per Diem. | | Infantry of the Line. per Diem. | |
|---|---|---|---|---|
|  | s. | d. | s. | d. |
| Serjeant Major | 2 | 8 | 2 | 0 |
| Quarter Master Serjeant | - | - | 2 | 0 |
| Serjeant | 1 | 8 | 1 | 4 |
| Corporal | 1 | 1½ | 0 | 10 |
| Do. having served more than seven years | 1 | 2½ | 0 | 11 |
| Do.  Do.  fourteen years | 1 | 3½ | 1 | 0 |
| Trumpeter | 1 | 1 | - | - |
| Drummer or Fifer | - | - | 0 | 7¼ |
| Private | 0 | 9 | 0 | 6 |
| Do. having served more than seven years | 0 | 10 | 0 | 7 |
| Do.  Do.  fourteen years | 0 | 11 | 0 | 8 |

44. The

| | |
|---|---|
| No. 44. Soldiers acting as Musicians. | 44. The General Orders of the 5th August, 1803, having signified His Majesty's pleasure, that in regiments having bands of music, not more than *one* private soldier of each troop or company shall be permitted to act as a musician, and that one non-commissioned officer shall be allowed to act as master of the band, the Paymasters and Adjutants are to distinguish in their Pay-lists and Adjutant's rolls respectively, all the private men and the non-commissioned officer acting as musicians as above-mentioned, by placing opposite to the name of each in the column of remarks, the word " Band." |

Of course no Pay is to be charged for men of the said description, exceeding the number limited.

| | |
|---|---|
| No. 45. Subaltern Officers of Infantry holding other appointments. | 45. When a Subaltern Officer of Infantry holds a staff, or other appointment besides his Subaltern commission, he is not entitled to receive the allowance of one shilling per diem in addition to his Pay; the said allowance being expressly limited to Officers holding only one appointment. The Pay of the Lieutenant of Infantry holding another appointment is therefore only 4s. 8d. and that of the Ensign only 3s. 8d. per diem. |
| No. 46. Officers of Militia when newly appointed. | 46. In the case of an Officer being newly appointed to a Corps of Militia,* the charge of his Pay from the date of his commission must invariably be supported by a special certificate, signed by the Commanding Officer and Paymaster, of the commission of such Officer having been produced to them, and of the date thereof agreeing with the commencement of the charge. |
| No. 47. Pay of Officers and other charges in the Agents monthly abstracts to be | 47. Regimental Agents are in future to annex to their monthly or supplementary abstracts, certificates in the following form: viz. " We do hereby certify, that we have carefully compared this abstract with the latest accompts and es- |

---

* As also if promoted.

timates

*vouched by a special certificate of the Agent.*

timates of the same Regiment, received from the regimental and district Paymasters, and that we have not inserted in this accompt any charge against the public which has been, or is proposed to be, defrayed by the said Paymasters on account of the Pay of Officers, or otherwise; nor the Pay of any Officer shewn by the accompts or estimates of the said Corps to be absent without leave, and who has not since obtained leave by the proper authority for the period for which the charge is herein made; we also certify, that the bills drawn by the Paymasters for the services of this corps are all duly credited in the accompts in which they should regularly appear, so far as the said accompts have been received."*

Addition in the case of Corps on foreign stations: "We further certify, that we have not charged the Pay of any Officer serving abroad who was not entitled to receive it from us, as being effective in the Corps for the period charged, and as not having received the same from the Paymaster, or otherwise, to the best of our knowledge and belief."

## RECRUITING.

*No. 48. Discharging men or casting horses.*

48. When men belonging to Regiments of the Line, or Fencibles at home, are discharged or troop horses are cast, the orders or authenticated copies of the orders, of His Royal Highness the Commander in Chief, (whose sanction for discharging or casting every man or horse, is indispensably necessary) are to be annexed invariably to the Pay-lists of the period. On foreign

---

* The following addition to the certificate has since been made:
"And that all the commissioned Officers, non-commissioned officers and privates for whom the additional allowances granted by His Majesty (commencing from the 25th June, 1806) are charged herein, are to the best of our knowledge and belief, after particular enquiry, entitled thereto."

stations

Part II.] *Regimental Accompts.* 177

stations the orders of the Officer commanding His Majesty's forces are to be annexed in like manner.

No. 49. Levy money in the second battalions of numbered Regiments.

49. The Paymasters of the second battalions of numbered Regiments are not to insert, in their Regimental estimates, any portion of the levy money of men of the additional force raised for limited service, the same not being to be drawn from the agent of the battalion, nor to be charged in their Regimental Pay-lists: but the bounty payable at the Head Quarters of the said second battalions for men inlisted at once for unlimited service, as also for those of the additional force volunteering for unlimited service, and for the boys authorized to be enlisted in the said battalions, is to be estimated and charged in their monthly estimates, and Pay-lists, respectively, except in the case of the first battalion of the same Regiment being on the establisment of Ireland, when of course the levy money for the men, whether enlisting at once, or volunteering, for unlimited service, is to be drawn from the General Agent, and to be charged in separate accompts, in order that the amount may be defrayed by Ireland.

Bounty of two Guineas retained from Volunteers of the additional force.

[In instances where men of the additional force volunteer for unlimited service in a battalion which is on a foreign station, the two Guineas ordered to be retained out of their bounty for necessaries, by the Adjutant General's letter of the 29th of November last, are to be paid to them on their arrival at the Army Depot, agreeably to a late order from His Royal Highness the Commander in Chief.*]

---

* See the Adjutant General's letter of 24th September, 1806, communicating a new regulation on this head (printed at the end of this series of Explanatory Directions.)

M

CONTIN-

## CONTINGENCIES.

**No. 50. Allowance for the maintenance of the horses of Adjutants and Surgeons.**

50. The allowance for the maintenance of the horses of Adjutants and Surgeons of Infantry in Great-Britain being regulated by that granted from time to time for the horses of Staff Officers in the districts, the rate of which is not ascertained until after the expiration of the half-yearly periods, ending on the 24th of June, and the 24th of December, the said rate, when fixed, will be notified officially to the Paymasters, who, on being acquainted therewith, will settle for any difference between the amount already issued to the Adjutants and Surgeons, and that to which they will have become entitled, according to the rate so notified, for the district in which the Corps shall have been stationed during the preceding half-year; charging, or deducting the difference in his Pay-lists, accordingly as the charges already made shall have fallen short of, or have exceeded, the proper amount of the allowance.

The *Monthly* issues and consequent charges for this allowance will continue to be made until further order, at 2s. a-day, and are to be supported by certificate in the following form, viz. for the Adjutant's horse—" I do hereby certify upon honour that Adjutant
did actually and necessarily keep a horse for the performance of his Regimental Duty, from the
to the                ; that
the same was his own property, and that no forage in kind has been drawn for the said horse at the public expence, nor any other allowance in lieu thereof, either as a bât horse, or in any shape whatever."

Commanding Officer.

For the Surgeon's horse,—" I do hereby certify upon honour, that Surgeon
did actually keep a horse for the performance of his Regimental Duty, from the        of
to the        of

that

that the same was his own property, and that no forage in kind, nor any other allowance in lieu thereof, has been drawn for the said horse at the public expence, either as a bât horse, or in any shape whatever."

Commanding Officer.

## INCREASED RATES TO INN-KEEPERS, &c.

No. 51. Beer Money not chargeable for Men on board Ship.

51. Paymasters will clearly understand that Beer Money is not chargeable for men on board ship, whether victualled by the public or not.

No. 52. Allowance to Men permitted to find their own Lodgings in South Britain.

52. The nature of the allowance granted to men permitted to find their own lodgings in South Britain, appearing to have been misconceived by district Paymasters in general, they are informed that this indulgence is limited to such men only of the party as, being married and of good character, are permitted by the Inspecting Field Officer to provide themselves with Lodgings.

## EFFECTS AND CREDITS.

No. 53. Men become Non-effective.

53. When men become non-effective by death or desertion, or by being delivered up in consequence of having been claimed as apprentices, or as deserters from other regiments, separate statements of particulars of their accompts are to be invariably annexed to the Pay-lists [of the Month,] which statements are to be made up from the latest period of settlement prior to their becoming non-effective, if the men shall have been present with the regiment above three months; otherwise from the date of enlistment, if recruited at head-quarters; or from the date of joining, if sent to the regiment from a detached party. These statements are to specify what articles of necessaries were remaining at the time the men became non-effective, and in what manner the same

same had been disposed of, and are to be vouched by certificates upon honour of the Officers commanding the Troops and Companies to which the men belonged, that they contain correct and complete accompts of the effects and credits, or debts, of the men.

This rule does not apply to the Militia.

## DIRECTIONS WHICH CANNOT BE CLASSED UNDER ANY PARTICULAR HEAD OF SERVICE.

No. 54. Paymasters of Cavalry to *muster* the Horses of the Officers.

54. The Paymasters of regiments of Cavalry are to muster the effective horses of the Officers of the regiments kept for regimental duty, as well as the troop horses, and to specify in the Pay-lists of the respective troops opposite to the name of each Officer, the number of his horses of the above description present, and the number absent.

No. 55. Paymasters to *muster* the Bat or Baggage Horses.

[55. The horses allowed by the existing Regulations to be employed as bât and baggage horses, for which any charge is made against the public, either for the supply of forage, or on account of farriery, are to be mustered on the 24th of each month, by the Paymasters of Corps of Cavalry, of Regular and Fencible Infantry, and of Militia; and the number of bât and baggage horses of each description is to be specified on one of the sheets of the Pay-lists not otherwise appropriated; or in the Militia, on a separate paper to be annexed to the [Monthly] Accompts. A declaration is also to be added to the Paymaster's affidavit in the [Monthly] Pay-lists or Accompts, of the number of bât and baggage horses actually present at the muster, and that the horses of this description borne on the [Monthly] Roll, are to the best of his knowledge and belief, exclusive of the horses kept by any Officer of the Corps for the performance of his duty or for other purposes.]*

No. 56. Paymasters how to

56. In conformity to the Direction contained in Article 14, of the Additional Instructions,

---

\* Since the issuing of the above order, the Baggage Horses of Officers have been discontinued—and the number of Bât Horses reduced to two per Regiment.—The declaration of the Paymaster in regard to the Bât Horses is now annexed to the Monthly Abstracts.

dated

## Part II.] Regimental Accompts.

specify in their Pay Lists the Regulations and Letters received relative to accompts.

dated 11th May, 1801, Paymasters are desired to specify in their Pay-lists the following particulars as to all regulations and letters relative to accompts, which shall have been received by the Commanding Officer or Paymaster, during the period of the pay-list, viz.

1st. The date of the regulation or letter.

2dly. From whom the same was received.

3dly. The purport thereof.

4thly. The date at which the same was received by the Commanding Officer or Paymaster.

Paymasters transmitting pay-lists or accompts to the Secretary at War will describe upon the corner of the cover what each packet contains.

No. 57. Commanding Officers and Adjutants to date their certificates in the Pay Lists

57. Officers Commanding regiments, and Adjutants, are in future to add to their general certificates, in the [Monthly] Pay-lists and Accounts, the dates on which the same shall have been signed by them respectively; and the Officers commanding Troops or Companies, are also to date their certificates at the foot of the pay-lists of their Troops or Companies.

Paymasters are required to take particular care that this direction be always attended to, before the Pay-lists are transmitted to the War-Office.

No. 58. Abstracts of examination and decisions, from the War Office as to accompts.

58. Regimental and district Paymasters are required invariably to acknowledge by return of post, the receipt of the abstracts of examination of their pay-lists, and of the official decisions, upon their answers, and are allowed the period of one month from that time for stating such circumstances as they may have to offer in explanation: but in case no such explanation shall have been received at the War-Office, or no sufficient reason for the delay shall have been assigned, within three days after the expiration of the above limited period, the objections made will be considered as acquiesced in by the Paymasters, and the charges objected to will be finally disallowed, without regard to any subsequent representations.

56. It

No. 59. When printed forms for accompts, &c. have not been received, the same to be made out in *Manuscript*.

59. It is to be clearly understood by regimental Paymasters and others, that when the printed forms for the regimental accompts, the books of general abstract, the Adjutant's rolls, estimates, &c. do not arrive in due time, and the regiment is stationed at such a distance from London as not to admit of obtaining them within a few days, by an application to the Secretary at War, the same are to be made up in *Manuscript*, agreeably to the forms in use.

*War-Office*, 25*th April*, 1805.

W. DUNDAS.

*Circular*

*Circular from the Adjutant General to General Officers commanding in Districts, relative to the Payment of Bounty for Men who volunteer for extended Service.*

Horse Guards, 24th September, 1806.

SIR,

THE following arrangement relative to the payment of bounty to men, who volunteer for extended service, which is applicable to all cases that may occur, and consolidates the former instructions on the subject, has received the Commander in Chief's approbation; and I am directed to signify His Royal Highness's pleasure, that, in order to make it effectually known to all concerned, the substance of this Letter shall be communicated to the troops in the district under your command.

In all cases where men extend their services in the same Regiment, they are to receive their full bounty on volunteering, with the exception of Two Guineas, which portion is to be retained until they join the first Battalion, if at home, or, if it is abroad, until the Officer commanding the second Battalion is satisfied that each man is provided with a complete stock of necessaries.

When men volunteer into another Regiment, than that in which they have been serving, they are immediately to receive Two Guineas from the Officer appointed to take charge of them, and the remainder of their bounty on joining the first Battalion of the new Regiment, if at home, or the second Battalion, if the first is abroad; due consideration as in the former case, being had by the Commanding Officer to the state of their necessaries.

Men, who may extend their services in Regiments abroad, consisting of only one Battalion, will be finally settled with for their bounty at the Army Depôt.

I am directed by His Royal Highness to add, that this arrangement is intended to apply, not only in cases of volunteering,

teering, which may take place from this period, but also in instances where a residue of bounty is still unpaid to men, who have extended their services.

I have the honor to be, with great respect, &c.

HARRY CALVERT,
Adjutant General.

Addressed to General Officers commanding Districts in Great Britain and the Islands.

Part II.] *Regimental Accompts.* 185

*Explanatory Directions for the Information and Guidance of Paymasters and others, continued from page* 182, *dated War Office,* 22*d August,* 1806.

## PAY.

No. 60. Soldiers permitted to commute their punishment for service abroad, to receive pay, &c.

60. SOLDIERS who, in consequence of desertion, or other crimes, have been permitted to commute their punishment for service abroad, are not precluded from receiving pay and beer money as other Soldiers, while under an escort in Great Britain, proceeding to the depôt or place of embarkation, in order to join the Regiment abroad, with which they are destined to serve; and if they are billetted upon, and victualled by the innkeeper on the march, the usual extra allowance may be charged on the route; but no charge for necessaries is to be made against the public, for men under such circumstances.

## RECRUITING.

No. 61. Parties on detachment or recruiting.

61. The Paymasters of districts, of detachments, and all other Officers concerned, are to take care, in future, that the Troop or Company to which each Non-commissioned Officer, Trumpeter, Drummer, Fifer, or Private Man, of a party or detachment belongs, be invariably specified opposite to his name on the Pay List thereof, as pointed out by the printed forms.

No. 62. Recruits not finally approved.

62. The dates of enlistment of all Recruits are, in every case, to be stated opposite to their names in each Pay List in which a charge is made for them, until finally approved.

No. 63. Recruits rejected.

63. When a Recruit is rejected, the reasons of rejection are always to be specified opposite to his name in the Pay List.

If

If rejected from a cause, as to which culpable inattention is imputable to the Recruiting Officer, it is to be clearly understood, that no charge whatever for such Recruit is to be made against the Public, either on account of levy money, pay, or allowance to carry him home; unless when specially authorized, by the Secretary at War, upon the recommendation of His Royal Highness the Commander in Chief.

The inlisting of Recruits, who are *under sized*, is to be considered as an instance of the above description.

No. 64. Expences of Recruiting Officers.

64. Expences incurred by Officers employed on the Recruiting Service on account of postage, or for the carriage of Pay Lists or Accompts from the Head Quarters of the Recruiting District to the stations of Recruiting Parties, are not to be charged against the Public, but are to be defrayed by the Recruiting Officer.

No. 65. Pay of Men discharged from Regiments transferred to the Irish establishment.

65. The pay of men discharged and recommended to Chelsea Hospital, who shall at the time of the transfer of a Regiment to the Irish Establishment, be waiting in this country for the first Chelsea Board to be held subsequently to their discharge, is, notwithstanding the said transfer, to be charged by the Agents in their accompts with this country to the period of the first meeting of the said Board. It is understood that the like rule will be observed in Ireland, in regard to men discharged there, and recommended to Kilmainham Hospital from corps transferred to the British Establishment.

## CONTINGENCIES.

No. 66. Receipts for the hire of waggons.

66. The receipts given by constables for the hire of waggons, and transmitted to this Office as vouchers for the charges of the extra rates, payable under orders of the Magistrates at the General Sessions, being frequently without stamps, although amounting to Two Pounds and upwards, Paymasters, and other Officers concerned,

concerned, are apprized that receipts of the above description are not exempted by law from the duties on stamps, except in the cases of *emergency,* specified in the Mutiny Act (Clause 53 of the present Mutiny Act); and that receipts not duly stamped, cannot therefore with propriety be admitted in support of such charges.

No. 67. Passage of Parties across the Thames from Gravesend to Tilbury, and *vice versâ.*

67. Claims having been made in some instances for the passage of parties across the Thames from Gravesend to Tilbury, and from Tilbury to Gravesend, Paymasters, and other Officers concerned, are apprized that no charge on that account can properly be admitted against the Public: a passage boat between the two places being established under the direction of an Officer of the Royal Engineers, by which parties of Troops, great or small, pass and repass, free of all toll or demand.

No. 68. Carriage of arms for corps in Great Britain.

68. The carriage of arms, for corps stationed in Great Britain, is, in all cases where the delivery takes place from the Tower, or from any other ordnance magazine, to be defrayed by the Board of Ordnance, upon proper vouchers being produced.

The expence attending the removal of arms, *subsequently to their arrival at the Head Quarters of Corps,* is liable to be paid out of the customary allowances granted for the carriage of regimental baggage.

No. 69. *Allowances to the wives of Non-commissioned Officers and Men who may not be permitted to embark with their husbands.*

69. When a Regiment in Great Britain is ordered to embark for service abroad, and the number of the wives of the Non-commissioned Officers and Men, exceed the proportion allowed to go with the corps, as limited by the orders of the Commander in Chief, each of the wives not permitted to embark is to receive an allowance of One Guinea for herself, and Five Shillings for each of her children, to enable her to proceed to the place of her intended residence in England or Wales: if she be desirous of proceeding to Ireland or Scotland, a passage may be immediately provided for her to the port where she wishes to land; but if no such passage

sage can be obtained at the place where the Regiment embarks, she is to receive the above allowances to enable her to proceed to the port where a passage can be most conveniently procured.

Upon her arrival in Ireland or Scotland, she is to receive the further sum of Ten Shillings for herself, and Three Shillings for each of her children, to enable her to proceed to her intended place in that country if it be not at the place of her landing.

In order that there may be no difficulty in regard to the payment of the above allowances, the Commanding Officer of a Regiment ordered to embark for a foreign station will be pleased to cause separate alphabetical lists to be made out, of the women whose intended residence is in England or Wales, Ireland or Scotland, respectively, specifying the allowances paid to each, and mentioning whether a passage has been found for any of them at the place of embarkation. These lists are to be immediately forwarded to the Secretary at War.

The allowances paid to the women at the Regiment, are to be drawn for by the regimental Paymaster, and to be charged in his public accompts as a contingency, an estimate of the amount thereof being previously transmitted to the War Office, with a duplicate for the use of the Agent; and the allowances to be paid at the ports in Ireland or Scotland, are to be paid by the District Paymasters under the orders of the Officers commanding at those places. The Paymasters will charge the same of course, regimentally in their accompts with the British War Office: those in Scotland drawing upon the regimental Agents: and those in Ireland upon the general Agent in Dublin, who will charge the amount against the general Agent in London, as a sum to be received from the British regimental Agent.

The women who may be entitled to this latter allowance are to be furnished by the Commanding

ing Officer with certificates according to the annexed form, which they should be instructed to preserve carefully, to prevent any difficulty in their obtaining the allowance, or in their being provided with a passage.

Printed forms of these Certificates will be furnished from the War-Office upon applications mentioning the numbers required.

## FORMS.

This is to certify that the bearer hereof            is the wife of            a            in the            Regiment of            , is entitled to a free passage from            to            and on her arrival is to receive the sum of Ten Shillings [for herself, and Three Shillings for each of her children] provided            be not the place of her intended residence.

*This is to be struck out or altered, where she has no child, or only one.*

The said            is *(here describe her)*

This is further to certify that the said            has signified her intention of proceeding to            from which place she is to embark for            and that she has received the sum of one Guinea [for herself, and five shillings for each of her children] to enable her to reach the former place.

*This is to be struck out or altered, where she has no child, or only one.*

*Commanding Officer.*

N. B. This latter certificate is unnecessary where a passage can be obtained at the place where the Regiment embarks, in a vessel bound for the port to which the woman wishes to go in Ireland or Scotland.

DIREC-

## DIRECTIONS WHICH CANNOT BE CLASSED UNDER ANY PARTICULAR HEAD OF SERVICE.

No. 70. Paymaster ceasing as such.

70. All Regimental and District Paymasters, or committees of Paymastership, when ceasing to act as such, are to balance their public accompts exactly to the termination of the respective periods for which the said accompts are to be rendered by them; except in the case of Paymasters going upon leave of absence, who of course will have engaged to remain responsible for the Officers doing the duties of the Paymastership, during their absence.

No. 71. Paymasters permitted to resign.

71. In the event of a Paymaster being permitted to resign, it is desired, when it can be effected without material inconvenience, that the public accompts shall be made up by him to the usual period of the termination of the quarterly accompts. But when this cannot be accomplished, he is to make up not only his monthly general abstracts, but a detailed Pay-list (similar to the one in use for quarterly accompts) for one month or two months, as the case may be, to the 24th of the month in which he ceases to act, which Pay List of course is to be closed and exactly balanced, in the mode pointed out in the form of Supplementary Pay Lists, made out after the termination of each year.

The same rule is to be observed, as far as circumstances will admit, in the event of a Paymaster ceasing to act from any other cause.

No. 72. Paymasters newly appointed.

72. Paymasters, or Committees of Paymastership, newly appointed, are to make up their first detailed Pay Lists (in the form adopted for Quarterly Accompts), for one, two, or three months, as the case may require, commencing of course from the date inclusive, subsequent to that on which the public accompts of the preceding Paymaster or Committee shall have terminated, and ending with the last day of
the

the quarterly period in which their duties shall have commenced.

When the preceding Paymasters, or Acting Paymasters, or Committee, have exactly balanced their public accompts, the totals of the expenditures and receipts of the then current year, are to be carried forward to the new accompts; but where the Paymasters from circumstances of incapacity or otherwise, shall not have been able to complete their public accompts, and to balance the same, the Officer, or Officers, taking upon themselves the functions of the paymastership, will not, in such case, be required to carry over the totals of expenditures and receipts, but they will be expected to use their best endeavours to get the former accompts stated, and if possible, exactly balanced; or if the same cannot be properly liquidated, then to ascertain, and make a just report of, the exact amount remaining to be accounted for.

No. 73. Decisions upon the Answers to the Official Abstracts of Examination.

73. Referring to Article 58 of these Directions, Commanding Officers and Regimental and District Paymasters and Agents, are apprized, that, in order that the intentions of the Legislature, in regard to the speedy settlement of Regimental Accompts, may be complied with, it has been determined, that the Decisions upon the Answers to the Official Abstracts of Examination, shall be considered as *final* with respect to the accompts of the period to which they relate; and that the accompts shall be closed accordingly.

The Paymasters will therefore be particularly careful to furnish at once every explanation and document, that shall be called for by the Abstracts of Examination, as it will only be in very special cases that any subsequent explanation will be received, and then only, upon the express recommendation of the Commanding Officer, to the Secretary at War. The greatest care should also be taken, in the first instance, that no charge be inserted in the accompts of Agents or Paymasters, except in strict conformity to the 21st Article of these Directions, and that in all cases such

such explanations may be given, as may seem requisite to establish the propriety of every charge.

The want of due attention in this respect has occasioned much inconvenience, and has very much impeded the settlement of the accounts.

Paymasters to deduct all Sums disallowed.

74. In consequence of the before-mentioned intimation, as to the Decisions being final, Paymasters and other Officers concerned are hereby strictly enjoined to deduct from their charges, in the mode pointed out by the 25th Article of these Directions, all such sums as shall be stated to remain disallowed in the Decisions received by them respectively from the War Office; and this without receiving any other special instruction from the Secretary at War for that purpose. The said deductions are to take place, when the charges disallowed belong to the same year, in the first Pay List made out subsequently to the receipt of the decisions; but when the charges belong to the public accompts of a former year, then in a separate manuscript Supplementary Pay List, to be made out as soon as the decisions conveying the result of the examination of all the public accounts rendered by the Paymaster for that year shall have been received by him.

No. 75. Accompts for former Periods not to be considered as settled.

75. Agents and Paymasters will understand, that, although it is judged proper to proceed more immediately with the examination of their accompts for the present year, those for former periods are not therefore to be considered as settled; but the examination of them will be proceeded upon, and the result communicated to them, as soon as practicable.

No. 76. Description and Period of the Accompts to be specified upon the Cover that encloses them.

76. When Regimental or District Accompts or Documents relative thereto, are transmitted to the War Office, it is requested that the description and period of the accompt, may in future be distinctly specified upon the left hand corner of the cover in which the same is enclosed.

No. 77. Forms of Monthly Abstracts.

77. Paymasters are apprized, that an alteration is intended to be made in the form of the General State of the Monthly Abstracts, in order

der that the totals of the expenditures and receipts may be carried over, from month to month throughout the year, and that the addition and deduction of errors may be made therein, in like manner as in the General States of the quarterly accompts.

When the new forms are circulated, the Paymasters are to make out their Monthly General Abstracts accordingly, (stating and adding together in the first instance, on a manuscript paper to be affixed thereto, the totals of each of the preceding months of the current year) and accompanying their Abstracts, in all cases where corrections are made, with a manuscript statement to shew the particulars of such corrections, and the heads of service to which they belong, in the mode adopted in the quarterly accompts.

It is not however expected that the totals of the Monthly Abstracts and Quarterly Accompts, terminating on the 24th March, 24th June, 24th September, and 24th December, should be made exactly to agree; therefore any omissions or errors that may have occurred in the Monthly General Abstracts, are not be noticed in the Quarterly Pay Lists, but the latter (being the Accompts to be principally examined) are to be made out as correctly as possible. Errors and omissions in the Monthly Abstracts are to be corrected in the first Monthly General Abstract, or Manuscript Supplementary Abstract of the same year, made out after the discovery thereof, and those occurring in the Quarterly Accompts are to be corrected in like manner, in the Quarterly or Supplementary Pay Lists of the same year.

The Paymasters will however take care that the totals of the expenditures and receipts for each year in the Monthly and Quarterly Accompts, shall ultimately be the same.

No. 78. Regiments ordered

78. The Paymasters of Regiments ordered for embarkation for service abroad, whether from Ireland

for Service abroad.
Ireland or England, are to apply by letter to the Secretary at War, London, for a supply in advance of the printed forms for making up their **Regimental Public Accompts**.

*War-Office*, 22d *August*, 1806.

R. FITZPATRICK.

*Circular*

*Circular Letter to Colonels of Regiments of Cavalry, Infantry of the Line, Militia, and Fencibles, on the British Establishment, relative to an Arrangement for the regular and punctual Settlement of Regimental Accompts.*

*War-Office, 27th February,* 1804.

SIR,

HAVING judged it proper, with the view of preventing any further accumulation of unsettled Regimental Accompts, to form an arrangement by which it is expected that the Pay-Lists and Agents' Abstracts for the current period, commencing from the 25th of *December* last, will be finally examined soon after the receipt thereof in this Office; and it being essential to the attainment of this object, that no delay should, in future, take place in the delivery of the Accompts of the Regimental Agents; I have the honour to request, that you will give particular orders for the observance of the necessary regularity in this respect, on the part of the Agent of the Regiment under your command.

I cannot omit this opportunity of mentioning to you, that, notwithstanding the explicit declaration contained in my Predecessor's Letter of the 29th of *May*, 1801, and the plain rule of conduct laid down for the Regimental Agents in the 3d Article of the instructions therein referred to, it has frequently happened, in cases where the Paymasters have drawn for larger sums than were obviously required for the use of the Corps, that the Agents, instead of addressing themselves immediately to the Commanding Officers, as required by the article abovementioned, have entered into an explanatory correspondence with the Paymasters, and have acquiesced in the temporizing expedients they have offered for adjusting their accompts; thereby defeating the object of the regulation, which was to ensure to the Commanding Officers the earliest information of the excessive demands of the Paymasters, and thus to enable them, by a prompt interference, to check the improper conduct of the Paymasters in this respect, and to prevent the accompts of the Corps from getting into confusion: and I am so fully convinced of the necessity of enforcing the strictest attention to this point, as well as to the other rules contained in the King's Regulations, that I think it proper to apprize you, that wherever any defalcation shall take place in the accompts of a Paymaster, which might have been prevented by the Agent's following the rules prescribed for his conduct, I shall most certainly decline taking any steps for relieving him (through the sureties of the Paymaster or otherwise,) from the loss to which he may be exposed.

Trusting that you will concur in the propriety of this determination, and that you will give proper instructions to your Agent accordingly, I shall hope, that, by his attention to this and the other parts of his duty, every facility will be afforded for the future regular and punctual settlement of the accompts of the Corps, and that no cause will arise to render it expedient to look to any material change in the present system of Regimental Finance.

I have the honour to be,

SIR,

Your most obedient

humble Servant,

CHARLES BRAGGE.

Colonel of the
    Regiment of

*Circular*

*Circular Letter to Regimental Agents, relative to Accompts.*

*War-Office, 28th February, 1804.*

IN conveying to you the enclosed copy of Mr. *Bragge's* Circular Letter, (27th Feb. 1804) addressed to the Colonels of Regiments, I am directed to acquaint you, with *The Secretary at War's* desire, that, immediately upon receiving the General States of the Paymaster of the Corps to which you are Agent, you will compare the bills therein credited, with those which you shall have accepted, or paid, or shall know to have been drawn, belonging to the period of the Accompt; and if you find that the Paymaster has omitted to give credit for any bill or bills that should have been inserted in his General States, you will immediately report the same to the Commanding Officer of the Regiment, and to this Department.

[In reference to the arrangement alluded to in Mr. *Bragge's* Letter above-mentioned, I am directed to apprize you, that, the Abstracts of the examination of the Regimental Pay Lists, will in future be sent to you, in the first instance, in order that you may take copies thereof, to be retained by you; you will then return the Abstracts to this Office, within three days, with any explanations you may have to give for the guidance of the Paymaster in answering the objections made to the charges in his Accompts, which will be forwarded to him from hence with the Abstracts.

The decisions upon the Paymaster's answers will also be sent to you to be copied, and are to be immediately afterwards returned.]*

Your own answers to the Abstracts of the examination of your Accompts are invariably to be given within ten days from the receipt thereof.

I am,
Your most
obedient Servant,
WILLIAM MERRY.

Agent of the

---

* These two paragraphs are not now applicable; the practice of sending to the Agents the Abstracts of examination and decision upon the Paymaster's Accompts having been discontinued.

*Circular Letter to Officers commanding Regiments of Cavalry, Infantry of the Line, Militia, and Fencibles, on the British Establishment, relative to the regular transmission of Pay Lists, &c.*

*War Office, 29th February,* 1804.

SIR,

HAVING judged it proper, with the view of preventing any further accumulation of unsettled regimental accompts, to form an arrangement by which it is expected that the Pay Lists, and Agents' Abstracts, for the current period, commencing the 25th of *December* last, will be finally examined, soon after the receipt thereof in this Office; and it being essential to the attainment of this object, that the regimental Pay Lists should be transmitted with the greatest possible regularity; I have the honor to request, that you will enforce the strictest attention to this point on the part of the Paymaster of the Corps under your command; and that if any circumstances should occur to render some delay unavoidable, you will be pleased to report the same to this Office.

With the view of enabling you to judge of the correctness of the credits given in the General Abstract of the accompts of the Corps, which the Paymaster is required to keep for your inspection, and which should agree with the credits in the General States of his Pay Lists, I have caused the instructions contained in the enclosed Letter, (28th February, 1804,) to be given to the regimental agent, which, I trust, will answer the desired purpose.

I have the honor to be,

SIR,

Your most obedient

Humble servant,

CHARLES BRAGGE.

The Officer commanding the
Regiment of

P. S. You will be aware that the last paragraph applies more particularly to Regiments on the home station.

*General*

## Regimental Accompts.

*General Orders relative to the transmission of Regimental Pay Lists and Accompts.*

*Horse Guards, 13th August, 1804.*

IT having been represented to the Commander in Chief by the Secretary at War, that the King's Regulations in regard to the early and proper authentication and transmission of the regimental Pay Lists and Accompts, are not duly attended to, (especially in the instance of Corps stationed abroad) His Royal Highness most strictly enjoins Officers in the command of Regiments, both abroad and at home, to cause the Pay Lists and other accompts of their respective Corps, to be prepared, duly authenticated, and transmitted to the War Office as soon as possible after the expiration of the periods at which, by the established regulations, it is required they should be made up; and in case of a delay being unavoidably incurred, His Royal Highness directs that an especial explanation as to the cause of it shall be made to the Secretary at War.

By order of His Royal Highness

The Commander in Chief.

HARRY CALVERT,
Adjutant General of the Forces.

*Circular to Commandants of Militia Corps relative to the adoption of Quarterly Pay Lists.*

*War Office,* 31*st December,* 1804.

SIR,

IT being judged expedient to dispense with the rendering of the Pay Lists of Militia Corps more frequently than once in three months, and to adopt, in lieu thereof, a more compendious form of Monthly Accounts, I have the honor to acquaint you therewith, and that the Paymaster of the             under your command will accordingly not be required to make up Pay Lists to the 24th of *January* and 24th of *February* next, but will receive, in due time, a Form of Pay List, to be used for the three months, ending the 24th of *March* following; and so, in like manner, for the quarters ending the 24th of *June,* 24th of *September,* and 24th of *December,* in each year.

It being, however, essentially necessary that the Corps should be mustered on the 24th of every month, the Adjutant is still to make up his rolls accordingly; and the Paymaster is to take the musters by the said rolls, which are to be transmitted to this Office, with the new Forms of Monthly Accounts above alluded to: duplicates of the rolls being retained, as at present, at the Head Quarters of the Corps.

These new forms will be furnished, as soon as printed, with such explanations as may be necessary upon the few points in which they will differ from the documents which the Paymaster is now accustomed to prepare.

I have the honor to be,

SIR,

Your most obedient servant,

W. DUNDAS.

Colonel of the
    of Militia.

*Circular*

*Circular to the Commandants of Militia Corps relative to the Transmission of the Quarterly Pay Lists.*

War Office, 15th March, 1805.

SIR,

THE new Forms of Three Monthly Pay Lists, alluded to in my Letter of the 31st December last, being about to be circulated, I have the honor to acquaint you, it is not desired that the same should be transmitted to this Office earlier than the 24th of next month, unless the Pay Master should be able to complete it sooner; in which case, it may be sent off as soon as it shall have been duly attested and certified.

I am further to apprize you, that, although the said form is necessarily calculated to include Officers and Men who have not actually received their pay for the periods set against their respective names, yet it is extremely desirable that every individual should be fully settled with before the Pay Lists are sent off, which, from the time allowed as above stated, may, it is hoped, be generally effected.

A separate statement of the pay of the Officers is to be transmitted with the Pay List for the use of the Agent.

I have the honor to be,

SIR,

Your most obedient servant,

W. DUNDAS.

Commandant of the ,
    of Militia

*Circular*

*Circular to Colonels of Militia Regiments relative to the adoption of a more compendious Form of Monthly Accompts, &c.*

*War Office, 3d January*, 1806.

SIR,

REFERRING to my Circular Letter of the 31st *December*, 1804, I have the satisfaction to acquaint you, that the result of the arrangement therein notified, and of the examination of the Militia Accompts of the current year, has been such, as not only to warrant the adopting a still more compendious Monthly Accompt, than the one alluded to in my said Letter, but to admit of my dispensing with the preparation of detailed accompts for the other services of the corps, as well as the pay, more frequently than once in three months.

In consequence of this measure, the only documents to be transmitted to this Office *monthly*, will be the Estimate; the new Accompt above alluded to; and the Adjutant's Roll; with duplicates of the two former for the use of the Agent; and I have particularly to request, that you will give the strictest orders for the regular and punctual transmission thereof, at the usual periods, in conformity to the General Order of His Royal Highness the Commander in Chief, dated the 13th August, 1804, explaining to the Commanding Officer, that the responsibility on this head will attach upon himself.

The new Monthly Accompt will be immediately printed, and sent to the Paymaster; and Forms of Accompts for the other services above mentioned, adapted to the extended period, will be prepared and furnished in due time.

I think it proper to mention, that although the distribution of the Non-commissioned Officers and Men, will not be required to be sent to this Office monthly; yet as it appears desirable, that it should be made up as soon after the expiration of each month as possible, the form will be adapted accordingly: I am at the same time to observe, it is essential that this most useful document should be prepared with all possible attention, and that it should properly be made up by the Adjutant, under the orders of the Commanding Officer,

and

Part II.] *Regimental Accompts.* 203

and not by the Paymaster; who is however to be supplied with a duplicate thereof, monthly, as it may serve to regulate his charges for the extra allowance to innkeepers, and the extra price of meat, as well as for other expenditures, depending upon the effective number of the Non-commissioned Officers and Men, at particular dates.

The accompts of the extra price of meat are also to be made out and certified by the General Officer *monthly*; but are only to be transmitted to this Office with the other accompts of the corps once in three months.

I am to add, that as the Quarterly Pay Lists of the Militia will probably be required to be made up, alphabetically, for the whole Regiment, instead of being divided into Companies, it may be useful for this object, to have an alphabetical list prepared of all the Non-commissioned Officers and Men, of the corps under your command, as they stood on the 25th December last, classed according to their respective ranks.

I have the honor to be,

SIR,

Your most obedient

Humble servant,

W. DUNDAS.

Colonel of the
  Militia.

*Circular*

*Circular to Agents of Regular Regiments of Cavalry and Infantry, Fencibles and Militia.*

*War Office,* 27*th January,* 1806.

SIR,

REFERRING to the Circular Letter from the Secretary at War, to the Colonels and Commandants of Militia Corps, dated 3d instant, I am directed to acquaint you, that you are to continue to make up and deliver your Monthly Abstracts as usual, but that the vouchers for your incidental payments are to be retained and transmitted with your Quarterly Accompts, the form of which will be communicated to you in due time.

I am,

SIR,

Your most obedient

Humble servant,

W. MERRY.

Agents
of Regulars, Fencibles, and Militia.

---

N. B. The Instructions contained in this Letter were intended to apply to the Regulars and Fencibles, although the previous Letter of the 3d January was addressed only to the Commandants of Militia Corps.

## Part II.] Regimental Accompts. 205

*Circular to Colonels of Regiments of Cavalry and Infantry of the Line, Fencible Infantry, and Royal Veteran Battalions on the Home Station, relative to the adoption of Pay-lists for the period of three Months.*

*War-Office, 29th January, 1806.*

SIR,

THE rendering of detailed statements of the regimental expenditures, so frequently as once a month, being considered to be unnecessary, in the present state of the accompts of the army, and being found to be in some respects inconvenient; I have the honour to acquaint you therewith, and that the Paymaster of the regiment under your command, will accordingly, not be required to make up Pay-lists to the 24th *February* next: but will receive, in due time, a form of Pay-list, to be used for three months, ending the 24th *March* following, and so on, in like manner, for the quarters, ending the 24th *June*, 24th *September*, and 24th *December* in each year.

It being, however, essentially necessary that the Corps should be mustered monthly, and that this Office, as well as the Commanding Officer and Agent, should be informed, as frequently as heretofore, of the state of the Paymaster's accompts; the Paymaster is to muster the Corps at the usual time, by the Adjutant's rolls (which are to be made up and transmitted to this Office as at present; duplicates of the rolls being retained at the Head-quarters of the Corps); and is to transmit, at the same time, a monthly abstract of his public accompts, with a duplicate for the use of the agent, retaining a triplicate at the regiment. The forms of these abstracts are printing, and will be furnished as soon as possible.

In consequence of this arrangement, the only documents relative to accompts to be transmitted from the regiment *monthly*, will be the Adjutants' roll, the abstract above alluded to, and the estimate; and it being essential to the regular proceedings of this department, that these documents should be received at the proper periods, I have particularly to request, that you will give the strictest orders for the punctual transmission thereof in conformity to the General Order

of

of his Royal Highness the Commander in Chief, dated 13th August, 1804;* explaining to the Commanding Officer that the responsibility for enforcing a due observance of the said order will attach upon himself.

I am to add, that in the case of the transfer of the Regiment under your command to the Irish Establishment, or of its embarking for service abroad, detailed pay-lists and accounts will still be required to be made up to the date preceding the transfer or embarkation, and that the Paymaster will be furnished with proper forms of account accordingly, upon his applying to this Office.

I have the honour to be,

SIR,

Your most obedient humble servant,

W. DUNDAS.

*PS. The Pay-list to the 24th instant is to be sent to this Office; but it will be returned, that it may be incorporated with the Quarterly Pay-list above alluded to.*

Colonel of the
    Regiment of


In the Circular of same date to Regiments on *foreign stations* the dates mentioned towards the conclusion of the first paragraph were varied according to the station of the Regiment; the postscript was omitted; and the last paragraph stood as follows:

" I am to add, that in the case of the arrival of the Regiment, under your command in Great-Britain, detailed Pay-lists and Accompts will still be required to be made up to the date preceding the disembarkation, and that the Paymaster will be furnished with proper forms of accompt accordingly, upon his applying to this Office.

---

* See page 199.

*Circu-*

*Circular to Paymasters of Regiments of Cavalry and Infantry of the Line* on the Home Station; *relative to the preparation of the New Monthly Accompts.*

*War-Office, 14th February, 1806.*

SIR,

I HAVE the Secretary at War's directions to transmit to you the enclosed printed forms of the Monthly Accompt alluded to in Mr. Dundas's Letter of the 29th ultimo, which you will take care to forward to this Office, by the time when the Monthly Pay-lists have been hitherto required to be sent off; reporting to the Commanding Officer the circumstances which may, in some instances, occasion a delay in this respect.

As this Accompt is for the most part nearly similar to Documents which you have been accustomed to prepare, it is not supposed that you will have any difficulty in making it up; and it seems only necessary to explain, that it is not to be accompanied by any vouchers, either for the pay of Officers, or for other charges, except such are pointed out in the new form; it being intended that every other usual and necessary receipt, or voucher, should be attached to the *Quarterly* Accompts; for which purpose all routes, receipts, or other documents, should therefore be carefully preserved: and as it may happen, that an Officer may not be present with the Corps so as to sign the Quarterly Accompts at the time of their being made up; in which case, unless you are in possession of a proper receipt, the charge for such Officer's pay would of course be disallowed; it will be essentially necessary, that with the view of preventing any embarrassment on this head, you should invariably take a receipt for each monthly issue of the pay of every Officer, which may be given up to him, upon his signing the Quarterly Accompt in which such pay shall be included.

The accompts of the extra price of Meat are to be made out and certified by the General Officers *Monthly* as heretofore, but are only to be transmitted to this Office with the other accompts of the Corps once in three months.

As

As you are in possession of a duplicate of the Pay-list for the month of January last, that Pay-list will not be sent back as was intended; but the vouchers are herewith enclosed, in order that such of them as shall be required may be annexed to the Quarterly Accompt.

I am,

SIR,

Your most obedient humble servant,

W. MERRY

Paymaster of the
    Regiment of

Circulars of the same date were addressed to the Paymasters of Regiments *on foreign stations* (the East Indies excepted) inserting in the first paragraph after the words " forward to this Office," the words " in original and duplicate:" omitting the word " Routes" in the 2d paragraph; and omitting altogether the two last paragraphs.

Part II.]  *Regimental Accompts.*  209

*Circular to the Agents, enclosing the new Form of Quarterly Accompts.*

*War-Office, 9th April,* 1806.

REFERRING to the Circular Letter from this Office of the 27th January last, I enclose herewith a printed form of the Quarterly Accompts therein alluded to, and am to acquaint you, that the same are to be rendered to this Office, within seven days, at the latest, from the dates of the receipt of the Duplicate General States of the Accompts of the Regimental Paymasters; and in order that there may be no delay in this respect, the Accompts of your own disbursements should be made up immediately after the expiration of the Quarterly period, so that upon the arrival of the Paymaster's Accompts, you will only have to compare the particulars of his credits with the bills which you shall have paid for the services of the same period.

The necessary vouchers are, of course, to accompany your Accompts, agreeably to the intimation contained in the Letter above referred to.

I am, &c.

WILLIAM MERRY.

PS. Your Monthly Abstracts are to be sent in as usual. You are requested to specify on the left hand corner of the cover transmitting your Accompts, of what description they are.

Agents of Regulars, Fencibles,
  and Militia.

*Circular to the Commanding Officers of Regiments, relative to the periods of transmitting the Quarterly Pay-Lists.*

*War-Office, 19th March,* 1806.

SIR,

REFERRING to the Circular Letter from my Predecessor, to the Colonels of Cavalry and Infantry of the Line, dated 29th *January* last, I have the honour to acquaint you that, agreeably to the intimation therein given, the Quarterly Pay-Lists and Accompts are preparing, and will be shortly circulated; and in order that the preparation of the Monthly Abstracts and Estimates may not interfere with the making up of the said Quarterly Accompts, the latter will not be required to be sent off before the 14th of the month, following the termination of each Accompt, viz. the 14th *April,* the 14th *July,* the 14th *October,* and the 14th *January,* in each year.

I have the honour to be,

SIR,

Your most obedient

humble Servant,

R. FITZPATRICK.

The Officer Commanding
Regiment of

*Memorandum*

Part II.] *Regimental Accompts.* 211

*Memorandum for the Information and Guidance of Paymasters of Militia, in making up the New Quarterly Accompts.*

*Dated War-Office, 19th March, 1806.*

THE pay of the Commissioned and Warrant Officers is to be stated and vouched as in the former Accompts.

The names of the Non-commissioned Officers, Drummers, Fifers, and Private Men, entitled to the full Rates of pay, are to be stated together for the whole Corps, instead of being divided into Companies, and are to be classed in their respective ranks accordingly as they shall have been effective for the complete period, or for broken periods, as follows, viz.

Those, who shall have been effective for the complete period of the Accompt, are to be stated in the first Class of each rank; in the second Class are to be placed, those who were effective at the commencement of the period, but who ceased to be so, before the termination thereof; in the third Class, those who became effective, after the commencement of the period, and remained so, to the termination; and in the fourth Class, those who became effective after the commencement, and ceased to be so before the termination, of the period.

Each of these Classes is to be stated in alphabetical order.

The three forms following that allotted for the insertion of the names of the Private Men entitled to full pay, seem to require no explanation; but it is hoped, that the second and third of these forms will not often be brought into use; as it is desirable, that every Non-commissioned Officer and Man should be settled with, when it can be done, before the Quarterly Accompts are made up.

The next form is, in some respects, similar to one included in the Monthly Accounts of the last year, and may be easily filled up.

The Abstract of the pay of the Non-commissioned Officers, Drummers, Fifers, and Private Men, is intended to produce a simple calculation of the amount thereof, founded upon the aggregate numbers of days of the respective ranks included in the preceding Statements.

o 2

The

The Contingent Accompt, the General Accompt of the increased rates paid to Innkeepers, &c. the Muster Roll of the Bât Horses, the Accompt of the carriage of baggage, and statement of marches, the state of the balance of effects and credits or debts of soldiers, and the General State of the Paymaster's Public Accompts, have not been altered since the former year, except in what was necessary to adapt them to the extended period.

The certificates of the Commanding Officer and Adjutant, and the affidavit of the Paymaster, have been framed, so as only to require their authentication of the Accompts in what appears properly to belong to their respective situations.

The Paymasters will take care to observe, whether the remarks placed opposite to the respective names in the Adjutants Rolls, contain all such explanations for elucidating the respective Charges, as would have been given when the Corps was mustered by the Pay-Lists, and will make such further observations as may be requisite for that purpose.

INSTRUCTIONS

#  SECTION III.

## PART III.

### SERIES OF INSTRUCTIONS

TO

*PAYMASTERS OF RECRUITING DISTRICTS.*

*Original Instructions to Paymasters of Recruiting Districts, dated 3d February, 1798.*

I. THE Paymaster of each Recruiting District is to draw from the Agents of Regiments on Foreign Stations, to which the several Troops, Companies or Parties within the same belong, the sums necessary for carrying on the different branches of that service, including the pay of all the Commissioned Officers actually employed therein, and is to issue the same in such proportions, as shall be requisite, to the Officers, who have the charge of the said parties.

II. His draughts for pay may be made every month in advance; but, for the other services, from time to time, and to such amount only, as occasion may require, and the Inspecting Field Officer shall approve; giving previous notice thereof to the Agent, and distinguishing, in his draughts, and in the notices given thereof, the amount for each head of service. The concurrence of the Inspecting Field Officer is to be expressed by the word "Approved," in his own writing, signed by himself on the face of the draught.

III. Re-

III. Recruiting Officers commanding Parties shall receive, from the Paymaster of the District, whatever money shall be wanted for the service, including the pay of Officers as well as of Men, and shall be accountable to him in the first instance for the same. They shall make out, and deliver to him Monthly Pay-Lists, containing the name of each individual of their Parties and Recruits (and, in the Cavalry, the number of Troop Horses) subsisted by them within the month; And shall also make up the Accounts of Bounty Money, &c. monthly. These Lists and Accounts shall be made to the 24th of each month inclusive, and regularly continued to the respective periods, when the Parties or Recruits shall cease to be subsisted by them, or to be under their command.

The form of the Pay-List, and of the authentication thereof, shall be such as may be prescribed by the Inspector General of the Recruiting Service, to whom the particular adjustment thereof has been referred.*

IV. Every such Officer shall settle with the Men under his Command, precisely on the 24th of each month, and shall annex to his Monthly Pay-List and Account, a state of the effects and credits, or debts of the Non-commissioned Officers and Private Men who may have died or deserted, within the said period.

V. The Paymaster, whose Office includes that of Mustermaster, is to muster, by the Pay-Lists, the several parties within his district, on the 24th of each month, if the same can be effected in one day; or if not, as soon afterwards as may be; the Pay-Lists are then to be examined, and further authenticated, by the Adjutant of the District, as well as the Paymaster; after which they are to be laid before the Inspecting Field Officer for his examination and signature.† [They are then (under cover to the Secretary at War) to be transmitted to the chief District Pay-master resident at Chatham, where they shall be examined, chequed, and further certified by the Inspector General; and from whence they shall be returned to the War-Office. Duplicates of these Accounts shall also be transmitted to the War-Office immediately from the Inspectors of Districts, which

---

* The established forms of Pay-lists and Accompts are now supplied by the War-Office through the District Paymasters.

† The remainder of this Article is now totally inapplicable.

Duplicates

Part III.]  *Regimental Accompts.*  215

Duplicates, after having been compared with, and, if necessary, altered in conformity to the originals received from Chatham, will be dispatched to the respective Agents.]

VI. The limitation of the time for transmitting the Pay-Lists and Accounts, and the Duplicates thereof, will be fixed by the Inspector General, as the details of the service may require.*

VII. The Pay-Lists, made out and authenticated as before-mentioned, will be deemed to have the full credit and authority of Muster Rolls, and to be entire and incontrovertible vouchers. The accounts will be settled upon them finally; and no subsequent appeal will be admitted on those parts to which they extend. As to the other parts, no alteration will be allowed after settlement; nor before, unless on the special recommendation of the Inspector General.

VIII. The Paymaster is to be amenable, in the ordinary course, to Martial Law, for every part of his conduct which may appear inconsistent with military discipline, or the rules of the service; but he shall not be liable to receive orders touching the manner of making up his Pay-Lists and Accounts, unless under a special Instruction in writing, from the Commander in Chief of the Forces, the Secretary at War, or the Inspector General of the Recruiting Service.

IX. The Pay-master, once appointed, shall not be removeable, except by Command of the King, or by the Sentence of a General Court-Martial.

X. In case of the Paymaster's death, or incapacity from accident, his papers of accounts shall be taken into possession of the Inspecting Field Officer and Adjutant of the district, who are to act as a committee of Paymastership, and to make up and transmit the several Pay-Lists and Accounts [above specified] at the same periods, and under the like Regulations, as are prescribed for the Paymaster, until further provision.

XI. Paymasters of Recruiting Districts will receive a special Military Commission, under the Sign Manual, and be allowed Lodging-money as a Captain, viz. eight shillings

---

* For the periods of transmission of the accounts, vide Memorandum of 13th June, 1806, p. 222.

per week; but they are in no shape whatever to have claim to military rank in the Army.

XII. Pay at the rate of fifteen shillings a day will be annexed to the Paymaster's commission.

XIII. Each Paymaster will be allowed twenty pounds per annum for postage and stationary;* and a clerk, who is to be an enlisted soldier, and to have the rank and pay of a Serjeant.

Given at the War-Office, this third day of February, 1798.

By His Majesty's Command,

W. WINDHAM.

---

* A further expenditure of postage and stationary is allowed when actually incurred.—See the Circular of 13th November, 1800, p. 220.

*Circular*

*Circular Letter from the Secretary at War to the Paymasters of Recruiting Districts, containing further Instructions for their Guidance.*

*War Office*, 31st *August*, 1798.

SIR,

I AM to signify to you the King's pleasure, that the following rules in addition to the regulations of the third of February last, be observed from the twenty-fifth instant inclusive.

When a Recruit is intermediately approved, the district Paymaster is to reimburse the Recruiting Officer the sum actually advanced by him, on account of Bounty for the said Recruit, not exceeding the amount authorized by the regulation, and is to charge the same in his accompt.

When a Recruit shall have been finally approved at [Chatham,]\* the chief district Paymaster shall draw upon the Regimental Agent, for the reserved bounty, and shall pay the same.

[He shall also, if the Recruiting Officer be present at Chatham, pay to him that part of the levy money to which he has a personal claim, on the final approbation of the Recruit, together with the reward to the party by which the recruit was enlisted, or to the person who brought him, and shall draw for the same likewise on the Regimental Agent:] †  and these respective sums the chief district Paymaster shall charge in his accompt.

But if the Recruiting Officer shall not be present at [Chatham,] the certificate of the final approbation of the Recruit, transmitted by the Inspector General of the Recruiting Service to the inspecting Field Officer, is to be immediately communicated by him to the district Paymaster, to whom it will be an authority and direction for paying to the Recruiting Officer his personal share of the levy money, together with the reward above mentioned, and for charging the same in his accompt.

For your further information and guidance, a statement

---

\* Now, the Isle of Wight.
† The proportion of bounty payable on attestation, is now paid and charged by the Recruiting Officer.

of

of the distribution of the levy money, specifying in what manner the several portions thereof may be charged in the public accompts, is annexed to this paper, and some printed forms of accompts to be observed by the district Paymasters, are sent herewith.*

You will communicate these orders to the Inspecting Field Officer of the district to which you belong.

I am,<br>
Sir,<br>
Your most obedient,<br>
Humble Servant,<br>
W. WINDHAM.

---

* The statement and forms referred to have been altered by later orders.

## Regimental Accompts.

*Circular containing additional Instructions to Paymasters of Recruiting Districts.*

SIR,  *War Office, 22 April,* 1799.

IT being at present thought expedient to dispense with the transmission to Chatham barracks of the Pay-lists made up by the district Paymasters, as had been required by the fifth clause of the instructions of the third of February, 1798, I am directed to acquaint you therewith, and to desire, that the Pay-lists may be forwarded immediately to this Office, under the address of the Secretary at War.

In consequence of this alteration, it will be unnecessary to make up duplicate Pay-lists; but abstracts of the lists, containing particulars, with names, dates, and sums for the Pay of Officers stated therein, and totals of the other charges, under their respective heads of service, must be regularly transmitted with the Pay-lists of the period.

The said abstracts, being for the use of the Agents, so far as they are severally concerned, are, of course, to be made out on separate papers for the staff, and for each of the Regiments having detachments within your district.

I am further directed to acquaint you, that, as previously to your drawing on the Agents, you must form certain estimates of the probable amount of the services to be supplied for the different Corps within your district, it is necessary in order to enable the respective Agents to place the sums so drawn to the several Regimental accompts, that they be furnished, before or at the time of drawing, with copies of such estimates; or that the draughts themselves should contain a distribution of the sums, specifying the Corps for which they are drawn, agreeably to the said estimates.

In the making of these allotments, a rigorous exactness will not be required, as the excess or deficiency may be corrected in a subsequent estimate; but the receipts and expenditures for each Corps are to be exactly balanced at the termination of the year.

In pursuance of these instructions, I enclose a new form of general state, to be made use of by you, in your monthly accompts, in lieu of the one formerly transmitted.

I am, Sir,
Your most obedient Servant,
W. WINDHAM.

*Circular Letter from the Secretary at War to Paymasters of Recruiting Districts, relative to the Allowance for Postage and Stationary.*

*War Office,* 13*th November,* 1800.

SIR,

HAVING taken into consideration the returns made to my Circular Letter of the 21st June last, to Paymasters of Recruiting Districts respecting their necessary expences in Postage and Stationary for the public service, I am to acquaint you, that the actual Payment of Stamps of Drafts on Agents is to be charged by the said Paymasters monthly, as the Drafts are credited, and the allowance for Postage and Stationary, half yearly, at the rate of 20*l.* per annum, and that at the end of three years, if the charge for Stationary (exclusive of Stamps) and for Postage taken together, shall upon an average be found to have exceeded the amount of 20*l.* per annum, the excess shall be charged by them at the termination of the said period, the same being vouched by a certificate upon honour to have been *bonâ fide* incurred for the public service, the first charge according to this regulation, is to be made up to the 24th December next, being the termination of the third year from the commencement of the present system; such Paymasters as may have had more recent appointments, are to make up their accompts to the same time from their respective dates.

I am, &c.

W. WINDHAM.

*Circular*

*Circular to Inspecting Field Officers of Recruiting Districts, enclosing Forms of Quarterly Accompts.*

*War Office, 30th June,* 1806.

SIR,

IT being judged expedient that the detailed accompts of the Paymasters of Recruiting districts should be made up for *Quarterly,* instead of *Monthly* periods in the same manner as those of Regimental Paymasters, I am to acquaint you therewith, and that the printed forms have been altered accordingly.

A set of these forms, and a memorandum explaining the alterations, the mode of preparing them, and signifying the periods when they should be transmitted to this Office, are enclosed herewith, for your information and guidance.

You will be pleased to instruct the Paymaster, to whom similar forms and memorandum are sent by this post, to pay due attention thereto.

I am,

SIR,

Your most obedient Servant,

R. FITZPATRICK.

To the Inspecting Field Officer
of the                           District.

*Memorandum for the Information and Guidance of Paymasters of Districts in making up the new Quarterly Accompts.*

*War Office, 13th June,* 1806.

Forms 5 and 6.

THESE accompts to be made up by District Paymasters, are, after the 24th instant, to be *three monthly,* viz. for the periods from the 25th June to the 24th September; from the 25th September to 24th December; from the 25th December to 24th March; and from the 25th March to the 24th of June.

The expenditures for pay and allowances within the three months, whether defrayed in the first instance by the District Paymaster, or by the Recruiting Officer, instead of being classed under two distinct heads, as heretofore, are to be consolidated by the District Paymaster, and to be placed together opposite to the name of each individual Officer, Soldier, or Recruit of the Party.

The Paymaster is to distinguish however, in a separate column allotted for that purpose, the proportion of the amount (if any) paid by himself to each individual, without passing into the hands of a Recruiting Officer.

The sums in this separate column being added in the proof table to the sums charged monthly by the Recruiting Officers, and vouched by their certificates, will shew clearly what proportion of the charge belongs to the accompts of the Recruiting Officer, and what is charged as paid by the Paymaster himself. If the accompts are correctly stated, the totals paid for the period of the accompt in the proof table will of course correspond with the totals of charge, as shewn by the accompts under the respective heads of service and the recapitulation.

The lines at the bottom of the proof table for the

the addition and deduction of sums short charged and overcharged, and the statement corresponding therewith on the back of the accompt, will afford a facility to the Paymaster in making his corrections, where they should properly be made, namely, in the accompts of the party for which the short charges or overcharges had occurred.

The addition of the total brought forward from the preceding accompt of each party is to be made, in order that the total expenditure for the same party within the current year, may be constantly shewn. The Paymaster when he completes, in this respect, his first quarterly accompts of a party to the 24th September, is to transmit therewith a recapitulation of the charges made for the same party in each of the six preceding months of the current year, shewing how the totals inserted at the foot of the accompt have been ascertained.

The Quarterly Pay Lists of parties are in future to be numbered on the back in red ink, in the order in which the same are charged in the Quarterly General State of the Public Accompts: the numbers to begin with No. 1, and to be continued in regular succession to the termination of the accompts of the year.

Forms 1, 2, 3, and 4. The accompts of the *Recruiting Officers* being to be made up and rendered *monthly* as heretofore, the new forms adopted are the same in substance as those now in use. The only material object of the alteration made therein, is, that the certificates, signed by the Officers commanding the parties, may be separated from the accompts of the Officers, to serve as vouchers for the Quarterly Accompts of the Paymasters, to which they are accordingly to be annexed. The accompts of the Officers are however to be carefully preserved by the several District Paymasters, until their Quarterly Accompts shall have been examined and passed at the War Office.

Forms 7 and 8. These new forms are for Monthly and Quarterly General States, in both of which the heads of of expenditures for the additional force are of course omitted: in other respects they are so little altered from the forms now in use as to require no particular explanation.

The Paymaster will however be aware that the *Monthly* General States are to be made up as before to the 24th of *every* month, and as they will not require much time for preparation, are to be regularly transmitted with the Agents' monthly abstracts, on or before the 8th of the month subsequent to that in which they terminate. The *Quarterly* General States, Pay Lists, and Agents' Abstracts, will not be required to be sent until the 22d of the month subsequent to that in which they terminate, but are in no case to be detained beyond that date.

<small>Period of transmitting the accompts to the War Office.</small>

The numbers to be placed in red ink on the Paymaster's accompts of parties as above directed are to be inserted in the first column of the Quarterly General State.

The certificates of the Inspecting Field Officer and Adjutant, and the Affidavit of the Paymaster at the back of the respective General States have been altered to render them conformable to those annexed to the Monthly and Quarterly Regimental Accompts, so as to require only their authentication of the accompts in what appears more peculiarly to belong to their respective situations.

<small>Forms 9 and 10, (also 11 for Scotland)—Form 12</small>
These forms being also for services to be stated monthly, are not altered, nor the estimate of Staff Pay.

<small>Form 13.</small>
The accompt for the Staff Pay is to be made up quarterly.

<small>No. 20. Monthly Abstracts.</small>
[The form of Monthly Abstract may be made up more expeditiously than before, the heads of service of the expenditures being no longer required to be stated therein.]*

<small>No. 20. Quarterly Abstracts.</small>
The form of Quarterly Abstract (which has been printed with the No. 20 also) will however

---

* This direction is annulled by the first paragraph of Article 77 of the Explanatory Directions to Paymasters.

require

require the services to be specified as formerly, but the totals only of the *receipts* as particularized in the Monthly Abstract, are to be stated therein. In these abstracts the totals of expenditures and receipts of the preceding months of the same year are to be brought forward.

In all other points it is conceived an attentive inspection of the forms themselves will shew how the accompts are to be made up.

It is not expected that any charges belonging to the additional force will occur after the 24th instant; if there should, they may be inserted in the General States in the usual manner, making the necessary manuscript alterations therein.

SECTION

# SECTION III.

## PART IV.

### INSTRUCTIONS TO PAYMASTERS

OF THE

### ADDITIONAL BATTALIONS

FORMED FOR LIMITED SERVICE.

*Extract of a Circular Letter to the Colonels of Regiments augmented by additional Battalions under the Defence Act, relative to the Appointment of Paymasters to the said Battalions, dated War Office, 1st October, 1804.*

["YOU will be pleased to recommend one of the Subalterns of the Battalion for the appointment of Paymaster thereto; who will be required to give security, himself for One Thousand Pounds, and two sureties for Five Hundred Pounds each. He will transmit to this Office the names of his proposed sureties, with two referees for each. From the period of the commencement of the establishment the pay of the said Paymaster will be made up to 15s. a day as in the Fencible Infantry; until which period an allowance, to be regulated by the numbers of the men at Head Quarters will be made to him. The appointment is to take place by Warrant under your signature and seal, agreeably to a form which will be sent to you from this Office, and is not on reduction to entitle the Paymaster to Half-pay. Until the appointment of a Paymaster shall have taken place, a committee of Paymastership may be formed, agreeably to the 25th Article of the Instructions for Paymasters herewith enclosed.]*

When the Corps is established, a Paymaster's Clerk is to be appointed from amongst the Non-commissioned Officers, and Privates; who, if one of the Serjeants, will continue to receive the Pay of that Rank, and, if one of the Corporals or Privates, will have his pay made up to that of Serjeant."

---

\* The footing of Paymasters in these Battalions was afterwards altered.—See page 227.

*Circular*

# Part IV.] *Regimental Accompts.*

*Circular to the Colonels of Regiments augmented by additional Battalions under the Defence Acts, relative to the Appointment of Paymasters.*

*War Office, 6th November, 1804.*

SIR,

HIS Royal Highness the Commander in Chief having represented, that, in consequence of the removals that may be expected to take place, of the Officers of the additional Battalion of the         Regiment of Foot under your command, to the First Battalion thereof, and vice versâ, considerable inconvenience would probably arise, as well to individuals as to the public, if the Paymaster of the additional Battalion should be required to hold a Subaltern commission, as directed in my Circular Letter of the 1st ultimo; and it being judged expedient, as well for the above reason, as upon a consideration of the peculiar constitution of the additional Battalions, that a different Regulation should be established in regard to the appointment of a Paymaster thereof, from what has been observed in the case of other Corps formed for limited service; I have the honor to acquaint you, His Majesty is pleased to order, that the Paymaster of the additional Battalion of your Regiment shall be appointed by commission, and shall not hold any other employment therein; that the pay of the appointment shall be Ten Shillings a day, and that, upon the disembodying of the corps, the Officer holding the employment shall receive such reduced allowance in the shape of half pay or otherwise, as shall be deemed reasonable with reference to the extent of his services. You will therefore be pleased to recommend a proper person for the said appointment in the usual manner.

If you should have already fixed upon a proper person for the employment, in pursuance of my Letter above referred to, there will be no objection to his being appointed, upon his resigning his regimental commission.

I am to add, that the above arrangement is not to occasion any alteration in the nature and amount of the security to be required from the Paymaster, according to my Letter of the 1st ultimo, before referred to.

I have the honor to be, &c.

W. DUNDAS.

Colonel of the
 Regiment of Foot.

*Circular*

*Circular to the Colonels of Regiments augmented by second Battalions from the Army of Reserve, relative to the future Appointments of Paymasters.*

*War Office, 26th November, 1804.*

SIR,

I HAVE the honor to transmit herewith for your information, a printed copy of a Circular Letter* from this department to the Colonels of the Regiments augmented by additional Battalions under the Defence Acts, relative to the appointment of Paymasters to the said Battalions; and to acquaint you, that whenever the Subaltern who is acting as Paymaster in the Second Battalion of your Regiment shall in the course of service be removed therefrom, you are to recommend a person to succeed him in the Office of Paymaster, upon the footing explained in the enclosed Circular.

I have the Honor to be,

SIR,

Your most obedient

humble Servant,

W. DUNDAS.

Colonel of the

---

* See the preceding page.

*Letter*

*Letter to Lieutenant Colonel Gordon, relative to granting an Option to Paymasters of Second Battalions to succeed to the Paymastership of the First Battalions of their own Regiment.*

War Office, 25th April, 1805.

SIR,

I AM directed to acknowledge the receipt of your Letter of the 18th instant, and to acquaint you, that the Secretary at War does not see any objection whatever, to the arrangement proposed by His Royal Highness the Commander in Chief, that the Paymasters of second Battalions, not holding Subaltern Commissions in the Corps, should have the option of succeeding to the Paymastership of the First Battalion of their own Regiments, upon giving the securities required for such appointments.

I have, &c.

F. MOORE.

Lieutenant Colonel Gordon,
&c. &c. &c.

*Extract of a Circular Letter from the Secretary at War to the Commanding Officers of Second Battalions of Infantry for limited Service.*

*Dated War Office, 5th February,* 1805.

["I think it proper further to acquaint you, in reference to the Adjutant General's Letter of the 29th November last, that the sum of Two Guineas therein desired to be retained from the Bounty of Men who Volunteer for General Service, is not to be drawn for by the Paymaster in the first instance, but is to be paid and charged by the Paymaster of the first Battalion, when the men shall actually join that Corps; and that if this proportion of the Men's Bounty should have been already charged, the amount is to be credited back to the public, by a deduction from the total charge for Recruiting in the Supplementary Pay-list of the last year. This instruction is not, however, to preclude the men from receiving the said sum of Two Guineas at the Head Quarters of the second Battalions, in special cases, when His Royal Highness the Commander in Chief shall think proper to recommend such a measure; in which event, however, due care is to be taken to apprize the Commanding Officer and Paymaster of the first Battalion thereof.]\*

These men are to be borne on the strength of the 2nd Battalion while they shall continue to serve therewith, but it is necessary, that they should be invariably distinguished in each monthly Pay-list and Adjutant's Roll of the 2nd Battalion, by the letters *U. S.* (meaning *Unlimited Service Man*) being placed in red ink in the column of remarks opposite to their respective names.

The Boys enlisted for the said Battalion, under His Majesty's late orders, are to be classed together under the head of "Boys;" their names being placed alphabetically in each company, after those of all the men, and the printed numbers being altered, so as to shew the number of Boys in each Company. In all Recruiting accompts they are to be distinguished either by the word Boy, or by the initial B, in red ink, placed opposite to their respective names.

The Levy-money of the Boys is already specified in the schedule published by the Adjutant General, dated the 28th

---

\* These Instructions, as far as they apply to a future Period, are affected by the Regulations stated in the Adjutant General's Circular printed in the former part of this Section.

December

Part IV.] *Regimental Accompts.* 231

December last, but it is necessary to explain, that the expence of one shilling for attesting, is to be paid out of the allowance to the bringer. The Pay of these Boys [Eight Pence]* *per diem*, and the several *allowances* of Beer money, allowance to Innkeepers, &c. are to be charged for them in the same manner as for the other soldiers of the Battalion.

The Pay of Officers belonging to the 1st Battalion, but serving with the 2nd Battalion, is not to be charged in the Pay-list of the latter; but is to be issued according to the following rule, which has been established, with the concurrence of the Lord Lieutenant of Ireland, viz. the Officers belonging to a Battalion in Ireland, but serving with a Battalion in this country, are to receive their pay, in British money, from the Paymaster of the Recruiting District in which the latter shall happen to be stationed, who will draw for the same through the General Agent of the Recruiting Service in London, and will make his charges on account thereof, in the same manner as for Officers of Irish Regiments employed on the Recruiting Service in Great Britain. The like rule will be observed in regard to Officers belonging to Battalions on the British establishment, but serving in Battalions stationed in Ireland; their pay being drawn through the General Agent in Dublin. For this purpose, the Paymaster of the Battalion in which the Officers are serving, is to make out separate monthly estimates of the Pay to be issued to such Officers, transmitting one Copy thereof to the District Paymaster, and two Copies to the Secretary at War; (one of which will be for the use of the General Agent.) The Monthly Pay-lists for this service are to be rendered by the Regimental Paymasters, through the Paymasters of the Districts, who supply the necessary funds; and should be confirmed by the certificates of the Commanding Officer, Adjutant, and Paymaster, care being of course taken, that no Officer be included therein, until it shall have been satisfactorily ascertained that he has not received Pay for the same period, either from the Agent, or Paymaster of the Battalion to which he belongs.

When both Battalions are on the same establishment, it will be requisite, that similar estimates and separate accompts

---

* Altered to Ten Pence.

of the Officers serving with the Battalion to which they do not belong, should be transmitted to this Office by the Paymaster thereof, the Pay of the Officers being, however, drawn for upon the Agents of the Battalions to which the Officers belong, and not upon the District Paymasters."

I have the honor to be,

SIR,

Your most obedient humble Servant,

(Signed) WILLIAM DUNDAS.

*Circular*

*Circular Letter from the Secretary at War, to the Commanding Officers of Battalions for limited Service stationed in Great Britain, relative to the Charges for Recruits raised for the 1st Battalions of the said Regiments when abroad, except in the East Indies.*

*War Office, 30th December, 1805.*

SIR,

REFERRING to the General Order of His Royal Highness the Commander in Chief, dated the 30th October last, I have the honor to acquaint you, that as all the Recruiting for the first Battalion abroad of a Regiment having a second Battalion *for limited service,* is to be carried on by the second Battalion only, the necessary funds for the levy money, pay, and other allowances, for the Recruits raised for the Regiment, even if engaged for unlimited service, are to be drawn for on account of such second Battalion, and the charges are to be made in the accompts thereof accordingly, so that there may be no separate Recruiting accompt rendered to this Office, for the first Battalion while stationed abroad, except where the first Battalion is ordered to the East Indies, in which case the charges for the Recruits engaged for unlimited service, must all be made in the accompts of the first Battalion. Due care is however to be taken that in all the Pay-lists of the Battalions for limited service, or of parties thereof, the men engaged for *unlimited* service are to be invariably distinguished as such by the initials U. S. placed opposite to their respective names.

In consequence of this arrangement, which will of course commence immediately after the Recruiting Parties of the first Battalion shall have been all called in, as required by the General Order above referred to, it is not thought expedient that the distinction which has hitherto subsisted between the Recruits for unlimited service and those of the additional Force, as to the extra price of meat, should be continued. The Recruits of the latter description are therefore

fore to receive the benefit of the said allowance previously to joining at the Head Quarters of the Battalion in like manner as other Recruits, from the 25th instant inclusive.

>I have the Honor to be,
>
>SIR,
>
>Your most obedient
>
>humble Servant,
>
>W. DUNDAS.

Officer Commanding the Second Battalion
of the             Regiment of Foot.

SECTION

( 235 ).

# SECTION III.

## PART V.

### MISCELLANEOUS INSTRUCTIONS

RELATIVE TO

### ACCOMPTS.

*Regulation relative to the Effects and Credits of Non-Commissioned Officers, and Privates, who die.*

Dated *War Office, 20th February,* 1799.

THE King having been pleased, by his Regulations of the 19th January, 1798, to order that a report of the effects and credits of non-commissioned Officers, and Privates, who may die or desert, shall be regularly made from each Regiment, in the Pay-list of the period; I have it now in command to acquaint you, what further measures are to be taken, relative to the said effects and credits, in the case of deceased Soldiers, and to signify to you His Majesty's Pleasure, that the following instructions be strictly observed by the Regiment under your Command.

Whenever a Non-commissioned Officer or Private shall die, his Regimental debts (which, considering the pay Soldiers at present receive, can be but few and small, if any, and ought not in any instance to exceed, except when increased by the sentence of a Court Martial, *Ten Shillings* for any Soldier in the Infantry, and *Fifteen Shillings* in the Cavalry) shall be liquidated out of the amount of his effects and

credits;

credits; the remainder of which shall then be placed in the hands of the Regimental Paymaster, and shall be duly paid over by him to the representatives of such Non-commissioned Officer or Private, if claimed antecedently to the respective periods hereafter prescribed for crediting the same to the public.

On the twenty-fourth of June, and twenty-fourth of December in each year, a general statement, shewing the several receipts and payments under this head, with the names of the respective men, shall be given on some blank leaf or leaves of the current Pay-list, for the six months terminating on the twenty-fourth of December and twenty-fourth of June preceding, respectively; so that six months, at the least, will have elapsed from the periods of the death of the men before the general statement is made up: and the balance of each statement shall be* then credited to the public, and carried to the general state of the said Pay-list, so as to be vouched by the general certificates and affidavit of the Commanding Officer, Adjutant, and Paymaster, respectively.

In the event of a change of the Paymaster, a general statement, made up and vouched in like manner, of the receipts and payments from the termination of the last half-yearly accompt, under this head, to the period when the person or persons doing the duty of Paymaster shall have ceased to act, shall be transmitted to this Office, and a duplicate thereof delivered to the new Pay-Master, to whom the Balance is to be paid, in order that he may account for the several sums, and include them in his general statement of effects and credits, as before directed.

These balances, though credited thus to the public, will still be considered as a deposit, and liable to be refunded at any subsequent period, when demanded by the proper representatives: and the Paymaster and Agent are hereby authorized and required to receive, examine, and report such demands accordingly to this Office, in order that the necessary directions may be given for satisfying the same.

Such Regimental debts of soldiers, who die, as may not be liquidated by their respective effects and credits, are to fall, as heretofore, on the Captains of the respective Troops or Companies to which they belong; except in cases where the

---

* This is altered as to Regiments abroad: see the following Circular.

deficiency

deficiency shall have been created by the sentence of a Court Martial, when the amount of such deficiency shall be considered as a public charge, and not to be made good by the Captain.

With respect to effects and credits of Non-commissioned Officers and Privates, deceased, and the appropriation thereof, from the 25th of December, 1797, to the twenty-fourth of December, 1798, the Regimental Paymaster will state them in one general accompt in the Pay-list to the twenty-fourth of June next.

Given at the War Office, this twentieth day of February, one thousand seven hundred and ninety-nine.

By His Majesty's Command,
W. WINDHAM.

*Circular*

*Circular to the Commanding Officers of Regiments relative to the Effects and Credits of deceased Soldiers, &c.*

*War-Office, 23d December, 1800.*

SIR,

IN order the better to answer enquiries relative to the existence or non-existence of Soldiers, I am to acquaint you with His Majesty's pleasure, that, in the Regiment under your command, when two or more Soldiers of the same name appear on the Monthly Roll at one period, the Adjutant should constantly insert, opposite each name, the Man's trade and place of birth; and also, when it can be done, the precise Regiment to or from which Men are drafted or received. A date, and place of muster, are also always to be inserted on the Adjutant's Roll—and, in the Column of Remarks opposite to the name of each Man who shall have died, the amount of his effects and credits (if any) is to be stated, as in the Pay-List.

I am further to signify to you His Majesty's pleasure, that when your Regiment is stationed out of Great Britain, the Paymaster, instead of retaining in his hands, the effects and credits of deceased Soldiers, as directed by His Majesty's Regulation of 20th February, 1799, is to credit the same at once in his [monthly]\* public Accompt of the period, unless in cases when it shall be known, that the Representatives of the deceased are residing in or near the station, where the Regiment is serving; which circumstance should in such case be noticed on the face of the Pay-List.

With respect to any balances of deceased Soldiers which may have accrued, and which, if the Regiment has been stationed out of Great Britain, may not have been included in the half-yearly general statement required by the Regulations above referred to, the same are to be credited in the first Pay-List made out after the receipt of this order—and balances which shall have accrued in like manner in the Re-

---

\* Quarterly.

giment, whenever ordered from this Country for Foreign Service, are to be credited to the public on the embarkation thereof.

I have the honour to be,

Sir,

Your obedient Servant,

W. WINDHAM.

The Officer Commanding
   the           Regiment of

---

N. B. For Regiments in the *East Indies*, there is a special Regulation on the above subject. See the Appendix.

*Circular*

*Circular Letter to the Commanding Officers of Regiments relative to establishing a Check on the Issues of Provisions, &c. on Foreign Stations.*

*War-Office, 6th May,* 1799.

SIR,

THE King having been pleased to order, that a check should be instituted on the issues of provisions, and other supplies, on Foreign Stations, and at Home, by means of the Regimental Paymasters, I am to signify to you His Majesty's pleasure, that the following Regulations be observed by you, and by the Paymaster of the      Regiment, under your Command.

When the Regiment is to receive Provisions, or other Supplies from Government, the Regimental Paymaster on the day preceding that fixed upon for the first delivery of the articles, shall certify to the Officer of the Commissariat, charged with making the issues thereof, the exact numbers of persons of each rank actually present with the Corps, as well as the number of horses; and, on the day preceding each subsequent delivery, he shall certify in like manner the number then present, and also the alterations since the former certificate; as far as they may affect the deliveries of provisions or other supplies to the Army.

The said several certificates are to be further vouched by your signature as Commanding Officer.

Where Detachments are stationed at a distance from the Head Quarters, and out of the reach of the Regimental Paymaster, like certificates are to be furnished by the respective Commanding Officers thereof, and the same shall be admitted as the Voucher to the Officer of the Commissariat on the deliveries to be made by him.

I have the honour to be,
SIR,
Your most obedient
humble Servant,
W. WINDHAM.

The Officer commanding the
    Regiment.

*Circular*

*Circular Letter from the Secretary at War to the Commanding Officers of Regiments, relative to the Transfer of Regiments to and from the Irish Establishment.*

*War-Office, 23d Oct.* 1802.

SIR,

I HAVE the honour to acquaint you, that, in order to prevent the inconvenience arising from the delay which has frequently occurred in ascertaining the precise dates of the commencement of Regiments upon the British and Irish establishment, an arrangement has been proposed to the Lord Lieutenant of Ireland, and has been approved by His Excellency, by which the transfer will always take place in future, from the first day of the military month, (viz. the 25th of the calendar month,) inclusive, that shall next ensue after the embarkation of the Regiment from Great Britain or Ireland, or after the landing of the Corps, if it arrive in Ireland from a Foreign Station.

I am further to acquaint you, that in pursuance of this measure, the following Rules are to be observed by the Paymasters and Agents respectively, in making up their Pay-Lists and Abstracts, viz.

In the case of a Corps proceeding to Ireland, the Paymaster and Agent will make up their Pay-Lists and Abstract to the last day of the military month, (viz. the 24th of the calendar month,) inclusive, that shall next ensue after the embarkation of the Corps, or of the first division thereof, if sent from Great-Britain; or after the disembarkation of the Corps, or of the first division thereof, if landed in Ireland from a Foreign Station; charging therein for the whole period, and in British Money, the pay of the Officers and Men, and the several fixed regimental allowances, specified in the annexed State, No. 1.

They will also charge therein the other usual and regular disbursements of the Corps, up to the day of embarkation of the respective divisions, if sent from England, or up to the day preceding the landing thereof, if from a Foreign Station, inclusive, and no further.—The above-mentioned Pay-Lists and Abstract are to be transmitted to the British War-Office, and the Paymaster is to account with the British

tish Agent for the sums that he shall have received for the several services included therein, and to balance his Accompt exactly with the Agent accordingly.*

The expenditures occurring *in Ireland*, after the landing of the Corps, and previously to its being placed on the Irish establishment, are not to be charged in the Accompts with the British War-Office, but separate statements thereof are to be annexed to the first Irish [Monthly] Pay-Lists and Agent's Abstract respectively; the Paymaster drawing of course upon the Irish Agent for the amount, in Irish money, of such of the said expenditures as shall be defrayed by him.

In the case of a Corps embarking from Ireland, the Paymaster and Agent are to make up their Pay-Lists and Abstract respectively, to the last day of the military month (viz. the 24th of the calendar month) inclusive, that shall next ensue after the embarkation of the Corps, or of the first division thereof, charging therein for the whole period, and in Irish money, the pay of the Officers and Men, and the several fixed regimental allowances, specified in the annexed State, No. 2.

They will also charge therein the other usual and regular Disbursements of the Corps, up to the day of embarkation, and no further.—The Pay-Lists and Abstract last mentioned, are to be transmitted to the Irish War-Office, the Paymaster drawing upon the Irish Agent for the necessary funds, and balancing his Accompts exactly with the said Agent.

The other expenditures, if any, occurring *after the embarkation of the Corps*, but previously to the termination of the military month during which the Regiment continues on the Irish establishment, are to be stated in separate Accompts to be transmitted to the British War-Office with the first British Pay-List, and Agent's Abstract respectively,

---

\* It is to be understood, however, that the District Paymasters are not to separate their expenditures for the month in which the Corps embarks; but are to render their accounts thereof, *including the levy money paid*, up to the ensuing 24th of the month, to the Government of the country which the Corps is quitting.

It has been since ordered that the sums paid at the Regiment to complete the levy money of Recruits, inlisted previously to the change of establishment, is to be charged to the Country on which establishment the Regiment was at the date of enlistment of the respective Recruits.

and

and the necessary funds for such of the last-mentioned expenditures as are defrayed by the Paymaster, are to be drawn for upon the British Agent; care being taken that estimates of the probable amount thereof are previously furnished in the usual manner.

In the case where, in consequence of the Corps proceeding from Ireland to a Foreign station, an advance shall be made by the Irish Government for a period beyond the termination of the last Irish Pay-List, the said advance, which will be distinctly issued in British Money, is to be drawn for separately upon the Irish Agent, but is, nevertheless, to be considered as made by Great Britain, and the Paymaster is to account for the same in his Pay-List with the British War-Office; it being intended that the Irish Agent shall be reimbursed by the Agent in this country. The said advance is to be regulated by the 13th Article of the Additional Instructions and Regulations dated the 11th of May, 1801, and two Copies, duly signed and certified, of the Paymaster's estimate, on which the Advance shall be founded, are to be transmitted to the Secretary at War in England.

I have the honour to be,

SIR,

Your most obedient

humble Servant,

C. YORKE.

To the Officer Commanding

State No. 1, of fixed Regimental Allowances, referred to in the preceding Letter.

### In the Regular Regiments of Cavalry.

Allowances to the Captains of Troops; and for the use of the Riding Masters, Rough Riders, and for incidental expences relating to the same.

Allowance for carriage of Ammunition.

Ditto   for fire and candles for Guards.

Ditto   to Paymaster for postage and stationary.

Regimental allowance for ditto.

*Extra allowance for Farriery.

### In the Regular Regiments of Infantry.

Allowances to the Captains of Companies.

Allowance for carriage of Ammunition.

Ditto   for fire and candles for Guards.

Ditto   to Paymaster for postage and stationary.

Regimental allowance for ditto.

Allowance for Ordnance articles.

Ditto   for Great Coats.

---

\* To these may now be added the allowance for saddle water-decks, and corn sacks.

State No. 2. of fixed Regimental Allowances in Ireland, referred to in the preceding Letter.

| *In the Regular Regiments of Cavalry.* | *In the regular Regiments of Infantry.* |
|---|---|
| The allowance to the Captains in lieu of the amount of their stock purse dividends. | The allowance to the Captains in lieu of the amount of their non-effective dividends. |
| The allowance to the Riding Masters, and for Farriery. | The allowance to the Captains in lieu of Contingent men. |
| Regimental allowance for postage and stationary. | Major's allowance for carriage of Ammunition. |
| Paymaster's ditto for ditto. | Ditto for fire and candles for Guards. |
| Allowance for carriage of ammunition. | Regimental allowance for postage and stationary. |
| Ditto for fire and candles for Guards. | Paymaster's ditto. |
| | Allowance for Ordnance articles. |
| | Ditto for Great Coats. |

*Extract*

*Extract of a Letter from the Secretary at War to Sir Edward Baker Littlehales, Bt. enclosing the preceding Regulation, dated War Office, 27th October, 1802.*

"IT being intended in the case of the extra advance of Pay, which may be made in Ireland on the embarkation of a Corps for service, and will be reimbursed by Great Britain, that any loss by discount on the Paymaster's draughts, or by exchange on the bills of the Irish agents, shall be made good here; and it being of course expected, that any profit on such draughts or bills should be credited to this country; I am further to request that you will move his Excellency to cause an official communication to be made to this department in every such case, specifying the period for which the advance shall have been made, the particulars of the loss or gain on the sum advanced, and the precise amount of the bill which the Irish agent will have to draw upon the British agent, in order that the necessary instructions for the payment thereof may be given accordingly."

Part V.]    *Regimental Accompts.*    247

*Regulation for subsisting Men belonging to Regiments in Ireland, and left behind in Great Britain; and in certain cases, Men of such Regiments coming over to this Country on Furlough.*

*Dated War Office, 21st May, 1803.*

MUCH inconvenience having been experienced from there not being any uniform rule established for subsisting Men belonging to Regiments in *Ireland*, and left behind in *Great Britain*, and, in certain cases, men of such Regiments coming over to this country on Furlough; the following regulation has been framed, with the view of remedying the inconvenience, and is to be strictly attended to by Regimental and district Paymasters, the General Agent, and all others whom it may concern.

───────────────

When from sickness, or any other cause, a party is left behind in this country, by a Regiment embarking for *Ireland*, their pay is to be issued by the Regimental Paymaster, up to the termination of the Military month in which the corps embarks.

The Regimental Paymaster is to make a report to the Paymaster of the Recruiting district in which the party is left, or to the Paymaster of detachments if in the neighbourhood of *Portsmouth* or *Plymouth*, or other place where a Paymaster of detachments should be stationed, as well of the numbers of each rank belonging to the party, as of the period to which they have been paid:—He is to make a similar report to the Agent of the Regiment in *Ireland*, apprizing him that the pay and allowances of such party are to be supplied in *England*, by means of the General Agent for Recruiting, in like manner as is prescribed for a Recruiting Party of a Regiment on the *Irish* establishment, and are to be charged in the Pay-lists of the district Paymaster, or Paymasters of detachments; which are of course to be transmitted to the War Office in *Dublin*.

The Regimental Paymaster is also to supply the Officer commanding the Party with the necessary information and

Q 4    proper

proper forms of accompt, to enable him to make up his Pay-lists for the district Paymaster, or Paymaster of detachments, respectively, as the case may be; the Officers and men of the Party continuing to receive the same rates of pay and allowances as are received by Troops on the *British* establishment in *England*, or *Scotland*, according as the Party shall happen to be stationed.—The form of the certificate at the foot of the accompts is to be as follows:

### *When applying to Cavalry.*

" I do hereby certify and declare upon my word and honor, as an Officer and a Gentleman, that on the
day of                   I mustered the party and horses under my command, belonging to the         Regiment of
at which time I saw such Commissioned, non-commissioned officers, trumpeters, privates and horses as are borne upon the preceding Muster-roll and Pay-list, excepting such of them as are therein stated to be absent; and that, according to the best of my knowledge and belief, the reasons of absence specified opposite to the respective names, and number of horses, in the said Muster-roll and Pay-list, are the true and actual reasons thereof.

I do further certify that the sum of
charged on account of pay has been actually and *bonâ fide* received for the Commissioned, non-commissioned officers, trumpeters and privates of this Party, as above stated, and paid to them, or to the persons who have supplied articles of subsistence:

That the sum of                                         charged
for the extra allowance to Innkeepers, &c. for men, and the sum of                        charged under the
same head for horses, as also the sum of
                    charged on account of subsistence for troop horses, have been duly received and applied."

*When*

Part V.] *Regimental Accompts.* 249

*When applying to Infantry.*

" I do hereby certify and declare, upon my word and honor, as an Officer and a Gentleman, that on the day of             I mustered the party under my command belonging to the             Regiment of             at which time I saw such Commissioned, non-commissioned officers, drummers or fifers, and privates as are borne upon the preceding muster-roll and Pay-list, excepting such of them as are therein stated to be absent; and that, according to the best of my knowledge and belief, the reasons of absence specified opposite to the respective names in the said Muster-roll and Pay-list, are the true and actual reasons thereof.

I do further certify that the sum of             charged on account of Pay has been actually and *bonâ fide* received for the Commisioned, non-commissioned officers, drummers or fifers, and privates of this party, as above stated, and paid to them, or to the persons who have supplied articles of subsistence:

And also that the sum of             charged for the extra allowance to Innkeepers, &c. has been duly received and applied."

The Paymaster of the Recruiting district, or Paymaster of detachments, is to continue the issue of the pay of the party, so long as they remain in his district, or in the neighbourhood of *Portsmouth, Plymouth,*\* or other place as before mentioned, and is to draw for the amount upon the General Agent for Recruiting in *London*, taking care to include the charge of the expenditures thereof in his Pay-lists with the *Irish* Government, and to transmit to the said General Agent distinct abstracts thereof, in like manner as is prescribed for a Recruiting Party in the 27th article of the Regulations and Instructions for carrying on the Recruiting Service, (dated 25th August, 1802.)†

When the party proceed to join the Regiment, they are to be supplied by the District Pay-Master, or Pay-Master of Detachments, with the necessary funds for their pay and allowances, [up to the termination of the Military month in which

---

\* Applies also to Bristol and Liverpool.
† The same directions are contained in the present Recruiting Regulations, dated 25th October, 1806.

they

they are expected to embark;]* and the Commanding Officer of the party is to account with the said Paymaster for the expenditure thereof, [annexing to his accompt the approving certificate of the Commanding Officer or Paymaster of the Regiment, of such of the disbursements included in the said accompt as shall have taken place after the arrival of the party in *Ireland*.

In special cases, where a further advance shall become necessary, the Officer commanding the party is to apply, in proper time, to the Secretary at War, for instructions, mentioning the strength of the party, and explaining the circumstances that shall have occasioned the application.]†

The District Paymaster, or Paymaster of Detachments, by whom the advance shall be made, is to furnish the Officer commanding the party with a certificate of the period to which the pay and allowances shall have been issued by him, transmitting a duplicate to the Agent in *Ireland*, through the General Agent in *London*, for the information and guidance of the Regimental Paymaster. The said District Paymaster, or Paymaster of detachments, is also to take care that the Commanding Officer of the Party balances his accompt exactly and with as little delay as possible.

In the case where a Party belonging to a Regiment in *Ireland* may happen to land in this country, they are to be subsisted, while they remain here, in the mode above prescribed, upon their shewing, by satisfactory documents, the period to which they had received pay from the Regimental Paymaster; as are also individual men, whether sick or on furlough; but it will be proper that the District Paymaster, or Paymaster of Detachments, should have the special authority of the Commanding Officer of the Regiment, for issuing the pay of such men, which he is to apply for accordingly through the General Agent.

Given at the War Office, this 21st day of May, 1803.

By His Majesty's Command,

C. YORKE.

---

\* To the days of Embarkation only: see article 41 of Explanatory Directions.

† These directions will not now apply.

*Circular*

*Circular to the Agents of Regiments on the British Establishment relative to the Mode of charging Fees.*

*War Office,* 23d *Nov.* 1805.

SIR,

I AM directed to acquaint you, that in future all Fees properly chargeable to the Public, in the Accompts with this Office, except the Fees of Debenture and Clearing Warrants, and other Annual Fees, are to be inserted in the Abstracts of the Agents for the period in which the same shall have been actually paid by them: and this although the service on which the Fees are taken may belong to former years.

I am,

SIR,

your most obedient

humble Servant,

Wm. MERRY.

*Declaration required to be made by Regimental Paymasters previously to their Appointment.*

I do hereby declare that my Recommendation to be Paymaster of the

hath been obtained, without any Recompense, Reward, or Gratuity, therefore given, paid, secured, or promised, or hereafter to be given, paid, secured, or promised, directly or indirectly, by or to, any Person or Persons whomsoever.

Witness,

SECTION

# SECTION IV.

# REGULATIONS

FOR THE

## *GOVERNMENT*

OF CERTAIN

# DISTINCT DEPARTMENTS

OR

# BRANCHES OF SERVICE.

( 255 )

# SECTION IV.

## REGULATIONS
### FOR THE
## *GOVERNMENT*
### OF
### CERTAIN DISTINCT DEPARTMENTS,
### OR BRANCHES OF SERVICE.

*Regulations to be observed with respect to the Pay, Clothing, and Allowance for Contingent Expences, in future to be granted to Corps of Volunteer and Yeomanry Cavalry, formerly subject to the Regulations dated June, 1803.*

*War Office, 12th July, 1806.*

#### PAY.

CONSTANT pay will be allowed for an Adjutant (if properly qualified) to Corps consisting of three Troops and upwards, at the rates specified in the margin.*

#### CLOTHING.

Three Pounds per man for each effective member, enrolled and serving on or before the 24th of July, 1806.

#### ALLOWANCE IN LIEU OF PAY FOR A SERJEANT AND TRUMPETER, AND FOR CONTINGENT EXPENCES.

An allowance of Two Pounds per annum will be granted to the Commanding Officer, for each effective member of the Corps, (Commissioned Officers excepted) out of which

---

* Pay, 6s. a day. Allowance for the keep of a horse, 2s. a day.

fund he is to pay his Drill Serjeant and Trumpeter, and to defray all contingent expences.

The Commanding Officers will also be allowed the actual expence of the stamps, upon which the bills are drawn upon the General Agent.

Where Corps are desirous of exercising for a number of successive days under the provisions of the 46th Section of the Volunteer Act, the Commandants thereof are to send a Return, in the manner therein directed, to His Majesty's Lieutenant of the County, and may immediately, upon having received a notification from him, that the Return has been transmitted to the Secretary at War, draw upon the General Agent for a sum, agreeably to the numbers therein contained, at the rate of 2s. for each Volunteer, and 1s. 4d. for each horse: and within ten days after such duty shall have been performed, the Commanding Officer is to make out and forward an accompt to the Secretary at War, the form of which he will be furnished with, and remit to the Bank of England the balance, (if any) which may remain in his hands.

N. B. It is to be clearly understood, that the exercise abovementioned is to be in addition to the usual drills, for which the men are not entitled to any pay; the above allowances of 2s. and 1s. 4d. are only granted where the Corps are actually assembled and billetted for a certain number of successive days.

If a Corps, or any part thereof, shall be called out in cases of actual invasion, or the appearance of an enemy on the coast, or for the suppression of any insurrection, riot, or disturbance, or to escort prisoners, or deserters, pay will be allowed at the rates, and in the manner specified in the memorandum of allowances granted when upon permanent duty;* the certificate of His Majesty's Lieutenant or Sheriff of the County, for the first mentioned services, and of the General of the district, for the two last, will be required as a voucher for the duty having been necessarily performed, and with their sanction.

---

\* Not reprinted; most of the substance of it being contained in one or other of this Collection of Regulations.

## GENERAL OBSERVATIONS.

The contingent allowance will be issued half-yearly in advance; the Commandant is to apply for it by letter, addressed to the Secretary at War, enclosing a certified return of the persons actually serving, and unless he shall hear to the contrary within ten days after the letter by usual course of post has reached the War Office, he may draw upon the General Agent for the same, by a bill at thirty days sight, taking care to advise him of such draught. The pay of the Adjutant (if any) is to be applied for, and drawn, in like manner.

The Commanding Officers who have not received the clothing allowance for the current year, may, upon filling up and forwarding to the War Office a certificate, the blank form of which is enclosed,* draw upon the General Agent for the same, in like manner as for the contingent allowance.

The bills for sums due, on account of exercise under the 46th Section of the Volunteer Act, or when called out as specified in the 6th Article of these Regulations, may be drawn at three days sight.

All Adjutants in future to be appointed, must be qualified as follows, viz.

> Adjutant, by four years service as a Commissioned Officer, or Serjeant Major in the Regulars, embodied Militia, Fencible forces, or East India Company's service.

To obtain pay for an Adjutant, application should be made through His Majesty's Lieutenant of the County, to the Secretary of State for the Home Department.

In case a Commandant shall have to remit any balance to the Bank of England, he may pursue the following mode; viz. pay the sum due into the hands of a banker in the country, and instruct him to direct his correspondent in London to pay the amount, in the name of the corps, to the account of the General Agent at the Bank: the Commandant will advise the General Agent of such instructions having been given, particularly stating in the letter the sum, as well as the year for which such balance is applicable. Should any dif-

---

* Not reprinted.

ficulty occur in complying with this Regulation, the sum overdrawn may be remitted directly to the General Agent.

Ammunition for exercise and practice is in future to be obtained through the medium of the General of the district.

In addition to the Returns of Effectives to be transmitted to this Office on the 24th December, and 24th June of each year, three Returns are to be transmitted each year to His Majesty's Secretary of State for the Home Department, viz. on the 1st April, 1st August, and 1st December, as required by the 9th Section of 44 Geo. III. Cap. 54. and Monthly Returns are to be sent to the Generals commanding in the districts.

The allowance for contingent expences will not be issued for supernumeraries exceeding the establishment, nor the clothing allowance for supernumeraries, or for any member who shall not have been enrolled, and serving, on or before the 24th July, 1806.

All bills must be advised by a letter signed by the drawer, and be drawn upon the stamps required by law, agreeably to the following schedule.

### BILLS AFTER SIGHT.

| | | | |
|---|---|---|---|
| If | 2 0 0 | 5 5 0 | One Shilling |
| Above | 5 5 0 | 30 0 0 | One Shilling and Sixpence |
| Above | 30 0 0 | 50 0 0 | Two Shillings |
| Above | 50 0 0 | 100 0 0 | Three Shillings |
| Above | 100 0 0 | 200 0 0 | Four Shillings |
| Above | 200 0 0 | 500 0 0 | Five Shillings |
| Above | 500 0 0 | 1000 0 0 | Seven Shillings and Sixpence |
| Above | 1000 0 0 | — — | Ten Shillings |

(and not exceeding)

# Volunteer and Yeomanry Corps. 259

*Regulations to be observed with respect to the Pay, and Allowance for Contingent Expences, in future to be granted to Corps of Volunteer and Yeomanry Cavalry, accepted subsequently to the 3d of August,* 1803.

*War Office,* 12*th July,* 1806.

PAY.

CONSTANT pay will be allowed for an Adjutant (if properly qualified) to Corps consisting of not less than 300 rank and file, at the rate specified in the margin; and for a Serjeant Major, to a Corps under 300 rank and file, but consisting of not less than three Troops of 40 rank and file, at the rate specified in the margin.*

ALLOWANCE IN LIEU OF PAY FOR A SERJEANT AND TRUMPETER, AND FOR CONTINGENT EXPENCES.

An allowance of Two Pounds per annum will be granted to the Commanding Officer for each effective member of the Corps, (Commissioned Officers excepted) out of which fund he is to pay his Drill Serjeant and Trumpeter, and to defray all contingent expences.

The Commanding Officers will also be allowed the actual expence of the stamps upon which the bills are drawn upon the General Agent.

Where Corps are desirous of exercising for a number of successive days, under the provisions of the 46th Section of the Volunteer Act, the Commandants thereof are to send a Return, in the manner therein directed, to His Majesty's Lieutenant of the County, and may immediately, upon having received a notification from him that the Return has been transmitted to the Secretary at War, draw upon the General Agent for a sum, agreeably to the numbers therein contained, at the rate of 2s. for each Volunteer, and 1s. 4d. for each

---

* Adjutant, Pay, 6s. a day. Allowance for the keep of a horse, 2s. a day.
Serjeant Major, 3s. 11d. a day, including 9d. for a horse.

horse: and within ten days after such duty shall have been performed, the Commanding Officer is to make out and forward an accompt to the Secretary at War, the form of which he will be furnished with, and remit to the Bank of England the balance (if any) which may remain in his hands.

N. B. It is to be clearly understood that the exercise abovementioned is to be in addition to the usual drills, for which the men are not entitled to any pay; the above allowances of 2s. and 1s. 4d. are only granted where the Corps are actually assembled and billetted for a certain number of successive days.

If a Corps, or any part thereof, shall be called out in cases of actual invasion, or the appearance of an enemy on the coast, or for the suppression of any insurrection, riot, or disturbance, or to escort prisoners, or deserters, pay will be allowed at the rates, and in the manner, specified in the memorandum of allowances granted when upon permanent duty; the certificate of His Majesty's Lieutenant or Sheriff of the County, for the first mentioned services, and of the General of the district, for the two last, will be required as a voucher for the duty having been necessarily performed, and with their sanction.

### GENERAL OBSERVATIONS.

The contingent allowance will be issued half-yearly in advance; the Commandant is to apply for it by letter, addressed to the Secretary at War, enclosing a certified Return of the persons actually serving, and unless he shall hear to the contrary within ten days after the letter by usual course of post has reached the War Office, he may draw upon the General Agent for the same by a bill at thirty days sight, taking care to advise him of such draught. The pay of the Adjutant, or Serjeant Major, (if any) is to be applied for, and drawn, in like manner.

The bills for sums due on account of exercise, under the 46th Section of the Volunteer Act, or when called out as specified in the 5th Article of these Regulations, may be drawn at three days sight.

All Adjutants and Serjeants Major in future to be appointed, must be qualified as follows, viz.

Adjutant, by four years service as a Commissioned Officer

## Volunteer and Yeomanry Corps. 261

cer, or Serjeant Major, in the Regulars, embodied Militia, Fencible Forces, or East India Company's service.

Serjeant Major, by three years service as a Non-commissioned Officer or Private in ditto.

To obtain pay for an Adjutant, application should be made through His Majesty's Lieutenant of the County, to the Secretary of State for the Home Department; but for a Serjeant Major, to the Secretary at War.

In case a Commandant shall have to remit any balance to the Bank of England, he may pursue the following mode, viz. pay the sum due into the hands of a banker in the country, and instruct him to direct his correspondent in London, to pay the amount in the name of the Corps, to the account of the General Agent at the Bank: the Commandant will advise the General Agent of such instructions having been given, particularly stating in the letter the sum, as well as the year for which such balance is applicable. Should any difficulty occur in complying with this Regulation, the sum overdrawn may be remitted directly to the General Agent.

Ammunition for exercise and practice is in future to be obtained through the medium of the General of the district.

In addition to the Returns of effectives to be transmitted to this Office on the 24th December, and 24th June, of each year, three Returns are to be transmitted each year to His Majesty's Secretary of State for the Home Department, viz. on the 1st April, 1st August, and 1st December, as required by the 9th Section of 44 Geo. III. cap. 54. and Monthly Returns are to be sent to the Generals commanding in the districts.

The allowance for contingent expences will not be issued for supernumeraries exceeding the establishment.

All bills must be advised by a letter signed by the drawer, and be drawn upon the stamps required by law, agreeably to the following Schedule.

### BILLS AFTER SIGHT.

| | | and not exceeding | | |
|---|---|---|---|---|
| If | 2 0 0 | | 5 5 0 | One Shilling |
| Above | 5 5 0 | | 30 0 0 | One Shilling and Sixpence |
| Above | 30 0 0 | | 50 0 0 | Two Shillings |
| Above | 50 0 0 | | 100 0 0 | Three Shillings |
| Above | 100 0 0 | | 200 0 0 | Four Shillings |
| Above | 200 0 0 | | 500 0 0 | Five Shillings |
| Above | 500 0 0 | | 1000 0 0 | Seven Shillings and Sixpence |
| Above | 1000 0 0 | | — | Ten Shillings |

*Abstract of the Regulations and Allowances applicable to Corps of Volunteer Artillery and Infantry formerly subject to the Regulations dated June,* 1803.

*War Office,* 12th *July,* 1806.

### PERMANENT PAY IS ALLOWED FOR

An Adjutant\* and Serjeant Major†
> To a Battalion of 10 Companies, or a Corps of from 250 to 500 Private Men and upwards.

A Serjeant Major
> To a Corps of from 150 to 250 Private Men.

### NECESSARY QUALIFICATIONS FOR THE APPOINTMENT OF

An Adjutant—Four Years Service as a Commissioned Officer or Serjeant Major in the Regulars, Embodied Militia, Fencibles, or East India Company's Service.

A Serjeant Major—Three years service as a Non-commissioned Officer or Private in the Regulars, Embodied Militia, Fencible, or East India Company's Service.

### PAY,

To the Non-commissioned Officers, Drummers and Privates, enrolled on or before the 24th July, 1806, for each day they shall be present at exercise, not exceeding 26 days in each year.‡

For Drill Serjeants.∥

Stamps upon Bills drawn on the General Agent.

### REPAIR, &c. OF ARMS.

An allowance for keeping of arms and accoutrements and maintaining them clean and in proper repair.§

---

\* Rates per diem.—Adjutant 6s. and 2s in addition for the keep of a horse.
† Serjeant Major 1s. 6d. per diem, and 2s. 6d. per week in addition.
‡ One Shilling per day.
∥ Sixpence per Company, per diem.
§ Rate per annum, 6s. 8d. per stand.

\*\*\* When

*⁎* When called out in cases of riot, &c. the pay will be the same as for the service of permanent duty.

NB. The above is a mere specification of the different allowances, and of the circumstances under which they are granted, the mode of obtaining them is pointed out in the accompanying Memoranda.

## MEMORANDA.

### HIS MAJESTY'S LIEUTENANTS OF COUNTIES.

His Majesty's Lieutenant of the County is the channel through which all matters for the consideration of his Majesty's Secretary of State for the Home Department, or the Board of Ordnance, respecting Volunteer Corps, should be conveyed.

It is indispensable that his Majesty's Lieutenant should be addressed on the following heads :*

To obtain an alteration in the title, or establishment of the Corps.

Forage allowance for Adjutant.

Arms and accoutrements, or to have them exchanged.

On the subject of the recommendation of Officers.

Officer's Commissions.

The authority of his Majesty's Lieutenants to sign commissions was retrospective;—the fee to the Clerk upon each commission is not to exceed five shillings, which is the whole expence, the stamp duty not being chargeable thereon.

In order that the names of Officers may be inserted in the Gazette, it is necessary that a list thereof, stating the dates of the commissions, and that they *have been signed* by his Majesty's Lieutenant, should be transmitted to the Gazette Writer; the list to be signed by his Majesty's Lieutenant or the Clerk of the Peace for the County.

---

* All these applications will be submitted by His Majesty's Lieutenant, if he approves thereof, to His Majesty's Secretary of State, except those for Arms, &c. which are to be referred to the Board of Ordnance, and for commissions, which are to be signed by the Lord Lieutenant.

## HIS MAJESTY'S SECRETARY OF STATE FOR THE HOME DEPARTMENT.

His Majesty's Secretary of State for the Home Department is the authority to whom all matters for consideration for which the existing regulations do not provide, and which are not connected with the immediate issue of allowances, should be referred through the medium of his Majesty's Lieutenant.

Returns of the effectives, in the usual form, signed by the Commandant, are to be transmitted *directly* to his Majesty's Secretary of State at three stated periods within the year, viz. on the 1st April, 1st August, and 1st December, in lieu of the monthly returns formerly required by that department.

When Companies or Corps are formed into Battalions, &c. the returns for His Majesty's Secretary of State are to be made up *as those of a Battalion*, and not for the incorporated companies *individually*.

## SECRETARY AT WAR.

The examination of all accounts, and the admission or disallowance of all charges therein, rest entirely with the department of the Secretary at War; who should consequently be addressed upon such subjects by the Commandant; all bills are therefore to be considered as drawn upon account until the Secretary at War shall have settled the amount to which the Corps is entitled, upon the vouchers furnished.

If a Corps or any part thereof is called out in case of actual Invasion, or the appearance of an Enemy on the coast, or for the suppression of any insurrection, riot, or disturbance, or to escort prisoners or deserters, pay will be allowed at the rates and in the manner specified in the memorandum of allowances granted when on permanent duty.* The certificate of His Majesty's Lieutenant or Sheriff of the county for the first mentioned services, and of the General of the district for the two last, must be transmitted to the Secretary at War as a voucher for the duty having been performed, and with their sanction.

---

* Not reprinted; most of the substance of it being contained in one part or other of this Collection of Regulations.

## Volunteer and Yeomanry Corps.

#### RECEIVERS GENERAL OF COUNTIES.

The Receivers General of the land tax in England, are to be applied to for the annual allowance granted for the keeping of Arms and Accoutrements, and maintaining them clean and in proper repair. The Arms are to be inspected by two Deputy Lieutenants, or one Deputy Lieutenant and a Magistrate, whose certificate, as to their being kept in good order, is necessary to obtain the allowance. In Scotland the Lord Chief Baron and Barons of Exchequer will issue the allowance above mentioned.

#### GENERALS COMMANDING DISTRICTS.

The Generals Commanding Districts are to defray the expence of fitting up, and numbering the Waggons attached to the Volunteer Force.

Haversacks and Canteens will, if desired, be supplied for the use of the Volunteers in the event of their being required to leave their homes, from the Government Depôt under the direction of the General of the District.

They are the channel through which Ammunition is to be obtained.

Returns of the effectives in the usual form, signed by the Commandant, are to be transmitted to the General of the District on the 24th of each month, in lieu of those formerly sent to the inspecting Field Officers.

#### COMMANDANTS

Are to sign all bills upon the General Agent, or to authorize some person to do so in their absence, by addressing in the latter case, a letter to the General Agent, stating the name, and transmitting the signature of the person so appointed. The necessity for this precaution is obvious from all sums being carried to the Debit of the Commandant, whose authority is in consequence requisite, before his account can be regularly charged with any bill drawn by another person, and before any such bill can be paid.

#### ADJUTANTS.

## ADJUTANTS.

Constant pay for an Adjutant is allowed upon the special application of the Lord Lieutenant to the Secretary of State, where properly qualified by former service, which must be distinctly specified in the recommendation. The pay to commence from the first period of his doing duty after his joining the Corps. The allowance in lieu of forage can only be obtained upon a similar application, and when granted, commences from the first period the Horse was necessarily kept, upon a certificate to that effect.

## SERJEANTS MAJOR

May be appointed by the Commandant, if qualified by former service, which must be detailed, in the first Pay-list transmitted to the War Office in which the pay is charged, which is to commence from the first period of their doing duty after the acceptance of the Corps.

## DRILL SERJEANTS.

Pay will be granted at the rate of sixpence per diem for each company of a volunteer corps 'for defraying the expence of Drill Serjeants, to be distributed as the Commandant shall direct.

## SERJEANTS.

One Serjeant is allowed to every twenty private men borne on the establishment.

## CORPORALS.

One Corporal is allowed to every twenty private men borne on the establishment.

## DRUMMERS.

Two Drummers per Company may be charged for on the establishment.

## SUPERNUMERARIES.

Supernumeraries exceeding the establishment, and *Recruits entering after the 24th July,* 1806, are not entitled to any allowance whatever.

ESTIMATES

## ESTIMATES

Are different from accounts, as they contain merely the presumptive calculations upon which the sums required are in the first instance issued; the accounts, viz. Pay-lists, forage certificates, and accounts current, are the vouchers for the application of the sums received upon estimate.

All estimates are to be transmitted to the General Agent. They are to be forwarded on the 1st December, March, June, and September respectively, for the quarter commencing on the 25th of those months, on which date the bills for their amount are to be drawn at thirty days sight, which allows of an interval sufficient for the receipt and examination of the estimate, and to admit of errors being notified before the bills are drawn, and if no such notification takes place, the Commandant may draw accordingly, advising the General Agent of his bill, by the post of the day on which he negociates it.

For the first quarter.—The pay and forage allowance of the Adjutant, the pay of the Serjeant Major, and allowance in lieu of pay for the Drill Serjeants for three months, and pay for seven days for the remainder of the corps, are to be included in the estimate by anticipation.

For the second quarter.—The pay and forage allowance of the Adjutant, the pay of the Serjeant Major, and allowance in lieu of pay for the Drill Serjeants: if between 24th December and 24th March, the Corps has performed more than seven days exercise, the excess may be included in the second estimate, not exceeding 26 days.

The third and fourth estimates will, in the event of the twenty-six days exercise being exhausted in the preceding Quarters, only include the pay and forage allowance of the Adjutant, the pay of the Serjeant Major, and Drill Serjeants, these allowances being issued quarterly in advance.

The foregoing arrangement admits of the Corps exercising at such periods as may be most convenient, and of drawing for the pay (for 26 days, or any proportion thereof,) at the expiration of the quarter, in which the number of days exceeding seven have been performed. The mode usually adopted, however, is to charge for 6 or 7 days for each quarter. The pay for 26 days need not be drawn for quarterly, but if it is preferred may be drawn for at once at the end of the year; but at all events an estimate must be sent

25 days

25 days previously to drawing; the allowances of the persons on permanent pay may, nevertheless, in the latter case be drawn for quarterly in advance.

It would save the Commandants the trouble of repaying sums overdrawn at the end of the year, (which generally occurs where the whole of the allowances are drawn for upon estimate) if they were to omit drawing for the allowance in lieu of pay to Drill Serjeants until their Pay-lists, in which it is to be charged, shall, at the expiration of the year, have been forwarded to the War Office, when they can readily ascertain, and draw for, the balance which may be due thereon.

It is to be observed, that the Commandant is not bound to issue the allowances in advance, although he draws for them, but is to exercise his own discretion in that respect, having in view the security of the public.

### BILLS.

All bills for the annual allowances are to be signed by the Commandant or some person regularly authorised by him, and are to specify the service, year, and name of the Corps to which they are applicable: they must be drawn at thirty days after sight, as the funds are issued to the Bank of England under the direction of the Secretary at War, upon a calculation of their being drawn at that period.

In the event of the Corps being called out in case of alarm, &c. the bills are to be drawn at the longest period after sight at which they can be negociated at par.

All bills must be advised by a letter signed by the drawer, and be drawn upon the stamps required by law, agreeably to the following schedule.

### BILLS AFTER SIGHT.

|  | *l. s. d.* |  | *l. s. d.* |  |
|---|---|---|---|---|
| If | 2 0 0 | and not exceeding | 5 5 0 | One Shilling. |
| Above | 5 5 0 | | 30 0 0 | One Shilling and Sixpence. |
| Above | 30 0 0 | | 50 0 0 | Two Shillings. |
| Above | 50 0 0 | | 100 0 0 | Three Shillings. |
| Above | 100 0 0 | | 200 0 0 | Four Shillings. |
| Above | 200 0 0 | | 500 0 0 | Five Shillings. |
| Above | 500 0 0 | | 1000 0 0 | Seven Shillings and Sixpence. |
| Above | 1000 0 0 | | - - | Ten Shillings. |

### ACCOUNTS.

The annual accounts, viz. the Pay-lists, the forage certificates, and Account current, should be made out and sent to the War Office as soon after the 24th December in each year as possible.

The Adjutant's pay is to be charged in the Pay-list from the first period of his doing duty, and the forage allowance (if granted) from the date of the horse having been kept, both subsequently to 24th December preceding.—The certificate applicable to the latter allowance, the form of which is annexed to the Pay-list, must be filled up and signed by the Commandant.

The Pay of the Serjeant Major must be charged in the Pay-list, and his qualification must be detailed in the first, in which it is certified to have been paid.

The allowance in lieu of pay for the Drill Serjeants is to be inserted in the contingent certificate at the foot of the Pay-list, which is to be filled up and signed.

The pay, and forage certificates, are to be filled up and signed, applicable to the sums paid for each of these services; *as credit is only given for sums certified to have been paid.*

The Account current on the Staff Pay-list should be filled up with a specification of the bills drawn, (which need not exceed one per quarter.) The object of this account is to ascertain if all the bills entered to the Debit of the Corps have been drawn by the Commandant, or with his authority, and if any irregularity exists, to enable the War Office to take the requisite measures accordingly. A duplicate of this account current should be sent to the General Agency Office, for which purpose forms will be sent with the blank Pay-lists, which being compared with the books in that department, enables it readily to discover any inaccuracy.

If it appears from the account current that there is a balance due to the Corps, it may be drawn for; if on the contrary, the sums drawn upon estimate exceed the sums certified to have been paid, such balance is to be paid into the *Bank of England*, and is not to be carried to the account of the succeeding year; this may be done by the Commandant paying the sum due into the hands of a banker in the country, and instructing him to direct his correspondent in London to pay the amount in the name of the Corps to the account of the General Agent at the Bank:—The Commandant will advise the General Agent of such instructions having been given, particularly stating in the letter, the *sum*, as well as the *service, year,* and *name* of the Corps to which such balance is applicable: without this letter of advice credit will not be given to him by the War Office for the amount. Should any difficulty occur in complying with this Regulation, a bill for the sum overdrawn may be remitted directly to the General Agent. The charge for the stamps is to be inserted in the account current, unless the bills have been drawn and the stamps obtained at the General Agency Office.—A memorandum of which should also be made in the account current.

When Companies or Corps are formed into a Regiment, Battalion, &c. the Commandant is required to make up the accounts for the year; the same will be settled *as for a Battalion*, and not for the incorporated Companies, *individually*. The Commandant will receive all balances in the hands of the Commanding Officers of the Corps, or Companies, forming the Regiment, Battalion, &c. and will draw for all arrears. Where a Commandant has been appointed previously to the 24th of December, to succeed another, the Commandant last appointed is to make up the accounts of the year.

All balances are to be drawn for in separate bills, applicable to each year, ending 24th of December, as the accounts are settled annually by the War Office, to which department Supplementary Pay Lists are to be transmitted applicable to each year, with the usual certificates filled up for the amount. *All sums are carried to the debit of the year wherein the service for which they are drawn was performed, without any reference to the date of the bill.* When balances are drawn for, an amended account current should be sent.

*No sum whatever can be issued after the 24th of December in each year until all the accounts up to that date shall have been balanced, as above detailed by the vouchers received at the* War Office, *or by remittances paid into the* Bank of England.

All letters for the General Agent should be addressed as follows:

" *The Right Honorable the Secretary at War,*

*War Office,*

" Volunteer Agency."

*London.*"

It

It is of importance that the rank of the Commandant and title of the Corps should be subjoined to the signature, and that the nearest post town, and the county in which it is situated, should be specified in the address.

The Returns for the Secretary of State should be addressed,

" *His Majesty's Secretary of State,*

*Home Department,*

*London.*"

*Abstract of the Regulations and Allowances applicable to Corps of Volunteer Artillery and Infantry, accepted subsequently to the 3d August,* 1803.

*War-Office, 12th July,* 1806.

#### PERMANENT PAY IS ALLOWED FOR

An Adjutant and Serjeant Major*
  To every Corps of 500 rank and file and upwards.
An Adjutant only
  To a Corps of not less than 300 rank and file.
A Serjeant Major only
  To a Corps of less than 300 rank and file, but composed of 3 Companies of 60 Privates.

#### NECESSARY QUALIFICATIONS FOR THE APPOINTMENT OF

An Adjutant—Four years service as a Commissioned Officer or Serjeant Major in the Regulars, embodied Militia, Fencibles, or East India Company's service.

A Serjeant Major—Three years service as a Non-commissioned Officer or Private in the Regulars, embodied Militia, Fencibles, or East India Company's Service.

#### PAY.

To the Non-commissioned Officers, Drummers, and Privates, enrolled on or before the 24th July, 1806, for each day they shall be present at exercise, not exceeding twenty-six days in each year.†

---

\* Rate per diem, Adjutant 6s. and 2s. in addition for the keep of a horse.
Serjeant Major, 1s. 6d. per diem, and 2s. 6d. per week in addition.
† 1s. per day.

For

## Volunteer and Yeomanry Corps. 273

For Drill Serjeants.*
Stamps upon bills drawn on the General Agent.

ALLOWANCE FOR CLOTHING.

One Pound per man at the expiration of three years from the original date of acceptance of the Corps, for such Non-commissioned Officers, Drummers, and Privates, as were enrolled, and serving on or before the 24th day of July, 1806.

REPAIR, &c. OF ARMS.

Where a depôt is kept.†
Where a depôt is not kept.‡

*\** When called out in cases of riot, &c. the pay will be the same as for the service of permanent duty.

N. B. The above is a mere specification of the different allowances, and of the circumstances under which they are granted; the mode of obtaining them is pointed out in the accompanying memoranda.§

---

* 6d. per Company per diem.
† Rate per annum, 6s. 8d. per stand.
‡ Rate per annum, 3s. 4d. per stand.

§ The same as those annexed to the Abstract of the Allowances, &c. applicable to the Corps formerly subject to the Regulations dated June, 1803.—See page 263 to 271.

*Regulations*

*Regulations and Instructions for carrying on the Recruiting Service of His Majesty's Forces in the United Kingdom of Great Britain and Ireland: dated 25th Oct. 1806.*

IT being judged expedient to adopt some alterations and amendments in the System established for the better Recruiting of His Majesty's Forces in the United Kingdom of Great Britain and Ireland, the following Regulations and Instructions for that purpose have been approved of by His Majesty, and are to be strictly observed by all Regiments of Cavalry and of Infantry respectively.

ART. I. Regiments of Infantry are to send their Recruiting Parties to those counties of which they bear the name; by which means it is hoped that they will acquire a local interest that may materially assist them in obtaining men. The Regiments of Cavalry, the Royal Regiments of Infantry, and such as do not bear the name of any particular county, will, on application to the Inspector General of the Recruiting Service, be permitted to recruit in such place as they may think most advantageous. The foregoing order is not, however, to preclude Corps in general from sending Recruiting Parties to the great manufacturing towns, or other parts of the United Kingdom; permission being previously obtained from the Inspector General: but Colonels and Commanding Officers of Regiments, having once fixed the quarters of the Recruiting Parties of their respective Regiments, are not to change them for the private convenience of Officers, who may be on the recruiting duty; nor for any cause but that of the absolute good of the service, when they will give one month's previous notice thereof to the Inspector General; neither is any Party to be withdrawn without his, or the Inspecting Field Officer's being previously apprized, and the Accompts of the Party being finally settled with the District Paymaster, to the satisfaction of the Inspector-General or Inspecting Field Officer. Whenever Recruiting Parties not belonging to Regiments of the Line are ordered on the recruiting duty to London, they will report their arrival to the Inspecting Field Officer, in order that the seal of his office may be affixed to their Beating Orders. This Regulation to extend to the Militia Regiments.

II. The

II. The stations of the Recruiting Parties are divided into districts, the Head Quarters, and extent of which are specified in the annexed State, (No. I.)—An Inspecting Field Officer is stationed in each district for the purpose of commanding them. When it happens that any Troops are stationed at the Head Quarters of a district, and the Inspecting Field Officer is the Senior Officer, he is not to interfere in the discipline, the interior œconomy, or regimental duties of any Corps; but he is in other respects to be considered as the Senior Officer, and may, upon any emergency, when the entire military force in that quarter is called out, assume the chief command.—In like manner, when the Officer commanding a Regiment or detachment is senior to the Inspecting Field Officer, he is on no account whatever to interfere in the interior arrangement of the Recruiting Parties; but he has the power of calling upon the Inspecting Field Officer for such Returns of the Parties in the place as he may judge proper.

III. The Inspecting Field Officers are authorized to give an intermediate approval of the Recruits whom they judge fit for service, except in cases where Regiments are so quartered as to render it, in point of distance, equally convenient for the Recruits to be sent at once to the Head Quarters of the Regiment to which they belong, for final approval; but special authority must be given for that purpose, by the Inspector-General of the Recruiting Service; a copy whereof is to accompany the accompt in which the Recruit so allowed to be raised, shall be included.

IV. The Senior Officer in each quarter is to report weekly to the Field Officer of the district, the number and strength of the Parties therein, specifying the names of the Commissioned Officers belonging to them, and whether they have been present, or absent during the week.

The names of the recruits, with a description of their persons, &c. are also to be inserted in this Weekly Return; the whole drawn up according to the Form hereunto annexed, (No. 2.)

V. No Party, for the purpose of Recruiting, is ever to be detached from the Head Quarters of a Regiment or a Recruiting Party without an Officer, unless by special authority for that purpose; and no Officer is to leave his station, even for one day, without reporting it to the Inspecting Field Officer of the district, or to be absent therefrom for more than one day, without the previous permission of the said Field

Officer; neither can two Officers of the same Corps be permitted to recruit in the same town.

VI. The Field Officers in their districts are to be responsible for the dress, regularity, and good conduct, of the Officers, Non-commissioned Officers, and Private Men of the several Recruiting Parties under their command: and, as a circumstance tending greatly to promote that discipline and regularity, which are necessary to be maintained on the Recruiting Service, it is His Majesty's pleasure, that the Officers employed thereon do constantly wear their uniforms; the punctual observance of which order is to be enforced by the Field Officers in their respective districts; and no Non-commissioned Officer, or Private Man, is to be allowed to deviate in the smallest degree from the established rules of their respective Regiments, in regard to their uniform and dress.

VII. Detachment courts-martial are to be ordered, at the discretion of the Inspecting Field Officers of districts, for the trial of such offences as may be committed by the Non-commissioned Officers and Soldiers of the Recruiting Parties under their command, and would be cognizable by a Regimental court-martial:—Such detachment courts martial are to be composed of the Recruiting Officers in their districts, of the usual number and ranks; their sentences are not to be carried into execution until they shall have been approved by the Inspecting Field Officer.

VIII. The Inspecting Field Officers of districts receive orders from the Inspector-General of the Recruiting Service, what Returns they are to send: all Letters, Returns, and Reports, as well as all applications whatsoever, are to come to the Inspector-General, through the Inspecting Field Officers, and nothing direct from the Recruiting Officers.

IX. In order to indemnify the Field Officers for the incidental expences to which they are liable in visiting the Recruiting Quarters under their respective commands, an allowance of Ten Shillings a day each, in addition to the Full Pay of their respective regimental ranks, is made to them;\* and the actual expence they are at for stationary and postage of

---

\* If the Inspecting Field Officer or Adjutant should be on the Half Pay of Cavalry, the Regimental Full Pay to be allowed to them will be only that of Infantry of the Line, of the same rank.

letters upon the Public Service (certified upon honor) is reimbursed.

X. Each Field Officer is allowed to appoint a Subaltern Officer to do the duty of Adjutant in the district, with an allowance of Three Shillings a day in addition to his Full Pay;* and two Serjeants, one to act as Serjeant Major, and the other as Clerk to the district; these Serjeants receive the pay of Staff Serjeants of Infantry; viz. 2s. 6d. a day, with the usual allowance for clothing. An Officer of the Hospital Staff is placed under the orders of each Field Officer, to examine the Recruits when brought for inspection, and to give such medical assistance as may be in his power to the several Recruiting Parties in the district he belongs to; but in case the Parties are so situated as to render the attendance of the district Staff Surgeon impracticable, a resident practitioner is to be employed, whose charges for such attendance must be transmitted by the Inspecting Field Officers to the principal Medical Officer of the Army Depôt, and such parts thereof as are approved by him will be admitted in the Accounts of the Recruiting Officers. All such bills are to be accompanied by a certificate written thereon by the Officer commanding the Party, stating that the expence incurred was unavoidable, and that no military medical person, or practitioner receiving a medical allowance, was stationed in the quarter.

No man is to be allowed to call for medical aid without an order from his Officer in writing, and the name of each man is to be specially entered on the face of the medical bill.

XI. All Recruiting Officers and Parties, whether belonging to Regiments at home or abroad, are to be subject to the control of the Field Officers appointed to superintend this service. They are to be supplied with the necessary sums, and to account for all their disbursements on this service, through the Paymasters of the Recruiting Districts, except in the case (mentioned in Article III.) where the Recruits by special permission are allowed to be sent at once to the Head Quarters of the Regiment to which they belong for final approval: in this case the Recruiting Officers are to be

---

* Vide Note in the preceding page. The Full Pay in this case, is, of course, not to include the additional allowances granted to Subalterns holding but one appointment.

supplied with money, and to account for their expenditures through their respective Regimental Paymasters; but they are strictly required to send Weekly Returns to the Inspecting Field Officer of the district, according to the directions in Article IV. of these Instructions.

Commanding Officers of Regiments are on no account to furnish private instructions to the Officers they may send on the Recruiting Service, directing them to send Recruits to Head Quarters, to avoid intermediate approval.

XII. Colonels of Regiments are not precluded from taking upon themselves, if they think proper, the whole direction of the Recruiting Service for their own Corps: but Officers recruiting for rank, as well as all others employed on the Recruiting Service, are strictly to conform to the Regulations which require Returns of the Men raised to be made to the Inspector-General of the Recruiting Service, and are to send Weekly Returns to the Inspecting Field Officer in whose district they are stationed, of the increase or decrease of their Recruits, as also of any casualties that may happen in their Parties, in order that the Inspector-General may be enabled to transmit an exact state of the Recruiting Service of the week to the Adjutant-General: and all Officers and Parties employed on the Recruiting Service of such Corps must equally be subject to the superintendance and control of the Inspecting Field Officer of the district where they are stationed, and will receive orders through him, from the Inspector-General of the Recruiting Service, when they are to send their Recruits to the *Army Depôt*, or any other quarter or place of embarkation: and when Colonels shall wish to remove the quarters of their Recruiting Parties, they are to communicate with the Inspector-General, who will inform them if the proposed change is likely to interfere with the general Recruiting Service. The Colonels of Regiments abroad are not to grant any leave of absence to Officers upon the Recruiting Service, without the concurrence of the Inspector-General: the leaves of absence so granted are to be notified through the Inspecting Field Officers of the districts to the Officers concerned; and such Officers may at any time be ordered by the Inspector-General to join their respective Parties.

In cases where the Colonels of Regiments serving abroad shall *occasionally* take upon themselves to approve Recruits raised for their Corps, they are strictly enjoined to require,

and

and to receive, sufficient chirurgical testimony of the fitness for service of such Recruits, and to certify the same, with their approval, on the back of the respective attestations: but the Inspecting Field Officer of the district, upon receiving the said Recruits, will nevertheless cause a further examination to be made of them by the *Officer of the Hospital Staff*: and if any men shall be found upon such examination to be unfit for service, he will dismiss them, informing the Colonel of the Regiment of the *Medical Officer's* objection, on which such dismission is grounded.

XIII. Regiments stationed abroad and not having a second Battalion at home, being deficient in Non-commissioned Officers to complete their Recruiting Parties, may be supplied on application to the Inspector-General at the *Army Depôt*.

When a Party of Recruits is to be sent from any Recruiting Quarter in *Great Britain*, or, having arrived from *Ireland*, marches through *England*, to the *Army Depôt*, their march is to be regulated in such manner as that they may arrive at *Southampton either on a Tuesday or Saturday morning by ten o'clock*, where they are to report themselves to the Inspecting Field Officer, and follow such directions as he may give them for proceeding to the *Depôt*.

Whenever a Recruiting Officer, either in Great Britain or Ireland, sends any Recruits to the *Army Depôt*, or to the Head Quarters of his Regiment, he must transmit an account in writing to the Inspector-General, or to the Commanding Officer of the Regiment, respectively, stating to what period such Recruits have received their subsistence, and beer money, which in regard to the Recruits sent to the *Army Depôt*, should be only to the day of their arrival at *Southampton* inclusive: the extra allowance to innkeepers should be charged only to the preceding day inclusive. And the accounts of the expenditure are to be rendered to the District Paymaster at that station accordingly.

XIV. The age and standard of Recruits shall be as stated in the Regulations herewith transmitted, (No. 3.)

The greatest care is to be taken that no man be enlisted who is not stout and well made; and that the lads and boys are perfectly well limbed, open chested, and what is commonly called long in the fork.

The lads and boys are to be enlisted as Privates, without any promise or expectation being held out to them that they are to be of the band, or put on Drummer's pay.

The greatest caution is to be taken in ascertaining that the lads who offer themselves are not apprentices, and every enquiry is to be made on this head, both by the Recruiting Officer, and the Inspecting Field Officer of the district.

It will be advisable, in all cases where it is practicable, to procure a certificate from the Parish Officers, to be annexed to the attestation, setting forth that the boy so enlisted is not, to their knowledge or belief, an apprentice, and likewise specifying his age.

XV. The Recruits wanted for *General Service* in His Majesty's forces, or in those of the East India Company, are to be enlisted by the Adjutants and Non-commissioned Officers of the Recruiting Districts; and by Half-pay Officers and others specially appointed to recruit by His Royal Highness the Commander in Chief; and the like allowances will be given to the said Adjutants and Non-commissioned Officers as are directed to be made to the Officers and Recruiting Parties of particular Corps: the utmost care is to be taken, as well by the Inspecting Field Officers as by the Adjutants, that the nature of the engagement be fully explained to these Recruits.

XVI. No Recruit is to be on any account enlisted, who has the least appearance of sore legs, scurvy, scald head, or other infirmity, that may render him unfit for His Majesty's service.

XVII. All Recruits are to be enlisted without limitation as to the place of service; and no Recruit is to be enlisted or attested in any other capacity, than as a Private Soldier.

XVIII. All Recruits are to be brought before a neighbouring Magistrate of the city, town, or county, where they are enlisted; within four days, but not sooner than twenty-four hours after enlistment; these times being prescribed by the law: the day of enlisting and place of enlistment are to be specified on the back of their attestations, which are to be precisely according to the forms annexed, marked No. 4, and No. 5, for Recruits for particular Corps, and for General Service respectively. The utmost care is to be taken in filling up the attestations correctly and legibly: the dates must not be inserted in figures but in words, and without any erasure. No Recruit is to be sent to his Regiment or to the *Army Depôt*, on any pretence whatsoever, whose enlistment and attestation have not been completely and finally executed, conformably to the above directions; and all the attestations

of

of Recruits raised within the month are to be invariably transmitted with the Monthly Accompts of the Party, if not before, to the Head Quarters of the respective Recruiting Districts, when, after the District Paymaster has inspected them, they will be forwarded to the *Army Depôt*, if for Regiments on Foreign Service; or to the Head Quarters of the Regiments, if in Great Britain or Ireland.

In the case of Recruits not passed by the Inspecting Field Officers, as mentioned in Articles III. and XI. the attestations are to be sent (within the like period,) at once to the Head Quarters of the respective Regiments.

XIX. When Recruits abscond, or refuse to go before a Magistrate to be attested within the time prescribed by law, an attested certificate of that fact is to be immediately sent to the Inspecting Field Officer of the district, and to be communicated by him to the District Paymaster, as likewise to the Inspector-General, and also to the Head Quarters of the Regiment if in Great Britain or Ireland; as no allowance will be made to the Recruiting Officer for Recruits so absconding or refusing to go before a Magistrate, and afterwards sworn in as deserters, although they should be sent under an escort to their Regiments if at home, or to the *Army Depôt*, if the Regiment is on foreign service, unless such certificate shall have been previously received.

XX. It being contrary to law, and highly injurious to the Recruiting Service, to permit money to be taken by any Non-commissioned Officer, or Soldier, under the name of *smart money*, and in consequence thereof to discharge any man who has received enlisting money, except such man shall have been carried before a Magistrate within the four days prescribed by the Mutiny Act, and in his presence shall have declared his dissent to such enlisting; Recruiting Officers are therefore ordered to give the necessary caution to their Parties, and to report any Non-commissioned Officer or Private Soldier guilty of this offence to the Inspecting Field Officer of the district, who will forthwith cause such Non-commissioned Officer or Soldier to be brought to trial for the same by a detachment court-martial.

XXI. No deduction is to be made from the bounty or subsistence of the Recruit, for enlisting money, attesting, or ribband cockade (commonly called *colours*.)

XXII. The distribution of the new rates of levy money for Recruits is to be made as specified in the state, hereunto annexed,

annexed, marked No. 6, and to commence from the 25th October, 1806, inclusive, and no other allowance than what is therein mentioned will be granted to Recruiting Officers; they not being liable to any loss arising from casualties, unless in cases of culpable inattention.—It will also be observed that the allowances formerly given to the Recruiting Party for a Recruit dying after having been intermediately but not finally approved are *discontinued*.

XXIII. The Pay and Beer Money issued to all Recruits, and the extra allowance to innkeepers in England, when *bonâ fide* paid for them *to the innkeepers themselves, and not otherwise*, will be allowed in the accompts from the dates of enlistment, including Recruits dying or deserting previous to any inspection; provided their attestations, with the dates of enlistment indorsed, shall be produced to the District Paymasters, or to the Regimental Paymasters, as the case shall require, and they shall be regularly borne on the Pay Lists of the detachment for the period, with the dates of deaths or desertions correctly stated thereon. In like manner the extra allowance for Soldiers when on a march in Scotland and Ireland, will be allowed.

If a Recruit shall have been *occasionally* approved by the Colonel of the Regiment for which he is raised, according to the forms prescribed in Article XII. and shall, afterwards, upon chirurgical examination, be dismissed by the Inspecting Field Officer of the district, on the report of the District Medical Officer, (to whom all Recruits must be sent for examination, unless enlisted at Head Quarters, or allowed to be sent thither at once for final approval,) the same allowance shall be made as in cases of intermediate approval by Field Officers of districts: but in any instance, where it shall not appear by the attestation that the Regulations prescribed in the Article above referred to have been observed, no part of the levy money or subsistence will be allowed, and the Colonel will be held responsible for the consequences of the omission. In the event of the arrival at the Head Quarters of any Regiment stationed in Great Britain or Ireland, of a Recruit who has been intermediately approved by an Inspecting Field Officer of a district, and of the Recruit's being objected to by the Commanding Officer of the Regiment, as unfit for the service, the man shall be retained at the Head Quarters until the Commander in Chief's pleasure be known, and the Commanding Officer shall immediately report to

the

the Adjutant-General, for His Royal Highness's information, the size, age, and date of attestation of the Recruit objected to, and the cause of the objection, which must be fully explained and ascertained, whether or not existing previous to the period of his intermediate approval;—in this report, the Officer by whom the Recruit was enlisted, and the Inspecting Field Officer from whom he received intermediate approval, must be named, in order that His Royal Highness, at the same time that he decides on the particular case submitted to him, may be enabled to form a judgment of the degree of attention with which this important branch of the service is conducted, with the view of preventing, by every possible means, any improper or unnecessary expence accruing therefrom to the Public.

XXIV. An allowance of Nine Pence per Mile will be made for the carriage of the Baggage of each Recruiting Officer in proceeding to, or returning from, his station, either with or without a Party; provided the same be approved by the Inspector-General of the Recruiting Service, when the Officers belong to Corps serving abroad, or by the Commanding Officers of Regiments, if stationed at home. This allowance not being to be granted in any case where the private accommodation of the Officer shall have been concerned, nor until the service has been actually performed, the certificates of approval in support of the charges in the Pay List are to be according to the annexed form.

*(Referred to in Article XXIV.)*

I DO hereby certify upon honor, that                of the                Regiment of is entitled to the allowance of Nine Pence per Mile, specified in the 24th Article of the Regulations and Instructions for carrying on the Recruiting Service, he having proceeded from                to                where he arrived on the                day of                being a distance of miles, and amounting to the sum of

I do further certify that the said journey has not taken place for the private accommodation of the above mentioned Officer, but was performed in consequence of orders for that purpose,

purpose, calculated solely for the benefit of His Majesty's service.

Dated at    this    day of

XXV. Allowances will be made for the passage of Recruiting Officers, and of the Non-commissioned Officers, Trumpeters, Drummers, and Private Men, and Recruits, to, and from, Great Britain and Ireland respectively, at the rates specified in the annexed state (No. 7.) These allowances are, in all cases where practicable, to be paid in Ireland by the Paymasters of the districts within which the Officers and Men shall embark, or land, in that country, and are to be charged by them in their Accompts of the Corps to which the Parties belong, or of the men raised for General Service, as the case may be. In cases where they cannot be so paid, special instructions will be given, on the application of the Officer or Non-commissioned Officer commanding the Party, to the Inspector-General of the Recruiting Service, or to the Deputy Inspector-General.

XXVI. Every Officer commanding a Recruiting Party shall make out Monthly Pay Lists, containing the name of each individual of his Party, and Recruits (and in the Cavalry the number of troop horses) subsisted by him within the month; and shall also make up the Accompts of Expenditures actually incurred by him, in conformity to the Regulations, under the respective Heads of Extra Allowance to Innkeepers, and Allowance to Men on a March; Bounty Money; Allowances for the Extra Price of Bread and Meat, (when paid by the Recruiting Officer); and, in the Cavalry, Allowances for Extra Feed, and for the Extra Allowance to Farriers for Troop Horses, if any.

These Pay Lists and Accompts are to be stated according to the forms which shall be prescribed from time to time in Great Britain and Ireland respectively, and will be furnished, by the District Paymasters, on the application of the Recruiting Officers: they are to be made up to the 24th of each month, being the precise day on which every Officer is required to settle with the men, or to the respective days, prior to the 24th, when the Party or Recruits shall cease to be subsisted by him, and are to be transmitted as follows, viz.— those for the District Paymasters are to be sent off so as to arrive at the Head Quarters of the district on, or before, the 1st of the month subsequent to that in which they terminate; and

and those for the Regimental Paymasters so as to arrive at the Regiment by the 28th of the current month, at the latest.

To each Pay List and Accompt is to be added a State of the effects and credits, or debts, of the Non-commissioned Officers and Private Men who may have died or deserted within the period. Every Officer commanding a Recruiting Party shall *muster* the same by his Pay List on the 24th of each month; or on the day of termination of his Accompts, as before mentioned.

If the District Paymaster is present, as his duty requires, the muster shall be taken under his authority and superintendence, and be deemed to be his muster; and a specification of his having mustered the detachment, and of the date on which the said muster was taken, is to be made accordingly in his affidavit: but, in case of his absence from any unavoidable or allowed cause, the same shall be admitted as authentic, without such authority or superintendence; the fact of the Party having been mustered by its Commanding Officer, and the day on which the muster was taken by him, being specified in his certificate; which, together with his Accompts, must, in such case, be transmitted to the War Office in Great Britain or Ireland, as the case may be, with the Monthly Accompts of the District, or Regimental, Paymaster.

XXVII. A General Agent is appointed in London, upon whom the District Paymasters in Great Britain will draw for the amount of the expenditures of Recruiting Officers belonging to Regiments stationed in *Ireland*, and they will account with him for the same accordingly. Separate Monthly and Quarterly Accompts of such expenditures, vouched in like manner with the other Public Accompts are to be made up by the District Paymasters in Great Britain, for the use of the Irish Government, and to be regularly transmitted by the post, addressed to the War Office in Dublin: and distinct Monthly and Quarterly Abstracts of the said Pay Lists *for each Regiment*, made out according to the forms prescribed, are to be sent at the same time to the General Agent in London, each of the said Abstracts being previously vouched by the signatures of the Inspecting Field Officer, Paymaster, and Adjutant, of the district.

Another General Agent is appointed in Dublin, upon whom the District Paymasters in Ireland are to draw, and with whom they will account for the expenditures of Recruiting Officers belonging to Regiments on the *British Establishment*. Separate Monthly and Quarterly Accompts and distinct Abstracts, as before described, are to be made up by the District Paymasters in Ireland, and are to be transmitted regularly; the former to the Secretary at War in London, and the latter to the General Agent in Dublin.

XXVIII. The expenditures on account of the Levy Money, Pay, &c. of Recruits enlisted for *General Service* are to be made through the General Agents, upon whom the District Paymasters, *both in Great Britain and Ireland*, are to draw for such parts as shall be paid by them: the remaining part payable by the Paymaster of the *Army Depôt*, is to be drawn for by him upon the General Agent in London. An arrangement will be made for enabling the General Agent to obtain repayment, from the Agents of the Corps in which the Recruits shall be placed, or from the East India Company, as the case may require.

Where Recruits for *General Service* shall die, desert, or be rejected, without being attached to any particular Corps, or transferred to the service of the East India Company, the General Agent will make his charge according to the Instructions, which he will from time to time receive, from the Secretary at War.

XXIX. Whenever a Non-commissioned Officer or Private shall die, his regimental debts, which, considering the pay soldiers at present receive, can be but few and small, if any, and ought not in any instance to exceed, (except when increased by the sentence of a court martial) Ten Shillings for any soldier in the Infantry, and Fifteen Shillings in the Cavalry, shall be liquidated out of the amount of his effects and credits; the remainder of which shall then be placed in the hands of the Paymaster of the district, and shall be duly accounted for by him to the representatives of such Non-commissioned Officer or Private, or in such other manner as is directed for Paymasters of Regiments, by the Regulations of the 20th February, 1799, or shall have been directed by subsequent Regulations.

XXX. The Inspecting Field Officers are by no means to allow any Officer to quit his Recruiting Station, without first settling his accompts with the District Paymaster. Should any Officer be guilty of a breach of this article, the same is to be immediately reported to the Inspector-General, in order that

*Recruiting Instructions.* 287

that the transaction may be laid before His Royal Highness the Commander in Chief.

XXXI. Recruiting Officers, Parties, and Recruits, whether belonging to the British or to the Irish Establishment, are to receive, in the currency of the country where they happen to be stationed, the like rates of pay and allowances as are received by the Officers and Men of His Majesty's Regiments serving in the same part of the United Kingdom, and no other.

XXXII. Officers belonging to Regiments at home, who are now employed on the Recruiting Service, or who may be hereafter ordered on that duty, will be furnished with a copy of Instructions by the Commanding Officers of the Regiments to which they belong, who will require the same to be returned, on the removal of any such Officer from the Recruiting Service.

Officers belonging to Regiments abroad, who may be employed on the Recruiting Service, will be furnished with a copy of Instructions by the Inspecting Field Officers of Recruiting Districts, who will in like manner require the same to be returned, on the removal of such Officers from the Recruiting Service.

XXXIII. All Officers engaged in new levies, or raising men under special Letters of Service, are to conform themselves to the foregoing Regulations, in all points, not otherwise stipulated in their Letters of Service, or directed by His Majesty's order. And they are to take the utmost care that no copies of beating orders be made use of, except such as are authenticated from the War Office, and endorsed by the Commandants or some of their Officers to Commissioned, or regularly attested Non-commissioned, Officers, by name, for whose conduct on the Recruiting Service, they, the respective Commandants, shall be held responsible.

The foregoing Regulations do not extend to the Regiments of Life Guards, Royal Horse Guards, and Foot Guards; Royal Artillery; Royal Military Artificers; or Marines; further than that the Inspecting Field Officer, or Senior Officer, in each town will, agreeably to the power vested in him by the Articles of War, take cognizance of any disorderly conduct, or breach of military discipline, among their Parties; and in case of disputes arising between their Non-commissioned Officers and Men, and those of His Majesty's other forces, the Commanding Officer will, when he finds it

absolutely

absolutely necessary, order a detachment court-martial, composed of Officers of the several Corps the persons to be tried belong to; except in regard to the Marines, among whom any misconduct is to be reported specially, that the same may be represented to the Lords Commissioners of the Admiralty.

By order of His Royal Highness

The Commander in Chief.

HARRY CALVERT,
Adjutant General.

*Adjutant General's Office*, 25th Oct. 1806.

## STATES REFERRED TO IN THE PRECEDING REGULATIONS FOR RECRUITING.

# No. 1.
*Referred to in Article II.*
### LIST OF RECRUITING DISTRICTS
*Shewing their Head Quarters and Boundaries.*

## ENGLAND AND WALES.

| No. | Head Quarters. | Extent of Districts. |
|---|---|---|
| 1. | DURHAM | Counties of Northumberland and Durham. |
| 2. | CARLISLE | —Cumberland and Westmoreland. |
| 3. | LEEDS | —Yorkshire. |
| 4. | MANCHESTER | —Lancaster and Chester. |
| 5. | NOTTINGHAM | Lincoln, Nottingham, Derby, Leicester, and Rutland. |
| 6. | IPSWICH | —Norfolk, Suffolk, and Cambridge. |
| 7. | SHREWSBURY | —Salop and North Wales. |
| 8. | BIRMINGHAM | Staffordshire, Worcestershire, and Warwickshire. |
| 9. | HEREFORD | Hereford and Monmouth, with the whole of South Wales. |
| 10. | BEDFORD | Bedfordshire, Northamptonshire, Huntingdon, and Hertford. |
| 11. | MAIDSTONE | —Kent and Essex. |
| 12. | MARLBOROUGH | —Gloucester, Wilts, Oxford, and Berks. |
| 13. | SOUTHAMPTON | —Dorset, Hants, and Sussex. |
| 14. | EXETER | —Devon, Somerset, and Cornwall. |
| 15. | LONDON | Middlesex, Bucks, Surrey, and 15 miles round London. |

## NORTH BRITAIN.

| Head Quarters. | Extent. |
|---|---|
| EDINBURGH | Dumfries, Roxburgh, Selkirk, Edinburgh, Haddington, Linlithgow, Peebles, Berwick, Stirling, Dumbarton, Clackmannan, Fife, Kinross, and Perthshire. |

ABERDEEN

| Head Quarters. | Extent of Districts. |
|---|---|
| ABERDEEN | —Aberdeen, Forfar, and Kincardine. |
| GLASGOW | Lanark, Kircudbright, Wigton, Air, Renfrew, Argyle, and Bute. |
| INVERNESS | Rofs, Caithnefs, Sutherland, Cromarty, Invernefs, Banff, Elgin, and Nairn. |

## IRELAND.

| | |
|---|---|
| DUBLIN | The Counties of Wicklow, Kildare, Queen's County, Eaft Meath, and Dublin City and County. |
| BELFAST | The Counties of Londonderry and Antrim, with the Towns of Downpatrick, Bangor, Killelagh, and Saintfield, and that part of the County of Down called the Ards, being North Eaft of Strangford Lake. |
| NEWRY | The remainder of the County of Down, the Counties of Louth, Armagh, and Monaghan, with the Town of Coote Hill, County of Cavan, and that part of the County of Tyrone which takes in from Dungannon to Cookftown, and to the Eaftward of thefe places to Lough Neagh. |
| ENNISKILLEN | The remaining part of the County of Tyrone, the Counties of Donegal, Sligo, Leitrim, Fermanagh, and Cavan, except the Town of Cootehill. |
| ATHLONE | The Counties of Mayo, Rofcommon, Galway, King's County, Weft Meath, and Longford, and the Towns of Rofcrea, and Nenagh, in the County of Tipperary. |
| LIMERICK | —The Counties of Clare and Limerick. |
| CORK | —The Counties of Cork and Kerry. |
| WATERFORD | The Counties of Waterford, Wexford, Kilkenny, Carlow, and Tipperary, except the Towns of Rofcrea, and Nenagh. |

No. 2.

## No. 2.

*Referred to in Article IV. of the*

**WEEKLY RETURN of the Recruiting Party, Commanded by            Regiment of            recruiting at**

| NAMES OF RECRUITS. | AGE | SIZE | | WHERE BORN | | WHEN INLISTED. | WHEN ATTESTED. | ALTERATIONS SINCE LAST RETURN | | | | |
|---|---|---|---|---|---|---|---|---|---|---|---|---|
| | | Feet. | Inches. | Parish. | County. | | | Inlisted. | Dead. | Discharged. | Deserted. | Sent to Head Quarters. |
| | | | | | | | | | | | | |
| | | | | | | | | | | | | |

| STRENGTH OF THE PARTY. | |
|---|---|
| Captains. | |
| Lieutenants. | |
| Cornets or Ensigns. | |
| Serjeants. | |
| Corporals. | |
| Trumpeters or Drummers. | |
| Privates. | |
| Number of Recruits with the Party. | |

# No. 3.

*Referred to in Article XIV.*

## THE AGE AND STANDARD OF RECRUITS
*shall be as follows, viz.*

IN the HEAVY CAVALRY, Men shall not be enlisted above *Twenty Five Years of Age*; their Height shall not be less than *Five Feet, Seven Inches*; Growing Lads, under *Eighteen Years of Age*, may be taken as low as *Five Feet Six Inches*, provided they are in every other respect strictly eligible.

In the LIGHT CAVALRY, the *Men* are not to be above *Twenty Five Years of Age*; and their Height is not to be less than *Five Feet Seven Inches*, nor to exceed *Five Feet Nine Inches*; Growing Lads, under *Eighteen Years of Age*, may be taken at *Five Feet Five Inches*.

In the Light Cavalry Regiments serving in the EAST INDIES, growing Lads, from *Sixteen to Eighteen Years of Age*, may be taken as low as *Five Feet Three Inches*; and *Boys*, under *Sixteen*, at *Five Feet Two Inches*.

In the INFANTRY, *Men*, enlisted for particular Corps, are not to be taken above *Thirty Years of Age*, nor less than *Five Feet Five Inches high*, but *Growing Lads*, from *Seventeen to Nineteen Years of Age*, may be taken as low as *Five Feet Four Inches*.

Men enlisted for GENERAL SERVICE, in His Majesty's Forces, or in those of the East India Company, are not to be taken above *Thirty Years of Age*, nor under *Five Feet Four Inches high*: Growing Lads, under *Eighteen Years of Age*, may be enlisted for the like Service at *Five Feet Three Inches*; and *Boys*, under *Sixteen Years*, at *Five Feet Two Inches*.

Boys enlisted under the Order of the 28th of December, 1804, by Regiments, specially authorised to receive them, are not to be taken above *Sixteen Years of Age*, nor under *Five Feet in Height*.

No. 4.

*Referred to in Article XVIII.*

## ATTESTATIONS FOR REGIMENTS.

I                            do make Oath, that I
am or have been                            and to the best of my Knowledge
and Belief, was born in the Parish of                            in the County of
                    and that I am of the Age of                    Years ; that I
do not belong to the Militia, or to any other Regiment, or to His Majesty's Navy or
Marines, and that I will serve His Majesty for the Period of *
Years, provided His Majesty should for so long require my Service; and also for such further
Term, not exceeding Six Months, as shall be directed by the Commanding Officer on any
foreign Station, and not exceeding Three Years as shall be directed by any Proclamation of
His Majesty ; Provided always, that in the latter case the said additional Period shall determine whenever Six Months of continued Peace, to be reckoned from the Ratification of
any Definitive Treaty, shall have elapsed subsequent to the Expiration of the said
Years.

Witness my Hand,

_____ { Signature of the Recruit.

Sworn before me, at
            Day of                One
Thousand Eight Hundred and

_____ { Witness present.

Signature of the } _____
Magistrate.      }

\* Seven Years for Infantry, Ten Years for Cavalry, Twelve Years for Artillery, if the Person enlisting is of the Age of Eighteen Years or upwards, but if under Eighteen Years, then the difference between his Age and Eighteen to be added to such Seven, Ten, or Twelve Years as the Case may be.

---

        to wit. { I                                    One of His
Majesty's Justices of the Peace of
do hereby Certify, that
appearing to be             Years old,         Feet
Inches high,                Complexion,         Eyes,           Hair
came before me, at                on the                Day of
                    One Thousand Eight Hundred and         and stated himself
to be of the Age of             Years, and that he had no Rupture, and was not
troubled with Fits, and was no ways disabled by Lameness, Deafness, or otherwise, but had
the perfect Use of his Limbs and Hearing, and was not an Apprentice; and acknowledged
that he had voluntarily Inlisted himself to serve His Majesty KING GEORGE the THIRD, in
the                                Regiment of
commanded by
and did engage to serve for the Period of             Years, provided
His Majesty should for so long require his Service; and also for such further Period
as His Majesty shall please to direct, not to exceed in any Case Three Years, and to determine whenever Six Months shall have elapsed of continued Peace subsequent to the Expiration of the Term of         Years. And I do hereby Certify, That, in my Presence
the Third and Fourth Articles of the Second Section, and the First Article of the Sixth
Section of the Articles of War, against Mutiny and Desertion, were read over to him; and
that he took the Oath of Fidelity mentioned in the said Articles of War, and also the Oath
above set forth; and that I have given to the said
a Duplicate of this Certificate, signed with my Name.

_____ { Signature of the Magistrate.

MEMORANDUM.—The above named Recruit stated that he Inlisted himself on the
            Day of                        One Thousand Eight Hundred and
            for the Bounty of                    ; and received in my
Presence the Sum of                        on being attested.

_____ { Signature of the Magistrate.

I have examined the above named Recruit, and find him         for His Majesty's
Service.

_____ { Signature of the Surgeon.

N. B. *The Magistrate is requested to cause the Dates of the Month in each Instance to be inserted in Words not in Figures, and to notice the Particulars contained in the Memorandum.*

# ARTICLES OF WAR.

### *Third and Fourth Articles of the Second Section.*

3. 'Any Officer, Non-Commissioned Officer, or Soldier, who shall *begin, excite, cause,* or *join in* any *Mutiny* or *Sedition*, in the Regiment, Troop, or Company, to which he belongs, or in any other Regiment, Troop, or Company, in His MAJESTY's Service, or in any Party, Post, Detachment, or Guard, on any Pretence whatsoever, shall suffer *Death,* or such *other Punishment* as by a General Court Martial shall be awarded.

4. 'Any Officer, Non-Commissioned Officer, or Soldier, who being present at any *Mutiny,* or *Sedition,* shall not use his utmost Endeavour to *suppress the same,* or coming to the *Knowledge of any Mutiny,* or *intended Mutiny,* shall not, without Delay, *give information thereof* to his Commanding Officer, shall suffer *Death,* or such *other Punishment* as by a General Court Martial shall be awarded.'

### *First Article of the Sixth Section.*

'All Officers, Non-Commissioned Officers, and Soldiers, in His MAJESTY's Service, who shall be convicted of having *deserted the same,* shall suffer *Death,* or such *other Punishment* as by a General Court Martial shall be awarded.'

### *Oath of Allegiance*—39 Geo. III. c. 109.

"I A. B. being inlisted to serve either in His MAJESTY's Troops, or in the Forces of the *East India* Company, according as His MAJESTY shall think fit, do swear, That I will bear true Allegiance to our *Sovereign* Lord KING GEORGE, and that I will, as in my Duty bound, defend HIM in HIS PERSON, CROWN, AND DIGNITY, against all His Enemies; and that so long as I shall remain in HIS MAJESTY's SERVICE, I will duly observe and obey HIS MAJESTY's Orders, and the Orders of the *Generals* and *Officers* set over me by HIS MAJESTY; and if HIS MAJESTY shall please to appoint me to serve in the Forces of the *United Company of Merchants of England trading to the East Indies,* then I swear that I will also be true to the said *United Company,* and will duly observe and obey all *their Orders,* and the Orders of *their Generals* and *Officers,* who shall be lawfully set over me."

Date,————

Name,————

297

No. 5.

*Referred to in Article XVIII.*

## GENERAL SERVICE.

I                                                              do make Oath, that I
am, or have been                                      and to the best of my Knowledge
and Belief, was born in the Parish of                              in the County of
                      and that I am of the Age of                   Years; that I
do not belong to the Militia, or to any other Regiment, or to His Majesty's Navy or Marines, and that I will serve His Majesty for the Period of         *Years,
provided His Majesty should for so long require my Service; and also for such further Term, not exceeding Six Months, as shall be directed by the Commanding Officer, on any foreign Station, and not exceeding Three Years, as shall be directed by any Proclamation of His Majesty; provided always, that in the latter Case the said additional Period shall determine whenever Six Months of continued Peace, to be reckoned from the Ratification of any Definitive Treaty, shall have elapsed subsequent to the Expiration of the said Years.

——————————————— } Signature of the Recruit.

Sworn before me at
   this         Day of                } ——————————————— } Witness present.
One Thousand Eight Hundred and

Signature of the } ———————————————
Magistrate.      }

* Seven Years, if the Person enlisting is of the Age of Eighteen or upwards, but if under Eighteen, then the Difference between his Age and Eighteen to be added to such Seven Years.

———

                     } I                                              One of His
   to wit.           }
Majesty's Justices of the Peace of
do certify, that
aged              Years              Feet                    Inches high,
                  Complexion         Eyes                    Hair, came
before me, at                        on the                         Day of
              One Thousand Eight Hundred and         and acknowledged
that he had voluntarily inlisted himself for the Bounty of
to serve either in His Majesty's Army, or in the Forces of the East India Company, according as His Majesty shall think fit to order. And I further certify, that, in my Presence, the Third and Fourth Articles of the Second Section, and the First Article of the Sixth Section of the Articles of War, against Mutiny and Desertion, were read over to him; that he took the Oath of Allegiance prescribed by the Act of 39 Geo. III. c. 109, to be taken instead of the Oath of Fidelity mentioned in the said Articles of War, and also the Oath above set forth; and that he received the Sum of
on being attested.

——————————————— } Signature of the Magistrate.

MEMORANDUM. The above named Recruit stated that he inlisted himself on the
         Day of              One Thousand Eight Hundred and                ;
and also declared that he had no Rupture, and was not troubled with Fits, and was no ways disabled by Lameness, Deafness, or otherwise, but had the perfect Use of his Limbs and Hearing, and was not an Apprentice.

——————————————— } Signature of the Magistrate.

I have examined the above named Recruit, and find him             for His Majesty'
ervice.

——————————————— } Signature of the Surgeon.

3. *The Magistrate is requested to cause the Dates of the Month to be inserted in each Instance in Words, not in Figures,*
          *and to notice the Particulars contained in the Memorandum.*

# ARTICLES OF WAR.

## *Third and Fourth Articles of the Second Section.*

3. 'Any Officer, Non-Commissioned Officer, or Soldier, who shall *begin, excite, cause,* or *join in* any *Mutiny* or *Sedition,* in the Regiment, Troop, or Company, to which he belongs, or in any other Regiment, Troop, or Company, in His MAJESTY's Service, or in any Party, Post, Detachment, or Guard, on any Pretence whatsoever, shall suffer *Death,* or such *other Punishment* as by a General Court Martial shall be awarded.

4. 'Any Officer, Non-Commissioned Officer, or Soldier, who being present at any *Mutiny,* or *Sedition,* shall not use his utmost Endeavour to *suppress the same,* or coming to the *Knowledge of any Mutiny,* or *intended Mutiny,* shall not, without Delay, *give information thereof* to his Commanding Officer, shall suffer *Death,* or such *other Punishment* as by a General Court Martial shall be awarded.'

## *First Article of the Sixth Section.*

'All Officers, Non-Commissioned Officers, and Soldiers, in His MAJESTY's Service, who shall be convicted of having *deserted the same,* shall suffer *Death,* or such *other Punishment* as by a General Court Martial shall be awarded.'

## *Oath of Allegiance*—39 Geo. III. c. 109.

"I A. B. being inlisted to serve either in HIS MAJESTY's Troops, or in the Forces of the *East India* Company, according as HIS MAJESTY shall think fit, do swear, That I will bear true Allegiance to our *Sovereign* Lord KING GEORGE, and that I will, as in my Duty bound, defend HIM in HIS PERSON, CROWN, AND DIGNITY, against all His Enemies; and that so long as I shall remain in HIS MAJESTY'S SERVICE, I will duly observe and obey HIS MAJESTY's Orders, and the Orders of the *Generals* and *Officers* set over me by HIS MAJESTY; and if HIS MAJESTY shall please to appoint me to serve in the Forces of the *United Company of Merchants of England trading to the East Indies,* then I swear that I will also be true to the said *United Company,* and will duly observe and obey all *their Orders,* and the Orders of *their Generals* and *Officers,* who shall be lawfully set over me."

## No. 6.

## DISTRIBUTION OF LEVY MONEY

*Referred to in Article XXII.*

|  | Men and Lads for the | | Boys for General Service enlisted under the Orders of Inspecting Field Officers of Recruiting Districts. |
|---|---|---|---|
|  | Cavalry. | Infantry and General Service. |  |

| | | £. s. d. | £. s. d. | £. s. d. |
|---|---|---|---|---|
| Bounty to the Recruit. | On being attested, in Money | 1 1 0 | 2 2 0 | 1 1 0 |
| | On intermediate { in Money | 1 1 0 | 2 2 0 | 1 10 0 |
| | Approval, { in Necessaries | 0 12 0 | 0 12 0 | 0 12 0 |
| | On final Appro- { in Money | 2 6 0 | 3 12 0 | 2 2 0 |
| | val, { in Necessaries | 3 3 0 | 3 3 0 | 3 3 0 |
| | Total Bounty to the Recruit | 8 3 0 | 11 11 0 | 8 8 0 |
| To the Officer, Churiate approved | For attesting | 0 1 0 | 0 1 0 | 0 1 0 |
| | For Surgical Examination | *0 2 6 | *0 2 6 | *0 2 6 |
| | For Postage, Stationery, &c. | *0 7 0 | *0 7 0 | *0 7 0 |
| | On final Approval, to cover all other incidental Expences | *0 10 6 | *0 10 6 | *0 10 6 |
| To the Party, on final Approval. | Reward | 1 1 0 | 1 1 0 | 1 1 0 |
| | For conducting the Recruit to the Place of final Approval | *0 5 0 | *0 5 0 | *0 5 0 |
| | To the Bringer of a Recruit, whether belonging to the Party, or otherwise, on final Approval | 3 3 0 | 3 3 0 | 0 0 0 |
| | Total Levy Money, British Currency | 13 13 0 | 17 1 0 | 10 15 0 |

The Charges marked thus (\*), are not allowed for Recruits raised at the Head Quarters of a Regiment: the Allowance of Five Shillings for conducting a Recruit to Head Quarters is not granted in the Case of a Recruit sent at once to Head Quarters for final Approval.

The Sum required in this Schedule to be expended in Necessaries, out of the Bounty of a Recruit on Final Approval, is intended to be laid out, under the Controul of the Commanding Officer, if the Regiment is at Home, in such Articles as are considered immediately requisite, after which his Stock of Necessaries (as detailed in His Majesty's Regulation for the Clothing and Appointments of the Army, dated 22d April, 1803) if there should yet appear any deficiency, is to be completed gradually, by Stoppages at the Rate of 1s. 6d. per Week, as directed by the said Regulation, as such Stoppages accrue.

Recruits for Corps Abroad, or for General Service, sent to the Army Depôt in the Isle of Wight, or to the Cavalry Depôt at Maidstone, are likewise to be completed in Necessaries, gradually, as the regulated Stoppages accrue, under the Controul of the Inspector General of the Recruiting Service.

The Necessaries allowed on intermediate Approval, are to be furnished under the Orders of the Inspecting Field Officers, and are to consist of One Shirt, and one Pair of Shoes, at the Price of 6s. each.

If the Recruit has of his own any of the above Articles fit to be included among his Regimental Necessaries, the Surplus of the Portion of Bounty, allotted for the Purchase of Necessaries, is to be paid to him in Money.

*N. B.* A Recruit signifying his Dissent after Twenty-four Hours posterior to his Inlistment, and within Four Days, can only be required to refund One Shilling, as enlisting Money, and Twenty Shillings for what is usually called "Smart Money."

### Distribution of the Levy Money allowed for each Boy raised under the Order of the 28th December, 1804, by such regular Regiments as have been specially appointed to receive them.

| | | £. s. d. |
|---|---|---|
| Bounty to the Recruit. | On Approval at the Regiment or by the Inspecting Field Officer, { in Money | 0 10 6 |
| | { in Necessaries | 2 2 0 |
| | Total Bounty | 2 12 6 |
| The Bringer or Parent of the Boy. | On Attestation | 2 2 0 |
| | Total Levy Money | 4 14 6 |

The Necessaries to be provided out of the Bounty of Boys, are to be furnished under the Orders of the Inspecting Field Officers of Recruiting Districts, and Commanding Officers of Battalions respectively, and are to consist of the Articles under-mentioned.

| | £. s. d. |
|---|---|
| Two Shirts, at 6s. each | 0 12 0 |
| Two Pair of Shoes, at 6s. per Pair | 0 12 0 |
| Pack | 0 6 6 |
| Leggings | 0 3 4½ |
| Two Pair of Stockings | 0 1 10 |
| Brushes and Black Ball | 0 1 1 |
| Two Combs | 0 0 4 |
| Straps for Great Coats | 0 2 4 |
| Stock and Clasp | 0 0 9 |
| Sundries | 0 1 9½ |
| | £. 2 2 0 |

If the Boy enlisted has of his own any of the above Articles fit to be included among his regimental Necessaries, the Amount herein specified for the same Article is to be paid to him in Money, unless required to complete his regimental Stock in any other manner.

The Charge of One Shilling for attesting is to be defrayed out of the Allowance to the Bringer.

## No. 7.
*Referred to in Article XXV.*

State of the Allowances for the Passage of Recruiting Officers, and of Non-Commissioned Officers, Trumpeters, Drummers, and Private Men and Recruits, to and from Great-Britain and Ireland respectively.

| | | For each Commissioned Officer | For each Non-Commissioned Officer, Trumpeter, Drummer, Private Man and Recruit. |
|---|---|---|---|
| From Port Patrick | To Donaghadee | Half a Guinea | Five Shillings |
| From Liverpool | { To Belfast | One Guinea and an Half | Five Shillings |
|  | { To Dublin | One Guinea and an Half | Six Shillings |
| From Holyhead | To Dublin | One Guinea and an Half | Five Shillings |
|  | { To Dublin | Two Guineas | Ten Shillings and Six-pence |
|  | { To Belfast | Two Guineas | Six Shillings and Six-pence |
| From Bristol | { To Waterford | One Guinea and an Half | Five Shillings |
|  | { To Cork | One Guinea and an Half | Seven Shillings and Six-pence |
|  | { To Limerick | Two Guineas | Half a Guinea |
| From Milford Haven | To Waterford | One Guinea and an Half | Five Shillings |
| From the Isle of Wight | { To Cork or Waterford | Two Guineas | Half a Guinea |
|  | { To Limerick | Three Guineas | Half a Guinea |

The same Rates of Allowance will of course be made for the like Voyages from the Irish to the British Ports.

*General Orders respecting the Bounty of Recruits deserting before final Approval.*

*Horse Guards, 29th Sept.* 1802.

HIS ROYAL HIGHNESS the Commander in Chief directs it to be made known to the Army, that in the event of *a Recruit deserting before final approval,* and afterwards returning, or being recovered to the Service, such part of his bounty as remains unpaid (and to which by his desertion he has in point of right forfeited all claim) shall in future be laid out for the man, at the discretion of his Commanding Officer, in such of the articles of necessaries as are allowed to be provided out of the Recruit's Bounty; and shall be accordingly charged in the Regimental accounts, under the head of "Recruiting Disbursements," the particulars of the expenditure being specified.

By Order of His Royal Highness,

The Commander in Chief.

HARRY CALVERT,
Adjutant General.

*General*

# Recruiting Instructions.

*General Orders relative to the Bounty of Boys, enlisted for the Purpose of being trained as Drummers or Fifers.*

*Horse Guards, May* 31st, 1805.

IT is His Majesty's pleasure, that in instances where by the special permission of the Commander in Chief, a certain proportion of *Boys*, under the regulated standard in age and size, are enlisted into Regular Regiments of Infantry for the purpose of being trained as Drummers or Fifers, no greater charge shall be admitted against the public, for Bounty, than the sum of two pounds two shillings, which is considered sufficient to provide such Boys with Regimental necessaries.

By Command of His Royal Highness,

The Commander in Chief.

HARRY CALVERT,
Adjutant General.

*Circular to Commanding Officers of Regiments of Dragoon Guards and Dragoons in Great Britain, relative to an Allowance of certain Articles of Equipment for Cavalry Recruits.*

*War Office, 9th June,* 1803.

SIR,

HIS MAJESTY having been graciously pleased to order that each Cavalry recruit, after having been finally approved at the Head Quarters of the Regiment, shall, as soon as the Commanding Officer may think fit, be furnished at the public expence, with the articles of Cavalry equipment mentioned in the margin,* I have the honor to acquaint you, that a charge may accordingly be made under the head of Recruiting in the Regimental Pay Lists, of the amount of the cost of the said articles, at the rates respectively set against them; the same being supported by certificates from the Commanding Officer, shewing that each man, for whom the charge has been made, has been finally approved, and has been actually furnished with all the said articles of a proper quality, in conformity to patterns approved by the Clothing Board, and lodged at the office of the comptrollers of Army Accompts.

I am however to apprize you, that in the case of the recruit dying, deserting, or being discharged, within six months after approval, and leaving at Head Quarters any of the articles furnished as above-mentioned, the articles so left are, if sufficiently good, to be given out to another recruit, and no charge is of

---

|   |   | s. | d. |
|---|---|---|---|
| * 1 | Pair of saddle bags, lock and key | 18 | 4 |
| 1 | Corn bag | 1 | 0 |
| 1 | Watering bridle | 5 | 6 |
| 1 | Horse log | 0 | 6 |
| 1 | Curry comb and brush | 3 | 5 |
| 1 | Mane comb and sponge | 0 | 8 |
| 1 | Horse picker | 0 | 2 |
| 1 | Lock cover | 1 | 0 |
| 1 | Water sponge | 1 | 0 |
| 1 | Pair of scissars | 1 | 6 |
| 1 | Horse cloth | 8 | 0 |
| 1 | Surcingle | 4 | 6 |

course

course to be made to the public for such articles; if the articles are not fit to be given out to the recruit, they are to be sold, and the produce thereof is to be credited to the public in the pay lists, by a deduction from the total charge for recruiting.

It will of course be understood, that although these articles of equipment are allowed in the first instance by Government, yet that they are liable to be replaced, as usual, out of the regulated stoppage from the pay of the men:

I have the honor, &c.<br>C. YORKE.

Officer commanding the
&c. &c. &c.

*Instructions to Officers and other Persons specially appointed to Recruit for the Infantry.*

*Adjutant General's Office*, 13th *October*, 1806.

THE following Regulations have been approved by His Majesty, and are to be strictly observed, by all persons acting under the authority of His Royal Highness the Commander in Chief, in the extraordinary Recruiting of the Infantry.

Art. 1. They are to be confined to enlist men within the limits specified in the authority given to them under the hand of the Commander in Chief.

2. The age, size, and description of the Recruit to conform to his Majesty's Regulations for Recruiting the Army.

3. The Bounty to the Recruit, and the distribution thereof, is to be according to the statement annexed.

4. Persons employed will not be entitled to any pay, but will receive the sum of five guineas, to cover all charges and incidental expences for each Recruit, in the proportion set forth in the annexed schedule.

5. They are to conform to all orders issued from time to time from the Commander in Chief, through the Inspector General, or Inspecting Field Officer of the district.

6. Persons so authorized, not receiving half-pay, must give security, themselves in the sum of 100*l.* and two securities in the sum of 50*l.* each.

7. The Inspecting Field Officers and District Paymasters to satisfy themselves of the responsibility of the securities.

8. The sum of 40*l.* to be advanced to persons so authorized, by the District Paymaster.

When 25*l.* of that sum shall have been satisfactorily accounted for to the Inspecting Field Officer, and District Paymaster, a further sum of 25*l.* may be advanced, and so on, without deviating from this rule, except in cases of the extraordinary success of an individual, when the District Paymaster, and Inspecting Field Officer, at their discretion, may advance further supplies.

9. It is to be distinctly certified on the back of each attestation, by the Officer or other person employed under these

Instructions,

*Recruiting Instructions.*

Instructions, that the Recruit was enlisted at on the      day of      180 by      having authority from the Commander in Chief to that effect, bearing date the      day of      180

10. All Recruits to be attested for General Service, or for the      Regiment of Infantry, or for such other Regiment of Infantry as the Recruit may select.

11. The Recruiting Regulations dated the      day of      to be strictly attended to, as far as they regard general Conduct and Discipline, and are applicable to this particular Service.

12. All Recruits raised are to be delivered to such Parties within the District as the Inspecting Field Officer may appoint.

By Command of Field Marshal

His Royal Highness

The Duke of York.

HARRY CALVERT,
Adjutant General.

Statement

Statement of the Distribution of Levy Money for Recruits raised in the United Kingdom by Officers and others, specially appointed to Recruit for the Infantry.

|  |  |  | Levy Money |  |  |
|---|---|---|---:|---:|---:|
|  |  |  | *l.* | *s.* | *d.* |
| Bounty to the Recruit. | On being attested, in Money |  | 2 | 2 | 0 |
|  | On intermediate approval | In Money | 2 | 2 | 0 |
|  |  | In Necessaries | 0 | 12 | 0 |
|  | On final approval | In Money | 3 | 12 | 0 |
|  |  | In Necessaries | 3 | 3 | 0 |
|  | Total Bounty of the Recruit |  | 11 | 11 | 0 |
| To the Extra Officer | On intermediate approval | For Attesting | 0 | 1 | 0 |
|  |  | For Surgical Examination | 0 | 2 | 6 |
|  |  | Reward | 3 | 3 | 0 |
|  | Reward on final Approval |  | 2 | 2 | 0 |
|  | To the Regimental or other Party, receiving and conducting the Recruit to the place of final approval |  | 1 | 6 | 0 |
|  | Total Levy Money, British Currency |  | 18 | 5 | 6 |

N. B. The above to take place from the 20th of *October*, 1806.

*Form*

*Form of a Bond to be given by the Person employed on the extraordinary Recruiting Service.*

KNOW all men by these presents, that I

am held and firmly bound unto our Sovereign Lord George the Third, of the United Kingdom of Great Britain and Ireland, King, Defender of the Faith, in the sum of One Hundred Pounds of good and lawful money of Great Britain, to be paid to our said Lord the King, his heirs and successors. To which payment, well and truly to be made, I bind myself, my heirs, executors, and administrators, and every of them, firmly by these presents, sealed with my seal. Dated the
Day of                               in the
Year of the reign of his said Majesty, and in the year of our Lord One Thousand Eight Hundred and

WHEREAS the above bounden
                is employed on the Recruiting Service:
and whereas the said
ought in all things well and faithfully to do, perform and execute, the duties of his said employment, as the same now are, or hereafter shall, or may, be prescribed, settled and established: and whereas the said
his heirs, executors and administrators, ought at all times when he, or they, shall be thereunto required, well and truly to account for all, and every, sums, and sum of money which shall, or may, be received by him the said
                or otherwise come to his hands by virtue of such employment, as aforesaid, and the balance, if any, found to be due from him, or them, to pay over to our said Lord the King, his heirs and successors, or unto such other person, or persons, as he, or they, shall in that behalf direct: now therefore the condition of this obligation is such, that if the said

do

do and shall, from time to time, and at all times, well and truly pay and apply, or cause to be paid and applied, to, and for, the uses and purposes of the said Recruiting Service, all and every sums, and sum of money, which shall, or may, be received by him the said                          or which shall otherwise come to his hands, or with which he shall, or may become justly chargeable, according to such orders, directions and instructions, as shall, from time to time, be given to him the said                          by, or as he shall, from time to time, receive from His Majesty's Secretary at War for the time being, the Inspector General of the Recruiting Service for the time being, the Inspecting Field Officer of the District in which he shall be employed, or by, or from, such other person, or persons as shall be duly authorized to give orders, directions and instructions, to the said                                          in that behalf; and also if the said                          his heirs, executors and administrators, shall and do from time to time, and at all times hereafter, when he, or they, shall be thereunto duly required, well and truly account for all and every, sums, and sum of money, which shall, or may, be received by him, or which shall otherwise come to his hands, by virtue of such employment as aforesaid, and well and truly pay, or cause to be paid, unto His Majesty, his heirs and successors, or unto such other person, or persons, as he, or they, shall nominate, or appoint, or as shall be duly authorized to receive the same, the balance which upon the examination and settlement of his accompts by the Paymaster of the District, with the concurrence of the Inspecting Field Officer thereof, shall, from time to time, appear to be due from him the said                          his executors, or administrators, thereon, and otherwise well and faithfully demean himself, in all matters relating to the duties and business of his said employment, then the above written obligation to be void, or else to remain in full force.

Sealed and delivered in } the presence of

*Regulation*

## Deserters.

*Regulation respecting Deserters, comprehending the several Points of their Apprehension, Inspection, Escort, and incidental Expences. Dated the* 1st *September,* 1801.

IT being essentially requisite from the numerous instances of collusion practised with respect to persons charged with Desertion, and of irregularity in the mode of arranging expences incurred on their account, that one general system, embracing the several points of their *apprehension, inspection, escort,* and *incidental expences* should as far as practicable, prevail in Great Britain and Ireland; the following instructions have been approved of by His Majesty, and are in future to be strictly observed throughout the United Kingdom.

### I. APPREHENSION.

Whenever a person shall be apprehended on suspicion of being a *Deserter*, he is to be taken before a Magistrate, who, if he find sufficient cause, will commit the man to prison, and transmit a report thereof, pursuant to the Mutiny Act, to the Secretary at War: and it would greatly tend to the furtherance of the public service, if the Magistrate would take the trouble of accompanying his report with a description of the man's person, briefly mentioning at the same time the evidence on which the commitment is made.

Commanding Officers of Regiments or Detachments are not, however, to permit the soldiers under their command who apprehend any person as *a Deserter*, to take him before a Magistrate, until such Commanding Officer shall have examined into the facts alledged, and ascertained that there is reason to believe the charge well founded.

After the report of the Magistrate is received, the station of the Corps to which the person apprehended is stated to belong, will of course decide the Official line of proceedings; if the party accused be taken up in Ireland, and belong to a Regiment in that part of the United Kingdom, the War Office in Dublin will make the necessary enquiry at the *Head Quarters of the Regiment;* but if the Corps be in Great Britain, or abroad, and the apprehension happen in Ireland, the particulars will be sent from Dublin to the Secretary at War in England,

England, who will investigate the case, and communicate the result to the Irish War Office: the like proceedings will be had, when persons charged with *Desertion* from Regiments in Ireland are apprehended in Great Britain.

The removal under *escort*, or release of the person accused, will of course depend on the issue of those proceedings; and the orders will be given accordingly, by the War Office in London, or in Dublin.

## II. INSPECTION.

In order to avoid *unnecessary expences*, when a *Deserter* under *escort* shall arrive at any place in the United Kingdom, where a Staff Surgeon may be stationed, he shall there undergo *a strict medical examination* as to his *fitness for Service*; and if *found unfit*, either from age or infirmity, an immediate report shall be transmitted by the Commanding Officer to the Secretary at War, who (in Great Britain, with the concurrence of the Commander in Chief, and in Ireland with that of the Commander of the Forces there) will cause the man to be *dismissed*; unless in any particular cases where circumstances appear to make it adviseable, for the sake of *discipline*, to forward men, even of this description, to the *Head Quarters* of their respective Corps: each man so *dismissed* is to have a reasonable proportion of pay to carry him back to his last place of residence, at the rate of *six-pence* British per diem, and such additional allowance as may be made for *Deserters* in confinement by any special regulation then in force:) the said *pay* (and *extra allowance* if any) to be *charged* on the *back* of the *Route*, to which is to be annexed a *certificate* from the Commanding Officer, that the man has been *dismissed* by order.

## III. ESCORT.

When an *order* shall be received by the Commanding Officer of any Corps or Detachment, for a party to take charge of a *Deserter*, and convey him to any place, the said Commanding Officer shall *advance*, or cause to be *advanced*, so much money on account of *pay* for the *Deserter* as will be sufficient to defray the arrears thereof during the time of his *confinement* and the expence of *medicines* and *attendance* (if any shall be due); he shall likewise cause such *necessaries* as

the

## Deserters.

man may be *absolutely* in *need* of to be *provided* and *paid for*, which in no case are to exceed *one shirt at* 5s. 6d.—*one pair of shoes, at* 6s.—*and one pair of stockings, at* 1s. 6d.— and the *sums* so *defrayed*, and *advanced* on account of *Pay, &c.* are to be stated distinctly on the *back* of the *route*; as likewise the particulars and actual *charge* of the *necessaries*, and to be *signed* by the Commanding Officer himself, or by the *Adjutant*, or *Paymaster*, by his direction. The Commanding Officer shall also cause to be *advanced a further sum* sufficient to *subsist* the *deserter* to the *next quarter* on the road; on arrival at which the Officer Commanding there is to *repay* the Non-commissioned Officer of the *Escort*, the *money disbursed* at the *first quarter*, and so much of the *sum advanced* for *subsistence*, as shall have been *expended*, and shall appear *properly accounted for* on the *route*, and is also to *advance the sum necessary to subsist the deserter* to the *next quarter* on his *route*: the *total* of the *sum disbursed* at the *second quarter*, and so much of the *sum advanced* there for *subsistence*, as shall have been *expended*, and shall appear *properly accounted* for on the *route*, are in like manner to be *repaid* by the Officer Commanding at the *third quarter*; and so on, *from quarter to quarter*, until the *deserter* shall arrive at his *final destination*.

The persons receiving the money, viz. the *Gaoler*, and the *Non-commissioned Officer* who takes charge of the *Deserter*, shall likewise *sign* to the *sums respectively received by them*.

When a *deserter* is delivered over from one party to another, the Commanding Officer of the Corps to which the *latter party* belongs, or the *Adjutant or Paymaster*, by his directions, shall carefully *inspect the route*, and see that the *money* which hath been received, is there *properly accounted for*;—If upon such inspection of the route any *improper charges* shall be found, they shall be *crossed out on the route*, and the amount only of what had been advanced (exclusive of such improper charges) shall be returned by the *Regiment receiving the Deserter*;—The *Non-commissioned Officer* under whom such *improper charges* shall have been incurred, is to be required by his Commanding Officer forthwith to *make good* the amount thereof, and in case of his failing so to do, is to be put under *stoppages* for the same.

No pay shall be *advanced*, nor shall any *necessaries be provided*, but by or under the *immediate direction* of the Commanding Officer, Adjutant, or Paymaster, who is to *sign his name*

*name* to the *charge*.—At those *stations*, where the *escort* is relieved by a *detachment* under the command of a *Quarter Master* or of a *Non-commissioned Officer*, such *Officer* is to *sign* for the *expenditure*; but in that case he is to subjoin to his signature and description the following words, " *No superior Officer at the station.*"

No more money shall be advanced on account of *Pay*, than the *time* and *distance* may *require*.

*Necessaries* shall be supplied but *once* for *any* march; *if destroyed or made away with*, the Officer commanding at the *next quarter* will order *a detachment court martial* to try the prisoner, *Non-commissioned Officer, or any of the escort*, who shall appear to be *in fault*, in order that an *immediate example* may be made of *the offender*; after which should the *punishment inflicted* render him *unable* to proceed, the same must be reported in *Great Britain* to the COMMANDER IN CHIEF; and in *Ireland* to the COMMANDER OF THE FORCES there.

No *horse* or *carriage hire* shall be *allowed*, except in the case of a *deserter* being taken so ill between one stage and another, as to be *incapable* of proceeding on foot; on such occurrence happening, the *necessity* that occasioned the *extra charge* must be *certified* on the *back* of the *route* by the Commanding Officer and a *Surgeon* at the next town; and should the *deserter* still be unable to proceed on foot, a report thereof is to be made to the War Office, for further instructions.

No fees shall be allowed at gaols; the Mutiny Act having expressly provided for the *admission of deserters without fees into gaols* as well on the road, as at the places where they are first committed; therefore all *Non-commissioned Officers*, commanding *escorts* with *deserters*, are to endeavour as much as possible, to march in such a manner as to lie in *towns* or *villages* having *public places of confinement*, or where *troops are stationed*; as they must otherwise be *responsible* for the *security* of the *deserters* in their own quarters.

## IV. EXPENCES.

The *Agent* of the *Regiment* to which a *deserter* belongs, or the *Paymaster* thereof, if the *deserter* is sent to his *Regiment*, shall *repay the money advanced* as above-mentioned, provided it is *properly accounted for on the route*, and shall *charge* the *same against the Public*; if in the *Regular* and
*Fencible*

## Deserters.

*Fencible Regiments*, as *Recruiting Disbursements*; and if in the *Militia* as *Contingent Disbursements*; and under the following heads, viz. the *subsistence*, at *sixpence per diem* for each *deserter*, whether from the *Cavalry* or *Infantry*, during the *period* of his *confinement*, and on the *march*; the *extra allowance* for the same time (now fixed at *three pence per diem*, but liable to be reduced, or discontinued, by future regulation, whenever the *price* of *provisions* may be thought to admit thereof);

*Necessaries*, not exceeding the limits prescribed by these Instructions; and *Handcuffs*;

*Medicines*, and other *necessary expences* in consequence of *sickness*; subject to the approval of the *Inspector* of *Regimental Hospitals*.

The *deserter* is not to be replaced on the *strength* of his *Regiment*, until *the day he joins.*

The *route* by which *deserters* are marched shall in no case include men belonging to *different Regiments.*—Each route shall be carefully preserved, and *deposited* with the *Agent*, or *Paymaster*, by whichever of them the several expenditures are finally reimbursed; in order to its being *transmitted* with their *Public Accompts*, as an indispensable *voucher* for the charges of such expenditures.

*Lastly*, It has been observed, that the *sums advanced* for *deserters* have, on many occasions, been only supported by the *signature of a Non-commissioned Officer*, without that of either the Commanding Officer, *Adjutant*, or *Paymaster*, to which may be chiefly attributed the *frequency* of *improper charges* for *necessaries*, *horse hire*, &c. &c. and the routes have in too many cases been found to be so *shamefully defaced and tattered*, as to be absolutely *illegible:*

It is expected that such instances of *irregularity*, and *want of care*, shall not occur in future; but if they should, it will be to the *certain loss* of the *Corps* under whose *escort* they shall have taken place.

> Given at the War Office, this 1st day of September, 1801.
>
> By His Majesty's Command.
>
> C. YORKE.

## Form of a Route for escorting a Deserter.

IT is His Majesty's pleasure, that you cause a proper *guard* to be made from

and convey      to the next *Regiment, Troop, Company,* or *Detachment*, quartered on the road to

And the said *Regiment, Troop, Company,* or *Detachment,* is hereby required to convey the said *Deserter* to the next *Corps*, and so from *Corps* to *Corps* upon that road until he arrive at
   there to be *delivered* to the

You are to cause *a sum to be advanced*, sufficient to defray the arrears of pay during the *confinement of the Deserter* , and such other expences as may be incurred, conformably to the Regulation; as also *a further sum*, sufficient to *subsist the Deserter* to the next *quarter* on the road: on arrival at which the Officer Commanding there, is to *repay the Non-commissioned Officer* of the *Escort*, the money disbursed at the *first quarter*, and so much of the sum advanced for     subsistence, as shall have been expended, and shall appear *properly accounted for, on the Route;* and is also to *advance the sum* necessary to *subsist* the *Deserter* to the *next quarter* on    Route: the *total* of the sum disbursed at the *second quarter*, and so much of the sum advanced there for subsistence as shall have been expended, and shall appear *properly accounted* for on the *Route,* are in like manner to be *repaid by the* Officer Commanding at the *third quarter*, and so on *from quarter to quarter*, until the *Deserter* shall arrive at    *final destination.*

It is His Majesty's further pleasure, that upon receiving the said *Deserter* , you cause a *full description* of    person to be inserted on the *back hereof,* together with a *particular account* of the *necessaries*     possessed of, or shall be furnished with: and the *Non-commissioned Officer commanding* each subsequent *Escort*, is hereby required and directed to *examine* the said *Deserter* and    *necessaries* by such *description* and *account; as every such Officer* is to be *answerable for the identity of the person committed to his charge,* and will be liable to *punishment* for suffering any *improper consumption* or *making away* of the *necessaries* of such *Deserter* upon the road.

                 Wherein

## Deserters.

Wherein *the civil Magistrates*, and all others concerned, are to be assisting, in providing quarters, and otherwise, as there shall be occasion.

    Given at the War Office the    day of

     By His Majesty's Command.

    In the absence of the Secretary at War,


To the Officer Commanding
 the

*Circular*

*Circular to Commanding Officers of Regiments relative to Charges for the Subsistence of Deserters on the March.*

*War Office,* 14*th April,* 1806.

SIR,

IT having been observed of late that Charges for the *Subsistence* of Deserters *on the March,* have been frequently struck out of the Routes, as not being vouched by the signature of the Commanding Officer, Adjutant, or Paymaster; and it being presumed, that this practice has obtained, from the supposition that the Regulation of the 1st September, 1801, requires such Charges to be so authenticated; I think it proper to explain to you, that the instructions on this head were not intended to preclude the admission of such Charges, if made at the proper rate, and for the proper periods; although the Payments thereof should not be confirmed by the Signature of an Officer.

Money *advanced* at the first, or any subsequent quarter on the road, must, however, still be not only properly accounted for, but must be sanctioned by the signature required in the Regulation above referred to.

I avail myself of this opportunity to add, that moderate Charges for unavoidable Repairs of Shoes, on a long March, will be admitted, the same being sanctioned by the signature of a Commissioned Officer.

I have the honor to be,

SIR,

Your most obedient

Humble servant,

R. FITZPATRICK.

Officer commanding
  the

*Warrant*

*Warrant for the gradual Abolition of Regimental Chaplaincies, and making more effectual Provision for the Performance of Religious Duties throughout the Army: dated 23d September, 1796.*

## GEORGE R.

WHEREAS we have taken into our most serious consideration the nearly universal want of personal attendance among the Chaplains of Regiments, and of care in providing proper deputies; as well as the difficulty of finding Clergymen to attend Corps serving abroad, upon such a stipend as is usually stopped from the pay of the Chaplains for that purpose, and left to the management of Commanding Officers; and it appearing to us, that by abolishing the office of Regimental Chaplain, as soon as the same may be practicable, and assigning an adequate pay to such Clergymen as shall attend our forces on foreign service, more effectual provision may be made for the regular performance of religious duties throughout our army, without bringing any additional charge upon the Public:—We have therefore thought fit hereby to signify our will and pleasure, that all Regimental Chaplains, who do not join their respective Corps on or before the 25th of December next, shall retire from our service on a reduced subsistence of Four shillings *per diem*, to commence from that day inclusive, and to be continued to them during the term of their natural lives; and that all future savings from the pay of Regimental Chaplains, as now borne on the establishment, shall be applied to the purpose of compensating such persons as may from time to time be employed in the actual performance of divine service to our forces, in the manner herein-after directed:

On the 25th of June, 1797, and at the end of every subsequent half-year, a certificate (according to the form annexed, No. 1.) shall be transmitted to the office of our Secretary at War, by the Commanding Officer of each Corps whose Chaplain shall have joined, stating that such Chaplain continues in the personal discharge of his duty; without which certificate the Chaplain's pay shall be respited on the settlement of the Accompts of the Regiment to which he belongs; unless

less it shall appear that such Chaplain has signified his desire of being placed on the Retired List: but any Chaplain failing in his personal attendance, and not having made such application, shall be superseded.

No Chaplain shall hereafter be allowed to appoint a deputy; no Chaplaincy which may become vacant by death, or resignation, shall be again filled up; no sale, exchange, or transfer of commissions by the present Chaplains shall be permitted after the 25th of December, 1796, unless the application for that purpose shall have been made previous to that day; and in the interval preceding it, no Chaplaincy shall be sold for more than was given for it by its present possessor; nor shall the purchaser have any claim to sell the same again.

And in order to provide for the regular performance of religious duties in future among the Regiments whose Chaplains may retire in consequence of these our Regulations, our further will and pleasure is, that wherever an army is formed, or a body of troops ordered to be assembled for service abroad, and in all garrisons or stations where several Regiments are near together, Chaplains shall be appointed according to the number of Corps, in the proportion of one to each Brigade, or to every three or four Regiments; which Chaplains shall receive Ten Shillings *per diem*, each, during the time of their actual continuance on foreign service, whether in the field, or in garrison; and that, after twelve years of real foreign service, every such Chaplain shall be permitted to retire on an allowance of Four Shillings *per diem*, payable in the same manner and subject to the same restrictions as the half-pay.

For such Regiments on foreign service as are in separate stations, or not more than two in one place or near together, an efficient Chaplain shall be appointed at each station, with an allowance of Seven Shillings per day; such Chaplains to be promoted to Brigades, with Ten Shillings per day, as opportunity may offer, and as they shall be found deserving; and likewise, after twelve years actual and foreign service, to be permitted to retire, with an allowance of Four Shillings *per diem*; subject to the same regulations as are observed in regard to the receipt of half-pay.

The necessary number of Chaplains for foreign service shall be borne on the staff of the different armies, and garrisons, at the rates above specified, and their pay shall be drawn by them

them monthly from the Agents of the respective Commanders in Chief, and Governors.

For every barrack in the British dominions, a neighbouring Clergyman is to be employed as the Curate to perform Divine Service every Sunday, and to be paid Twenty-five Pounds *per annum.*

The Commanding Officer of every separate Regiment in quarters will attend with his Regiment at some parish church; or employ a neighbouring Clergyman to perform Divine Service to the men: and he will empower the Clergyman whose parish church he may attend, or who has done the duty of the Regiment, to draw on the [Agent of the Regiment]* for such sum, as he may think a just compensation, provided that for any single Regiment the sum so drawn does not exceed Ten Shillings per week for the actual time of service performed: the Clergyman's draft to be accompanied by a certificate agreeable to the annexed form, No. II.

*Lastly,* We do hereby subject all regular Chaplains, desiring to be continued in our service, to the orders of the person whom we shall hereafter appoint to be Chaplain-General of our army, and who is to govern himself by such instructions as we shall from time to time think fit to give him through our Secretary at War.

>Given at our Court at St. James's this 23d day of *September*, 1796, in the thirty-sixth year of our reign.

By His Majesty's Command.

W. WINDHAM.

---

* Altered: see page 330.

*Certificates*

*Certificates referred to in the foregoing Warrant.*

## No. I.

I *A. B.* commanding His Majesty's           Regiment, do certify upon my honour, that the Reverend
          bearing the commission of Chaplain in this Regiment, has been personally resident, and performed his duty as Chaplain constantly during the last six months from
          to
In witness whereof I have signed this certificate.

## No. II.

WE the Commanding Officer and Paymaster of His Majesty's           Regiment, do hereby certify upon our honour, that the Reverend           (Rector or Curate) of           has personally attended and performed the duty of Chaplain to this Regiment, now in quarters at           during the space of           weeks from
to           and we do therefore authorise him to draw upon the [Agent of the Regiment]* for
accompanying his draft with this certificate.

(Signed)

---

\* Altered, as before-mentioned.

*Extract*

## Chaplains.

*Extract of a Circular Letter from the Secretary at War to the Colonels of Regular Regiments, respecting the Abolition of Regimental Chaplaincies, dated 30th September, 1796.*

"As the Colonels of Regiments have heretofore been allowed to recommend to the Chaplaincies, of which eventual benefit they will be deprived by the new system, His Majesty is graciously pleased to order, that in case any Chaplain, whether continuing on full pay, or placed on the Retired List, should die in the life time of the present Colonel of his Regiment, such Colonel shall receive the sum of 700*l.* if in the Cavalry, or 500*l.* if in the Infantry, by the sale of a Cornetcy, or one or more Ensigncies; the difference, with interest at 5 per cent. per annum on the principal until discharged, to be made good by the Public.

His Majesty is at the same time pleased hereby to make known his determination that this indulgence shall be confined to the present Colonels of Regiments, and not be extended to those Officers who may be appointed to the command of Regiments after the date of the Regulation."

*Extract of a Circular Letter from the Secretary at War to the Chaplains of Regular Cavalry and Infantry Regiments, respecting the abolition of Regimental Chaplaincies, dated 30th September, 1796.*

" FROM the nearly universal want of personal attendance among the Chaplains of Regiments, and of care in providing proper deputies, as well as from the difficulty of finding Clergymen to attend Corps serving abroad upon such stipends as are usually stopped from the pay of the Chaplains for that purpose, and left to the management of Commanding Officers, His Majesty seeing the inutility and inexpediency of bearing a Chaplain on the establishment of every Corps in his service, has been induced to order, that some more effectual means shall be forthwith taken to provide for the due performance of religious duties throughout the army, and that the office of Regimental Chaplain shall be gradually abolished. In regard to the present possessors of these Commissions, who are generally understood to have purchased, it is His Majesty's pleasure, that such as belong to established Regiments shall have their option either to join their Corps before the 25th December next, and continue to serve therewith, (as no Chaplain will hereafter be permitted to employ a deputy) or to retire from the service, and be placed at that time upon an allowance for life, of Four Shillings per diem, which is to be paid them in the same manner as their present subsistence, and as such will be tenable with every species of ecclesiastical benefice."

## Chaplains.

*Circular from the Chaplain General, in explanation of the Warrant for abolishing Regimental Chaplaincies.*

*War Office, 3d February,* 1797.

SIR,

AS it appears necessary to give some explanation of the manner of distributing the allowance of 10s. per week mentioned in the latter part of His Majesty's Regulation respecting the Performance of Religious Duties throughout the Army; I am desired by the Secretary at War to acquaint you, that where Regiments are much divided, and in places where the Soldiers have hitherto attended the different parish Churches without any inconvenience to the Clergymen, or the parishioners, and without any expence being incurred to the Regimental Chaplains, it is not to be doubted but that the practice will be allowed to continue without any demand being now made on that account, notwithstanding Government has agreed to admit of the expenditure of a certain sum per annum in those cases where a particular attention, or considerable increase of duty, may be required of the Clergy: to such cases, the Commanding Officer of each Corps in quarters is requested to confine his distribution of the said allowance, so as not to exceed 10s. per week for the whole Corps, nor even to expend that sum unnecessarily.

I have the honor to be,

SIR,

Your most obedient humble servant,

J. GAMBLE,
Chaplain General.

*PS.* Any Letters which you, or the Clergy in your neighbourhood, may have occasion to write to me, are to be put under cover to the Secretary at War.

Officer commanding the
    of

*Circular to Commanding Officers of Regular and Fencible Corps, in further explanation of the Warrant for abolishing Regimental Chaplaincies.*

*War Office, 9th October,* 1798.

SIR,

IT having been found by experience, that, notwithstanding my Circular Letter of the 3d February, 1797, great misapprehension continues to exist on that part of His Majesty's Warrant for the gradual Abolition of Regimental Chaplaincies, dated 23d September, 1796, which relates to the distribution of the allowance of the Ten Shillings per week, mentioned in the latter part of the said Warrant; I have the Secretary at War's directions to transmit to you the following explanation, for the future guidance of the Regiment under your command:

By the latitude allowed a Commanding Officer in the paragraph alluded to, either to attend with his Regiment at some parish church, or employ a neighbouring Clergyman to perform Divine Service to the men, it was by no means intended to authorise an equal and indiscriminate allowance in both cases, but merely to leave it to the discretion of the Commanding Officer, to apportion a suitable compensation, where a particular attention was required; and it never ought to have been understood, that the mere customary attendance of the military in the vacant part of churches, during parochial service, was to be paid for at a rate equal to what was to be allowed where a separate service was indispensably requisite.

This distinction, which I have endeavoured to make as evident as possible, leads me to the regulations which result from it, and of which the most scrupulous observance will be in future expected:

1st. Where a Regiment is so situated that a *separate service, solely for their use,* is required and performed, the same is to be duly certified by the Commanding Officer and Paymaster, the latter of whom is thereupon to pay to the Clergyman the allowed sum of Ten Shillings per week for the period certified, which will be reimbursed to him in the manner hereafter specified.

2dly.

## Chaplains.

2dly. If, in the case of a Regiment in quarters, or in temporary barracks, either in or near to cities or large towns, where, from the size or number of the churches, a separate service becomes unnecessary, it shall appear to the Commanding Officer that the Clergyman has paid a particular attention to his Corps, and has had his parochial duty considerably increased, by visiting their sick, a certificate of the fact is to be signed by such Commanding Officer and the Paymaster of the Corps; the Commanding Officer at the same time recommending such a portion of the limited allowance as he shall think proper; which, *if admitted by me*, is, in the first instance, to be defrayed by the Paymaster, and afterwards repaid to him as hereinafter directed; but it is requested that Officers will carefully distinguish between *a separate service* and the attendance of a Regiment during the parochial course of duty, as the full allowance of Ten Shillings per week is confined to the former.

3dly. All certificates referred to in the regulation, and which are for duty in Great Britain, are to be presented at the War Office, within three months of the latest day of the period comprehended in the certificate.

4thly. Certificates for short periods (except where a separate service is performed) will be received with the utmost caution; and as the allowance is weekly, if any odd days are included in the demand, the same will be rejected.

5thly. As frequent enquiries have been made respecting payment for the occasional duties of marriage, baptism, and burial, it is to be observed, that the regulation only provides for such duties as could have been performed by the Regimental Chaplain, had he been present with his Regiment; under which description such occasional duties would not be included, as in England they must always have been performed by the parochial minister, or with his consent; *and to him* the fees, when required, must have been paid: on the two former by the parties themselves, and on the latter by the Captains of Troops or Companies, as one of the articles for which they receive a contingent allowance.

6thly. Where, from the particular situation of Corps, any arrangement, not provided for in the Regulation, or Circulars, may appear eligible, it will be proper to send such information as will enable me to submit the same to the Secretary at War, for his consideration; without which previous communication, no deviation whatever will be admitted.

To

To the foregoing Regulations I am to add, that, as many defective certificates have been presented, which have unavoidably been disallowed, it can hardly be necessary to suggest to Commanding Officers to use the utmost caution in giving the authority of their names to charges not strictly conformable to the Regulations.

Mr. Windus, of the War Office, being appointed cashier of the monies appropriated for this service, all future draughts upon accompt thereof, whether from Paymasters or others, are to be made on him, at ten days after sight, instead of on the Agents, as directed by the general Warrant.

I have the honour to be,

Sir,

Your most obedient

humble servant,

J. GAMBLE,
Chaplain General.

*P.S.* Any Letters which you, or the Clergy in your neighbourhood, may have occasion to write to me or Mr. Windus, are to be put under cover to the Secretary at War.

Officer Commanding
the

*Circular*

## Chaplains.

*Circular to Commanding Officers of Militia Corps, relative to an Explanation of some Parts of the Warrant for abolishing Regimental Chaplaincies.*

War Office, 9th October, 1798.

SIR,

HAVING, by order of the Secretary at War, addressed a Circular Letter of this date to the several Commanding Officers of Regular and Fencible Corps, in explanation of some parts of His Majesty's Warrant for the gradual abolition of Regimental Chaplaincies, dated 23rd September, 1796, which have not been correctly understood; I am directed to enclose, for your information, three printed copies of my said letter; and to desire that you will govern yourself thereby, in as far as respects the various limitations to be in future observed in all certificates for the performance of Divine Service to the Military: the like certificates as are therein prescribed being required to accompany any charges on that head in the contingent accompts of the Regiment under your command.

I have the honour to be,

SIR,

Your most obedient,

Humble Servant,

J. GAMBLE,
Chaplain General.

Officer commanding
the         Regiment of Militia.

*Extract*

*Extract from the Instructions given by the Secretary at War to Arthur Windus, Esq. Agent for paying the Allowances to retired and Officiating Chaplains: dated War Office, 8th August, 1806.*

"IN pursuance of a plan approved by the Lords Commissioners of His Majesty's Treasury for consolidating and placing in the hands of one person, the duty of paying the allowances to the retired and officiating Chaplains, with the pay of the Chaplain General, and the usual contingencies, I hereby appoint you to that office, in performing the duties of which, you will strictly govern yourself by the following instructions.

The allowance of four shillings a day to the retired Chaplains, is to be issued, in general, by quarterly payments, and not before the expiration of the quarter.

In addition to their drafts, which are to be at ten days after sight, and which on accepting, are to be made payable by you at the Bank of England, you are to require from each retired Chaplain, as the voucher to accompany your accompt, a receipt according to form No. 1. Previously also to paying the allowance to the 24th December in each year, you are to be furnished with a certificate of the existence of the party, agreeable to form No. 2.

It may occur that the retired Chaplain may himself be the minister of the parish, or that there may be only one Churchwarden, Heritor, or Elder; in the former instance, the signature of the Churchwardens (Heritors or Elders, as the case may be) will be sufficient, and in the latter, a certificate signed by the Minister and only one Churchwarden (Heritor or Elder) may be accepted, but in both cases, the reason of the deviation is to be stated in the margin.

As a considerable time has unavoidably elapsed in preparing your final instructions, during which, several payments, from 25th December, 1805, may have been made by the Regimental Agents, upon receipts different from those prescribed, and in some instances, upon drafts only, the same are first to be submitted to me through the Chaplain General, and where no objection shall occur, you shall be furnished with my special authority for repaying and charging the same

## Chaplains.

in your accompts; the like authority shall also be granted on the recommendation of the Chaplain General, for charging in your accompts, any other payments that may properly have been made since the 25th December, 1805, although the vouchers may not be in strict conformity to these your instructions.

With regard to future compensations to officiating Chaplains, and other incidental expences, the issue thereof is to be preceded by a certificate, according to the forms 3 and 4, sent, under cover to the Secretary at War, to the Chaplain General, who, after examining the same, is to sign a recommendation No. 5, which on being countersigned by the Secretary at War, Deputy Secretary at War, or Chief Examiner of Army accompts, will be put into your hands, as the authority whereon to make the payment therein directed; you are then to apprize the parties of your holding such authority, with directions to transmit to you a receipt (duly stamped) for the amount, and in addition thereto, to draw upon you a correspondent bill at ten days after sight.

The receipts of the retired Chaplains are to be without stamps, the payments to them being for reduced subsistence in lieu of the full pay attached to their former commissions.

In the event of the death of any of the parties, you are to require a certificate thereof from the Minister and Churchwardens of the parish in which the decease took place, and also the production of the requisite letters of administration, if the sum to be received exceed five pounds.

You are to continue to advance to those Chaplains who subsequently to their retirement in this country were transferred to the Irish establishment, their reduced subsistence of four shillings a day; and the difference between the remittances made from Ireland on that account, and the actual amount advanced by you, is to be charged and allowed in your accompts.

Each and every of the payments to be made by you under these instructions, are to have a retrospect from the 25th December, 1805."

*Forms referred to in the preceding Instructions.*

### No. 1.

RECEIVED of Arthur Windus, Esq. Agent, for paying the allowances to retired and Officiating Chaplains, the sum of
*(to be inserted in words,)* being (with the undermentioned deduction for the duty on property) for          days reduced subsistence at four shillings per diem, from
          180   to                              180   both inclusive

£

of the

A. B.
Retired Chaplain
Regiment of


### No. 2.

WE the Minister and Churchwardens, (Heritors or Elders, as the case may be,) of the parish of
in the county of                              do hereby certify, that the Reverend
is now living in this parish; that he appears to be about the age of                    and to the best of our knowledge and belief, was Chaplain of the         Regiment of
   As Witness our hands this                    Day of

*Forms*

## Chaplains. 333

*Forms of Regimental Certificates, as the Case may be; to be transmitted to the Chaplain General, under cover to the Secretary at War.*

### No. 3.

*(For Troops attending Divine Service at Parish Churches.)*

WE the Commanding Officer and Paymaster of His Majesty's            Regiment of
do hereby certify upon our honour, that the Reverend
has from
to
been very attentive to the Soldiers of this Regiment, by visiting the sick, and that in the period above mentioned, the Regiment has regularly attended Divine Service with the parishioners at            Church, where the said Mr.            officiated. We do therefore recommend, that an allowance at the rate of
*per Week, be made to him accordingly.

Commanding Officer.

Paymaster.

---

*(For a separate Service.)*

WE the Commanding Officer and Paymaster of His Majesty's            Regiment of
do hereby certify upon our honor, that the Churches in this neighbourhood not being sufficiently large to accommodate the Soldiers with the parishioners at the time of parochial service, the Reverend            has
from            to
performed a separate service solely for the use of this Regiment, now in Quarters at
and has also been very attentive to the Soldiers by visiting the

---

* Not to exceed 10s. per week.

sick: we do therefore recommend that an allowance, at the rate of * per week, be made to him accordingly.

Commanding Officer.

Paymaster.

*Forms of Certificates for Barracks, large or small, as the case may be, to be transmitted to the Chaplain General, under Cover to the Secretary at War.*

### No. 4. LARGE BARRACKS.

———————— Barracks     1806.
THIS is to certify, that the Rev.
has from            to
constantly discharged all the duties required of him, by visiting the sick, and performing a separate service solely for the Troops occupying these Barracks, consisting of

> To be signed by the Commanding Officer alone, if a General Officer, but if of inferior Rank, by the Commanding Officer and Barrack Master.

### SMALL BARRACKS.

———————— Barracks     1806.
THIS is to certify, that the Rev.
has from            to
regularly visited the sick in these Barracks, when required; and that the Troops occupying the same, consisting of
have constantly attended Divine Service at the Parish Church of
where the said Rev.
did in the above interval officiate.

> To be signed the same as preceding Certificate.

---

\* Not to exceed 15s. per Week.

No. 5.

It is recommended to His Majesty's Secretary at War, by the Chaplain General, that Arthur Windus, Esq. Agent for paying the allowances to retired and officiating Chaplains, be authorised to pay to
the sum of
*(to be inserted in words)* conformably to the annexed Certificate.

> To be signed by the Chaplain General, and afterwards by the Secretary at War, Deputy Secretary at War, or Chief Examiner of Army Accompts.

All Letters on the above Service addressed to the Chaplain General, or to Mr. Windus, are to be put under cover to the Secretary at War, directed as follows:

On His Majesty's Service.
Right Honourable
The Secretary at War,
War Office,
London.

Chaplain General's Department.

# SECTION V.

## PAY & ALLOWANCES

OF

*GENERAL*

AND

## GENERAL STAFF OFFICERS.

# SECTION V.

## PAY AND ALLOWANCES

OF

## GENERAL AND GENERAL STAFF OFFICERS.

*State of the Rates of Pay and Allowances borne on the Establishment for certain Classes of General and General Staff Officers.*

|  | Nominal or Gross Pay, per diem. | | | Nett Pay for 365 Days as borne on the Establishment. | | |
|---|---|---|---|---|---|---|
|  | *l.* | *s.* | *d.* | *l.* | *s.* | *d.* |
| General | 6 | 0 | 0 | 2,074 | 10 | 0 |
| Lieutenant General | 4 | 0 | 0 | 1,383 | 0 | 0 |
| Major General | 2 | 0 | 0 | 691 | 10 | 0 |
| Brigadier General | 1 | 10 | 0 | 518 | 12 | 6 |
| Adjutant General | *1 | 0 | 0 | 345 | 15 | 0 |
| Deputy Adjutant General | *0 | 10 | 0 | 172 | 17 | 6 |
| Quarter Master General | *1 | 0 | 0 | 345 | 15 | 0 |
| Deputy Quarter Master Gen. | *0 | 10 | 0 | 172 | 17 | 6 |
| Major of Brigade | 0 | 10 | 0 | 172 | 17 | 6 |
| Aide de Camp | 0 | 10 | 0 | 172 | 17 | 6 |

N. B. The rates above specified, marked thus*, are those *usually* allowed on the establishment, for Officers of the respective departments. The Adjutant General and Quarter Master General at *Head Quarters*, and their deputies, as also the Deputy Adjutant General and Deputy Quarter Master

Master General in *North Britain*, receive, under special arrangements in their favour, higher rates of pay.

A further deduction of 6d. in the pound, calculated on the gross rates, is made from the above Pay, at the Pay Office.

A General is allowed *three* Aides de Camp; a Lieutenant General, *two*; and a Major General, *one*.

*General and Staff Officers.* 341

*State of the Rates of Forage Money allowed in Time of War, to Officers serving on the Home Staff.*

| | Number of Rations of Forage per diem. | Amount for 200 days, at 6d. per ration, after deducting 1s. in the Pound. |
|---|---|---|
| | | *l. s. d.* |
| General | 40 | 190 0 0 |
| Lieutenant General | 30 | 142 10 0 |
| Major General | 24 | 114 0 0 |
| Brigadier General | 20 | 95 0 0 |
| Major of Brigade | 4 | 19 0 0 |
| Aide de Camp | 4 | 19 0 0 |

## MEMORANDUM.

The Adjutant General and Quarter Master General, and their Deputies and Assistants, at *Head Quarters*, receive Forage Money at the rate attached to their Rank in the Army. The Assistant Adjutants General, and Assistant Quarter Masters General in the *Districts*, are allowed the same at the rate of 6 Rations per diem, each; being for 200 days 28*l*. 10*s*.

The period of each annual Campaign, for which the above allowances of 200 days Forage Money are granted, is considered to extend from the 1st May to the 16th November. Officers serving on the Staff upon the 1st May, receive the full allowance: those subsequently appointed, a proportion thereof, calculated from the respective dates of their appointments to the 16th November.

*Extract*

*Extract\* of a Circular Letter from the Secretary at War to General Officers commanding in Districts relative to the Forage and Lodging Money of the Staff.*

*Dated War Office, 11th August, 1803.*

"I HAVE the honour to acquaint you, that in consequence of the recommendation of his Royal Highness the Commander in Chief, the General and Staff Officers serving in the several districts in Great Britain, will be entitled to Forage for their effective horses, not exceeding the proportion specified in the annexed state, No. I, from the 25th June last inclusive, and that where Forage shall not be issued in kind, the respective Officers will be allowed to make a charge for the same in their contingent Accompts, according to the rules prescribed in His Majesty's Regulation of the 29th May, 1801,† and at a rate which will be fixed half yearly, upon the report of the Commissary General, and will be notified in proper time from this Office to the General Officers commanding in the districts.

I am further to acquaint you, that upon consideration of the various and indeterminate charges made by General and Staff Officers, under the head of Rent of Houses or Lodgings, it has been thought proper to establish a fixed rate of Lodging Money for each rank, agreeably to a scale herewith enclosed (No. 2).

This Regulation is considered as commencing from the 25th December last, inclusive, and the allowances may be charged in the contingent Accompts accordingly from that date, being supported by certificates upon honor, signed by the respective Officers, declaring that during the whole period for which the charge shall have been made, they had not been furnished with a house or apartment under the orders of Government, but had provided the same at their own ex-

---

\* The Paragraph omitted related to the Medical Staff.
† Superseded by the Regulation of 13th Dec. 1804: See p. 344.

pence.

## General and Staff Officers.

pence. The allowance will be granted without any deduction on account of the period of the Campaign.

The expenditures for Travelling, and for Postage and Stationary, are to be stated and vouched as directed in the Statement above referred to."

---

For the Rates of Allowance specified in the Enclosure of the above Letter, see pages 345 and 346.

*Regulations relative to the Contingent Accompts of General and other Staff Officers.*

THE Contingent Accompts of General and other Staff Officers are to be made up half-yearly, viz. from 25th December to 24th June, both days inclusive; and from 25th June to 24th December, both days inclusive, and agreeably to the annexed form, No. I.

The Contingent Accompts of Assistant Adjutants General, Aides de Camp, and Majors of Brigade, are to be included in those of the General Officers, to whom they are respectively attached; those of Assistant Quarter Masters General are to be transmitted to the Quarter Master General, by whom they will be presented to the War Office.

Majors of Brigade, not attached to any General Officer, are permitted to make up, and to certify, their own accompts.

When General or other Staff Officers are desired by the Secretary at War to issue money on account of Government, and directed to charge the amount of such disbursements in their Contingent Accompts, they are to produce as a voucher for each payment, a receipt from the party to whom the payment is made, according to Form No. II. which receipt is to be accompanied by a copy of the order authorizing the expenditure.

Should the exigencies of the service compel a General Officer to incur an expence by his personal authority, which cannot be classed under any of the heads specified in the "Form of a Contingent Accompt" (No. I.) it will be disallowed, unless sustained by a subsequent authority from the Secretary at War, copy of which, and of a receipt, according to the prescribed Form, No. II. are to accompany the Contingent Accompt, as vouchers for the charge.

No contingent accompt, receipt, or other voucher, will be admitted, in which any erasure, correction, or addition, shall appear, affecting the amount and date of the expenditure, or altering the purport of the document.

The travelling expences of General and other Staff Officers, which are only allowed in case of their being ordered upon particular service, requiring more than ordinary expedition,

## General and Staff Officers. 345

dition, and which cannot be performed with their own horses, consistently with the purposes for which they are required to be kept, will not be admitted, unless a copy of the order from the Commander in Chief's department be annexed as a voucher to the account of such expences; which expences are to consist only of the actual and bonâ fide expenditure for horses, carriages, and turnpikes.

Receipts for stationary are to be invariably accompanied by the bills of particulars.*

It will be seen by the tenor of the voucher required for the charge of postage, that the charge must be strictly confined to letters or packets received *on the public service.*

The amount of the Duties paid by General and other Staff Officers for horses actually and bonâ fide kept by them for the public service only, will be allowed, if accompanied by the Collector's receipt and by a certificate as specified in Form, No. I.

Given at the War Office, the 13th of December, 1804.

W. DUNDAS.

---

Statement of the Number of Horses, for which, if Effective, the General and other Staff Officers serving in Great Britain, may draw Forage in Kind, or receive an Allowance in lieu thereof, during the Continuance of Hostilities.

| RANK OF OFFICERS. | No. of Horses allowed for, *if effective.* |
|---|---|
| General | 16 |
| Lieutenant General | 12 |
| Major General | 10 |
| Brigadier General | 8 |
| Assistant Adjutant General | 4 |
| Assistant Quarter Master General | 4 |
| Aid de Camp | 3 |
| Major of Brigade | 3 |

---

* The Form of the Certificate annexed, shews that the Stationary charged for, must be applied to the public service only.

For a specification of the articles to be charged to the Public under the head of Stationary, see page 348.

As the rates of allowance in lieu of forage are regulated agreeably to the contracts entered into by the Commissary General, which of course vary in different Districts, the accompts are not to be made up until the necessary information on that head shall have been received from the War Office, by the General Officer commanding in each district, who will communicate the same to the several Staff Officers under his command, as soon as possible after the receipt thereof.

N. B. Officers of the undermentioned descriptions are also allowed Forage, for the number of horses (if effective) specified against each.

| | |
|---|---|
| Deputy Commissary General | 4 |
| Assistant Commissary | 3 |
| Chaplain of Brigade | 1 |

Their claims for the said allowance are to be settled in the departments to which they respectively belong; but must be confirmed by the Certificate of the General Officer, commanding in the district in which they may have served.

---

Statement of the Rates of Lodging Money allowed to General and other Staff Officers, in cases where they are not furnished with a House, or Apartments, belonging to, or under the Orders of Government, but actually provide the same at their own Expence.

| RANK OF OFFICERS. | Annual Allowance for Lodging. | |
|---|---|---|
| | *l.* | *s.* |
| General | 300 | 0 |
| Lieutenant General | 250 | 0 |
| Major General | 200 | 0 |
| Brigadier General | 150 | 0 |
| Assistant Adjutant General | 81 | 18 |
| Assistant Quarter Master General | 81 | 18 |
| Aid de Camp | 54 | 12 |
| Major of Brigade | 54 | 12 |

*346

## No. I.

### FORM OF A GENERAL OR OTHER STAFF OFFICER's CONTINGENT ACCOMPT.

Accompt of Contingent Expences incurred by _____
from _____ to _____ both days inclusive.

| Name of Claimant. | Number of Voucher. | Description of Accompt. | Amount. | | |
|---|---|---|---|---|---|
| | | | *l.* | *s.* | *d.* |
| A. B. | | **Accompt of Forage.** Forage for ____ Horses from the _____ 180 to the _____ 180 both Days inclusive. ____ Days, at _____ each Horse per Day ............... | | | |
| C. D. | | (Assistant Adjutant General, Aide De Camp, or Brigade Major, as the Case may be) Ditto ____ Horses from _____ to _____ both Days inclusive, ____ Days at the like Rate ............................ | | | |
| | | hereby certify upon ____ Honor, that the Number of Horses specified in the foregoing Accompt were *effective* during the *whole period* for which Forage is charged, and that they were actually and bonâ fide kept for the *Public Service only*, and that ____ did not draw, or cause to be drawn, any Forage from any Contractor, or other Person, authorised to issue Forage, belonging to Government, within the said Period. Dated at _____ this ____ Day of _____ 180 | | | |
| A. B. | | **Accompt of Lodgings.** Lodgings for myself, from _____ 180 to _____ 180 both Days inclusive, ____ Days, at _____ per Annum .................... | | | |
| C. D. | | Ditto for (Assistant Adjutant General, Aide De Camp, or Brigade Major, as the Case may be) ____ Days from _____ to _____ at ____ per Annum ...... | | | |
| | | hereby certify upon ____ Honor, that during the *Whole* of the above-mentioned Period, for which Lodgings are charged, ____ not furnished with a House, or Apartments, belonging to, or under the Orders of Government, but that ____ actually provided the same at ____ own expence. Dated at _____ this ____ Day of _____ 180 | | | |
| A. B. | | **Accompt of Stationary, Postage, and Carriage of Letters.** Stationary as per Accompt ................................. | | | |
| C. D. | | Postage and Carriage of Letters and Packets, on the Public Service ............... | | | |
| | | hereby certify upon ____ Honor, that ____ have paid the Sum for Stationary, and the Sum for Postage and Carriage of Letters and Packets, as specified against ____ Name ; and that the *Whole* of the said Stationary has been, or will be applied to the Public Service only ; and that the said Letters and Packets were all on the Public Service. Dated at _____ this ____ Day of _____ 180 | | | |
| A. B. | | **Accompt of Travelling Expences.** Travelling Expences from _____ to _____ as per Accompt of Particulars, vouched by the Order of The Commander in Chief, dated _____ a Copy whereof is annexed ............................ | | | |
| C. D. | | hereby certify that the Duty on which ____ employed, on the occasions above referred to, required more than ordinary Expedition, and could not have been performed with ____ own Horses, consistently with the Purposes for which they are required to be kept. Dated at _____ this ____ Day of _____ 180 | | | |
| A. B. | | **Accompt of Duties paid for Horses.** Amount of Duties on _____ Horses belonging to me and (Assistant Adjutant General, Aide de Camp, or Brigade Major, as the Case may be) from _____ to _____ | | | |
| | | hereby certify upon ____ Honor, that the Number of Horses for which ____ have paid the Sum set against ____ Name ____ were actually and bonâ fide kept by ____ for the Public Service only. Dated at _____ this ____ Day of _____ 180 | | | |
| C. D. | | For so much paid by me to _____ as per Order of the Secretary at War dated _____ a Copy of which is annexed ........................................ | | | |
| | | Total £ | | | |

### GENERAL ABSTRACT OF THE FOREGOING ACCOMPT.

Amount of Accompt of Forage............................
Lodgings ...............................
Stationary, &c............................
Travelling Expences ............................
Duties on Horses ............................

Total Amount £

I hereby confirm this Accompt, the several Disbursements specified, and Sums charged therein, amounting in the whole to _____ Pounds, _____ Shillings, and _____ Pence, appearing to be faithfully and correctly stated. Dated at _____ this ____ Day of _____ 180

*General and Staff Officers.*

No. II.

*Form of a General Receipt for Cash Payments.*

*Place and Date.*

RECEIVED by the Hands of [General, Lieutenant General, Major General, Assistant Adjutant General, Aid de Camp, or Brigade Major, as the case may be] the Sum of being
in full for
for the use of his Majesty's Service.

*Signature.*

£⸺

*Circular*

*Circular to General Officers commanding Military Districts in Great Britain, specifying the Articles of Stationary allowed to be charged against the Public, in the Contingent Accompts of General and Staff Officers.*

*War Office, 24th January, 1805.*

SIR,

IT appearing on examination of the Contingent Accompts of General and other Staff Officers, that charges are frequently made in the stationary bills for articles which neither come properly within that description, nor were ever intended to be allowed at the public expence, I have the honor to transmit herewith a list of the only articles which are allowed to be charged at the public expence, under the head of stationary, and to request that you will communicate the same to the several General and Staff Officers serving in the district under your command.

I have, &c.

(Signed) W. DUNDAS.

---

*List of Articles of Stationary, referred to in the Secretary at War's Letter of the 24th January, 1805.*

Paper, including books for entry of letters.
Pens.
Ink.
Tape.
Wafers.
Sealing Wax.
Cards for Returns.
Pencils.
Rulers.
Ink Stands.
India Rubber.
Pen Knives.

SECTION

# SECTION VI.

## MEDICAL DEPARTMENT

OF THE

## ARMY:

INCLUDING THE

## *VETERINARY BRANCH.*

# SECTION VI.

## MEDICAL DEPARTMENT

OF THE

## ARMY:

INCLUDING THE

## *VETERINARY BRANCH.*

*New Arrangement of the Medical Department of the Army; dated 12th March, 1798.*

HIS Majesty is pleased to order that the establishment of an Army Medical Board for conducting the general business of the Medical Department of the Army, shall be discontinued; and that in future the Physician General, Surgeon General, and Inspector of Regimental Hospitals, shall each have his distinct province of business, and of recommendation; and be each made openly and solely responsible for his own acts, according to the following distribution of departments and patronage.

### THE PHYSICIAN GENERAL

To recommend Physicians, when required to be added to any establishment, and to give his opinion, as well on any proposed appointment of Physician to a vacancy in the hospitals abroad, as on any other matters which may be referred to him, separately or jointly with other Officers of the Hospital Staff, by the Commander in Chief, or the Secretary at War.

To continue (with the Surgeon General) to inspect the medicines of the army, and to examine and check the bills of the Apothecary General; stating from time to time to the Secretary at War, such observations as may occur to them on the mode of carrying on that branch of the service.

When applied to by Officers in London for a certificate of their ill health, as a ground for soliciting leave of absence, to consider it as a part of his official duty, to examine into the case (if not a surgical one) and to certify his opinion thereof, for the information of the Commander in Chief.

To preside at the medical examination of Candidates for Regimental or Staff Commissions, as required by the regulations after stated.

### SURGEON GENERAL.

To recommend Staff and Regimental Surgeons and Assistants; to select from the Staff Surgeons on full pay at home, such as may be necessary to be employed in the *general* hospitals, camps, or districts, in this kingdom; to make his requisitions to the Inspector for Apothecaries and Hospital Mates; and to appoint the inferior Officers and attendants in the said hospitals, for the management of which he is to be responsible.

To correspond with the heads of hospitals abroad, and to attend to all matters that are to be transacted at home in relation thereto.

To be the channel of application for extending the leave of Officers absent from hospitals abroad; and of orders for their return to their duty.

To continue (with the Physician General) in the duty regarding the Apothecary General; and (with the Inspector) in that which respects the claims of Officers for bounty or indemnification for loss of limbs, and cure of wounds.

To certify, when applied to by Officers in town, in surgical cases, in like manner as before specified for the Physician General in medical cases.

To assist at the medical examination of Hospital mates.

INSPECTOR

## INSPECTOR OF REGIMENTAL HOSPITALS.*

To recommend all Hospital Mates, Apothecaries, Purveyors, and Deputies; and the inferior Officers, on the formation of any new establishment.

To inspect regimental hospitals at home; to correspond with the Regimental Surgeons; and to be responsible for all matters relative to the supply of their medicines, and management of their hospitals.

To act with the Surgeon General relative to the claims of wounded Officers; and to certify when applied to, in surgical cases, as above.

To assist at the medical examination of Hospital Mates.

---

General Rules relative to Qualifications for Appointments in the Medical and Chirurgical Branches of the Service, and to other Matters regarding the Medical Department of the Army.

ALL *Mates*, as at present, to pass an examination *for Surgeon of a Regiment*, before the Court of Examiners at Surgeon's-Hall: and none of those entering into the service after the present period, to be deemed eligible to a regimental commission, unless they shall have also passed a *medical* examination; if at home, by the Physician General, assisted by the Surgeon General and Inspector, or one of them, or, if abroad, by a Board of Hospital Officers, as prescribed by the standing Regulations.

The *Assistant Surgeons*, to be taken from among the Hospital Mates; *the Surgeons of Regiments* from the Assistant Surgeons, who are to be preferred according to length, or merit of service; and not, on the recommendation of their Commanding Officer, to succeed regimentally, unless they otherwise have reasonable pretensions to the promotion.

The half-pay to be first resorted to, for the supply of *all* Officers of the Hospital Staff; such as have been placed on

---

* Mr. Knight, the present Inspector, is commissioned as " Inspector General of Army Hospitals."

half-pay in the course of the present war, not to be allowed an option (unless in case of ill health) if their services should be again deemed necessary.

When new appointments must be made, *the Apothecaries* to be selected from the Assistant Surgeons, or Hospital Mates; the *Purveyors* to be taken from among the Senior Staff, or Regimental Officers, whose pay is only ten or twelve shillings a day, if any are found among them properly qualified for the duties of that department.

In the case of *Physicians*, a medical degree at Oxford or Cambridge, or a license from the College of Physicians in London, although always desirable, not to be deemed *indispensable* requisites: if the candidate should otherwise have strong pretensions from military service, local knowledge and experience, or other circumstances of special cogency; or if he should be a medical graduate of *any* University in Great Britain or Ireland, and be found properly qualified in other respects, on one or more examinations by the Physician General, assisted by two Army Physicians to be associated with him on such examinations, by his Majesty's order through the Commander in Chief, or the Secretary at War.

No person hereafter obtaining the Commission of Physician, Staff Surgeon, Apothecary, Purveyor, or Deputy Purveyor, shall be deemed to have any title to half-pay by virtue thereof, unless after three years service abroad, or five years service at home, [reckoned from the date of such Commission.*]

The line respecting appointments abroad, where the Commanders in Chief are empowered to grant commissions, to be duly observed.

The Monthly Reports of the Sick of the Army to continue to be made up, and signed as usual by the Physician General, Surgeon General, and Inspector of Hospitals, who shall meet for that purpose once a month, or oftener if necessary: at which meetings they are expected to communicate their observations to each other on any matters regarding this branch of the service, and to offer any remarks in relation thereto, which they may think proper, for the consideration of the Commander in Chief, or the Secretary at War.

---

* Altered.—See the following Letter of 19th March, 1801.

*Medical Department.*

All Regulations which have taken place during the existence of the Army Medical Board, to continue in force, and not to be deviated from without his Majesty's previous authority, signified by the Commander in Chief, or the Secretary at War.

Given at the War-Office, this 12th day of March, 1798.

By His Majesty's command,

W. WINDHAM.

*Letter from the Secretary at War to the Principal Officers of the Army Medical Department: relative to the Term of Service entitling Medical Staff Officers to be placed on Half-Pay.*

*War Office,* 19*th March,* 1801.

GENTLEMEN,

SOME late representations from Officers of the Medical Staff, having directed the attention of His Royal Highness the Commander in Chief, to the effect of that article in the regulation concerning the arrangement of the Medical Department of the Army, dated 12th March, 1798, which expresses, that—" No person hereafter obtaining the " Commission of Physician, Staff Surgeon, Apothecary, " Purveyor, or Deputy Purveyor, shall be deemed to have " any title to Half-pay, by virtue thereof, unless after three " years service abroad, or five years service at home; " reckoned from the date of such commission." And His Royal Highness having thereupon thought proper humbly to represent to the King, that under this limitation His Majesty's gracious intention of rewarding such Officers as are of long service and merit, might not in all cases be fulfilled; and having submitted therefore that Officers of the descriptions above particularized, might be deemed entitled to the Half-pay of the respective Commissions they may hold at the period of their reduction, after three years service abroad, or five years service at home, *not reckoning from the dates of such Commissions only, but including the whole of their services:* to which His Majesty has been graciously pleased to accede:

I am to acquaint you therewith for your information and guidance, and that the above quoted part of the Regulation in question is to be considered as altered accordingly.

I am, &c. &c.

C. YORKE.

Sir Lucas Pepys, Bart.
T. Keate, Esq.
F. Knight, Esq.

*Circular*

*Circular to the Colonels of Regiments of Dragoon Guards and Dragoons, relative to granting an additional Allowance of 1s. a Day to Assistant Surgeons.*

*War Office,* 12th *Jan.* 1801.

SIR,

HIS Majesty having taken into consideration, that the Assistant Surgeons of Regiments of Cavalry, being required to be mounted, are liable to an expence for the maintenance of their Horses, to which those of Infantry Regiments are not, although the rate of their Pay is the same, has been graciously pleased to order, that from the 25th ult. inclusive, an Allowance of 1s. a day, free of deduction, shall be made to each Assistant Surgeon of Cavalry for the maintenance of his Horse, and that the same shall be issued with his Pay; but His Majesty has expresly signified his Commands, that the said Officers shall not be entitled to a higher rate of Half-pay on Reduction, than they would have received if the above Allowance had not been granted to them.

I have the Honor to be,

SIR,

Your most obedient

Humble Servant,

W. WINDHAM.

Colonel of the
Regiment of Dragoons.

*Circular to the Commandants of the Corps of embodied Militia in Great Britain, relative to the Appointment and Situation of Surgeons' Mates.*

*War Office,* 27th *June,* 1803.

SIR,

DOUBTS appearing to be entertained in some cases relative to the appointment and situation of Surgeons' Mates in the Militia, I have the honor to acquaint you that in every corps, at an establishment of not less than three hundred rank and file, the Commandant may appoint a Surgeon's Mate; and in Corps, at an establishment of not less than *seven hundred and fifty rank and file, when effective to two thirds at least of that number, a second Surgeon's Mate; for whom Pay will be allowed at the rate of five shillings a day each, if they do not hold Subalterns' commissions; or at the rate of three shillings and six pence a day, if they likewise hold Subalterns' commissions, from which they are not precluded.

I have the honor to be,

SIR,

Your most obedient,

Humble servant,

C. YORKE.

---

\* On special application from the Commandant, a second Surgeon's Mate is now allowed to any Militia Corps, whose effectives exceed 500 rank and file, although its establishment may not be so high as 750 rank and file.

*Regulation*

*Regulation for encreafing the Advantages and improving the Situation of the Medical Officers of the Army, dated 22d May, 1804.*

## GEORGE R.

WHEREAS we have approved of an arrangement for encreafing the advantages, and improving the fituation of the Medical Officers of our Army; with the view of encouraging able and well educated perfons to enter into, and continue in, that line of our fervice; our will and pleafure is, that from the 25th *December* laft, inclufive, the following Regulations do take place on the above head.

I. Hofpital Mates for General Service fhall be appointed by commiffion from us; and fhall have the Full Pay of Six Shillings and Six pence a day, nett, while employed at Home, and of Seven Shillings and Sixpence a day, nett, while employed on Foreign Stations: with Half Pay on reduction at the rate of two fhillings a day, fubject to the ufual deduction.

The Widows of fuch as fhall have ferved as Hofpital Mates with our Land Forces Abroad, and fhall die on Full Pay, fhall be allowed the Penfion of Sixteen Pounds per Annum: the Children of fuch Hofpital Mates, and the Widows and Children of thofe who fhall die on Half Pay, fhall be eligible to Allowances from the Compaffionate Fund, according to the Rules eftablifhed for the diftribution of that bounty.

Hofpital Mates appointed for temporary and local fervice, fhall not receive Commiffions, nor be entitled to any of the other above-mentioned advantages; but fhall remain in all refpects on their prefent footing.

II. The Affiftant Surgeons of our Regiments of Dragoon Guards, and Dragoons, Foot Guards, and Infantry of the Line, fhall, without diftinction as to their having ferved at Home or Abroad, have the Full Pay of Seven Shillings and Sixpence a day, nett: with Half Pay when reduced at the rate of Three Shillings a day, fubject to the ufual deduction: The Affiftant Surgeons of our Regiments of Dragoon Guards and Dragoons, fhall, while on Full Pay, receive the further Allowance of One Shilling a day for a Horfe, as at prefent.*

---

* The Affiftant Surgeon has his choice of quarters according to his ftanding in the Regiment, with refpect to the Subaltern Officers.

III. The Apothecaries to our Forces, and the Surgeons attached to the respective Recruiting Districts in Great Britain, shall continue on their present footing; the rate of their Full Pay being Ten Shillings a day, and that of their Half Pay Five Shillings a day, subject to the usual deductions.

IV. The Pay borne on the Establishment for the Surgeons of our Regiments of Regular Infantry, shall be encreased to the same rate as that now allowed to the Surgeons of Cavalry, viz. Eleven Shillings and Four-pence a day, nett: and in the Infantry, as well as in the Cavalry, the Surgeon shall be required to keep a Horse at his own expence, to enable him the better to perform his Regimental Duty. The Half Pay of Regimental Surgeons, both of Cavalry and Infantry, shall be encreased to Six Shillings a day, subject to the usual Deduction.*

Every Regimental Surgeon of our Regular Forces, after Seven Years service as such, or Ten Years service with our Army in the whole, in a Medical Capacity, on Full Pay, shall have his Pay augmented to Fourteen Shillings and One Penny per diem, nett, but is not to be entitled on that account to any additional Half Pay when reduced.

Every Regimental Surgeon of our Regular Forces, after Twenty Years service with our Army in the whole, on Full Pay, shall have his Pay augmented to Eighteen Shillings and Tenpence a day, nett, and shall have a claim to retire on Half Pay at the before mentioned rate of Six Shillings a day; but if the cause of his retirement be ill health contracted in the service, and shall be so certified by the Army Medical Department, the rate of his Half Pay on retiring after the above

---

* Under the authority of a previous Warrant, dated 30th November, 1796, the Regimental Surgeon has his choice of quarters according to his standing in the Regiment with respect to the Captains: and in time of war is allowed the same baggage and forage money as Captains; but in no shape whatever is he to have any claim to military rank in the army different from what Surgeons of Regiments were formerly entitled to.

It was directed by the same Warrant that, in regular Corps of Cavalry and Infantry, all allowances on account of medicines and hospital expences, (as well the annual, as the occasional allowances during encampment), together with perquisites or gratuities of every kind, should cease and determine on the 25th of December, 1796: and that, from the said date, medicines should be supplied to the respective Corps by the Apothecary General; and the hire of hospitals, and all medical expences attending Detachments and Recruiting Parties, be defrayed at the public charge.

length

length of service, shall be Ten Shillings a day, subject to the usual deduction.

Every Regimental Surgeon of our Regular Forces, after Thirty Years service with our Army, in the whole, on Full Pay, shall have the unqualified right of retiring on Half Pay at the rate of Fifteen Shillings a day, subject to the usual deduction.

The Widows of Regimental Surgeons of our Regular Forces permitted to retire after Twenty Years service on Full Pay, shall not be precluded from the Pension on account of the retirement of their husbands.

The Pay of the Surgeons of our Militia Corps, when embodied, shall be encreased, as in the Line, to Eleven Shillings and Fourpence a day: and the Militia Surgeons shall be under the same obligation to keep a Horse.

V. The Full Pay borne on the Establishment for the Surgeons to our Forces, shall be encreased to Fifteen Shillings a day; and their Half Pay to Six Shillings; subject to the usual deductions.

Every Surgeon to our Forces shall derive the same advantages as a Regimental Surgeon, from completing the respective terms of Twenty and Thirty Years service on Full Pay, as above specified.

VI. The Physicians, Purveyors of Hospitals, and Deputy Purveyors of Hospitals, to our Forces, shall remain in all respects on the same footing as at present.*

VII. The Full Pay annexed to the appointment of Deputy Inspector of Hospitals to our Forces, shall be Twenty-five Shillings a day, and the Half Pay Twelve Shillings and Sixpence; subject to the usual deductions. But after Twenty Years service with our Army in the whole, on Full Pay, a Deputy Inspector of Hospitals shall have a claim to Full Pay at the rate of Thirty Shillings a day, and to Half Pay at the rate of Fifteen Shillings a day; subject to the usual deductions.

---

|  | Per Day. |
|---|---|
|  | l. s. d. |
| * The Pay of Physicians to the forces is | 1 0 0 |
| Of Purveyors | 1 0 0 |
| and 5s. more for a Clerk if one be actually employed. |  |
| Of Deputy Purveyors | 0 10 0 |

All these Rates are subject to the usual deductions of poundage and hospital.

VIII. The Full Pay annexed to the appointment of Inspector of Hospitals, shall be Two Pounds a day, and the Half Pay One Pound a day; subject to the usual deductions.

The several appointments undermentioned, shall be hereafter discontinued in our service; as superfluous and embarrassing, and holding out the idea of Distinctions in Rank and Duty not easy to be defined, viz.

>Field Inspector.
>Assistant Inspector.
>Deputy Inspector General.
>Inspector General.
>Superintendant General.

Given at our Court at St. James's, this 22nd Day of *May*, 1804, in the Forty-fourth Year of our Reign.

By His Majesty's Command.

W. DUNDAS.

# Medical Department.

*Circular to the Colonels of Regiments of Dragoon Guards and Dragoons on the British Eftablifhment, enclofing the King's Warrant of 22d May, 1804.*

SIR,                                      *War Office*, 28th *May*, 1804.

I HAVE the honor to tranfmit herewith, for your information, two printed copies of His Majefty's Warrant for increafing the advantages and improving the fituation of the Medical Officers of the Army; bearing date the 22d inftant.

Agreeably to the directions of the faid Warrant, the Pay of the Surgeon and Affiftant Surgeon of your Regiment, will from the 25th *December* laft inclufive, be borne on the Eftablifhment, at the Nett Daily Rate undermentioned, viz.

|  | Nett Daily Rate. |  |
|---|---|---|
|  | s. | d. |
| SURGEON. Grofs Daily rate 12s. reduced by the ufual deductions to | 11 | 4 |
| ASSISTANT SURGEON | 7 | 6 |

Should the Surgeon of your Regiment, by length of Service, have acquired a title to any of the farther advantages mentioned in the 4th Article of His Majefty's Warrant, and prefer his claim accordingly, you will be pleafed to make a Report thereof to the Principal Officers of the Army Medical Department; upon whofe joint recommendation the additional Pay to be allowed in confequence will be iffued through the Agent for Army Hofpitals.

The Report muft fpecify the dates of the feveral Commiffions or Appointments which the Surgeon has held, and the fituations and Corps in which he has ferved: and is to be authenticated by your certificate of fuch of the facts as come within your knowledge.

I have the honor to be,
SIR,
Your moft obedient humble fervant,

Colonel of the                          W. DUNDAS.
Regiment

*Circular to Colonels of Regiments of Infantry of the Line, enclosing His Majesty's Warrant of 22d May, 1804, for encreasing the Advantages and improving the Situation of the Medical Officers of the Army.*

*War Office*, 28th May, 1804.

SIR,

I HAVE the honor to transmit herewith, for your information, two printed copies of His Majesty's Warrant for increasing the advantages and improving the situation of the Medical Officers of the Army; bearing date the 22d instant.

Agreeably to the directions of the said Warrant, the Pay of the Surgeon and Assistant Surgeon of your Regiment will, from the 25th December last inclusive, be borne on the Establishment, at the nett daily rate undermentioned, viz.

|  | Nett Daily Rate. |  |
|---|---|---|
|  | s. | d. |
| Surgeon.—Gross daily rate 12s. reduced by the usual deductions to | 11 | 4 |
| Assistant Surgeon | 7 | 6 |

[But as the augmentation of the Pay of the Surgeon, viz. 1s. 11d. a day, is granted to him for the express purpose of enabling him to keep a horse for the better performance of his regimental duty, he will, of course, not be entitled to the above difference, except upon a special certificate from the Commanding Officer of his having actually kept a horse, for Public Service, during the period for which the charge shall be made: the Paymaster will therefore insert in the column allotted for the Pay of the Surgeon, only the former rate of 9s. 5d. a day, and he will charge the difference in a distinct sum under the same head of service, taking care to have it supported by the certificate above-mentioned.]* It being, however, intended to place the Surgeon of Infantry on the same footing with the Surgeon of Cavalry, who contributes no more than $8\frac{1}{2}d.$ a day towards the maintenance of his horse, an allowance will be made for the horse kept by the Surgeon of Infantry, at the same rate, and in the same manner, as that granted for the horse of

---

* All charges for periods prior to 25th December, 1805, are regulated by this Order.—For subsequent periods a new rule is established. See the Circular, page 368.

the Adjutant; deducting the above proportion of $8\frac{1}{2}d.$ a day; this allowance being of course charged for the same Period as the augmentation of his Pay.

Should the Surgeon of your Regiment by length of service have acquired a title to any of the farther advantages mentioned in the 4th article of His Majesty's Warrant, and prefer his claim accordingly, you will be pleased to make a report thereof to the principal officers of the Army Medical Department; upon whose joint recommendation the additional Pay to be allowed in consequence will be issued through the Agent for Army Hospitals.

The report must specify the dates of the several commissions or appointments which the Surgeon has held, and the situations and Corps in which he has served: and is to be authenticated by your certificate of such of the facts as come within your knowledge.

I have the honor to be,

SIR,

Your most obedient

Humble servant,

W. DUNDAS.

Colonel of the
    Regiment of Foot.

*Circular to Commandants of Militia Corps, enclosing His Majesty's Warrant of 22d May, 1804, for encreasing the Advantages and improving the Situation of Medical Officers of the Army.*

*War Office, 28th May, 1804.*

SIR,

I HAVE the honor to transmit herewith, for your information, two printed copies of His Majesty's Warrant for increasing the advantages and improving the situation of the Medical Officers of the Army; bearing date the 22d instant.

Agreeably to the directions of the said Warrant, the Pay of the Surgeon of your regiment, will, from the 25th *December* last inclusive, be borne on the establishment, at the nett daily rate undermentioned, viz.

|  | Nett Daily Rate. |
|---|---|
|  | *s. d.* |
| SURGEON. Gross Daily rate 12*s*. reduced by the usual Deductions to | 11 4 |

[But as the augmentation of the Pay of the Surgeon, viz. 1*s*. 11*d*. a day, is granted to him for the express purpose of enabling him to keep a Horse for the better performance of his regimental duty, he will, of course, not be entitled to the above difference except upon a special certificate from the Commanding Officer of his having actually kept a Horse, for public service, during the period for which the charge shall be made: the Paymaster will therefore insert in the column allotted for the Pay of the Surgeon, only the former rate of 9*s*. 5*d*. a day, and he will charge the difference in a distinct sum under the same head of service, taking care to have it supported by the certificate abovementioned.]*

It being, however, intended to place the Surgeon of Infantry on the same footing with the Surgeon of Cavalry, who contributes no more than 8½*d*. a day towards the maintenance of his Horse, an allowance will be made for the Horse kept by the Surgeon of Infantry, at the same rate, and in the same manner, as that granted for the Horse of the Adjutant; deducting the above proportion of 8½*d*. a

---

\* See the note, page 364, and the Circular, page 368, which equally apply to the Militia as to the Line.

day; this allowance being of courfe charged for the fame period as the augmentation of his pay.

I have the honor to be,

SIR,

your moft obedient

humble Servant,

W. DUNDAS.

Commandant of the
Regiment of Militia.

*Circular to Colonels of Regiments of Infantry of the Line, and Militia, relative to the Pay of Regimental Surgeons.*

*War Office,* 14*th Nov.* 1805.

SIR,

I HAVE the honor to acquaint you, that, notwithstanding the instructions contained in my Circular of the 28th May, 1804, the distinction of the Pay of Regimental Surgeons into 9*s.* 5*d.* Pay, and 1*s.* 1 1*d.* additional Pay, will, from the 25th of next Month inclusive, be considered as no longer subsisting. From the said period, the Surgeon's Pay is to be charged in the pay list in one sum, at the rate of 11*s.* 4*d.* a day.

It is, however, to be clearly understood, that the Surgeon is not, in consequence, released from the obligation imposed upon him by His Majesty's Warrant of the 22d May, 1804, of keeping a horse for regimental duty; which regulation the Commanding Officers of Regiments are responsible for enforcing.

The daily allowance for the maintenance of the Surgeon's horse, subject to the usual deduction of $8\frac{1}{2}d.$ will be continued under the same circumstances, and the charges on that head must be supported by the same certificate, as heretofore.

I have the honor to be,

SIR,

Your most obedient,

Humble servant,

W. DUNDAS.

Colonel of the
    Regiment of

## Medical Department.

*State of the Rates of Forage Money allowed in Time of War to Medical Staff Officers serving in Great Britain.*

|  | No. of Rations of Forage per Diem. | Amount for 200 Days at 6d. per Ration, after deducting 1s. in the Pound. |
|---|---|---|
|  |  | *l.* *s.* *d.* |
| Inspector of Hospitals | 4 | 19 0 0 |
| Deputy Inspector of Hospitals | 3 | 14 5 0 |
| Physician | 3 | 14 5 0 |
| Surgeon | 2 | 9 10 0 |
| Apothecary | 2 | 9 10 0 |
| Purveyor | 3 | 14 5 0 |
| Deputy Purveyor | 2 | 9 10 0 |

The period of each annual Campaign, for which the above allowances of two hundred days Forage-money are granted, is considered to extend from the first of May to the sixteenth of November. Officers serving on the Staff upon the first of May, receive the full allowance; those subsequently appointed a proportion thereof, calculated from the respective dates of their appointments to the sixteenth of November.

Rates of Lodging Money allowed to Medical Staff Officers in the Districts in Great Britain, from the 25th December, 1802, inclusive, in Cases, where they are not furnished with a House, or Apartments, belonging to, or under the Orders of Government, but actually provide the same at their own Expence. (Extracted from the Enclosures of the Circular of 11th August, 1803, p. 542).

|   | per Ann.* |   |   |
|---|---|---|---|
|   | l. | s. | d. |
| Inspector of Hospitals, Deputy or Assistant Inspector of Hospitals, or Physician | 54 | 12 | 0 |
| Purveyor | 54 | 12 | 0 |
| Surgeon | 39 | 0 | 0 |
| Apothecary | 39 | 0 | 0 |
| Deputy Purveyor | 39 | 0 | 0 |
| Hospital Mate | 27 | 6 | 0 |
| Purveyor's Clerk | 15 | 12 | 0 |

N. B. The above Allowances are to be settled in the Department to which they respectively belong, but the Claims are to be confirmed by the Certificate of the General Officer of the District in which they have been serving during the period.

* These Allowances are usually issued at *weekly* Rates; as specified in page 374.

Number of Horses for which, if effective, Medical Staff Officers in the Districts in Great Britain, may draw Forage in Kind, or receive an Allowance in lieu thereof, during the Continuance of Hostilities.* (Extracted from the Enclosures of the Circular of 11th August, 1803, page 342).

| | |
|---|---|
| Inspector of Hospitals | 4 |
| Deputy or Assistant Inspector of Hospitals | 3 |
| Physician | 3 |
| Surgeon | 2 |
| Apothecary | 2 |
| Hospital Mate | 1 |

N. B. The above Allowances are to be settled in the Department to which they respectively belong, but their claims on this head are to be confirmed by the Certificates of the General Officer of the District in which they shall have been serving during the period.

---

* The Taxes upon the effective Horses for which Forage is allowed by the Regulation are paid by the Public.

*Letter to the Surgeon General, stating the Allowances of Lodging Money, and for Travelling Expences, to Officers of the Medical Staff.*

War Office, 15th August, 1803.

SIR,

HAVING laid before the late Secretary at War your Letter of the 25th ultimo, and its enclosure, I received Mr. Yorke's directions to acquaint you that he had no objection to granting the Allowances for Lodging Money, and Travelling Expences to the Medical Officers therein mentioned, according to the Rates you have recommended; except that it appeared to Mr. Yorke, that the Lodging Money of the Purveyor's Clerk should be only six shillings a week, and that the allowance for the Travelling Expences of the Hospital Mate and Purveyor's Clerk should be only ninepence per mile, being the same as is made to Officers employed on the Recruiting Service. You will therefore be pleased to grant your recommendations for the payment of the said Allowances accordingly, commencing from 25th December last inclusive.

I am however to apprize you, that Mr. Yorke was of opinion, that all the Claims of Medical Staff Officers to Lodging Money should be supported by their Certificates, upon honour, that during the whole period for which the charge shall have been made, they had not been furnished with a house or apartments under the orders of Government; but had provided the same at their own expence, and should be confirmed by the General Officer, commanding the District in which the Officers have been serving during the period.

Mr. Yorke was further of opinion, that the Recommendations of Allowances for Travelling Expences should invariably specify the circumstances under which the allowance was proposed to be granted; and that care should be taken that no Officer should receive the allowance in the case where his proceeding from one station to another arose from his own desire, or where he was taken from Half-Pay, or obtained a step by promotion. It is also proper to mention that His Royal Highness the Commander in Chief having recommended that the Medical Staff Officers should, in the Districts, receive an allowance for the Forage of a certain

number

## *Medical Department.*

number of effective horses, not exceeding the proportion specified in the annexed State, the payment of the said allowance may be recommended accordingly from 25th June last inclusive; the claims of the Officers being supported by the certificate prescribed by his Majesty's Regulation of 29th May, 1801,* a copy of which is herewith annexed. It will of course be understood that in consequence of this allowance, the said Medical Officers will not be entitled to travelling expences upon any occasion, where the service shall not be so pressing, as to render it impracticable to perform the duty with their own horses.

I am, &c.

W. MERRY.

T. KEATE, Esq.

---

* Superseded by the Regulation of 13th December 1804. See p. 344.

Scale of *Lodging Money and Travelling Expences proposed by the Surgeon General, to be allowed to Medical Officers, on Home Duty, who come under the following Circumstances.*

| Ranks. | Lodging Money when not allowed Barrack Rooms.* | Travelling Expences when not allowed Forage. | Cases where the Allowance of Travelling Expences in lieu of Forage appears necessary. |
|---|---|---|---|
| Class I. { Inspector, Assistant Inspector, Physician, Purveyor, } | 1 Guinea per Week. | 1s. 6d. per Mile. | 1. To all Hospital Officers not on leave of Absence who are ordered to repair to the Coast to embark for a Foreign Station. |
| Class II. { Surgeon, Apothecary, Deputy Purveyor, } | 15s. per Week. | 1s. 2d. per Mile. | 2. To all Hospital Officers not on leave of Absence who are ordered to repair to any of the Home General Hospitals, or to any of the Home Stations. |
| Class III. { † Hospital Mate, and Purveyor's Clerk. } | † 10s. 6d. per Week. | 10d. per Mile. | 3. To all Hospital Officers not on leave, who are ordered on specific Duties at Home. |

Arlington Street, 25th July, 1803.

T. KEATE.

\* N. B. It has been subsequently decided, that Lodging Money is not to be allowed to a Medical Officer for a period during which he continued in his usual Residence, and did not incur any additional Expence on account of other Lodgings.
† Six Shillings per Week only allowed to the Purveyor's Clerk for Lodging; and Nine-pence per Mile for Travelling Expences for Hospital Mate and Purveyor's Clerk.

## Medical Department.

*Letter to the Surgeon General, relative to the Allowances for Travelling Expences to Medical Officers.*

*War Office, 24th November, 1803.*

SIR,

HAVING laid before the Secretary at War, your Letter of the 11th instant, I am directed to acquaint you, that Mr. Bragge is convinced, by the reasons you have therein stated, that the distinction you contend for may be fairly taken in favor of Medical Officers, who having been placed on half pay, and being settled as practitioners, are called upon for service, without obtaining an additional step of rank; and the Secretary at War therefore approves of your recommending an allowance for travelling expences to be made to such Officers, according to their rank, from the respective places of their residence, to the stations to which they may be ordered to repair for duty.

I am, &c.

W. MERRY.

Thomas Keate, Esq.
&c. &c. &c.

*Letter to the Surgeon General relative to the Lodging Money of Medical Officers.*

*War Office, 5th June, 1805.*

SIR,

I AM directed to acknowledge the receipt of your Letter of the 29th ultimo, and to acquaint you that the allowance of Lodging Money cannot be granted to any Medical Officer whose usual residence is in the metropolis, unless with the sanction of the Lords Commissioners of His Majesty's Treasury, to whom the Secretary at War would refer officially upon a special case that should be stated to this department.

I am, &c.

W. MERRY.

Thomas Keate, Esq.

*Letter to the Surgeon General, relative to Recommendations for the Travelling Expences of Medical Officers.*

*War Office, 9th December,* 1805.

SIR,

YOUR Letter of the 4th instant, having been laid before me, I am to acquaint you, that according to the original Instructions from this Office, dated 15th August, 1803, no allowance for travelling was to be granted to Medical Officers, who had received forage money for their horses, except where the service should be so pressing as to render it impracticable for them to proceed with their own horses: I am therefore to apprize you, that in all future recommendations for travelling expences of Medical Officers, it is to be stated, either that no allowance for forage has been, or will be recommended during the half year, in which the allowance for travelling shall have been claimed, or that the service (which is to be described) could not be performed with the horses allowed to the said Officers, consistently with the purposes for which they are required to be kept.

I am, &c.

W. DUNDAS

T. Keate, Esq.
&c. &c. &c.

*General Order prefixed to the Regulations for Regimental Hospitals.*

*Horse Guards, Jan. 1st,* 1806.

His Majesty having been pleased to approve the following Regulations for the use of Regimental Hospitals, His Royal Highness the Commander in Chief, hereby enjoins Commanders of Regiments, of every description, and all Regimental and Assistant Surgeons, to govern themselves, in their respective Duties, touching the care of the sick Soldiers, and the management of the Regimental Hospitals, in strict conformity thereto.

By order of His Royal Highness

The Commander in Chief.

HARRY CALVERT,
Adjutant General.

*Extract*

*Extract* * *of the Regulations for Regimental Hospitals, signed by the Physician General, Surgeon General, and Inspector General of Army Hospitals, and referred to in the preceding General Order.*

" HIS Royal Highness the Commander in Chief having issued the most positive Orders to all Officers commanding Brigades and Regiments, to give very particular attention to the management of Regimental Hospitals, it becomes our duty to introduce such Rules and Regulations for the interior economy of the same, as may best provide for the health and comfort of the Soldier, and generally secure to his Majesty's Service all the advantages to be expected from our care and superintendance.

The following Instructions, *duly attended to*, will be found conducive to those desirable and important objects.

The reports of the visiting Officer, and of the Surgeon, will afford such information to the Commanding Officer, as will satisfy him, with the help of his own occasional visits, that the several duties of the Hospital are duly performed.

It is required of the Surgeon, that he shall keep a correct Journal of all cases; which will furnish to the Inspector General, or his Deputies, the best evidence of the Surgeon's diligence, and of his professional skill.

All Regimental Hospitals are under the immediate direction of their respective Surgeons, subject nevertheless to the general superintendance and controul of the Inspector General of Army Hospitals, and of any other Officers of the Medical Staff, who may be ordered to inspect the same from time to time. They are to see that every part of the Hospi-

---

* The parts *omitted* are such as appear to be intended exclusively for the guidance of the Surgeon in his professional capacity, and therefore not to be necessary for the information of General Officers, or Commanding Officers of Regiments; for whose use this Collection is more particularly designed.

tal Regulations has been observed,—to assist with their advice the attending Surgeon,—to correct errors, and to propose to the Officers commanding Brigades or Regiments, such further improvements as they may deem necessary for the benefit of the sick and of the service.

When a Regiment is divided and stationed in different quarters, the Medical Staff is to be equally distributed; that as few detachments as possible may be left to the care of country practitioners.

Each Regiment of Five Hundred effective men and upwards, should be provided with a Surgeon and two Assistant Surgeons.

The station of the Surgeon is always to be at the Head-quarters of his Regiment. If the regiment be divided in cantonments, the first Assistant Surgeon is to be placed with the strongest detachment, and the second with the next in succession in point of numbers; and in no case, where the Regiment is thus divided, and the Surgeon present, should either of the Assistants be allowed to remain at Head-quarters.

The spirit of this regulation should extend to the divisions of a Regiment on its march; and it is here of consequence that the Surgeon himself should accompany the *last* division; as well to ascertain the diligence of the Assistant Surgeons who have gone before, as to give the best directions for the Sick who may from *necessity* be left behind.

The Quarters of one of the Medical Officers of the Regiment should be always near the Hospital, and, when encamped, one of them is to sleep in Camp.

Leave of absence to the Medical Staff of Regiments must be regulated by the Commander in Chief's order of the 3d February, 1803.

When a Regiment is in Barracks, a Hospital is required to be provided and properly supplied with furniture, bedding, and utensils, by the Barrack Department, according to the regulation, and the established Schedule from that office. In other situations, the Surgeon will resort to his own Regimental Stores, which he is on no account to increase or replenish without previous permission; and, once a year at least, he will make a report of the state of them to the Inspector General.

When in Quarters, the Surgeon must look out for a house suitable

suitable to the strength of the Regiment, in a dry situation and with good water; but, before he engages it, he must state to the Inspector General of Army Hospitals, its rent and situation, with the number and size of the rooms—what wards have fire-places, and how many beds each room will contain.—Without this preliminary measure and the sanction of the Inspector General first obtained, no charge for a hired house will be allowed, unless very pressing emergency shall justify a departure from this regulation, and which must be stated in the first Weekly Return.

In Barrack Hospitals, straw to fill the paillasses is to be provided by the Barrack Department; but in the hired Hospitals, it is to be purchased by the Surgeon, and to be charged as a Contingency in his next Weekly Return.

No Hospital is to be engaged for a longer term than by the week; and to obviate every unnecessary increase of Hospital Baggage, the Landlord should be required to provide the equipments of fire-irons, tables, and forms, or they must be hired elsewhere at a weekly charge.

The establishment of Hospital Servants gives for a Regiment of 500 men and upwards, one Nurse at 1s. one Serjeant at 6d. and one Orderly at 4d. per day:—this is understood to be the maximum of Expence to be generally brought against the Public under that head. In battalions of inferior numbers, the expence of Hospital Attendants must be regulated in due proportion to their strength. If, from unusual sickness, further assistance be necessary, application must be made to the Inspector General for his approval of it, unless the pressure of the moment will not wait for such sanction; but the necessity must be then stated in the next Weekly Return.

This regulated allowance is intended for an entire Regiment: when the Regiment is separated, the Surgeon is expected to exercise his discretion in dividing and apportioning the ordinary expence of the whole, in such a way as to meet the exigencies of all. Thus, in the situation of a Regiment detached in three parts, it is adviseable to discontinue the Nurse, and to employ three Orderlies in her stead; and, by so doing, to give a due proportion of assistance to each Detachment.

The Serjeant is to take charge of the bedding, utensils, and other Hospital Stores, and be himself answerable to the Surgeon,

Surgeon, who of course is responsible to the Public, for any damage or loss.

This non-commissioned Officer should be very active and of good character. He should be selected by the Surgeon, with the approbation of the Commanding Officer, and be exempted from other military duties; nor should he be removed, except in cases of misconduct or inefficiency.

The Commanding Officer should be applied to for a guard, in order to furnish Sentries to the Regimental Hospital, or to the Hospital Tent; which Sentries are to be directed to admit no person but the Staff, the Officers of the Regiment, and those immediately employed in the Hospital;—they are to be particularly careful in preventing liquor or any other articles from being carried into the Hospital, without the Surgeon's permission; nor are they to allow any Patient to go out (to the Necessary excepted) without a Ticket of Leave from the attending Surgeon.

When a Regiment is encamped, a Hospital Tent will be allowed, unless a convenient house for the purpose can be procured in the vicinity; and when the Hospital Tent is the sole accommodation for the Sick, a Hut ought to be constructed by a fatigue party of the regiment, to answer the purposes of a cooking and messing room. A trench is to be dug round the Tent, for carrying off the water.

Bedsteads are too heavy an incumbrance for the ordinary equipment of a Regimental Hospital; which either in the field, or in a hired house, may be otherwise accommodated.

In a hired house, where the floors are kept clean by the use of the dry scrubbing brush, the Sick may be sufficiently protected by one or more straw mats between the floor and the paillasse; and in the Hospital Tent, the Patients may, within a short space of time, and at the most trifling expence, be placed on *temporary* bedsteads, after the manner that has of late been recommended. Some faggot-wood, drawn from the Commissary by a requisition from the Commanding Officer, with a few nails, is all that is required.

The regimental Surgeon, or Assistant Surgeon, must regularly visit the Hospital, at least twice every day, and keep a book of the admissions, discharges, and the cases of the Patients; in which the name, age, disease, diet, and treatment, are to be fully inserted, subject to the call of the Inspector

spector General of Army Hospitals, or Commanding Officer of the Regiment.

To obviate contagion, or check its spreading influence, the Surgeon should make frequent inspections into the state of the Barracks, and of their environs :—he should see that all due cleanliness be preserved *within*, and that no nuisances exist *without*; that the ventilators or air-barrels be not shut or obstructed, and that the mess-rooms be not made use of for washing or drying Linen.

It is likewise an essential part of the Surgeon's duty, when the Regiment is accommodated by billets, to examine the men's quarters, to ascertain that the apartments are free from damp ; that the bedding is clean, and the air pure.—As these health-inspections are of much consequence to the welfare of the Regiment, the Surgeon is enjoined to report the same to his Commanding Officer, with such observations as may arise out of his official visits.

By general orders of His Royal Highness the Commander in Chief, the stoppage to be drawn from men in hospital is fixed at 10d. per day ; but for boys subsisted at 10d., the stoppage of 8d. is to be drawn.

The above stoppage and the general expenditure of the hospital are under the immediate direction of the Surgeon, who will check and controul the Serjeant's accounts, being himself responsible for the due appropriation of the money, as well as for the general conduct of the hospital, and of the servants under his authority.

For the comfort of the Sick, and the simplicity of accompts, the late regulation, respecting the extra price of meat and bread to the Sick in hospital, is hereby done away ; and henceforward the necessary supplies of those articles, whether in quarters or in camp, are to be provided under the responsibility of the Surgeon at the *actual market-price*, and to be so charged in the Weekly Returns, without any reference to, or demand on the Paymaster.—The meat should be of prime quality, and the bread of the best household sort : the *actual market-price* to be ascertained and verified by the Commanding Officer, whose approving signature is required to be attached to the Weekly Returns transmitted by the Surgeon to the Inspector General.

When a Detachment is without a Regimental Assistant, and is not within reach of any Military Surgeon, the country practitioners may be employed. The regulated allowance has been at 1d. per man per week, for medicines and attendance; but, where the number is under *fifty*, and the contract cannot be made for that sum, it is allowable to give 6d. per month. Every Officer commanding a Detachment should be apprised by the Regimental Surgeon of this Regulation, and of the necessity for certifying in the Bill the precise number of men, the period of attendance, and that there was no Military Medical Officer on the spot, or within a reasonable distance; as, without this certificate, the charge will be rejected. When from the pressure of the moment, (on a march, or on sick furlough) such agreements cannot be made, the country practitioner will be allowed to charge his Medicines at a price suited to such class of Patients. It must here be well understood, that men are not to be sent on *sick* furlough without the previous approval of the Inspector General of Army Hospitals; and that no medical expences can be allowed for men on other than sick furlough.

When smaller numbers are under the command of a Serjeant, it should be his duty to have the bills certified by the proper Officer of his company, as soon as he joins the Regiment.

On the removal of Regiments or Detachments from one quarter to another, should an absolute necessity prevail for leaving any sick behind, either in charge of a Military Surgeon, or of a country practitioner, it is most positively required, that the respective Medical Staff should report to the Inspector General the names of the sick so transferred, with the particular circumstances that called for such a measure.—The medical expences for Sick not so reported will be uniformly rejected.

The bills of practitioners, and other bills, must be early sent for approval to the Inspector General; and when paid must be inserted in the next Weekly Return. A half yearly accompt, in duplicate, is to be made up on the 24th June, and 24th December, both copies are to be transmitted to the Inspector General without Delay, and the accompt must *close* the expences of the half year; as all charges or bills in arrear will be positively rejected.—The Abstract, when approved, will be returned to the Surgeon, to be by him delivered

livered to the Paymaster, that the amount may appear in his public accompts.

N. B. All bills above 40s. should be receipted on a proper stamp, at the expence of the party receiving the money.

The Surgeon is to deposit in the hands of the Paymaster, monthly, any growing surplus of the Hospital Fund, either *detached* or Regimental, taking his Receipt for the same; and when deficiencies shall call for an advance of money to the Surgeon for Hospital uses, the Paymaster, by an Order from the War Office, is allowed to issue it on account, under the authority of the Commanding Officer.

Every Surgeon, before he quits his situation or leaves the kingdom, must make up his accompts from the last half yearly settlement, and transmit the same to the Inspector General, or he will be charged by the Paymaster to the whole amount of the uncertified expenditure.

All Regimental Surgeons and Assistant Surgeons are expected to take care of the sick of any other Regiment, Detachment, or Recruiting Party, men on furlough, &c. whose Regiments are at a distance.

This duty is not confined to the Line and Militia alone, but extends itself to every class of military, either in the Guards or in the Ordnance Department.

When a Regiment is ordered to change its Quarters, the Surgeon is to transfer such of his Sick as cannot be moved in possible safety with the Baggage, to the nearest General Military or Regimental Hospital, accompanied with a detail of the cases and of the treatment, for the information of the Surgeon, to whose care they are to be transferred.—The Expence attending the removal is to be charged in the Contingencies of the first Weekly Return *of the Regiment removing*, and the circumstances of the case are to be detailed as a voucher for the necessity of removal.

The removal of Hospital Stores is not a charge on the Hospital Fund; they are considered as part of the Regimental Baggage, and must be conveyed according to the War Office regulations.

All Letters and Returns to the Inspector General, or any other member of the Army Medical Board, must be sent under cover to the Right Honourable the Secretary at War, War Office, with the words "*Medical Department*," on the left-hand corner.

The foregoing Instructions are to be strictly observed by the Regimental Surgeon; all former Rules and Regulations being revoked."

L. PEPYS.<br>
T. KEATE.<br>
F. KNIGHT.

## Medical Department.

### General Orders relative to Leaves of Absence to Medical Officers.

*Horse-Guards, 3d February, 1803.*

THE Commander in Chief has observed, that the benefit to be expected to the Service from the increased Establishment of the Regimental Medical Staff Officers, has been in many instances entirely lost by these Officers having been permitted to go on leave of Absence in common with other Officers of the Regiment, without a due attention to the particular nature of their Employment, and to the importance and necessity of their constant attendance; nor has the expence to the Public, for the extra Attendance of Country Practitioners, been diminished in the proportion which might have been expected, from the increased medical aid which has been afforded to Regiments.

His Royal Highness recommends these Observations to the serious consideration of Officers, in the command of Regiments, and enjoins them to be very circumspect in the Leaves of Absence which they hereafter recommend for their Regimental Surgeon and Assistant Surgeon: the applications can be proper only in one of the following Instances, either that from the Regiment being assembled in one or two Quarters, and remarkably healthy, the attendance of one of the Medical Staff Officers can for a time be dispensed with; or else, that from particular circumstances the indulgence of Leave of Absence to an Officer of this description, becomes an object of most material importance to his private concerns.

Officers commanding Detachments, not having any Medical Staff Officer attached to them, are immediately on arrival at their stations, to enquire whether there are any means of obtaining Medical Assistance from a Military Staff Officer in the vicinity, and it is only in cases when such aid cannot be obtained, that they are justified in having recourse to the practitioners of the country, of which a special Report is immediately to be made to the Officer commanding the Regiment, who will state the same to the Inspector General of Regimental Hospitals; hereafter, no charge will be admitted, for extra Expences incurred for Medical Assistance, the necessity of which has not at the time been reported in the manner above directed.

By Order of His Royal Highness

The Commander in Chief.

HARRY CALVERT,<br>Adjut. Gen. of the Forces.

## Medical Department.

**General Orders relative to the Stoppage from the Pay of Men in Regimental Hospitals.**

*Horse-Guards, 31st August, 1802.*

THE Regulation for improving Regimental Hospitals, bearing date in the month of September, 1799,* having directed that the sum of four shillings per week should be retained out of the pay of the Soldier, for his maintenance while in the Regimental Hospital, and for the incidental expences of the said Hospital; and it being thought proper to establish a new rate of Stoppage applicable to the above purposes, and to the other purpose hereafter mentioned.—It is His Majesty's pleasure, that, from the 25th September next inclusive, the sum of Tenpence a day shall be retained by the Paymaster, or Acting Paymaster, out of the Pay and Beer-money of each Non-commissioned Officer, Trumpeter, Drummer, and Private Man of his Majesty's Regiments of every description, during the time of their being in the Regimental Hospital; and that the same be paid over to the Regimental Surgeon, as a Fund, to be applied by him, under the superintendance of the Commanding Officer, to the maintenance of the men, and the general Expences of the Hospital.

It is His Majesty's further order, that regular Accompts of the expenditure for the above Services, be kept by the Regimental Surgeons of the Regiments of Cavalry and Infantry of the Line, to be furnished by them (being previously certified by the Commanding Officer) to the Inspector-General of Army Hospitals, at such times and in such forms as shall be prescribed, through the said Inspector General, in order that, in the case of a deficiency of the said Fund, the same may be made good; and that, in the case of a Surplus, the same may be applied to the general Medical expences of the Corps.

By order of His Royal Highness
The Commander in Chief.

HARRY CALVERT,
Adjutant-General.

---

* Superseded by the preceding amended Regulations: page 879, &c.

*General Order prefixed to the Instructions for General Hospitals.*

*Horse Guards, 31st March,* 1800.

HIS Majesty having been pleased to approve the following Regulations for the use of General Hospitals, in Great Britain, and the Islands of Guernsey, Jersey, Alderney, Sark, and Man, His Royal Highness the Commander in Chief, hereby enjoins all persons concerned to govern themselves in their respective duties, touching the care of the sick Soldiers, and the management of Hospitals, in strict conformity thereto.

By order of His Royal Highness

The Commander in Chief.

HARRY CALVERT,
Adjutant General.

*Extract*

## Medical Department.

*Extract\* from the Instructions for General Hospitals, signed by the Physician General, Surgeon General, and Inspector General of Regimental Hospitals: dated 31st March, 1800.*

A COMMISSIONED Medical Officer is to visit the Hospital at least twice in the twenty-four hours.

The visiting duty of the Medical Officer is to commence, from Lady-day to Michaelmas, precisely at 9 o'clock, and from Michaelmas to Lady-day, at 10 o'clock in the morning; the evening visit is to be made at 8 o'clock, and the utmost punctuality is required to the hours of attendance, from the Commissioned Officers, and Hospital Mates.

A written Report of the state of the Hospital is to be made every morning; also a Monthly Return of the Hospital, to the Military Superintendant.

By command of His Royal Highness the Commander in Chief, no Medical Officer is to absent himself from the Hospital, without leave from the General commanding the district, obtained through the Military Superintendant, and with the concurrence of the Surgeon General.

Every Medical Officer doing duty in the Hospital is to leave his name and address, in writing, with the resident Mate; and any one going away on leave of absence, is to leave directions where he may be found.

A specific Return of the Patients, according to the usual form, is to be sent by the 20th of each month to the Secretary of the Army Medical Board, under cover to the Secretary at War, for the information of His Royal Highness the Commander in Chief.

An Orderly Hospital Mate is to be on duty, from the hour of attendance in the morning, to the same hour the following morning; to visit the wards frequently; and to be constantly during that period in the Hospital:—this duty to be done in rotation, according to seniority.

The Orderly Mate, coming off duty, is, when relieved, to

---

\* The parts omitted are chiefly such as relate to the professional duties of the Officers; to the conduct of the *servants* of the Hospital; and to other matters of minute detail.

report to the Commissioned Officer in charge of the Hospital, who will report to the Military Superintendant, its present state, with the alterations during the preceding day, according to the annexed Form, in which he will mention his having visited the Hospital at 8 o'clock in the evening, with any other remarks that may occur; viz. admissions, discharges, or deaths.

---

I VISITED the Hospital at eight o'clock last night, and make the following Report this morning.

*Hospital*       180

To the Senior Medical Officer
   Hospital

                          Orderly Mate.

| Regiment. | Name. | Company. | Admitted. | Discharged. | Died. | Disease. | REMARKS. |
|---|---|---|---|---|---|---|---|
| | | | | | | | |

He

## Medical Department.

He will also inform the resident Mate of any admissions, discharges, or deaths, during the time of duty, that they may be entered in the register by the resident Mate.

He is to take the night duty; to see that every thing is quiet and regular; and, if any thing extraordinary occurs, he is to report it to the Commissioned Officer in charge of the Hospital.

The name, regiment, and company of every Patient, with the dates of admission and discharge, or death, are to be entered in the register by the resident Mate.

The Apothecary, resident Hospital Mate, or Medical Store Keeper, who has the charge of, and is responsible for, the medical stores, is not to deliver out any medicines to Patients, unless prescribed for them by name in the day book; he is to see the Dispensary locked after the hours of business, and to keep the key of it himself.

The Purveyor, Deputy, or Acting Purveyor, is to take under his charge, and to keep an exact account of, all hospital stores, provisions, utensils, &c. except medicines; and to see that the Hospital is perfectly furnished with every article wanted, as well as the diet, &c. that shall be directed by the attending Medical Officer.

The Purveyor is to make a Weekly Return of the state of the Hospital to the Officer in charge of the Hospital, and to keep an exact copy of the Monthly State sent to the Army Medical Board and Surgeon General: he is to report all kinds of misbehaviour in the Patients or Servants, to the head of the Hospital, who will report to the Military Superintendant: he is to give a Return to the Military Superintendant of every article of necessaries furnished to the Soldiers, at the time the same is given, with the price thereof, and no articles are to be furnished to the Soldiers, except such as are mentioned in the list of necessaries specified in His Majesty's Regulations.

The wages of the attendants and servants of the Hospital, are to be paid by the Purveyor, according to the annexed scale.

SCALE

SCALE OF WAGES *to be paid to the Officers not Commissioned, and the Servants, in all General Hospitals.*

| QUALITIES. | Rations, viz. *full Diet.* | Pay per Diem. |
|---|---|---|
| | | s. d. |
| Acting Deputy Purveyor | 1 | 5 0 |
| Resident Mate | 1 | 5 0 |
| Orderly ditto | 1 | 5 0 |
| Clerk and Store-keeper | 1 | 3 0 |
| Matron | 1 | 2 6 |
| Head Nurse | 1 | 1 0 |
| Sempstress | 1 | 1 0 |
| Steward, if a Soldier | 1 | 1 0 |
| Ditto, if not a Soldier | 1 | 2 0 |
| Surgery Man, if a Soldier | 1 | 0 6 |
| Ditto, if an Out Pensioner | 1 | 1 1½ |
| Ditto, if not a Soldier | 1 | 1 6 |
| Ward Master, if a Soldier | 1 | 0 6 |
| Ditto, if an Out Pensioner | 1 | 1 1½ |
| Ditto, if not a Soldier | 1 | 1 6 |
| Cook | 1 | 0 9 |
| Nurse | 1 | 0 9 |
| Washer-woman | 1 | 1 0 |
| Orderly Man, if a Soldier | 1 | 0 3 |
| Ditto, if an Out Pensioner | 1 | 0 8 |
| Ditto, if not a Soldier | 1 | 1 0 |

The senior Medical Officer, Physicians, and Purveyors, are to be allowed the same proportion of rooms, furniture, coals, and candles, if resident in the Hospital, as a Field Officer in barracks.

The Surgeons, Apothecaries, Deputy and Acting Purveyors, as Captains; and the Hospital Mates and Clerks, as Subalterns:—The Barrack Department to provide the furniture, coals, candles, &c.

All extra disbursements are to receive the previous sanction of the Secretary at War, through the Surgeon General, in writing, except upon an emergency; and then, such emergency and the nature and extent of the disbursement, are to be be immediately stated to the Secretary at War, through the Surgeon General.*

The Purveyor's Weekly Accounts of Provisions, and expenditure of every denomination, are to be minutely examined and signed by the Military Superintendant, and the senior Medical Officer, who are also to examine and sign the Quarterly Accounts.

All requisitions for stores, made to the Surgeon General, by the Purveyor, are to be approved, and countersigned, by the senior Medical Officer.

No order for the issue of stores is to be regarded by the Purveyor, unless in the hand writing of the senior Medical Officer.

The Purveyor is to send in his accounts within three weeks after every quarter day; and his accounts of the men's stoppages to the War Office, [every month.]†

He is to keep an exact account or register of every Soldier sent to the Hospital, his Regiment, Company, Name, Admission, Discharge, or Death, which he is to report to the Military Superintendant, through the head Medical Officer; from which an account must be made out, and sent to the Regimental Agent, and to the War Office, at the end of every month, that a stoppage of [Sixpence]‡ per diem may be made from such Soldier's pay, while in the Hospital.

The Ward Master is to lock the gates of the Hospital at eight o'clock in the evening in Winter, and nine in Summer, after which no person, except the Resident Mate, Orderly Mate, or a Commissioned Officer, is to visit or remain in the Hospital, but by the particular order of the head of the Hospital: and he is to report any irregularities he may witness in the Patients or Servants of the Hospital, to the Officer at the head of the department, who will report to the Military Superintendant.

---

* All extra disbursements not so authorised will be invariably deducted from the accounts, and the expence thrown on the Purveyor, unless the urgency of the case demanded it, and then it must be reported with the Weekly Return, or it will be rejected.

† Since the introduction of Quarterly Pay Lists, the accompts of stoppages are only required to be sent in once a quarter.

The quarter should be considered as ending on the 24th March, 24th June, 24th September, and 24th December, in each year.

‡ Now 10d.

The Patients are to comply with the Regulations of the Hospital; those who are able, must assist in cleaning or airing the Hospital, and by every means in their power lend their aid to the helpless.

Any Patients, who behave disorderly, are to be reported to the Commanding Officer in charge of the Hospital; and if their cases will allow of it, they are to be put on low diet, or confined as their offences may deserve, until they are properly reported to the Military Superintendant, which report must be made without delay; and no Soldier is to be continued on low diet beyond 24 hours, as a punishment, without the knowledge and consent of the Military Superintendant.

The General commanding in the district should be applied to, by the Military Superintendant, for a suitable guard."

L. PEPYS.<br>
T. KEATE.<br>
J. RUSH.

*Copy*

## Medical Department. 397

*Regulations relative to the Pay and other Charges for Soldiers while in General Hospitals; dated 30th April, 1809.*

IT appearing that the application of the present system of accompts, in regard to the pay, and other charges, for Soldiers while in General Hospitals, has been variously understood; and it being indispensably requisite that one uniform mode of settling the expenditure under this head, should be pursued, it is the King's pleasure that the following Rules, which have been adopted for that purpose, be observed.

As only the nett sum paid to the men, is to be charged in the Regimental Pay Lists, the Purveyors in their accompts, will not be required to specify the amount of the hospital stoppages, but are to state the names, ranks, corps, troops, or companies, of the respective patients, dates of their admission, and discharge, or death, with the particulars of necessaries furnished to each man, and the prices thereof. Also the amount of the advances made to the men, on quitting the hospital, and the stations to which the said men shall have been sent.

Duplicates of these accompts are to be made out by the Purveyors of Hospitals, as directed by the Instructions for General Hospitals, issued 31st past, and are to be transmitted monthly, (or, with regard to men discharged from the hospitals, immediately after such discharge,) one copy to the Secretary at War, and the other copy to the Regimental Paymaster, if the men on quitting the hospital are destined to join the Regiments to which they belong; otherwise to the Agent of the Corps; and the Paymaster, or Agent, on receipt thereof, is to reimburse the charges for necessaries and advances, accordingly, out of the pay of the men, and to take the proper steps for causing them to be correctly accounted with, for the remainder of their pay, after the further deduction of the stoppage, for the time they shall have been in the hospital, at the rate of *[Sixpence per day for each Non-commis-

---

* Altered to Tenpence as before-mentioned.

sioned Officer and Private Man, as fixed by His Majesty's Warrant, dated 6th February, 1799.]

Thus, the only charges to be made in the Regimental Accompts, are to be the specific sums for necessaries and advances to the men, on leaving the hospital, actually paid by, and reimbursed to, the Purveyors; together with the remainder of the nett subsistence paid on the settlement with the men; and the hospital stoppage, not having been drawn, will not make a part of the charges in the Regimental Accompts, or of the credits in the accompts of the General Hospitals.

The expence for burials will be charged, as heretofore, against the Captains of the respective Troops or Companies.

If any Non-commissioned Officers or Soldiers are permitted to be employed as Stewards, Surgery Men, Ward Masters, or Orderly Men, their names, rank, corps, and troop or company, are to be specified distinctly in every Return made by the Purveyors; as also, the dates of their having been so employed, from which their title to their regimental pay, free of deduction of the hospital stoppage, may be clearly ascertained.

Given at the War Office, this 30th day of April, 1800.

By His Majesty's Command.

W. WINDHAM.

*Letter*

*Letter from the Secretary at War to the Surgeon General, relative to Contracts for Supplies for General Hospitals.*

*War Office, 20th January,* 1801.

SIR,

IT having been found necessary to establish some new Regulations respecting the modes of contracting for the supplies of General Hospitals at home, and of drawing bills for the expenditures thereof, I am to acquaint you, that the following instructions are to be strictly and minutely observed in those respects, and am to signify to you the King's pleasure that you do use all possible exertion and attention to enforce and promote the due execution thereof.

1. When any new contract is to be made, public notice is to be given, and all tenders are to be delivered in, sealed, and are not to be opened, but in the presence of the Military Superintendant, who is to preside at the examination thereof; and no contract is to be entered into by the Purveyor, without the express concurrence of the said Superintendant, who, if he should entertain any doubts, is to report thereupon to the Military Superintendant of Hospitals in South Britain and to wait his directions. The Superintendant and Purveyor will each of them be held responsible for the propriety of any contract entered into in future.*

All contracts, bonds, &c. are to be made according to a general and approved form: no verbal agreements are to be admitted.

To furnish a check on the quality of the articles delivered by the Contractors, the Military Superintendant is to visit, and examine the Purveyor's stores, whenever he (the Superintendant) shall see occasion. And in case the Purveyor, or any Medical Officer, shall propose to condemn any articles of the Purveyor's stores, such condemnation shall not take place without the previous examination and concurrence of

---

* As the Surgeon General has to examine and approve the accompts of all hospitals, a copy of any contract ought to be sent to him for his guidance, at least, if not for his approbation: the original should accompany the accompt.

the Military Superintendant, who is to take care that articles which may be fit for other purposes, shall be converted thereto.

2. Bills drawn by the Purveyor on the Agent of hospitals, for sums in advance on account of contingencies, shall not be accepted by him, unless they have on the face of them the approving signature of the Military Superintendant. [And bills for payment of Contractors, or others, on settled accompts, shall either be drawn by the respective persons to whom the accompts are due, and be authenticated by the signatures of the Military Superintendant, and of the Purveyor, or, if drawn by the Purveyor, shall be made payable to the persons to whom the sums are due, or their order, and shall be authenticated by the signature of the Military Superintendant.]\*

I am, &c.

W. WINDHAM.

T. Keate, Esq,

---

\* The signature of the Military Superintendant is not now considered necessary to be affixed to the draught for the balance of an account.

*Letter*

## Medical Department. 401

*Letter from the Secretary at War to the principal Officers of the Army Medical Department, relative to the formation of Boards of Inspection, &c.*

War Office, 8th July, 1801.

GENTLEMEN,

HAVING paid due attention to the suggestions contained in Mr. Keate's Letter of the 29th April last, for establishing a proper controul over the supply and expenditure of medicines and hospital stores, and to the several points, which on a further consideration of the subject, have appeared most necessary to be provided for, I submitted to the Commander in Chief the following Regulations for the future conduct of this branch of the public service; and with His Royal Highness's approbation, I am now to communicate them to you for your information and guidance, and to be by you circulated to the respective Officers of the Medical Department abroad and at home.

No orders shall be given to the Apothecary General, or Messrs. Trotter, for supplies for the *General* Hospitals at home or abroad, except through the Surgeon General, nor for *regimental* supplies, except through the Inspector of Regimental Hospitals.

Those Officers shall sign the respective invoices, and enter them in books kept for that purpose, before they are sent to the Apothecary General, or to Messrs. Trotter for execution.

In the case of supplies for General Hospitals, the Apothecary General, and Messrs. Trotter, who, it is presumed, of course send invoices with every parcel of medicines and stores, shall transmit duplicate invoices to the Surgeon General, to be compared with the original orders entered in his book; and, if found correct, to be forwarded by him to the senior Officer of Hospitals, on the station for which the medicines and stores are destined.

Duplicates of the invoices of medicines and stores furnished regimentally, are in like manner to be sent to, and entered, and forwarded by the Inspector of Regimental Hospitals.

The bills of the Apothecary General, and of Messrs. Trotters, for articles delivered, are to be compared with the books of orders kept by the Surgeon General, and Inspector General, without whose respective signatures of approval, the certificate of the Secretary at War, in the case of the Apothecary

cary General, and of the order for payment, in the case of Messrs. Trotter, will not hereafter be given.

The Packers shall make a Return to the Surgeon General of the periods at which any medicines and stores have been shipped, and of the vessels they are on board.

Upon the arrival of any supplies abroad, the senior Hospital Officer on the station shall appoint a Medical Board, (consisting of not less than three Commissioned Officers, if that number can conveniently be had) whose duty it will be to examine the condition in which they are received; to ascertain whether they correspond with the invoices forwarded by the Surgeon General; to notice any omissions of articles, or deficiencies in their quantity, or defects in their quality; and where they find any damage sustained, to endeavour to learn whether the same has proceeded from want of care on board ship, or in the original packing and shipping of the articles.

Of these several particulars, a report is to be made by the said Board to the senior Hospital Officer on the station, who will transmit a copy thereof with his own remarks to the Surgeon General, in order that it may be laid before the Secretary at War.

The like method is to be pursued in regard to the stores received at the General Hospitals at home, for their own consumption.

[When supplies are to be deposited at Deal, Gosport, or Plymouth, for the future exigencies of foreign service, on their arrival at those ports, the packages are to be carefully inspected by a Medical Board, constituted as above directed: any that appear damaged are to be opened, and their contents more minutely examined; and a report is to be made accordingly, in the same manner as is before specified: when they are required to be shipped for foreign service, a fresh inspection into the state of the packages is to be made by a Board as before directed.

The supplies deposited at Deal, Gosport, and Plymouth, for foreign service, are to be put into stores entirely apart from those for the use of the hospital there, although in charge of the same Storekeeper, and separate books are to be kept of their receipt and expenditure.

No special appointments are deemed necessary for that purpose, as the requisitions from abroad will only be occasionally answered from the depôts of Deal, Gosport, and Plymouth, and then chiefly by sending the supplies in divisions already packed and invoiced. The Resident Mates therefore, it is conceived, may very well receive, arrange, and forward, these stores, assisted, if necessary, at the times of receiving and shipping, by the Deputy Purveyors, or some of the other Mates.

Whenever an inspection or embarkation of these stores is about to take place, previous notice thereof shall always be given by the senior Medical Officer to the resident Military Superintendant, who may attend as he shall see fit: any negligence in the receiving or stowing them on board ship, is to be immediately reported to him, in order that he may

apply

apply to the Commissary General, or make such other representation as may be necessary; and the expences attendant on such receipt, inspection, and shipping of supplies, at the General Hospitals, are not to be deemed admissible, unless vouched by the approving signature of the Military Superintendants.]*

No articles which have been used, or kept a long time in store, shall be sent to foreign stations.

At each General Hospital at home, a Board, consisting of at least two Commissioned Medical Officers, to be named by the senior Hospital Officer, shall once in every month inspect the stores, and the manner in which they are arranged; examine the Apothecary's and Purveyor's Returns of receipts, expenditure, and remains, and compare them with the vouchers; and shall deliver their reports of the result of every such inspection, together with a statement of such articles as may be required to supply deficiencies, to the senior Hospital Officer. The Military Superintendant shall be apprized when every such monthly inspection is to take place, and it is to be expected that both he, and the senior Hospital Officer, shall attend the same, the former for the purpose of communicating his observations, particularly in respect to the Purveyor's department, to the Military Superintendant General at Chelsea; and the latter, in order to receive the Report and Statement of the Board, and to transmit the same to the Surgeon General, accompanied by any observations or further information that he may think necessary thereupon. But it is to be clearly understood, that the monthly inspection herein directed, is not to be considered as substituted for, or in any degree interfering with, that controul over the expenditure and accompts of the hospitals, which has been assigned to the Military Superintendants by preceding Regulations, particularly by the Secretary at War's Letter, dated 28th January, 1801.

The view and approval of all the medicines by the Physician and Surgeon General will of course continue, as required by His Majesty's patent to the Apothecary General; and it is expected that the duty shall be performed with the most unremitting and scrupulous attention.

I am, &c.

C. YORKE.

Sir Lucas Pepys,
T. Keate, Esq.
John Rush, Esq.

---

* The General Hospitals at the Ports above-mentioned being broken up, the Instructions no longer apply.

*Letter from the Secretary at War to the Surgeon General, relative to the Disposal of condemned Hospital Stores, &c.*

*War Office,* 12th *September,* 1801.

SIR,

YOUR Letter of the 22d ultimo having been laid before me, I have deemed it expedient to prepare the following Instructions, in addition to those contained in my predecessor's Letter to you of the 20th January last, and have to signify to you the King's pleasure that you do cause them to be strictly and minutely attended to by such Medical Officers and others as they may concern.

I have, &c.

C. YORKE.

T. Keate, Esq.

---

*Instructions to be observed in the Disposal of condemned Hospital Stores, &c. by the Officers composing the Hospital Boards, and others, whom the same may concern.*

IT appearing that my predecessor's Letter of the 20th January last, contained no directions in regard to the disposal of unserviceable hospital stores, condemned from time to time by the Board appointed to inspect them at the General Hospitals; or to the periods at which the condemnation of such stores should take place: I have to desire, that the following Instructions be strictly attended to on this head.

The

The condemnation of unserviceable stores, medicines, and instruments, at the several General Hospitals in Great Britain, is to be made twice only in one year.

All tents, and other camp equipage, wood, pewter, brass, copper, iron, or tin, condemned as useless, are (by the Purveyor of the hospital, with the concurrence of the Military Superintendant) to be disposed of *on the spot*, except where Messrs. Trotter may have a resident Agent, in which case they are to be delivered to him; except also where (there being no Agent at the place) the magnitude of the stores may justify their being sent in a transport to London consigned to Messrs. Trotter.

The stores of the above description condemned at York Hospital, are invariably to be sent to Messrs. Trotter.

Bedding and dresses, no longer applicable as such, are to continue to be appropriated, as far as practicable, to other useful purposes in the hospital.

Condemned medicines are to be burnt or buried, in presence of the Board that condemn them; any part thereof excepted that may be judged saleable, under which head may be considered the grease contained in ointments or otherwise.

All chests, bottles, or other vessels, in which medicines may have been sent down; and also all instruments found useless, are to be forwarded to Messrs. Trotter, for sale, in London.*

The whole of the above is to be under the controul of the Military Superintendants at the different hospitals, who, with respect both to the articles that are saleable, and to those which are to be destroyed, will be considered responsible, that none of them be brought forward again, in any shape, to the prejudice of government.

Given at the War Office, this 12th day of September, 1801.

C. YORKE.

---

* Except (of course) where the value is not worth the freight.

*General Orders relative to the Stoppage from the Pay of Soldiers in General Hospitals.*

*Horse Guards,* 23d *February,* 1804.

WHEREAS by a General Order dated the 31st August, 1802,* the stoppage from the Pay of each Non-commissioned Officer and Private Man, when in a Regimental Hospital, was fixed at ten pence per diem, and whereas the reasons for establishing the said rate of stoppage apply equally, if not more forcibly, to the case of the Soldier in a *General Hospital*; it is His Majesty's Pleasure, that from and after the 25th instant inclusive, the sum of *ten pence* a day shall be retained out of the Pay of each Non-commissioned Officer, Trumpeter, Drummer, Fifer, and Private Man, of His Majesty's Regiments of every description, while in *a General Hospital in Great Britain,* on account of the expences incurred by the Public in maintaining the Soldiers, and in providing the necessary comforts and attendance for them in that situation.

His Majesty is further pleased to signify His Royal Pleasure that, in order that the Soldier in a General Hospital, may be placed upon the same footing in regard to the residue of his Pay, as when in a Regimental Hospital, the allowance of *one penny* per diem, called "*beer money,*" shall from the date above-mentioned, be granted to each Non-commissioned Officer, Trumpeter, Drummer, Fifer, and Private Man, in *a General Hospital,* in addition to his Pay, and shall be accounted for to him, in the settlement of his Hospital Accounts.

By order of His Royal Highness the Commander in Chief.

HARRY CALVERT,
Adjutant General.

---

* See page 389.

*General Orders relative to the Supply of Bread and Meat to Soldiers in Regimental Hospitals.*

*Horse Guards, 22d Jan.* 1806.

WITH a view to assure the necessary supply of Provisions to the Sick, and to simplify the Hospital Accounts, it is His Royal Highness the Commander in Chief's command, that, notwithstanding any former orders on the subject, bread and meat for the Soldiers, who are in Regimental Hospitals, whether in camp or in quarters, shall be provided under the superintendence of the Surgeon, at the actual market price, and shall be so charged in the Weekly Returns; and as the Men in the hospital, in obedience to this regulation, will no longer be included in the Weekly Regimental Returns for Meat and Bread, no charge is hereafter to be made by the Paymaster on their account for the extra price thereof, the Surgeon being responsible for the accuracy of the account, and for the quality of the articles provided by his direction.

The Meat must be of prime quality, and the Bread the best household.

The actual market price of both is to be ascertained, and verified by the Commanding Officer of the Regiment, whose approving signature is required to be attached to the Weekly Returns transmitted by the Surgeon to the Inspector General of Army Hospitals.

It will be clearly understood, that this Regulation, which is to take place from the 25th of February next inclusive, is not to affect the stoppage to which the Soldier is liable in Regimental Hospitals.

By order of His Royal Highness the Commander in Chief.

HARRY CALVERT,
Adjutant General of the Forces.

*General Orders, relative to the Stoppage from the Pay of Boys in General Hospitals.*

*Horse Guards, 12th November,* 1805.

HIS Majesty having been graciously pleased to direct, that the daily rate of pay, allowed to boys belonging to Regiments specially authorised to enlist boys for unlimited service, shall be encreased from *Eight Pence* to *Ten Pence,* from the 25th October, 1805; it is hereby directed, that a stoppage of *Eight Pence* a day shall be retained out of the pay of each boy recruit, while in a General or Regimental Hospital in Great Britain, on account of the expences incurred by the Public in their maintenance, and in providing the necessary comforts and attendance for them in that situation.

The usual allowance, called beer money, granted by His Majesty's command, to soldiers in General or Regimental Hospitals, is in like manner to be made to boys of the above description.

It is clearly to be understood, that this rule applies only to the case of boys receiving the pay of Ten Pence per diem, and that the order now issued is intended to cancel the one upon the same subject, bearing date the 1st of March last.

By Order of His Royal Highness

The Commander in Chief.

HARRY CALVERT,
Adjutant General of the Forces.

## Medical Department.

*General Orders relative to the Accommodation of the Sick of the Ordnance Department abroad.*

Horse Guards, 24th July, 1806.

HIS MAJESTY having been pleased to approve of the following Regulations, for the accommodation of the Sick of the Ordnance Department abroad, His Royal Highness the Commander in Chief hereby enjoins all Officers in Command, and all Medical Officers, on foreign stations, to govern themselves in their respective duties, in regard to the care of the Sick of the Ordnance Department, in strict conformity thereto.

By Order of His Royal Highness
The Commander in Chief.

HARRY CALVERT,
Adjutant General of the Forces.

---

On foreign stations, all sick Soldiers of the Artillery, Engineers, Royal Military Artificers, and Labourers, and other Ordnance Military Corps, and such persons belonging to the Civil Branch of the Ordnance, as may be considered by the superior Officers of that department, to be entitled to Military Medical Attendance, and Medicines; such as Storekeepers, Clerks, Artificers, Labourers, and other persons belonging to the department, shall be admitted into General and Regimental Hospitals, (or attended in their Quarters, according to their situations,) and supplied with diet, medicines, wine, porter, and all other allowances, and necessaries, and whether in Hospitals, or attended in Out Quarters, shall be treated in every respect precisely in the same manner, and be subjected to the same Regulations and Controul, as the sick Officers, Non-commissioned Officers, and privates of the other parts of His Majesty's Army.

The same stoppages are to be made from their pay, both

in regard to Hospital Charges, and Rations, the application of which is to be governed by the same Regulations; and in lieu of all other expences incurred by Government, for medicines, stores, attendance, wine, porter, freight, &c. a further sum of 2s. 2d. per diem, is to be paid for every Artilleryman, or person attached to the Ordnance, while he remains in General or Regimental Hospital, or is attended in Quarters, which sum is to be paid at home, by the Ordnance department, to the orders of the Secretary at War; the account to be grounded on quarterly detailed returns, which it will be the duty of the Inspector of Hospitals, or principal Medical Officer on the station, to transmit to the Secretary at War, founded on the Purveyor's and Regimental Surgeon's books, certified as to the correctness by himself, and by the Commanding Officer of Artillery, Engineers, or other superior Officer of the Ordnance, who will require regular reports from all stations within the Command, of the number of Sick in Hospital, or in Quarters, whereby he may check the returns.

These returns are to be minutely investigated, in the proper departments abroad, particularly in the Office of Accompts, and are to be further sanctioned and verified by the certificate of the Commander of the Forces on the station, by whom one set is to be transmitted to the Secretary at War, and another set by the principal Officer of the Medical department to the Surgeon General.

A Military Medical Staff will be sent out, by the Ordnance department, to the Windward and Leeward island station; each Surgeon and Assistant Surgeon will be furnished by that department, with the proper surgical instruments: one Surgeon, and one Assistant Surgeon, will be the Ordnance establishment at Barbadoes; and one Assistant Surgeon at each other island, or colony in that Command. A Surgeon and two Assistants will be stationed at Jamaica; a Surgeon and Assistant Surgeon at Quebec; and an Assistant, if necessary, at each station in British North America; one Surgeon and two Assistants will be stationed at Gibraltar; one Assistant Surgeon at Malta; a Surgeon and Assistant at Ceylon; and a Surgeon and Assistant at the Cape of Good Hope. Also in any other foreign possessions, which may eventually be captured, and where such Medical Assistance will be requisite. These Medical Officers of the Artillery will be in every respect subject to the Controul of the Inspector of Hospitals, or other Staff Officers, directing the Medical Concerns of the respective stations.

The

## *Medical Department.*

The aforesaid Ordnance Medical Officers will be chiefly occupied in attendance on the Sick of the Artillery in Hospitals, and in Out Quarters or Detachments, and on the Civil Officers of the Establishment, for whom they will be allowed to draw Medicines from the General Stores of the Army. They are, however, not to consider this attendance upon persons belonging to the Ordnance, their sole and exclusive duty; but they are hereby strictly enjoined to give assistance and attendance to all Sick Officers, Non-Commissioned Officers, and Soldiers, whether in or out of Hospitals; as the Medical Officers of the Line are enjoined to give mutual aid to the Ordnance department, whenever required so to do.

Each Medical Officer of the Ordnance will make his usual return to the superior Officers of his own department, as well Military, as Medical, according to the orders he may from time to time receive through the Chief of the Medical department on the station.

By order of His Royal Highness,
The Commander in Chief.

HARRY CALVERT,
Adjutant General of the Forces.

*Circular to the Colonels of Cavalry Regiments, respecting the Appointment of Veterinary Surgeons.*

*War Office, 24th May,* 1796.

SIR,

His Majesty having approved of the plan suggested by a Board of General Officers assembled to take into consideration (among other matters) the means of improving the present practice of Farriery in the Corps of Cavalry; I have the honor to acquaint you that agreeably to the said plan, His Majesty has been pleased to order, that a person properly educated at, and having received a certificate from the Medical Committee of the Veterinary College shall be attached to each Regiment, under the name of Veterinary Surgeon; that he shall be appointed by warrant from the Colonel, after being attested to serve in the Army in the capacity aforementioned for such limited period as shall be agreed upon, not less than seven years; and that, during the continuance of his service, he shall have exactly the same pay as a Quarter Master of Cavalry, viz. 5s. 6d. per diem.

As however, the College cannot at present furnish the whole number of Veterinary Surgeons requisite for the Cavalry, each Regiment not so supplied is permitted to send a student to the College, to be instructed in the Veterinary Science, for whose maintenance and education, half of the above pay will be allowed; the name of such student to be inserted at the foot of the Monthly Returns of each Regiment; and his allowance to be charged in the contingent half yearly accompts, accompanied by a Certificate from the Colonel or Commanding Officer, and the professor of the Veterinary College, of his attendance on his studies, during the period for which the allowance is charged.

The Students previously to their admission to the College, are to be attested to serve in the Army as above mentioned, for any period not under seven years, to be reckoned from the day of their commencing the duty of Veterinary Surgeons in the Regiments to which they shall be respectively attached; and from the date of their attestations, both the Surgeons and Students are to be considered as liable to be tried and punished by a General Court Martial for disobedience of Orders, or any other offence against the Established Rules of Military Discipline.

It will rest with his Royal Highness the Duke of York, to determine to which Regiments the Pupils who are now stated to have nearly completed their education at the College shall be assigned: should your's not be of the number, you will be pleased to apply to Mr. Coleman, the Professor, as well in regard to the admission of a Student for its future service, as for any other information which you may wish to obtain upon the nature of the Institution.

I have, &c.

W. WINDHAM.

N. B. The plan detailed in the above Letter was departed from in the sequel:—see the following page.

*Second*

*Second Circular to Colonels of Cavalry Regiments, relative to the Appointment of Veterinary Surgeons.*

*War Office, 21st Sept. 1796.*

SIR,

UPON attempting to carry into effect the plan stated in my Circular Letter of the 24th May last, for supplying the Cavalry with Veterinary Surgeons, it has appeared that much difficulty and delay must unavoidably occur in finding proper persons to go through a regular course of studies for that purpose at the College, under the engagements prescribed in the plan, without any certainty of their future services in the Army proving adequate to the expences bestowed by the public on their education; whereas, by appropriating the sum which had been intended for the education of the pupils during three years, to an encrease of the daily pay of the Surgeons, and by putting the institution itself upon a more respectable footing than had been originally proposed; it is to be hoped that a sufficient number of persons already well educated in Surgery, and who if not now conversant in the Veterinary Art, may be able in a very moderate space of time to qualify themselves for the practice of it, will be immediately induced to turn their views to the obtaining these appointments in His Majesty's Service.

From these considerations, His Majesty has been pleased to order, that laying aside the idea of charging the public with any expence for their education, the Veterinary Surgeons shall have the pay of seven shillings per diem, (six shillings to be issued as subsistence, and one shilling as arrears) and that they shall receive their appointments by commission under His Royal Sign Manual.

Instruments and Medicines will be supplied to them (free of cost) by the principal Veterinary Surgeon, who will have an allowance of three shillings a year for each horse for providing the same, which allowance is to be paid monthly, by the Regimental Agent, according to a return to be sent of the number of horses present with the Regiment, on the first of each month, including such horses belonging to the Commissioned and Warrant Officers as are *bonâ fide* kept at quarters for Military Service, the same to be signed by the

Commanding Officer, and by the Veterinary Surgeon. The amount of this charge for the horses of the non commissioned officers and private men, is to be deducted from the Fund for Farriery, and the allowance for those of the Commissioned Officers is to be charged against their respective accounts. The Veterinary Surgeons (in addition to the returns required by their Colonels and Commanding Officers) are regularly to send such reports as the Principal Surgeon may think necessary, relative to the state of the horses under their care, the expenditure of their stores, and the nature and success of their practice.

That there may be no question as to the good quality of the medicines furnished by the Principal Veterinary Surgeon, it is stipulated, that they shall be constantly purchased at Apothecaries Hall, but in order to guard against the improper expenditure of them, it is His Majesty's express order, that the Veterinary Surgeons shall be restrained from private practice of every kind; and His Majesty expects the Colonels and Commanding Officers to be particularly careful in preventing any the smallest deviation from this order.

I have to add, that Mr. E. Coleman, Professor of the Veterinary College, is appointed by His Majesty to be Principal Veterinary Surgeon to the Cavalry, with an allowance of ten shillings per diem, and that he has been desired to use his utmost exertions to procure persons qualified to serve as Veterinary Surgeons in the respective Corps of Cavalry, whose names, accompanied with a certificate of their competency, signed by himself and two of the examining committee of the College, he is from time to time to transmit to the Colonels of the Corps not yet provided, in order that they may be recommended in the usual course to commissions.

As some time will, however, unavoidably elapse before all the Regiments of Cavalry can be supplied with Veterinary Surgeons, Mr. Coleman has undertaken to furnish each Corps to which a Surgeon shall not have been appointed, with a Chest of Horse Medicines, ready prepared, with ample directions, describing the symptoms of common diseases, and pointing out the preparation adapted to each particular complaint.

The Chest is to be placed under the care of the Commanding Officer, who is to cause the Medicines to be administered by the Farriers according to the directions above referred to.

Pattern

Pattern Hoofs, shod according to the new principle, will also be sent with the Medicine Chest, in order that the Farriers may be able immediately to adopt the mode of Shoeing recommended by the Principal Veterinary Surgeon.

I have, &c.

W. WINDHAM.

P. S. Besides the pay allowed to the Veterinary Surgeon, he will have a further allowance of one shilling a day for the maintenance of his horse, which will be issued as subsistence; and he will be considered as entitled to extra feed for his horse, in the same manner as the other Commissioned Officers of the Regiment.

*Circular to Colonels of Regiments of Cavalry, relative to the supply of Horse Medicines, &c.*

*War Office, 26th May,* 1803.

SIR,

MR. COLEMAN, principal Veterinary Surgeon, having submitted for consideration certain Regulations respecting the conduct of the Farriers in the several Regiments of Cavalry in this country, which have been approved by His Royal Highness the Commander in Chief, I have the honor to acquaint you therewith, and to signify to you the King's Pleasure, that you do cause the said rules as undermentioned to be duly observed in the
Regiment of Dragoon         under your Command.

The Farriers at out-posts are to receive supplies of Medicines from the Veterinary Surgeon at Head Quarters, or where the distance is so considerable as to render a regular supply in that mode difficult or impracticable, the Medicines will be sent from the Principal Veterinary Surgeon upon the application of the Farriers through the Regimental Veterinary Surgeon. But as it may sometimes happen that the Drugs will be consumed before a fresh supply can be received, the Farriers under these circumstances may purchase simple Medicines on the spot, but they are not to purchase compounded, useless, or obsolete Medicines, or any other articles than the following, viz. *Spirits of Turpentine, Soft Soap, Cape or Hepatic Aloes, Calomel, Cantharides, Euphorbium, Corrosive-Sublimate, Nitre, Sulphur, Antimony, Tartar-Emetic, Extract of Lead, Opium, Arsenic, Blue Vitriol, Fox-Glove, Allum, White-Vitriol, Common-Turpentine, Tar, Vitriolic-Acid, Tow, Rosin, Common-Oil, Common Ointment* for Blisters, or *Lard, Bole-Ammoniac,* and *Linseed-Meal.*

The above Medicines, &c. are of course only to be purchased between the periods of sending the requisition and receiving the supply of Drugs either from Head Quarters, or from the Principal Veterinary Surgeon.

The bills for proper Medicines so purchased are to be examined and checked by the Regimental Veterinary Surgeon, and certified by the Commanding Officer, and sent to the Principal Veterinary Surgeon, who will pay the amount unless it be made to appear that the charges are immoderate.

I am

I am further to acquaint you that in consequence of a representation from Mr. *Coleman*, of the expences to which the Veterinary Surgeons are subjected when ordered to attend Horses at distant out-posts, an allowance of sixpence per mile both in going and returning, will be granted in aid of those expences, to commence from the 25th of last month, in all cases where the distance of the out-posts shall exceed twenty-five miles from the Head Quarters of the Regiment, upon the charge being vouched by a special certificate from the Commanding Officer.

It appearing that the rule under which the expence for the carriage of Horse Medicines has been allowed is not generally understood, I am to explain to you that the charge on this head will be admitted for the Medicines sent by the Principal Veterinary Surgeon to the Head Quarters of the Regiment, or to the Out-posts in the cases mentioned in the preceding Regulation, but that no expence is to be brought against the public for the conveyance of the Medicines from one Division of the Regiment to another.

The charge for this service must be invariably supported by the receipts of the Carriers.

I have the honor to be, &c.<br>C. YORKE.

# SECTION VII.

## *REGIMENTAL*
## FIELD ALLOWANCES.

# SECTION VII.

## REGIMENTAL
## FIELD ALLOWANCES.

*Memorandum relative to the Field Allowances of Regiments serving in Great Britain, or embarking therefrom for Foreign Service.*

WHEN Regiments of *Infantry* encamp in Great Britain, an allowance of Baggage and Forage-money, at the Rates undermentioned, is usually ordered to be issued by Warrant, for the complete establishment of Officers, viz.

| REGIMENTAL APPOINTMENTS. | Rates of Baggage & Forage-money. |
|---|---|
| | *l. s. d.* |
| Colonel | 36 5 0 |
| Lieutenant Colonels, each | 30 0 0 |
| Majors, each | 25 0 0 |
| Captains | 20 0 0 |
| Lieutenants } each Ensigns | 12 10 0 |
| Paymaster } each Adjutant | 20 0 0 |
| Quarter-master | 12 10 0 |
| Surgeon | 20 0 0 |
| Assistant Surgeon, or Surgeon's Mate, each | 12 10 0 |

The

The Paymaster of Militia, being also a Subaltern Officer, does not receive the above allowance for each appointment, but only an allowance of 20*l.* in the whole. The same Rule applies to the Surgeon's Mate of Militia, when he is also a Subaltern.

---

When Regiments of Infantry embark from Great Britain for Foreign Stations, (the East Indies excepted) not having previously received Field Allowances in the same year, the like Allowances of Baggage and Forage Money, with the addition of 20*l.* per Company, and 10*l.* for the Surgeon, under the denomination of Bât-money, are ordered by Warrant, for the full establishment.

Regiments of Cavalry encamping in Great Britain are not entitled to Field Allowances.

When Regiments of Cavalry embark for Foreign Stations, (excepting as before, the East Indies) an allowance of Bât and baggage-money, amounting to 30*l.* per Troop, is ordered to be issued by Warrant, for the complete establishment of the Regiment. The Surgeon is also allowed 10*l.* as Bât-money.

---

Some of the General Principles by which the Issue and Distribution of Field Allowances are governed, are the following :—

1. The Allowances are never granted twice to a Corps within the same year.

2. They are issued into the Agent's hands, and are not to be charged in the Pay-master's Accompts; nor is it expected that the Pay-master should correspond with the War Office on the subject thereof.

3. When Field Allowances have been granted for the complete establishment of a Regiment, the Distribution of the same to individual Officers rests with the Commanding Officer; who in making such Distribution should be guided by *the custom of the Service*; consulting the Regimental Agent, when necessary.

4. After the Allowances are once granted for the Establishment

blishment of a Regiment, no further Allowance is issued for individual Officers subsequently appointed, or ordered to join.

---

The Issues of Field Allowances to the Troops *serving abroad* are regulated by the Generals commanding in the respective Stations; and do not *in any shape* come under the Cognizance of the War Office.

---

N. B. Last War, Regiments that had received the Full Allowance of Baggage and Forage Money, on taking the Field in Great Britain, for the first time, were allowed for the three following years of Home Encampment, *Forage Money only*, at the Rates after mentioned, in lieu of Baggage and Forage Money, viz.

| Ranks. | Rates of Forage Money. |
|---|---|
| | *l. s. d.* |
| Colonel | 27 10 0 |
| Lieutenant Colonel | 22 10 0 |
| Major | 17 10 0 |
| Captain and Staff classed as such Staff | 12 10 0 |
| Subalterns and other Staff | 8 8 0 |

This Reduction in the Rate of Allowance after the first Campaign, has not been made in the present War.

*Extract*

*Extract of a Circular from the Secretary at War to the Commanding Officers of Regiments in Great Britain, relative to the Mode of Foraging Bât Horses: dated War Office, 20th Sept. 1803.*

"I HAVE the honour to acquaint you, that the whole expence of Forage for the Bât Horses ordered to be provided by you for the Service of the Regiment under your command, is to be defrayed under the orders of the Commissary-General, as well when in Barracks and Quarters, as when in Camp; and that the Regimental Paymaster is to draw upon the Commissary-General on, or immediately after the 24th of each month, for the amount of the charges on this head.

It is to be clearly understood, that none of the above charges are to be inserted in the Regimental accompts; but, it being thought proper to grant an allowance of one penny per diem for each of the said horses for the expence of farriery, the amount thereof may be stated in the pay-lists, under the head of Contigencies, the same being supported by special certificates from the Commanding Officer, shewing that the horses were effective during the whole of the period for which the charges shall be made."

---

N. B. At present the number of Bât-horses maintained on home-service is only two per Regiment, one for carrying the Surgeon's medicines, and one for carrying the intrenching tools. The subjoined Extract of a Circular, dated the 11th June, 1804, prepared when a greater number of horses was allowed, will serve to shew the footing on which the two above-mentioned are maintained.—The Extract is taken from a Letter to the Infantry of the Line; but Letters to a similar effect were addressed to the Cavalry and Militia.

" The Bât-horses provided for the purpose of carrying camp kettles, the Surgeon's Medicine Chest, and the Paymaster's Public Papers, are to be considered as under the immediate care of the Captains, Surgeon, and Paymaster, respectively; who will be held responsible that the horses are, at all times, perfectly ready for service; and, in order to compensate for all the charges attending these Bât-horses, except their Forage) and for the expence of replacing them as hereafter mentioned, the said horses will, at the conclusion of the War, or whenever the original Orders for holding the Regiment in readiness to take the Field are superseded, be left to the disposal of the Captains, Surgeon, and Paymaster for the time being.

" Should

"Should the Regiment remain in this country, and be kept for more than four years in a state of readiness to take the field, new allowances will be granted at the beginning of the fifth year for providing Bàt-horses for the above services.

"The Regimental Bàt-horses allotted for the carriage of ammunition and intrenching tools, are of course to be under your superintendance as Commanding Officer; but may be placed more immediately under the care of the Quarter-master: the contingent expences of farriery, stable utensils, &c. attending their maintenance, as also the charge of replacing them, when absolutely necessary, will be borne by the Public, for whose benefit these horses are, in all cases, to be ultimately disposed of.

"Should your Regiment be ordered to embark for *Ireland*, for the Islands of *Guernsey* and *Jersey*, or for Foreign Service, the bàt-horses, and the baggage-horses of the Officers, will most probably be ordered to be left behind; and in that case, the Bàt-horses of the Captains, Surgeon, and Paymaster, will be at the disposal of the Public; unless three complete years shall then have elapsed from the time when the allowance for purchasing them was granted, in which case they may be sold for the benefit of the Captains, Surgeon, and Paymaster. The personal Bàt-horses of Officers will, of course, belong to the Officers.

"The usual allowance will be granted by the public for replacing the Bàt-horses, for carrying camp kettles, medicines, and the Paymaster's public papers, in cases where they shall be ordered to be shot for the glanders; or shall be lost in action, or taken by the enemy, under circumstances evidently not the fault of the Officers; in all other cases, they are to be replaced by the Officers in whose charge they are."

---

It was explained by a subsequent Circular, dated 4th October, 1804, that the Allowance of one penny a day per horse for Farriery, was not to be considered as discontinued; but to be charged in the Accompts as usual.

*Extract of a Circular Letter from the Secretary at War to the Commanding Officers of Regiments of Infantry, stationed in England and Wales, relative to the Ration of Forage for Bât Horses.*

"IN pursuance of Instructions from His Royal Highness the Commander in Chief, I have the honor to acquaint you, that the ration of Forage to be allowed to the *Bât Horses,* of the Regiment under your command, is not to exceed *six pounds of oats,* and *fourteen pounds of hay.*

"This rule is not however to apply to the *hay* furnished to the bât horses *billetted in quarters,* which is to be supplied in the same quantity as heretofore."

MEMORANDUM.—In the Circular to the Regiments in Scotland, the last of the above Paragraphs was omitted.

# SECTION VIII.

## CLOTHING AND APPOINTMENTS.

( 429 )

# SECTION VIII.

# CLOTHING

AND

# APPOINTMENTS.

*Warrant eſtabliſhing certain Regulations with reſpect to Clothing and Regimental Appointments, dated the 15th Auguſt, 1781.*

GEORGE R.

WHEREAS the General Officers of our Army, to whom we were pleaſed to refer the conſideration of ſome proper method for the preventing of diſputes between Colonels of Regiments and their predeceſſors, with reſpect to Clothing and Regimental Appointments, have, in their ſeveral Reports, bearing date the 19th of March, 1774, the 6th of February laſt, and the 22d of May laſt, ſubmitted to us ſundry Regulations to the effect hereunder mentioned; we, having thought fit to approve thereof, are pleaſed hereby to authorize and direct, that the ſame may be duly obſerved and put in execution, as follows.

That the Commanding Officer preſent with every Regiment of Horſe, Dragoons, and Infantry, together with the Officer next in ſeniority, not under the rank of Captain, do annually, between the 25th day of December, and the 25th day of January,

ary, make a strict inspection into the state and condition of the different Appointments and Accoutrements of the Regiment, and do cause to be drawn out an accurate State, under the several Heads, of such Accoutrements and Appointments as shall be wanting at that time; and likewise of such as will, in their opinion, be necessary to compleat the Regiment for service against the *review to be made of such Regiment by one of our General Officers in the ensuing spring, or as soon after as our service will permit; and that such State be entered in the Regimental Book.

That the Colonel do provide and send to the Regiment all such Accoutrements or Appointments, agreeable to the said State, early in the Spring; or, in the case of Regiments on Foreign Stations, as soon as the same may be practicable.

That the Commanding Officer do certify to the Reviewing General, what articles have been furnished by the Colonel, and delivered to the Regiment.

That the Reviewing General do mention in his Report to us, whether the several articles necessary for compleating the Regiment for service have been provided.

And that, besides the inspection and entry herein before directed to be made, with respect to the Accoutrements and Appointments necessary to compleat the Regiment to the next Review, a State be also drawn out at the same time, or as soon after as convenient may be, and in like manner entered in the Regimental Book, of such as, in the opinion of the like Inspecting Officers, may become liable to be cast before the expiration of the assignment.

And we hereby think proper to declare, agreeable to the humble recommendation of our said Board of General Officers, that it is our royal intention, that the necessary articles for compleating our Regiments for service having been provided agreeable to such respective States and Entries, the Colonel and his Representatives shall be exempted from any further Claim in respect of Accoutrements or Regimental Appointments during the period for which the Off-reckonings are assigned, and the same shall be conclusive, in case of a vacancy, as well against any demands which may be made by the succeeding Colonel, as otherwise.

---

* The General Officers serving on the Staff, and commanding in camps or districts, are considered as Reviewing Generals.

And

## Clothing and Appointments. 431

And whereas our said Board of General Officers have given their opinion, that if an annual supply shall be effectually made in the manner herein before specified, the Regulations now subsisting, and particularly those established by a Warrant of our Royal Grandfather, bearing date the 30th of May, 1736, which have been found, by late experience, to be not adapted to the present circumstances of our service, may, without detriment or hazard, be abrogated; and that it will be unnecessary to ascertain any stated periods for the providing of the usual different species of Appointments and Accoutrements; we do hereby revoke and annul the said Warrant,* and likewise such parts of any other Warrants now in force, as relate to the providing of Appointments and Accoutrements at stated periods.

[And as the 9th day of November, annually, is, according to the present Regulation, fixed for the viewing and sealing of patterns for the Clothing of our Army, from which Act the several Colonels become entitled to the assignment of their respective Off-reckonings; our will and pleasure further is, that with respect to Regiments raised previous to the 27th day of June, 1779, if it shall happen that our Clothing Board shall be prevented from meeting, or if by any means, other than by the Colonel's own default, proper patterns shall not have been exhibited on the 9th day of November in any year, the Colonel, or his Representatives, shall be permitted, upon exhibiting proper patterns, to make an assignment; and such assignment, when made, shall vest the like interest in the Colonel and his Representatives, and his or their Assigns, and they shall respectively be entitled to the benefit of the assigned Off-reckonings, in like manner as if the assignment had been actually made on the said 9th day of November.

And in regard to the Regiments raised since the 27th day of June, 1779, the commencement of whose Off-reckonings is regulated by the date of their respective establishments, our will and pleasure is, that patterns of their Clothing be exhibited, and the same being approved and sealed in the usual manner, that an assignment of their Off-reckonings be permitted to be made eight months before the respective times at which the New Clothing for such Regiments is to be delivered to the Soldiers, being the usual space of time allowed for the providing of Clothing for our Army in general; and we do hereby also allow to the Colonels of such Regiments, or their Representatives, the like privilege of assigning, and the benefit of the Off-reckonings, during the period for which the same might have been assigned from the respective days whereon they are authorized to exhibit patterns to the Clothing Board, notwithstanding the Board shall not have then met

---

* According to the Clothing Regulations of the 22d April, 1803, the Scale of Duration of Appointments, established by the Warrant above quoted, is still to be *held in view* so far as relates to the Cavalry. See page 448.

met to view and seal the said patterns, and unless the not exhibiting of proper patterns shall have proceeded from his or their own default.]*

Given at our Court at St. James's, this 15th day of August, 1781, and in the 21st year of our reign,

By His Majesty's Command.

C. JENKINSON.

---

\* These Orders are, in several particulars, rendered inapplicable to the present circumstances of the Army, by the alteration of the Clothing Period. See page 445.

## Clothing and Appointments.

*Regulation for the Clothing and Appointments of the Army, dated 22d April, 1803.*

## GEORGE R.

WHEREAS it hath been represented unto us by the Commander in Chief of our forces, and the General Officers composing, with him, our permanent Clothing Board, that certain alterations in the clothing of our army, and in the mode in which the soldiers' necessaries are at present supplied, would be attended with much benefit to the soldier and with advantage to our service; which alterations the Board have suggested, upon the principle, that the desirable objects in clothing a soldier, are, that the articles with which he is furnished shall be no more in number than his necessities require, but that each shall be durable, and unexceptionable of its kind; that the soldier shall receive them at ready money prices, purchased from the first hands, as far as circumstances will admit; and that the charges made for them shall not be complicated, but such as admit of being explained in the most simple and satisfactory manner: And whereas we, entirely approving of the suggestions of the Board, have thought fit to direct, that the existing regulations touching the clothing and appointments of our forces should be altered accordingly; and have moreover deemed it advisable, that the whole clothing regulations, as so amended, should be comprized in one warrant, and published for the guidance of our army: Our will and pleasure therefore is, that instead of our warrants severally bearing date the 23d April 1801, the 20th May 1801, and the 22d December 1802, this our warrant be considered as the sole standing regulation for our service, in regard to the species of clothing to be provided, and the claims of soldiers on account thereof; the provision of necessaries; the period of the delivery of clothing; the species and duration of Cavalry appointments; and the supply of great coats for the Infantry.

*Species*

## SPECIES OF CLOTHING TO BE PROVIDED, AND CLAIMS OF SOLDIERS ON ACCOUNT THEREOF.

### CAVALRY.

**I.** In a Regiment of Dragoon Guards or *Heavy* Dragoons, each Serjeant, Corporal, Trumpeter, and Private Man, shall have for clothing,

*Annually,*
One hat; and
One pair of gloves; and
*Once in every Two Years,*
One coat;
One waistcoat, and
One pair of breeches.

**II.** In a Regiment of *Light* Dragoons, each Serjeant, Corporal, Trumpeter, and Private Man, shall have for clothing,

*Annually,*
One pair of gloves:
*Once in every Two Years,*
One upper jacket,
One under jacket,
One flannel waistcoat, and
One pair of leather breeches;
*Once in every Three Years,*
One helmet; and
*Once in every Four Years,*
One watering cap.

The colour of the jacket for regiments serving in the East Indies is to be grey, instead of blue.

**III.** In our Royal Waggon Train, each Serjeant shall have for clothing,

A leather cap, laced with silver, to be supplied only when actually required; and

*Once in every Two Years,*
A blue jacket, with silver lace;
A blue waistcoat, with sleeves; and
A pair of blue plush breeches.

Each Corporal shall have for clothing,

A plain leather cap, to be supplied only when actually required; and

*Once*

## Clothing and Appointments.

*Once in every Two Years,*
A blue jacket, silver lace on cuff and collar;
A blue waistcoat, with sleeves: and
A pair of blue plush breeches.
Each Private shall have for clothing,
A plain leather cap, to be supplied only when actually required; and

*Once in every Two Years,*
A plain blue jacket;
A blue waistcoast, with sleeves; and
A pair of blue plush breeches.

Sealed patterns of all the above-mentioned articles are to be placed in the charge of the Inspectors of Army Clothing, who are hereby authorized to renew, from time to time, such of the patterns as are damaged or worn out; and the clothing is to be made up in strict conformity thereto. But it is not required that the leather breeches and gloves should be shewn to our Clothing Board at the biennial Exhibitions of Patterns, previous to the passing of Assignments.

## INFANTRY.

IV. It is represented by our Clothing Board, that the breeches furnished as regimental clothing are made of materials inferior in quality, and ill calculated to stand hard service, or long marches: that the annual delivery of a waistcoat front to Soldiers in Europe and North America, is attended with less comfort to the men, than the practice of delivering a complete waistcoat with sleeves, which has been adopted in the West Indies; and that, although a very great and acknowledged advantage is derived to the Service from the delivery of shoes under the inspection of the Clothing Board, yet that the arrangement in its present form is liable to objection in two points of view; inasmuch as, in the case of Regiments at home, the Colonels, not having the means of making prompt payment for the shoes which they supply, are under the necessity of delivering to their Regiments, an article of an inferior quality, to that which the men can themselves purchase at the same, perhaps at a lower, price, for their ready money; and as, in the case of Regiments abroad, the Colonels experience great difficulty, and, frequently, losses, in recovering from the Soldiers that portion of the cost of shoes, which, according to the Regulation hitherto in force, each individual is to repay to his Colonel.

In order, therefore, to remedy these evils, we are pleased to direct, that the Clothing of our Corps of Infantry shall in future consist of the articles undermentioned, viz.

V. In a Regiment of Foot Guards, each Serjeant shall have for clothing,

*Annually,*

A coat; the sleeves unlined;

A waistcoat with sleeves;

A pair of breeches, made of materials of the same quality as the coat and lined;

A pair of military shoes;

A pair of gaiters; and

A pair of buck or doe skin gloves:

*Once in every Two Years,*

A lackered felt cap, with a cockade, and feather or tuft:\*

Each Corporal, Drummer, and Private Man, shall have for clothing,

*Annually,*

A coat, the sleeves unlined;

A waistcoat, with sleeves of milled serge;

A pair of breeches; made of materials of the same quality as the coat;

A pair of military shoes;

A pair of gaiters; and

A pair of mitts: and

*Once in every Two Years,*

A cap as above.

VI. In a Regiment of Infantry of the Line serving in Europe, North America, or New South Wales, (Highland Corps excepted) each Serjeant shall have for clothing,

*Annually,*

A coat, the sleeves unlined;

A pair of breeches, made of materials of the same quality as the coat;

---

\* Respecting the use of Lacquered Felt Caps by the Infantry in general, see a subsequent Circular from the Adjutant-General, dated 20th October, 1806.

*Clothing and Appointments.*

A cloth waistcoat, lined, with sleeves of milled serge; and
A pair of military shoes; and
*Once in every Two Years,*
A cap, as above:
Each Corporal, Drummer, and Private Man, shall have for clothing,
*Annually,*
A coat, the sleeves unlined;
A pair of breeches, made of materials of the same quality as the coat;
A kersey waistcoat, with serge sleeves, and
A pair of military shoes: and
*Once in every Two Years,*
A cap, as above.

VII. In a Highland Corps on the above stations, each Serjeant shall have for clothing,
*Annually,*
A jacket, the sleeves unlined;
A cloth waistcoat, with serge sleeves; and
A pair of military shoes:
The Colonel is also to be at the charge of Highland appointments, viz. bonnet, feathers, plaid, and purse.

Each Corporal, Drummer, and Private Man, shall have for clothing,
*Annually,*
A jacket, the sleeves unlined;
A kersey waistcoat, with serge sleeves; and
A pair of military shoes:
The Colonel is also to be at the charge of Highland appointments, viz. bonnet, feathers, plaid, and purse.

VIII. In a Regiment of Infantry serving in the West Indies, (except the 5th Battalion of our 60th Regiment, and the Regiments composed of People of Colour) each Serjeant shall have for clothing,
*Annually,*
A coat, partly lined;
A serge waistcoat, with sleeves;
Two pair of Russia linen trowsers;
A pair of flannel drawers: and
A pair of military shoes; and
*Once in every Two Years,*
A cap, as above.

Each

Each Corporal, Drummer, and Private Man, shall have for clothing,

*Annually,*

A coat, partly lined;
A serge waistcoat, with sleeves; with cuff and collar the colour of the facing of the Regiment;
A pair of Russia linen trowsers;
A pair of military shoes: and
A foraging cap; and

*Once in every Two Years,*

A lackered felt cap, &c. as above;

IX. In the 5th Battalion of the 60th Regiment, and the 95th Regiment of Foot, (or Rifle Corps,) each Serjeant shall have for clothing,

*Annually,*

A jacket, the sleeves unlined:
A waistcoat, with serge sleeves;
A pair of pantaloons; and
A pair of military shoes; and

*Once in every Two Years,*

A cap, as above;

Each Corporal, Drummer, and Private Man, shall have for clothing,

*Annually,*

A jacket lined, but not laced; the sleeves unlined;
A kersey waistcoat, with serge sleeves;
A pair of blue pantaloons, made of cloth of the same quality as the jacket; and
A pair of military shoes; and

*Once in every Two years,*

A cap, as above;

The men are to be stopped the extraordinary charge of two shillings and threepence on this clothing, in consequence of receiving *pantaloons* instead of *breeches.*

X. In the Regiments composed of People of Colour, serving in the West Indies, each Serjeant shall have for clothing,

*Annually,*

A jacket, the sleeves unlined;
A serge waistcoat, with sleeves:
Two pair of Russia linen trowsers; and
A pair of military shoes; and

*Once*

## Clothing and Appointments.

*Once in every Two Years,*

A cap, as above; and

A grey great coat, of the same quality as now worn, but distinguished from the Privates' great coats, by cuffs, collar, and buttons, of Serjeant's quality, conformably to the facings, &c. of the Regiment.

Serjeants being Europeans shall also have one pair of flannel drawers annually.

Each Corporal, Drummer, and Private Man, shall have for clothing,

*Annually,*

A round jacket, partly lined;
Two pair of Russia linen trowsers; and
A pair of military shoes; and

*Once in every Two Years,*

A cap, as above; and
A grey great coat.

XI. In a Regiment of Infantry serving in the East Indies, each Serjeant shall have for clothing,

*Annually,*

A coat, partly lined; and
Two pair of military shoes; and

*Once in every Two Years,*

A cap, as above:

In lieu of other articles, clothing adapted to the climate is to be supplied at the discretion of the Commanding Officer, to the amount of Eighteen Shillings and Eight Pence per annum; which will become an annual charge against the Colonel.

Each Corporal, Drummer, and Private Man, shall have for clothing,

*Annually,*

A coat, partly lined; and
Two pair of military shoes; and

*Once in every Two Years,*

A cap, as above:

In lieu of other articles, clothing adapted to the climate is to be supplied, at the discretion of the Commanding Officer, to the amount of Six Shillings and Seven Pence Halfpenny per annum; which will become an annual charge against the Colonel.

Certificates that articles to the amount above-stated, have actually been delivered, to the Serjeants, Corporals, Drummers,

mers, and Privates, respectively, of Regiments in the East Indies, are to be signed by the respective Commanding Officers, and to be transmitted half-yearly, through the Adjutant General, to our Clothing Board, care being taken to provide against accidents, by sending a duplicate of each certificate by a subsequent opportunity.

Highland Corps serving in the East Indies, are to discontinue, while serving there, the Highland appointments.

XII. In our Staff Corps, each Serjeant, Corporal, Drummer, and Private Man, shall have for clothing,

*Annually,*

A coat;
A waistcoat, or waistcoat front;
A pair of blue cloth pantaloons; and
A pair of half-boots; and

*Once in every Two Years,*

A cap as above;

And further, in consideration of the laborious nature of their Service, each Serjeant, Corporal, Drummer, and Private Man, shall have,

*Annually,*

A Russia Duck waistcoat, with sleeves, and a pair of Russia Duck pantaloons.

Sealed Patterns of all the above-mentioned articles of clothing are to be placed in the charge of the Inspectors of Army Clothing, who are hereby authorized to renew from time to time such of the Patterns as are damaged or worn out, and the clothing is to be made up in strict conformity thereto.

XIII. And whereas we have been pleased to order, that the whole clothing of our army should be viewed by two permanent Inspectors of Clothing, instead of being viewed, as heretofore, by a General Officer of the Clothing Board; and have appointed Two Inspectors of Clothing accordingly: We do hereby authorize and direct the said Inspectors, or the Inspectors for the time being, to view, and compare with the Sealed Patterns, the clothing of our several Regiments of Cavalry and Infantry, as soon as the same shall have been prepared by the respective Clothiers; and if the said clothing appear to be conformable to the Sealed Patterns, to grant two Certificates of their view and approval thereof; one of which Certificates is to be delivered to the Clothier, to be sent with the clothing to the Head Quarters of the Corps,

and

## Clothing and Appointments.

and the other to be lodged with our Clothing Board, as the necessary voucher for passing the assignment of the allowance for the said clothing.

It is our further will and pleasure, that the clothing be viewed, and Certificates be signed by both the Inspectors; except in cases where the absence of one of them shall be unavoidable: in all which cases, the cause of such absence is to be stated by the other Inspector, in his Certificate of the view of the clothing.

The Inspectors shall follow such further instructions as they may from time to time receive from the Commander in Chief of our Forces, our Secretary at War, or our Clothing Board.

XIV. Sealed Patterns of the Clothing shall in future be sent to, and remain deposited at the Head Quarters of every Corps, whether abroad or at home; in order that the new clothing may be compared therewith, at any convenient time, by the General Officers commanding on the respective stations abroad, and in the several Districts at home; or by the Officers who may be appointed to inspect the said clothing: And Certificates of the conformity thereof to the sealed Patterns, and of the same having been delivered in due time to the men, shall be in future transmitted by such General, or other officers, as aforesaid, through the Adjutant General, to our Clothing Board. And to obviate any inconveniencies that might otherwise arise from the want of such view of the clothing being taken at an early period, it is hereby directed, that in each Regiment abroad, or at home, the Commanding Officer present with the Corps when the clothing is received, together with the two Officers next in seniority, not under the rank of Captain, do immediately on its arrival make a strict inspection into the same, and do cause to be drawn out an accurate state of the quality, quantity, and condition, thereof; which state he shall transmit, through the Adjutant General of our Forces, to our Clothing Board: And it is our pleasure, that such state shall be entered in the Regimental Books, for the future inspection of such superior Officer, as may be ordered from time to time to inspect or review the Regiment.

XV. The clothing of Regiments on foreign stations is not to be furnished in materials, but is to be sent out made up; except in instances where we shall be pleased to grant a special

cial dispensation through our Commander in Chief, or Secretary at War.

XVI. And whereas it appears highly expedient, that an uniform rule thould be laid down, in regard to the claims of Soldiers to clothing, at stated times, or broken periods; and to the rates at which compensation shall be made in such cases as shall admit of payment in money, in lieu of the articles in kind, under the restrictions herein after mentioned: We do hereby declare, and make known, that Non-commissioned Officers and Soldiers, dying, or discharged, before the completion of the period for which the clothing is assigned to last, reckoned from the usual day of delivering the same, have no demand whatever on account thereof.

If a Serjeant is reduced to the ranks, his clothing is to be given in for the use of his successor; and he himself will receive Privates' clothing, equally worn (or as nearly as may be) with the clothing he has given in.

A Recruit who comes into the Regiment after the proper time of the delivery of the clothing (if not raised for an augmentation, in which case he is to be furnished with new clothing, complete, as hereinafter directed) shall be immediately entitled to clothing as good as that in wear by the rest of the Regiment: and he shall be entitled to new clothing at the next period of general delivery to the Regiment.

XVII. It is the duty of the Colonels, and of those employed by them, to take especial care that the clothing be forwarded and delivered to their respective corps at the exact period when it is due; and few cases ought to arise, in which it should become a question whether an allowance in money might not be substituted by the Colonels, in lieu of delivering in kind the articles which by our Regulations they are required to furnish: but if from any extraordinary circumstances of the Service, such an instance should be supposed to have occurred in any of our Regiments, or detachments of Regiments, serving abroad, the ground on which a commutation of money is proposed, shall be fully stated to the Commander in Chief of our Forces, or (when there is no Commander in Chief) to our Secretary at War; in order that our Pleasure may be previously taken thereupon.

If we should think proper to signify our approbation of the measure, the following sums, being the estimated amount

of

## Clothing and Appointments. 443

of what the Colonels would have paid to their Clothiers, after a reasonable deduction for incidental charges to which they are liable, shall be given to the Men:

*In the Dragoon Guards and Dragoons.*

| To each Serjeant, in lieu of | *l.* | *s.* | *d.* |
|---|---|---|---|
| Coat } Waistcoat } Breeches } | 5 | 12 | 0 |
| 2 Hats } 2 Pair of Gloves } | 0 | 12 | 0 |
| | 6 | 4 | 0 |

| To each Corporal, Trumpeter, and Private, in lieu of | *l.* | *s.* | *d.* |
|---|---|---|---|
| Coat } Waistcoat } Breeches } | 3 | 0 | 0 |
| 2 Hats } 2 Pair of Gloves } | 0 | 9 | 0 |
| | 3 | 9 | 0 |

Although some of the articles of clothing above specified belong exclusively to the Dragoon Guards and *Heavy* Dragoons, it is to be understood, that the total rate of compensation applies equally to the *Light* Dragoons.

*In the Infantry.*

To each Serjeant, in lieu of clothing complete, 3*l.* 12*s.*

To each Corporal, Drummer and Private, in lieu of clothing complete, 1*l.* 16*s.* 6*d.**

PROVISION OF NECESSARIES.

XVIII. Whereas by our Warrant of the 25th of May 1797, for encreasing and regulating the pay and allowance of Noncommissioned Officers and Private Men of Corps of Cavalry and Infantry respectively, serving at home, we therein ordered, that a sum not exceeding, in the Dragoon Guards and Dragoons, Two Shillings and Seven Pence Halfpenny per week, and in the Infantry of the Line, One Shilling and Sixpence per week, for Necessaries, should be retained from the

---

* The Rates of Compensation to Serjeants, Corporals, Drummers, and Privates of Infantry, above specified, were altered by His Majesty's Warrant of the 15th April, 1805. See Page 469.

Pay of Soldiers; and whereas Lists of the Necessaries to be provided out of the said stoppages, were by our order annexed to our Clothing Regulations of the 20th May 1801, and 22d December 1802; which Lists now require alteration; we are pleased in lieu thereof to cause Schedules to be annexed to this our warrant, containing a specification of the articles, both of Clothing and Necessaries, with which a Soldier, serving at home, is to be provided, and in which he is to be kept at all times complete: and we do hereby also authorize the like stoppage of One Shilling and Sixpence a week, for Necessaries of the same description, from the Pay of Soldiers of Infantry serving in any part of Europe, or North America.

It is expected that all the Articles of Necessaries specified in the said Schedules can be furnished of unexceptionable materials, and be kept in complete repair, by the stoppages above-mentioned; but in particular instances where the same shall not be found adequate, a Regimental Court of Enquiry, or Court Martial, as the circumstances of the case may require, is to be convened, for the purpose of authorizing such further stoppage as may be judged expedient. And it is our express will and pleasure, that no further stoppage for Necessaries be made from the Pay of Soldiers serving at home, or in any part of Europe or North America, without the sanction of such Regimental Court of Enquiry, or Court Martial.

We are further pleased hereby to authorize the like stoppage of One Shilling and Sixpence a week, for necessaries, from the Pay of Soldiers of Infantry serving in the West Indies; to be expended on articles suitable to that station.

XIX. The prices of the Articles mentioned in the said Schedules of necessaries are now purposely omitted, as liable to variation in a certain degree from temporary or local circumstances; but we do expect, that every Officer in the command of a Regiment, and every Captain or other Officer commanding a Troop or Company, will feel it to be a most important part of his duty to take care that all articles are purchased for the Soldiers, on the most advantageous terms, and at ready money prices; and that they are delivered to the men at prime cost, without any other extra charge than what, on some occasions, may unavoidably be incurred for carriage, and, when Regiments are on foreign stations, for freight and insurance.

*Clothing and Appointments.*

If * ~~in the course of the year~~ any of the articles specified in the said Schedules should not be wanted for the Soldier's use, the money stopped for such articles shall be repaid him.

We do further think proper to declare, that without derogating in any degree from the general controul and responsibility of the Commanding Officers of Regiments, both in the Cavalry and Infantry, or precluding them from directing the purchase of Articles agreeably to our Regulations, and charging the same to the different Troops and Companies, whenever it evidently tends to the benefit of the Soldier, it is, nevertheless, to the Captains or Commanding Officers of Troops and Companies, that we do more immediately look for the due and punctual execution of our Royal Intentions, in what regards the care of the clothing, and the provision and care of the necessaries, of the Men of their respective troops and companies. And the Captains, or Commanding Officers of troops or companies, are accordingly hereby made responsible, that the necessaries provided for their men be of a fit and proper quality; that their complement be at all times complete; and, above all, that such purchases as are necessary be made in the manner most likely to leave no cause of complaint to the Soldier.

The Captains, or Commanding Officers of troops and companies, are also responsible that the persons furnishing the articles be settled with regularly and punctually, as the stoppages accrue.

PERIOD OF DELIVERY OF CLOTHING.

XX. Whereas by our warrants of the 23d April 1801, and the 22d December 1802, we were pleased to establish a precise period for the delivery of clothing to our regiments of Dragoon Guards and Dragoons, Foot Guards, and Infantry of the Line, and to regulate the assignments of the clothing allowance in conformity thereto: And whereas we have since directed, that our Royal Regiment of Horse Guards should be subject to the provisions on the above heads, contained in our last mentioned warrant: we do hereby enjoin, that the special directions contained in our said warrants, in regard to the intermediate assignments to be made for periods terminating on the 24th December 1801, and 1803, respectively; to the amount of compensation to

---

* See the Circular, Page 470.

Soldiers for clothing during the said periods; and to the claims of Colonels arising from the alteration of the period of clothing, be in every respect duly attended to and fulfilled.

XXI. In further conformity to the provisions of our said warrants; it is our pleasure, that the 25th December 1803, shall be the day on which the next complete clothing of our Royal Regiment of Horse Guards, and of our Regiments of Dragoon Guards and Dragoons, Foot Guards, and Infantry of the Line, shall be considered to be due; and upon the said day, or as near thereto as possible, the same shall actually be delivered to the men of our said corps, wherever stationed: In subsequent years also, the 25th day of December shall be the date of delivering the articles of clothing for our said forces, as the said articles become due respectively, according to the periods assigned for their duration.

XXII. In order to correspond with the period of delivery, the next assignments of the allowance for the clothing of our said corps, extending for two years in the Cavalry, and for one year in the Infantry, shall commence on the 25th December 1803: and the future annual or biennial assignments shall in like manner commence on the 25th December in succeeding years.

XXIII. The 25th of this instant April shall be the day upon which the then Colonels of our said corps shall be entitled to make an assignment for the period commencing the 25th December 1803, and on which they and their representatives shall have a vested interest therein. In future years also, the 25th of April preceding the commencement of the New Assignment, shall be the day on which the Colonels' title to such assignment shall become a vested interest.

XXIV. Whenever augmentations to existing corps, or new levies, are placed on the establishment, the like allowance as heretofore, of twenty-four months off-reckonings in the Cavalry, and twenty months off-reckonings in the Infantry, shall be made to the Colonel or Commandant; the proportion accruing between the date of the commencement of the augmentation, or new levy, on the establishment, and the next general clothing period, being uniformly granted under an assignment, and the remainder issued in money.

XXV. Every man raised for such augmentation, or new levy, shall, upon being finally approved, be furnished with complete new clothing: and at the commencement of the

next

*Clothing and Appointments.* 447

next assignment of the clothing allowance for the whole corps, every man, without regard to the period at which he may have received his first clothing, shall become entitled to, and be supplied with, another complete clothing; with the exception of such articles only, as, in the Infantry, are appointed to last more than one year, and in the Cavalry more than two years.

SPECIES AND DURATION OF CAVALRY APPOINTMENTS.

XXVI. The Appointments to be furnished to the Cavalry, exclusive of clothing and necessaries, shall consist of the undermentioned articles; which are to be provided in strict conformity to patterns lodged in the charge of the Inspectors of Army Clothing.

*To the Dragoon Guards and Heavy Dragoons.*

Boots shod with iron, and nails at the toe.
Cloaks with Sleeves.

Sadlery.
- Saddle with pannel and pad in one—A web-girth, with six roller buckles—pair of strap flaps.
- Martingale, breast plate, with roller buckles.
- Leather surcingles, with roller buckles.
- Pair of stirrup leathers, with roller buckles.
- Pair of stirrup irons.
- Bit and bridoon complete, with head reins and nose band.
- Pair of double forage straps ⎫
-     Single ditto.             ⎪
- Pair of cloak straps          ⎬ With roller buckles.
-     Single ditto              ⎪
- Firelock strap                ⎪
- Pair of holster straps        ⎪
- Holster and shoe case         ⎭
- Carbine bucket, with picket ring.
- Carbine bucket strap.
- Cover for holsters.
- Leather cloak cover.
- Horse collar with iron chain.

Buf

**Buff Accoutrements.**
- Pouch curved for thirty rounds.
- Pocket behind ditto.
- Roller buckles.
- Carbine belt, 3 inches wide.
- Buckles with two brass tongues and tip.
- Pair of straps for the pouch to hang by.
- Brass slider and swivel.
- Sword waist belt, 2 inches wide.
- Brass plate and slide with a bar and double tongue.
- Bayonet frog with buff leather.
- Sword knot of buff leather.

### *To the Light Dragoons.*

Cloak with sleeves.
Boots.
Saddlery.—Saddle complete, as for the Dragoon Guards, and Heavy Dragoons.

**Buff Accoutrements.**
- Pouch curved for thirty rounds.
- Pocket behind ditto.
- Roller buckles.
- Carbine belt $2\frac{1}{2}$ inches wide.
- Buckles with two brass tongues and tip.
- Pair of straps for the pouch to hang by.
- Brass slider and swivel.
- Sword waist belt $1\frac{1}{4}$ inch wide.
- Sword carriage.
- Bayonet frog, of buff leather.
- Sword knot, of buff leather.

### *To the Royal Waggon Train.*

Cloak; and
Boots.

XXVII. And whereas, upon the Report and Representation of our Board of General Officers, we were pleased, by our warrant bearing date the 15th August 1781, to annul the Regulation, dated the 20th May 1736, by which fixed periods of duration had been assigned for certain articles of Cavalry Appointments; as undermentioned, viz.

## Clothing and Appointments. 449

| Years of Duration. | Appointments. |
|---|---|
| 16 | Saddles. Holster pipes. Buckets. Stirrup leathers. Stirrup irons. |
| 12 | Bits. |
| 6 | Head Stalls. Reins. Breast plate. Cruppers. Girths. Surcingles. Straps. |
| 12 | Cloaks. |
| 6 | Boots. |
| 20 | Buff accoutrements. |

And whereas in process of time, great and unexpected inconvenience was found to arise in the service from the disuse of such rule of conduct; under a sense of which inconvenience the Board of General Officers of our Cavalry, who were assembled in the year 1796, to consider of means for the better regulation of the clothing and appointments of the Cavalry, did, in their report made to us, humbly remark, " That although it is the duty of a Colonel at all times to " keep his Regiment complete in its different appointments, " yet it ought still to be expected, that the several species " should last nearly the time prescribed by his late Majesty's " warrant in the year 1736," and did humbly recommend the revival of the said regulations " as tending greatly to " promote care and attention both in Officers and Men, and " to uphold an idea of what may be expected in the ordinary " course of home service." And whereas, since that time, the General Officers composing our permanent Clothing Board, sensible of the continuance and bad effects of the same inconvenience, have also humbly submitted unto us their opinion, that the revival of such a scale of duration as may reasonably be expected of Cavalry appointments, on home service, and as the Colonels may be enabled to comply with, would serve for a general guide in all future inspections, would assist much in checking negligence and abuse, and would restore that care, responsibility, and attention, of Officers and Men, for their appointments, which at all times, the service so essentially

sentially and necessarily demands, and without which, no expence whatever can, in the field, preserve troops in an effective state: we are therefore pleased to order, that, in conformity to the experience of past times, and to ensure that care and attention which our military service so essentially requires, the Regulation of 1736 above-recited, with regard to the expected duration of the before-mentioned appointments, shall be held in view in all annual inspections, and be acted upon, as far as possible, in relation to the care and regimental œconomy of appointments, during the ordinary course of home service: and as the duty of the Colonel demands that he should at all times keep his regiment complete in its different appointments, so is the most strict attention to their proper care and preservation required from Commanding and Troop Officers; which they are to enforce by every means in their power; and to cause individuals immediately to repair, or replace, such appointments, as are lost or materially damaged, by their neglect or mismanagement; or otherwise than in the fair course of service.

## SUPPLY OF GREAT COATS FOR THE INFANTRY.

XXVIII. And whereas by our warrant of the 23d April 1801, we were pleased to direct, that each man of our regiments of Foot Guards and Infantry of the Line (the regiments composed of people of Colour, in which great coats form a part of the clothing supplied by the Colonel, and corps serving in the East Indies, excepted) who was not then possessed of a great coat in good and serviceable condition, should forthwith be furnished with one, according to a pattern lodged in the Office of the Comptrollers of the Accompts of our army; and that great coats of the like species should be supplied to the rest of the men of our said regiments, as soon as the coats then in use became unserviceable: for which effect we were pleased to authorise the Colonels to provide at that time one complete set of great coats of an approved quality for the full numbers borne on the establishment of their respective regiments: It is now our pleasure, that the following regulations be observed in the future supply of the said article.

XXIX. The great coats provided as aforesaid, shall be renewed at the expiration of every three years from the time of their delivery, if necessary, (but not oftener) agreeably

to

*Clothing and Appointments.* 451

to certificates to be from time to time transmitted to our Secretary at War, specifying the number wanted, and the periods at which those required to be replaced were originally delivered to the men.

XXX. The expence of the future supplies of great coats shall be defrayed out of the fund established by our warrant above referred to, viz. an allowance from the Public (commencing from the 25th December 1801, and to be issued half yearly into the hands of the Regimental Agents) of Three Shillings per man, per annum, and, in the case of corps using Highland clothing, of four shillings per man per annum, for the full establishment of Non-commissioned Officers, Drummers, and Private Men, of each Regiment of Foot Guards and Infantry of the Line at home and abroad, (excepting, as above-mentioned, Regiments composed of People of Colour, and Corps serving in the East-Indies): and a contribution from the Colonels of the said Regiments, (commencing also from the 25th December 1801) in Corps using Highland clothing, of Ten Pence, and in other Corps, of One Shilling and Ten Pence per annum,* for every man included in their assignments, except warrant and contingent Men: which allowance and contribution are to be continued as before.

XXXI. The fund so arising in each Regiment shall be lodged in the hands of the Regimental Agent, subject to the care and management of the Commanding Officer (not being under the rank of a Field Officer) who is to be accountable to us for the proper expenditure of the same.

XXXII. With a view of preventing great coats from being prematurely worn out by abuse or neglect, we do hereby declare our pleasure, that they are to be considered as regimental appointments or necessaries: and that the Soldiers are liable to make good by stoppage from their pay, any loss or damage of the great coats (arising from misconduct) which may occur during the period of three years herein-before assigned for their duration.

XXXIII. As soon after the 24th of December in each year, as may be practicable, the Commanding Officer of each Regiment shall render to our Secretary at War an accompt, certified

---

* See the Circular, page 466, relative to a further Contribution on the part of the Colonel, towards the Cost of Great Coats for *Serjeants.*

upon

upon honor, of the produce of, and charges against, the Great Coat Fund of the Regiment under his command, within the preceding year, terminated on the above day: and we do enjoin and require the General Officers who shall from time to time review and inspect our Forces, particularly to notice in their Reports the state of the great coats in wear; adding such observations as they may think fit to make, respecting the attention which shall appear to have been paid to their preservation.

XXXIV. In order to be secure that the articles supplied shall be invariably of the quality and form best adapted for the use of our Army, it is our further pleasure, that patterns of the great coats shall be exhibited by the clothiers, and sealed by our Clothing Board at their Annual Meetings, each clothier being required to exhibit three pattern coats, agreeing in form and quality with the pattern deposited in the Comptrollers' Office, but made up of three several sizes, and (for distinction) to be numbered, 1, 2, 3; and that our Inspectors of Clothing shall examine the great coats, in like manner as the annual clothing, and observe that they are, in respect of material, form, and size, equal to the patterns sealed by our Clothing Board; as an accurate criterion of which, each coat is to be of the full weight of the sealed pattern, of the corresponding size. The view certificate of the Inspectors, and a certificate by the clothier, setting forth that "the material of all the coats is *Kersey wove*" are to accompany the bill of the clothier, as indispensable vouchers. Every successive supply of great coats is to contain an equal proportion of the three sizes; and our Inspectors of clothing, out of every parcel submitted to their inspection for any regiment, are to select and seal one coat of each size; which coats so sealed by the Inspectors are to be sent with the rest to the quarters of the regiment, where they will afford a standard for judging, whether the accompanying articles are of the proper quality and size.

XXXV. The Serjeants' great coats are in future to be of the same quality as now worn; but to be distinguished from the privates by cuffs, collar, and buttons, of Serjeants' quality, conformable to the facings, &c. of their respective regiments.

XXXVI. Finally, we do declare it to be our intention, that all Colonels, Commanding Officers, or other Officers, who shall direct, or knowingly permit, any alteration whatsoever

## Clothing and Appointments. 453

soever to be made in any part of the clothing or appointments, so that the same shall differ in the smallest degree from the patterns of the several articles sealed by our Clothing Board, and sent to the respective regiments; or shall allow any deviation from our existing Regulations for the clothing and appointments of our Forces, except in case of unavoidable necessity, which must always be especially reported for our information, shall be considered guilty of disobedience of orders, and be liable to such punishment for the same, as by a General Court Martial shall be awarded. And to prevent ignorance of these Regulations being pleaded in excuse of not having conformed thereto, it is our pleasure, that a copy of the same be inserted in the Orderly Book of every Regiment in our Service.

And for the due performance of the several matters herein before expressed, this shall be to the Pay-Master General of our Land Forces, to the General Officers of our Clothing Board, and to all others whom it doth or may concern, a sufficient warrant, authority, and direction.

Given at our Court at St. James's, this 22d day of April 1803, in the Forty-third year of our Reign.

By His Majesty's Command,

C. YORKE

*SCHEDULE*

## SCHEDULE, No. 1.

### CAVALRY.

List of Articles of Clothing and Necessaries with which a Soldier of Dragoon Guards or Dragoons is to be at all times provided, and in which he is to be kept complete, by sundry Articles furnished by the Colonel as expressed in the foregoing Regulations, and by the Stoppage of Two Shillings and Seven Pence Half Penny a week from his pay, sanctioned by the preceding warrant.

### ARTICLES OF CLOTHING.

*Dragoon Guards or Heavy Dragoons.*

Furnished in the first Instance by the Colonel:
- Annually — { 1 Hat
             { 1 Pair of gloves.
- Once in every Two Years — { 1 Coat
                            { 1 Waistcoat
                            { 1 Pair of breeches

*Light Dragoons.*

Furnished in the first Instance by the Colonel:
- Annually — 1 Pair of gloves
- Once in every Two Years — { 1 Upper jacket
                            { 1 Under jacket
                            { 1 Flannel waistcoat
                            { 1 Pair of leather breeches
- Once in every 3 Years - - - - 1 Helmet
- Once in every 4 Years - - - - 1 Watering cap.

ARTICLES

*Clothing and Appointments.* 455

### ARTICLES OF NECESSARIES.

Paid for by the Men.
- An extra pair of breeches of the same quality, and to be in wear with those furnished by the Colonel.
- A pair of breeches' slings;
- A stable jacket, trowsers and foraging cap;
- A nose bag, watering bridle and log;
- Three shirts;
- One night cap;
- One stock and clasps;
- Three pair of worsted stockings;
- One pair of long black gaiters;
- Two pair of shoes;
- One pair of shoe clasps;
- Three shoe brushes;
- Two combs, razor and soap;
- One clothes brush, worm and picker;
- Mane comb and spunge, curry comb and brush;
- Horse picker and scissars;
- Emery, oil, pipe clay, whiting, and blacking;
- Button stick and hook;
- Powder bag, powder and puff;
- Carbine lock case;
- A pair of saddle bags.

The actual expenditure for horse cloths, and surcingles, not exceeding One Shilling and Eight-pence per Annum for each man, will be defrayed by the Public, as expressed in the warrant for establishing a consolidated allowance at a daily rate for Soldiers of Cavalry and Infantry, bearing date the 1st of September 1795.*

---

* The Article of the Warrant referred to is as follows :—
" That the actual Expence of Horse Cloths and Surcingles for the Cavalry, not exceeding 1s. 8d. per Man annually, and the actual Expence of altering Clothing in the Infantry, not exceeding 2s. 6d. per Man, annually; be made extra Charges in the Public Accompts of the Regiments respectively, and annexed, with proper Certificates, to the Charge of Allowance for Clothing."

*SCHEDULE,*

## SCHEDULE, No. 2.

### INFANTRY.

List of Articles of Clothing and Necessaries with which a Soldier of Infantry of the Line, serving in Europe or North America, is to be at all times provided, and in which he is to be kept complete by sundry articles furnished by the Colonel, or at the expence of the Public, or by the Stoppage of One Shilling and Sixpence a week from his pay, sanctioned by the preceding warrant.

#### ARTICLES OF CLOTHING.

Furnished in the first Instance by the Colonel.
- One regimental cap, with cockade, and feather or tuft.
- One regimental coat.
- One waistcoat.
- One pair of breeches.
- One pair of shoes.

#### ARTICLES OF NECESSARIES.

Furnished in the first Instance at the Expence partly of the Colonel and partly of the Public. } One regimental great coat.

These Articles with oil, emery, and brick dust, are allowed for by the Public to the extent of 2s. 9d. per Annum, for effectives, in corps at home: on other stations they are paid for by the men ------- } Turnscrew, brush, and worm.

*Clothing and Appointments.*

Paid for by the Men.
{
One pair of shoes.
One pair of black cloth (long) gaiters.
Three shirts.
Three pair of worsted or yarn socks.
Worsted or yarn mitts during the winter.
One black stock.
One foraging cap.
One knapsack.
One clothes brush.
Three shoe brushes.
Black ball.
Hair ribbon and leather.
Two combs.
Straps for carrying the great coat.
}

## MEMORANDUM.

The breeches, and any other articles of clothing or necessaries, which it may be requisite to *replace* from the Soldiers' stoppages, are to be made exactly of the same material and pattern as those originally furnished by the Colonel.

All Soldiers' shoes are to be made in conformity to the shoes furnished by the Colonel, according to the patterns approved by the Clothing Board and sealed by the Inspectors of Clothing.

It is recommended as a matter of œconomy, that the shirts furnished to Soldiers should hereafter be of a rather better quality than those which were supplied when the price was limited to Five Shillings and Sixpence.

In Highland Regiments, and other Corps authorized by the foregoing warrant to wear *Clothing* of a description different from that of the Army in general, the articles of such peculiar *Clothing* are to be substituted for those specified in the above list.

In Corps that wear *Pantaloons*, short black gaiters are to be provided as Necessaries, instead of long black gaiters.

In Highland corps, hose are to be provided as necessaries, instead of gaiters as above.

In Regiments serving in the West Indies, in lieu of cloth gaiters, and breeches, a pair of flannel drawers, and a second pair of Russia linen trowsers, are to be substituted.

---

In corps serving at home, the actual expenditure for altering clothing, not exceeding Two Shillings and Sixpence per Annum, each man, will be defrayed by the Public, as expressed in the warrant for establishing a consolidated allowance at a daily rate, for Soldiers of Cavalry and Infantry, bearing date the 1st September 1795.*

---

* See page 455.

## Clothing and Appointments.

*Regulation for the Clothing of the Embodied Militia: dated 8th August,* 1803.

## GEORGE R.

WHEREAS by our Warrant, bearing date the 22nd April, 1803, we have been pleased to establish certain new Regulations in regard to the clothing and necessaries of our Regiments of the Line: and whereas we think it for the good of our service to extend the like Regulations to our Militia forces, so far as the same are applicable thereto: our will and pleasure therefore is, that from and after the 25th December next, our Warrant for regulating the clothing and half mounting of the embodied Militia, dated the 26th June, 1801, shall cease to be in force; and that, in lieu thereof, this our Warrant, shall be considered as the standing Regulation for our Regiments, Battalions, Corps, and Independent Companies of Militia, when embodied.

I. Each Serjeant shall have for clothing,

### Annually,

A coat, the sleeves unlined;
A pair of breeches, made of materials of the same quality as the coat;
A cloth waistcoat, lined, with sleeves of milled serge; and
One pair of military shoes: and

### Once in every Two Years,

A lackered felt cap, with a cockade, and feather, or tuft.

Each Corporal, Drummer, and Private Man, shall have for clothing,

### Annually,

A coat, the sleeves unlined;
A pair of breeches, made of materials of the same quality as the coat;
A kersey waistcoat, with sleeves of milled serge; and
One pair of military shoes: and

Once

*Once in every Two Years.*

A cap, as above.

Each of the above-mentioned articles of clothing is to be made up in strict conformity to the pattern approved by us, and lodged in the charge of our Inspectors of Army Clothing.

II. Previously to the preparation of the annual clothing of each Corps, two pattern suits thereof shall be exhibited, on the part of the Commandant, to our Clothing Board; who, if they approve the same, will cause their seal to be affixed thereto: one of the pattern suits so sealed shall remain deposited in the Office of the Adjutant General of our forces: and the duplicate pattern suit shall be sent to, and remain deposited at, the head quarters of each Corps: in order that the new clothing may be compared therewith at any convenient time, according as the same shall be ordered by the General Officers commanding in the several districts: and certificates of the conformity of the new clothing to the sealed pattern, and of the same having been delivered in due time to the men, shall be in future transmitted by the said General Officers, through the Adjutant General, to our Clothing Board, and duplicates thereof to our Secretary at War, as necessary vouchers for the due passing of the accompts of such clothing. And to obviate any inconvenience that might otherwise arise from the want of such view of the clothing being taken, under the orders of a General Officer, at an early period, it is hereby directed, that, in each Corps, the Commanding Officer present therewith when the clothing is received, together with the two Officers next in seniority, not under the rank of Captain, shall, immediately on its arrival, make a strict inspection into the same, comparing it with the sealed pattern; and shall cause to be drawn out, an accurate state of the quality, quantity, and condition thereof; which state he is to transmit through the Adjutant General of our forces, to our Clothing Board: and it is our pleasure, that such state shall be entered in the Regimental Books, for the future inspection of such superior Officer as may be ordered from time to time to inspect or review the Corps.

III. And whereas it is highly expedient that an uniform rule should prevail in regard to the claims of Soldiers to clothing, at stated times or broken periods; we do hereby declare and make known, that Non-commissioned Officers and Soldiers of the Militia, dying, or discharged, before the completion

## Clothing and Appointments.

pletion of a full year from the appointed day of delivering the annual clothing of their Corps, have no demand whatever on account thereof.

If a Serjeant is reduced to the ranks, his clothing is to be given in for the use of his successor; and he himself will receive Privates' clothing, equally worn (or as nearly may be) with the clothing he has given in.

A man who comes into the Corps after the proper time of the delivery of the clothing, shall be immediately entitled to clothing of that year, as good as that in wear by the rest of the Corps: and he shall be entitled to new clothing at the next period of general delivery to the Corps.

IV. Whereas by our Warrant of the 25th May, 1797, for encreasing and regulating the pay and allowance of Non-commissioned Officers and Private Men of Corps of Infantry serving at home, we therein ordered, that a sum, not exceeding One Shilling and Sixpence a week, for necessaries, should be retained from the pay of Soldiers: and whereas a list of the necessaries to be provided out of the said stoppage, was, by our order, annexed to our Clothing Regulation for the Militia Service, dated the 26th June, 1801; which list now requires the like alteration as hath been made in the list of necessaries for Soldiers of the Line by our before-mentioned Warrant of the 22d April, 1803; we are pleased, in lieu thereof, to cause a Schedule to be annexed to this our Warrant, containing a specification of the articles, both of clothing and necessaries, with which a Militia Soldier is to be provided, and in which he is to be kept always complete.

It is expected that all the articles of necessaries specified in the said Schedule can be furnished of unexceptionable materials, and kept in complete repair, by the stoppage above mentioned; but in particular instances where the same shall not be found adequate, a Regimental Court of Enquiry, or Court Martial, as the circumstances of the case may require, is to be convened for the purpose of authorizing such further stoppage as may be judged expedient. And it is our express will and pleasure, that no further stoppage for necessaries be made, without the sanction of such Regimental Court of Enquiry or Court Martial.

If ~~in the course of the year~~ * any of the articles of neces-

---

* See the Circular, page 471.

saries

saries specified in the said Schedule should not be wanted for the Soldier's use, the money stopped for such articles shall be repaid him.

V. The prices of the articles mentioned in the said Schedule of necessaries are now purposely omitted, as liable to variation, in a certain degree, from temporary or local circumstances; but we do expect, that every Officer in the command of a Corps, and every Captain, or other Officer, commanding a Company therein, will feel it to be a most important part of his duty to take care that all the articles be purchased for the Soldiers on the most advantageous terms, and at ready money prices; and that they be delivered to the men at prime cost, without any other extra charge than what on some occasions may unavoidably be incurred for carriage.

We do further think proper to declare, that without derogating in any degree from the general controul and responsibility of the Commanding Officers of Corps, or precluding them from directing the purchase of articles agreeably to our Regulations, and charging the same to the different Companies, whenever it evidently tends to the benefit of the Soldier, it is, nevertheless, to the Captains or Commanding Officers of Companies, that we do more immediately look for the due and punctual execution of our royal intentions, in what regards the care of the clothing, when once delivered, and the provision and care of the necessaries, of the men of their respective Companies. And the Captains, or Commanding Officers of Companies, are accordingly hereby made responsible, that the necessaries provided for their men be of a fit and proper quality; that their complement be at all times kept up; and, above all, that such purchases, as are necessary, be made in the manner most likely to leave no cause of complaint to the Soldier.

The Captains, or Commanding Officers of Companies, are also responsible, that the persons furnishing the articles be settled with regularly and punctually, as the stoppages accrue.

VI. The 25th December, 1803, shall be the day on which the next complete clothing of our Corps of Embodied Militia, as herein before described, shall be considered to be due; and upon the said day, or as near thereto as possible, the same shall actually be delivered to the men of our said Corps, wherever stationed: in like manner, in every subsequent year, the 25th day of December shall be the general period of clothing

## Clothing and Appointments. 463

thing our Militia forces, so long as they shall continue embodied.

VII. And whereas we have been graciously pleased to approve of each Non-commissioned Officer, Drummer, and Private Man of our Embodied Militia, being provided with a great coat of an approved pattern, in like manner as the Soldiers of our other Infantry forces, without suffering any deduction from his personal pay on that account; and have signified our orders, through our Secretary at War, for providing accordingly a complete set of great coats for the establishment of our respective Militia Corps; the cost of which, together with the expence of the package and carriage, is to be made good by our Warrants to the clothiers who shall have furnished them, upon accompts to be rendered to our Secretary at War by the said respective clothiers: it is now our pleasure, that the following Regulations be observed in the management of the said article.

The great coats, being provided at the sole expence of the Public, and calculated to last three years from the time of delivery, are to be returned into the stores of Government upon the disembodying of the Militia; and, in order to prevent their being prematurely worn out by abuse or neglect, we do hereby declare our pleasure, that they are to be considered as regimental appointments or necessaries, and that the Soldiers are to be responsible for, and liable to make good by stoppage from their pay, any loss or damage of the great coats (arising from misconduct) which may occur before the expiration of the period of three years assigned for their duration: and we do enjoin and require the General Officers who shall from time to time review and inspect our Militia forces, particularly to notice in their Reports the state of the great coats in wear, and the degree of attention which shall appear to have been paid to their preservation.

The Serjeants' great coats are to be distinguished from the Privates', by cuffs, collar, and buttons of Serjeants' quality, conformable to the facings, &c. of their respective Regiments.

VIII. The allowances to the Colonels of Militia for clothing shall continue to be issued at the rates established\* by our Warrant of the 26th June, 1801, namely, 5*l*. 12*s*. 9*d*. for each

---

\* The rate of the Clothing Allowance for *Serjeants* of Militia has been altered.—See Circular, page 467.

Serjeant, 2*l*. 18*s*. 7*d*. for each Drummer, and 2*l*. 8*s*. 7*d*. for each Corporal and Private Man; the surplus of which allowances, after providing the clothing, will continue liable as heretofore to defraying the occasional expence to which Commandants of Militia Corps are subject, on account of the difference between the price of buff accoutrements, and the allowance in lieu of tan leather accoutrements, granted under the directions of our Board of Ordnance.

---

And of all and each of the foregoing Regulations, every Colonel, Commanding Officer, Adjutant, Paymaster, and Agent, of our Embodied Militia, and all others whom it shall or may concern, are to take diligent notice, and govern themselves accordingly.

> Given at our Court at St. James's, this 8th day of August, 1803, in the forty-third year of our reign.

By His Majesty's command.

C. YORKE.

---

## SCHEDULE.

LIST of Articles of Clothing and Necessaries with which a Soldier of the Embodied Militia is to be at all Times provided, and in which he is to be kept complete by sundry Articles furnished by the Commandant, or at the Expence of the Public, or by the Stoppage of One Shilling and Sixpence a Week from his Pay, sanctioned by the preceding Warrant.

### ARTICLES OF CLOTHING.

*Furnished in the first instance by the Commandant.*
- One Regimental Cap, with Cockade, and Feather or Tuft.
- One Regimental Coat.
- One Waistcoat.
- One Pair of Breeches.
- One Pair of Shoes.

ARTICLES

*Clothing and Appointments.* **465**

ARTICLES OF NECESSARIES.

Furnished in the first instance at the expence of the Public. } One Regimental Great Coat.

These articles, with oil, emery, and brick dust, are allowed for by the Public to the extent of 2s. 9d. per annum, for each effective man. } Turnscrew, Brush, and Worm.

Paid for by the Men.
{
One Pair of Shoes.
One Pair of Black Cloth (long) Gaiters.
Three Shirts.
Three Pair of Worsted or Yarn Socks.
Worsted or Yarn Mitts during the Winter.
One Black Stock.
One Foraging Cap.
One Knapsack.
One Clothes Brush.
Three Shoe Brushes.
Black Ball.
Hair Ribbon and Leather.
Two Combs.
Straps for carrying the Great Coat.
}

MEMORANDUM.

THE breeches, and any other articles of clothing or necessaries, which it may be requisite to *replace* from the Soldiers' stoppages, are to be made exactly of the same material and pattern as those originally furnished by the Commandant.

The shoes, supplied as necessaries, are to be made in strict conformity to the shoes furnished by the Commandant, according to the patterns approved by the Clothing Board, and sealed under their direction.

It is recommended, as a matter of œconomy, that the shirts furnished to Soldiers should hereafter be of a rather better quality than those which were supplied when the price was limited to five shillings and sixpence.

The actual expenditure for altering clothing, not exceeding two shillings and sixpence per annum, each man, will be defrayed by the Public, as expressed in the Warrant for establishing a consolidated allowance at a daily rate, for Soldiers of Cavalry and Infantry, bearing date the 1st September, 1795.*

---

* See page 455.

*Circular*

*Circular Letter to the Colonels of Regiments of Infantry of the Line, relative to the Contribution to be made out of the Off-Reckonings towards the Cost of Great Coats for Serjeants.*

*War Office*, 12th *Jan.* 1804.

SIR,

IT appearing by a communication from the Adjutant General, that in adopting the new regulations for Infantry Clothing, established by His Majesty's Warrant of the 22d April, 1803, a saving of eightpence to the Colonel arises on each suit of Serjeant's clothing, in addition to the one shilling and ten pence saved by the alteration in the pattern of Army Clothing, which took place in the year 1798; and it being thought proper that this further saving should be applied in aid of the charge of making the additional distinctions in the Great Coats for Serjeants, mentioned in the 35th article of the Warrant above referred to; I have the honor to acquaint you therewith, and, that, from the 25th ultimo, inclusive, the sum of *two shillings and sixpence (instead of one shilling and ten pence) per annum, for every Serjeant included in your assignments of off-reckonings, is, by His Majesty's Order, to be contributed accordingly to the Great Coat Fund of your Regiment.

I have the honor to be,

SIR,

Your most obedient

Humble Servant,

C. BRAGGE.

Colonel of the
    Regiment of Foot.

---

\* Memorandum.—In Highland Corps, the new rate of contribution will be one shilling and six pence, instead of ten pence as formerly.

*Circular to the Colonels of the Regiments of Militia, respecting a new Rate of Clothing Allowance for Serjeants.*

War Office, 12th January, 1804.

SIR,

IT appearing by a communication from the Adjutant General, that in adopting the new Regulations for Infantry Clothing, established in the Line by His Majesty's Warrant of the 22d *April*, 1803, and extended to the Militia by His Majesty's Warrant of 8th *August*, 1803, there arises a saving of Eightpence to the Colonel on each Suit of Serjeant's Clothing, in addition to the One Shilling and Tenpence saved by adopting the new pattern of Militia Clothing, established by His Majesty's Warrant of the 26th *June*, 1801:[*] and it being thought proper that this further saving should be applied in aid of the charge of making the additional distinctions in the Great Coats for Serjeants, mentioned at the conclusion of the 7th Article of the Warrant of the 8th *August*, 1803, above referred to; I have the honor to acquaint you therewith, and that in the issues on account of the Clothing of your Regiment for the year commencing the 25th ultimo, and in future, the Allowance for each Serjeant of the establishment, will, by His Majesty's order, be granted at the rate of 5l. 12s. 1d. only; being Eightpence less than the present Allowance; which deduction will be carried in aid of the Public Charge as above mentioned.

I have the honor to be,

SIR,

Your most obedient

Humble servant,

C. BRAGGE.

---

[*] This Warrant is not reprinted, it being superseded by the Warrant of the 8th August, 1803.

*Letter from the Adjutant General, relative to the Description of Clothing to be furnished to Paymasters' Clerks, or Armourers, in the Militia.*

*Horse Guards, 11th February, 1805.*

SIR,

HAVING submitted to the Commander in Chief your Letter of the 7th instant, I am directed by His Royal Highness to acquaint you, for the information of the Secretary at War, that Soldiers who are employed as Paymaster's Clerks or Armourers, are to be clothed according to the station they hold in the Regiment, whether Serjeants, Corporals, or Privates.

I have, &c.

H. CALVERT.

F. Moore, Esq.

## Clothing and Appointments.

*Warrant for altering the Rate of Compensation to Soldiers of Infantry, in lieu of Clothing: dated 15th April, 1805.*

## GEORGE R.

WHEREAS it hath been represented by our Clothing Board, that the rate of compensation to Soldiers of Infantry, in lieu of Clothing, established by our Warrant of 22d April, 1803, includes the full value of a lacquered felt cap; and whereas, according to our Clothing Regulations, the Soldier is not entitled to be supplied with a cap of the above description oftener than once in two years, and has therefore a claim to a moiety only of the value thereof, in part of compensation for his annual clothing; our will and pleasure is, that by a deduction of half the value of a cap, viz. 3s. 6d. the rate of compensation to Corporals, Drummers, and Privates, fixed by our Warrant above-mentioned, be reduced from 1l. 16s. 6d. to 1l. 13s.; and, that by the like deduction of half the value of a Serjeant's cap, viz. 4s. the rate of compensation to Serjeants be reduced from 3l. 12s. to 3l. 8s.

It is our further pleasure, that, on the like account, the rate of compensation to Soldiers of our West India Regiments, (in which great coats form part of the clothing supplied by the Colonels, and are calculated to last two years) shall be reduced in the case of Corporals, Drummers, and Privates, to 1l. 7s. 6d. by a deduction of half the value of a great coat, being 5s. 6d. in addition to the before-mentioned deduction of 3s. 6d. for the cap; and in the case of Serjeants, to 3l. 1s. 9d. by the deduction of half the value of a Serjeant's great coat, being 6s. 3d. in addition to the before mentioned deduction of 4s. for the cap.

Given at our Court at St. James's, this 15th day of April, 1805, in the 45th year of our reign.

By His Majesty's command,

W. DUNDAS.

*Circular*

*Circular to the Colonels of Regiments of Cavalry and Infantry of the Line, enclosing an amended Copy of the Clothing Regulations.*

*War Office, 18th April,* 1806.

SIR,

I AM directed to transmit for your guidance a printed copy of the Clothing Regulations of the 22d April, 1803, in which the words, "*in the course of the year*," on the 45th page,* are struck out by His Majesty's authority, it appearing that from a misconstruction of these words, Commanding Officers have, in some instances, delayed until the conclusion of the year to account to Soldiers for the surplus (if any) of the weekly stoppage for necessaries; instead of causing them to be settled with for the same, monthly, in the Infantry, and every two months in the Cavalry, agreeably to His Majesty's intention, and former orders.

I have, &c.

W. DUNDAS.

---

* See page 445 of this Collection.

*Clothing and Appointments.*

*Circular to the Commandants of Militia Corps, enclosing an amended Copy of the Clothing Regulation.*

*War Office,* 18th *April,* 1805.

SIR,

I AM directed to transmit herewith, for your guidance, a printed copy of the Regulation for the Clothing of the Embodied Militia, dated 8th August, 1803; in which the words, "*in the course of the year,*" on the 13th page, are struck out, by His Majesty's authority:* it appearing that from a misconstruction of these words, commanding Officers have, in some instances, delayed until the conclusion of the year to account to Soldiers for the surplus (if any,) of the weekly stoppage for necessaries, instead of causing them to be settled with for the same monthly, agreeably to His Majesty's intention, and former orders.

I have the honor to be,

SIR,

Your most obedient,

humble servant,

W. DUNDAS.

Colonel of the
　　　Regiment of Militia.

---

* See page 461, of this collection.

*Circular*

*Circular to Agents of Infantry Regiments on the British Establishment, relative to the Provision of Great Coats.*

*War Office,* 24th *May,* 1805.
GENTLEMEN,

L EST from any misunderstanding of His Majesty's Regulations, it should be conceived that Great Coats are to be provided under the immediate orders of the Commanding Officers of Regiments, or Captains of Companies (in like manner as some other articles of Regimental Necessaries); I am directed to explain to you, for the information of the corps in your agency, that according to the intent of the King's Regulations, it rests exclusively with the Colonels of Regiments to give orders for the provision of Great Coats, as well as the Clothing of their respective Regiments.

I am, &c.

F. MOORE.

Agent of the

*Regulation*

*Regulation for the Supply of Bear Skin Caps to the Grenadiers of Militia Corps, dated 28th November, 1805.*

## GEORGE R.

WHEREAS it has been our intention, that in our corps of Embodied Militia, in like manner as in our Regiments of the Line,* Bear Skin Caps should be considered as a part of the dress of the Grenadiers; and whereas it is represented that our corps of Militia are not, in every instance, acquainted with this our intention; we are pleased hereby to order, that in all our corps of Embodied Militia, Bear Skin Caps, according to a pattern approved by us, and lodged in the Office of the Comptrollers of the Accompts of our Army, be supplied to the Grenadiers, and replaced as often as shall be found necessary.

Of which the Colonels of Regiments, and all others whom it may concern, are to take due notice, and govern themselves accordingly.

Given at our Court at St. James's, this 28th day of November, 1805, in the forty-sixth year of our reign.

By His Majesty's Command,

W. DUNDAS.

---

* The authority for supplying Bear Skin Caps to Grenadiers of the Line is understood to be a Warrant of the 27th July, 1768, obsolete in other respects, which enjoins that "Black Bear Skin Caps" be supplied to the "Fusileer Regiments, Companies of Grenadiers, and Drummers, as often as shall be necessary."

*Regulation for the Inspection of Great Coats; dated* 19*th March,* 1806.

## GEORGE R.

WHEREAS, at the desire of the Commander in Chief of our forces, the General Officers composing our Permanent Clothing Board have taken into consideration the Regulations prescribed by our Warrant of the 22d April, 1803, in regard to the Inspection of Great Coats; and have reported unto us their opinion, that it will scarcely be practicable for our Inspectors of Clothing to make the Inspections therein prescribed at the precise periods when they may be required; and that, even if such Inspections could in all cases be made, the Inspectors have no means of ascertaining that the Great Coats viewed by them are actually those which are sent out and delivered to Regiments; and whereas the Board have humbly suggested an amendment of the Regulations, of which we are pleased to approve: our will and pleasure therefore is, and we do hereby authorise and direct, that our Inspectors of Army Clothing do seal and deliver to each Army Clothier a sufficient number of Great Coats of the three Regulation Sizes; which, after due examination, shall be found to be in every respect conformable to the Patterns approved and sealed by the General Officers of our Clothing Board; that no Delivery of Great Coats, whether greater or less, be, on any occasion, made by the Army Clothiers, without one set of such sealed Patterns, forming part of the supply; and that the Commanding Officers of Regiments, both at Home and Abroad, immediately on the arrival of the Great Coats at their Head Quarters, do assemble a Board, consisting, in each Regiment, of the Commanding Officer, and two Officers next in seniority, not under the rank of Captain, and do cause the bales to be opened and inspected in the Presence of the said Board; and a Report, signed by the Members thereof, to be transmitted to the Office of our Adjutant General, specifying whether the Great Coats are in every respect strictly conformable to the sealed Patterns which accompany them. Duplicates of the said Reports are to be sent to the Regimental Agents.

And in order to obviate the inconvenience that would be

sustained

sustained by the Furnishers of Great Coats, if payment for the same were, in the cases of Regiments on *Foreign Stations*, to be withheld until the receipt of the above-mentioned Reports; we are pleased to direct, that, whenever Great Coats are about to be shipped for a Regiment serving abroad, a careful and minute Inspection of the same be made at the Packer's, by such person or persons, not exceeding two (being Commissioned Officers), as the Inspectors of Clothing shall, from time to time select and appoint, under their responsibility; for which service, such person or persons shall be remunerated, at the rate of Ten Shillings per day, each, for the days on which they are respectively so employed to perform this service; whose Reports, being approved by our Inspectors of Clothing, shall be acted upon in discharging the Accompts of the Clothiers by whom the Great Coats may have been provided.

And it appearing to us, that the above measures are calculated to secure to our Army, on all occasions, the supply of Great Coats of a proper quality; we are pleased to dispense with any other Inspection thereof by our Inspectors of Army Clothing.

And our Inspectors of Clothing, the Colonels, and Commanding Officers of Regiments, and all others, whom it doth, or may, concern, are to take due notice of these our Orders, and govern themselves accordingly.

Given at our Court at St. James's, this 19th Day of March, 1806, in the Forty-sixth Year of our Reign.

By His Majesty's Command,

RICHARD FITZPATRICK.

*Circular to Regimental Agents relative to the Inspection of Great Coats.*

*War Office, 5th May,* 1806.

GENTLEMEN,

I TRANSMIT herewith some printed copies of His Majesty's Regulation for the inspection of Great Coats, bearing date the 19th March last. In conformity to the said Regulation, you will not in future discharge any Clothier's accompt for Great Coats furnished to Regiments in your Agency, until you receive, *in the case of Regiments at home,* Reports from the Commanding Officers, specifying that the Great Coats are strictly conformable to the sealed Patterns; and in the case of *Regiments on Foreign Stations,* certificates to the like effect, signed by the Officers appointed for the particular service of inspecting Great Coats, and bearing the approving signature of one of the inspectors of Clothing.

I am to add, that in future the accompts for the original supplies of Great Coats, the charge of which is to be defrayed by Warrant, must invariably be accompanied by Reports or Certificates of the above description, as the case may require.

I am, &c.

F. MOORE.

Agent of the

*Form*

*Form of the Certificate to be signed by Commanding Officers of Regiments, when Great Coats are required to be replaced.*

Great Coats.

I do hereby certify that Great Coats will be required for the Regiment of Foot, on the        18    ; to replace the like Number delivered to the Men of the said Regiment, on the        18    .

Of the above number of Great
    Coats        are for Serjeants.

Commanding Officer.

N. B. According to His Majesty's Regulations, Great Coats are not to be replaced within a shorter period than three years from the time of delivery; and then only, *if necessary*, in consequence of the unserviceable state of the Great Coats in wear.

*Circular Letter from the Adjutant General to General Officers commanding Districts in Great Britain, relative to the Clothing to be taken with Men transferred from one Corps to another.*

Horse Guards, 11th September, 1806.

SIR,

IT having been referred for the opinion of a Board of General Officers what clothing men enlisted for limited service should take with them when they volunteer for general service into other Regiments than those to which they originally belonged; and the Board having submitted for the approbation of the Commander in Chief the following Regulations on that head, viz. "That such Soldiers should take with them the clothing which they received, or ought to have received, on the 25th day of December preceding, and which clothing would become the property of such Soldiers on the next 24th December; that the Colonel receiving such Soldiers should pay to the Colonel of the Regiment from which they volunteered a sum for each Soldier on account of his clothing, equal to the allowance which the Soldier would be entitled to receive for his clothing (if a compensation is received by him in lieu of clothing) for the remainder of the year, ending the 24th December, at the rate *per month* established under the Regulation of His Majesty of the 15th April, 1805, viz. Five Shillings and Eight-pence for Serjeants, and Two Shillings and Nine-pence for Corporals, Privates, and Drummers." I have the honor to signify to you that His Royal Highness has been pleased to approve thereof, and to direct that they may be duly notified for the information of the several Regiments stationed in the district under your command.

I have the honor, &c.

HARRY CALVERT,
Adjutant General.

N.B. A similar communication was made to Regimental Agents, for the information of Colonels of Regiments.

*Circular*

## Clothing and Appointments. 479

*Circular Letter from the Adjutant General to Agents of Regiments, relative to Payment for Caps taken with Soldiers transferred from one Regiment to another.*

Horse Guards, 2d October, 1806.

SIR,

I HAVE the honor to signify that the Circular Letter addressed to you on the 22d ultimo,\* relative to the sum to be paid for the Non-commissioned Officers' and Soldiers' caps, by the Colonels of the Regiments receiving men who volunteer general service, having been written under a misconception with respect to the allowance for the cap not being included in the sum fixed by His Majesty's Warrant of 15th April, 1805, is in consequence hereby cancelled, and the following is to be observed, in addition to the Regulation recommended by the Board of General Officers, and approved by the Commander in Chief, as communicated in my Circular Letter of the 11th ultimo.

When any Non-commissioned Officer or Soldier, having volunteered as aforesaid, shall be transferred within the first year after the issue of the cap, (which is to last two years) a further sum, than that fixed by the Board, is to be paid, of Four Shillings for Serjeants, and Three Shillings and Sixpence for Corporals, Drummers, and Privates, being the remaining moiety of the value of the cap for the second year.

It follows of course if the transfer takes place any time during the second year of the cap being issued, at the expiration of which period it becomes the property of the Soldier, that the rate per month of Five Shillings and Eight-pence for Serjeants, and Two Shillings and Nine-pence for Corporals, Drummers, and Privates, as fixed by the Board, only is to be paid.

I am in consequence to signify the Commander in Chief's commands, that you take the earliest opportunity of communicating the subject hereof for the information of the several Regiments within your agency.

I have, &c.
HARRY CALVERT.

---

\* Not printed.

*Circular Letter from the Deputy Adjutant General to Regimental Agents, relative to the Discontinuance of lacquered Felt Caps.*

Horse Guards, 20th October, 1806.

SIR,

IT having been represented to the Commander in Chief, that the use of the lacquered cap, which has been adopted for the Infantry of the Army, has been found from experience to be attended with much inconvenience and prejudice to the troops, His Royal Highness has submitted the same to the King, and His Majesty has been graciously pleased to command, that those Regiments of Infantry which are entitled to caps for the year, commencing 25th December, 1806, shall have them made of felt, in strict conformity to a pattern cap, which is lodged at the Office of the Comptrollers of Army Accompts, the leather parts of which, and brass plate, are to be supplied once in two years, and the felt crown, and tuft, annually, as heretofore. You will be pleased to make an early communication of the substance of this Letter to the Colonels of the Regiments in your agency.

I have, &c.

W. WYNYARD,
Deputy Adjutant General.

*Letter*

*Letter from the Adjutant General to the General Officers, Commanding Districts at Home, and Stations abroad, and also to Regimental Agents, relative to the Distinction to be made in the Great Coats of Non-commissioned Officers.*

Horse Guards, 27th October, 1806.

SIR,

APPLICATION having been made to the Commander in Chief to authorize a difference to be established between the Great Coats of Non-commissioned Officers and Privates, and His Royal Highness approving as a mark of distinction, that Serjeants should be allowed to wear on their present uniform Great Coats, Collar and Cuffs of the colour of the facings of their respective Regiments, with the Chevrons on the right sleeve, the same as on their Regimental Coats, and that Corporals should wear the Chevrons without any other distinction on their Great Coats: I have in consequence, the honor to notify the same to you, for the information of the several Regiments within your Command (or Agency) observing that Regiments which adopt what is now proposed, or the individuals themselves, must be at the expence attendant, as the Commander in Chief cannot undertake to recommend any alteration in this respect in the established Regulations.

I have the honor, &c.

HARRY CALVERT,

Adjutant General.

# SECTION IX.

## MISCELLANEOUS ORDERS.

# SECTION IX.

## MISCELLANEOUS ORDERS.

*Circular Letter from the Secretary at War to General Officers commanding Districts, relative to Allowances to Deputy Judge Advocates.*

*War Office, 6th April,* 1802.

SIR,

GREAT difficulty having been constantly found in determining what Allowance should be made to the Officers, or others, who have occasionally officiated as Deputy Judge Advocates; and in judging how far it might be proper to comply with their demands for Contingent Expences; I have the honor to acquaint you that in consequence thereof, His Majesty has thought fit to order, that a positive Regulation shall be formed, in regard to the performance of the said duty in future, limiting the Pay of every Person officiating as a Deputy Judge Advocate, to two Guineas for each Day the Court Martial shall actually sit, and allowing the like Pay for the intervening Sundays; but not more than two days Pay for the whole of any Adjournment, which may take place during the Trial, whether for the sake of referring to the Public Departments, or for any other purpose.

The Deputy Judge Advocate's Account of Expences actually incurred on any Court Martial for Stationary, Hire

Hire of Rooms, Fire and Candle, &c. is to be submitted (with Vouchers) to the President of such Court Martial, who is to decide on the necessity, as well as the reasonableness of the charges, and to certify to the Judge Advocate General, the sum proper to be admitted under each head.

In communicating to you His Majesty's orders for the future arrangement of this branch of the service, I cannot, Sir, too strongly recommend, that, whenever a Court Martial is to be held in your District, you should exert your best endeavours to prevail on some Military Officer acquainted with this particular duty, or at least well informed on the General Rules of the service, who may be stationed at or near the place of Trial, to accept a deputation from the Judge Advocate General, such mode being far more eligible, than the employing of a gentleman of the law, or other Person, throughout a whole district, by which means very heavy expences have, in some instances, been incurred for travelling.

This Regulation respecting the Pay, and Contingent Charges of Officiating Judge Advocates, you will be pleased on every occasion to cause to be communicated to the persons concerned, previously to the assembling of the Court Martial; in order that no question may arise on those points after the duty shall have been performed.

I have &c.

C. YORKE.

P. S. You will be pleased to communicate this Letter to each of the General Officers serving in the District under your Command.

## Miscellaneous Orders. 487

*Letter to the Surgeon General and Inspector General of Regimental Hospitals; enclosing a Paper stating the leading Rules to be observed in Cases where Officers apply to them for their Certificates relative to Charges for curing Wounds.*

*War Office, 11th July, 1798.*

GENTLEMEN,

IT having been represented that on the Official Applications made to you, for certifying expences incurred by Officers of His Majesty's Army, for the cure of Wounds, received in Action, circumstances are not unfrequently met with, which induce much uncertainty from the want of some regulated line of discrimination; I enclose herewith for your information and guidance a paper, specifying what are understood to have been the principal objects of enquiry, and modes of proceeding, upon which the recommendatory certificates of the Surgeon General and Inspector of Regimental Hospitals, were intended to be, and have been usually given, in such cases, conformably to the scope of the Regulation.

I am, &c.
W. WINDHAM.

Surgeon General, and Inspector
General of Regimental Hospitals.

---

WHEN an Officer applies to the Surgeon General, and Inspector of Regimental Hospitals, for their certificate relative to a charge for curing a Wound received in Action, he is first to produce to them a certificate, signed by the Officer commanding the Corps he served in at the Action, or from a General Officer present, or exercising a Command on the Station, shewing the time, place, and manner, in which the Wound was received.

The

The Officer is next to produce proof that he could not be attended by Medical Officers serving on the station in a public capacity.

These points being clearly made out to the satisfaction of the Surgeon General, and Inspector of Regimental Hospitals, they are to proceed by inspection, as well as enquiry, to inform themselves of the nature and state of the Wound.

They are next to examine the accompt of expences for the cure thereof; together with the vouchers; and in so doing they are first to ascertain the period of time comprehended in it, which is not to exceed six months from the receipt of the Wound. They are next to see that no charge is made but for Medical and Surgical Treatment; and lastly, they are to estimate the charges, not by the Rank, or Situation of the Wounded persons, nor by the allowed skill and reputation of the professional persons employed, but merely by the circumstances of the Wound, and by the treatment absolutely required; according to which they are to take care that the charges are moderate and reasonable.

The certificate of the Surgeon General, and Inspector of Regimental Hospitals, is to contain specific information on each of the points above-mentioned. It is not to be in the form of a letter nor addressed to any particular person, but it is to be transmitted with the other necessary documents to the War Office.

If no vouchers can be obtained for the accompt, or only such as are defective, the Surgeon General and Inspector of Regimental Hospitals, are to inform themselves as exactly as possible, of the causes thereof, and to report the same in their certificate. They are also in such cases, not to regard the accompt or demand stated to them, but to recommend on their own judgment a sum reasonably to be allowed, according to the circumstances of the case, which may appear to them sufficiently ascertained, and for which they are willing to be responsible.

If any very extraordinary case should occur, to which the entire application of these general Rules might be deemed inexpedient; the Surgeon General and Inspector of Regimental Hospitals, are in such cases to make a special Report on the circumstances before they frame their certificate.

*State*

## Miscellaneous Orders.  489

*State of Allowances and Regulations, in Cases where Officers lose an Eye, or a Limb, or are killed in Action.*

IF a Wound shall be received in Action, by any Commissioned Officer, which shall occasion the loss of an Eye, or a Limb, or the total loss of the use of a limb, he shall receive a Gratuity in Money, of one year's full pay, and be further allowed such expences relating to his cure (if not performed at the King's Charge) as shall be certified to be reasonable, by the Surgeon General of the Army, and Inspector General of Regimental Infirmaries, upon examination of the vouchers which he shall lay before them.

If the Wounds received shall not amount to the loss of a Limb, the charge of cure only shall be allowed, certified as above.

When any Commissioned Officer shall lose an Eye, or a Limb as aforesaid, the Commanding Officer of the Corps, in which he serves, shall deliver to him a certificate, specifying the time when, and the place where, the said accident happened; a duplicate of which certificate shall likewise be transmitted with the next monthly return.

When any Commissioned Officer shall be killed in Action, his Widow, and orphan Children (if he leaves any) shall be allowed as follows:

To the Widow, a full year's pay, according to her Husband's Regimental Commission.

To each Child, under age, and unmarried, one third of what is allowed to the Widow.

Posthumous Children to be included.

All Persons dying of their Wounds, within six months after the Battle, shall be deemed slain in Action.

The Commanding Officer of the Corps in which the slain Officer served, shall on demand, give a certificate of his being killed in Action to his surviving Wife and Orphans respectively, specifying the time when, and the place where, the said accident happened, a duplicate of which certificate shall likewise be transmitted by the next Monthly Return.

*Regulation*

*Regulation for the Indemnification of Losses sustained by Officers and Soldiers of His Majesty's Forces on Actual Service.*

*Dated War Office, 1st March,* 1796.

THE King having been pleased to direct and order, that the following Regulations shall be observed with respect to indemnification for losses of Baggage and Camp equipage, unavoidably sustained by Officers and Men of, or attached to His Majesty's Forces on actual Service; viz.

### INFANTRY.

|  | *l.* | *s.* | *d.* |
|---|---:|---:|---:|
| 1st. The whole of the personal Baggage of a Subaltern Officer to be valued at | 60 | 0 | 0 |
| —— Camp Equipage between two Subalterns, | 35 | 0 | 0 |
| 2nd. The Baggage of a Captain to be valued at | 80 | 0 | 0 |
| —— Camp Equipage, | 35 | 0 | 0 |
| 3rd. Field Officer's Baggage, | 100 | 0 | 0 |
| —— Camp Equipage, | 60 | 0 | 0 |
| 4th. Colonel's Baggage, | 120 | 0 | 0 |
| —— Camp Equipage, | 80 | 0 | 0 |

### CAVALRY.

|  | *l.* | *s.* | *d.* |
|---|---:|---:|---:|
| 5th. The whole of the personal Baggage of a Subaltern Officer to be valued at | 70 | 0 | 0 |
| —— Camp Equipage, | 45 | 0 | 0 |
| 6th. Captain's Baggage | 90 | 0 | 0 |
| —— Camp Equipage, | 45 | 0 | 0 |
| 7th. Field Officer's Baggage | 120 | 0 | 0 |
| —— Camp Equipage | 90 | 0 | 0 |
| 8th. Colonel's Baggage | 140 | 0 | 0 |
| —— Camp Equipage | 90 | 0 | 0 |

9th. Officers giving Certificates signed by themselves and the Commanding Officers of their Regiments, that they have lost the whole of their Baggage and Camp Equipage, and that at the time it was lost they were in no respect deviating from the Orders of the General Officer Commanding in Chief relative to Baggage, shall receive the whole of the sums above allotted, according to their Ranks.

10th.

10th. Officers losing any part of their Baggage are to give in similar certificates according to the best of their belief and judgment, without entering into particulars, but estimating their loss at one-fourth, one-half, or three-fourths, of the whole value, according to which they shall be paid the like proportion of the above sums.

11th. The whole Baggage of a Quarter Master of Cavalry shall be estimated at 40l. A Quarter Master losing the whole or any part of his Baggage, must produce certificates from the Officer Commanding, and from his Captain, as to the quantity of his Baggage, which to the best of their belief and judgment has been lost, according to which he will receive the whole, or a proportion of the above sum of 40l.

12th. The Baggage, and Camp Equipage of all Staff Officers of both Cavalry and Infantry are to be valued as those of Subaltern Officers, except for such as are allowed a Tent to themselves, whose Camp Equipage in that case will be valued as that of a Captain.

13th. A Serjeant of Cavalry losing his Necessaries, without any fault of his own, shall receive - - - - 2 15 0
14th. Corporal, Trumpeter or Private - 2 10 0
15th. Serjeant of Infantry - - - 2 10 0
16th. Corporal, Drummer, or Private - 2 2 0
17th. A Servant, not being a Soldier - 3 8 0

The certificates in these five cases to be the same as in the case of the Quarter Master.

The King has also been pleased to order, that the Officers of His Majesty's Forces on actual Service, whose Horses shall be killed or taken by the Enemy, or shall be shot for the Glanders, shall receive allowances by way of indemnification for them, according to the following rates, viz.

## CAVALRY.

|   | l. | s. | d. |
|---|---|---|---|
| Heavy Dragoons, 1st Charger, | 47 | 5 | 0 |
| Light Dragoons, 1st ditto, | 36 | 15 | 0 |
| Heavy or light ditto, 2nd ditto, | 31 | 10 | 0 |
| Quarter Master's Horse, | 29 | 8 | 0 |

## INFANTRY.

| | | | |
|---|---|---|---|
| Field Officer's Charger, | 31 | 10 | 0 |
| Adjutant's ditto, | 31 | 10 | 0 |

Chaplain's

Chaplain's and Subalterns Horses, each          18 18 0

Bât Horses (both Cavalry and Infantry)     -    18 18 0
General Officers, 1st Charger,    -    -    47 5 0
                 2nd ditto,    -    -    -    31 10 0

Aides de Camp, Brigade Majors, and other Staff Officers, whose situations require their keeping good Horses, receive as the light Dragoons.

Staff Officers for whom inferior Horses are deemed sufficient,    -    -    -    -    -    -    18 18 0

Certificates, stating the particular circumstances and causes of the loss of the horses, are to be signed by the Officers themselves and by the Commanding Officers of their Regiments.

And the General Officers Commanding in Chief on the different Foreign stations, are hereby required to decide on the claims preferred in their respective Districts of Command upon the ground of this Regulation, and to grant payment accordingly.

> Given at the War Office, this first day of March, 1796. By His Majesty's Command,
>
> W. WINDHAM.

*Circular*

*Circular to Generals Commanding on Foreign Stations, relative to the Claims of Officers for Losses incurred on Actual Service.*

War Office, 8th May, 1797

SIR,

IN addition to my Letter of the 30th April, 1796,* I have the honor to signify to you the King's Pleasure, that no claims of Officers for Losses incurred on Actual Service in the Districts under your Command, or on the Seas adjacent, be referred home for indemnification, except under very particular circumstances; and that, in case of such reference, you do furnish the respective Officers with certificates, stating the amount of the allowance you would have thought proper to grant, and the reason of the same not having been granted in the mode prescribed by His Majesty's Warrant.

This rule is not only to govern future references, but is also to extend to such as may already have taken place, upon fresh application being made to you by the Officers concerned; as no allowance can be granted here for losses sustained abroad, but upon a certificate of the kind above stated.

I have, &c.

W. WINDHAM.

---

* The Letter referred to merely enclosed the preceding Regulation.

*Circular to Colonels of Regiments, communicating a new Rule in regard to Indemnification for Appointments lost on Service.*

*War Office,* 15th *July,* 1805.

SIR,

In pursuance of instructions from the Lords Commissioners of His Majesty's Treasury, I have the honor to acquaint you that, in future, all claims for indemnification or compensation for Accoutrements and Appointments, lost on Service, or delivered over for the public use, are to be settled according to the actual value of the several articles at the time of their being lost or delivered over, and not according to the expence that may be incurred in replacing them; and in order that such claims may be rendered with uniformity and precision, I enclose a Form of Statement which is to accompany every application that shall be made on the above account.

I am further to acquaint you, that the claims for Accoutrements and Appointments lost or delivered over on Foreign Service, are to be settled according to the above rule, by the General Officers commanding at the several Stations abroad.

I have the honor to be,

SIR,

Your most obedient

humble Servant,

W. DUNDAS.

Colonel of the
    Regiment of

Statement

## Miscellaneous Orders.

Statement of Articles lost on Service, (or delivered over for the public use, as the case may be) for which a compensation is claimed on behalf of the Colonel of

| No. of each Article. | Description of each Article. | Date of Delivery. | Expected Duration of the Article, according to His Majesty's Regulations. | Actual Duration. | Actual Cost. | Proportionate Deduction for Wear and Tear. | Actual Value. |
|---|---|---|---|---|---|---|---|
| | | | | | | | |

We do hereby certify, upon honor, that the above articles were *(here describe the circumstances under which the Articles were lost, or delivered over)* and that the above statement, by which the value of each Article is ascertained, is just and true, according to the best of our knowledge and belief.

Commanding Officer.

Quarter Master.

---

N. B. Some difficulties having occurred in carrying the above Regulation into effect, it is not for the present acted upon.

*General Orders relative to an Indemnification to be granted to Officers for the Loss of Appointments belonging to glandered Horses.*

*Horse Guards, July 1st, 1805.*

IT is His Majesty's pleasure, that, in cases where it may be found indispensably necessary to destroy articles of Appointment belonging to glandered Horses, in order to prevent infection, the Colonels of the regiments concerned shall be indemnified for the loss of such Appointments, by an adequate Allowance, appreciated on the value of the articles destroyed, upon application to His Majesty's Secretary at War, accompanied by proper vouchers for the real value of the articles destroyed, and the absolute necessity of their destruction, signed by the Commanding Officers and Veterinary Surgeons of their respective regiments.

By Command of His Royal Highness

The Commander in Chief.

HARRY CALVERT,
Adjutant General.

*Circular*

*Circular to the Colonels or Commanding Officers of Regiments on the British Establishment, relative to the Mode of obtaining Arms.*

*War Office, 1st May,* 1799.

SIR,

IT having been represented to His Royal Highness the Commander in Chief, by the Lieutenant-General and Board of Ordnance, that much irregularity has occurred in the manner of obtaining the authorities for Arms, and in the indiscriminate receipt thereof from the stores of ordnance; regard having rather been had to the complete establishment than to the effective numbers of the corps for whose service they were required; and that, in cases of augmentations and otherwise, Arms have been delivered, which, after a lapse of many years, and remaining the whole of the time in the Packer's warehouses, have been returned to the Tower in a state unfit for any service, without a considerable expence being incurred to restore them to proper order: and His Royal Highness having in consequence deemed it essential that such directions should be given as may serve to prevent, as far as practicable, a continuance of the same inconveniences and expence; I have the honour to enclose, for your information and guidance, certain Regulations to be adopted on the above heads in future, and to which His Royal Highness expects the most scrupulous regard and attention in all applications that may hereafter be made for the delivery of small Arms.

I have the honor to be,

SIR,

Your most obedient

Humble servant,

W. WINDHAM.

P. S. Your Agent may be supplied with more copies of the Regulations, upon application to this Office.

Colonel             , or
  Commanding Officer of the

*Regulations*

*Regulations to be observed in applying for, and procuring Deliveries of Small Arms, for the Regiments and Corps in His Majesty's Service.*

I. All applications for Arms, for any Regiments or Corps in His Majesty's service, shall be made according to the form hereunto annexed; and shall be addressed in the first instance to the Commander in Chief, who (except when the demands are made for augmentations to Regiments) will call upon the Ordnance for such information respecting former supplies of Arms that may have been delivered to those Regiments, as will enable him to judge whether the deficiencies, which the demands transmitted are intended to make good, have been owing to want of care of the Arms, or to the length of the period in which they have been in use, or to any unavoidable accidents in the course of service.

II. The demand being approved by the Commander in Chief, will be transmitted to the Secretary at War, that His Majesty's Warrant may be obtained as the Authority to the Ordnance in making the delivery of the Arms.

III. In order to prevent the heavy contingent charges which are now made for the package and warehouse-room of Arms, and also to put an end to the accumulation of such articles in the storehouses belonging to private individuals; the service of packing and dispatching Arms to the stations of the Regiments for which they are designed, will, in lieu of being conducted by the Agents or Packers as heretofore, be undertaken and performed by the Board of Ordnance; except in regard to the procuring of freight, which is to be done by the Agents, as heretofore.

IV. When His Majesty's Warrant, authorising any supplies of Arms, shall have been obtained and transmitted to the Ordnance, the delivery of them is not to take place, until the Colonel or Commanding Officer of the Regiment shall signify to the Board, either in writing or through his Agent, whether he is desirous of receiving the whole number specified in the Warrant immediately, or what proportion of them, and at what time; also the place to which he wishes them to be conveyed. If the Regiment is not in Great Britain, the Colonel or Agent will signify to the Board the name of the ship in which freight for

the

*498

## CAVALRY.

Form of Return to be transmitted to the Commander in Chief, by the Colonels or Officers commanding Regiments of Cavalry in His Majesty's Service, when it shall be necessary to make Application for a fresh Supply of Arms.

| Establishment of the Regiment. | | | Whether completed in Arms to the Establishment, and when: or to what Extent the Regiment has been supplied. | Effective Strength of the Regiment. | | | NUMBER OF ARMS IN POSSESSION: AND THEIR STATE. | | | | | | Number of Arms required. | | | | | Causes of the Deficiencies. Whether lost upon Service: or by Deserters: worn out by Length of Service: or damaged, or deemed unfit for Service, by Causes which are to be specified. |
|---|---|---|---|---|---|---|---|---|---|---|---|---|---|---|---|---|---|---|
| Serjeants. | Trumpeters. | Rank and File. | | Serjeants. | Trumpeters. | Rank and File. | State of the Arms. | Swords. | Carbines. | Bayonets. | Pistols. | Trumpets. | Swords. | Carbines. | Bayonets. | Pistols. | Trumpets. | |
| | | | | | | | GOOD - - - | | | | | | | | | | | |
| | | | | | | | REPAIRABLE - | | | | | | | | | | | |
| | | | | | | | BAD - - - | | | | | | | | | | | |

Head Quarters,

Day of

# INFANTRY.

**Form of Return** to be transmitted to the Commander in Chief, by the Colonels or Officers commanding Regiments of Infantry in His Majesty's Service, when it shall be neceffary to make Application for a frefh Supply of Arms.

| Establishment of the Regiment. | | | Whether completed in Arms to the Eſtabliſhment, and when: or to what Extent the Regiment has been ſupplied. | Effective Strength of the Regiment. | | | NUMBER OF ARMS IN POSSESSION; AND THEIR STATE. | | | | | | | | Number of Arms required. | | | | | | | Cauſe of the Deficiencies. |
|---|---|---|---|---|---|---|---|---|---|---|---|---|---|---|---|---|---|---|---|---|---|---|
| Serjeants. | Drummers. | Rank and File. | | Serjeants. | Drummers. | Rank and File. | State of the Arms. | Pikes. | Fuſils. | Bayonets. | Firelocks. | Bayonets. | Drums. | Hangers. Drummers | Pikes. | Fuſils. | Bayonets. | Firelocks. | Bayonets. | Drums. | Drummers Hangers. | Whether loſt upon Service; or by Deſerters; worn out by Length of Service; or damaged, or deemed unfit for Service, by Cauſes which are to be ſpecified. |
| | | | | | | | GOOD - - - | | | | | | | | | | | | | | | |
| | | | | | | | REPAIRABLE - | | | | | | | | | | | | | | | |
| | | | | | | | BAD - - - | | | | | | | | | | | | | | | |

*Head Quarters,*
*Day of*

the Arms has been engaged; and the port at which she is to receive her cargo.

V. The above Regulations apply not only to His Majesty's Regular Forces, but also to the Embodied Militia, Fencibles, and Embodied Provisional Cavalry.

Given at the War Office this 1st day of May, 1799.

By His Majesty's command,

W. WINDHAM.

*Extract from His Majesty's Warrant of the 25th June, 1806, containing Instructions to the Paymaster of the Pensions to Widows of Officers of the Land Forces and Royal Marines.*

"WHEREAS by our Orders and Instructions, dated 27th April, 1770, and by our Warrants dated 15th June, and 24th October, 1796, and 27th July, 1797, and 3d December, 1798, and 30th April, 1800, we were pleased to declare the rates at which the Pensions of Widows of the several Officers therein specified should be allowed, which pensions, by reason of the great increase in the price of the necessaries of life, and from other causes, are, in many instances, become inadequate to the support of certain classes of the said Widows in a manner anywise suitable to the appointments which their husbands held in our army: and whereas we think it may be of essential benefit to our service to make a more competent provision for the Widows, so circumstanced, of such Officers as have died, or been killed, or shall hereafter die, or be killed therein: and whereas the distressed situation of Widows of Officers, dying on Half-pay, having been most humbly represented unto us, we think it also reasonable to make a similar provision for them in case their husbands have died, or shall die, on or after the 25th June, 1806, and were placed on Half-pay subsequently to their marriages with the said Widows, in consequence of the reduction of the Corps to which they belonged, or of being incapable of further service; our will and pleasure therefore is, that from and after the 25th day of June, 1806, instead of the Regulations contained in our said Orders and Instructions, and in our Warrants above referred to, the following shall be observed by you in the payment of this our royal bounty, viz.

We do hereby declare it to be our intention that the Pensions to the said Widows shall be allowed according to the commissions by which their respective husbands did receive pay, and not according to brevets, unless we shall think fit in any case expressly to direct otherwise, and that they shall be paid at the following rates, viz.

*To*

## Miscellaneous Orders.

|  | To the Widow of a | Rates per Annum. £. |  | To the Widow of a | Rates per Annum. £. |
|---|---|---|---|---|---|
| Regimental Appointments. | Colonel | 80 | Staff Appointments. | Physician having died previously to 25th June, 1806, or dying on, or subsequently, without having served abroad as such | 30 |
|  | Lieutenant Colonel | 60 |  |  |  |
|  | Major | 50 |  |  |  |
|  | Captain | 40 |  |  |  |
|  | First Lieutenant | 30 |  |  |  |
|  | Second Lieutenant | 26 |  |  |  |
|  | Cornet | 26 |  |  |  |
|  | Ensign | 26 |  | Purveyor | 30 |
|  | Paymaster | 30 |  | District Paymaster | 30 |
|  | Adjutant | 30 |  | Surgeon | 30 |
|  | Quarter Master | 26 |  | Apothecary | 26 |
|  | Surgeon | 30 |  | Deputy Purveyor | 20 |
|  | Assistant Surgeon | 26 |  | Hospital Mate, who has served abroad as such | 20 |
|  | Veterinary Surgeon | 20 |  |  |  |
|  | Chaplain | 20 |  |  |  |
| Staff Appts. | Physician dying subsequently to the 24th June, 1806, after having served abroad as such | 40 |  | Commissary, at 20s. per day | 30 |
|  |  |  |  | Ditto, at 15s. per day | 26 |
|  |  |  |  | Ditto, at 10s. per day | 20 |

That every Widow of any Officer of our Land Forces, who shall hereafter claim our bounty, shall produce to our Secretary at War, for the time being, a certificate signed by the Colonel, or in his absence, by the Commanding Officer and Agent of the Regiment in which her husband served; and every Widow of any Officer of the Hospital Staff of our Army shall produce a certificate signed by the Physician General, Surgeon General, or Inspector of Hospitals, certifying to the best of their knowledge that such Widow was the lawful wife of the Officer deceased, in which certificate shall likewise be expressed the time when such Officer was killed or died in our service, and where, together with the situation and circumstances of the Widow, and period when such Officer and Widow were married; to which certificate shall be subjoined an affidavit sworn to by her before a Justice of the Peace, or other Magistrate, that she was the lawful wife of the Officer deceased, that she is his Widow and has no Pension, Allowance, or other provision from Government either in Great Britain or Ireland.

That every Widow of a Marine Officer who shall hereafter claim our bounty, shall produce to you a Warrant made out and signed by the Commissioners for executing the office
of

of our Lord High Admiral, (while our Marine Forces are under that Board) requiring you to pay such Widow or Widows of Marine Officers, our bounty according to the same rate of yearly Pensions as you are hereby authorised to pay to the Widows of Officers of our Land Forces, bearing equal rank in our service; in order that such Widow or Widows may be inserted in a Warrant to be signed by us, empowering you to pay her, or their, respective Pensions accordingly. But in case it shall happen that our Marine Forces shall cease to be under the direction of our Admiralty Board, you are then to observe and follow the same instructions for making payment of the Pension to Widows of Marine Officers who may hereafter claim our bounty, as are hereby given concerning the Widows of Officers of our Land Forces.

That every Widow, before she receives her Pension, shall deliver to you an affidavit, sworn to by her before a Justice of the Peace, or other Magistrate, that she was the lawful wife of the Officer deceased; that she is his Widow, and has no Pension, allowance, or other provision from Government, either in Great Britain or Ireland.

That as any Regiment shall be transferred to that part of our United Kingdom called Ireland, the Widow of any Officer who did belong to such Regiment shall cease to be paid otherwise than in Ireland.

That in case any Widow shall not appear to receive her Pension, her Attorney shall, before payment, produce an affidavit sworn to by the said Widow in the form herein-before directed, together with a certificate under the hands of the Minister and Churchwardens of the parish where such Widow resides, that she is living, and to the best of their knowledge and belief still a Widow.

That as any of the said Widows shall die or marry again, their Pensions shall cease and determine from the time of such death or marriage."

## No. I.

*Required for placing a Widow on the Pension.*

WE do hereby certify to the best of our knowledge, that

was the lawful wife of

who*

wherefore we humbly recommend her as an object of His Majesty's royal bounty. Given under our hands this
day of

{ *The Colonel to sign here.*

{ *The Agent to sign here.*

came this day before me, and made oath that she was lawfully married to
late a  in the
commanded by
and ever since his decease she has continued a Widow, and is so at this present time; and that she has no pension, allowance, or provision made her by Government.

{ *The Widow to sign here.*

*Sworn before me, at
this  day of*

N. B. *The Magistrate is to state the name of the place of his residence. When the Colonel's signature cannot be procured, that of the Commanding Officer is required. Widows of Staff Officers are to be recommended by their late husbands' respective Commanding Officers.*

---

\* Insert where and when the Officer died, or was killed; together with the situation and circumstances in which the Widow is left, and date of marriage; and annex certificate of marriage, or a copy thereof, certified by the Minister of the parish, in which the ceremony was performed.

## No. II.

*Required for receiving the Pension when the Widow does not employ an Agent, but appears in person.*

                                                came this day before me, and made oath that she was lawfully married to                late a                   in the        commanded by and ever since his decease she has continued a Widow, and is so at this present time; and that she has no pension, allowance, or provision made her by Government.

*Sworn before me, at*
    *this    day of*

N. B. The above affidavit is administered to the Widow at the War Office.

## No. III.

*Required for receiving the Pension when the Widow employs an Agent.*

WE, the Minister and Churchwardens of the parish of
           in the county of          do
hereby certify, that         is now living, and to the best of our knowledge and belief, is the Widow of
     late a         in the
commanded by
   As witness our hands, this     day of    180

         ——————————— *Minister.*

         ———————————
         ——————————— } *Churchwardens.*

                        came this day before me, and made oath that she was lawfully married to
     late a         in the
    commanded by
and ever since his decease she has continued a Widow, and is so at this present time; and that she has no pension, allowance, or provision, made her by Government, except the pension she receives by His Majesty's bounty as an Officers's Widow.

         ——————————— → { *The Widow to sign here.*

*Sworn before me, at*
  *this*     *day of*
*the certificate having previously been executed.*

———————

   I do attest and declare that I verily believe the above certificate and affidavit to be genuine and authentic.

         ——————————— → { *The Agent to sign here.*

*N. B. The Magistrate is requested not to administer the oath, unless the certificate shall have been regularly executed: both certificate and affidavit to be executed on or after the 24th of April, 24th August, and 24th December in every year. The Magistrate is to state the place of his residence at the time of administering the oath. No erasures, alterations, or interlineations admitted. Should there be no Churchwarden, or only one, the Minister is to certify the same on the face hereof.*

State

*State referred to in the Secretary at War's Circulars, relative to encreasing the Pay of the Army, &c. dated in 1806. (See Section I.)*

RATES of the increased PENSIONS to WIDOWS of Officers of the Land Forces; commencing from the 25th June, 1806.

| APPOINTMENTS. | Rate of Pension. £. |
|---|---|
| Lieutenant Colonel | 60 |
| Major | 50 |
| Captain | 40 |
| Lieutenant, Adjutant, Surgeon | 30 |
| 2d Lieutenant, Cornet, Ensign, Quarter Master, Assistant Surgeon | 26 |
| Chaplain, Deputy Purveyor, and Hospital Mate occasionally | 20 |

N. B. The Pension to Widows of *Half Pay* Officers, is only granted to such as may become Widows subsequently to the 24th June, 1806.

*Letter*

*Letter from the Adjutant General, relative to Officers absent without Leave.*

*War Office,* 19*th April,* 1800.

SIR,

I HAVE received His Royal Highness the Commander in Chief's directions to inform you, that in consequence of the representation made to the King of the frequent instances which occur of Officers being guilty of neglect of duty, by being absent without leave, and not joining their respective Regiments, it is His Majesty's pleasure, that in future the pay of all Officers who are absent *without leave,* or who, having obtained leave of absence, overstay the period of it, (of whom I have received His Royal Highness's commands to make, from time to time, special Returns to the War Office) shall be stopped in the hands of their Agents, nor shall it, in any instance, be afterwards paid to such Officer, except upon a very strong and full representation from the Commanding Officer, stating some unavoidable cause for this apparent breach of duty, in which particular case, His Majesty's further pleasure will be notified, through the Commander in Chief, to the War Office.

His Royal Highness the Commander in Chief will feel it incumbent upon him to submit the name of any Officer who continues absent without leave, and whose absence is not accounted for, to His Majesty, for the purpose of being superseded.

I am commanded to request you will cause this information to be transmitted to the Agents of the Army, directing them to give it the most extensive circulation in the Regiments in their agency, and that you will enjoin them in every instance to give immediate notice to Officers appointed to Regiments in their agency, whether by original appointment, exchange, or promotions, directing them at the same time to have recourse to the readiest means of joining their respective Regiments, whether at home or on foreign service.

I have the honor to be, &c.

H. CALVERT,
Adjutant General.

Right Hon. W. Windham.

*Circular*

*Circular to the Agents of Regiments, relative to the Pay of Gentlemen first obtaining Commissions.*

*War Office, 24th July, 1805.*

SIR,

I N pursuance of the recommendation of his Royal Highness the Commander in Chief, I have the Secretary at War's directions to acquaint you, that notwithstanding the instructions contained in the Adjutant General's letter of the 19th of April, 1800 *, the Pay of Gentlemen first obtaining Commissions in the Regular or Fencible Regiments, or Militia, will be allowed up to the 24th of the military month following that in which their Commissions shall be dated; although they shall not have joined, or have been returned absent with leave, in the course of such period.

I am,

SIR,

Your obedient servant,

W. MERRY.

Agent

---

* See Page 507.

*Miscellaneous Orders.*

*Circular to Generals commanding on foreign Stations, relative to the Mode of Application when regimental Paymasters have Occasion for Leave of Absence.*

War Office, 7th August, 1800.

SIR,

IT being found expedient to establish a certain rule to be observed when Paymasters of regiments, stationed abroad, have occasion to request a leave of absence; I have it in command to acquaint you, that in such cases they are to make application in writing to the Commanding Officer of the corps to which they belong, accompanied with a statement of the means by which the duty of Paymaster is to be supplied during their absence, and a declaration that they shall consider themselves equally responsible with regard to any accounts to be made up for the period they may be absent, as if the whole business of the paymastership had been transacted by themselves. This statement and declaration are to be transmitted by the Commanding Officer to the General Officer commanding in chief on the station; who, provided he is satisfied as to the propriety of the application, and sees no objection to the person or persons recommended to act during the Paymaster's absence, may give the necessary leave accordingly.

I have, &c.

W. WINDHAM.

General
Commanding the forces.

*Circular to Agents of Regular Regiments, relative to the Advance of Pay to Officers embarking for Service.*

War Office, 9th September, 1805.

SIR,

Doubts appearing to be entertained in regard to the period from which individual Officers, embarking for foreign service, should receive the advance of pay allowed to them upon such occasions; I am directed to acquaint you, that the same is to be allowed from the day following that of their embarkation, and may be drawn for when the proper Officer at the Army Depôt shall have reported that they are entitled thereto.

In the cases where the Officers shall not embark from the Isle of Wight, the advance will be permitted to be drawn for upon the recommendation of the Adjutant General.

I am, &c.

F. MOORE.

Agent of the

*Circular*

*Circular to Agents of Regular Regiments on the British Establishment, relative to the Pay of Officers embarking for Foreign Service.*

*War Office, 6th June,* 1806.

SIR,

IT having been represented that great inconvenience is felt by officers arriving at foreign stations without any proper notification of the period to which their pay had been advanced on embarking, I am to desire that you will, in future, take care that every officer who shall receive his pay from you on proceeding to a foreign station, be furnished with a regular certificate of the date to which he shall have been paid in this country.

I am, SIR,

your most obedient

humble servant,

R. FITZPATRICK.

Agent of the

*Circular to Paymasters of Regiments abroad, respecting the Nature of the Services to be defrayed by the Deputy Paymasters General on Foreign Stations.*

*War Office,* 31st *October,* 1806.

SIR,

IN pursuance of a suggestion from the Paymaster General, I have the Secretary at War's directions to acquaint you, that when the Corps to which you belong shall be stationed abroad, you are not to receive from the Deputy Paymaster General any sums for other services than the Pay of the Officers and Men, but are to draw upon the Regimental Agent for such other services, which you will be aware are limited to the half yearly allowances to Field Officers and Captains, and for postage and stationary, with the addition, in the Cavalry, of the allowance for Riding Masters, &c. and, occasionally, bounty of Recruits.

All other incidental expences are to be defrayed out of the extraordinaries of the army, under the orders of the General Officers commanding.

I am, &c.

Paymaster of the

W. MERRY.

*General*

*General Orders respecting the Number of Women allowed to accompany Regiments embarking for Foreign Service, and the Allowances to Wives and Children of Soldiers not permitted to embark with the Men.*

Horse Guards, 29th October, 1800.

HIS Royal Highness the Commander in Chief is pleased to direct, that the following Regulations respecting the number of women allowed to accompany Regiments embarking for foreign service, shall in future be most strictly adhered to.

Except on occasions when circumstances may render it necessary for troops to embark entirely without women, (which in such cases will be particularly notified) His Royal Highness permits women, being the lawful wives of Soldiers, to embark in the proportion of six to a hundred men, (Non-commissioned Officers included,) but in order to obviate the distress to which the families of Soldiers are liable to be exposed, the women exceeding the above number, being the lawful wives of Non-commissioned Officers or Soldiers, shall, if natives of England, on their husbands embarking for foreign service, receive for themselves one guinea each, and for each child born in lawful wedlock, under ten years of age, the sum of five shillings to enable them to return home. And all women and children in the same situation, and under the description above-mentioned, being natives of Scotland or Ireland, shall receive the same allowance, and should they require it, be provided with a passage by sea, to the nearest port of the country to which they belong.

The General and other Officers who are directed to superintend embarkations, will be authorised by the Secretary at War, to advance the sums necessary for carrying the above arrangement into effect.

By order of His Royal Highness
The Commander in Chief.

HARRY CALVERT,
Adjutant General.

---

MEMORANDUM.

The mode of issuing the allowances to the wives of Soldiers not permitted to embark with their husbands, was explained in a Regulation from the War Office, dated 20th August, 1806; which is printed in the Explanatory Directions to Paymasters, No. 69. [Section III. page 187 to 189.]

*Circular*

*Circular to Generals Commanding in Districts, relative to the mode of defraying the Expence of the Hire of Ground for Encampments.*

*War-Office, 6th June,* 1805.

SIR,

I HAVE the honor to transmit herewith for your information and guidance, an Extract of a Report from the Comptrollers of Army Accompts, respecting the mode of defraying the Expence of the Hire of Ground for Encampments, &c. which has been approved of by the Lords Commissioners of His Majesty's Treasury.

You will of course be aware that in consequence of this Arrangement, no charges of the above description are in future to be included in the Contingent Acompts of General Officers rendered to this Department.

I have, &c.

General                                         W. DUNDAS.

---

*Extract of a Report from the Comptrollers of Army Accompts to the Lords Commissioners of His Majesty's Treasury, dated* 15th *May*, 1805.

" Considering that the General Officers at present grant Warrants on the Commissary General for Military Expenditure, under the denomination of Field Works, Beacons, &c. We are of opinion, that it may be most adviseable to adopt the same method in paying for the hire of Ground used for the Encampments, &c. of His Majesty's Troops, and that the Commissary General be authorized to pay to the Parties owning and letting such Ground, the Monies which shall be due to them, upon their producing a Warrant, directing the Payment from the General Officer
                                        commanding

commanding in the District where the ground is hired, with the following Papers annexed, viz. A Statement of the quantity and nature of the Land so hired; together with a specification of the Agreement made with the Party letting the same, whether Owner or Occupier, in which is to be stated the time for which it is engaged, and the price to be paid; and to be signed by the Quarter-Master General, and the principal Officer of Engineers attending such Camp; which Documents, with the Receipt of the Party entitled, should be admitted as sufficient Vouchers in the Accompt of the Commissary General."

*Circular Letter to the General Officers commanding Districts, containing further Information, relative to the Hire of Ground for Encampments.*

*War Office, 31st July,* 1805.

SIR,

IN addition to my Letter of the 6th ultimo, I have the honor to acquaint you that the Lords Commissioners of His Majesty's Treasury, have been pleased to approve of the Agreements for the Hire of Ground for Encampments, being signed by the Senior Officer on the Staff commanding in the District, and by an Assistant Quarter-Master General, in the absence of his Principal; all claims sanctioned in this manner, will consequently be paid by the Commissary General, without the intervention of this Office.

I am further to acquaint you, that where it may be necessary to hire Ground for the Exercise of particular Corps, the same is to be reported by the Commanding Officer to the General Officer commanding in the District, who will, if he thinks proper, convey the application to the Quarter-Master General, upon whose Recommendation an Authority will be given, from this Office, to the Regimental Pay-Master, to charge the Amount in the contingent Accompts of the Corps.

I am, &c.

W. DUNDAS.

*General Orders, relative to Men Sleeping out of Quarters.*

*Horse-Guards,* 13*th April,* 1800.

HIS Royal Highness the Commander in Chief, is pleased to signify His Pleasure, that in future no Man is to be allowed to sleep out of his Quarters, except such as have Families, who are, together with their Wives, of good character, and who (if not married previous to enlistment) have married with the consent of their Commanding-Officers.

By order of His Royal Highness
The Commander in Chief.

HARRY CALVERT,
Adjutant General of the Forces.

*General Orders relative to the Number of Men permitted to Sleep out of Quarters.*

Horse Guards, 4th September, 1801.

SIR,

IN addition to the General Orders of the 13th of *April*, 1800, respecting the Indulgence granted to married Men of good Character being permitted to sleep out of Quarters, I am directed to acquaint you, for the information of Officers Commanding Regiments in the District under your Command, that the permission is to be limited to Ten Men for every Hundred, which, by His Royal Highness the Commander in Chief's positive Orders, is never to be exceeded, and only granted to Men answering the Description above specified.

I have, &c.

W. WYNYARD,

Deputy Adjutant General.

To Generals
Commanding Districts.

*Circular*

*Circular to the Agents of His Majesty's Regiments serving in the East Indies; relative to the Accommodation of Officers proceeding to India on Board the Company's Ships.*

War Office, 14th May, 1805.

SIR,

THE Court of Directors of the East India Company having lately adopted some resolutions in regard to the accommodation of His Majesty's Officers proceeding to India on board the Company's ships; which have been acquiesced in by the Commander in Chief, and by the Secretary at War; I am directed to communicate to you, for the information of the Colonels and other Officers of the Regiments in your Agency, the following arrangements founded upon the resolutions above-mentioned, viz.

No Officer holding the regimental commission of Colonel, Lieutenant-Colonel, Major, Captain, Surgeon, or Paymaster, belonging to the Regiments mentioned in the margin* (being those which were serving in India when the said resolutions were passed) will, in future, be accommodated at the tables of the Commanders of the Company's ships free of expence to himself.

For Subalterns, Adjutants, Quarter Masters of Infantry, and Assistant Surgeons, the usual allowance of 95 *l.* will be ordered into the Agent's hands as heretofore.

In the event of any other of His Majesty's Regiments proceeding to India, free accommodation will be provided by the Company for the established complement of Officers of the respective ranks. When the full establishment shall have been once sent out, the Colonels, Lieutenant Colonels, Ma-

---

\* 8th Light Dragoons.  
19th do.  
22d do.  
24th (late 27th) do.  
25th (late 29th) do.  
12th Foot  
22d do.  
33d do.  
34th do.  
65th do.  
73d Foot.  
74th do.  
75th do.  
76th do.  
77th do.  
78th do.  
80th do.  
84th do.  
86th do.  
94th do.

jors, Captains, Surgeons, and Paymasters, respectively, who may subsequently embark, will be under the necessity of defraying themselves the expence of their accommodation at the Captain's table during the voyage (the passage being provided at the public expence:) for Subalterns, Adjutants, Quarter-Masters of Infantry, and Assistant Surgeons, an allowance of 95 *l.* will be issued in the usual manner.

No order for receiving on board one of the Company's ships an officer whose passage may be applied for individually, will, in future, be given, by the Court of Directors, until the regulated sum, for his accommodation at the Captain's Table, shall have been actually deposited in the hands of the Company's Paymaster at the India House, agreeably to the rates specified in the margin hereof.*

When a detachment consisting of Officers and recruits embarks from the Army Depot in the Isle of Wight, with a general order for their reception on board the Company's ships, in which the rank only is specified, and not the names of the Officers, the Commanders of the Company's ships will be instructed not to receive on board any of the Officers, until the regulated allowance for their accommodation during the voyage as above specified, shall be paid to the Commander, either in the current coin of the Realm, or in notes of the Bank of England. In these cases the payment will be made to the Commander by the Staff Officer of the Army Depot, superintending the embarkation; and the chief Paymaster at the Depot will draw upon you, in the case of Subalterns, Adjutants, Quarter Masters of Infantry, and Assistant Surgeons, for the 95 *l.* allowed to defray the expence of their passage; and in the case of Colonels, Lieutenant Colonels, Majors, Captains, Surgeons and Paymasters, for the amount of Pay, usually advanced to them on embarking; which advance of Pay is to be invariably applied in satisfying the demands of the

---

\* Colonel — £ 185
  Lieutenant Colonel — 135
  Major — 135
  Captain — 110
  Lieutenant — 95
  Ensign or Cornet — 95
  Paymaster — 110
  Adjutant — 95
  Quarter-master of Infantry — 95
  Surgeon — 95
  Assistant Surgeon — 95

## Miscellaneous Orders. 621

Captains. In order that the pay advanced may more nearly cover the above charge, the advance for the ranks mentioned in the margin,* will be increased from six to seven months; and where even with this addition the advanced pay is not sufficient to defray the sum which the Commanders are authorised to claim, the difference is to be made up by the Officers themselves in the presence of the Staff Officer.

You are of course not to suffer any circumstances to prevent your honoring the bills of the chief Paymaster, for the amount of the passage money, and advance of Pay as above-mentioned.

It will be your duty to make the Officers of the Regiments in your Agency, fully aware of the purport of the above regulations.

I am, Sir,

Your most obedient,

Humble Servant,

F. MOORE.

---

* Majors of Infantry.
 Captains   do.
 Paymasters  do.

*Extract from an Advertisement, dated General Post-Office, 1st August, 1806, containing the Substance of the Regulations under which Soldiers are allowed to send and receive Letters at a low Rate of Postage.*

"NO single Letter sent by the Post, on his own private concern only, from any Serjeant, Corporal, Trumpeter, Drummer, Fifer, and Private Soldier, in His Majesty's Army, within any part of His Majesty's dominions, shall, whilst such Soldier shall be employed on His Majesty's Service, and not otherwise, be charged with a higher Rate of Postage than the Sum of One Penny for the conveyance of each such Letter; such Postage to be paid at the time of putting the same into the Post-Office of the town or place from whence such Letter is intended to be sent by the Post, provided that upon every such Letter so to be sent, the Name of the Writer, and his class or description in the Regiment, Corps, or Detachment to which he shall belong, shall be superscribed, and provided that upon every such Letter there shall be written in the hand-writing of, and signed by, the Officer having at the time the Command of the Regiment, Corps, or Detachment,\* his name, and the name of the Regiment, Corps, or Detachment commanded by him.

No single Letter, directed to any such Soldier, upon his own private concern only, within any part of His Majesty's dominions, whilst such Soldier shall be employed on His Majesty's Service, and not otherwise, shall be charged with a higher Rate of Postage than One Penny, provided that such Penny be paid upon putting the Letter into a Post-Office, established under the Authority of His Majesty's Postmaster-General; and provided also, that every such Letter shall be directed to such Soldier, specifying on the Superscription thereof the Regiment, Corps, or De-

---

\* Any person *not having at the time the Command of the Regiment, Corps, or Detachment*, who shall write his name on a letter, as above, in order that the same may be sent at a low rate of postage, is liable, by law, to the penalty of Five Pounds.

tachment

tachment to which he shall belong, and provided that it shall not be lawful for the Deputy Postmaster to deliver such Letter to any Person, except the Soldier to whom it shall be directed, or to some Person appointed to receive the same, by writing under the hand of the Officer having the Command of the Regiment, Corps, or Detachment to which the Soldier shall belong.

Nothing in these Instructions is to be construed to extend to Letters sent by or to Commissioned or Warrant Officers in the Army."

*Circular to the Commanding Officers of Regiments on the British Establishment, relative to the Mode of addressing Applications to the War Office.*

*War Office, 12th September, 1804.*

Sir,

FROM the frequent irregularities which take place in the mode of addressing applications to this office, and which, besides being the cause of considerable trouble to this department, and to those who make the applications, are also productive of delay in the conduct of the public service, I am induced to transmit the following instructions on the above head, for the information and guidance of yourself and the other officers of the regiment under your command.

Officers belonging to regiments stationed in *Great Britain*, *Guernsey*, and *Jersey*, (not being commanding officers) are not, unless in extraordinary cases of special and obvious necessity, to address themselves directly to this department; but are to apply, in the first instance, to the commanding officers of their respective regiments, whose experience and information on military subjects, will, it is presumed, in most cases, prevent the necessity of further reference. Where the application is of such a kind as not to admit of a decisive answer from the commanding officer, it is expected that in forwarding the same, either for the consideration of the general commanding in the district, or immediately to the War Office, as the case may be, the commanding officer will furnish at the same time, every information of a regimental or local nature, which may assist in determining the point in question, and state the opinion which he is himself inclined to form thereupon.

Every application, whether brought before the commanding officer of a regiment by any of the inferior officers, as above-mentioned, or originating with himself, relating to any unusual regimental expenditure incurred or proposed, which from its nature may be likely to have occurred, or to occur, in other corps, is to be submitted by the commanding officer, in the first instance, to the general commanding in the district; who will, if necessary, forward the same to this office, accompanying it with his authentication of the

facts

facts contained therein, and with his opinion upon the propriety of assenting to what is desired.

On other points, including all pecuniary claims that are merely of a personal nature, or evidently affecting the particular corps only in which the claim occurs, the commanding officer's application may be addressed immediately to this department.

Officers in this country belonging to regiments on *foreign stations* (the colonels excepted, in whose discretion it will rest to correspond with this office either directly, or through their agents), are to consider the agents of their respective regiments as the channel of communication with the War Office. Whenever the object of the application can be answered without a reference to this department, it will be the duty of the agents to apprize the officers accordingly: in other cases, the agents are to forward the application, transmitting therewith every explanation and document that may be necessary.

Officers on service with regiments on foreign stations are of course to apply, through the commanding officers, to the general commanding in chief on the station.

The instructions contained in this letter are not to be considered as extending to points connected with the particular line of duty of paymasters, as marked out in the instructions to paymasters—They will therefore, on such points, continue to correspond directly with the department of Accompts in the War Office.

All applications made contrary to the above instructions, will be returned unanswered.

I have the honor to be,

Sir,

Your most obedient

humble servant,

W. DUNDAS.

Officer commanding the
Regiment of

# APPENDIX.

# APPENDIX.

*Circular to Commanding Officers of Regiments of Cavalry, and Marching Regiments of Foot; relative to the Description of previous Service which entitles Soldiers to additional Allowances: And also respecting the Allowance to Lieutenant Colonels and Majors of Infantry at Home, for the Keep of a Horse.*

*War Office, 25d September,* 1806.

SIR,

IT appearing by some recent enquiries of Commanding Officers and Paymasters, that it is not completely understood in what manner the late orders for encreasing the pay and allowances of the Army apply to the battalions of Infantry formed for limited service; I have the honor to explain to you, that the advantages therein held forth, can be claimed only by men liable to serve abroad; and consequently that Non-commissioned Officers and Privates engaged *and serving* under the Terms of the Army of Reserve Act, and the additional Force Act, in like manner with the Militia, and the Fencibles not liable to serve out of the United Kingdom or the Islands in the Channel, are not to receive any Part of the Encrease of pay and allowance granted from the 25th June last.

Upon the same principle, previous Service *under the Terms of the said Acts,* is not to be taken into account in estimating the claims of Soldiers of Infantry (now attested for General Service) to the additional allowances granted to men after seven and fourteen years' service respectively.

I think

I think it proper also to make you fully aware, that the period during which Soldiers *may have been actually absent* from their regiments, in a state of desertion previously to 25th June last, is to be deducted in estimating their length of service. You are already apprized, that Desertion occurring subsequently to that period, will deprive a Soldier of all title to benefit arising from antecedent service.

I take this opportunity of annexing a List (No. 1) of Fencible Corps, which, according to the terms of their letters of service, were liable to serve out of the United Kingdom and the Islands in the Channel; together with a List (No. 2) of certain Fencible Corps raised for home service, but which are understood to have volunteered for Foreign service. In the case of the latter, the precise dates of their volunteering cannot, in every instance, be at this time ascertained: according to a communication, however, from the Adjutant-General, the general period may be fixed from 1st November 1799.

Previous service in the said Corps will, therefore, be considered as giving Soldiers a title to the additional allowances above mentioned, from the dates of the letters of service, and the general period of volunteering, respectively; regard being of course had to the time and nature of the engagement of men enlisted after the said period. Service in the Royal Artillery and Marines is also to be taken into account.

I am farther to add, in reference to the allowance granted to Lieutenant-Colonels and Majors of Infantry Regiments, at home, for the Keep of a Horse, that in cases where the said Officers are absent on leave the allowance will not be permitted to be charged, unless the horses are left at the Head-Quarters of the Regiment, so as to be all times ready for the Public Service.

I have the Honor to be,<br>
SIR,<br>
Your most obedient<br>
humble Servant,<br>
RICHARD FITZPATRICK.

Officer Commanding
    Regiment of

No. 1.

## No. 1.

List of Corps of Fencible Infantry, raised for Service out of the United Kingdom.

| Corps. | Names of Commandants. | Dates of Letters of Service. | Dates of Disbandment. |
|---|---|---|---|
| Newfoundland | Colonel Skinner | 25th April, 1795 | 12th August, 1802 |
| Prince of Wales's Own | Sir William Johnstone | 10th July, 1798 | 24th May |
| Lochaber | Colonel Cameron | 17th Ditto | 26th June |
| Third Argyll | Colonel M'Neil | | 3d July |
| Princess Charlotte of Wales's | Colonel M'Leod | 19th Ditto | 11th June |
| Wallace | Sir Thomas Wallace Dunlop | 20th Ditto | 3d Feb. 1800 |
| Banffshire | Colonel Hay | 26th Ditto | 10th May, 1802 |
| Clan Alpine | Colonel A. Macgregor Murray | 31st Ditto | 24th July |
| Ross and Cromarty | Colonel Lewis Mackenzie | 8th August | 27th Ditto |
| Cambrian Rangers | Colonel Edwards | 22d Ditto | 20th May |
| Surry Rangers | Colonel Pollen | 26th November | 13th November |
| Royal Birmingham | Colonel Rann | 6th December | 24th Dec. 1799 |

# No. 2.

**List of Corps of Fencible and Provisional Cavalry, and Fencible Infantry, raised for Home Service, which are understood to have Volunteered for Service out of the United Kingdom.**

### FENCIBLE CAVALRY.

| Regiments. | Names of Commandants. | Dates of Disbandment. |
|---|---|---|
| Ayrshire | Colonel Dunlop | 17th April, 1800 |
| Berwick | Sir Alexander Don | 15th September |
| Cambridge | Colonel Adeane | 22d Ditto |
| Cinque Ports | Lord Hawkesbury | 25th March |
| Dumfries | Colonel Maxwell | 15th September |
| Fifeshire | Colonel Thomson | 26th March |
| First Regiment | Colonel Villiers | 22d September |
| Hampshire | Colonel Everitt | 13th May |
| Lanark and Dunbarton | Lord Belhaven | 17th Ditto |
| Lancashire | Colonel Bisshop | 22d September |
| Lothian, East and West | Colonel Hamilton | 1st May |
| Lothian, Mid | Earl of Ancram | 22d September |
| Norfolk | Colonel Harbord | 10th May |
| Oxford | Colonel Parker | 19th October |
| Pembroke (Detachment) | Colonel Dunne | 31st August |
| Perthshire (Ditto) | Colonel Moray | 7th April |
| Princess of Wales's | Earl of Darlington | 22d September |
| Princess Royal's Own (Detachment) | Colonel M'Dowall | 3d April |
| Roxburgh and Selkirk | Sir John Scott | 27th September |
| Rutland | Colonel Craufurd | 7th May |
| Somerset | Earl Poulett | 26th March |
| Sussex | Sir James St. Clair Erskine | 7th April |
| Warwick (Detachment) | Colonel Churchill | 5th Ditto |

## PROVISIONAL CAVALRY.

| Regiments. | Names of Commandants. | Dates of Disbandment. |
|---|---|---|
| Worcester | Colonel Cocks | 12th April |

### FENCIBLE INFANTRY.

| Regiments. | Names of Commandants. | Dates of Disbandment. |
|---|---|---|
| Princess of Wales's, or Aberdeen | Colonel Leith | 11th April, 1803 |
| Breadalbane, 3d Battalion | Earl of Breadalbane | 28th July, 1802 |
| Cheshire | Colonel Courtenay | 12th Ditto |
| Devon and Cornwall | Colonel Hall | 14th Ditto |
| Dunbarton | Major General England | 5th October |
| Durham | Colonel Skerret | 22d May |
| Elgin | Earl of Elgin | 15th October |
| Fraser | Colonel Fraser | 12th July |
| Loyal Irish | Colonel Handcock | 7th Ditto |
| Limerick | Sir Vere Hunt | 1st November, 1800 |
| Nottingham | Colonel O'Connor | 28th February, 1803 |
| Rothsay and Caithness | Sir John Sinclair | 26th July, 1802 |
| Suffolk | Colonel Robinson | 13th October |
| Tarbert | Sir Edward Leslie | 24th June |
| Ancient Irish | Colonel Fitzgerald | 10th August |
| York | Colonel Stapylton | 30th June |

N. B. Since the above Communication was prepared, it has been ascertained, that the Loyal Essex Fencible Infantry, commanded by Lieutenant General Urquhart, volunteered for Service out of the United Kingdom. The said Regiment should therefore be added to the above List, No. II.

*Warrant establishing certain Orders and Regulations, for the better ordering of the Army, and for improving the Condition of Non-commissioned Officers and Soldiers, and for fixing the Pensions, Allowances and Relief to which Non-commissioned Officers and Soldiers are to become entitled on their Discharge, by reason of the Expiration of certain Periods of Service, or as invalid, disabled, or wounded.*

## GEORGE R.

WHEREAS in pursuance, and in furtherance of the Provisions of certain Acts of Parliament, passed during the last Session, we are pleased to issue the following Orders and Regulations, for the better ordering of our Army, and for improving the condition of Non-commissioned Officers and Soldiers, and for fixing the Pensions, Allowances and Relief to which Non-commissioned Officers and Soldiers are to become entitled on their Discharge, by reason of the Expiration of certain Periods of Service, or as Invalid, disabled, or wounded:

Our will and pleasure therefore is, that the same be duly observed by all whom it may concern.

Given at our Court at Saint James's, this 7th Day of October, 1806, in the Forty-sixth year of our Reign.

By His Majesty's command,

RICHARD FITZPATRICK.

## *Appendix.*

*Orders and Regulations referred to in His Majesty's Warrant of the 7th of October, 1806.*

*Periods and Terms of Inlisting.*

In the Infantry - - - 7 Years
   Cavalry - - - 10 Do.
   Artillery - - - 12 Do.

*Men willing to engage for a Second Period of Service will be re-inlisted,*

In the Infantry for - - 7 Years,
   Cavalry - - - 7 Do.
   Artillery - - - 5 Do.

*Men willing to engage for a Third Period of Service will be re-inlisted,*

In the Infantry for - - 7 Years.
   Cavalry - - - 7 Do.
   Artillery - - - 5 Do.

No Non-commissioned Officer or Soldier to be allowed to re-inlist for a Second Period of Service, until within twelve months of the end of his first period, nor for a third, until within two years of the end of his second. The new period in each case not to be considered as commencing until after the expiration of the one preceding.

No Non-commissioned Officer or Soldier to be allowed to re-inlist, or engage to re-inlist, into any other than his own Regiment, until after his complete discharge.

Non-commissioned Officer or Soldier, changing from one service to another, viz. from Infantry to Cavalry, Cavalry to Artillery, &c. to engage for a term of years equal to the first period of the service into which he enters.

For young men inlisting under eighteen years of age, the time wanting to complete eighteen to be added to the seven, ten, or twelve years.

Periods of service may be extended by the Commanding Officer of the Government, Colony, Island, or Station, as to Non-commissioned Officers and Soldiers serving abroad, for six months; and by the King, with respect to Non-commissioned

missioned Officers and Soldiers serving either at home or abroad, until six months shall have elapsed of continued peace, subsequent to the expiration of the period of service for which they were serving, provided always that no such extension of service shall in any case exceed three years.

No Non-commissioned Officer or Soldier having inlisted for, and serving in his last period of service, to be compelled to serve under any such extension of service beyond six months after the expiration of such last period.

Non-commissioned Officers and Soldiers may be transferred from one Battalion to another, of the same Regiment; or, if disabled, to a Veteran Battalion; but not otherwise drafted from one Regiment to another without their consent.

Every Non-commissioned Officer or Soldier entitled to his Discharge, if then serving abroad, to be sent to Great Britain or Ireland, free of Expence, and to receive the pay allowed to Non-commissioned Officers and Soldiers, on a March, from the place of his being landed, to the parish or place in which he shall have been originally inlisted, at the rate of twelve miles for each day's march, with the usual number of halting days; and every Non-commissioned Officer and Soldier, so entitled to his Discharge, who shall be discharged at any place in the United Kingdom, other than that to which he belongs as above, to have the like pay, from the place of discharge to the place of his attestation as aforesaid.

*Rates of Pensions of Men who shall have inlisted for, and be discharged after having served the second and last Periods of Service.*

## CAVALRY AND INFANTRY.

*After Second Period.*  per Diem.
                        l. s. d.

Serjeant-Major, Quarter-Master-Serjeant, Serjeant,
  Corporal, and Private  - - - - - - -  0 0 5

*After Third Period.*

Serjeant-Major and Quarter-Master-Serjeant, having served three years as such, so much in addition to his claim for Pension as Serjeant, as will make in the whole - - - - - - - 0 2 0

Serjeant

*Appendix.*

|  | | *per Diem.* | | |
|---|---|---|---|---|
|  |  | *l.* | *s.* | *d.* |
| Serjeant | from | 0 | 1 | 0 |
|  | to | 0 | 1 | 10 |

One halfpenny a day to be added to the shilling for every year of Service as a Corporal, and one penny for every year of service as a Serjeant, but the pension in no case to exceed 1s. 10d.

| Corporals | from | 0 | 1 | 0 |
|---|---|---|---|---|
|  | to | 0 | 1 | 6 |

One halfpenny a day to be added to the shilling for every year of service as a Corporal, but the Pension in no case to exceed 1s. 6d.

Private - - - - - - - - - - - - - - - 0 1 0

To Serjeant-Majors, Quarter-Master-Serjeants, Serjeants, Corporals, or Privates, serving after Third Period, one halfpenny a day to be added to the Pension for every year of service after the expiration of the last period, without limit as to the amount.

*Soldiers discharged before the Expiration of their Periods of Service.*

Non-commissioned Officer or Soldier, discharged during First Period, and re-inlisting into his own Regiment, or into any other Regiment into which he may be permitted to inlist, to be allowed to reckon, for the purpose of claiming Pay and Pension, all years of former service.

Non-commissioned Officer or Soldier, discharged during Second Period, to be allowed to reckon, for Pay and Pension, all former service, and one year for every two of absence, subsequent to such discharge, and to be entitled to pension of five pence on the expiration of the period so computed.

Non-commissioned Officer or Soldier, discharged during Third Period, and not receiving a Pension, as invalid, wounded, or disabled, shall immediately receive the Pension due at the expiration of the Second Period, and for obtaining the difference between it and the Pension due on the expiration of the Third Period, be allowed to reckon one year for every two years of absence subsequent to such discharge, so as to be entitled to the full Pension of one shilling a day at the expiration of the Third Period so computed.

*Soldiers*

*Soldiers quitting at the Expiration of their Periods of Service.*

Non-commissioned Officer or Soldier quitting the Service, and afterwards re-inlisting into his own Regiment, not to reckon, for the Purpose of claiming any Increase of Pay, the first two years after re-inlisting.

Non-commissioned Officer or Soldier so quitting, and re-inlisting into any other Regiment, not to reckon, for the Purpose of claiming Increase of Pay, the first three years after re-inlisting.

*Service in East or West Indies.*

Non-commissioned Officer or Soldier, to be allowed to reckon three years for every two years of Service in the East or West Indies, for the Purpose of claiming Increase of Pay, and Pension in case of discharge, but not for the purpose of claiming discharge, before the actual expiration of the Second Period of Service.

*Increase of Pay and Pensions, how forfeited.*

Non-commissioned Officers and Soldiers, discharged before completion of service, and not conforming to any Rules or Regulations, prescribed by the Commissioners of Chelsea Hospital, as to registering their names and places of abode, and notifying the same from time to time; or not offering themselves on any Proclamation of His Majesty, or not joining any garrison or veteran Battalion, if required by the Commissioners of Chelsea Hospital, to forfeit all claim to Increase of Pay, or to Pension, on account of Service; but no Soldier to be liable to be so called upon to serve, either under any Proclamation, or under any Order of the Commissioners of Chelsea Hospital, who shall have completed his Three full Periods of Service, as computed under these Regulations.

Non-commissioned Officer or Soldier may be deprived, by Sentence of General Court Martial, of all, or any proportion, of claim to Increase of Pay, or to Pension, on account of former years of Service.

*Rates of Pensions of Non-commissioned Officers and Soldiers discharged as disabled or unfit for Service.*

|  | Per Diem. |
|---|---|
|  | s. d. |
| If incapable of contributing to earn a livelihood — from | 1 3 |
| to | 1 6 |

|  | s. | d. |
|---|---|---|
| If disabled, but able to contribute something towards their livelihood - - - - - - | 1 | 0 |
| If disabled, but able materially to assist themselves - - - - - - - - - - - | 0 | 9 |
| If unfit for Service, but able to earn a livelihood | 0 | 6 |

Men who, in respect merely to their disability, would be placed on either of the two lower Classes, shall, if discharged during the Third Period of Service, be entitled to the Pension of one shilling.

No Non-commissioned Officer or Soldier to be allowed to claim, of right, any such Pension, whose disability or unfitness has arisen from vice or misconduct.

Commissioners of Chelsea to determine to which Class of Pension each man belongs, with power of removing from one class to another.

Non-commissioned Officers or Soldiers, having had such pension allowed, may, by the Commissioners, be required again to serve till they shall have completed their Periods of Service.

---

*The foregoing Orders and Regulations are to be understood as referring to those Non-commissioned Officers and Privates only, who have inlisted subsequently to the 24th of last June; but Non-commissioned Officers and Soldiers having inlisted (for General Service) previously to that period, are to be entitled, in virtue of their former services, to the full benefit of what is therein contained, in all that relates to Pay and Allowances, and also to Pensions, if discharged as Invalid, Disabled, or Wounded, or after a period of service of not less than Fourteen Years.*

---

By His Majesty's command,
R. FITZPATRICK.

---

The above Orders and Regulations were communicated to the Army in a Circular from the War Office, dated 23d October, 1806: which contained the following paragraph:

" You will observe, that, under one article of the Orders and Regulations, men are to be allowed, in regard to Pay and Pension, to reckon three years for every two years of service in the East or West Indies. The further increase of Pay to which any of the men of your Regiment may, in consequence, have a claim, is to be issued upon their own statements, when you have not the means of immediately ascertaining the correctness thereof; the men being, of course, liable to refund any part to which it shall afterwards appear they were not entitled."

*Circular*

*Circular from the Secretary at War to Colonels of Regiments of Cavalry; relative to allowing an Augmentation or Diminution of the Feed of Cavalry Horses in certain Cases.*

*War-Office, 24th June, 1805.*

SIR,

IT having been judged expedient to establish a Regulation for allowing an augmentation, or a diminution, of the Feed of the Horses of the Cavalry, in certain cases, according to the state of their health, and the duties on which they may be employed; and the subject having been referred to the consideration of a Board of Cavalry Officers, I enclose herewith for your information and guidance a Copy of their Report, which has been laid before the King, and has received His Majesty's approbation. The Regulation is to come into operation as soon as the Commissary General shall have made his arrangements with the Contractors for furnishing the Articles, which, when required, may be substituted for Oats. As this measure does not affect the pecuniary concerns of the Regiment, it seems only necessary for me to explain, that in all cases where His Royal Highness the Commander in Chief shall authorize the turning out any Horses to grass, the Commanding Officer is to report to this Department, through the General Officer commanding in the District, the terms on which the Grass can be procured; and he is not to enter into any agreement on that head, until he shall have received the necessary authority, through the said General Officer.

The forms of Accompts will be furnished from this Office. One of the Monthly Accompts is to be annexed to the Regimental Pay List, and another is to be sent up at the same time for the Commissary General, under cover to the Secretary at War.

I have, &c.

W. DUNDAS.

Colonel of the

*Report*

## Report on Cavalry Forage, December 1804.

### CAVALRY—OATS.

IN consequence of His Royal Highness the Commander in Chief's Directions, signified by the Adjutant-General, November 15th, 1804,

That General Sir David Dundas, together with Major-Generals Staveley and Cartwright, shall take into their consideration, and report upon, a proposed measure—" for al-
" lowing a certain latitude to Commanding Officers of Ca-
" valry Regiments, in commuting the Feed of the Horses
" of their Regiments, and for framing such a regulation
" thereon, as they shall judge best calculated to answer the
" end proposed,"

They proceeded to peruse and examine the several Papers on the subject, that accompanied the Adjutant-General's Letter; and having maturely considered the whole, *humbly Report*—

That to avoid intricate detail, and to be at a certainty of Expence, the Public allows a certain fixed Ration of Hay, Straw, and Oats, for each Cavalry Horse, per Diem, *sick* or *well*; and under the direction of the Commissary-General, the same is delivered in each District or Quarter, according to the demands of Commanding Officers, and for existing numbers, which are frequently mustered by the Paymasters, and agreeably to weekly and monthly Returns.

Although this allowance may be, on the whole, very liberal and sufficient, yet great inconvenience has arisen from no provision having been made for the varying circumstances of the service, that do always occur, and do require that a different proportion and quality of food shall be administered to horses, that come under a certain description:—As when at grass; sick, or in hospital; on marches, or extra duties; young, or ill-thriving horses, &c. This it is necessary should be so regulated, that no additional complicated Accompts shall arise between the Regiment and the Public, or the Commissary-General and Contractors; that such a degree of notoriety shall be adopted as to be perfectly satisfactory to the public; and prevent the suspicion of any individual deriving advantage from it; and that no expence shall accrue to Government, exceeding the annual Forage Allowance made for the effective Horses of each Regiment.

To accomplish this end it is proposed—

1. That the full quantity of the Hay and Straw Ration for each Horse present (sick included, those at grass excluded) is always to be drawn for; but the Commanding Officer is to use his discretion in directing the distribution of it among the Horses, as circumstances may require.

2. That the Ration of *Oats* for Troop Horses may be diminished from time to time (but not exceeding one pound and a half) at the discretion, and by order, of the Commanding Officer of a Regiment of Cavalry; and a saving Accompt kept of this, in order, in some cases, to commute for the food of sick Horses; and in other seasons and situations, to be enabled to add to the feed of effective ones. Half of the Oats of the sick Horses may also be reserved, and no Oats to be drawn for Horses while at grass.

3. Whenever any alteration is made by the Commanding Officer of the Regiment in the Ration of Oats to be issued to the whole, or any part, encrease or decrease, the same to be notified at the time in a Regimental Order.

4. The Commissary-General will settle with the Contractors in their Contracts, that when required, they shall furnish such and such quantities of Malt, or Bran, or Oatmeal, or Barley, as shall be deemed equivalent to one pound of Oats in value. The said quantities to be notified to the Regiment, and the Accompts to be still kept in lbs. of Oats, without entering into a specification of the other articles.

5. In a Regimental Monthly State, Hay and Straw will be drawn and accounted for, as at present, for sick and effective Horses.—Oats demandable, according to the regulated feed, will be stated for existing Horses (exclusive of those at grass.) Against this will be placed pounds of Oats, actually drawn for, including the commuted proportion of Bran, Oatmeal, Barley, and Malt. The difference will be a balance in favour of the Regiment, to be carried on from month to month.

6. The balances of each month will make out the annual state of the Reserve Fund. The annual settlement with the Commissary General to be made to the 24th October in each year, and any balance in favour of the Regiment to be carried on to its credit.

7. From this Reserve Fund, on proper occasions, the Commanding Officers of Regiments will, therefore, be enabled, by drawing from the Contractors (Oats in kind, or commuta-

## Appendix. 543

commutation), to provide food for Sick Horses; encrease of feed on marches and other duties, and in the season of exercise: also extra feed for young and ill-thriving horses.

8. Each Troop and Regiment will keep an accurate Diary, expressing the number of horses at grass, in barracks, in quarters, which will tend to regulate Accompts.

9. The Commissary General will state the form of such Accompts as are necessary, on this occasion, between him and each Regiment.

10. Monthly and Weekly Returns between the Troops and Commanding Officer of a Regiment are required. Forms applicable to the Cavalry in general are herewith transmitted,* for the approbation of His Royal Highness the Commander in Chief, and Commanding Officers will establish such further Regimental Regulations as are necessary to facilitate the effective operation of this Order.

11. The Regimental Stoppage will be in general equal to the expence of Grass Horses. Where more is to be incurred, previous Application must be made to the Secretary at War, that it may be allowed in the Paymaster's Accompts.

12. The annual Accompt is of such a nature, and made of such notoriety, as to require no Official controul, so as to create delay, difficulty, and embarrassment to Commanding Officers. Reviewing Generals may inspect it; and Abstracts, if thought necessary, given in periodically.

13. Each Troop will, on the back or face of its Regimental Weekly Return, mention the number of pounds of Oats, for which it has drawn commuted Articles; and will also mention the Rate of Stoppage per week.

D. DUNDAS, General.

December 24th, 1804.

---

* It has not been thought necessary to print the Forms referred to.

*Circular Letter to Colonels of Regiments of Cavalry, referring to the preceding Circular, and enclosing the Copy of a Clause inserted in the new Contracts for supplying Forage to the Troops in Barracks.*

*War Office, 31st October, 1805.*

SIR,

REFERRING to the Regulation communicated to you in my Letter of the 24th June last, for allowing an augmentation or a diminution of the feed of the horses of the Cavalry, in certain cases, according to the state of their health, and the duties on which they may be employed; I have now the honor to enclose herewith for your further information, a copy of a clause which the Commissary General has caused to be inserted in the new contract for supplying forage to the Cavalry in barracks, which takes place from the 25th instant, inclusive.

I have, &c.

W. DUNDAS.

Colonel of the

---

*Clause inserted in the new Contracts for supplying Forage to the Cavalry when in Barracks. To commence 25th October, 1805.*

WHENEVER, and as often as the Officers commanding each Regiment, Troop, or Detachment, shall think it proper, and for the good of the service, that green forage should be supplied in stables, instead of hay, and shall require the same, such Commanding Officer shall, on application to the Commissary General, when the same can be conveniently procured, be supplied therewith instead of hay, and in quantity not exceeding the value of the hay allowed by the contract

for

## Appendix. 545

for each horse. And whenever such Officers may deem it proper to reduce the allowance of oats to any extent, but not exceeding one pound and a half short of the allowed ration, and demand at any future period, or from time to time, as may be found necessary, the whole or any part of the quantity of oats, which may be so short drawn, the same shall be supplied accordingly. Or should it be thought proper to have delivered in lieu thereof, barley, malt, oatmeal, or bran, such articles shall be supplied in the following proportions:

In lieu of every pound of oats } Of barley, one pound.
Ditto      Of malt, three eighths of a pound.
Ditto      Of oatmeal, one third of a pound.
Ditto      Of beans, one eighth of a pound.

Which substitution shall be charged in the Monthly Accompt as oats, and paid for accordingly.

*Circular to Commanding Officers of Regiments, inclosing Forms of Returns, &c. for stating the length of Service of Soldiers.*

*War Office*, 31st *Dec.* 1806.

SIR,

Referring to the concluding paragraph of my Circular Letter of the 29th July last, I enclose herewith a Form of Return, calculated to shew the length of Service of the Non-commissioned Officers,* and Privates of the Regiment under your command, which I am to request that you will cause to be made up according to the Service of each man *as it stood on the 24th June last inclusive.* In cases where the men shall not be able to prove satisfactorily the actual duration of their Service in other Corps, either now stationed abroad or discontinued, you will be pleased to cause them to be settled with in conformity to their own Statements, if you should not be aware of any objection thereto: inserting the precise dates thereof, if possible, against their names in *red ink*, in the beforementioned Return, with such explanatory Remarks as may enable this Office to judge what further steps are necessary to be taken to corroborate the said statements: the result of such further enquiry will be communicated to you. It will, however, be proper, that you should explain to the men that if it should be found, that their statements are incorrect, they will be required to refund the additional Pay which they shall have received; and if any case shall appear where an unfounded claim shall have been preferred with a fraudulent Intent, the offender will be liable to punishment, according to the nature and extent of his offence.

With the Return above-mentioned, you will transmit a certificate in the Form No. 1, sent herewith. A duplicate of the said Return should be made out, to be kept at the Regiment, and to be corrected from time to time, in which it may be convenient, for the purpose of ascertaining correctly the claims of the men to the respective allowances on the

---

* The blank is intended to be filled up with the words "Trumpeters" or "Drummers and Fifers," as the case may be.

## Appendix. 547

Out-Pension, that the dates of the appointment of Non-commissioned Officers should be inserted in the column of Remarks.

In order that the services of the men may in future be clearly ascertained, you will be pleased to transmit to this Office with all convenient dispatch for the Quarter ending the 24th of September last, and immediately after the end of each succeeding Quarter, Returns according to the accompanying Form No. 2, of the Non-commissioned Officers and Privates that shall have been brought upon the strength of the Corps, during the Quarter, with the other particulars pointed out in the said Form, and with any additional Remarks that you shall think likely to assist this Department in keeping a complete and correct Register of the Services, &c. of each Soldier now belonging, or who shall hereafter belong, to the Corps.

I am further to acquaint you, that, in the case of men sent to stations where they will receive their Pay through another channel than that of the Regimental Pay-master, it will be essentially necessary that each individual Soldier already entitled, or likely to become entitled, previously to rejoining his Regiment, to an additional allowance, in consequence of the length of his Service, shou d be furnished with a certificate to that effect; the said certificate to be signed by the Commanding Officer or Adjutant, and to specify in the former case the rate of his augmented pay, and in the latter case the date on which he will be entitled to additional pay. The Pay-master should likewise furnish the same information in the Reports, which he will have to make in pursuance of the Instructions conveyed in the 41st Article of the Explanatory Directions.

Printed Forms of the Returns and Certificate abovementioned, will be furnished from this Office in the first instance, and more will be supplied, upon application, when wanted.

I am further to acquaint you, that so much delay is experienced in ascertaining the former Services of Men, who, having been discharged or discontinued, have again entered the Army, that, in order to save trouble to Public Departments, and to obtain a speedy decision on the claims of the men in general, it is judged expedient, that each Corps should make up a return, agreeably to the enclosed Form No. 3, of such

such of the men who have been discharged therefrom, or struck off the Roll, as are not actually known to be dead or totally disqualified for any Military Service; during the period from the 25th December 1783, to the 24th of June 1806, both inclusive. I am therefore to request that a Return may be accordingly prepared, by the Regiment under your command, and transmitted to this Office with as little delay as possible.

I have the honor to be,

SIR,

Your most obedient servant,

R. FITZPATRICK.

PS. In order to assist the Regiment in making up the return first mentioned, a Form partly filled up, is sent as an Example, No. 4:

To the Officer Commanding
    the             Regiment of

---

It has not been thought necessary to reprint at length the Forms of Returns enclosed in the above Circular. The Heads of the Columns of the first of them, are annexed, together with the Certificates referred to.

(No. I.)

STATEMENT of the Periods of Service of all the Non-Commissioned Officers, Trumpeters,* and Privates, of the _____ Regiment of _____ † on the 24th June, 1806, made out according to the late Rules and Regulations.

| Names, beginning with | | Trades and Places of Birth where more than one of the same Name. | In the present Corps. | | Former Service, if any, on this or other Corps; or whole Period on the Out-Pension. | | | Periods of Service, or on the Out - Pension. | | | | | | | | | Whether East Indies or West Indies. | Whole Period of Service in the East or West Indies. | | | | Numbers entitled to the respective Rates of Pay depending upon length of Service. | | | | | | REMARKS |
|---|---|---|---|---|---|---|---|---|---|---|---|---|---|---|---|---|---|---|---|---|---|---|---|---|---|---|---|---|
| RANKS. | Christian Names. | Surnames. | | Dates of Enlistment. | Corps, or Out-Pension. | From | To | Dates of Birth. | In each Corps, when in more than one, to 24th June, 1806, or half the Period of the Out-Pension. | | While Absent by Desertion, (if any) previously to 24th June, 1806. | | Amount of Deduction. | | Total Amount of Deduction | | | | From | To | Earn Period (Years of Service in the East or West Indies.) | | | | | | | | | |
| | | | | | | | | | Years. | Days. | From | To | Years. | Days. | Years. | Days. | | | | | Years. | Days. | Years. | Days. | Corporals | Privates | Corporals | Privates | Corporals | Privates | |

N. B. The above is a Form for the Cavalry.—The Alterations for the Forms for the Infantry are as follows:—
At * for " Trumpeters," substitute " Drummers or Fifers."
† Insert the words " who have failed to serve Abroad"
For Quadrants of the Columns marked (1) (2) and (3) respectively, substitute

(1) Having served 14 years.
(2) Having served 1? years, but not 14.
(3) Not having served 12 years.

## No. 1.

*Certificate referred to in the Circular Letter of the Secretary at War of 31st December, 1806.*

WE do hereby certify, upon honour, that to the best of our knowledge, information, and belief, the Statement sent herewith, of the periods of Service of each Non-commissioned Officer,            and Private Man of the         Regiment of               which has been examined by us, is correct in every particular; except in the instances stated in *red ink*, which we are not competent to decide upon.

_____ Commanding Officer.
_____ Adjutant.
_____ Pay-Master.

*Certificate for Corporals and Privates actually entitled to an Additional Allowance in consequence of length of Service. (Referred to in the Secretary at War's Circular of 31st December, 1806.)*

              Rank.  Surname.  Christian Name.  Comp,  Regt.
I Certify that
is *actually* entitled to an additional allowance of \*
a day in consequence of the length of his Service.
       Dated at       this      of      180

    † _____

\* Insert in words.
† To be signed by the Commanding-Officer or Adjutant.

---

*Certificate for Corporals and Privates expected to become entitled to an Additional Allowance in consequence of the length of their Service. (Referred to in the Secretary at War's Circular of 31st December, 1806.)*

              Rank.  Surname.  Christian Name.  Comp.  Regt.
I Certify that
will become entitled on the        18  inclusive,
to an additional allowance of \*        a day, in
consequence of the length of his service.
       Dated at       this      day of      180

    † _____

\* Insert in words.
† To be signed by the Commanding-Officer or Adjutant.

*Statement*

*Regulations to be observed in the supplying of the Troops with the several Articles to be furnished to them, under the Direction of the Commissary General, in the Home Encampments.*

### BREAD.

EACH Soldier is to receive as his allowance for four days, a well-baked loaf, weighing six pounds, made of flour prepared with a twelve shilling seamed cloth from good wheat; for which loaf the Soldier is to be charged five pence; to be paid by the Regimental Paymaster, at every settlement, to the Contractor, or to such other person as the Commissary General may appoint to receive it. Servants not being Soldiers, in the proportion of two per troop or company, and washer-women for each troop or company, in the proportion of one to every twenty men, are permitted to receive Bread at the same price, to be paid also by the Paymaster.

### WOOD.

Each Soldier is to be allowed three pounds of wood per day, to be delivered in rations of twelve pounds for every four days; and to prevent unnecessary waste in this article, it is to be delivered only for the effectives present in the field, according to the Morning Reports, on the days of delivery.

Servants and Batmen not being Soldiers, in the proportion of two to each troop or company, and washer-women for each troop or company, in the proportion of one to every twenty men, are permitted to draw wood at the rate of twelve pounds each for four days. The sick in the Regimental Hospital are to be allowed six pounds each per day.

The Colonel, or Commanding Officer of a Regiment, is to be allowed eight rations of twelve pounds each, for four days; the Field Officers, four rations each [*]; and the Officers of each troop or company, eight rations for their own use, and the supply of the sutler.

---

[*] The Paymaster and Surgeon, each four: the Adjutant, Assistant Surgeon, and Veterinary Surgeon, each two.

General Officers are to draw what wood they may have occasion for, not exceeding one hundred rations per day, of three pounds each, for a General, seventy for a Lieutenant General, fifty for a Major General, and forty for a Brigadier General.

Other Officers of the Staff, when by order attached to, and while resident at the camp, are allowed to draw wood, if necessary, for their own bona fide consumption, not exceeding the following rates per day, viz.

|  | Rations of 3 lb. |
|---|---|
| Adjutant General and Quarter Master General each | 50 |
| (But if General Officers they may draw according to their rank.) | |
| Deputy Adjutant General and Deputy Quarter Master General, each | 12 |
| Assistant Adj. Gen. and Assistant Q. M. Gen. each | 6 |
| Aid-de-Camp | 4 |
| Major of Brigade | 6 |
| Engineer | 6 |
| Commissary General | 50 |
| Deputy Commissary General | 12 |
| Assistant Commissary | 6 |
| Resident Commissary | 4 |
| Physician or Inspector of Hospitals | 10 |
| Assistant ditto ditto ditto | 6 |
| Surgeon, Apothecary, and Purveyor, each | 4 |
| Deputy Purveyor and Mate to General Hospital, each | 2 |
| Provost Marshal | 6 |
| Assistant to ditto | 2 |
| Chaplains of Brigade | 4 |

When wood cannot be procured, coal may be issued at the rate of one pound, for a pound of wood.

## STRAW

IS to be allowed at the rate of one truss of thirty-six pounds to each paillasse for two men, *being a full bedding;* at the expiration of sixteen days to be refreshed with half a truss to each paillasse; and at the expiration of thirty-two days the whole is to be removed, and a fresh bedding of one truss is to be given, and so on every succeeding period of sixteen and thirty-two days.

For

## Appendix. 553

For the sick in the Regimental Hospital, the straw is to be changed as often as it may be deemed necessary.

Two trusses per Troop or Company are to be allowed for Bâtmen, or Servants not being Soldiers; and three trusses per Troop or Company, for the Washer-women, not having paillasses, to be renewed every sixteen days.

Thirty trusses per Troop or Company are allowed on first taking the field, for thatching the womens' huts.

Regiments *not having paillasses* are allowed straw at the following rates.

On taking the field, two trusses of 36lb. each to every five men, at the end of eight days to be refreshed by one truss, and at the end of eight days more to be refreshed again by the same quantity. At the end of twenty-four days the whole to be removed, and an entire new bedding to be given, and refreshed as before, viz. two trusses for every five men, &c.


## FORAGE.

THE ration is to consist of fourteen pounds of hay, and ten pounds of oats, and is only to be issued from the magazines for the effective horses, actually belonging to, and standing at the pickets, or in the stables of the camp, according to Returns to be signed upon honour, by each individual Officer inserting in his own hand-writing, the number of effective horses he actually has in camp.*

Four pounds of straw are to be added to the ration of forage for the Cavalry and Artillery horses only.

The Returns above mentioned are to be transmitted to the Resident Commissary, certified by the Commanding Officer of Corps, on their respectively entering the camp, and regularly every day preceding the issuing morning afterwards.

The General Officers and Staff, are to draw forage (strictly upon honour), only for their effective horses; and are required to cause Returns of the horses they have with them in the field, to be as early as possible sent to the Resident Commissary, on the Troops going into camp, and regularly on every day preceding the issuing morning afterwards, as above directed.

---

* The ration for bât horses is 14lbs. hay—and 6lbs. oats.

Six pounds of straw are to be allowed to the General Officers and Staff, in addition to the prescribed ration of forage.

The General Officers, their Aides de Camp and Staff, are not to exceed the number of rations stated in List No. I.—nor Regiments of Dragoons, that in List No. II.—nor Regiments of Infantry, that in List No. III.

## STAFF. List, No. I.

|  | Horses. |
|---|---|
| His Royal Highness the Commander in Chief | 30 |
| General commanding a District | 16 |
| Lieutenant General | 12 |
| Major General | 10 |
| Brigadier General | 8 |
| Adjutant General, Quarter Master General, and Barrack Master General, each | 8 |
| (But if General Officers, according to rank.) | |
| Secretary to the Commander in Chief, Deputy Adjutant, Quarter Master, and Barrack Master General, each | 5 |
| Assistant Adjutant, and Assistant Quarter Master General, each | 4 |
| Aid de Camp to the Commander in Chief | 4 |
| Aids de Camp, and Majors of Brigade, each | 3 |
| Commissary General | 6 |
| Deputy Commissaries General | 4 |
| Assistant Commissaries | 3 |
| Inspector General of Hospitals | 4 |
| Assistant Inspector of Hospitals | 3 |
| Physicians and Purveyors, each | 3 |
| Surgeon, Apothecary, and Deputy Purveyor, each | 2 |
| Assistant Surgeon | 1 |
| Chaplain of Brigade | 1 |
| Provost Marshal | 2 |
| Assistant to ditto | 1 |

## CAVALRY. List, No. II.

| | |
|---|---|
| Colonel | 8 |
| Lieutenant Colonel | 7 |
| Major | 6 |
| Captains, each | 4 |

Subalterns.

*Appendix.* 555

|  | Horses. |
|---|---|
| Subalterns, each | 3 |
| Paymaster | 2 |
| Adjutant | 3 |
| Quarter Masters, each | 1 |
| Surgeon | 1 |
| Assistant Surgeon and Veterinary Surgeon, each | 1 |
| Sutler | 2 |

## INFANTRY. List, No. III.

| | |
|---|---|
| Colonel | 7 |
| Lieutenant Colonel | 6 |
| Major | 5 |
| Captains, each | 3 |
| Subalterns, each | 1 |
| Paymaster | 2 |
| Adjutant | 2 |
| Quarter Master | 1 |
| Surgeon and Assistant Surgeon, each | 1 |
| Sutler | 2 |

N. B. Regimental Officers having brevet rank, are only to draw forage according to their regimental rank.—And Officers having two commissions, to draw only for one.

The Field Officers, and Captains of Cavalry, are to pay sixpence per ration for the forage, and eight-pence halfpenny per ration is to be paid by the Paymaster, or acting Paymaster, for the troop horses of the Non-commissioned Officers, Trumpeters, and Privates. The Subalterns, Paymasters, Adjutants, Surgeons, Assistant Surgeons, and Quarter Masters of Cavalry, are to receive forage without payment, as are all the Officers of the Infantry, and the Sutlers both of Cavalry and Infantry.

Articles, bad in their kind, or deficient in weight, are not to be received by the Troops; the badness or deficiency to be ascertained before taken from the magazine in the presence of a Commissioned Officer of Cavalry, and a Quarter Master of Infantry, and the Resident Commissary; but articles once taken from the magazine cannot be returned but with the approbation of the Resident Commissary.

After

After four deliveries of bread, wood, and forage, and one of straw have been issued, making a period of sixteen days, a settlement is to be made: and the Regimental Paymasters or acting Paymasters, are to pay to the Contractors, or other proper persons, by bills on the Agents, (in the presence of the Resident Commissary,) the above mentioned proportions of the pay of the men, and of the subsistence of the troop horses, applicable to the provision of bread for the men, and of forage for the said horses, viz. five-pence for each loaf of six pounds, and eight-pence halfpenny for each ration of forage. The Paymasters of Cavalry will also take care, that the sums due from the Field Officers and Captains for the forage supplied to their horses, and from the Servants not being Soldiers, and Washerwomen for bread, be punctually paid to the Contractor, or other proper persons, at the regular periods of settlement. A Commissioned Officer in the Cavalry, and the Quarter Master in the Infantry, are at the same time, to sign a general receipt for all the articles of supply delivered from the magazine to their respective Corps, during that period. The settlement for the Generals and Staff is to take place at the period of thirty-two days. The Aids de Camp to sign receipts for the supplies delivered to the respective Generals and suites. Physicians or Surgeons to sign receipts for the supplies delivered for the use of the General Hospital.

The Commissary General will take care that these Regulations are observed by all persons employed in deliveries to the troops; and printed copies thereof are to be sent to the Generals commanding districts, and be by them distributed to the Regiments that encamp, that they may be made acquainted with the Regulations with which they are required to comply.

The above Regulations respecting the articles to be issued by the Commissary General to the troops in the home encampments, have received the Commander in Chief's approbation.

By Command of His Royal Highness.

HARRY CALVERT,
Adjutant General.

*Horse Guards, June 25, 1803.*

*General*

*Appendix.*

*General Orders relative to Soldiers acting as Musicians.*

*Horse Guards, 5th August,* 1803.

IT is His Majesty's pleasure, that in Regiments having bands of music, not more than *one* Private Soldier of each Troop or Company shall be permitted to act as Musicians, and that one Non-commissioned Officer shall be allowed to act as Master of the Band. These men are to be drilled and instructed in their exercise, and in case of actual service, are to fall in with their respective Troops or Companies completely armed and accoutred.

His Royal Highness the Commander in Chief desires that General Officers commanding in districts will immediately communicate the above order to the several Regiments under their command, and strictly enforce its observance.

By order of His Royal Highness
The Commander in Chief.

HARRY CALVERT,
Adjutant General of the Forces.

*General Orders relative to the Mode of conducting the Recruiting Service of Second Battalions.*

*Horse Guards, 8th December,* 1806.

HIS Majesty is pleased to direct, that the Recruiting Service of the Second Battalions of Regiments of the Line, shall be conducted, in every respect, in strict conformity to the Orders and Regulations for the general Recruiting Service of the Army. Commanding Officers of Regiments will immediately communicate to the Inspector General of the Recruiting Service, the arrangements they propose making of their Recruiting Parties; and they will enjoin the Officers, employed on this service, to be very exact and punctual in transmitting the Returns required by the King's Regulations, in order that an estimate may, from time to time, be made of the success with which this levy is attended in each Regiment. No Recruit can be counted effective, until he has been finally approved at the Head Quarters of one of the Battalions of the Regiment.

The Commander in Chief permits in every hundred Recruits raised for this levy, the proportion of fifteen lads, who are of the height of Five Feet Two Inches, and not above Sixteen years of age, provided they are of a promising appearance.

It is recommended in arranging the Recruiting Parties, that attention shall be paid to the local interests which Officers may derive from their connections, or other circumstances, and the Commander in Chief approves of Field Officers being employed in the superintendance of the Recruiting Parties of their respective Regiments, subject, however, to the general controul of the Inspector General of the Recruiting Service, and of the Inspecting Field Officers of Districts.*

Commanding Officers of Regiments will transmit to the Adjutant General, for the Commander in Chief's information, the dislocation of their Recruiting Parties, a duplicate of which they will transmit to the War Office, for the information of the Right Honourable the Secretary at War.

The Commander in Chief looks with confidence to the best

---

* See page 569.

exertions of the Officers employed on this service, and entertains the most sanguine expectations that the levy will be completed at the expiration of six months from this time.— In instances where this object is obtained previous to that period, His Royal Highness desires that no relaxation of exertion may arise from that circumstance, but that each individual, until he receives orders to the contrary, will continue his best endeavours in promoting the further success of the Recruiting Service of the Regiment to which he belongs.

By order of His Royal Highness
The Commander in Chief.

HARRY CALVERT,
Adjutant General.

*General Orders relative to the Enlistment of* Lads.

*Horse Guards, 14th January, 1807.*

IT is His Royal Highness the Commander in Chief's pleasure that the proportion of *Lads* who are permitted to be enlisted by the additional Battalions of *certain* Regiments under the authority of the General Order of the 8*th December last,* shall be of the same description as those enlisted under the Circular Order of the 28*th December,* 1804, viz. *not above Sixteen Years of age, nor under Five Feet in height,* and who are classed under the head of *Boy* Recruits, and that the same rate of bounty and pay shall be allowed to these boys as have been prescribed in former orders.

By command of His Royal Highness,
The Commander in Chief.

HARRY CALVERT,
Adjutant General.

*Circular to Generals commanding on Foreign Stations; relative to an alteration in the mode of receiving and communicating His Majesty's Decisions on the Proceedings of Courts Martial.*

*War Office, 22d August,* 1806.

SIR,

His Majesty having signified his pleasure that his decisions upon proceedings of courts martial shall be received and communicated by the Commander in Chief, or in his absence by the Adjutant General, and not, as heretofore, by the Judge Advocate General; I avail myself of the opportunity of sending the annual Warrant authorizing you to hold courts martial, to apprize you of the above-mentioned alteration, and which is recognized in the said Warrant.

You will be pleased to observe, that the proceedings are, as usual, to be transmitted in the first instance to the Judge Advocate General, to be laid before His Majesty.

I have, &c.

R. FITZPATRICK.

---

N. B. The alteration has equally taken place, in the mode of receiving and communicating His Majesty's decisions on the proceedings of courts martial held on the home station.

*Letter from R. H. Crew, Esq. to the Deputy Secretary at War, relative to the Supply of Forge Carts.*

*Office of Ordnance, 15th December, 1806.*

SIR,

I HAVE the Board's commands to acknowledge the receipt of your Letter of the 24th ultimo, respecting the issue of forge carts by this department, and I am, in answer, to acquaint you, for the information of the Secretary at War, that the Board do consider forge carts for Cavalry Regiments an ordnance store; and upon receipt of the proper authority of His Majesty's Warrant, will, from time to time, as they may be required, direct forge carts to be supplied to Cavalry Regiments, in the proportion of one forge cart to a Squadron, consisting of two Troops; I am further to state that it is expected forge carts should be kept in repair by the Regiment twelve years after they are delivered from the ordnance magazines.

I have the honor to be, &c.

R. H. CREW.

F. Moore, Esq. &c. &c. &c.
 War Office.

*Circular*

*Circular to the Commanding Officers of Regiments in the East Indies relative to the transmission of Adjutants' Rolls and the Mode of stating the Amount of the Effects and Credits of deceased Soldiers.*

SIR,

*War Office, 6th April,* 1803.

IT being thought proper that Monthly Adjutants' Rolls should be transmitted to this Office from the Regiments stationed in the East Indies, in order that the enquiries of the relations of Soldiers belonging to those Regiments may be answered with the same facility as in the case of Corps on every other station abroad, I have the honor to acquaint you therewith, and to signify to you the King's pleasure, that you do cause Adjutants' Rolls according to the printed form, which will be furnished from hence, to be made out monthly, and forwarded to this Office, by the earliest proper opportunities, with duplicates thereof, to serve in the event of the originals being lost. The Adjutant will of course understand that when, through accident, a sufficient supply of printed forms should not have reached the Regiment, he is to make out the Rolls in manuscript, according to the accustomed form. Enclosed herewith I send a copy of the Regulation (23d December, 1800)* prescribing the mode in which the amount of the effects and credits of deceased Soldiers are to be stated on the Adjutants' Rolls, and am to desire that you will give instructions to the Paymaster to prepare Monthly States of the effects and credits, or debts of Non-commissioned Officers, Drummers, or Fifers, and Private Men dead, or deserted, according to the annexed form, which you will cause to be transmitted to this Office, with duplicates for the use of the Agent, taking care that the amount of the effects and credits of deserters, and the sums to be paid in this country to the representatives of deceased Soldiers, be remitted to the Agent by every proper opportunity.

I have, &c.

C. YORKE.

---

* See page 238.

564 *Appendix.*

*State of the Effects and Credits, or Debts, of the Non-commissioned Officers, Drummers or Fifers, and Private Men of the Regiment of             who have died, or deserted, from the 25th of         to the 24th of         following, both days inclusive.*

| Company. | Names. | How become Non-effective. | Amount of Effects and Credits. | Amount of Debts. | Remarks shewing whether the amount of the Effects and Credits of each of the Persons deceased has been or will be paid to their Representatives abroad, or is to be paid through the Agent in this Country. | Amount remitted, or to be remitted to the Agents in England. |
|---|---|---|---|---|---|---|
|   |   |   |   |   | Total Brought forward from preceding State - - -  In all from 25th December to the 24th  *£ |   |

We certify to the best of our knowledge and Belief that the above State is Correct.

_____Commanding Officer.
_____Adjutant.
_____Paymaster.

---

\* The Paymaster will explain particularly on the back of this Paper, whether the whole of this Sum, or what part thereof, shall have been remitted by him to the Agent, also when, and by what means remitted.

## Appendix. 565

*Extract of a Letter to Lieutenant General Vyse, relative to an Allowance to the Inhabitants of North Britain upon whom Soldiers may be quartered: dated War Office, 20th September,* 1803.

" THE Lords Commissioners of His Majesty's Treasury having signified their approbation of an allowance of 9d. per week for each man, being made to the inhabitants of Scotland, without discrimination, upon whom Soldiers may be billetted, I have the honor to request that you will signify the same in General Orders to the Troops under your command in North Britain, and take such steps for notifying the measure to the inhabitants in that part of the kingdom as you shall think most adviseable.

I beg leave to add, that if you are satisfied that the allowance need not be granted in the cases where the men are not billetted upon the inhabitants for a complete week, the Regulation may be so established; but that I should see no objection, if you thought it expedient, to allow the sum of one penny for each man who shall also be billetted upon the inhabitants for any number of days less than a week, or exceeding that period."\*

---

\* This allowance of 1d. a day for broken periods has been established accordingly.

*Memorandum stating some Peculiarities in the Situation of Soldiers in North Britain.*

THE Soldier in North Britain, when billetted *in stationary quarters*, being only entitled to be supplied with a bed, is allowed, in addition to his beer money, one halfpenny per diem, in lieu of the articles furnished by innkeepers to billetted Soldiers in South Britain.

When permitted to find his own lodgings he receives the further sum of one halfpenny a day, making (with his beer money) two-pence a day in the whole.

The allowance to innkeepers for Soldiers victualled on the march in South Britain, does not attach in Scotland, but the men find their own provisions in that situation; an extra allowance of three pence a day being made to each Non-commissioned Officer, Trumpeter, and Private Man of Cavalry, and five pence a day to each Non-commissioned Officer, Drummer, and Private Man of Infantry, in addition to his pay and beer money.

Troops in all situations in North Britain purchase their own bread, the extra price above sixpence for each 4 pound loaf being charged in the Regimental Pay Lists.

In places in Scotland where bread is not the food of the ordinary class of the Inhabitants, the Soldiers may be supplied with oatmeal in lieu thereof, in the proportion of one pound and one eighth of a pound of oatmeal to one pound of bread.

The horses of Officers and the troop horses of Regiments of Cavalry in North Britain, when stationed in *barracks*, are supplied with the complete ration of hay, straw, and oats, under the orders of the Commissary General.

When stationed in *quarters*, these articles are purchased under the direction of the Commanding Officer, and the extra expence, after deducting eight-pence halfpenny for each daily ration, is charged against the Public in the Regimental Pay Lists.

*Circular*

*Circular from the Secretary at War to Generals commanding on Foreign Stations, requiring the transmission of Half-yearly Staff Returns.*

*War Office, 24th July, 1799.*

SIR,

GREAT inconvenience having, in many instances, arisen, as well to the public service as to individuals, in consequence of this department not receiving timely and complete information in regard to the situation of the Military Staff and Garrison Officers employed with the British Forces on foreign stations; and His Majesty, in order to remedy this inconvenience, having been pleased to direct that the Commandants of his forces, on the several stations abroad, should be required to furnish regular Half-yearly Returns, agreeably to the enclosed form, of the Officers of the above description attached to the troops under their command; I have the honor to acquaint you therewith, and to signify to you the King's pleasure that you do accordingly forthwith transmit to this Office a Return of the General and Staff Officers, and Officers of Hospitals, (including Garrison Officers) serving with the forces in          or considered as attached thereto, although absent with leave, or otherwise, from 25th December, 1798, to 24th June last, inclusive, made up according to the said form; and that you do in future, as soon after the 24th June, and 24th December, in each year, as may be practicable, transmit similar Returns for the preceding half year, terminating on the above days respectively.

You will be pleased to cause this to be registered as a Standing Order; to be observed by every Officer upon whom the command of the troops in          may hereafter devolve.

I have the honor, &c.

W. WINDHAM.

*Return*

Return of the General and Staff Officers, and Officers of the Hospitals (including Garrison Officers) attached to the Forces from 25th to 24th both inclusive.

| Names. | Employments. | Periods for which entitled to Pay, as being present and serving, or as absent with leave. | | Periods for which the Pay has been or will be issued abroad. | | Periods for which the Pay is to be issued in Great Britain. | | Remarks. |
|---|---|---|---|---|---|---|---|---|
| | | From | To | From | To | From | To | |
| | | | | | | | | |

N. B. The Column for Remarks is designed to contain Notices of Casualties, the absence or presence of Officers, or such other Particulars as may appear proper to be communicated, and are not adverted to in the preceding Columns.

*Circular relative to the Allowances to Field Officers employed in superintending the Recruiting Service of Second Battalions.*

War Office, 7th February, 1807.

SIR,

REFERRING to the Letter from the Adjutant General, dated the 8th December last, signifying the orders of His Royal Highness the Commander in Chief, that a Field Officer of the Battalion under your command, should be employed in superintending the Recruiting Parties of the Corps; I have the honour to acquaint you, that to enable the said Field Officer the better to perform his duty, in visiting the quarters of the several parties, the allowance for the forage of his horse will be continued to him, notwithstanding his absence from the Battalion: and the Regimental Paymaster may charge the same accordingly, upon receiving a Certificate from the Field Officer, according to the following Form.

I am to add, that the extra expences actually and necessarily incurred by the Field Officer so detached, on account of postage and stationary for the public service, may be reimbursed to him by the District Paymaster, and may be charged in his account of the contingencies of the Staff of the District; the accompts thereof being vouched in the same manner as those of the General and Staff Officers.

I have the honor to be,

SIR,

Your most obedient

Humble servant,

(Signed) R. FITZPATRICK.

Officer Commanding
2d Battalion        Regiment of Foot

*Certificate for the Charge of the Allowance to a Field Officer, for the Maintenance of his Horse when detached on the Recruiting Service, under the Order of His Royal Highness the Commander in Chief, dated 8th December, 1806.*

I DO hereby certify upon honour, that I did actually and necessarily keep a horse, for the performance of my duty in superintending the Recruiting Service of the Battalion of the Regiment of Foot, from to ; that the said horse was my own property; and that no forage in kind has been drawn for the same, at the public expence, nor any other allowance in lieu thereof, as a bât horse, or in any shape whatever.

———————— { *Field Officer Superintending the Recruiting Parties of the 2d Battalion of the*

*General*

*Appendix.* 571

*General Orders, substituting New Regulations for those formerly in force, relative to the incidental Expences of Officers on the Recruiting Service.*

*Horse Guards, February 1st,* 1807.

HIS Majesty has been pleased to command, that the Regulations at present existing for covering the incidental expences of Officers employed on the Recruiting Service shall be cancelled; and that, in lieu of the Ten Shillings and Sixpence now granted out of the Levy Money for a Recruit, and of the Ninepence per mile hitherto issued for Travelling, and of all other Charges for Incidental Expences (such only excepted as are mentioned in the annexed Schedule), an Allowance shall be made to the Recruiting Officer, at the Rate of Two Guineas for every Recruit (Man or Lad), on final Approval, from this date inclusive.

The substance of this Order cancels the 24th Article of the General Recruiting Regulations, dated the 25th October, 1806, and the 25th Article as far as relates to the Passage of Officers to and from Ireland: but His Majesty has graciously thought fit to direct, that in the event of special Cases arising, where from particular circumstances, the Recruiting Officer may be liable to peculiar hardships from the non-allowance of any charge for travelling, on the same being explained and certified to the Commander in Chief by the Officer Commanding, if the Regiment is at home, or by the Inspector General of the Recruiting Service if the Regiment is abroad (through the medium of His Royal Highness's Military Secretary), such Remuneration shall be granted as may appear equitable, not exceeding the Ninepence per mile hitherto allowed :—A Form of the Certificate to be used on these occasions is herewith enclosed.

The amount of Levy Money for Recruits enlisted in the United Kingdom, will be as stated in the annexed Schedule, and the Appropriation of the several Sums is to be made in strict conformity thereto.

It is to be observed that this Order has no reference to such Officers and other persons as have been specially appointed to Recruit, under the Orders of the 27th October, 1806.

By Order of His Royal Highness

The Commander in Chief,

(Signed)          HARRY CALVERT,

Adjutant General.

## DISTRIBUTION OF LEVY MONEY.

|  | Cavalry | | | Infantry and General Service. | | | Boys for General Service, enlisted under the Orders of Inspecting Field Officers of Recruiting Districts. | | |
|---|---|---|---|---|---|---|---|---|---|
| **Bounty to the Recruit** | | | | | | | | | |
| On being attested, in money | 1 | 1 | 0 | 2 | 2 | 0 | 1 | 1 | 0 |
| On intermediate Approval, in money | 1 | 1 | 0 | 2 | 2 | 0 | 1 | 10 | 0 |
|    in necessaries | 0 | 12 | 0 | 0 | 12 | 0 | 0 | 12 | 0 |
| On final Approval, in money | 2 | 6 | 0 | 3 | 12 | 0 | 2 | 2 | 0 |
|    in necessaries | 3 | 3 | 0 | 3 | 3 | 0 | 3 | 3 | 0 |
| Total Bounty to the Recruit | 8 | 3 | 0 | 11 | 11 | 0 | 8 | 8 | 0 |
| **To the Officer** | | | | | | | | | |
| For Attesting | 0 | 1 | 0 | 0 | 1 | 0 | 0 | 1 | 0 |
| On intermediate approval { Surgical Examination | 0 | 2 | 6 | 0 | *2 | 6 | 0 | *2 | 6 |
| Postage, Stationary, &c. | 0 | *7 | 6 | 0 | *7 | 6 | 0 | *7 | 0 |
| On final Approval, to cover all other incidental Expences | 0 | 2 | 0 | *2 | 2 | 0 | 0 | 10 | 6 |
| **Party on final approval** | | | | | | | | | |
| Reward | *2 | *5 | 0 | *2 | *5 | 0 | 0 | *5 | 0 |
| For conducting the Recruit to place of final approval | 1 | 1 | 0 | 1 | 1 | 0 | 1 | 1 | 0 |
| To the bringer of a Recruit, whether belonging to the party, or otherwise, on final approval | 3 | 3 | 0 | 3 | 3 | 0 | 0 | 0 | 0 |
| Total Levy Money, British Currency ............£. | 15 | 4 | 6 | 18 | 12 | 6 | 10 | 15 | 6 |

The

*The Allowance of* Two Guineas *to the Officer on final Approval, is not to be paid when the Party happens to be commanded by a Non-Commissioned Officer: nor the* Guinea and a Half *(the addition now granted) to the* Recruiting Staff, *for Recruits for General Service.*

*The Charges marked thus* (\*) *are not allowed for Recruits raised at the Head Quarters of a Regiment; nor are the Two Shillings and Sixpence to be charged for Surgical Examination, if a Recruit is enlisted at the Head Quarters of a Recruiting District; nor in Cases, where it is practicable to obtain the Examination of a Recruit by a Military Medical Officer.*

*The Allowance of Five Shillings for Conducting a Recruit to Head Quarters, is not granted in the Case of a Recruit sent at once to Head Quarters for final Approval.*

The sum required in this Schedule to be expended in Necessaries, out of the Bounty of a Recruit on Final Approval, is intended to be laid out, under the controul of the Commanding Officer, if the Regiment is at home, in such Articles as are considered immediately requisite; after which his Stock of Necessaries (as detailed in His Majesty's Regulation for the Clothing and Appointments of the Army, dated 22nd April, 1803) if there should yet appear any deficiency, is to be completed gradually, by Stoppages at the rate of 1s. 6d. per week, as directed by the said Regulation, as such stoppages accrue.

Recruits for Corps abroad, or for General Service, sent to the Army Depôt in the Isle of Wight, or to the Cavalry Depôt at Maidstone, are likewise to be completed in Necessaries, gradually, as the regulated Stoppages accrue, under the controul of the Inspector General of the Recruiting Service.

The Necessaries allowed on intermediate approval, are to be furnished under the orders of the Inspecting Field Officers, and are to consist of one shirt, and one pair of shoes, at the price of 6s. each.

If the Recruit has of his own any articles fit to be included among his Regimental Necessaries, the surplus of the portion of Bounty allotted for the purchase of Necessaries, is to be paid to him in money.

N. B. A Recruit signifying his Dissent after twenty-four hours posterior to his enlistment, and within four days, can only be required to refund one shilling, as enlisting money, and twenty shillings for what is usually called "Smart Money."

## Appendix. 575

*Distribution of the Levy Money allowed for each Boy raised under the Order of 28th December 1804, by such Regular Regiments as have been specially appointed to receive Boys.*

|  |  |  | *l.* | *s.* | *d.* |
|---|---|---|---|---|---|
| Bounty to the Recruit { On Approval at the Regiment Or by the Inspecting Field Officer } | In money | 0 | 10 | 0 |
|  | In necessaries | 2 | 2 | 0 |
| Total Bounty |  |  | 2 | 12 | 6 |
| To the Bringer, or Parent of the Boy } On Attestation |  |  | 2 | 2 | 0 |
| Total Levy Money |  |  | 4 | 14 | 6 |

The Charge of One Shilling for Attesting is to be defrayed out of the Allowance to the Bringer.

The necessaries to be provided out of the Bounty of Boys are to be furnished under the orders of the Inspecting Field Officers of Recruiting Districts, and Commanding Officers of Battalions respectively, and are to consist of the Articles under mentioned.

|  | *l.* | *s.* | *d.* |
|---|---|---|---|
| Two Shirts, at 6s. each | 0 | 12 | 0 |
| Two Pair of Shoes, at 6s. per pair | 0 | 12 | 0 |
| Pack | 0 | 6 | 6 |
| Leggings | 0 | 3 | 4½ |
| Two Pair of Stockings | 0 | 1 | 10 |
| Brushes and Black Ball | 0 | 1 | 1 |
| Two Combs | 0 | 0 | 4 |
| Straps for Great Coats | 0 | 2 | 4 |
| Stock and Clasp | 0 | 0 | 9 |
| Sundries | 0 | 1 | 9½ |
|  | 2 | 2 | 0 |

If the Boy enlisted has of his own any of the above Articles fit to be included among his Regimental Necessaries, the Amount herein specified for the same Article is to be paid to him in money, unless required to complete his Regimental Stock in any other manner.

---

The Bounty to be given to *Boys*, who, by the special permission of the Commander in Chief, are enlisted for the purpose of being trained as *Drummers* or *Fifers* is to continue the same as specified in the General Order of the 31st May 1805; viz.—*Two Guineas.*

*Certificate referred to in the preceding Regulation.*

I DO hereby certify upon honour, that
of the                         Regiment of
proceeded from                 to
where he arrived on the        day of
being a distance of            miles; and was recalled
on the         of                        in consequence of

I do further certify that the said journey has not taken place for the private accommodation of the above Officer, but was performed in consequence of orders for that purpose, calculated solely for the benefit of His Majesty's Service; and being removed from that station before it was possible to cover the expence of his journey, by the Two Guineas allowed for each Recruit on final approval; I hereby recommend his case for the consideration of the Commander in Chief, for such remuneration as His Royal Highness may judge equitable.

The number of Recruits raised by the Officer above-mentioned, and finally approved, was

Dated at            this          day of


To His Royal Highness the
    Commander in Chief's
    Military Secretary, &c. &c.

*Circular*

*Circular to Commanding Officers, relative to the General Registry of the Army being kept in the War Office.*

War Office, 21st February, 1807.

SIR,

REFERRING to my Letter of the 31st December last,* I have the honor to acquaint you it is judged expedient, that the General Registry of the Non-commissioned Officers and Soldiers of the Army should be kept in this Office: and I am accordingly to signify to you the King's Pleasure, that you do transmit the Quarterly Return required by my said Letter, to the War Office in London; whether the Corps be on the British or Irish Establishment at the time.

I have the honor to be,

SIR,

Your most obedient

Humble servant,

(Signed) R. FITZPATRICK.

Officer Commanding
 the         Regiment of

---

* See page 546.

*Circular*

*Circular to Agents, limiting the Period within which they are to furnish the Explanations required of them, on the Examination of their Accompts.*

*War Office, 3d March,* 1807.

GENTLEMEN,

IT being found that, notwithstanding the Instructions contained in the Circular Letter from this Office, dated 28th February, 1804,\* the Regimental Agents do not furnish the explanations required of them, on the examination of their accompts, with due regularity and punctuality; I think it proper to apprize you, that, in future, the rule, prescribed in the 58th Article of the Explanatory Directions,† as to the deciding on the articles specified in the Abstracts of Examination, will be observed in the case of Regimental Agents; and the charges objected to will be finally disallowed, unless the necessary explanations be given within three days after the period of ten days limited by the said Circular; or a satisfactory reason be assigned for the delay, which may in some special instances be unavoidable.

I am,

Gentlemen,

Your most obedient

Humble servant,

(Signed) R. FITZPATRICK.

Agent of the
    Regiment

---

\* See page 197.
† See page 181.

*Circular*

*Circular to Agents, relative to the Re-payment of Advances made, in certain Cases, by Regimental and District Paymasters; and other Persons in known Public Trust.*

*War-Office, 24th February,* 1800.

GENTLEMEN,

THE exigencies of the Service requiring frequently, that advances of Public Money should be made by Regimental and District Pay-masters, and other Persons in known Public trust, on account of Corps with which they are not immediately connected; and it appearing, that the recovery of such Money is in many instances rendered difficult by unnecessary objections and delays; I have it in command to signify THE KING's Pleasure, that all Agents do without demur pay the demands for such advances, unless they can shew from satisfactory evidence in their own hands the impropriety thereof; and in case it should appear after Payments have been so made, that the charges were without proper foundation, HIS MAJESTY expects, that every attention shall be given by the Parties, who have received Payment, to facilitate the return of the Money.

I am,

Gentlemen,

Your most obedient Servant,

(Signed)   W. WINDHAM.

Agent of the
          Regiment

*General*

*General Orders, relative to the Accompts of Soldiers who are sent to General Hospitals.*

*Horse-Guards*, 1st *August*, 1800.

IN order to obviate the inconveniences and difficulties which have occurred in the Settlement of the Accounts of Soldiers, who, having been received into General Hospitals, are found from Wounds or other causes incapable of further Service; and to prevent the delay in granting their Discharges (which has been the necessary consequence;) His Royal Highness the Commander in Chief is pleased to direct, that the Accounts of every Soldier who is sent into a General Hospital, whether at home, or abroad, shall be made up to the succeeding 24th of the month, and transmitted to the Regimental Agent, properly authenticated by the Signatures of the Regimental Pay-master, and the Commanding Officer of the Troop or Company to which the Man belongs; and that it shall therein be particularly stated, whether the man has, or has not, any claim for Clothing, or on any other account.

It is His Royal Highness's Pleasure, that this shall be regarded as a standing Order, and accordingly be entered in the Orderly Book of every Regiment.

By order of His Royal Highness

The Commander in Chief.

(Signed)      HARRY CALVERT,
Adjutant General of the Forces.

---

This Order is to be considered as extending equally to Prisoners of War.

*Appendix.*

*Memorandum pointing out the Authority upon which Payments for Hospital Contingencies are to be made.*

BY a Regulation, dated 23d June, 1801, it is determined that no Payment shall be made by the Agent for Army Hospitals, on Account of Hospital Contingencies, until he is in possession of a proper Document, according to the annexed Form, recommending such Payment; confirmed by the approving Signature of the Secretary at War, Deputy Secretary at War, or Chief Examiner of Army Accompts: viz.

*It is recommended to his* MAJESTY's *Secretary at War, by the* [Surgeon General, or Inspector General of Army Hospitals, as the case may be] *that          Agent for Army Hospitals, be authorized to pay to                 the Sum of* [to be inserted in words] *for* [specify the Service, and the Period.]

*Dated this                Day of*

*Signature of the Surgeon-General, or Inspector-General of Army Hospitals* (as the Case may be.)

See Section VI.

*Circular*

*Circular to Agents, relative to the Mode of crediting the Allowances issued on account of Great Coats.*

*War Office,* 18*th August,* 1803.

Gentlemen,

THE allowances issued half-yearly on account of Great Coats,\* having been in a great many Instances omitted to be credited by the Agents of Infantry Corps in their Monthly Abstracts; I am directed by the Secretary at War to acquaint you, that this Credit is to be invariably given, in a distinct Sum, in the same Column with the Allowances to the Captains of Companies; but that a Charge may be made in the same Abstract, of the amount of the said Allowances, as " carried to a separate Accompt."

I am,

Gentlemen,

Your most obedient

humble servant,

(Signed) W. MERRY.

Agent of the
    Regiment.

---

The above Rule applies equally to the Allowances issued for Saddle Water Decks and Corn Sacks in the Cavalry.†

---

\* See Page 451.
† See Page 89.

*Circular*

*Circular to the Inspecting Field Officers of Recruiting Districts, relative to the regular Transmission of District Pay Lists.*

*War Office, 5th March*, 1804.

SIR,

HAVING judged it proper, with the view of preventing any further accumulation of unsettled Regimental Accompts, to form an Arrangement, by which it is expected that the Pay-Lists, and Agents' Abstracts, for the Current Period, commencing the 25th of December last, will be finally examined, soon after the Receipt thereof in this Office; and it being essential to the attainment of this object, that the District Pay-Lists should be transmitted with the greatest possible regularity;[*] I have the honor to request, that you will enforce the strictest attention to this point on the part of the Pay-master of the District under your command; and that if any Circumstances should occur to render some delay unavoidable, you will be pleased to report the same to this Office.

I have the Honor to be,

SIR,

Your most obedient,

humble Servant,

(Signed)   CHARLES BRAGGE.

The Inspecting Field
  Officer of the
  Recruiting District.

---

[*] See SECTION III. Part III.

*Extract*

*Extract of a Circular Letter from the Secretary at War, to the Commanding Officers of Corps of Militia, dated War Office, 19th February, 1805: requiring a Monthly Distribution of the Men, in support of the Charges for Innkeepers Allowance.*

"It being extremely desirable, that the Pay-Lists of Militia Corps, which are to be rendered in future at the end of every three months,* should contain no other charge whatever than for the Pay of the Officers and Men: and it being necessary with a view to this Object, that some Additional Document should be furnished in support of the Charges made in the Monthly Accompts under the head of ' Increased Rates paid to Innkeepers;' I have the honor to transmit to you the enclosed Form † of a Distribution of the Non-commissioned Officers and Men on each day of the Month, which it is conceived may answer this purpose, and may enable this Office to settle finally the Charges above referred to, without requiring the Particulars to be stated so much in detail as heretofore in the Regimental Pay-Lists.

" I am accordingly to request that you will cause the above Forms (which will be furnished from this Office) to be completed and transmitted with the [‡Monthly] Accompts."

---

\* See Page 200.
† Not reprinted.
‡ Quarterly.

*Circular*

## Appendix. 585

*Circular to Pay-Masters of Corps of Militia, relative to the adoption of a New Form of Monthly Accompt, &c.*

War Office, 14th January, 1806.

SIR,

IN transmitting to you the enclosed Copy of a Circular Letter,* from the Secretary at War, to the Commandants of Militia Corps, I am directed to acquaint you, that the Monthly Accompts therein alluded to, are to be sent to this Office, at the usual Periods; but are not to be accompanied by any Vouchers, either for the Pay of Officers, or for other Charges, except such as are pointed out in the New Form of Monthly Accompt; it being intended that every other usual and necessary Receipt, or Voucher, should be attached to the *Quarterly* Accompts, for which purpose all Routes, Receipts, or other Documents, should, therefore, be carefully preserved: and as it may happen, that an Officer may not be present with the Corps so as to sign the Quarterly Accompts at the time of their being made up; in which case, unless you are in possession of a proper Receipt, the Charge for such Officer's Pay would of course be disallowed; it will be essentially necessary, that, with the view of preventing any embarrassment on this head, you should invariably take a Receipt for each Monthly Issue of the Pay of every Officer, which may be given up to him, upon his signing the Quarterly Accompt in which such Pay shall be included.

I am,

SIR,

Your most obedient
humble Servant,

(Signed)   W. MERRY.

Pay-Master of the
              of Militia

---

* See Page 202.

*Circular relative to the mode of issuing the Half-Pay of Officers employed on the Extraordinary Recruiting for the Infantry.*

*War-Office,* 19*th February,* 1807.

SIR,

IT having been determined, that the Officers on Half-pay, who are employed on the Extraordinary Recruiting of the Infantry, under the Regulations from Head Quarters, dated 27th October, 1806,\* and who consequently cannot receive their Half-pay in the usual manner, from their inability to take the Oath required by Law, shall receive an Allowance in lieu of the same, at the Periods when the Half-pay is in general course of payment, from the Pay-masters of the Recruiting District in which they respectively reside; I am directed to acquaint you therewith, and to desire, that you will call upon the Officers of the above description who are employed in the District, forthwith to render to you Statements of their respective Claims for Half-pay, for the Period ending 24th December last, which Statements you will transmit to this Office, in order that the same may be investigated, and the necessary authority given for the payment thereof.

I have the honor to be,
SIR,
Your most obedient humble Servant,
(Signed)          F. MOORE.

P. S. It is proper to explain that *in Cases where the Officers shall not have raised any Recruits, and will not have derived any Emolument from their Appointments as Recruiting Officers,* their Half-pay should be received at the Pay-Office, upon their rendering the usual Affidavit.

Inspecting Field Officer
  of the
  Recruiting District.

---

The above order applies only to Officers on the *War Office List* of Half Pay; who are paid by the Paymaster General of the Forces.

---

\* See Page 306.

*General*

*Appendix.* 587

*General Orders issued to the Troops in North Britain, relative to Charges for the Extra Price of Meat, Bread, and Oatmeal for the Men; and, in the Cavalry, of Corn, Hay, and Straw for the Horses.*

*Adjutant General's Office, Edinburgh, 13th May,* 1801.

THE Secretary at War having signified to Lieutenant General Vyse, that it was understood at the War Office, that the Pound Weight of Butcher's Meat varied considerably in different parts of Scotland; and it being proper that the Regulation on this Head should be acted upon according to one uniform Rule; it is the General's Order, that the extra price of Meat is to be charged in every part of North Britain, for the regulated proportion only of the English Pound Avoirdupois of sixteen ounces, and the same is to be expressed accordingly, in the heads of the third and fourth columns of the Accompts that are rendered of the Charge of the said Allowance.

The same standard of the English Pound Avoirdupois to be applied in like manner, and expressed accordingly in the Accompts of the other Articles supplied to the Troops in North Britain, upon which an Allowance is made by the Public upon certain proportions of their weight, viz. Bread and Oatmeal for the men; and in the Cavalry, Corn, Hay, and Straw for the Horses.

(Signed) ALEXANDER MACKAY,
Deputy Adjutant General.

See page 566.

*Circular*

*Circular to Agents, pointing out the Forms of Accompts to be rendered by them.*

*War Office, 28th September,* 1801.

Gentlemen,

THE inclosed Forms of Public Accompts to be made up by the Regimental Agents (No. 1, 2, and 3), having been approved, I am to signify to you The KING's Pleasure, that they be invariably observed in the Accompts to be transmitted by you, for each of the Corps within your Agency, agreeably to the Rules hereafter specified.

No. 1 is the Form of a Monthly Abstract of Disbursements and Receipts, to be substituted for the one now in use, and to be sent monthly to this Office, on, or before, the 1st of the Month subsequent to that, in which the Accompt is terminated. This Form is to be adopted for the Accompts commencing on the 25th instant, and to be accompanied with an abstract Statement, made out in like manner, of the Sums paid and received by you, for the nine preceding months of this year; which will of course exhibit at one view the Totals brought forward into the first Accompt, made out agreeably to the new Form.

No. 2 is the Form of a Supplementary Abstract of Disbursements and Receipts, that shall have occurred subsequently to the termination of the year to which they belong, and shall not, therefore, have been included in the last [Monthly] Abstract of that year.* In this Accompt deduction is to be made of any Sums that shall have been erroneously inserted in the former Abstracts for the said year, either

---

* In the Supplementary Abstract now to be rendered, the Disbursements and Receipts not included in the last *Quarterly* Abstract of the year, are to be stated, and the Totals are of course to be brought over from that Accompt. Should the Totals of the last Quarterly and last Monthly Abstract differ, the Agent is in such case to annex to his Supplementary Abstract a special Memorandum signed by himself, accounting particularly for such difference.

*Appendix.*

on account of the pay of Officers, or otherwise; and also of such Sums, if any, as shall have been drawn by the Paymaster beyond the amount of Sums expended, as shewn by their Public Accompts for the year. The said Supplementary Abstract is in future to be made up, and sent to this Office, on, or before, the 24th April.*

No. 3 is the Form of a General Annual State of the Public Accompts, for the Service terminating on the 24th of December in each Year. This is to be made up and transmitted to the War-Office, with the Supplementary Abstract No. 2, as above mentioned.

I am further to desire that you will, with as little delay as possible, make up, and transmit to this Office, Supplementary Abstracts and General Annual Accompts, agreeably to the said Forms No. 2 and 3, of the respective Corps to which you are, or have been Agent, for each of the years that have elapsed since the Commencement of the new System of Accompts: you will annex thereto such Vouchers, in regard to Contingent Charges made in your Monthly Abstracts for the said Period, as have not yet been given in to this Office, together with Receipts for the Allowance paid to the retired Chaplains, and for the sums paid into the hands of the Cashier of the Chaplain's Fund.

You will also take care that like Vouchers (retaining Duplicates thereof) shall always in future be sent in with the [Monthly] †Accompts, in which the charge to which they respectively belong shall be inserted.

[And as it is proper, as well from a regard to the Security of the Public, as to the established practice of Government on similar occasions, that the retired Chaplains should be required, at least once a year, to produce authentic Certificates of their Existence, I enclose herewith a Form, No. 4, of the Certificate, which it is expected you will obtain from each retired Chaplain of Corps in your Agency, previously to your paying him the Allowance up to the 24th of December in each year.

You will also obtain proper Certificates of the days of the Death of such retired Chaplains as may happen to die in the course of the Year.‡]

---

* If the Duplicate general State of the Supplementary Accompts of the Regimental Paymaster shall not have been received seven days before the 24th of April, then the transmission of the Agent's Supplementary Abstract is to be postponed until seven days after the receipt thereof, in conformity to the Rule laid down in the Circular to Agents, page 209.

† Now with the Quarterly Accompts.

‡ The Allowances to retired Chaplains are not now paid by the Regimental Agents. Vide page 330.

The above Certificates are to be annexed to your Accompts in support of your Charges on this head.

I am further to mention, for your Information, that the necessary Issues of Monies to cover the expected Regimental Expenditures will be directed of course by this Office, as well for Recruiting and Contingencies, as for the usual Monthly Services, without waiting, as heretofore, for the Applications from the Agents; which it is therefore conceived will not often be necessary. Should the case occur, I am to desire, that, for the purpose of enabling this Department to decide upon the propriety of the Claims, and to pay early attention thereto, your applications be invariably accompanied by a Statement prepared in the Form sent herewith No. 5, shewing the Total of the supposed Insufficiency of the Funds ordered to be imprested into your hands for the various heads of Service taken generally. I think it proper at the same time to recommend to you, to keep your Accompts of the Expenditures and Sums directed to be issued in such a manner, as may enable you, on all occasions, to judge of the propriety of answering Regimental Requisitions, and to furnish without delay to this Office, whenever called upon for that purpose, comparative Statements of the General Accompts of the Corps in the Form last mentioned.

I am,
    Gentlemen,
        Your most obedient Servant,
          (Signed)     C. YORKE.

Agents of the
    Regiment

---

*N. B. It has not been thought necessary to reprint here the several Forms alluded to in this Letter: but the same may be purchased as since altered, and printed by authority, at Mr. Egerton's Military Library, near Whitehall.*

*Appendix.* 591

*Circular relative to the Issues of Pay and Contingencies for the Staff of the Recruiting Districts in Great Britain.*

*War Office, 17th December,* 1802.

SIR,

IT being thought proper, that the Pay and Contingencies of the Staff of the Recruiting Districts in Great Britain, should from the 25th Instant inclusive, be issued through the General Agent for Recruiting, resident in London; I have the honor to acquaint you therewith, and to desire that you will instruct the Paymaster of the District under your Inspection, that he is to draw upon Mr. Ridge, instead of Messrs. Cox, Greenwood and Cox, for the said Services, from the above date.

I am further to acquaint you, that agreeably to the tenor of the Communication made to the Inspector General of the Recruiting Service in my Letter of the 23d ultimo, the Paymaster is not to issue his Draft, for the Pay and Allowances of the Commissioned Officers, belonging to the Staff of the District, until the *end* of the military month, except in the case of any individual Officer, who may cease to belong thereto, in the course thereof; and that he is to prepare a separate Estimate of the Pay and Contingencies of the Staff, for each month, with a duplicate for the use of the General Agent: and to transmit the said Estimate and Duplicate to this Office, so that the same may be received here, on or before the 12th of each month, in order that the issues may be regulated accordingly.

I have the honor to be,
SIR,
Your most obedient servant,
(Signed)     C. YORKE.

Inspecting Field Officer
of the       District.

*Circular respecting the Allowance to be granted to Men enrolled for Militia Corps, and rejected at Head Quarters; to carry them back to their Homes.*

*War Office, 31st March, 1804.*

SIR,

THERE being no established regulation for the guidance of Paymasters in issuing to Men enrolled for Militia Corps, and rejected on joining at Head Quarters, a proper allowance to carry them back to their respective homes; and it being necessary that some precise rule should be laid down in this respect: I have the honor to acquaint you, that, in future, the allowance to a man of the above description is to be the same as that which he was entitled to receive from the Clerk of the Subdivision Meeting, to enable him to join the Regiment, in pursuance of the 119th Section of the General Militia Act, (42d Geo. III. Cap. 90);* with the addition of a further gratuity of three days pay for his support, during the period that may elapse between his arriving at home, and his resuming his usual occupation.

I am to add, that where it shall appear that the man himself has been guilty of any fraudulent concealment of his unfitness for service, he should be dismissed without any allowance whatever.

I have the honor to be,

SIR,

Your most obedient servant,

(Signed)      C. BRAGGE.

Officer Commanding
   the     of
       Militia.

---

\* Scotch Militia, Cap. 91. Sect. 115.

*Circular enclosing a Memorandum respecting the New Forms of Monthly Accompts for Militia Corps.*

*War Office, 18th January, 1805.*

SIR,

IN transmitting to you the enclosed new Forms of Monthly Accompts, which you will be pleased to cause to be delivered to the Paymaster, with the accompanying Memorandum *, I think it proper to apprize you, that the alteration which you will perceive in the General Certificate of the Commanding Officer, and which is approved by His Royal Highness the Commander in Chief, has been adopted with the view of calling the attention of the Commanding Officer particularly to those points, which are considered more peculiarly within his Province. I make no doubt, however, of your enforcing, so far as may be in your power, a due regard to the established regulations on every other point connected with the Public Accompts of the Corps under your command.

I beg leave to add, that, as the Pay-Lists will not be furnished so frequently as heretofore, it will be essential, that the Remarks of the Adjutant upon his Rolls should contain every explanation that may tend to facilitate the examination and settlement of the Accompts in this Office : and I am to request that you will give him Instructions for this Purpose accordingly, desiring him, among other things, to take care to specify the reason why every individual is borne for the *first* time, or *ceases* to be borne upon the Roll ; and to explain, what has been the situation of each Non-commissioned Officer and Private Man, who shall not have been actually present on duty during the whole period.

---

* This Memorandum is not reprinted. The 46th Article of the Explanatory Directions of 25th April, 1805, being, however, particularly connected with the Subject, the Paymaster is desired to give the strictest attention thereto, by not including in the Statement the Name of any Officer *newly appointed, until he shall have actually seen his Commission.* See Page 175.

If an Officer should have been absent without leave in the course of the period, it is also to be noticed.

I have the honor to be,

SIR,

Your most obedient

humble servant,

(Signed) W. DUNDAS.

Officer Commanding
 the
  of Militia.

## Appendix. 595

*General Orders relative to Officers of Second Battalions becoming, from Promotion or other Causes, effective in the First Battalions of their Regiments.*

Horse Guards, 12th August, 1805.

THE Commander in Chief is pleased to direct, that whenever Officers belonging to second Battalions shall, from promotion, or other causes, become effective upon the establishment of the first Battalions of their Regiments, they shall be *immediately* ordered to join those Battalions, if stationed in any part of the United Kingdom, or the Islands in the Channel.

In instances where the first Battalions are serving on foreign Stations, it is His Royal Highness's pleasure, that the Officers becoming effective therein, shall remain with the second Battalions until opportunities offer for them to proceed to join the Battalions to which they properly belong: of which they will be timely apprized by the Inspector General of the Recruiting Service; for whose information Officers commanding second Battalions of Regiments, of which the first Battalions are abroad, are in future regularly to transmit (under cover to the Secretary at War) a Report on the first of each month, of the rank and names of Officers serving with their respective Battalions, who from seniority belong to the first Battalions, and likewise of the number of rank and file serving in the second Battalions, who are engaged for unlimited service. They are also to specify the same on the back of the Regimental Monthly Returns, transmitted to this Office, for the Commander in Chief's Information.

In order to enable them to comply with the foregoing Regulation, Officers Commanding Battalions are enjoined to require constantly from their Regimental Agents, the most prompt Communication of any casualty which may affect the appropriation of their Officers.

It is the Commander in Chief's further pleasure, that Officers, who may be removed by Promotion from first to second Battalions, shall, if present with the first Battalions, remain until the arrival of the Officers, who by reason of such promotion, become effective; and are to replace them

in

in the first Battalions; they are then, without fail, to be immediately ordered to join the second Battalions, and the time of their receiving such Orders is to be communicated by the Officers Commanding the regiments, to the Commanding Officers of the second Battalions:—the preference being thus given, in the interchange of Officers, to the first Battalions.

Officers on their removal from one Battalion to the other, will be allowed their travelling expences, in the same manner as when ordered upon the Recruiting Service; provided such removal does not take place, at their own request, or in consequence of their own personal promotion. All applications for travelling expences are to be made through the Officers Commanding the Regiments to the Commander in Chief's Military Secretary.

By Order of His Royal Highness
The Commander in Chief.

(Signed)      HARRY CALVERT,
Adjutant General of the Forces.

*Appendix.* 597

*General Orders, relative to the Recruiting for First Battalions, when ordered on Foreign Service; in Cases where the Second Battalions are for limited Service.*

*Horse Guards, 30th October,* 1805.

IT is His Majesty's Pleasure, in the event of the first Battalion of a Regiment of Infantry composed of two Battalions (of which the Soldiers of the second Battalion are engaged for Limited Service) being employed on Foreign Service, that the Recruiting Service of the regiment shall be conducted, exclusively, by Officers, Non-commissioned Officers, and Soldiers belonging to the second Battalion, especially nominated to that duty.

The intention of the arrangement prescribed by the above Order from His Majesty, being to render the First Battalions of Regiments as effective and complete as possible, it is the Commander in Chief's command, that on the first Battalion of a Regiment of the above description receiving Orders to hold itself in readines for embarkation, all Recruiting Parties shall be ordered to join the Battalion; care being taken, that they are timely relieved by Parties from the second Battalion: the Commanding Officer of the Regiment is enjoined, immediately, to make a communication to the Inspector General of the Recruiting Service (under cover to the Secretary at War), of the Exchange of the Officers and Parties, which may take place in consequence of this Regulation.

In some few instances, an immediate compliance with this Regulation to its full extent (which requires that, at least one Captain, two Subaltern Officers, with Non-commissioned Officers in proportion, belonging to the second Battalion, shall be employed on the Recruiting Service of the First,) may not be possible; but 'His Royal Highness strictly commands, that it shall on all Occasions be carried into immediate effect, as far as Circumstances will permit, and that the earliest opportunity shall be taken of supplying any unavoidable deficiency, in the Number of Officers and

Non-commissioned Officers, furnished by the Second Battalion for this duty.

This Order makes no Alteration in the existing Regulations respecting the Recruiting Service of Regiments composed only of one Battalion, nor of those Regiments which have two or more Battalions composed wholly of men engaged for unlimited service.

By Order of His Royal Highness,

The Commander in Chief.

(Signed)          HARRY CALVERT,

Adjutant-General of the Forces.

*Circular*

*Appendix.*

*Circular from the Adjutant General, relative to the Provision of a New Description of Pioneers Appointments.*

Horse Guards, 17th December, 1805.

SIR,

HIS MAJESTY having been pleased to approve of appointments, on an entire new principle, being established for the Pioneers of the Infantry of the Army, as was communicated for your information by a Letter addressed to your Regimental Agent on the 25th February, 1805;* and the Commander in Chief having been pleased to direct, that no Regiments shall henceforward, on any account, be considered prepared for service, without having their Pioneers completely equipped, in obedience to HIS MAJESTY's Commands; I am directed to desire that you will cause the Regiment under your Command, to be immediately provided with Pioneer Appointments of the very best materials, and made in strict conformity to the Patterns which are lodged in the Office of the Comptrollers of Army Accounts.

I am authorized further to inform you, that if the Regiment, under your Command, is now in possession of a Set of Pioneer Accoutrements of the old Description, the charge of replacing them by a new Set (amounting, according to the computation made by Messrs. Learmouth and Beazley, to 32*l.* 10*s.* 9*d.* per Battalion) will, on being duly certified to the Secretary at War, be allowed as a charge against the Public; the Colonels of Regiments being responsible to

---

\* The purport of this Letter was to apprize Colonels of Regiments, that Sealed Patterns of Pioneers Accoutrements, and Tools, as approved by the King, are lodged in the Office of the Comptrollers of Army Accompts.

have the tools and appointments specified, at all times in a complete State.

You will please to comply with the Secretary at War's Directions, with respect to the Disposal of the Pioneer Appointments, which have heretofore been in use, which must of course be considered as the property of the Public.

I have the honor to be,

SIR,

Your most obedient

humble servant,

(Signed) HARRY CALVERT.

Colonel of the
Regiment of Foot.

*Appendix.* 601

*General Orders, relative to Men transferred from regular Regiments to the Veteran Battalions.*

*Horse Guards, 10th February, 1806.*

IT is His Royal Highness the Commander in Chief's command, that whenever soldiers are transferred to any of the Royal Veteran Battalions, the Commanding Officers of the Regiments, from which they are removed, shall invariably transmit with them, a Return (agreeably to the annexed Form) stating an exact account of the age, services, and general character of each man, and assigning the cause of his Discharge from the more active part of the service.

The object of this Regulation is, to secure to the deserving old soldier, the full effect of HIS MAJESTY's most gracious Benevolence, announced to the Army by the General Order, dated the 18th of April, 1804,* and at the same time to prevent the Royal Bounty being bestowed on unworthy Objects, by enabling the Commanding Officers to decide, as to the description of Discharge, to which each man is entitled on being finally discharged from the service of the Royal Veteran Battalions. A consideration, therefore, for the Soldier's interests, and justice towards the Public, equally require the most strict observance of this Order, and His Royal Highness commands the Colonels, or Officers in the Command of each of the Royal Veteran Battalions, to make an especial Report of any Man who may hereafter arrive at their Head Quarters, for the purpose of being received into their Battalions, without this requisite Document of his former services.

By His Royal Highness
The Commander in Chief's Command.
(Signed) HARRY CALVERT,
Adjutant General to the Forces.

---

* By this order it was notified to the Army that, " hereafter Soldiers discharged from any of the Royal Veteran Battalions, *with especial recommendatory discharges*, as being disabled from further military duty, either from length of service, or from wounds received in the service, shall be in all cases allowed the Out-pension of Nine-pence per day: and, if totally incapacitated, by infirmities or wounds, from providing for themselves, that they shall be allowed a pension of One Shilling per day." Later Instructions are however contained in His Majesty's Warrant of 7th October, 1806.—See page 534.

RETURN

## Appendix.

RETURN of MEN who have been directed by His Royal Highness the COMMANDER IN CHIEF, to be transferred from the ——— Regiment of ——— to the ROYAL VETERAN BATTALION.

*Dated*

| NAMES. | Date to which subsisted by the ——— Regiment. | By what General, or other Officer, inspected. | Period of Service, stating also in what Corps. | Cause of being deemed unfit for active Service. | REMARKS. On the General Character as well as Services, of the Men transferred. |
|---|---|---|---|---|---|
| | | | | | |

*Appendix.* 603

*General Orders, requiring Quarterly Returns to be made of the Names of Officers whose Pay has been suspended, in consequence of their having been absent without Leave.*

Horse Guards, 1st July, 1806.

IT is His Royal Highness the Commander in Chief's Command, that Officers in the command of Regular and Militia Regiments, and corps of every description (with the exception of those serving in Ireland), shall in future transmit to the Adjutant-General's Office in London, as soon as possible after the 24th of March, June, September, and December, in each year, a Return (made up agreeably to the annexed Form) of the Names of those Officers of their respective Corps, whose Pay has been suspended in the course of the preceding three months, in consequence of their having been absent from their Regiments without leave.

In this Return it is necessary that the Commanding Officers should specify the period during which each Officer has been absent without due authority; and in the column of Remarks, it must be stated whether such Officer has accounted satisfactorily for his absence, and whether the Respite on his Pay has, or has not, been removed by the authority of the Commander in Chief.

His Royal Highness desires, that Commanding Officers of Regiments will be most particular in preparing and transmitting these Returns, when circumstances render them necessary; and when no such Circumstances occur, they are required to express the same, in a convenient space, in the Regimental Monthly Returns, of the 1st of the following Month.

Returns of the Description above-mentioned, for the two Quarters of the present year, ending on the 24th of March and June last, respectively, are required to be transmitted as soon as possible.

By Order of His Royal Highness,
The Commander in Chief.

(Signed) HARRY CALVERT,
Adjutant-General of the Forces.

## Appendix.

**QUARTERLY RETURN** of *Officers belonging to the* Regiment of *who have been absent without Leave for any Period during the preceding Three Months.*

Head Quarters, 25th of

| RANK and NAMES. | Period of being Absent without Leave. | | REMARKS. |
|---|---|---|---|
| | From | To | |

N. B. This Return is to be made out on Paper of the Foolscap Size, and to be folded in Four, and docketted as under:—

Regt. of

**QUARTERLY REPORT**
OF
**ABSENT OFFICERS,**
25th of

*Circular to the Commanding Officers of Regiments at Home, relative to advertising Deserters in the Hue and Cry.*

*War Office,* 13*th March,* 1794.

SIR,

IT being conceived, that much Advantage may be derived to His Majesty's Service by regularly advertising all Deserters therefrom in one particular Paper, and by circulating that Paper to the Head Quarters of the respective Regiments at Home, and to every Recruiting Party, free of Expence; I have the honour to acquaint you, that the Weekly Paper called " the Hue and Cry" has been fixed upon, as the best adapted for this Plan, which is to be carried into execution in the following manner.

Commanding Officers of Regiments at Home are to transmit to the War Office, an Account of all Deserters that, from the date of this Letter, shall Desert after joining, together with a description of their Persons, according to the Form* annexed: and to direct their Recruiting Officers to send like Returns to the War Office, in regard to such as shall hereafter Desert from their Parties.

The Inspector General is to give the like Orders to the Officers Recruiting for Regiments Abroad.

Commanding Officers of Regiments Abroad are to send their Account and Description of Deserters by every opportunity that occurs.

Descriptions so received will be severally inserted three times, with the Agent's Name and Place of Abode specified against the Regiment.

Commanding Officers of Regiments at Home, and Inspector General, are to furnish an Account of the present Recruiting Stations, and of such Alterations as may, from time to time, take place therein; that, agreeably to the Plan, the Publisher may regularly send the Paper to each Station, free of Expence.

The Publisher will send also to the Head Quarters of each Regiment at Home two Papers, free of Expence: which Papers are to be carefully preserved at Head Quarters, and

---

* Not reprinted: a later Form having been circulated by the Adjutant General. The mode of transmitting Reports of Deserters to the War Office, is explained on page 26 of the " General Regulations and Orders," dated 1st November, 1804.

at each Recruiting Party, wherever the same shall be stationed: and no Officer is in future to have any Recruit attested, without a previous strict Examination of his Person, and also a previous Inspection of the Paper, hereby directed to be transmitted as aforesaid; and if, on such Examination, or Inspection, it shall appear that the Person inlisted is described as a Deserter in such Paper, he shall be forthwith apprehended as such, and carried before a Magistrate accordingly.

The Reward for Apprehension, exclusive of the Parliamentary one*, is to be Twenty Shillings, payable by the respective Agents†: [excepting, in cases, where a Recruit shall Desert before Approval, when, if he be recovered to the Service, and Approved, the Reward is to be paid by the Recruiting Officer; who will, in future, be allowed the Levy Money, upon the Approbation of such Recruit.]

You will, in conformity to the above Regulations, cause the necessary Returns to be transmitted from Head Quarters; and direct the several Recruiting Parties of the ——————— Regiment of ——————————— under your Command, to pay the most invariable Attention to the sending of such as may appertain to their respective Stations.

I take this opportunity of desiring, that the deviations from the direct road, occasionally specified in the Orders for escorting Deserters, may be strictly attended to; as they are constantly allotted through places where there may be other Deserters for the same destination, who frequently remain a considerable time in Gaol for want of this Attention; or, where Troops are stationed, which, without such directions, would, according to the Tenour of the Order, be exempted from taking a Share in the Escort.

     I have the honour to be, Sir,
      Your most obedient Servant,
      (Signed)   GEO. YONGE.

Officer Commanding
 the    Regiment of

---

* This is paid under the Authority of the Mutiny Act, by the County in which the Deserter is seized.

† Or Pay Masters, due care being taken that it is not paid by both, and *provided the Deserter shall have been advertised in the Paper abovementioned and not otherwise.* This Reward is now chargeable to the Public for Recruits before and after Approval; the Direction contained in the latter part of the Paragraph in the Letter, having been annulled by subsequent Regulations.

*Circular*

*Appendix.*

*Circular from the Military Secretary to the Commander in Chief, addressed to Generals Commanding on Foreign Stations, relative to the Stoppages to be made from the Pay of Soldiers in General Hospitals Abroad.*

Horse Guards, 9th July, 1805.

SIR,

THE Secretary at War having represented to the Commander in Chief, that it would be extremely desirable for the purpose of maintaining one uniform System, relative to General Hospital Stoppages, that the same residue only should be left from the Soldier's Pay, while in General Hospital, in the Station under your Command, as is left to him in this Country; viz.

Threepence, from the Pay of a Private,
Fourpence three farthings, from that of a Drummer,
Fivepence one farthing, from that of a Corporal,
Ninepence three farthings, from that of a Serjeant.

I have His Royal Highness's Commands to desire that you may be pleased to carry this Suggestion into effect, and to direct the Paymasters of Regiments and others, to annex to their Pay-Lists and Accompts, the Receipts of the Officers of the Commissariat Department, to whom the Stoppages for the Men in General Hospital shall have been paid.

I have the honor to be,
SIR,
Your most obedient servant,
(Signed) J. W. GORDON.

To
Commanding His Majesty's Forces
at

*Circular relative to the Allowance of Pay and Marching Money to be granted to Soldiers discharged from the Veteran Battalions, and replaced on the Out Pension, without being required to make their appearance at the Chelsea Board; to carry them to their Homes.*

*War Office*, 16th *March*, 1807.

SIR,

REFERRING to the Orders and Regulations lately established for improving the situation of the Soldiers of the Army, dated 7th October last,* I have the honour to acquaint you, that in the case of Men discharged from a Veteran Battalion, and replaced on the Out Pension without being required to make their appearance at the Chelsea Board, they are to receive the same allowance of Pay and Marching Money to carry them home, as Non-commissioned Officers and Soldiers entitled to their Discharge from other Corps; but that a Deduction is to be made therefrom, of the Amount of the Out Pension of the Men for the period for which the advance shall be made. It will therefore be necessary, that, in every case where a Non-commissioned Officer or Private Man of the Veteran Battalion under your command shall be about to be Discharged, the Pay Master should apply to the proper Officer at Chelsea Hospital for Information, as to the Amount of the Nett Out Pension of the Man for the number of Days for which the pay and allowance on the March is proposed to be issued, so as to ascertain the exact amount of the difference, which should be charged in the Accompts rendered to this Office. The Pay Master should also annex to his Accompt the report which he shall have received from Chelsea Hospital on this Head.

I have the honor to be,

SIR,

Your most obedient Servant,

(Signed)　　R. FITZPATRICK.

Officer Commanding
   the     Royal Veteran Battalion.

---

* See page 534.

*Circular*

*Appendix.* 609

*Circular to Pay Masters of Recruiting Districts relative to Charges for Stamps on Bills drawn upon Agents: to the Mode of crediting the Effects and Credits of Soldiers belonging to Recruiting Parties, &c.*

*War Office, 24th March,* 1807.

SIR,

IN pursuance of an Arrangement adopted with the concurrence of the Lord Lieutenant of Ireland, I am to acquaint you, that all proper Charges of the actual Expence of Stamps upon Bills drawn by District Pay Masters in Great Britain on the Agents, whether the Service for which they shall have been drawn belong to the British, or Irish Establishment, are to be charged under the head of Contingent Disbursements, in the District Staff Pay Lists rendered to this Office, in the Form whereof the necessary Alterations will be made.

The Pay Masters are in each case to state distinctly the particulars of the Bills credited in each Quarterly General State with Great Britain and Ireland respectively, and for the future, are to insert them only in the Accompts of the period, in the General State of which, the Bills are credited.

I take this opportunity of enclosing a printed form of Supplementary General State, in which are to be inserted all such Expenditures and Receipts as from particular circumstances could not be included in the last Quarterly Accompts of the year to which they belong: the said General State and the Recapitulation on the back thereof, (which is calculated to shew at one View the total Annual Amount expended and received for the Staff, and for each Party, and how the Accompts for each Regiment have been balanced,) are to be made up and to be transmitted for the year 1806, immediately after the 24th of April next,* and for future years within three Months of the termination of the Annual period of the Accompts.

---

* In consequence of this direction, the Agents will not be required to send in their Supplementary Abstracts for such Corps as shall have had Parties recruiting in the districts for the year 1806, until after the receipt of the District Paymaster's Supplementary Abstracts.

I also

I also send a form of Supplementary Pay List which is to be used separately for each Party, and to be rendered to this Office with the said Supplementary General State; on the back thereof is to be inserted a general Statement of the Amount of Effects and Credits of Non-commissioned Officers, Trumpeters, Drummers or Fifers, Privates, and Recruits of each Party, who have Died or Deserted, or have been delivered up in consequence of being Apprentices, or Deserters belonging to other Corps within the year, shewing the several receipts and payments under this head, with the names of the respective Men. The balance of such Statement, after deducting the sums, if any, paid to Representatives of deceased Soldiers, it is thought proper should in regard to District Accompts be accounted for Annually, by a deduction thereof from the Expenditures at the foot of the Supplementary Pay Lists of the Party for the year, in which the Men shall have ceased to be effective; this deduction is to be made in the place allotted for Corrections, under the head of Pay of Men.

Care is to be taken that the charges of expenditures incurred on account of Levy Money of Recruits enlisted on or before the 24th of December in each year, and not included in the Quarterly Accompts of that period, are inserted in the Supplementary Pay List thereof, unless in cases where the payment shall not have taken place until after the expiration of the period limited for transmitting the said Pay List: when the charge may be made in the Pay Lists of the ensuing year, the cause of delay in this case, as is requisite in all cases of retrospective charges, being particularly explained in the column of Remarks.

I am to add, that the Balances due to you on the account of the year 1806, from the Officers employed to recruit under the late Regulations of 13th October last, are to be deducted from your Credits in the Supplementary General State, and in your Supplementary Abstracts for the Agents, (if not deducted in those to 24th December last) as not having been expended for the service of 1806: and the same are to be re-credited in your first General State for the current year.

I am,
SIR,
Your most obedient servant,
(Signed) R. FITZPATRICK.

Paymaster of the
  Recruiting District.

*Additional*

# ADDITIONAL NOTES.

IN reference generally to the Circulars respecting the encrease of Pay and Allowance from the 25th June, 1806, it is proper to mention, that in estimating the Claims of *Corporals* to the Additional Allowance depending on length of service, their previous service as Privates is to be taken into Account. It is also to be observed, that *service in the Troops of the East India Company*, does not give a claim to additional pay.

Page 39.—In pursuance of a Communication from Head Quarters, the following Rule has been laid down in regard to the Appropriation of the Allowance of 3s. a day to the Commanding Officers of Battalions: viz.—" The Officer who signs the Monthly Return is to be considered as in command of the Regiment, and as such, entitled to the Allowance of 3s. a day, although he may have been absent at intervals during the preceding month: if he is absent beyond the date of that Return, the Officer next in Command will sign the Return, and be entitled to the Pay from the period, on which his predecessor absented himself."

Page 51.—The Lieutenants of the Foot Guards, who have the Brevet of Major, or any superior Rank, are allowed the additional 2s. a day given to Captains of the Line in similar circumstances.
The Quarter-Masters of the Foot Guards have also been placed on the same footing with Quarter-Masters of the Line, in regard to the encrease of Pay and Allowance from 25th June, 1806.

Page 83.—Since the Alteration in the footing of Adjutants in 1802 (as explained in Pages 9 and 10), the Adjutants of Cavalry are allowed Forage for *three* Horses.

Page 141.—The 13th Article of the Additional Instructions to Paymasters, &c. dated 11th May, 1801, does not warrant the including in the Paymasters' Estimate the advance of pay for any Officer, Non-commissioned Officer, or Private, who is not to go abroad with the Corps.

Page 149—Officers on the *Staff* abroad, are not liable to any stoppage from their Regimental Pay on account of Rations.

Page 151, Article 9.—The Non-effective Allowance is not chargeable for a Captain, during the period of his being absent without leave.

Page 202.—The *Distribution* mentioned in the fourth paragraph should be transmitted to the War Office, in a separate cover, with the word "Distribution," written in the corner of the Cover.

Page 219, Fourth Paragraph.—The Rule contained in the four last lines is now indispensably requisite.

Pages 276 and 277.—Field Officers and Adjutants of Recruiting Districts, who are on the Half-Pay of Infantry, receive through the District Paymasters the difference between the Half and Full Pay of their respective Commissions, at the undermentioned daily Rates; being the nearest to which the annual amount is reducible.—The remainder is made good to them at the end of each year.

|  | Difference of Half and Full Pay per Annum. | | | Rate per Diem. | |
| --- | ---: | ---: | ---: | ---: | ---: |
|  | *l.* | *s.* | *d* | *s.* | *d.* |
| Lieutenant Colonel | 139 | 4 | 7½ | 7 | 7 |
| Major | 123 | 11 | 4½ | 6 | 9 |
| Captain | 82 | 17 | 9 | 4 | 6 |
| Lieutenant | 43 | 13 | 0 | 2 | 4 |
| Ensign | 34 | 5 | 11 | 1 | 10 |
| Adjutant | 37 | 8 | 3 | 2 | 0 |
| Quarter Master | 49 | 11 | 7 | 2 | 8 |

The difference per annum between Half and Full Pay, and the daily Rate of Issue, will not be the same, if the Officer be on the Half Pay of *Cavalry*. In that case the proper Amount should be ascertained by a reference to the War Office.

Pages 283, 284.—The allowances to Recruiting Officers mentioned in these pages are done away. *Vide* page 571.

Page 285, Fourth Paragraph of Art. XXVI.—The words "together with his Accompts," are inapplicable. *Vide* page 223.

Page 299.—Schedule 6—cancelled by the General Order of 1st February, 1807. *Vide* page 571.

Page 301.—Partly annulled. *See* the reference to the preceding note.

## Additional Notes.

Page 306.—The following alterations have taken place. Date of Instructions altered from 13*th* to 27*th* October, 1806.
Article 1.—For the words "under the hand of," the word "by," is substituted.
Article 5.—Before "Inspector General," introduce Adjutant General.

Page 307.—The date of the Recruiting Regulations, is the 25th October, 1806.

Page 308.—Omit the N. B.

Page 397, Third Paragraph.—If the Men on quitting the Hospital are sent to the depôt in the Isle of Wight, to a Recruiting District, or to any other station where there is a Paymaster of Detachments, who will have to settle with them for the remainder of their pay, while in Hospitals, the duplicate Accompts are to be sent to the Paymaster at such station.
The Accompts are now only required to be transmitted Quarterly, instead of Monthly. *Vide* Second Note on page 395.

Page 458.—The Allowance for altering Clothing is, of course, granted only to *Corps of Infantry serving at home.*

Pages 478, 479.—By a Circular to Agents, from the Adjutant General, dated 4th December, 1806, it is ordered, that the rule laid down in these Letters shall be adopted in regard to the Clothing of Men transferred from the Royal Veteran Battalions, to Regiments of the Line, or vice versâ. Claims occurring on the part of the Royal Veteran Battalions are to be adjusted by the Agents of those Corps.

Page 501.—By a recent Arrangement, the Widows of Inspectors of Hospitals are in certain circumstances to be allowed Pensions at the Rate of Fifty Pounds per Annum each; and those of Deputy Inspectors, the Pension of Forty-five pounds per Annum.

Page 509.—The applications for leave of absence for Paymasters of Corps at home, including Jersey and Guernsey, are to be made, through the regular channel, to the Adjutant General; each application being accompanied by the declaration of the Paymaster, in writing, that he will hold himself responsible for the Officer proposed to do his duty; who is not, however, to be a Field or Staff Officer.

Page 533.—The Loyal Essex Regiment of Fencible Infantry was disbanded on the 10th July, 1802.

The Inverness-shire Regiment of Fencible Highlanders, commanded by Colonel John Gordon Cuming, is also considered as one of the Corps that volunteered for extended service, from 27th August, 1801: and is therefore to be added to the List No. 2. This Corps was disbanded on the 25th August, 1802.

Page 571.—This Regulation is to be understood as applying to Officers who may have been actually on the journey to their Recruiting Stations, on the 1st February, 1807.

Page 595 to 598.—Various passages in these Orders have become inapplicable, since the Second Battalions have ceased to include men for *limited* Service.

( 615 )

# INDEX.

## A.

| | | |
|---|---|---|
| *Absence* - - - | Without leave. See *Leave*. | |
| *Abstracts of Pay-masters Accompts* | Alteration in the form, | 192, 193 |
| | Transmission of | 205 |
| *Accompts* - - - | Regimental. Section III. *passim.* | |
| *Accoutrements* | Carriage of | 95. 164 |
| | No charge for, to be included in the Pay Lists | 164 |
| | Provision and Inspection of | 430, 431 |
| | Specification and duration of, for Cavalry | 447 to 449 |
| | Indemnification for, when lost on service | 494 |
| *Act of Parliament* | For encreasing the Rates of Subsistence to Innkeepers, &c. | 75 |
| | Extract from the Pay Office Act | 109 |
| *Action,* - - - | Officers wounded or killed in | 489 |
| *Additional Force Acts* | Pay of Corps raised under | 53 |
| | Levy Money of Men ditto | 177 |
| | Recruiting charges for ditto | 225 |
| | Instructions to Paymasters of Battalions raised under | 226 to 234 |
| | Men serving under the terms of, not entitled to additional Pay | 529 |
| | Service under, excluded, in estimating claims to ditto | *ibid.* |
| *Additional Pay,* | Granted for length of service 30 to 55. | 529 to 539. 611 |
| | How forfeited | 533 |
| *Adjutant General,* | Pay and Allowances of | 339 to 341 |
| *Adjutants of Recruiting Districts* - - | To authenticate District Pay Lists | 214. 224 |
| | Appointment and Pay of | 277. 612 |
| *Adjutants of Regiments* - - | Pay and Rank of | 6 to 10. 39 |
| | Forage for the Horses of | 63. 178. 611 |
| | Monthly Rolls of | 124. 202. 205. 233. 563 |
| | Personal Baggage and Camp Equipage of | 401 |
| *Advance of Pay,* | To Regiments proceeding on Foreign Service | 112 |
| | To individual Officers ditto | 510, 511 |
| *Agency,* - - - | Deduction for | 4 to 8 |
| *Agent of Army Hospitals,* | Bills drawn on, by Purveyors for Contingencies | 400 |
| | Authorities to, for the Payment of Contingencies | 581 |
| *Agent (General) of the Recruiting Service in Dublin,* - - | Expenditures of British Parties in Ireland | 285, 286 |
| | Ditto—for Recruits for General Service | *ibid.* |

*Agent*

| | |
|---|---|
| *Agent (General) of the Recruiting Service in London, -* | When Pay of Officers may be drawn from him 231 |
| | Subsistence of Soldiers of Regiments in Ireland 247 |
| | Expenditures of Irish Parties in Great Britain 285 |
| | Ditto—for Recruits for General Service 286 |
| | Effects, Credits, and Debts of ditto — *ibid.* |
| | Pay and Contingencies of the Recruiting Staff 591 |
| *Agents of Regts.* | Allowance to, for postage and stationary — 97 |
| | Required to render periodical Accompts, &c. 110 to 113 |
| | Penalty on, for disobeying established Regulations *ib.* |
| | Security for — — — 114 |
| | Duty of, in regard to Paymasters 129. 136. 139 to 143. 195. 197 |
| | When to be accounted with, for Stoppages for Provisions — — — 149 |
| | When to remit Bank Notes to Paymasters — 158 |
| | Fees of Commission to be paid by 162. 169. 251 |
| | To be apprized of the names of Officers absent without leave — — — 165. 507 |
| | Pay, &c. charged by, to be specially vouched 176 |
| | Punctual delivery of the Regimental Accompts of 195. 197. 198. 578 |
| | Particular Instructions to, relative to Bills — 197 |
| | Abstracts of Examination of their Accompts, to be answered within a limited period — *ibid.* 578 |
| | Monthly Abstracts of — — 204 |
| | New Forms of Quarterly Accompts of — 209 |
| | Bills of District Paymasters on 213. 219. 609 |
| | Bounty of Recruits finally approved, when drawn for on — — — 217 |
| | Abstract of District Pay Lists for — 219 |
| | Communications to, on the following subjects: |
| |     Great Coat Fund — 451. 582 |
| |     Provision of Great Coats — 472. 477 |
| |     Inspection of ditto — 474. 476 |
| |     Clothing transferred with Soldiers — 478 |
| |     Caps ditto — — 479 |
| |     Discontinuance of Lacquered Felt Caps 480 |
| |     Distinction in the Great Coats of Serjeants and Corporals — — 481 |
| |     Pay of Gentlemen first obtaining Commissions 508 |
| |     Advance of Pay to Officers embarking for Foreign Service — 510, 511 |
| |     Ditto——for India — 519 to 521 |
| |     Repayment of Advances made by Persons in Public Trust — — 579 |
| |     Credits for the Allowance for Great Coats, Saddle Water Decks, and Corn Sacks 582 |
| |     Forms of Accompts to be rendered by them 588 |
| |     Clothing of Men transferred from the Line to the Veteran Battalions, or vice versâ 613 |
| *Aide de Camp,* | Pay and Allowances of — 339 to 348 |
| | Number of Horses allowed to — *ibid.* |

# INDEX.

| | | |
|---|---|---|
| Aid de Camp, | Allowance for the loss of a Charger | 492 |
| America, | Pay of Troops in | 22 |
| | Regimental Contingencies in | 94 |
| | Pay in advance to Regiments embarking for | 142 |
| Ammunition, | Carriage of — — 95. 157. 244, | 245 |
| Apothecary General | Medicines supplied by the | 401 |
| Apothecary, | Appointment of, how made | 354 |
| | Title of, to Half Pay — 354. | 356 |
| | Pay of | 360 |
| | Forage Money of | 369 |
| | Lodging Money of — 370. 372 to 374. | 376 |
| | Horses of | 371 |
| | Travelling Expences of — 372 to 375. | 377 |
| Apprehension | Of Deserters — — 311. | 606 |
| Apprentices, | Soldiers if claimed as, their Effects and Credits | 179 |
| | Not to be enlisted | 280 |
| Armourer, | In the Militia, Appointment and Pay of | 26. 55 |
| | Ditto,——Clothing of | 468 |
| | In the Line, Pay of — | 47 to 52 |
| | —— Fencible Infantry, ditto | 55 |
| Arms, | Expence of Articles for cleaning | 19. 154. 456 |
| | Carriage of — — | 95. 187 |
| | Mode of obtaining Issues of | 497. 498 |
| Army Depôt, | Recruits proceeding to — 172. 279, | 280 |
| | Principal Medical Officer at, to examine bills for Medical Assistance to Recruiting Parties in certain cases | 277 |
| | Paymaster of. See *Paymaster (Chief) of Recruiting Districts.* | |
| Army Medical Board, | } See *Medical Department.* | |
| Army Hospitals | Agent for. See *Agent of Army Hospitals:* and *Hospitals.* | |
| Arrears | Abolished — — | 3 to 8 |
| Artificers (Royal Military,) | } Recruiting Regulations inapplicable to | 287 |
| | Sick of, when abroad — | 409 to 411 |
| Artillery, | Recruiting Regulations inapplicable to | 287 |
| | Sick of, when abroad | 409 to 411 |
| Assignments | Of Clothing Allowance | 445 to 447 |
| Assistant Adjutant General | } Forage Money of | 341 |
| | Number of Horses allowed to | 345 |
| | Lodging Money of | 346 |
| Assistant Quarter Master General, | } Forage Money of | 341 |
| | Number of Horses allowed to | 345 |
| | Lodging Money of | 346 |
| Assistant Surgeon | Pay of — 46 to 52. 357. 359. 363, | 364 |
| | When two may be appointed in a Regiment | 380 |
| | Personal Baggage and Camp Equipage of | 491 |
| Attestations, | Expence of | 91 |
| | Forms of, and mode of filling up 280. 295. | 297 |
| | To be sent to the Head Quarters of Recruiting Districts, &c. | 281 |

Q Q        Baggage,

## B.

| | | |
|---|---|---|
| Baggage, Regimental, | Carriage of | 91. 99 to 105. 153 |
| | Of Recruiting Officers, Allowance for the Carriage of | 283 |
| | Of Officers, if lost on Service, Allowance for | 490 |
| Bât, Baggage, & Forage Money, | Not to be charged in the Pay Lists | 165 |
| | Rates and Distribution of | 421 to 423 |
| Bât & Baggage Horses, | To be mustered by Paymasters | 180 |
| | Mode of foraging | 424 to 426 |
| | Indemnification for the loss of | ibid. 492 |
| | Ration of Forage for, in Camp | 553 |
| Battle | Officers wounded or killed in | 489 |
| Bear Skin Caps | For Grenadiers in the Militia | 473 |
| Beating Orders | To be authenticated | 287 |
| Beer | In Barracks and in Camps | 12. 17 |
| | Allowance in lieu of | 66 |
| | Ditto—not granted to men on board ship | 179 |
| | Ditto—granted in General Hospitals | 160. 406 |
| Bills, | Negociation of, by Paymasters, when abroad | 129. 143 |
| | Drawn by Paymasters, to express for what Services | 139 |
| | Ditto—to be payable *after sight* | ibid. |
| | Ditto—abroad, to express the rate of exchange | 143 |
| | Ditto—Agents to be advised of | ibid. |
| | Ditto—at *par* from Foreign Stations | 165 |
| | Ditto—drawn from Ireland | 246 |
| Bonds, | For Officers, &c. employed in the Extraordinary Recruiting | 309, 310 |
| Books, Regimental, | Expence of | 91 |
| Bounty of Recruits, | See *Levy Money*. | |
| Boys, | Pay and Beer Money of | 27 to 29. 231. 408. 560 |
| | Bounty of | 27 to 29. 303. 560. 573. 575 |
| | How to be classed in Pay Lists | 230 |
| | Expence of attesting | 231 |
| | Standard and Age of | 279, 280. 293. 560 |
| | Parish Officers to certify whether the Boys are Apprentices | 280 |
| | Enlisted for Drummers or Fifers | 303. 575 |
| | Stoppage from the Pay of, in Hospitals | 408 |
| Bread, | Extra price of 11 to 17. 170. 284. 383. 407. 566. 587 | |
| | Supplied by contract | 69. 166 |
| | Proportion of Soldier's Pay applicable for | 146. 166 |
| | Deliveries of, in Camp | 551 to 556 |
| Brigade Major, | See *Major of Brigade*. | |
| Brigadier General on the Staff, | Pay and Allowances of | 339 to 348 |
| | Number of Horses allowed to | ibid. |
| Bristol | Paymaster of Detachments at, Instruction for | 173 |
| | Ditto—Issues by | 247 to 250 |
| Bugle, | Pay of | 54 |
| Burials of Soldiers, | Expence of, charged to Captains | 398 |

## C.

| | | |
|---|---|---|
| Campaign, Annual, | Period of | 341 |
| Camp Equipage, | If lost on Service, Allowance for | 490 |

*Camps,*

## INDEX.    619

| | | |
|---|---|---|
| Camps, - - - | See *Encampment*. | |
| *Candle for Guards,* | Allowance for | 95. 157 |
| *Cape of Good Hope,* | Contingencies of Regiments at | 94 |
| | Pay in advance to Regiments embarking for | 142 |
| Caps - - - - | Of Bear Skin, for Grenadiers in the Militia | 473 |
| | Transferred with Soldiers | 479 |
| | Of Lacquered Felt, discontinued | 480 |
| Captain, - - - | No longer generally responsible for Regimental Accompts | 3 |
| | Pay of | 5. 39. 47 to 52 |
| | Non-effective and Contingent Allowance to | 59 to 62. 151. 244, 245. 612 |
| | Lodging Money for | 64, 65 |
| | Responsible for the Application of Sums issued for his Troop or Company | 140 |
| | Debts of deceased Soldiers and Deserters, when chargeable to | 235 to 239 |
| | Burials of Soldiers, expence of, charged against | 398 |
| | Personal Baggage and Camp Equipage of | 490 |
| Carriage - - | Of Regimental Baggage | 91. 99 to 105. 153 |
| | Of Arms, Clothing, &c. | 95. 187 |
| Cavalry, - - | Pay | 5. 30 to 34. 47 to 50. 148 |
| | Allowance to Field Officers, Captains, &c. | 59 to 62 |
| | Extra Feed for Horses of Officers and Men | 83 |
| | Purchase of Troop Horses | 84, 85 |
| | Farriery | 87, 88 |
| | Saddle Water Decks and Corn Sacks | 89 |
| | Horses to be mustered by Paymasters | 180 |
| | Age and Standard of Recruits of | 293 |
| | Equipment for Recruits of | 304 |
| | Species of Clothing, and claims on account of it | 434 |
| | Species and duration of Appointments for | 447 to 450 |
| Chaplains - - | Regulations relative to | 319 to 335 |
| *Chaplain General* | See *Chaplains.* | |
| Chargers - - | Of Officers, if killed by the enemy, &c. Allowance for | 491 |
| *Chelsea Hospital,* | Out Pension of, encreased | 30 to 43. 534 to 539 |
| | Pay of Men waiting for a Board | 186 |
| | Out Pension of, how forfeited | 538 |
| *Children of Officers who may be killed in Action* | Allowance to | 489 |
| *Children of Soldiers* | No Stoppage required for their Provisions | 150 |
| | Conveyance for, to their homes | 187 to 189. 513 |
| Clothing, - - | Altering of | 19. 154. 164. 458. 613 |
| | Carriage of | 95 |
| | Not to be charged in the Pay Lists | 164 |
| | Regulations relative to | 429 to 481 |
| | Compensation in lieu of | 469 |
| | Of Men transferred from one Corps to another | 478. 613 |
| *Collectors of the Revenue,* | To supply Cash or Bank Notes for Paymasters Bills | 158 |
| Colonel - - - | Pay of | 5 |

Q Q 2    *Colonel.*

| | | |
|---|---|---|
| Colonel, | Responsible for his Agent | 113, 114 |
| | May take charge of Recruiting Parties | 273. 282, 283 |
| | May approve Recruits | 278. 282 |
| | Personal Baggage and Camp Equipage of | 490 |
| Commanding Officers, | Allowance to | 39. 611 |
| | Duty of, in regard to Paymasters 119 to 133. 138 to 143. 195. 205. 563. 593 | |
| Commissary General, | Regulation of the Supplies to be made by 551 to 556 | |
| Committee of Regimental Paymastership, | When to be apointed | 119. 130 |
| | Duty of, on ceasing to act as such | 190 |
| Compassionate Fund | Widows and Children of Hospital Mates eligible to the | 359 |
| Compensation | In lieu of Clothing | 442, 443. 469 |
| Confinement | Pay of Soldiers under | 163 |
| Consolidated Allowance | Abolished | 11. 15 |
| Constables | Demands of, for the hire of Waggons | 93 to 104 |
| Contingent Accompts | Of Staff Officers | 344 |
| Contingent Allowances | To Field Officers | 59, 60 |
| | To Captains and Riding Masters, &c. | 59 to 62. 151 |
| | For Captains, when the command of a Company is vacant | 151 |
| Contractors | For Bread | 69 |
| | Duplicates of their Accompts to be annexed to Pay Lists | 166 |
| | How to be paid by Paymasters | 166 |
| | For the Supplies of General Hospitals | 399 |
| Cornet, | Pay of | 6, 7. 47 to 50 |
| | Personal Baggage and Camp Equipage of | 490 |
| Corn, | See *Oats*. | |
| Corn Sacks, | Regulation for the Supply of | 89. 244. 582 |
| | Expence of, for Cavalry Recruits | 304 |
| Corporal, | Pay of | 11 to 25. 32 to 39. 47 to 55. 148. 174 |
| | Loss of his Necessaries, Allowance for | 491 |
| Courts Martial | For Detachments | 276. 288 |
| | Decisions of the King upon the Proceedings of | 561 |

D.

| | | |
|---|---|---|
| Debts | Of Soldiers | 126. 214. 235 to 239. 285, 286. 563 |
| Deduction | For Poundage, Hospital, and Agency | 4 to 8 |
| | — Provisions | 21. 23. 148 to 150 |
| | From the Pay of Soldiers in General Hospitals | 23. 148. 607 |
| | —— Staff Pay | 340 |
| | —— Forage Money | 341 |
| Defence Act, | See *Additional Force Acts*. | |
| Delivery of Clothing, | Period of | 415 |
| Deputy Adjutant General, | Pay and Allowances of | 339 to 341 |

*Deputy*

# INDEX.

| | | |
|---|---|---|
| Deputy Inspector General of the Recruiting Service | See *Inspector General.* | |
| Deputy Inspector of Hospitals, | Pay of | 361 |
| | Forage Money of | 369 |
| | Lodging Money of | 370. 372 to 376 |
| | Horses of | 371 |
| | Travelling Expences of | 372 to 377 |
| Deputy Judge Advocates, - | Allowances to | 485. 486 |
| Deputy Paymaster Generals, | When to issue Regimental Pay, &c. | 129. 143 |
| | Nature of Services defrayed by | 512 |
| Deputy Purveyor | Title to Half Pay | 354. 356 |
| | Pay of | 361 |
| | Forage Money of | 369 |
| | Lodging Money of | 370. 372 to 376 |
| | Travelling Expences of | 372 to 377 |
| Deputy Quartermaster General | Pay and Allowances of | 339 to 341 |
| Deserters - - | Escort Allowance for, abolished | 11. 15 |
| | Effects and Credits of | 126. 214, 285. 563 |
| | Passage of Escort for, to and from the Isle of Wight | 153 |
| | Charges for | 163. 314 |
| | Regulation respecting | 311 to 318 |
| | When deprived of benefit from antecedent service | 33. 41. 530 |
| | To be advertised in the *Hue and Cry* Weekly Paper | 605 |
| | Reports of, to be transmitted to the War Office *ibid.* | |
| | Parliamentary Reward for the Apprehension of | 606 |
| Detachments, - | Carriage of Baggage for | 91 to 105 |
| | Stoppage for Provisions for, when on board ship | 149. 173 |
| | How to be mustered and paid | 163 |
| | Paymasters of, advances by | 172. 247 to 256 |
| | Courts Martial for | 276. 288 |
| Discharges, - - | Expence of | 91 |
| | Rules to be observed in granting | 153. 176. 601 |
| | Periods when Soldiers become entitled to | 534 to 539 |
| Discount - - - | On Bills, when allowed | 158 |
| District Adjutant, | See *Adjutant of Recruiting Districts.* | |
| District Paymasters | See *Paymasters of Recruiting Districts.* | |
| Districts, Recruiting, - | Head Quarters and Extent of | 275. 289. 290 |
| District Surgeon, | See *Surgeon on the District Staff.* | |
| Dragoon Guards and Dragoons, | See *Cavalry.* | |
| Drummer or Fifer, | Pay of | 11 to 25. 29. 51 to 55. 148. 174 |
| | Bounty of Boys enlisted for | 303 |
| | Loss of Necessaries, allowance for | 491 |
| Duration - - | Of Cavalry Appointments | 449 |
| Drum Major, - | Pay of | 51 |

Q q 3           *East*

## E.

| | | |
|---|---|---|
| *East India Company,* | Recruits enlisted for the Service of | 280. 286. 611 |
| *East Indies,* | Pay of Soldiers on passage to | 23 |
| | — In advance to Regiments embarking for | 142 |
| | Recruiting for Battalions serving there | 233 |
| | Effects and Credits of deceased Soldiers and Deserters of Regiments there | 239. 563 |
| | Bât, Baggage, and Forage Money not allowed to Regiments embarking for | 422 |
| | Accommodation of Officers proceeding to, in the Company's ships | 519 to 521 |
| | Encrease of Pay, &c. for service there | 538, 539 |
| | Adjutants' Rolls of Regiments there | 563 |
| *Effects and Credits* | Of deceased Soldiers and Deserters, &c. | 126. 179. 214. 235 to 239. 286. 563 |
| | — Recruiting Parties and Recruits | 285. 609 |
| | Debts of Soldiers to be defrayed out of | 235. 286 |
| *Emery, &c.* | Allowance for | 456 |
| *Encampments,* | Hire of ground for | 514 to 516 |
| | Issues of Bread, Wood, Forage, &c. during | 551 to 556 |
| *Engineers,* | Sick of, when abroad | 409 to 411 |
| *Enlistment* | Periods and terms of | 535 |
| *Ensign* | Pay of | 6, 7. 39. 44. 51 to 55 |
| | Personal Baggage and Camp Equipage, of | 490 |
| *Equipment,* | Articles of, for Cavalry Recruits | 304 |
| *Escort* | Of Deserters | 312 |
| *Estimates, Monthly* | To be rendered by Paymasters | 138. 202 |
| *Examination* | Of Paymasters' Accompts, Abstracts of | 181, 191 |
| | — Agents' Accompts—ditto | 197. 578 |
| *Exchange* | On bills drawn by Paymasters when abroad | 129, 143 |
| | Ditto—from Ireland | 246 |
| *Existence of Soldiers* | Enquiries relative to | 238 |
| *Expences, Extraordinary,* | Not to be incurred without authority | 159, 191 |
| *Extra Feed* | For Dragoon Horses | 83. 284. 540 to 545 |
| *Extraordinary Recruiting,* | Regulations for | 306 to 310. 586 |
| *Eye,* | If lost by wounds in action, claim for | 489 |

## F.

| | | |
|---|---|---|
| *Furriery,* | Extra allowance for | 87, 88. 110. 150. 244. 284 |
| | For Bât and Baggage Horses | 425 |
| *Fees* | Of Commissions | 162. 169 |
| | When chargeable in the Public Accompts | 251 |
| *Fencible Cavalry,* | Pay | 5, 6 |
| | Appointment, Pay, and Duties of Paymasters. (See also *Paymasters of Regiments.*) | 121 to 129. 131 |
| | List of Corps of, formerly liable to serve abroad | 532, 533 |
| *Fencible Infantry,* | Pay | 5. 7. 53. 55 |

*Fencible*

## INDEX.

| | | |
|---|---|---|
| *Fencible Infantry,* | Appointment, Pay, and Duties of Paymasters. (See further under the head of *Paymasters of Regiments.*) — — 121 to 123. 131. 133 | |
| | For Home Service, Men of, not entitled to additional Pay — — — | 529 |
| | List of Corps of, formerly liable to serve abroad 530 to 533. | 613, 614 |
| *Field Allowance,* | Rates and Distribution of — | 421 to 423 |
| *Field Officers* - | No longer generally responsible for Regimental Accompts — — — | 3 |
| | New Rates of Pay for — — | ibid. 39 |
| | Contingent and Non-effective allowance for | 59 |
| | Lodging Money of — — | 64, 65 |
| | Personal Baggage and Camp Equipage of | 490 |
| | Forage for a Horse, &c. allowed to, when on the Recruiting Service — — | 569 |
| *Fifer,* - - - - | See *Drummer.* | |
| *Fire and Candle,* | Allowance for — 95. 157. | 244, 245 |
| *Foot Guards,* - | Pay — — 17. 35. | 51 |
| | Deduction for Necessaries — | ibid. |
| | Not affected by the Pay Office Act — | 113 |
| | Recruiting Regulations inapplicable to | 287 |
| | Period of Delivery of Clothing — | 445, 446 |
| | Allowance to Lieutenants in the, having Rank superior to that of Captain — — | 611 |
| | Pay, &c. of the Quarter Masters of — | ibid. |
| *Forage,* - - - | For the Horses of Lieutenant Colonels, Majors, and Adjutants — — 39. 63. 569. | 611 |
| | Supplied by Contract, how paid for — | 166 |
| | Issues of, on Foreign Stations — | 240 |
| | For Horses of Staff Officers — | 345. 553 |
| | Regulation for augmenting or diminishing the Issues of — — — | 540 to 545 |
| | Issues of, in Camp — — | 553 to 556 |
| | For Horses in Scotland — — | 566 |
| *Forage Money* - | For the Home Staff — | 341. 369 |
| *Foreign Stations,* | Allowance to Captains of Troops on — | 61 |
| | Regimental Contingencies on — | 94 |
| | Pay in advance of Corps embarking for | 141, 142 |
| | Paymaster's Bills, how to be drawn from | 143. 165 |
| | Deputy Paymaster General to issue the Pay of Regiments upon — — — | ibid. |
| | Issues of Provisions on — — | 240 |
| | Corps proceeding to, from Ireland | 241 to 246 |
| | Field Allowances on, not cognizable by the War Office — — — | 423 |
| | Claims for loss of Baggage, &c. upon, not to be referred home — — | 493 |
| | Pay in advance for Officers proceeding to | 510, 511 |
| | Nature of Services defrayed by Deputy Paymaster General on — — — | 512 |
| | Number of Women allowed to embark with Regiments for — — — | 513 |
| | Half Yearly Returns of the Staff upon | 567, 568 |

*Foreign*

| | | |
|---|---|---|
| *Foreign Stations,* | Stoppages from the Pay of Soldiers in General Hospitals, on | 607 |
| *Forge Carts,* | Supply of | 562 |
| *Forms of Accompts* | May be made out in Manuscript | 182 |
| | Supply of for Regiments embarking for Service abroad | 193, 194 |
| *Furlough* | For Men on, periods, &c. to be stated | 166 |

## G.

| | | |
|---|---|---|
| *General on the Staff* | Pay and Allowances of | 339 to 348 |
| | Allowed Three Aides de Camp | *ibid.* |
| | Number of Horses allowed to | *ibid.* |
| *General Hospitals,* | See *Hospitals.* | |
| *General Orders,* | Pay of Boys | 29 |
| | Extra price of Meat | 72 |
| | Punctual payment for Articles of Subsistence | 168 |
| | Punctual transmission of Regimental Accompts | 199 |
| | Bounty of Recruits deserting before Final Approval | 302 |
| | Bounty of Boys enlisted for Drummers or Fifers | 303 |
| | Prefixed to the Regulations for Regimental Hospitals | 378 |
| | Leaves of Absence to Medical Officers | 387 |
| | Stoppage from the Pay of Men in Regimental Hospitals | 389 |
| | Regulation for General Hospitals | 390 |
| | Stoppage from the Pay of Soldiers in ditto | 406 |
| | Supply of Bread and Meat in Regimental Hospitals | 407 |
| | Stoppage from the Pay of Boys in General ditto | 408 |
| | Sick of the Ordnance Department abroad | 409 |
| | Number of Women allowed to embark with Regiments | 513 |
| | Men sleeping out of Quarters | 517. 518 |
| | Soldiers acting as Musicians | 557 |
| | Recruiting Service of Second Battalions | 558 |
| | Enlistment of Lads | 560 |
| | Incidental Expences of Recruiting Officers | 571 |
| | Accompts of Soldiers sent to General Hospitals | 580 |
| | Extra Price of various Articles in North Britain | 587 |
| | Officers of Second Battalions becoming Effective in the First Battalions of their Regiments | 595 |
| | Recruiting for a First Battalion serving abroad, when the Second Battalion is engaged for limited Service | 597 |
| | Men transferred to Veteran Battalions | 601 |
| | Quarterly Returns of Officers absent without Leave | 603 |
| *General Service,* | Recruits for, by whom to be enlisted | 280 |
| | Ditto——expenditures on account of | 286 |
| | Effects, Credits, and Debts of Men raised for | *ibid.* |
| | Age and Standard of Recruits for | 293 |

*General*

# INDEX.

| | | |
|---|---|---|
| General State | Of Paymasters' Accompts, when to be rendered | 126. 128 |
| | Ditto—when to be balanced | 135 |
| | Ditto—Additions and Deductions how to be made in | 161 |
| Gibraltar, | Pay of Troops at | 22, 23 |
| | Regimental Contingencies at | 94 |
| | Pay in advance to Regiments embarking for | 142 |
| Glanders | Indemnification for Officers' Chargers shot for | 491 |
| | Ditto—for Appointments of Horses shot for | 496 |
| Grass | For Dragoon Horses | 540 to 543 |
| Gravesend | Passage of Parties from, to Tilbury | 187 |
| Great Coats, | Annual allowance for | 110. 166. 244. 245 |
| | Supply of | 450 |
| | Fund for providing | 451. 582 |
| | Contribution towards the cost of, for Serjeants of Infantry | 466 |
| | To be provided by *Colonels* | 472 |
| | Regulation for their Inspection | 474 |
| | Certificate for, when required to be replaced | 477 |
| | Of Serjeants and Corporals, distinction in | 481 |
| Ground, | Hire of | 514 to 516 |
| Guard Rooms, | Allowance for | 91 to 96 |
| Guernsey, | Postage, Stationary, &c. in | 93 |

## H.

| | | |
|---|---|---|
| Half Pay | Of Subalterns, &c. | 7. 37. 39. 52 |
| Half Pay Officers | Appointed to Recruit for the Infantry | 280 |
| | Ditto—Instructions for | 306 to 310 |
| | Ditto—Mode of issuing their Half Pay | 586 |
| Half Yearly Allowances, | Not to be issued abroad, by Deputy Paymasters General | 143. 512 |
| | Drafts for | 164 |
| Hay, | Supply of | 79. 587 |
| | Green Forage substituted for | 544 |
| | Issues of, in Camp | 553 to 556 |
| Hire of Ground | For Encampments | 514 to 516 |
| Horse Appointments | Not to be charged for, in Pay Lists | 164 |
| | Indemnification for, when destroyed to prevent Infection of the Glanders | 496 |
| Horse Cloths, | Expence of | 14. 157. 304. 455 |
| Horse Guards, Royal Regt. of | Pay | 13. 31. 48 |
| | Not affected by the Pay Office Act | 113 |
| | Recruiting Regulations inapplicable to | 287 |
| | Period of Delivery of Clothing to | 445, 446 |
| Horse Medicines, &c. | How supplied | 412 to 417 |
| Horses, | Number of, allowed for Officers in the Cavalry | 83 |
| | Purchase of | 84, 85 |
| | Casting of | 84. 153. 176 |
| | Of Officers, Duties levied on | 158. 345 |
| | Subsistence of, how applied | 166 |
| | To be mustered by Paymasters in the Cavalry | 180 |

*Horses*

| | | |
|---|---|---|
| *Horses*, - - - | Issues of Forage for, on Foreign Stations | 240 |
| | Number of, allowed to be kept by Staff Officers | 345, 371 |
| | Of Officers, allowance for, when killed by the enemy, &c. | 491 |
| | Regulation for augmenting or diminishing the feed of | 545 |
| | Forage for, in Camp | 553, 556 |
| | Ditto———North Britain | 566 |
| *Hospital*, - - | Deduction for | 4 to 8 |
| *Hospital Mates*, | Qualifications of | 353 |
| | Appointment of, by Commission, &c. | 359 |
| | Lodging Money for | 370. 372 to 376 |
| | Horses of | 371 |
| | Travelling Expences of | 372 to 377 |
| *Hospitals*, - - | Pay of Soldiers in | 23. 170. 397. 406. 607 |
| | Beer Money———ditto | 66. 160 |
| | Regulations for Regimental | 378 |
| | Ditto for General | 390. 580 |
| | Bread and Meat for sick Soldiers in, extra price of | 383 |
| | Surplus of Hospital Funds | 385. 389 |
| | Wages of Hospital Servants | 394 |
| | Contracts for the Supplies of | 399 |
| | Supplies of Medicines for | 401 |
| *Hospital Stores*, | Carriage of | 385 |
| | When condemned | 404, 405 |

## I.

| | | |
|---|---|---|
| *Jamaica*, - - - | Pay of Troops there | 22, 23 |
| *Jersey*, - - - | Postage, Stationary, &c. at | 93 |
| *Inn-Keepers Allowance* - - | When paid to Soldiers | 12. 160 |
| | Contribution of Soldiers towards | 66 |
| | Encreased Rates of | 75 |
| | Ditto—how to be charged | 160. 284. 584 |
| | For Recruits sent to the Army Depôt | 279 |
| *Inspecting Field Officer in London*, - - - | His Seal to be affixed to Beating Orders | 274 |
| *Inspecting Field Officers, Duties of, and points relating to, as specified in the Recruiting Instructions, &c.* | To approve the Drafts of District Paymasters | 213 |
| | To authenticate District Pay Lists | 214. 224 |
| | Change of Stations of Recruiting Parties | 274 |
| | When Senior Officers in their Districts | 275 |
| | Commanding Officers of Regiments, &c. if senior to them | ibid. |
| | Intermediate approval of Recruits | ibid. |
| | Reports of Senior Recruiting Officers in Districts | ib. |
| | Absence of Recruiting Officers | ibid. |
| | Dress, regularity, and conduct of Recruiting Parties | 276 |
| | Detachment Courts Martial | ibid. |
| | Orders of the Inspector General | ibid. |
| | Returns, &c. to be sent to ditto | ibid. |
| | Pay, Stationary, and Postage | ibid. 591. 612 |

*Inspecting*

# INDEX. 627

| | |
|---|---|
| *Inspecting Field Officers, Duties of, and points relating to, as specified in the Recruiting Instructions, &c.* | Appointment of District Adjutants and Serjeants 277 |
| | District Surgeons placed under the Orders of *ibid.* |
| | Medical Practitioners, when to be employed *ibid.* |
| | Officers Recruiting for Rank — — 278 |
| | Parties under the Charge of Colonels of Regiments *ibid.* 282, 283 |
| | Recruits for General Service — 280 |
| | ———— for the East India Company's Service *ibid.* |
| | ———— absconding, or refusing to go before a Magistrate 281 |
| | Distribution of Levy Money for Recruits *ibid.* 573 |
| | Recruits objected to by Commanding Officers after District approval — — 282 |
| | Expenditures of Irish Parties in Great Britain 285, 286 |
| | ——————— of British Parties in Ireland *ibid.* |
| | Recruiting Officers to settle with District Paymasters before quitting their Stations — 286 |
| | When to furnish Recruiting Instructions 287 |
| | Recruiting by Half Pay Officers, &c. 280. 306 to 310 |
| *Inspection* - - | Of Deserters — — 312 |
| | — Medicines, &c. — 402, 403 |
| | — Clothing — — 441 |
| *Inspector General of Army Hospitals,* | Charge of Medical Expences to be submitted to the 157 |
| | Duties of — — — 353 |
| | Supplies of Medicines for Regimental Hospitals ordered by 401 |
| | Certificate of, relative to Expences for Cure of Wounds — — 487 |
| *Inspector General of the Recruiting Service, Duties of, and points relating to, as specified in the Recruiting Instructions, &c.* | Duty of in regard to District Paymasters 215 |
| | Stations of Recruiting Parties — 274 |
| | Intermediate approval of Recruits by Inspecting Field Officers — 275, 281 |
| | Inspecting Field Officers under his Direction 276 |
| | Officers recruiting for Rank — 278 |
| | Parties under the Charge of Colonels of Regiments — *ibid.* 282 |
| | Recruits sent to the Army Depot — 279 |
| | ———— absconding, or refusing to go before a Magistrate — — — 281 |
| | Allowance to Recruiting Officers for carriage of Baggage — — 283. 571 |
| | Passage of Recruiting Parties, &c. to and from Ireland — — 284. 571 |
| | Recruiting Officers quitting their Stations 286 |
| | Recruiting by Half-Pay Officers, &c. 306 to 310 |
| | Pay and Contingencies of the Recruiting Staff 276, 277. 591. 612 |
| *Inspectors of Clothing,* | Appointment and Duties of 440, 441, 474 |
| *Inspector of Hospitals,* - | Pay of — — — 362 |
| | Forage Money of — — 369 |
| | Lodging Money of — 370, 372 to 376 |
| | Horses of — — 371 |
| | Travelling Expences of — 372 to 377 |

*Invalids*

## INDEX.

| | | |
|---|---|---|
| *Invalids* - - - | Pay — — — | 6, 7 |
| *Ireland* - - - | Allowances for Officers and Men of Regiments on the British Establihment, when serving there | 159. 287 |
| | Allowances to the Wives and Children of Soldiers proceeding thither — | 187 to 189 |
| | Pay of Soldiers proceeding to, or coming from | 172, 173 |
| | —— of Officers of Regiments on the Irish Establishment, serving in Great Britain — | 231 |
| | General Agent of the Recruiting Service in Dublin — — — | *ibid.* 285 |
| | Transfer of Corps to the Establishment of | 241 to 246 |
| | Subsistence of Men belonging to Regiments in, when serving in Great Britain — | 247 to 250 |
| | Allowance to Recruits on a March | 282 |
| | Passage of Parties to and from | 284. 301. 571. 613 |
| | Expenditures of Irish Parties in Great Britain | 285 |
| | Stamps for Bills drawn by District Paymasters upon Agents — — — | 609 |
| *Judge Advocate General,* - | Allowance for Deputies — | 485, 486 |

### K.

| | | |
|---|---|---|
| *Kettle Drummer,* | Pay of — — — | 47, 48 |

### L.

| | | |
|---|---|---|
| *Lacquered Felt* | Caps of, part of Clothing — | 436 |
| | Ditto, to be discontinued — — | 480 |
| *Lads,* - - - | See *Boys.* | |
| *Leave of Absence,* | Officers absent without Leave, Pay of | 147. 165. 507. 603 |
| | For Medical Staff Officers | 387 |
| | Mode of Application for, by Paymasters | 509. 613 |
| *Length of Service,* | Additional Pay for — — | 30 to 55 |
| | Of Soldiers, Forms of Returns, &c. for stating | 546 to 550 |
| *Levy Money,* - | Of Boys — — | 27. 230. 303. 573. 575 |
| | In the Second Battalions of Numbered Regiments — — | 177 |
| | Of Men volunteering for extended Service | 183, 230 |
| | For Recruits intermediately, or finally approved, | 217 |
| | No deduction to be made from, for Ribbands for Colours — — — | 281 |
| | Distribution of, for Recruits | *ibid.* 299. 573. 613 |
| | For Recruits deserting before final approval | 302 |
| *Lieutenant,* - | Pay of — — | 6, 7. 39 to 55 |
| *Lieutenant Colonel,* | Pay of — — | 5. 39. 47 to 55 |
| | Forage for a Horse — | 39. 530 |
| *Lieutenant General on the Staff,* | Pay and Allowances of — | 339 to 348 |
| | Two Aides de Camp allowed to — | *ibid.* |
| | Number of Horses ditto — — | *ibid.* |

*Life*

| | | |
|---|---|---|
| *Life Guards,* - | Pay | 13. 31. 47 |
| | Not affected by the Pay Office Act | 113 |
| | Recruiting Regulations inapplicable to | 287 |
| *Limbs,* - - - | Claims for Loss of | 352. 489 |
| *Limited Service,* - | Pay, &c. of Volunteers from, for General Service | 230 |
| | Battalions for, Recruits raised by | 233 |
| | Men engaged for, not entitled to encrease of Pay, &c. | 529 |
| *Liverpool,* - - | Paymaster of Detachments at, Instructions for | 173 |
| | Ditto——issues by | 247 to 250 |
| *Lodging Money,* - | To Soldiers in South Britain, finding their own Lodgings | 12, 17, 179 |
| | For Regimental Officers | 64, 65 |
| | —— Staff Officers | 342. 346. 370 |
| | To the Inhabitants of North Britain on whom Soldiers may be quartered | 565 |
| | To Soldiers in North Britain, finding their own Lodgings | 566 |
| *Losses,* - - - | Of Baggage, &c. Allowance and Regulations for | 490 to 495 |

## M.

| | | |
|---|---|---|
| *Magistrates,* - | To fix the Rates for the Hire of Waggons | 98. 104 |
| | To attest Recruits | 280 |
| | Recruits refusing to go before them | 281 |
| *Major* - - - | Pay of | 39. 47 to 55 |
| | Forage for a Horse | 39. 530 |
| | Allowance to for Carriage of Ammunition | 245 |
| | Ditto——Fire and Candle for Guards | ibid. |
| *Major General on the Staff,* | Pay and Allowances | 339 to 348 |
| | One Aide de Camp allowed to | ibid. |
| | Number of Horses ditto | ibid. |
| *Major of Brigade,* | Pay and Allowances of | 339 to 348 |
| | Number of Horses allowed to | ibid. |
| | Allowance to, for the loss of a Charger | 492 |
| *March,* - - - | Allowance to Men upon the | 75. 160. 284. 566 |
| *Marines,* - - - | Pay of Soldiers employed as such | 21. 23. 148. 149 |
| | Recruiting Regulations inapplicable to | 287, 288 |
| *Meat,* - - - | Extra price of | 11, 12. 71 to 74. 170. 203. 207 283. 284. 383. 407. 587 |
| | Proportion of Soldiers, Pay applicable to the Expence of | 146 |
| *Medical Department,* - - | New arrangement of | 351 to 355 |
| *Medical Expences,* | How to be charged | 157 |
| | For the Examination of Recruits | 277. 282 |
| | Of Country Practitioners | 384 |
| *Medical Staff,* - | Qualification for the | 353 |
| | Situation of improved | 359 to 362 |
| | Lodging Money and Travelling Expences of | 372 to 377 |
| *Medicines,* - - | How supplied | 401 |
| | To be inspected | 402, 403 |

Medicines

| | | |
|---|---|---|
| *Medicines,* | When condemned | 404, 405 |
| *Mediterranean,* | Pay in advance to Regiments embarking for | 142 |
| *Mess,* | Contribution towards | 11. 15. 67 |
| *Military Superintendant of Hospitals,* | Duty of | 391 to 396. 399 |
| | Inspection of Medicines, by | 402, 403 |
| | To superintend the Condemnation of Hospital Stores | 404, 405 |
| *Militia,* | Pay | 43 to 46. 55 |
| | Contingent Allowances | 95. 102 |
| | Appointment and Duty of Paymasters, (See also *Paymasters of Regiments*) | 121 to 123. 133 |
| | Expence of altering Clothing | 164 |
| | Carriage of Clothing and Accoutrements | ibid. |
| | Pay of Officers, newly appointed, or promoted | 175 |
| | Quarterly Pay Lists and new Monthly Accompts, adopted | 200 to 204. 211 |
| | Pay and Appointment of Surgeons' Mates | 358 |
| | Pay of Surgeons | 361. 366. 368 |
| | Regulation for the Clothing of | 459 to 465. 471 |
| | Clothing Allowance for Serjeants, new Rate of | 467 |
| | Clothing for Paymasters' Clerks, or Armourers | 468 |
| | Supply of Bear Skin Caps for Grenadiers | 473 |
| | Men serving in, not entitled to additional Pay | 529 |
| | Innkeepers Allowance | 584 |
| | New Form of Monthly Accompt | 585. 593 |
| | Allowance to enrolled Men, when rejected at Head Quarters | 592 |
| *Monthly Abstracts,* | Alteration in the Form of | 192, 193 |
| | Transmission of | 205 |
| *Monthly Rolls* | To be prepared by Adjutants | 124. 202. 205. 230. 238. 563 |
| *Musicians* | Soldiers acting as such | 175. 557 |
| *Musters* | Of Detachments | 163 |
| | Of Recruiting Parties | 214. 285 |
| *Mutiny Act,* | Provisions of, respecting the Hire of Waggons | 98 to 104 |
| | Period allowed by, for a Recruit to dissent to enlisting | 281 |

### N.

| | | |
|---|---|---|
| *Necessaries,* | Stoppage for, &c. | 11 to 19. 454. 456. 464 |
| | Provision of | 443 to 445 |
| | Indemnification for the loss of | 491 |
| | For Recruits | 299. 308. 574, 575 |
| *New South Wales,* | Pay of Troops there | 22. 23 |
| *Non-effective Allowance* | To Field Officers and Captains | 59 to 62 |
| | Not chargeable when the command of a Company is vacant | 151 |
| | Not chargeable for a Captain, when absent without Leave | 612 |
| *North Britain,* | Lodging Money for Officers in | 64 |
| | Beer Money in | 67 |
| | Medical Expences incurred in | 157 |

*North*

## INDEX.

| | | |
|---|---|---|
| North Britain, - | Allowance in certain cases to the Wives and Children of Soldiers proceeding thither | 187 to 189 |
| | Pay of Soldiers in, belonging to Regiments in Ireland | 247 to 250 |
| | Allowance for Recruits on a March in | 282 |
| | ———— to the Inhabitants in, on whom Soldiers may be quartered | 565 |
| | Peculiarities in the Situation of Soldiers there | 566 |
| | Forage for Horses in | ibid. |
| | Extra Price of various Articles in | 587 |
| Nurses (for Hospitals), - | Allowance for | 381 |

### O.

| | | |
|---|---|---|
| Oatmeal, - - - | Occasionally supplied to Soldiers in North Britain | 566 |
| Oats, - - - - | Supply of | 81. 587 |
| | Articles substituted for | 540 to 545 |
| Officers, - - - | Deduction for their Provisions | 149 |
| | Killed in Action, Allowance to their Widows and Orphans | 489 |
| Off-reckonings. - | See Assignments. | |
| Orderly Men (for Hospitals), | Allowance for | 381 |
| Orders and Regulations, - | (As laid before Parliament) for the better ordering of the Army, &c. | 534 to 539 |
| Ordnance Articles, | Charge for | 244, 245 |
| Ordnance Department, - | Carriage of Arms defrayed by | 187 |
| | Sick of the Artillery, &c. abroad, to be admitted into Military Hospitals | 409. 411 |
| Out Pension, - | See Chelsea Hospital. | |

### P.

| | | |
|---|---|---|
| Package - - - | Of Arms, Clothing, &c. | 95 |
| Passage Money - | For Parties and Recruits to and from Great Britain and Ireland | 301. 571. 612 |
| | For Officers proceeding to the East Indies | 519, 520 |
| Pay, &c. - - - | Rates of, as encreased in 1797 | 5 to 22, 148. 174 |
| | Ditto,— from 25th June, 1806 | 30 to 55. 174. 529. 534 to 539 |
| | Of Officers and Men, when to be drawn and issued by Paymasters | 145 |
| | Of Officers removed from one Corps to another | 146 |
| | Ditto ——— absent without Leave | 147. 165. 507 |
| | Of Soldiers in Confinement | 163 |
| | —Subalterns of Infantry holding other appointments | 175 |
| | —Soldiers commuting Punishment for Service abroad | 185 |
| | —Men waiting to pass the Chelsea Board | 186 |
| | —Volunteers from limited service Battalions | 230 |
| | —Officers of a first Battalion serving with the second | 231 |

*Pay*

| | | |
|---|---|---|
| Pay, &c. | Of Soldiers in General Hospitals | 397 |
| | —Gentlemen first obtaining Commissions | 508 |
| | In advance for Officers embarking for Service | 510, 511 |
| | Ditto —— proceeding to India | 519 to 521 |
| | Of Soldiers when discharged | 536. 608 |
| Pay Lists, | When to be rendered | 124. 127. 141 |
| | How to be vouched | 127 |
| | Of Detachments, &c. | ibid. |
| | Of Regiments abroad | ibid. |
| | Expence of | 128 |
| | Regular transmission of | 198 |
| | Quarterly ones, adopted in the Militia | 200 to 204. 211 |
| | Ditto — in the Cavalry, and Regular, and Fencible Infantry | 205 to 210 |
| | Ditto—periods of transmission of | 210 |
| | Effects and Credits of deceased Soldiers and Deserters, how to be included in | 235 to 239 |
| | Of Corps transferred to or from Ireland | 241 to 246 |
| | Of Recruiting Districts, transmission of | 215. 583 |
| Paymaster General, (See Deputy Paymaster General.) | Agents to render Accompts to | 109 to 113 |
| | Controul of, over Agents | ibid. |
| Paymasters of Recruiting Districts, Duties of, &c. | Original Instructions for | 213 to 216 |
| | To muster Recruiting Parties | 214. 285 |
| | Amenable to Martial Law | 215 |
| | Case of Death or Incapacity of | ibid. |
| | Pay and Allowances of | 215, 216 |
| | Pay and Rank of a Clerk for | 216 |
| | Allowance to, for Postage, Stationary, and Stamps | 216. 220 |
| | Further Instructions for | 217 |
| | Additional Instructions for | 219. 222 |
| | Pay of Officers of Irish Regiments in Great Britain, and *vice versâ*, when issued by | 231 |
| | Allowance in certain cases to the Wives and Children of Soldiers | 187 to 189 |
| | Transfer of Regiments to and from Ireland | 241 to 245 |
| | Subsistence of Men belonging to Regiments in Ireland | 247 to 250 |
| | Subsistence for Recruiting Parties | 126. 214. 277 |
| | To examine Attestations of Recruits | 281 |
| | In Ireland, to pay Passage Money of Recruiting Parties, &c. | 284. 571 |
| | Expenditures of Irish Parties in Great Britain | 285, 286 |
| | Ditto —— British Parties in Ireland | ibid. |
| | Effects and Credits of deceased Soldiers | ibid. 609 |
| | Recruiting Officers before quitting their Stations, to settle with | 286 |
| | Recruiting by Half Pay Officers, &c. | 306 to 310 |
| | Supplementary General States, and Pay Lists, Directions in regard to | 609 |

*Paymasters*

# INDEX. 633

| | | |
|---|---|---|
| *Paymasters of Regiments, Duties of, &c. (See Committee of Paymastership)* | Pay, Allowances, and Rank | 46. 53. 55. 117. 131 |
| | Appointed by Commission | 116 to 123. 133 |
| | By whom to be recommended | 116 to 123 |
| | Security for | ibid. |
| | Original Instructions for | 124 to 132. 135 |
| | In the Militia and Fencibles, liable to certain Military Duty | 123. 132 |
| | Explanatory Directions for | 145 to 194 |
| | Amenable to Martial Law | 129, 130 |
| | Death of, or Incapacity of from accident | 130 |
| | When to commence receiving Pay | ibid. |
| | Additional Instructions for | 136 to 143 |
| | Allowance in certain cases to the Wives and Children of Soldiers | 187 to 189 |
| | When ceasing to act as such, or being permitted to resign | 190 |
| | When newly appointed | 190 |
| | Disallowances by the War Office | 192 |
| | Accompts of particular periods preferably examined | 192 |
| | Case of drawing larger sums than are required | 195 |
| | Instructions to, relative to Quarterly Accompts | 211 |
| | Ditto——Effects and Credits of deceased Soldiers and Deserters | 235 to 239. 563 |
| | Ditto——Exchange on Bills drawn from Ireland | 246 |
| | Ditto——Subsistence of Men belonging to Regiments in Ireland | 247 to 250 |
| | Declaration by, previously to being appointed | 252 |
| | Advance of Pay to Soldiers quitting General Hospitals | 397 |
| | Mode of Application for Leave of Absence | 509. 613. |
| | Pay in advance for Regiments, how to be estimated | 611 |
| *Paymasters of Detachments,* | See *Detachments.* | |
| *Paymaster Serjeant, or Paymaster's Clerk,* | Appointment and Pay of | 46. 49 to 55. 117 to 121 |
| | Ditto——in Battalions for limited Service | 226 |
| | Clothing for, in the Militia | 468 |
| *Pay Office Act,* | Extract from | 109 |
| *Pensions* | To Officers' Widows. See *Widows of Officers.* | |
| | For discharged Soldiers. See *Chelsea Hospital.* | |
| *Physician General,* | Duty of | 351 |
| *Physician,* | How appointed | 354 |
| | Title of, to Half Pay | 354. 356 |
| | Pay of | 361 |
| | Forage Money of | 369 |
| | Lodging Money of | 370. 372 to 376 |
| | Horses of | 371 |
| | Travelling Expences of | 372 to 377 |
| *Pioneers' Appointments,* | Provision of | 599 |
| *Plymouth,* | Paymaster of Detachments there, issues by | 247 to 250 |
| *Portsmouth,* | Paymaster of Detachments there, issues by | 247 to 250 |
| *Portugal,* | Pay in advance to Regiments embarking for | 142 |

R R *Postage,*

# INDEX.

| | | |
|---|---|---|
| Postage, | Allowance for | 91 to 97. 117. 131. 157 |
| | Of Soldiers' Letters | 522 |
| Poundage, | Deductions for | 4 to 8 |
| Previous Service, | Description of, entitling Soldiers to additional Pay, &c. | 529 to 539. 611. 614 |
| Prisons, | Soldiers in. See *Confinement*. | |
| Prisoners of War, | Pay of | 25 |
| | Accompts of | 580 |
| Private, | Pay of | 11 to 25. 32 to 55. 39. 148. 174 |
| | Loss of Necessaries, Allowance for | 491 |
| Provisions, | Deductions for | 21. 23. 148 to 150 |
| | Issues of, on Foreign Stations | 240 |
| Purveyor, | How appointed | 354 |
| | Title of, to Half Pay | *ibid*. 356 |
| | Pay of | 361 |
| | Forage Money of | 369 |
| | Lodging Money of | 370. 372 to 376 |
| | Travelling Expences of | 372 to 377 |
| | Advances by, to Soldiers quitting General Hospitals | 397 |
| | Duty of, in regard to Contracts for Supplies of General Hospitals | 399 |
| | Ditto—on the condemnation of Hospital Stores | 404, 405 |
| Purveyor's Clerk, | Pay of | 361 |
| | Lodging Money of | 370. 372 to 376 |
| | Travelling Expences of | 372 to 377 |

## Q.

| | | |
|---|---|---|
| Quarter Master General, | Pay and Allowances of | 339 to 341 |
| Quarter Master | Of Cavalry, Pay of | 47, 48, 49 |
| | Ditto,——personal Baggage of | 491 |
| | Of Infantry, Pay of | 7. 39. 51 to 54 |
| | Ditto,——personal Baggage and Camp Equipage of | 491 |
| Quarter Master Serjeant, | Pay of | 39. 51 to 55. 148. 174 |
| Quarters, | Men sleeping out of | 517, 518 |

## R.

| | | |
|---|---|---|
| Rank, | Officers recruiting for | 278 |
| Ration of Provisions | Stoppage for | 149. 611 |
| Recruits, | When to be included in the Regimental Pay Lists | 126 |
| | Proceeding to the Army Depôt, Pay of | 172, 279 |
| | Proceeding to or coming from Ireland, ditto | *ibid.* |
| | When rejected, Causes of to be stated in the Pay Lists | 185 |
| | Dates of Enlistment to be specified in ditto | *ibid.* |
| | When rejected, charges for | 186 |
| | Bounty of, when intermediately approved | 217. 275 |

*Recruits*

# INDEX.

| | | |
|---|---|---|
| Recruits | Bounty of, when finally approved | 217 |
| | Certificate of final Approbation for | ibid. |
| | Raised for First Battalions serving abroad | 283 |
| | Intermediate Approval of | 275. 282, 283 |
| | Approval of, by *Colonels* of Regiments | 278, 279, 282, 283 |
| | Age and Standard of | 279. 293 |
| | Apprentices not to be enlisted | 280 |
| | For General Service | 286 |
| | — the East India Company's Service | ibid. |
| | When considered unfit for Service | ibid. |
| | To be inlisted without limitation of Service | ibid. |
| | Ditto,——only as Privates | ibid. |
| | When they may be attested | 280. 281 |
| | Attestations of, to accompany Monthly Accompts | ibid. |
| | Absconding, or refusing to go before a Magistrate | 281 |
| | Smart Money for | 281 |
| | No Deduction to be taken from, for Ribbands for Colours | ibid. |
| | Distribution of Levy Money for | ibid. 299. 573 |
| | Pay, Beer Money, &c. of | 282 |
| | Dying previous to Attestation | ibid. |
| | Objected to by Commanding Officers, after District Approval | ibid. |
| | Objected to by Inspecting Field Officers, after approval by Colonels of Regiments | ibid. |
| | Passage of, to and from Ireland | 284 |
| | Effects, Credits, and Debts of | 285 |
| | Deserting before final approval, Bounty of | 302 |
| | Bounty of Boys enlisted for Drummers or Fifers | 303 |
| | Of Cavalry, Articles of Equipment for | 304 |
| | Allowance for, to Recruiting Officers | 571 |
| Recruiting Districts | Appointment and Duties of Paymasters for | 126. 213 |
| | Pay of Parties when removed from one District to another | 171 |
| | Pay Lists of, Period of Transmission | 215. 533 |
| | Committee of Paymastership in | 215 |
| | Additional Instructions for Paymasters of | 217. 219 |
| | Forms of Accompts,&c. rendered by Paymasters of | 222 |
| | Inspecting Field Officers, if senior Officers in | 275 |
| | Commanding Officers of Regiments, &c. stationed in, if senior to the Inspecting Field Officers | ibid. |
| | Senior Recruiting Officer in, to make Weekly Reports | ibid. |
| | Serjeants appointed to | 277 |
| | Medical Assistance required in | ibid. |
| | Adjutants, &c. of, to enlist Men for General Service | 280 |
| | Attestations of Recruits, sent to the Head Quarters of | 281 |
| | Head Quarters, and Extent of | 275. 289, 290 |

*Recruiting*

*Recruiting Dis-tricts,* Pay and Contingencies of the Staff of, how issued 591. 612

*Recruiting Parties,* How supplied with Subsistence Money, &c. 126. 214. 277

 Officers in the command of, to transmit Pay Lists, Attestations, &c. to Regimental and District Paymasters    126. 223, 284, 285

 Stations of Officers and Men of, to be specified 166

 Pay of, when proceeding from one District to another 171

 Ditto—to the Army Depôt, or to and from Ireland 172, 279

 Troops and Companies to which the Men of belong, to be stated in the Pay Lists  — 185

 Expences of Recruiting Officers of  — 186, 222

 Mustered by District Paymasters, and Recruiting Officers  —  — 214. 285

 To be sent to the Counties of which their Regiments bear the name  — 274

 Change of Stations of  —  — 274

 Senior Recruiting Officer of, in Districts, to make Weekly Reports  — 275

 Weekly Returns of Recruits of  — *ibid.*

 Not to be detached by Regiments without an Officer *ib.*

 Officers of, not to be absent without leave *ibid.*

 Two Officers of one Corps not to recruit in the same town  —  — 276

 Dress, Regularity, and Conduct of  — *ibid.*

 Offences of, may be tried by Detachment Courts Martial  —  — *ibid.*

 Reports of, to be sent to Inspecting Field Officers *ibid.*

 Medical Assistance for  — 277

 Under the Controul of Inspecting Field Officers *ibid.*

 Colonels of Regiments may take charge of them 278. 282

 Attestations of Recruits, to accompany Monthly Accompts  —  — 280, 281

 Allowance for Recruits dying  — 282

 Allowance to Recruiting Officers for carriage of baggage  —  — 283. 571

 Passage of, to and from Ireland 284. 301. 571

 Effects, Credits, and Debts, of men of 285. 609

 Expenditures of Irish Parties in Great Britain 285, 286

 Expenditures of British Parties in Ireland *ibid.*

 Officers of, to settle with District Paymasters before quitting their Stations  — 286

 To be paid in the Currency of the Country in which they serve  —  — 159. 287

 How to be furnished with Instructions  — 287

 Beating Orders for  — *ibid.*

 Allowances to Field Officers, having the Charge of 569

*Recruiting*

# INDEX.

*Recruiting Service*, Regulations and Instructions for the—[See *Recruiting Districts, Recruiting Parties, and Recruits*] 274 to 301. 571
   Half-Pay Officers and others specially appointed to recruit — — 306 to 310. 613
   Of Second Battalions — — 558, 559. 569
   Travelling Allowance, &c. of Recruiting Officers on, abolished — — — 571. 612
   New Allowance for incidental Expence of Recruiting Officers on — — — *ibid.* 614
   Of First Battalions serving Abroad — 597

*Recruiting Service (General) Agent for)* See *Agent, (General.)*

*Regimental Accompts,* See *Accompts, and Paymasters of Regiments.*

*Regimental Appointments,* See *Accoutrements and Clothing.*

*Regimental Baggage,* See *Baggage.*

*Regimental Books,* Expence of — — — 91

*Regimental Debts,* See *Debts.*

*Regimental Hospitals,* See *Hospitals.*

*Register,* - - Of the Services of Soldiers, to be kept at the War Office — 33. 41, 42. 546 to 550. 577

*Reserve Acts,* - See *Additional Force Acts.*

*Returns* - - - Charge for — — — 91
   Of the Staff abroad — — 567, 568

*Revenue,* - - Collectors of, to supply Cash or Bank Notes, for Paymaster's Bills — — 158

*Riding Masters,* Annual Allowance for — — 61, 110

*Rough Riders,* - See *Riding Masters.*

*Route,* - - - For Deserters, Form of — — 316

## S.

*Saddle Water Decks,* Allowance for — — 89. 582

*Scotland,* - - See *North Britain.*

*Serjeant,* - - - Pay of — 11 to 25. 36. 39. 49 to 55. 148. 174
   Loss of Necessaries, Allowance for — 491

*Serjeant Major,* - Pay of — — 39. 51 to 55. 148. 174

*Servants of Officers,* Stoppages for their Provisions — 149
   Pay of when Soldiers — — 150
   Loss of their Necessaries, Allowance for — 491
   Straw for, in Camp — — 553

*Service,* - - - Length of, Additional Pay to Soldiers for 30 to 55
   Description of, giving a Title to Additional Pay, &c. 529 to 539. 611. 614
   Of Soldiers, Forms of Returns, &c. for stating 546 to 550

*Settlement,* - - Of Regimental Accompts, Arrangement for the 195

*Small Beer,* - - Allowance, in lieu of — — — 66

*Smart*

| | | |
|---|---|---|
| *Smart Money,* | For Recruits when to be taken | 281. 574 |
| *Southampton,* | Recruits for the Army Depôt sent to | 279 |
| *Staff Corps,* | Pay | 54 |
| *Staff Officers,* | Pay and Allowances of | 339 to 348 |
| | Contingent Accompts of | ibid. |
| | Allowance for the Loss of Chargers of | 492 |
| | Forage for the Horses of, in Camp | 553, 554 |
| | Serving abroad, Half-yearly Returns of | 567, 568 |
| | Ditto—not liable to Deductions for Rations | 611 |
| *Stamp Duties,* | Charge of | 98. 158 |
| *Standard,* | Of Recruits | 279. 293 |
| *Stationary,* | Regimental Allowance for | 91 to 97. 117. 131. 157 |
| | Articles of, allowed for Staff Officers | 345. 348 |
| *Stock Purse Dividends,* | Allowance to Captains in lieu of | 245 |
| *Stoppages,* | For Provisions | 21. 23. 148 to 150 |
| | In Hospitals 23. 148. 170. 383. 389. 406 to 408. 607 | |
| | For Necessaries | 11 to 19. 444, 445 |
| | — Washing | 12. 15 |
| | — Articles of Cavalry Equipment | 305 |
| | From the Pay of Soldiers of the Ordnance Department in Hospitals abroad | 409 to 411 |
| | From the Subsistence of Horses | 543 |
| *Store Rooms,* | Allowance for | 91. 95 |
| *Stores,* | Of Hospitals when condemned | 404. 405 |
| *Straw,* | Supply of | 79 |
| | Regulation for the Issue of, in Camp | 552 |
| *Subalterns,* | Pay of | 6 to 8. 47 to 55 |
| | Lodging Money of | 64, 65 |
| | Personal Baggage and Camp Equipage of | 490 |
| *Subsistence,* | Encreased Rates of, for Innkeepers | 75, 160 |
| | Articles of, Demands for to be punctually settled | 161. 168 |
| | Of Men and Horses; proportion of to be paid to Contractors for Bread and Forage | 166 |
| | Of Soldiers in Great Britain, belonging to Regiments in Ireland | 247 to 250 |
| | Of Deserters | 313. 318 |
| *Surcingles,* | Expence of | 14. 157. 304. 435 |
| *Surgeon on the District Staff,* | One attached to each Recruiting District | 277 |
| | To Examine all Recruits, except when raised at Head Quarters | 282 |
| | How appointed | 352 |
| | Pay of | 360 |
| *Surgeon General* | Duty of | 352 |
| | Supplies of Medicines for General Hospitals ordered by | 401 |
| | Certificate of, relative to Expences for cure of Wounds | 487 |
| *Surgeon's Mate* | Pay and Appointment of | 46. 53. 55. 353 |
| | Qualification of | 353 |

*Surgeon*

# INDEX.

| | | |
|---|---|---|
| *Surgeon (Regimental)* | Pay of | 5. 47 to 55. 360, 361. 363 to 368 |
| | Forage for a Horse | 170. 173. 361. 363 to 368 |
| | Qualification of | 353 |
| | Personal Baggage and Camp Equipage of | 491 |
| *Surgeon on the General Staff* | Pay and Allowances of | 360, 361. 369 to 377 |

## T.

| | | |
|---|---|---|
| *Taxes,* | On Officers Horses | 158. 345. 371 |
| *Tilbury,* | Passage of Parties from Gravesend, to | 187 |
| *Transfers* | Of Soldiers from one Troop or Company to another | 125 |
| | — Corps to and from the Irish Establishment | 241 to 246 |
| *Transports* | Pay of Soldiers embarked in | 22, 23. 148. 173 |
| *Travelling Expences,* | Of newly purchased Troop Horses | 85 |
| | — Recruiting Officers | 283, 571. 576. 614 |
| | — Staff Officers | 344 |
| | — Officers removed from one Battalion to another | 596 |
| *Triplicates,* | Of Vouchers to be taken, by Regiments abroad | 164 |
| *Trumpeter* | Pay of | 11 to 25. 47 to 50. 148. 174 |
| | Loss of Necessaries, Allowance for | 491 |
| *Turnscrew, &c.* | Allowance for | 456 |

## V.

| | | |
|---|---|---|
| *Veteran Battalions,* | Pay of | 53 |
| | Ditto for Men of, discharged, and replaced on the Out Pension | 608 |
| | Clothing of Men transferred to, or from, the Line | 613 |
| *Veterinary Surgeon (Principal)* | Horse Medicines, &c. supplied by | 87, 412 to 417 |
| *Veterinary Surgeon,* | Pay, and Appointment of | 46, 412 to 417 |
| *Volunteer Corps,* | Regulations for | 255 to 273 |
| *Vouchers,* | For the Pay of Officers | 146 |
| | Not to be altered or erased | 164 |
| | Duplicates and Triplicates to be taken | *ibid.* |
| *Unlimited Service,* | Pay, &c. of Volunteers for, from limited Service | 230 to 232 |
| | Recruiting for, by limited Service Battalions | 233. 597 |

## W.

| | | |
|---|---|---|
| *Waggons,* | Hire of | 98. 104 |
| | Ditto, Expence of Warrants for | 100. 103 |
| | Ditto, Receipts for | 186 |
| *Waggon Train,* | Pay of | 50 |
| | Clothing of | 434 |
| *War Office* | Mode of addressing Applications to | 524 |
| *Washerwomen,* | Bread, Straw, &c. for, in Camps | 551. 553. 556 |
| *Washing,* | Stoppage for | 12. 16 |
| *Watch Coats,* | Expence of | 19. 450 |

*Water*

| | | |
|---|---|---|
| *Water Decks* | Allowance for | 89. 582 |
| *West Indies,* | Pay of Troops there | 22, 23 |
| | Regimental Contingencies of Ditto | 94 |
| | Pay in Advance to the Regiments embarking for | 142 |
| | Encrease of Pay, &c. for Service there | 538, 539 |
| *Widows of Officers,* | Allowance to, when their Husbands are killed in action | 489 |
| | Rates of Pension for, &c. 30 to 37. 500 to 506. | 613 |
| *Wives of Soldiers* | No Stoppage required for their Provisions | 150 |
| | Allowance to, when not permitted to embark with their Husbands | 187 to 189, 513 |
| | To be provided with Certificates, by Commanding Officers | *ibid.* |
| | Number of, allowed to accompany Regiments on Service | 513 |
| *Wood,* | Deliveries of, in Camps | 551. 556 |
| *Wounds* | Claims for Cure of | 352, 487. 488 |
| | Loss of an Eye or a Limb occasioned by | 489 |

## Y.

| | | |
|---|---|---|
| *York Hospital* | Medical Stores condemned at | 405 |

ERRATA.

# ERRATA.

Page 49—Line 16—*for* 11s. *read* 11s. 4d.

143—Note, last line—*for* in the Appendix, *read* in Section IX.

182—Lines 3 and 4, the words " Books of General Abstract," should have been printed in a smaller Type; such books not being now kept.—*Vide* last Note of Page 140.

217—Last Note—the reference is misplaced: it should have been inserted at the termination of the second Paragraph.

Fourth Paragraph—the lines beginning, " He shall also," &c. and ending " Regimental Agent," should have been printed in the same Type as the Letter generally, and without the Brackets.

219—The signature to the Letter should have been— " R. TAYLER."

224—In the Note of Reference—*dele* " By the first Paragraph of Article 77, of the Explanatory Directions to Paymasters."

256—Note—*for* in one or other, *read* in one part or other.

339—In the Title of the State,—*after* " Rates of Pay," *dele* and Allowances.

423—Line 10 of the N. B.—*after* " classed as such," *dele* Staff.

470—Date of the Circular—*for* 18th April, 1806, *read* 18th April, 1805.

www.ingramcontent.com/pod-product-compliance
Lightning Source LLC
Chambersburg PA
CBHW060357230426
43663CB00008B/1301

*9781845748081*